Programming

Microsoft®

Access

2000

Rick Dobson

PUBLISHED BY
Microsoft Press
A Division of Microsoft Corporation
One Microsoft Way
Redmond, Washington 98052-6399

Library of Congress Cataloging-in-Publication Data
Dobson, Rick, 1944-
    Programming Microsoft Access 2000 / Rick Dobson.
      p.   cm.
    ISBN 0-7356-0500-9
    1. Microsoft Access.   2. Database management.   I. Title.
    QA76.9.D3D587   1999
    005.75'65--dc21   99-13032
                                          CIP

Printed and bound in the United States of America.

1 2 3 4 5 6 7 8 9   QMQM   4 3 2 1 0 9

Distributed in Canada by Penguin Books Canada Limited.

A CIP catalogue record for this book is available from the British Library.

Microsoft Press books are available through booksellers and distributors worldwide. For
further information about international editions, contact your local Microsoft Corporation
office or contact Microsoft Press International directly at fax (425) 936-7329. Visit our Web
site at mspress.microsoft.com.

EZ Access Developer Suite and Yes! I Can Run My Business are registered trademarks of
Database Creations, Inc. Total Access Agent, Total Access Analyzer, Total Access Compo-
nents, Total Access Memo, Total Access Statistics, Total VB SourceBook, and Total VB
Statistics are registered trademarks of FMS, Inc. ActiveX, FoxPro, FrontPage, IntelliSense,
JScript, Microsoft, Microsoft Press, Outlook, PowerPoint, Visual Basic, Windows, and Win-
dows NT are either registered trademarks or trademarks of Microsoft Corporation in the
United States and/or other countries. Other product and company names mentioned herein
may be the trademarks of their respective owners.

The example companies, organizations, products, people, and events depicted herein are
fictitious. No association with any real company, organization, product, person, or event is
intended or should be inferred.

Acquisitions Editor: Ben Ryan
Project Editor: Alice Turner
Manuscript Editor: Ina Chang

When I was a kid, one popular song was "This Is Dedicated to the One I Love." That song title really fits my purpose in this section. The one person on earth that I love the most is my wife, Virginia, and this book is dedicated to her. Without her support, encouragement, and help, you would be reading a different book—maybe by a different author.

Virginia was a major force behind the book from the beginning. When Ben Ryan from Microsoft Press approached me to write a book, Virginia urged me to say yes. When the time frame for completing chapters collapsed into a shorter than expected period, it was Virginia who stepped into the gap to relieve me of all household responsibilities. She also supported me as I worked long hours to complete the book. When I needed an extra pair of eyes to proofread chapters before submitting them to Microsoft Press, Virginia rose to the occasion again. Finally, when I gave all that I could to the book but felt that still more was required, it was Virginia who said a prayer to remind me that I can do all things through Christ, who strengthens me.

Contents

Acknowledgments

As the author, I am responsible for this whole book. Feel free to blame me for all that you do not like. However, when it comes to things that you do like, I remind you that I received plenty of valuable input.

I would not be the author of this book were it not for the great folks at Microsoft Press. My acquisitions editor, Ben Ryan, initially approached me and signed me to write the book. Later, I worked with the book's editorial team, including Alice Turner, Jim Fuchs, and Ina Chang. These folks gave unselfishly of their genius so that you could have a better book.

I received technical support from multiple sources. The Microsoft folks who added to the book by sharing their technical wisdom with me include Charles Allard, Michael Brotherton, Neil Charney, Russell Christopher, Debra Dove, Keith Fink, Alyssa Henry, and Kevin Mineweaser. Debra deserves special praise for her patience in answering an unending barrage of questions over the winter holiday season. A pair of training firms, Kizan Technologies and ExecuTrain, jointly sponsored my attendance at a Microsoft SQL Server 7 training seminar. The knowledge that I acquired there helped me immeasurably with the content on the Microsoft Data Engine and Microsoft Access Projects and with SQL language tips.

Introduction

This book is for database developers who want to use Microsoft Access 2000 to build custom applications. It covers the features that make Access a perennial favorite with developers, as well as the innovations in Access 2000 that you are most likely to use in your programming projects. Numerous programming samples demonstrate the core development techniques and rapid application development tools. The sample designs have been kept simple so you can easily adapt them for your custom applications or apply the techniques in your development work. The book's companion CD contains all the samples in the book as well as many others.

Access is a popular development platform in large measure because it is part of the Microsoft Office suite. Many clients want their Access systems to interoperate with the rest of Office, and they want systems that are transparent and easy to maintain without developer assistance. The techniques described in this book will help you meet these expectations. (For additional support, you can consult two Microsoft World Wide Web sites: www.microsoft.com/office/, which covers Access capabilities in general, and www.microsoft.com/officedev/, which covers the product's developer features.)

This book was written to meet the needs of a variety of readers. Longtime Access developers will find the essential information on the advances introduced in Access 2000. Another target readership is developers who primarily use non-Microsoft technologies, such as dBASE or Paradox. They know all of the development concepts, but they do not necessarily know how to implement those concepts with Access. Finally, this book is for highly motivated power users who want to graduate to developing solutions for others and want to ramp up quickly.

The book's presentation style has the aim of making you productive as a developer, and productive in using the new features in Access 2000. The presentation style is *look, see, do!* The many code samples throughout the book illustrate concepts that you can readily put to use in your applications. Think of them as recipes for performing specific development tasks. Try them "as is" from the book's CD. Then, modify them to work with your data and in the context of your custom application requirements. The samples are purposefully uncomplicated, easy to understand, and easy to reuse, so that you will be motivated to apply them in your own applications.

WHAT'S NEW WITH ACCESS 2000?

Access 2000 makes major strides in many areas. Microsoft has created a profoundly new product that still feels like the Access you know. This book highlights five specific areas of innovation: ActiveX Data Objects (ADO), enhanced SQL Server interoperability, Visual Basic for Applications (VBA) and packaging enhancements, Microsoft Jet engine improvements, and improved Web interoperability.

ActiveX Data Objects

ADO replaces nearly all of the data access functions that you previously performed with Data Access Objects (DAO). Access 2000 offers ADO functionality via three libraries: ADODB, ADOX, and JRO.

The ActiveX Data Objects 2.1 (ADODB) library offers core data access processing functions. The main ADODB objects include the *Connection*, *Recordset*, and *Command* objects. You can use these objects, along with their properties and methods, to connect to and manipulate a data source. The *Connection* object offers an interface to the new OLE DB provider technology. This technology is critical to the Microsoft Universal Data Access (UDA) architecture that provides high-performance access to a variety of data formats (both relational and nonrelational) on multiple platforms across the enterprise. UDA facilitates the integrated processing of traditional data sources, such as Jet and SQL Server data sources, with non-traditional sources, such as mail, file directories, and even video. UDA represents an evolutionary advance beyond today's standard data interfaces, such as Open Database Connectivity (ODBC), Remote Data Objects (RDO), and DAO.

The Microsoft ADO Extensions 2.1 for DDL and Security (ADOX) library offers an object-based approach to data definition and user-level security. It provides the traditional Jet user-level collections of *Users* and *Groups*. It ties permissions in database files to members of the *Users* and *Groups* collections in a workgroup information file. The ADOX model for this library tackles data definition chores using such objects as *Tables*, *Columns*, *Indexes*, *Keys*, *Views*, and *Procedures*. You can use these objects to dynamically define new tables, indexes, and relationships among tables. You can also define queries on the tables.

The Microsoft Jet and Replication Objects 2.1 (JRO) library primarily delivers Jet engine replication services through an ADO interface. This new ADO model lets you take advantage of all the new programmatic Jet database replication features. In addition, this model includes Jet engine functions such as compacting databases and refreshing the cache.

Enhanced SQL Server Interoperability

With Access 2000, you can process enterprise databases as easily as you work with Microsoft Jet databases. ADO connectivity is a part of the reason. However, integration is even tighter for SQL Server 6.5 and SQL Server 7 with the new Access Project. This new file type (.adp) works with SQL Server and Microsoft Data Engine (MSDE) databases in much the same way that .mdb files facilitate the processing of Jet databases. MSDE is a new database engine built on the SQL Server 7 model; it is meant for small workgroup solutions and complements the traditional Jet database engine. You can use either Jet or MSDE to develop solutions.

Access Projects explicitly expose views and procedures in the familiar database container framework. You can instantly connect to remote SQL Server databases, with the same graphical simplicity that you have with Jet databases. You can also use the SQL Server data with Access forms and reports (just as you do Jet data).

You also have seamless OLE DB interoperability with SQL Server and other back-end data sources. Using the ADO *Connection* object and OLE DB providers, you can connect to remote data sources and easily reference them programmatically for your custom applications.

VBA and Packaging Enhancements

Access continues to move toward VBA parity with the rest of Office. Access 2000 introduces a Visual Basic Editor (VBE) that has the same user interface as the one in Microsoft Word, Excel, and PowerPoint. You can transfer your code management and development skills directly to these other packages and thus enrich non-Access applications with data access functions.

The Office 2000 Developer Edition offers improved packaging and deployment options. For example, you can deploy solutions with MSDE and solutions that rely on a SQL Server–like database. You get the richness of views and procedures from the graphical interface as well as the programmatic interface. This is particularly important if an application might grow to require the capabilities of a full-fledged SQL Server database.

A new deployment option lets you deploy custom setup packages for your solutions via the Internet. You can thus vastly extend the range of clients that you serve. Your pool of potential development clients expands to include anyone around the globe with an Internet connection.

Jet Engine Improvements

Access 2000 ships with version 4 of the Jet database engine, which offers improvements in several areas of functionality. Particularly attractive is the availability of row-level page locking. Prior versions of Access performed locking at no lower than the page level. One reason for the introduction of row-level locking is the availability of Unicode support for text characters. You can now represent text data in different languages in multilingual applications. The new coding for text-based fields expands the space requirements for each character from 1 to 2 bytes and the page size from 2 to 4 KB. Since the page size has grown, Microsoft has enabled row-level locking to reduce the possibility of concurrent locks on the same page in multi-user applications.

Database replication has also improved in several areas. One improvement is the availability of column-level replication. In previous Jet versions, conflicts were detected at the row level so two replicas conflicted even if they changed different fields for the same record. Column-level replication improves performance by eliminating such conflicts. Access 2000 also introduces two-way replication between Jet and SQL databases. The prior version permitted only one-way replication from SQL Server to Jet.

Another praiseworthy improvement is programmatic control for changing the value of AutoNumber fields. You can set the initial and step values for AutoNumber fields when you create a table. You can also change these values for the next record in a table. In an Access Project, you can set AutoNumber fields from Table Design view. You can also change these values after a table is initially created.

Jet also offers SQL-level access to views and procedures. The Jet SQL improvements let you create and alter both types of database object models.

Improved Web Interoperability

One of the most significant new features of Access 2000 is data access pages, which act like Access forms and reports on the Web. You can design Web pages that bind directly to Jet or SQL Server data sources. With pages that act like forms, users can edit, add, and delete records graphically from a page. You can use design-time tools to programmatically control these features as well as sorting and filtering capabilities. While these pages do not enable subforms, you can create grouped data access pages that expand conditionally based on user input.

Data access pages can also serve as a host for the new Office 2000 Web Components, which you can use to create pages that contain interactive spreadsheets, dynamic charts, and pivot tables. You can also tie the spreadsheet and charting Web components to data displayed in grouped and ungrouped data access pages. This means that you can present calculations and charts that change dynamically as you move from one record to the next. Data access pages with pivot tables do not interact with other data sources on a page, but they do offer Excel-style "pivoting"—graphically moving parts of the data for a different view. In addition, pivot tables can be used for the analysis of multiple kinds of data, including SQL Server, Jet, and online analytical processing (OLAP) data sources.

Chapter 1

An Introduction to VBA

Over a decade ago, Bill Gates proposed a universal macro language for desktop applications. Microsoft Visual Basic for Applications (VBA) is the fulfillment of that dream and more. The VBA in Microsoft Access 2000 is common to all Microsoft Office components as well as scores of third-party packages. Its syntax is also consistent with the stand-alone Visual Basic programming language. VBA's ubiquity enables developers to use a single programming language in dozens of contexts simply by learning a new object model. VBA is like glue for an Access application. VBA holds everything together and gives an application form.

Access 2000 includes a new interface, the Visual Basic Editor (VBE), that brings it more in line with other Office components. However, you'll probably find yourself inserting VBA code behind the familiar Access forms instead of behind the user forms used in the rest of Office. This marriage of technologies will feel very natural.

This chapter will introduce VBA in Access 2000 and review VBA fundamentals as they relate to developing Access 2000 applications. It will also showcase major VBA innovations and demonstrate code-behind-form techniques. While this is a traditional Access development topic, there are some new twists to how you do it with VBE.

This chapter will cover seven aspects of VBA in Access, listed below, and will conclude with a brief discussion of macros.

- Collections, objects, properties, methods, and events
- Procedures and modules
- The VBE interface
- Jet, data types, and declarations
- Conditional logic and looping constructs
- Built-in functions
- Debugging and error trapping

COLLECTIONS, OBJECTS, PROPERTIES, METHODS, AND EVENTS

Access 2000 supports VBA, which facilitates object-oriented development. The following sections will introduce object-oriented development in the context of VBA and Access 2000. The information is targeted at power users migrating to programmatic application development and at mid-level developers who want to review object-oriented programming with VBA.

Collections and Objects

Access 2000 is an object-oriented development environment. Its Database window facilitates user access to tables, queries, forms, reports, modules, and macros. VBA makes these available along with a broad array of programmatic constructs, such as recordsets and *TableDef* objects. To get the most out of VBA in Access, you have to understand objects and a number of related concepts.

An object is a thing. Things can be as diverse as cars, phones, and videos. All objects have properties. Cars, for example, are defined by color, door, and engine properties, among others. Properties can define instances of generic objects. This object-oriented behavior allows you to specify unique instances of objects based on their properties. For example, a red car and a black car define two unique instances of the car object.

Object properties vary according to the object class to which they refer. A car has a different set of properties than a phone. Both have a color property, but a phone can also have a speaker property. Cars, on the other hand, have engines of different sizes. Some objects are containers for other ones.

Contained objects can also have properties. Engines come in various sizes and configurations, for example, while speakers come with volume controls and fidelity ratings. Properties can also define unique instances of contained object classes. A speakerphone has a different set of properties than a standard phone.

In addition to properties, objects also have methods. An object's methods are the behaviors that it can perform. A phone makes connections. A car moves. Many objects have multiple methods. Phones let you make local calls and long-distance calls, for example.

Access developers do not manipulate physical objects. We manipulate programming constructs such as forms, tables, and queries that can represent objects and their behaviors. The Access 2000 Database window shows some of its database object classes on its Microsoft Outlook–style toolbar. (See Figure 1-1.) Clicking the Forms button on the toolbar opens a view of form objects and displays two options for creating new forms. Form objects can contain other objects called controls. Contained objects define an object just as controls on a form define its look and behavior.

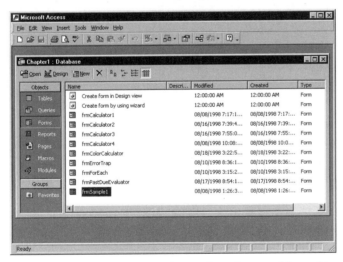

Figure 1-1. *The Database window with a selection of form objects and two options for creating new forms.*

Figure 1-1 shows several form objects. These objects comprise a *collection*. Access applications typically have collections of forms, tables, queries, and other objects. The Database window automatically sorts selected objects into classes. Clicking the toolbar on the left reveals the objects in each collection.

Collections are like objects. All Access collections have a *Count* property, which specifies the number of instances in the collection. Collections can also have an *Item* property. You can use the read-only *Item* property to return an individual form from the *AllForms* collection. Since a collection's members are individual objects, they do not have a *Count* property. The objects of a collection serve different purposes. A convertible car can serve different purposes than a family sedan, but they can both belong to the car collection in a household.

Properties and Methods

Properties and methods characterize the appearance and behavior of objects. The syntax for referencing these is *object.property* or *object.method*. The term *object* can refer to either an individual object or a collection of objects. For example, *txtInput1.BackColor* specifies the background color property of a text box on a form, and *AllForms.Item(0)* refers to the first form in the forms collection. If this form has the name *frmSample1*, you can refer to the form as *AllForms.Item("frmSample1")*.

You can see the properties of a database object by selecting it in Design view and clicking the Properties button on the toolbar. Figure 1-2 shows a form in Design view along with the form's property sheet. The property sheet shows a custom entry, *My Default Caption*, in the Caption property box. The *Close Button* property is selected. You can click the Close Button box and select No. The new *Close Button* property grays out the Close button when a form appears in Form view. Notice that the property sheet has multiple pages. Figure 1-2 shows the Format tab selected. These pages organize the properties into groups for fast retrieval.

Figure 1-2. *A simple form in Design view with its property sheet.*

NOTE In Access 2000, the property sheet is available in both Design view and Form view instead of only in Design view. This means that you can quickly modify and refine a form's appearance as you work with its design in Form view.

The *DoCmd* object is a rich source of methods for all levels of Access developers, but beginners find it especially helpful for getting started with methods. The *DoCmd* object has many methods, including *Close*, *OpenForm*, *GoToControl*, *FindRecord*, and *RunCommand*. Many *DoCmd* methods require arguments that specify how the method performs. Other methods have required and optional arguments. If you do not specify values for an optional argument, the method uses the default settings. *RunCommand* is particularly attractive to power users who are upgrading to programmer status; you can use it to execute the commands that are available on the Access menus and toolbars.

You can close a form in Access using the *Close* method of the *DoCmd* object. This method has two required arguments and one optional one. The first required argument specifies the type of object to close. When you close a form, use *acForm*. (*acForm* is a built-in Access constant whose value tells the *Close* method that you want to close a form. See the section titled "The Object Browser" on page 23 for more information about built-in Access constants.) The second argument is the form's name. This entry appears in the *Name* property of the form's property sheet. Enclose the name in quotes. The optional argument tells Access whether to save any changes to the form. The default setting is to prompt for whether to save. Use either *acSaveYes* or *acSaveNo* to close the form with or without saving any changes. You can invoke the *Close* method for a form using the following syntax:

```
DoCmd.Close acForm, "formname", acSaveNo
```

Many *DoCmd* methods apply directly to individual objects. For example, the *GoToControl* method assigns the focus to a specific control on a form. You can achieve the same result using the *SetFocus* method, which selects a control. Either method is convenient when your application needs to move the focus for entering new information or correcting faulty information.

Events

Events are very important in VBA programming. You can use events to make applications dynamic and interactive. Objects and collections have events, which serve as launching points for a developer's custom code. When you work with forms, you can use events for such tasks as data validation, enabling or disabling controls, changing the control that has the focus, opening a form, and closing a form.

You must understand when each event fires as well as the order in which the events fire. When a form opens, it triggers a sequence of events: *Open*, *Load*, *Resize*, and *Current*. The *Open* event occurs when a form starts to open but before it displays any records. The *Load* event occurs after the *Open* event. When the *Load* event fires, a form shows its records. Any code that causes a form to change its size or location by means of the *MoveSize, Minimize, Maximize,* or *Restore DoCmd* methods fires the *Resize* event. The *Current* event is the last one that normally occurs as a form opens. It marks the moment at which a particular record is current or available. It also fires when a user navigates to a new record or requeries or refreshes a form.

You access the events for forms and their controls by selecting the form or control in Design view and then clicking the Event tab of the property sheet. Clicking the Build button next to an event opens a dialog box that you can use to open the code module behind a form. Choosing Code Builder opens an event procedure in VBE. The event procedure is named *Objectname_Eventname*, where *Objectname* is the name of the object and *Eventname* is the name of the event. If you select a form and click the Build button for the *Close* event, for example, your event procedure will have the name *Form_Close*. If you create an event procedure for the *On Click* event of a label named *lblTitle*, VBA automatically names it *lblTitle_Click*.

The following are three event procedures for the form shown in Figure 1-2: *Form_Open, Form_Load*, and *lblTtitle_Click*. When you first open the form in Form view, a message box opens that reads, "The form opened." When you click OK, you see a second message that says, "The form loaded." After the form completes its loading cycle, clicking the label opens a third message box that says, "Hello from the label."

```
Private Sub Form_Open(Cancel As Integer)
    MsgBox "The form opened.", vbInformation, _
        "Programming Microsoft Access 2000"
End Sub

Private Sub Form_Load()
'This is s simple statement.
    MsgBox "The form loaded.", vbInformation, _
        "Programming Microsoft Access 2000"
'This sets a property.
    Me.Caption = "New Caption"
'Here are two methods for giving a control focus.
'    DoCmd.GoToControl "txtMyTextBox"
    Me.txtMyTextBox.SetFocus
'Now that the method worked, VBA sets a property.
    Me.txtMyTextBox.Text = "Hi, there!"
End Sub

Private Sub lblTitle_Click()
    MsgBox "Hello from the label.", vbInformation, _
        "Programming Microsoft Access 2000"
End Sub
```

The event procedures cause the message boxes to appear. Clicking the label invokes the *lblTitle_Click* event procedure. This procedure has a single statement that presents a message box. (The underscore at the end of procedure's first line is a continuation character.) The *Form_Open* event procedure also has a single statement. The *Form_Load* event procedure has several statements besides the one for its message box. This event procedure dynamically sets the caption for the form, which is particularly helpful when you have a form that has two or more roles in an application. It also sets the focus to the text box named *txtMyTextBox* and then assigns "Hi, there!" to the control's *Text* property. This event procedure demonstrates two different techniques for setting the focus. One relies on the *SetFocus* method, and the other uses the *GoToControl* method for the same purpose. The apostrophes at the beginning of some lines of code mark them as comments. Notice that one of the two techniques is a comment line.

PROCEDURES AND MODULES

Procedures are containers for VBA code. There are three types of these containers: subprocedures, function procedures, and property procedures. Although their functions overlap in some areas, each type has a specific and unique purpose. Access offers two basic kinds of containers for procedures: standard modules and class modules. Class modules can be custom classes for forms and reports. You can also use them to define your own classes to simplify reuse of code for such routine tasks as adding new employees, making a deposit to an account, or withdrawing money from an account.

Sub Procedures

Sub procedures can perform actions, compute values, and update and revise built-in property settings. ("Sub procedure" is usually shortened to "subprocedure" or simply "procedure.") As you have seen, Access 2000 automatically invokes procedures for events, but you can use them more broadly. Procedures never return values. They also do not define custom properties for form, report, or class modules.

A procedure consists of a series of VBA statements between *Sub* and *End Sub* statements. The *Sub* statement must declare a name for the procedure. While event procedures have very stylized names (such as *object_event*), procedure names generally follow standard variable naming conventions. They must begin with a letter, cannot exceed 255 characters, cannot include punctuation or spaces, and should not include a VBA keyword, function, or operator name. Procedures can take arguments, which you insert after the procedure name. If there is more than one argument, you separate them with commas.

One way to gain a basic familiarity with procedures is by using the Command Button wizard, which writes VBA code for more than 30 functions. All you have to do is make a few selections in dialog boxes. The procedures written by the wizard are generally simple, so they make good learning models. Even intermediate and advanced developers can benefit from the wizard because it generates a good skeleton for adding code with more specifics. Beginners can use the wizard to quickly automate record navigation, database maintenance, general form and report operations, invoking of other applications, and miscellaneous tasks such as running a query or dialing a phone number.

You invoke the Command Button wizard from the toolbox in Form Design view. Select the Control Wizards button and then drop a button on the form. This opens the dialog box shown in Figure 1-3. You can select from about a half dozen actions in each category. After completing all the dialog boxes for the action you select, you can view the code in Access 2000 VBE. Click the Code button on the Form Design toolbar to switch to VBE.

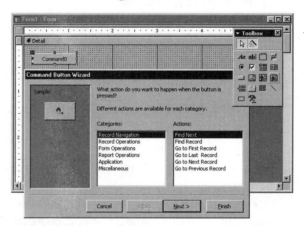

Figure 1-3. *Using the Command Button wizard, you can create a whole event procedure by replying to a few dialog boxes.*

Many developers prefer to write their procedures from scratch. You can open a code window for an event procedure as described above, or you can create an ordinary procedure. There are two ways to start this kind of procedure, depending on where you put it. If the procedure is to reside behind a form or report, click the Code button on the Design toolbar. If the code is to exist in a standard module that is not behind any specific form or report, choose Tools-Macro-Visual Basic Editor or press Alt+F11. In either case, you end up in VBE. Choose Insert-Procedure, and in the Add Procedure dialog box enter a name and confirm the selection of the Sub option button. This creates a shell for a procedure with a *Sub* and an *End Sub* statement. You can then add code to it.

Use your knowledge of the Access object model to code some actions. Recall that the *DoCmd* object has many methods. Type *DoCmd* and then press the period key. This opens a drop-down list box that displays all the legitimate entries after *DoCmd*. As you type an entry, Access converges on the subset of responses that match your entry. (See Figure 1-4.) If you are unsure what to type, you can scroll through the entries to find a method. This technique works for all objects, not just *DoCmd*. Microsoft calls this feature IntelliSense because it intelligently senses the subset of appropriate replies. IntelliSense actually does two things: It lists the properties and methods that are legitimate at any point in the construction of a VBA statement, and it provides syntax information about the content for the fields required for selected VBA statements. This dramatically reduces errors and helps you get started quickly.

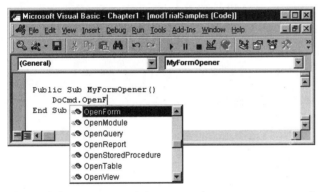

Figure 1-4. *IntelliSense helps to complete a VBA statement for the* DoCmd *object. You type the beginning of a statement, and it shows a list of legitimate replies for the balance of that portion of the statement.*

The following is a simple procedure consisting of three lines. The first line reserves a memory location for a calculated result. The second adds two constants. The third prints the result in the Immediate window. This window is like a work pad for storing intermediate results as you check your code. You can open it from VBE by choosing View-Immediate Window. You can run the procedure from VBE by clicking anywhere in the procedure and then clicking the Run Sub/UserForm button on the Standard toolbar.

```
Sub MyFirstCalculator()
Dim Result
    Result = 1 + 2
    Debug.Print Result
End Sub
```

In a more typical situation, you can call a procedure in either of two ways. You can include its name on a line by itself; if the procedure has any arguments, you can include them after the name, separated by commas. Alternatively, you can precede the procedure name with *Call*. This is a VBA keyword for invoking a procedure. When you use *Call*, enclose arguments in parentheses after the procedure name.

The following is a slightly more flexible version of the initial calculator function. The calculator consists of a pair of procedures. The one named *MySecondCalculator* adds any two numbers and prints the result to the Immediate window. It determines what numbers to add from the two arguments that it receives. The other procedure calls the procedure that performs the sum. You can vary the numbers the second procedure adds by altering the value of the two arguments in the first procedure. In a more sophisticated application, you might tie these argument values to variables or form fields.

```
Sub CallSecondCalculator()
    MySecondCalculator 1, 3
End Sub

Sub MySecondCalculator(First, Second)
Dim Result
    Result = First + Second
    Debug.Print Result
End Sub
```

Function Procedures

Function procedures—usually called "functions"—differ from procedures in a couple of ways. First, they can return a value, so you can use them in expressions just as you use variables. Second, they do not serve as event procedures. Both procedures and functions can perform tasks. With the exceptions noted, functions and procedures are generally interchangeable.

A function is a collection of VBA statements bounded by *Function* and *End Function* statements. It can accept arguments in the same way that a procedure accepts arguments. A function can include one or more expressions. At least one of these can set the function's name equal to a value. You can terminate a function after setting its value by using an *Exit Function* statement. Any function can contain one or more *Exit Function* statements.

Although a function can return a value, it does not have to. A function can be a collection of statements that invoke methods and set properties without ever setting the function name equal to a value. This is one way in which functions and procedures are similar.

You start a function just like you do a procedure, but you select the Function option button instead of the Sub option button in the Add Procedure dialog box. You can invoke a function procedure by clicking the Run Sub/UserForm button on the Standard toolbar in VBE. You can also invoke a function from the Immediate window: Type a question mark followed by the function name. If the function has arguments, you place these in parentheses, separated by commas. You can run your own custom functions as well as built-in Access functions from the Immediate window.

Figure 1-5 shows a view of VBE with a simple function that determines whether the date submitted as an argument is in the third millennium. To match popular conventions, we'll compute this millennium to start in the year 2000 rather than 2001. The function *Year2KTest* accepts a date and returns *3* if the date is in the third millennium, or returns *0* otherwise. The Immediate window below the code window shows the outcome for running the function with two different dates. The Immediate window in Figure 1-5 confirms this result by returning a *3* for the first day in 2000 and a *0* for the first day in 1999. Notice that you must enclose a date between pound signs.

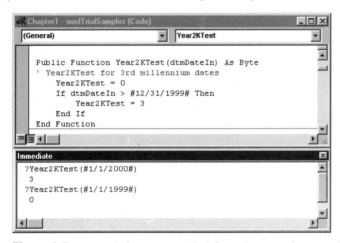

Figure 1-5. *A simple function invoked from the Immediate window.*

The procedure on the following page is a more sophisticated approach to millennium assessment. The function starts by declaring the range of dates for which it is accurate. Then it tests its argument against two millennium milestones. If the date does not fall within the first or second millennium, the function assumes that it belongs in the third millennium. The initial message box statement indicates the range of dates for which the function is accurate.

```
Public Function PopularMillennium(dtmDateIn) As Byte
    MsgBox "This works for dates after 12/31/0099" & _
        " and before 1/1/3000.", _
        vbInformation, _
        "Programming Microsoft Access 2000"
    If dtmDateIn <= #12/31/999# Then
        PopularMillennium = 1
    ElseIf dtmDateIn <= #12/31/1999# Then
        PopularMillennium = 2
    Else
        PopularMillennium = 3
    End If
End Function
```

Access 2000 dates are valid from 1/1/100 through 12/31/2999. This range is sufficient for the vast majority of desktop applications. If you need a range beyond these dates, you should consider coding dates independently of the Access serial date system.

> NOTE   Access 2000 is Year 2000-compliant. Like previous versions, it stores dates with the full four digits. Access 2000 also handles leap years correctly: Years divisible by 4 are leap years unless they are divisible by 100. However, if they are divisible by 400, they are leap years. Since 2000 is divisible by 400, it is a leap year. This rule is critical for computing the difference between two dates. The General Date and Short Date formats in Access use the operating system's short date format options to determine the correct display. If you set your Regional settings in the Control Panel to show dates with four-digit years, all of the General date formats will show the full four digits.

The above rules do not force you to program in such a way that Y2K issues cannot emerge. Therefore, any Access application can have a Y2K bug even though Access 2000 is Year 2000-compliant. Visit www.microsoft.com/technet/topics/year2k/default.htm for Microsoft's overview of the topic along with specific product and version Y2K compliance reviews. The FMS site (www.fmsinc.com/tpapers/index.html#Year 2000 Papers) has a different perspective on some Y2K/Access issues. FMS markets a product called Total Access Inspector 2000 that specifically detects Y2K issues in Access applications.

You can often use both procedures and functions to develop a solution to a problem. Figure 1-6 shows a form that relies on both kinds of functions to develop answers. The form allows a user to type values in the text boxes labeled Number 1 and Number 2. Clicking a function button of /, *, −, or + computes a corresponding outcome in the Result text box.

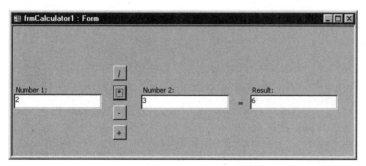

Figure 1-6. *This form serves as a simple calculator. VBA functions enable the form's buttons and populate the Result text box based on entries in the other two text boxes.*

The VBA code to implement the form in Figure 1-6 uses just four pairs of procedures, as shown below. Four procedures act as the event handler for a click to the four function keys on the form. These event handlers simply call a function that pulls the values from the two text boxes, executes the computation indicated by the function button, and returns that value to the event procedure. The event procedure, in turn, assigns the return value from the function to the third text box on the form. Notice the optional use of the *Me* prefix before the text box names. Since the code is behind the form with the text box, specifying the form name is optional. The event procedures use *Me* instead of the form's longer, more formal class name (*Form_frmCalculator1*).

```
Option Compare Database
Option Explicit
Dim dblResult As Double

Private Sub cmdAddition_Click()
    Me.txtResult = MyAdder
End Sub

Private Function MyAdder()
    dblResult = CDbl(txtNumber1) + CDbl(txtNumber2)
    MyAdder = dblResult
End Function

Private Sub cmdSubtraction_Click()
    Me.txtResult = MySubtractor
End Sub

Private Function MySubtractor()
    dblResult = CDbl(txtNumber1) - CDbl(txtNumber2)
    MySubtractor = dblResult
End Function
```

(continued)

```
Private Sub cmdMultiplication_Click()
    Me.txtResult = MyMultiplier
End Sub

Private Function MyMultiplier()
    dblResult = CDbl(txtNumber1) * CDbl(txtNumber2)
    MyMultiplier = dblResult
End Function

Private Sub cmdDivision_Click()
    Me.txtResult = MyDivider
End Sub

Private Function MyDivider()
    dblResult = CDbl(txtNumber1) / CDbl(txtNumber2)
    MyDivider = dblResult
End Function
```

The function and the procedures reside in the code module behind the form. The *Dim* statement at the top of the module declares a variable that all of the procedures in the module can use. Since users can click only one function key at a time, this sharing of *dblResult* works. The *Option Explicit* statement forces the declaration of variables before their use. This helps to guard against typographical errors, which are a common source of errors in programs. *Option Compare Database* is a module-level specification that designates string variables sorted in an order determined by the locale ID in the Control Panel.

The following pair of procedures illustrates much of what we have covered about procedures, functions, and methods. The form, *frmCalculator2*, has just two controls: a text box named *txtInput* and a command button named *cmdSquarer*. The form computes the square of the entry in the text box when the user clicks the button. The procedures display the result in a message box.

```
Option Compare Database
Option Explicit
Dim dblResult As Double

Private Sub cmdSquarer_Click()
    MySquarer Form_frmCalculator2.txtInput
End Sub

Public Sub MySquarer(MyOtherNumber As Double)
    dblResult = MyOtherNumber * MyOtherNumber
    MsgBox dblResult, vbInformation, _
        "Programming Microsoft Access 2000"
```

```
'Optional statements illustrating the use of methods
'    DoCmd.GoToControl "txtInput"
'    txtInput.SetFocus
'    DoCmd.Close acForm, "frmCalculator2", acSaveNo
End Sub
```

The *cmdSquarer_Click* event procedure invokes the *MySquarer* procedure and passes the contents of *txtInput* as an argument. *MySquarer* computes its result and then displays the result in a message box.

Three more comment lines suggest additional actions that you can perform. A line calling the *GoToControl* method shows how to move the focus from the button to the text box. The *SetFocus* example on the next line illustrates an alternative way to achieve the same result. The *Close* method shows how to close a form. Notice that this line uses yet another name, *frmCalculator2*, to refer to the form. Using the *acSaveNo* constant is important because it allows the form to close without a prompt asking whether to save the form.

Property Procedures

You use property procedures to define custom properties for forms, reports, and class modules. We will discuss class modules in the next section, and we will look at samples of property procedures in Chapter 7.

There are three types of property statements: *Property Get*, *Property Let*, and *Property Set*. You can use these statements to add special properties to forms. The *Property Get* statement and its matching *End Property* statement can return a value, just like a function procedure. If you define a property with only a *Property Get* statement, that property is read-only. A read-only property is convenient when you have the right to view a quantity but not to alter it—think of your 401K balance or your grades.

With some properties, it is important to be able to change them without being able to read them. For example, database security administrators do not necessarily need to be able to read the user passwords that they supervise. They only need to be able to write over them when users forget their password. Use the *Property Let* statement with its matching *End Property* statement to set a password.

The *Property Set* statement works similarly to the *Property Let* statement. Both create a setting for a property. The *Property Let* statement sets a property equal to a data type, such as a string or integer. The *Property Set* statement sets a property equal to an object reference. You use the *Property Set* statement with object references, such as references to a form or a report.

Since many properties are both read and write, you will frequently use both *Property Get* and either *Property Let* or *Property Set*. In this case, the pair of *Property* statements must have the same name so that they refer to the same property.

Modules

A module is a container for procedures and declarations such as *Option Explicit* and *Dim*. There are two basic kinds of modules. First, there are standard modules. These are listed under Modules in the Database window. The procedures in a standard module are independent of existing objects in an Access database file. This means there are no references to *Me* or control names without appropriate prefixes for the controls. However, your applications can reference procedures in standard modules readily from any other object.

The second kind of module is a class module. There are three basic varieties of these: form class modules, report class modules, and custom class modules. The procedures within a module are generally accessible to other modules. You can take a procedure out of this general scope by using the *Private* keyword when you initially specify the procedure. (See Figure 1-7 for sample syntax.) You can also explicitly declare procedures to have global scope by using the *Public* keyword.

A form module is the module for any form that has at least one declaration or procedure. Creating an event procedure for a form or a control on a form creates a form class module. Report class modules work about the same as form class modules, but the *Report* events are different from those for forms and you are unlikely to have the same mix of controls on a report as a form. You can create custom class modules that comprise method functions and procedure functions for a concept, such as an employee or an account. You can reference the methods and properties for custom class modules much as you do for built-in Access classes.

You use custom class modules like cookie cutters to make new instances of a class. Access offers two ways to accomplish this. First, you can use a single *Dim* statement to both declare the class and create a new instance of it. The syntax for this type of statement is

```
Dim objInstance As New objClass
```

The second approach relies on a pair of statements. The first member of the pair declares the object instance. The second member sets a reference to the object. The syntax for these statements is

```
Dim objInstance as objClass
Set objInstance = New objClass
```

The *objClass* name refers to a class module populated with property procedures and public method functions. These method functions act as methods for the class just as the property procedures serve to define properties. Chapter 7 shows how to create and use custom class modules.

THE VBE INTERFACE

Perhaps the most noticeable change to the Access development environment is the new VBE interface. This interface brings Access 2000 more in line with Microsoft Word, Excel, and PowerPoint from a development interface perspective. This section will explore the use and layout of the windows and show how to use them for debugging. It will also review the use of the Object Browser.

VBE Windows

Access 2000 offers at least three routes to VBE for modules that are not behind a form or a report. First, those familiar with development in other Office components can choose Tools-Macro-Visual Basic Editor from the Database window. A convenient shortcut for this is Alt+F11. This takes you immediately to VBE. You can use Alt+F11 to toggle back and forth between the Database window and VBE. Second, if you already have any standard modules, click the Modules button in the Database window and then double-click any standard module that you want to view. This opens VBE with that module displayed. Third, if you want to create a new standard module, click the Modules button in the Database window and then click New on the toolbar. This opens a blank module in VBE.

> **NOTE**   The Office development team is working on a fourth route to VBE that will be familiar to some Access developers. You will be able to click a Code button in the Database window with a standard module, form, or report selected. The Code button will open VBE with the corresponding module.

To get to the module behind a form or a report, you must first open the object in Design view. You can click the Code button on the Design toolbar. This opens the module and positions your display at the top of the module. You can move directly to the event procedure for a specific object on a form or a report by clicking the Build button next to the event in the property sheet. If there is no event procedure for an object, clicking the Build button and choosing Code Builder will move you to a blank event procedure for the object.

Once you navigate to VBE, you'll probably want to open the Project and Properties windows. These are convenient for opening and inspecting the other modules in an application. The Project window displays modules that are not behind a form or a report in the Modules folder. Modules behind forms and reports appear in the Microsoft Access Class Objects folder. You can select a folder associated with a form or a report to view and set the objects associated with the class. To open the Project or Properties window, choose the appropriate command from the View menu or use the keyboard and toolbar shortcuts.

> **NOTE** In order for the Properties window to show the objects for an Access class object, that object must be open in Design view. Double-clicking a module or a class in the Project window displays the corresponding instructions and declarations in the corresponding Code window, but the objects appear only if the class object is also open in Design view.

Figure 1-7 shows the code for this chapter's sample database loaded into VBE. The Project window shows the *Form_frmSample1* class selected. Below it, the Properties window shows the label control for the form's title selected. This window also shows that the label control has an event procedure associated with its *OnClick* event. The Code window to the right of the Project and Properties windows shows the code for this event procedure. You can move, resize, and dock any of these windows.

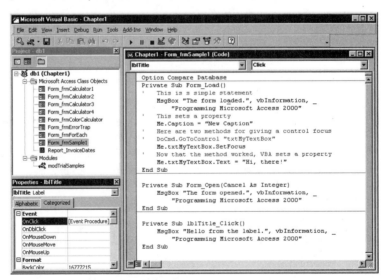

Figure 1-7. *VBE's Project, Properties, and Code windows showing the code for this chapter's sample database.*

Double-clicking any other Access class or *Module* object in the Project window opens the corresponding Code window. There you can inspect, edit, or copy the code. The Code window has a familiar layout, with Object and Procedure drop-down list boxes at the top. You can use these to navigate around a large module or open new procedures in an existing one. The Properties window shows the properties for the currently selected Access class or module. While you can edit object properties in this window, it is usually more convenient and flexible to edit object properties for a form or a report in Design view.

Debugging

You can use the Code window to debug and examine your code. You can add or remove a breakpoint on a statement by clicking the margin to the left of the statement. VBE marks the breakpoint with the traditional round dot in the left margin. Figure 1-8 shows the debugger stopped on the second of four lines of code in a procedure; the arrow in the left margin indicates the next line of code that will execute.

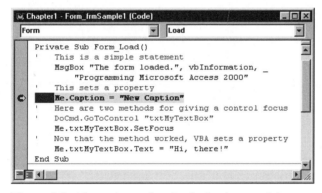

Figure 1-8. *The Code window for the load event of the* Form_frmSample1 *class at a breakpoint, with an arrow pointing to the next line that will execute.*

You choose Continue from the Run menu to restart code execution after a breakpoint. Figure 1-9 on the next page shows the result of executing the rest of the code in the *Form_frmSample1* procedure. Notice that the form's caption reads, "New Caption." The text box reads, "Hi, there!"

You can use the arrow shown in Figure 1-8 to skip over one or more lines of code in the execution path. For example, Figure 1-10 on the next page shows the result of dragging the arrow to the line that invokes the *SetFocus* method and choosing the Continue command from the Run menu. This procedure skips over the assignment of "New Caption" to the form's *Caption* property, so the form looks almost the same as in Figure 1-9 but its caption reads, "My Default Caption."

Figure 1-11 shows the result of dragging the arrow in Figure 1-8 to the final line of code that makes an assignment to the text box. This, of course, generates an error message because of the attempt to assign a property value without the object having focus.

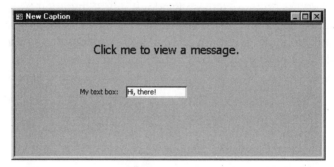

Figure 1-9. *The outcome of running all three remaining lines in Figure 1-8.*

Figure 1-10. *The outcome of skipping over the second remaining line in Figure 1-8 and continuing execution.*

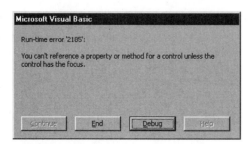

Figure 1-11. *The outcome of skipping to the last line in Figure 1-8 and continuing execution.*

Much of the functionality of the Microsoft Access 97 Debug window is available in Access 2000. The Debug window in Access 97 had a Watch page and a Locals page; each had a split screen in which the Immediate window was available as .part of the page. Access 2000 has separate Watch, Locals, and Immediate windows. You open these windows in VBE by using the View menu. You can drag, drop, and resize any of these windows alongside your Code, Project, and Properties windows. Choose Tools-Options and use the Docking page to designate which windows are dockable.

You can use the Watch window to track the values of expressions, variables, and objects as your code executes. After opening a Watch window, you can add variables to watch by choosing Debug-Add Watch. Select a variable to watch before invoking the command. When the Add Watch dialog box opens, select a Watch type and then click OK to close the dialog box. The value of the variable is shown in the Watch window as your code executes. If you step through your code in break mode, you can verify the value of critical variables after each step.

Figure 1-12 shows the value of *frmSample1*'s *Caption* property immediately after a line of code changes it from "My Default Value" to "New Caption." The Watch window shows the value of *txtMyTextBox* as Null since the code has not yet executed its assignment statement.

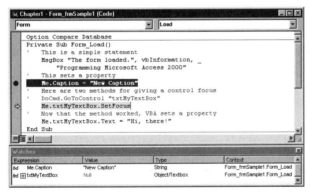

Figure 1-12. *A Watch window showing the status of expressions as an event procedure executes.*

The Locals window can display all the variables in scope while your code executes in break mode. When execution stops on a breakpoint, the Locals window contains a *Me* object. You can successively expand *Me* and its selected components to search out the values of all properties and variables. This can be helpful if you require exhaustive detail to help you determine how a program performs.

The Immediate window might be the most convenient tool for code development and debugging. From this window, you can run any function or subroutine that is in scope. You can also evaluate expressions and different ways of writing functions. Before the availability of Watch expressions, the Immediate window was a convenient place to print intermediate results in break mode, and it can still serve related functions in special circumstances.

Figure 1-13 shows three uses of the Immediate window. Our initial discussion of procedures described these functions, but it did not show their output to the Immediate window. Typing *MyFirstCalculator* invokes the procedure of the same name. When you press Enter in the Immediate window, it runs the procedure and prints the result, *3*, in the window. The same is true for the *CallSecondCalculator* procedure. In this case, the result is *4*. The last sample demonstrates how to specify arguments for the *MySecondCalculator* function—you just type the name, a space, and the arguments separated by a comma. This sample is critical because it shows how to use the arguments passed to a procedure or function to calculate a return value.

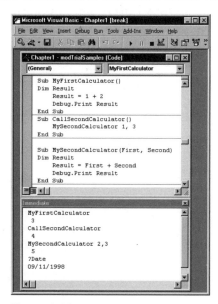

Figure 1-13. *The Immediate window showing how to run procedures and built-in functions.*

You can also use the Immediate window to run built-in and custom functions. With a function, you must specify a print command to return the result of the function. You can use the keyword *Print* or simply *?* followed by the function name and a carriage return. The last sample in the Immediate window shows how to call the built-in *Date* function.

The Object Browser

The Object Browser, shown in Figure 1-14, is a powerful tool for learning about object models. It is especially important to Access 2000 developers because of the many significant new object model innovations. For example, Access 2000 introduces a new data access development language—ActiveX Data Objects (ADO)—that will eventually make Data Access Objects (DAO) obsolete. At least three object models underlie the Access 2000 implementation of ADO.

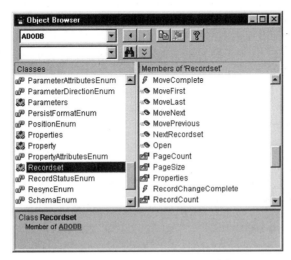

Figure 1-14. *The Object Browser view of the* ADODB Recordset *class and a select set of its members.*

Before viewing the ADO object classes in the Object Browser, you must set a reference to the appropriate library. Choose Tools-References to verify or create links to ADO type libraries. Open the Object Browser by clicking its button on VBE's Standard toolbar. You can also open it using the View menu or by pressing the F2 shortcut key. One of the ADO libraries has the name ADODB. Select this from the drop-down list at the top of the Object Browser. This changes the contents of the Classes list and the Members list in the browser. Figure 1-14 shows the *Recordset* class selected in the Classes list and a mix of properties, methods, and events appearing in the Members list. Select a member entry and click the ? button for detailed Help on that topic. The Object Browser can also search for specific classes and members with its search engine. Use the second drop-down list box to specify a search criterion. This sometimes returns result sets in several different libraries. The Object Browser lets you examine these separately.

JET, DATA TYPES, AND DECLARATIONS

You must specify data types in many places within Access, including variables within procedures and tables of stored data on a storage device. The following sections cover some development issues pertaining to data types from Jet 4 and the use of variables in procedures.

Jet

Access 2000 natively supports two database engines. Historically, Access was tied to the Jet database engine. Access 2000 introduces built-in database support for SQL Server 7. Access 2000 SQL Server compatibility is covered in Chapter 12. This section deals with the effects of Jet 4 innovations on Access 2000 application design. These innovations can affect the size of database files and record locking, how you work with selected field data types (including Memo, Hyperlink, and auto-incrementing key fields), and links to external data sources.

Access 2000 stores all text and memo data in Unicode format. This replaces the multi-byte character set (MBCS) format used in previous versions of Access for Japanese, Chinese, and selected other languages. Unicode is a subset of the ISO 10646 standard, which provides digital encoding for all written languages. This new standard requires 2 bytes, instead of the previous 1 byte, to represent a character. This can nearly double the size of databases that rely heavily on character-based fields. To offset this increase, Jet automatically compresses and decompresses these data types whenever possible. It compresses memo fields that are 4000 characters or less in length. Within a field, this can result in compression for some but not all rows in a memo data field. Both Access and ADO automatically compress Unicode characters, but DAO does not support compression for string data types. Developers who program in Jet SQL have available a WITH COMPRESSION clause for specifying tables.

In addition to the new format for character data types, the page size has doubled to 4 KB. This can lead to reduced concurrency due to more page-lock conflicts. Jet addresses this by offering single-row locking. You can minimize the concurrency issue by locking individual records instead of whole pages. Access 2000 lets users update two records on the same page concurrently.

NOTE The new page size increases the maximum database size from 1.07 GB to 2.14 GB.

Single-row locking is the overall default option, but users and developers can fall back to traditional page locking. Memo fields and indexes never support single-row locking. Data access via ADO or Jet SQL enables the optional fallback to page-level locking. Data access via Access forms and DAO is always via single-row locking.

While single-row locking is desirable for minimizing concurrency conflicts, it requires an overhead cost for setting and removing record locks. The impact of this overhead depends on record size relative to page size as well as the number of locks necessary for a task.

The transition to Unicode also enables Microsoft Windows NT–compatible sorting. This improves compatibility and performance because Access 2000 can deliver consistent sorting performance on both Microsoft Windows 95 and Windows NT systems. This is possible because Windows 95 supports sorting on just the default system language, while Windows NT supports correct sorting on multiple languages. In addition, Visual Basic 6 and SQL Server 7 support this same sorting standard, which provides cross-product standardization. Access 2000 sorting is 50 percent faster for most languages, but the increase in sorting speed is even greater for certain languages, such as Thai.

Jet 4 supports indexing for the first 255 characters of Memo data types. Prior versions of Access and Jet did not support any indexing for Memo fields. While the limited length of the index is not appropriate for all Memo field applications, it has special significance for the Hyperlink data type, which is a derivative of the Memo data type. The new indexing can enhance the sorting and searching of Hyperlink fields.

Jet 4 also enables developers to specify a start value and a step value for auto-incrementing fields. In addition, a new ALTER TABLE statement enables Jet SQL developers to reset both the start and step values. You use another new SELECT @@IDENTITY statement to recover the last value for the auto-incrementing column. You pass the SQL statement value along as the SQL text for the *Open* method of the *Recordset* object in an ADO statement. DAO does not support the new statement.

Jet 4 has enhanced installable ISAM technology in several areas, which can affect Access development opportunities with external data sources. The new Text/HTML ISAM lets you read Unicode-formatted web documents. The new Exchange ISAM offers enhancements in several areas. First, it reads indexes from Exchange Server. This dramatically speeds up searches for records in Exchange data sources. Second, the new ISAM supports the Windows Address Book for the Microsoft Outlook Express client. In smaller business environments in which the mail focus is external rather than internal, this offers significant benefits (if only in personal productivity). Third, Jet can retrieve custom-defined Outlook clients as well as those for the Outlook Exchange client. Users of dBase and Paradox databases can continue to enjoy read/write access to these databases through Jet 5. Those requiring support for a more recent version must obtain a copy of the Borland Database Engine from a third-party source.

Data Types

VBA regularly uses variables to save computed outcomes, set properties, designate arguments for methods, and pass values between procedures. To perform efficiently, VBA uses a set of data types for its variables. Several other Access tasks, such as defining tables and function arguments, use data types. This section focuses on data types for variables. Other data types are generally similar. Nevertheless, Access allows different data types for each task.

The following table lists the major types of variables and their storage requirements in VBA programs. Developers who need high levels of precision in their numerical computations can use the Decimal data type as a subtype of the Variant data type. Decimal data types are unsigned 12-byte integers scaled by a variable power of 10. You cannot declare a Decimal data type with a *Dim* statement, but you can store a Decimal data type by transforming a Variant with the *CDec* function. It is generally a good idea to use the smallest possible data type to leave the maximum amount of memory for other variables and application logic. However, when you need the precision for numerical computations, the Decimal data type is available.

VARIABLE DATA TYPES

Name	Number of Bytes	Range
Byte	1	0 through 255
Boolean	2	True or false
Integer	2	-32,768 through 32,767
Long	4	-2,147,483,648 through 2,147,483,647
Single	4	-3.402823E38 through -1.401298E-45 for negative values 1.40129E-45 through 3.402823E38 for positive values
Double	8	-1.79769313486232E308 through -14.94065645841247E-324 for negative values 4.94065645841247E-324 through 1.79769313486232E308 for positive values
Currency	8	-922,337,203,685,477.5808 through 922,337,203,685,477.5807
Date	8	January 1, 100 through December 31, 9999
Object	4	A reference to an object (see *Set* statement in the online help)
String (fixed)	Length	Up to approximately 64,000 characters
String (variable)	10 + length	Up to approximately 2 billion characters

Name	Number of Bytes	Range
Variant (with numbers)	16	Same as Double
Variant (with characters)	22 + length	Same as String (variable)
User-defined	Depends on elements	Sum of the constituent elements for the custom data type

When you fail to declare a variable as a specific type, Access assigns it the Variant data type. This data type is flexible because Variants can assume both numeric and string values. The Variant data type can hold all the other data types except user-defined types (which are a superset of all the other data types). When VBA performs an operation on two Variants, it must first retrieve the contents of the second Variant and convert the result to the data subtype of the first Variant. This makes processing Variants slower than processing other data types. In addition, the data subtype returned by the operation might be incorrect for your application.

You can use the *VarType* function to determine the data subtype of Variant. The *VarType* function takes a Variant data type and returns a VBA constant that indicates the subtype of the value in the Variant data type. For example, if *varMyVariable* contains "Hi, there!", *VarType(varMyVariable)* returns *vbString* (8). Similarly, if *varMyVariable* contains #1/1/2000#, *VarType(varMyVariable)* returns *vbDate* (7). Check the online documentation or the Object Browser for a complete list of the Variant subtype constants returned by the *VarType* function.

VBA conversion functions let you convert a Variant data type to a specific data subtype and they let you specify the type of result that you expect. For example, *CDbl(varMyVariable)* returns the contents of *varMyVariable* as the Double data type.

Despite its potential for error and its need for extra processing, Variant is a popular data type. The data in table, query, report, and form fields is Variant by default. If you leave a field in a table unspecified, the field returns a Null value when queried (assuming it has not been assigned data), which is one of two special Variant data values. A Null indicates missing, unknown, or inapplicable data. You use the *IsNull* function in VBA to test for Null values, and you use the *Is Null* operator in query criterion statements to do the same for a field. Be careful how you process variables with Null values because Nulls propagate. Any combination of a variable that equals Null with any other variable always returns a Null.

NOTE Since only Variant data types can assume Null values, you must use this type when your application can benefit from it. Nulls avoid the need for arbitrary values for specifying missing data from a field or variable type.

The *Empty* keyword is used as a Variant subtype and represents an uninitialized variable value. You use the *IsEmpty* function in VBA to determine whether a variable has this value. Empty, Null, 0, and zero-length strings ("") are different from each other. When VBA transforms a Variant variable that is equal to Empty, it transforms the variable to either 0 or "" depending on whether a number or string is most appropriate.

When you need to call Windows API functions through dynamic link libraries (DLLs), you sometimes need a user-defined variable. You must declare user-defined variables between *Type* and *End Type* statements. The individual lines between these two statements should define the elements of a custom variable type. You can think of a book, for example, as a collection of elements, including an ISBN, a title, author(s), a publisher, and pages. You can specify this custom data type as follows:

```
Type Book
    ISBN as Long
    Title as String
    Authors as String
    Publisher as String
    Pages as Integer
End Type

Sub MyBook
Dim udvMyBook as Book
    udvMyBook.ISBN = 1234567890
    udvMyBook.Title = "Programming Microsoft Access 2000"
    udvMyBook.Authors = "Rick Dobson"
    udvMyBook.Publisher = "Microsoft Press"
    udvMyBook.Pages = 550
End Sub
```

You insert the *Type...End Type* statement pair in the general declarations area of a module. The procedure *MyBook* creates an instance of the Book user-defined variable.

Declarations

Variables and constants can be declared. (A *constant* is a special variable whose value cannot be changed after it's set using a *Constant* statement.) A declaration serves two roles: It designates the variable's *scope* (the area within the application that can reference the variable), and it specifies a data type for the variable. These are good reasons for declaring variables before using them. You can require a variable declaration using the *Option Explicit* statement in the General area of a module.

You use the *Public* statement in a module's Declaration area to declare variables that your applications can use from any procedure within the application, including other modules. You can use the *Private* statement to explicitly define a variable as having local scope within a module. (This is not strictly required because the *Dim* and *Static* statements declare variables that are private to a module by default.)

The *Dim* statement reserves memory for a variable only until the procedure in which the variable is declared ends. This means that variables declared using a *Dim* statement lose their value from one call of the procedure to the next. Variables declared using a *Static* statement are preserved for the life of the module or until an application resets or restarts the module. (One use for static variable declarations is for running sums or determining the number of times that a procedure is called.)

> **NOTE** You can clear the values from the static variables in a procedure by choosing Reset from the Run menu in VBE.

You can use the *Static* keyword in function and procedure declarations as well as in variable declarations. This keyword works identically for functions and procedures; it preserves all the local variables in the function or procedure for the life of the module.

You use the *As* keyword with either the *Dim* or *Static* statement to specify a data type for a variable. The statement *Dim intMyNumber As Integer* declares the *intMyNumber* variable to be an integer data type.

Arrays

Access permits you to declare *arrays*. Arrays are variables that contain lists of values of the same type. An array can be multidimensional, up to as many as 60 dimensions. For example, the statement *Dim aryScores(2, 1) As Integer* reserves a two-dimensional array of six elements: three rows and two columns of integers.

By default, arrays are zero-based. The statement *Dim aryMyName(1)* has two elements, which your code can reference as *aryMyName(0)* and *aryMyName(1)*. You use the *Option Base 1* statement in the Declarations area to designate an array as one-based. The following procedure declares an array of two elements, defines its values, and prints its elements and the sum of those elements to the Immediate window.

```
Sub ArrayTest()
Dim aryMyExpenses(1) As Currency, Total As Currency
    aryMyExpenses(0) = 10.5
    aryMyExpenses(1) = 22.25
```

(continued)

```
      Total = aryMyExpenses(0) + aryMyExpenses(1)
      Debug.Print aryMyExpenses(0) & " + " & aryMyExpenses(1) _
         & " = " & Total
End Sub
```

The *aryMyExpenses* array contains two elements of the Currency data type. Because the Currency data type is 8 bytes, the *aryMyExpenses* array is a total of 16 bytes. Since you can use arrays with many dimensions and variable-length strings, arrays can rapidly consume large blocks of memory.

You use the *Dim*, *Static*, *Public*, and *Private* keywords as you do with scalar variables to define the scope of an array. You use the *ReDim* keyword to dynamically change the dimensions of a multidimensional array.

CONDITIONAL LOGIC AND LOOPING CONSTRUCTS

Conditional code execution and looping are at the heart of many code-based solutions. VBA offers a rich choice of options for implementing this kind of logic. The following sections review the major statement types that enable conditional program execution and looping and provide practical examples.

If...Then

Many procedures cannot achieve their objective by progressing sequentially through lines of code. It is often desirable to execute code conditionally—to skip some lines and perform others. One flexible and robust way to achieve conditional execution in VBA procedures is with the *If...Then* statement. There are actually three major variations of this basic statement. The first variation conditionally performs a simple block of code. The syntax is

```
If condition Then
    'Statements
End If
```

One or more statements can reside within an *If...End If* block. The terminating *End If* marks the end of the block. VBA executes the statements within the block only when the condition evaluates to *True*. You can nest multiple *If...End If* blocks within one another.

A second variation of the *If...Then* statement enables your code to execute either of two blocks of code. It has this syntax:

```
If condition Then
    Statements1
Else
    Statements2
End If
```

This form of the statement executes one of two blocks of code. When the condition is true, the statements in the first group execute. Otherwise, the statements in the second block execute.

While this design is more flexible than the first format, it's still limiting because you have only two options. You can, in fact, nest *If...Then* statements to enable more options, but VBA offers a third design that simplifies execution of any one of three or more statement blocks. The syntax is

```
If condition1 Then
    'Statements
ElseIf condition2 Then
    'Statements
Else
    'Statements
End If
```

This form of the *If...Then* statement incorporates multiple conditions and three or more groups of statements. You can easily add new statement groups and conditions by inserting new *ElseIf* clauses with their own conditions and statements. This design is more powerful than the second variation not only because it can accommodate more conditions but because it restricts the execution of each statement block (except the last) to the case in which there is a precise match to a condition test. The second *If...Then* statement executes its second statement block whenever the condition for the first statement block is not true. When failing a match to the first condition does not automatically serve as a basis for executing the second statement block, you need the third style of the *If...Then* statement.

Consider the form shown in Figure 1-15. The form includes a text box, an option group, and a command button. The option group allows a user to designate a square or a cube operation on the numerical value in the text box. To compute the square of a number, you type the number in the text box, select Square It in the Compute Type option group, and then click Compute.

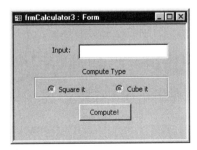

Figure 1-15. *A form for calculating squares or cubes of numbers.*

The following code shows the two procedures that make this squaring operation possible. The *cmdComputer_Click* event procedure responds to the click. If the option group *(opgComputeType)* equals 1, the user selected the Square It option button. The procedure calls *MySquarer* when the option group equals 1. Otherwise, it ends without performing any computations.

```
Sub cmdComputer_Click()
    If opgComputeType = 1 Then
        MySquarer txtInput.Value
    End If
End Sub

Sub MySquarer(MyOtherNumber As Double)
    dblResult = MyOtherNumber * MyOtherNumber
    MsgBox dblResult, vbInformation, _
        "Programming Microsoft Access 2000"
End Sub
```

This *cmdComputer_Click* procedure uses the first *If...Then* structure. It merely conditionally executes a single statement block. In this case, the block consists of just one line. If the user selects Square It, *MySquarer* multiplies the text box's value by itself and presents the result in a message box.

If the user selects Cube It before clicking the command button, the code does nothing. The option group returns a value of 2, but there is no condition to detect this. In fact, it is all or nothing when the option group equals 1. The following code shows a new version of the event procedure along with the code to handle the situation in which the user does not select Square It.

```
Sub cmdComputer_Click()
    If opgComputeType = 1 Then
        MySquarer txtInput.Value
    Else
        MyCuber txtInput.Value
    End If
End Sub

Sub MyCuber(MyOtherNumber As Double)
Dim dblResult As Double
    dblResult = MyOtherNumber ^ 3
    MsgBox dblResult, vbInformation, _
        "Programming Microsoft Access 2000"
End Sub
```

The *cmdComputer_Click* procedure uses the second form of the *If...Then* statement. It calls *MySquarer* if *opgComputeType* equals 1 but otherwise calls *MyCuber*. This works correctly if the user selects Cube It. However, at least one problem remains: The form opens with neither option button selected. If a user enters a number in the text box and then clicks the command button, the form returns the cubed value of the number despite the fact that the user selected neither option button. The fault lies in the design of the *If...Then* statement. We need the third variation with two separate conditions—one for squaring and the other for cubing. The following code shows this design:

```
Sub cmdComputer_Click()
    If opgComputeType = 1 Then
        MySquarer txtInput.Value
    ElseIf opgComputeType = 2 Then
        MyCuber txtInput.Value
    Else
        MsgBox "Click a computation type", _
            vbCritical, _
            "Programming Microsoft Access 2000"
    End If
End Sub
```

This sample includes two conditions. One tests whether the option group equals 1, and the other tests whether the option group equals 2. If the option group fails both tests, the procedure displays a message box reminding the user to click a computation type. If you add new option buttons to the option group for different computations, you can easily accommodate them. Just insert a new *ElseIf* clause with a special condition for each new button.

As you can see, the *If...Then* statement is very flexible. You can use it to handle many possible options, but it handles one or two items even more easily. Its syntax also changes slightly depending on what you are trying to accomplish.

Select Case

The *Select Case* statement does one thing: It evaluates an expression and conditionally executes one block of statements. When you work with more than one or two conditional options, the *Select Case* statement can be simpler to set up and easier to maintain than the *If...Then* statement. The general syntax for *Select Case* is

```
Select Case test expression
    Case expression list-1
        'Statements
    Case expression list-2
        'Statements
    Case Else
        'Statements
End Select
```

Notice that *Select Case* evaluates an initial test expression. This can be as simple as a passed parameter or as complicated as a rocket science expression. *expression list-1* and *expression list-2* are ranges (or specific values) for the test expression. Some options for specifying expression lists include constants, delimited items in a series, or expressions that evaluate to *True* or *False*. When an expression list is true because it matches the test expression, the corresponding block of statements execute. The syntax sample above shows just two lists, but you can add more by inserting additional *Case* statements. The *Case Else* clause is optional, but it is good programming practice. This option captures any test expression values not trapped by the preceding *Case* clauses. You can nest *Select Case* statements within each other; each instance must start with *Select Case* and terminate with *End Select*.

Figure 1-16 shows a *Select Case* statement used in a function procedure. This procedure can perform one of four numerical operations on a pair of numbers passed to it. A string argument specifies the operation, and the Immediate window shows the result of the operation. As you can see from the Immediate window, the expression list tests are not case sensitive.

A misspelled operation causes the *Case Else* clause to operate. In this situation, the function prints a message in the Immediate window announcing that the operation is not valid.

Figure 1-16. *A function procedure and output illustrating the use of the* Select Case *statement.*

For...Next

The *For...Next* statement is most obviously used for looping through a block of statements a known number of times. Since you can conditionally branch out of this kind of loop with an *Exit For* statement, you can also use the *For...Next* statement when you are not sure how many times to run before stopping. However, you must specify a maximum number of loops. The general syntax for the statement is

```
For counter = start To stop Step step
    'Statements
    If condition Then
        Exit For
    End If
    'Statements
Next counter
```

The *For* loop extends from the *For counter* line to the *Next counter* line. The *For...Next* statement initializes *counter* to the value of *start* and then executes the statements between *For* and *Next*. The flow of execution then returns to the top of the *For* loop, where *counter* is incremented by the optional *step*. (*counter* is incremented by 1 if *step* is not specified.)

The statements in the *For* loop are executed repeatedly until the value of *counter* exceeds *stop* (or when *counter* is less than *stop* if *step* is a negative number). Control then passes to the statement immediately following the *Next counter* statement. The optional *Exit For* statement causes the *For* loop to terminate prior to *counter* exceeding *stop*.

You can nest *For...Next* statements within one another. An inner loop passes control to an outer one when *counter* exceeds *stop*. VBA can generate a run-time error if it encounters a *Next* statement without a matching *For* statement, but you are likely to get a syntax error as you design your procedures.

The *CountFor* procedure (see below) applies *For...Next* logic while reinforcing techniques for working with arrays and *Static* declarations. (The array *aryMyArray* has five elements. Recall that array indexing begins with 0 unless your code explicitly specifies otherwise.) Next, the code declares an *Integer* variable to serve as a counter. The *For...Next* statement successively assigns the values 1–5 to the counter variable, *intIndex*.

Two statements execute for each pass through the loop. First the value of an element in *aryMyArray* accumulates the current value of *intIndex* to its current value. Since the code declares *aryMyArray* with a *Static* statement, the array elements retain their values on successive runs through the procedure.

After the first pass through the procedure, the array elements are the successive values of *intIndex*. After the second pass through the procedure, *aryMyArray* elements are twice the successive values of *intIndex*—and so on for each successive pass through the procedure. The second statement prints the current value of *intIndex* and the associated element of the array. Recall that you can reinitialize the value of the array elements to 0 by choosing Run-Reset from the VBE Run menu.

```
Sub CountFor()
Static aryMyArray(4) As Integer
Dim intIndex As Integer
    For intIndex = 1 To 5
        aryMyArray(intIndex - 1) = _
            aryMyArray(intIndex - 1) + intIndex
        Debug.Print intIndex, aryMyArray(intIndex - 1)
    Next intIndex
    Debug.Print vbLf
End Sub
```

Figure 1-17 shows Immediate window output for three successive runs through the procedure. The first column shows the successive values of *intIndex*, and the second column shows the corresponding values of the array elements. On the first run through the procedure, the array elements exactly match *intIndex*. On the second and third passes, the array element values are twice and three times the *intIndex* values. This accumulating outcome shows the impact of a *Static* variable declaration. The values of *intIndex* and *aryMyArray* exactly match each other on all passes through the procedure if you change the *Static* keyword in the *aryMyArray* declaration to *Dim*.

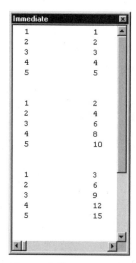

Figure 1-17. *The Immediate window showing the result of running the* CountFor *procedure three successive times.*

For Each...Next and *With...End With*

The *For Each...Next* and *With...End With* statements can work together nicely for form data validation and classic enumeration tasks. *For Each...Next* iterates through any collection (such as the controls on a form) or array. It does not require that your application know the number of elements in the collection or array. The *With...End With* statement can complement *For Each...Next* by simplifying how you code multiple controls in a statement block.

The *For Each...Next* statement is both similar to and slightly less complicated than the *For...Next* statement. It is similar to *For...Next* in that its loop starts with a line that begins with *For* and ends with a line that begins with *Next*. However, the design of the *For* and *Next* lines are different for both versions of the *For* loop. The *For Each...Next* statement is less complicated than the *For...Next* statement because you do not have to track three separate parameters (*counter*, *start*, and *stop*) or worry about a positive or negative *step* value. The *For Each...Next* statement always starts at the beginning and loops forward until it reaches the end of a collection or the elements in an array. The general syntax for the statement is

```
For Each element In group
    'Statements
    If condition Then
        Exit For
    End If
    'Statements
Next element
```

The *group* term in the first line of the *For Each...Next* statement refers to the collection or the array name. The *element* in both the first and last lines designates individual objects in a collection or elements in an array.

The *For Each...Next* statement repetitively executes the statements in its body for each element in the specified collection or array. You will often want an *Exit For* or other conditionally executed statement somewhere in the body of the *For* loop. This enables your code to respond dynamically to a special outcome in its environment. The condition test identifies this special outcome, and the *Exit For* or other conditionally executed statements engage only when the outcome occurs.

As with the *For...Next* statement, *For Each...Next* statements can nest inside one another. At the conclusion of a *For Each...Next* loop, control passes to the first statement following the loop.

The *With...End With* statement simplifies the referencing of several different properties or methods of the same object. You specify the object whose properties or methods you want to reference in the beginning *With* line, and you close the reference to that object with the *End With* line at the end of the block. Between the *With* and the *End With* lines you can access the object's properties or methods without specifying the object name. The following code shows the general syntax of the *With...End With* statement:

```
With object
    .propertyname1 = "new value1"
    .propertyname2 = "new value 2"
    .method1
    .method2
End With
```

object is the name of an object, a reference to an object, or an array name. *propertyname1* and *propertyname2* are properties of the object, and *method1* and *method2* are methods of the object. As you can see, the *With...End With* statement facilitates access to an object's properties and methods.

Figures 1-18, 1-19, and 1-20 show a data validation form in action. Although the form has only a pair of text boxes that require validation, the form's code uses a *For Each...Next* loop that can be expanded to accommodate more text box controls. You can make a slight change to include other types of controls in the validation procedure. Figure 1-18 shows the layout of the basic Input form with a pair of text boxes and a command button.

Clicking the Do It! command button invokes an event procedure that checks the text boxes to make sure they do not contain Nulls. If either control contains a Null, the event procedure displays a message box reminding the user to enter information in both text boxes.

The event procedure also calls a procedure that changes the background of each text box that contains a Null from white to yellow. The procedure also moves the focus to the last text box that contains a Null. The background stays yellow until the user updates the data in the text box.

Figure 1-19 shows a text box that contained a Null but now contains 1. The background of the text box changes back to white as soon as the user enters some information and moves the focus off the text box. Figure 1-20 shows the form after the new value updates the text box's value.

The following pair of procedures—named *cmdSubmit_Click* and *MarkFieldsToEdit*—examines the text boxes and yellow-highlights any text box that contains a Null. The *Click* event procedure for the command button loops through all the controls on the form. This includes text box as well as non–text box controls. The event procedure uses a *TypeOf* keyword to detect which control is a text box. Failure to take this measure can result in a run-time error because not all controls have a *Value* property. If the event procedure detects a text box control, it queries the control's *Value* property to determine whether it contains a Null. Any control with a Null triggers the code inside the *If...Then* statement. This code displays the message box and calls the procedure to highlight the control with the missing entry.

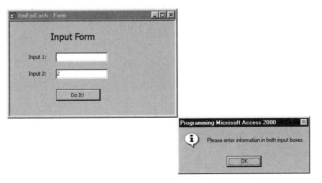

Figure 1-18. *The result of clicking the Do It! command button when at least one text box contains a Null.*

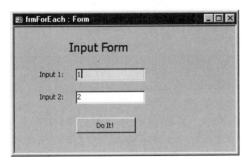

Figure 1-19. *A yellow-highlighted text box that contained a Null but now contains 1.*

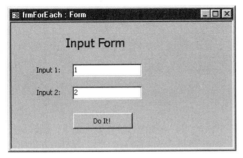

Figure 1-20. *After the user enters information and moves the focus, the text box's background color is reset to white.*

```
Private Sub cmdSubmit_Click()
'Check for valid entries.
    For Each ctl In Screen.ActiveForm.Controls
        If TypeOf ctl Is TextBox Then
            If IsNull(ctl.Value) Then
                MsgBox "Please enter information " _
                    & "in both input boxes.", _
                    vbInformation, _
                    "Programming Microsoft Access 2000"
                MarkFieldsToEdit
                Exit For
            End If
        End If
    Next ctl
End Sub

Public Sub MarkFieldsToEdit()
    For Each ctl In Screen.ActiveForm.Controls
        If TypeOf ctl Is TextBox Then
            If IsNull(ctl.Value) Then
                With ctl
                    .BackColor = RGB(255, 255, 0)
                    .SetFocus
                End With
            End If
        End If
    Next ctl
End Sub
```

The *MarkFieldsToEdit* procedure also uses the *TypeOf* keyword to identify text boxes. When it detects a text box that contains a Null, it uses a *With...End With* statement to change the control's background color and moves the focus to the control. This ensures that the last text box that contains Null has the focus at the end of the procedure.

Each of the event procedures in the code below fires on the *AfterUpdate* event. Each procedure uses a *With...End With* block to change the associated control's background color back to white if the background color is currently yellow. The *AfterUpdate* event occurs independently for both text boxes, but the code in each procedure is identical except for the name of the associated object (either *txtInput1* or *txtInput2*).

```
Private Sub txtInput1_AfterUpdate()
    With txtInput1
        If .BackColor = RGB(255, 255, 0) Then
            .BackColor = RGB(255, 255, 255)
        End If
    End With
End Sub
```

```
Private Sub txtInput2_AfterUpdate()
    With txtInput2
        If .BackColor = RGB(255, 255, 0) Then
            .BackColor = RGB(255, 255, 255)
        End If
    End With
End Sub
```

Do...Loop

The *Do...Loop* statement is yet another variety of looping statement available with VBA. The *Do...Loop* statement is a more flexible alternative to the *While...Wend* statement—it has all the functionality of the *While...Wend* statement and more. VBA retains *While...Wend* for backward compatibility.

You can use a *Do* loop to repeatedly execute a group of statements until a condition evaluates to either *True* or *False*. The *Do...Loop* statement syntax explicitly supports performing its test of a condition either before executing a block of statements or immediately after executing the block. As with the other looping statements, there is also a special statement for exiting a block in the midst of its execution. The two variations of syntax for the *Do...Loop* statement are as follows:

```
Do {While | Until} condition
    'Statements
    If condition Then
        Exit Do
    End If
    'Statements
Loop
```

And:

```
Do
    'Statements
    If condition Then
        Exit Do
    End If
    'Statements
Loop {While | Until} condition
```

The first variation performs its condition evaluation before executing the statements in the loop. The other format evaluates the condition immediately after executing the statements. The condition test can use either a *While* keyword or an *Until* keyword. The *While* keyword causes the loop to continue executing as long as the condition is true; the *Until* keyword causes the loop to continue executing as long as the condition is false. Most experienced Access developers have written many *Do* loops for navigating through the records in a recordset until the detection of an EOF (end of file) or a BOF (beginning of file). As with the other VBA looping statements, you can exit *Do* loops in the middle of a statement block by using an *Exit Do* statement.

Figure 1-21 shows a pair of function procedures and their output to illustrate how to program *Do* loops. The *DaysToNextMonth* function accepts a date and returns the number of days from that date to the first of the next month. If you enter the current date, the procedure counts it as one of the days to the beginning of the next month. For example, there are two days (2/28/2000 and 2/29/2000) from 2/28/2000 to the first day of the next month. The function starts by computing *dtmNextMonth*, which is the input date plus one month. (In this sample in Figure 1-21, the date is 3/28/2000.) The procedure then sets the function's name, which serves as a counter variable, equal to 0. The third line launches a *Do* loop with a condition that tests for the inequality of the next month vs. the input date plus the quantity in the function's name. As long as they are unequal, the loop executes its block, which consists of one statement that increments the function's value by 1.

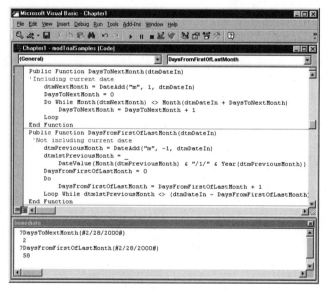

Figure 1-21. *A pair of function procedures that use condition tests at the beginning and end of a Do loop.*

The *DaysFromFirstOfLastMonth* function shows the effect of a condition test at the end of a *Do* loop. The output shows the number of days from 2/28/2000 to the first day of the previous month (1/1/2000). This equals 58 days, based on the 28 days in February and the last 30 days in January. This function begins by computing the previous month for the specified date. The function then passes that month to the *DateValue* function to determine the first day of that previous month. Just before starting the *Do* loop, the code sets *DaysFromFirstOfLastMonth* to 0. The code enters the loop without a condition test and increments *DaysFromFirstOfLastMonth* by 1. The condition test on the *Loop* line permits another pass through the loop as long as the input date minus *DaysFromFirstOfLastMonth* is less than the first of the previous month. In this way, the function counts 58 days from the input date to, but not including, the previous month's first day.

BUILT-IN FUNCTIONS

As many of the previous samples demonstrate, Access 2000 has a rich library of built-in functions. They can help you speed up development of custom solutions by minimizing and simplifying the original custom code you need to prepare. You can use the built-in functions in the same manner that you use your own custom ones, in procedures, queries, forms, and reports. By familiarizing yourself with the potential uses for built-in functions, you can discover new and innovative ways to apply your own custom functions.

This section includes three samples that use built-in functions: one for a query, one for a form, and one for a report. You can, and probably will, merge all three approaches in your applications. The third example shows how to make a control on a report act as a source for VBA code in a report module by using built-in functions. All three samples work with a small invoice table and demonstrate ways to report on invoices that are past due.

Figure 1-22 shows the original *InvoiceDates* table on the left and a query showing a view of the table on the right. The query selects 2 of the 10 rows in the *InvoiceDates* table and computes a new column called *Past Due Days*. (The date of the screen shot is 9/12/98.)

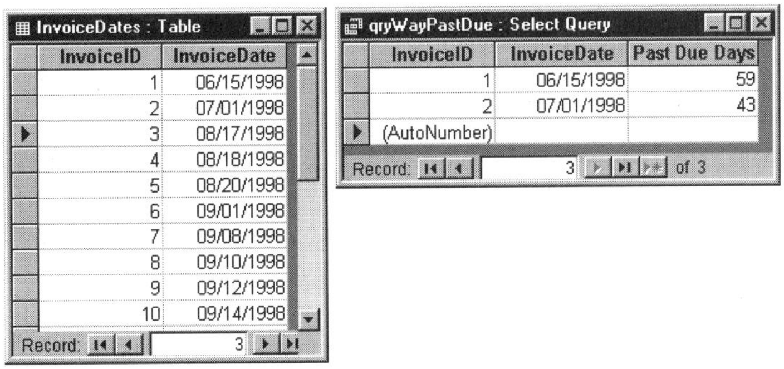

InvoiceDates : Table

InvoiceID	InvoiceDate
1	06/15/1998
2	07/01/1998
3	08/17/1998
4	08/18/1998
5	08/20/1998
6	09/01/1998
7	09/08/1998
8	09/10/1998
9	09/12/1998
10	09/14/1998

Record: 3

qryWayPastDue : Select Query

InvoiceID	InvoiceDate	Past Due Days
1	06/15/1998	59
2	07/01/1998	43
(AutoNumber)		

Record: 3 of 3

Figure 1-22. *An* InvoiceDates *table and the results of a query that selects rows and computes new fields with built-in functions.*

You can find the current date using one of two built-in functions: the *Date* function and the *Now* function. (The return value of the *Now* function also includes the current time. If you are working with dates only, it doesn't matter which one you use.)

The query includes both columns from the original *InvoiceDates* table. The criterion for the *InvoiceDate* column is *<Date()-30*. Since the current date at the time of the query is 9/12/98, any invoice from before 8/13/98 is past due. Therefore, the query returns the invoices from 7/01/98 and 6/15/98.

Past Due Days merit their own column. This computed field uses a pair of built-in date functions: *DateDiff* and *Now*. The *DateDiff* function is ideal for computing the difference between two dates. You can specify the difference in days, months, quarters, years, and various other units of time. The *DateDiff* function for the *Past Due Days* column returns the difference in days. The expression that calculates the field is *DateDiff("d", [InvoiceDate]+30,Now())*. This expression determines the current date using the *Now* function (although the *Date* function would work equally well). The term *[InvoiceDate]* refers to the table, which acts as a record source for the query. The *+30* designates the grace period during which an invoice is not considered late.

The query is a start for generating some useful business results, but it has a number of drawbacks. An obvious one is that Datasheet view does not tell you what the current date is. Therefore, you might wonder what the basis is for computing past due bills. The *frmPastDueEvaluator* form object in Figure 1-23 solves this problem by presenting the more user-friendly Form view of the data. In this view, three fields on the form provide the critical information. The *Invoice Date* field shows the creation date of the invoice. The next field shows the current date. The third field computes the number of days that an invoice is past due. This field displays a *0* if the invoice age is less than or equal to 30 days.

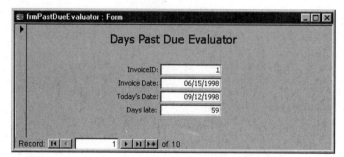

Figure 1-23. *A form for computing the days that invoices are past due.*

The last two fields on the form use built-in functions to compute their values. The *Today's Date* field uses *Date*. In this case, *Date* is better than *Now* because *Now* causes the date and time to show unless you explicitly format the field. If you set the field's *Control Source* property to *=Date()*, no formatting is necessary. The *Days Late* field uses an *IIF* (*Immediate If*) function. You write expressions with this function in a way that former spreadsheet developers will find very natural. For example, the expression for the last field on the form is *IIF(Date()-[txtInvoiceDate]>30,Date()-[txtInvoiceDate]-30,0)*. The expression has three arguments, like the spreadsheet *If* function. The first argument evaluates to *True* or *False*; it is a condition. If the condition is true, the *IIF* function returns the value of the second argument; if the condition is false, the *IIF* function returns the value of the third argument. Therefore, if the date in the text box with the invoice date, *txtInvoiceDate*, is more than 30 days before current date, the *IIF* function returns the number of days the invoice is beyond the 30-day grace period. Otherwise, the *IIF* function returns *0*.

The report in Figure 1-24 shows another approach to summarizing past due bills. The report includes three columns. The last column is a computed one that calculates the number of days an invoice is past due. For any given invoice row, this column is blank if the invoice is not past due. The report's header reminds the user of the report date so that the user knows what date defines the invoices as past due.

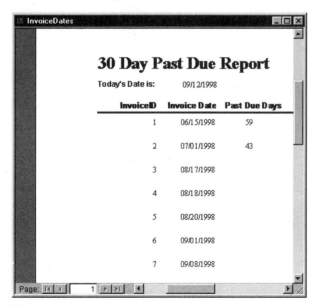

Figure 1-24. *A report that conditionally shows the number of days that an invoice is past due. If the invoice is less than or equal to 30 days old, the last column is blank.*

A formula is used to compute the last column in the report. You should be able to write the formula based on the previous two samples. What makes the report special is that the last column is sometimes blank. The *OnFormat* event procedure for the form's Detail section makes this possible by conditionally manipulating at run time the *Visible* property of the control for the report's last column. The event procedure logic is as follows:

```
Private Sub Detail_Format(Cancel As Integer, FormatCount As Integer)
Dim ctlD As Control
    For Each ctlD In Me.Detail.Controls
        If ctlD.Name = "txtPastDueDays" Then
            If ctlD.Value >= 0 Then
                ctlD.Visible = True
            Else
                ctlD.Visible = False
            End If
        End If
    Next ctlD
End Sub
```

The event procedure uses a *For Each...Next* statement to loop through the controls for each record, looking for the *txtPastDueDays* text box. This text box contains the number of days that an invoice is past due. If the quantity is positive, the invoice is past due and the code sets the control's *Visible* property to true. Otherwise, the invoice is not past due and the code sets the control's *Visible* property to false. These few lines of code generate the flexible report formatting at run time.

Summary of Selected Functions

Access 2000 has over 170 built-in functions that perform a broad range of tasks, including conversion between data types, date/time processing, statistical analysis of content in tables and queries, mathematics, and text processing. You can learn about the functions by first developing a general appreciation for what they do. This can save you from writing new code for a task when Microsoft has already written the code for you. Next, you can try to decipher how the functions complement one another. You can also learn the characteristics of the return values. For example, the *Hex* function returns a string representing the hexadecimal equivalent of a decimal number, and the *Oct* function performs a similar conversion to an octal representation. The output of both functions is suitable for string concatenation and comparisons but not for arithmetic operations.

You can also explore the impact of a function's optional arguments on the function's return value. Failure to understand these arguments can sometimes lead to misleading or confusing results. For example, the *StrComp* function compares two strings. The first two arguments are the strings to be compared. A third, optional argument specifies the type of comparison that is to be performed on the strings. You can specify a case-insensitive comparison, a case-sensitive comparison, or an alternative based on the New Database Sort Order option on the General page of the Access 2000 Options dialog box. If you do not specify this optional comparison, the function falls back to the comparison method specified by the *Option Compare* statement in a module's Declaration area. (If no method is specified, Access uses a binary comparison.)

The following table shows a selection of function categories and describes the purpose of selected functions in each category. There are more categories than those shown in the table, and there are generally more functions in each category. Any categorization is arbitrary since many functions can fit into more than one category. For example, the *DateSerial* function processes dates by returning date serial numbers based on non–date/time arguments, but it can also convert string dates to serial numbers. It therefore fits into both the date/time and conversion categories.

SELECTED FUNCTION CATEGORIES

Function Category	*Representative Functions*	*Purpose*
Conversion	*CDbl, CSng, CInt, CCur, CDec, Str, Val, Hex, Oct*	Determining the type of arithmetic an expression does and converting between data types
Date/time	*Date, Now, DateAdd, DatePart, DateDiff, Year, Month, Day, Hour, Minute, Second, Weekday, DateValue, DateSerial, MonthName, WeekdayName, FormatDateTime*	Expressing, computing with, and extracting date and time values from date serial numbers and string representations of dates and times
Domain aggregate	*DLookup, DCount, DSum, DAvg, DVar*	Computing statistical results, such as the count for a domain (such as a table or a query)
Error handling	*Error, CVErr, IsError*	Error trapping and custom error codes

(continued)

Selected Function Categories *continued*

Function Category	*Representative Functions*	*Purpose*
Inspection	*IsDate, IsTime, IsNumeric, IsNull, IsEmpty, VarType*	Programmatically assessing data types
Math	*Rnd, Sqr, Exp, Log, Sin, Cos, Tan*	Performing mathematical calculations
Messages	*MsgBox, InputBox*	Issuing messages and gathering input from the keyboard
Text	*Left, Right, Mid, Trim, UCase, LCaseStrReverse, Replace, InStr, InStrReverse*	Processing strings
Miscellaneous	*Sum, Count, RGB, FV, NPV, CreateObject, GetObject, SysCmd*	Aggregating statistical results, setting color properties, computing financial results, creating or getting references to ActiveX objects, presenting progress meters, and more

These functions perform a variety of tasks. String functions can extract, transform, and truncate unwanted parts of a text string, but you can also use the built-in functions to calculate financial results or mathematical values. Inspection functions are useful for determining data types before you attempt to compute expressions. Wise use of these functions and the conversion functions can enable your code to branch around potential data type mismatch errors. (Error processing is an essential part of any complete solution. Without it, your solutions cannot trap run-time errors or raise custom run-time errors.) Domain aggregate functions are not very fast, but they can replace a whole query or a more complicated SQL statement. For example, your applications can use the domain aggregate functions in VBA procedures as well as in queries and forms. SQL aggregate functions, such as *Count* and *Sum*, can also generate statistical results for record sources. These functions are not as widely applicable as domain aggregate functions. For instance, you cannot use them in VBA procedures.

Figure 1-25 shows a procedure and the Immediate window to illustrate the behavior of the *Hex* function. The procedure initially transforms both arguments to hexadecimal strings and then prints the results in the Immediate window.

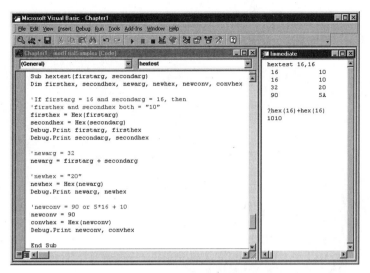

Figure 1-25. *A procedure that tests the* Hex *function.*

The string returned by the *Hex* function is not appropriate for arithmetic. The *hextest* function works around this by performing arithmetic with its decimal arguments and then transforming the result with the *Hex* function. The next several lines of the procedure demonstrate this approach. They add *firstarg* and *secondarg* and save the result in *newarg*. Then the procedure transforms *newarg* to a hexadecimal string and stores it in *newhex*. The procedure then prints *newarg* and *newhex* in the Immediate window.

The last transformation in *hextest* converts decimal 90 to the hexadecimal equivalent of *5A*. The comment lines before the transformation indicate that 90 is 5 × 16 + 10.

The last pair of lines in the Immediate window show that the *Hex* function returns string values. Actually, *Hex* returns a Variant data type, but the Variant's subtype is a string. The arithmetic operation hex 16 + hex 16 should yield hex 20. However, the Immediate window returns 1010. This shows that the plus sign in the *newarg = firstarg + secondarg* line performs a string concatenation instead of a numerical sum.

You should always look for techniques that minimize processing time. This is especially important for solutions that have a long lifetime of use or that perform essential business tasks. Figure 1-26 on the next page shows a procedure that can serve as the basis for timing the performance of your code. It computes the time that it takes to run a loop a fixed number of times. You can extend this basic design to compare the time it takes to perform a task with two different coding solutions. As you can see from the Immediate window, the simple code block runs quickly. On my test computer, it took just 2 seconds to pass through the loop two million times.

Figure 1-26. *Timing the completion of a task. This* TimedLoop *procedure also shows how several built-in functions operate.*

The *TimedLoop* procedure accepts a single argument that specifies how many times to run its loop. You can often discern performance differences better if you run a loop for a reasonable number of iterations. This simple loop has just two short statements. Note that before the procedure starts the loop, it saves the current time (*Now*) in *dtmStartTime*. After all the iterations have completed, the procedure saves the completion time in *dtmEndTime*. The *DateDiff* function computes the difference between these two values in seconds. (You previously saw this same function compute the difference between dates in days. It works with many time units, including years, quarters, hours, weeks, and even weekdays.) The *DateDiff* function handles the conversions to seconds and any peculiarities that arise from passing through midnight, and extracts the relevant quantities from the start and end times.

Since this particular timing test uses such a large number of iterations, it is particularly convenient to express the number of iterations with commas. The use of the *Format* function reveals how to accomplish this.

The domain aggregate functions are another distinct class of functions. They return statistical and lookup information about a domain (a set of records). The records can reside in either a table or the result of a select query. The functions can return count, sum, average, variance, and standard deviation statistics about a domain. You can also use the domain aggregate *DMin* and *DMax* functions to return the smallest or largest value from a column in the domain. The *DFirst* and *DLast* domain aggregate functions return a random record rather than the first or last record from the records sorted on one or more fields. The *DLookup* domain aggregate function is very popular; it returns one or more records that match a criterion. All domain aggregate functions share a format similar to the one shown here:

```
DFunctionName("fieldexpression", "domainname", "criteria")
```

All domain aggregate function names begin with *D*. Notice that the syntax embraces all three arguments in quotes. You can optionally place brackets around the field name in the first and third arguments. The first two arguments are mandatory, and the third is optional. The *fieldexpression* argument names a field on which to report. The *domainname* argument is the name of a record source. The optional third argument specifies a criterion statement for designating elements that you want in the return set. To return the company name from the first record in the *Shippers* table from the Northwind database, you use the following *DLookup* function:

```
DLookup("CompanyName", "Shippers", "ShipperID = 1")
```

The criterion in this sample specifies the record in the table with a *ShipperID* field of one. This is an AutoNumber field with a table data type of Long Integer. When this type of criterion is acceptable for your solution, it simplifies the use of domain aggregate functions. This *DLookup* function returns the field value from the single record that matches the criterion. If more than one record matches the criterion for a *DLookup* function, *DLookup* returns the first matching record in the domain source.

Other domain aggregate functions, such as *DSum*, *DCount*, and *DAvg*, compute results based on one or more records. The following VBA statement prints the number of past due invoices to the Immediate window based on a *DCount* function calculation:

```
Debug.Print DCount("InvoiceDate", "InvoiceDates", _
    "InvoiceDate < Now()-30")
```

This sample computes a count of invoices that are past due and prints the result. When used on the *InvoiceDates* table in the sample file for Chapter 2 on 9/12/98, this *DCount* function returns two records. You might want to add new records to the table or change some dates to get a different count when you try this sample.

Figure 1-27 shows a form that allows the user to enter the red, green, and blue values for a color and then displays the color when the user clicks the text box on the right. The red, green, and blue values for a color can range from *0* through *255*. If all three numbers are *0*, the color is black. If all three numbers are *255*, the color is white. Making any single number *255* while setting the other two to *0* creates an intense red, green, or blue color. The settings on my computer display the color for Figure 1-27 as a pale red or pink.

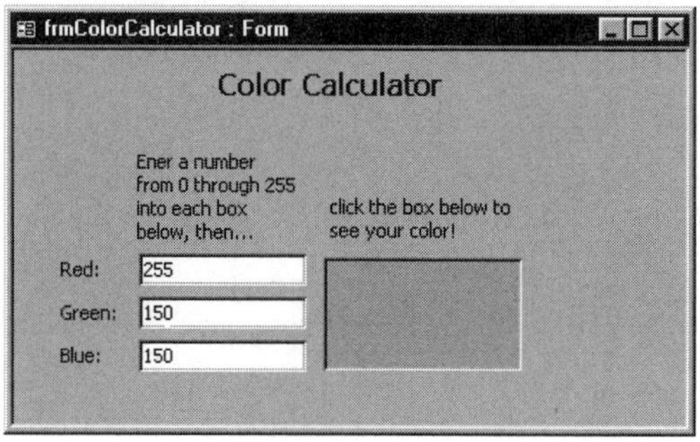

Figure 1-27. *A form showing a color viewer.*

The following event procedure for the text box on the right in Figure 1-27 does the simple processing for this color viewer. Aside from checking for Null entries in the color number text boxes, the procedure consists of a single statement. The statement uses the *RGB* function to set the *BackColor* of the large text box on the form's right.

```
Private Sub txtColorMe_Click()
'If null color field, set a default value.
    If IsNull(Me.txtRed.Value) Then
        Me.txtRed.Value = 0
    End If
    If IsNull(Me.txtGreen.Value) Then
        Me.txtGreen.Value = 0
    End If
    If IsNull(Me.txtBlue.Value) Then
        Me.txtBlue.Value = 0
    End If
'Set BackColor property.
    Me.txtColorMe.BackColor = RGB(Me.txtRed.Value, _
        Me.txtGreen.Value, _
        Me.txtBlue.Value)
End Sub
```

Checking for Null values is essential since a Null value can cause the *RGB* function to fail. There are many ways to tackle this issue, and the code in *txtColorMe_Click* is only one of them. For example, making the default value

0 if a color value is not specified is arbitrary. It could easily be *255* or some quantity between *0* and *255*. Another option is to not compute the *RGB* function but to merely send a message box that reminds the user to enter a value in all three text boxes on the left. Finally, you can actually let the run-time error occur for a Null value. Then you can trap the error and solve the problem. The next section explores ways of doing this.

DEBUGGING AND ERROR TRAPPING

If you write code, your code will contain errors. Aside from the normal variety of syntax errors and faulty logic in coding solutions, you can often get run-time errors for code that you think will work correctly. These errors can result from someone failing to enter a value in a text box or from the entry of an out-of-bound value in a text box. With trial deployments, you can solve many of these issues, but users can still enter an unanticipated value or click a button at the wrong time.

Error trapping is the process of catching run-time errors in your code before they cause abnormal termination of your application. Error trapping puts you in control. Your code can examine the error and sometimes even fix the problem without any action on the part of the user. If your code determines that user intervention is necessary, you can display an explanatory message. You can even gather new input in a set of custom dialog boxes and then proceed with the application. Even if you cannot gracefully recover from an error, you can terminate the program under prescribed conditions. Your solution can automatically save information about where the application failed as well as the error code, its description, and any other pertinent information. Then you can instruct the user to report the error to the proper person.

Because Access permits developers to respond to run-time errors, you should consider raising your own custom errors to trap special application logic errors, such as the entry of an out-of-bounds field value. In fact, Access lets you generate custom errors in a variety of ways. Your code can then recover from these custom errors just as it does from Access errors. You'll probably have a better idea of how to respond to your custom errors since you created them in the first place.

Essential Syntax for Error Trapping

You need to understand the *On Error* statement, the *Err* object, and the *Resume* statement to implement error trapping. They work together to enable error trapping and help you process errors after you trap them.

There are three versions of the *On Error* statement, but you are most likely to use this one, which enables error trapping:

```
On Error GoTo linelabel
```

When Access detects an error, this line allows your program to take control so that Access does not perform its default error handling. The *linelabel* argument is the name of the line to which you want to transfer control. Your code, starting with this line, is executed in place of the standard Access error processing code. Your code should determine and decipher the error number so that your program can take appropriate action. If you cannot fix the problem, you can at least get some information about the error before your code ends gracefully.

The *Err* object tells you about the error. It has two properties. The *Number* property precisely defines the error. The numbers stored in the *Number* property do not change from one version of Access to the next. This means that you can use the property as a robust error identifier. The other clue about the error is the *Err* object's *Description* property, which contains a textual description of the error. You should display these descriptions in the Immediate window or a message box.

When you initially design a program, the *Err* object descriptions can help you improve your design and develop appropriate responses to normal run-time errors, such as an out-of-bounds input value. An operational version of your program can also save descriptions of errors to a log file. This can help you design fixes expeditiously over the lifetime of the application. However, you typically will not want to detect errors by their descriptions, which are longer than their error numbers. (Microsoft might also reword descriptions even though the error numbers remain the same.)

The *Resume* statement is used to indicate where to resume running an application after the error. Use *Resume* without an argument if you want control to return to the same statement that caused the error. This approach can make sense when you fixed the problem that initially generated the error, such as a missing field value. If your error processing determines that it cannot fix the error, you might still want to continue at the line after the one that caused the error. Use the *Resume Next* statement for this. As long as the error does not affect the validity of these remaining code lines, this approach is at least possible. You will sometimes want to simply abort an application when your application uncovers an error that it cannot fix. In this case, transfer control after processing the error with the *Resume linelabel* statement. When you do error trapping, you will frequently include an *Exit Function* or *Exit Sub* statement with a label. It is convenient to use this label as the argument for the *Resume linelabel* statement when you want to exit the procedure after an error.

Error Trapping Samples

This section presents two error trapping samples. The first one is a basic application of error trapping logic. It shows error trapping for a function procedure in the Module folder. It also shows how to raise custom error codes. This sample shows how easy it is to process your application's internal errors with the same logic that you use for trapping Access errors. The second example uses error-trapping logic in the code behind a form. A distinguishing feature of this application is that it responds differently to each of two classes of errors.

The following function procedure builds error trapping into the more basic example shown earlier in Figure 1-16 on page 34. Recall that this routine performs one of four arithmetic operations. You pass the procedure three arguments: two operands and a string that specifies what arithmetic operation to perform on the numbers you pass the function.

At least two errors can crop up in this code at run time. First, a user can attempt to divide a number by 0. This generates error number 11. Second, the operation can generate a result larger or smaller than the data type permits. Access calls this an overflow error; its error number is 6. This procedure's error trapping logic catches these two errors explicitly, and it implicitly sets a trap for every other kind of error. The error handler helps the user by suggesting a fix for division by 0, and it explains what an overflow is in friendlier language than Access uses. Since you will often write applications for an audience that you know, your application can address that audience more directly than a general program like Access can.

```
Public Function Computer2(dblNumber1, dblNumber2, _
    Operation As String)
On Error GoTo Computer2Handler

    Select Case Operation
        Case "Addition"
            Computer2 = dblNumber1 + dblNumber2
        Case "Subtraction"
            Computer2 = dblNumber1 - dblNumber2
        Case "Multiplication"
            Computer2 = dblNumber1 * dblNumber2
        Case "Division"
            Computer2 = dblNumber1 / dblNumber2
    End Select
```

(continued)

```
Computer2Exit:
    Exit Function

Computer2Handler:
    If Err.Number = 11 Then
        MsgBox "Can't divide by zero. Change second number from 0.", _
        vbInformation, "Programming Microsoft Access 2000"
    ElseIf Err.Number = 6 Then
        MsgBox "Result exceeds data type value limits.", _
            vbInformation, "Programming Microsoft Access 2000"
    Else
        MsgBox Err.Number & ": " & Err.Description, vbInformation, _
            "Programming Microsoft Access 2000"
    End If
    Resume Computer2Exit
End Function
```

The *On Error* statement appears immediately after the start of the program. You want it there so that it can trap errors as soon as possible. If another program calls this one, it might make sense to use error trapping in that program so that it can use error trapping for its arguments to the *Computer2* function.

If you type *?Computer2(2, 4, "multiplication")* in the Immediate window and press Enter, the function returns *8*. Change multiplication to division, and the return value is *.5*. Next, enter *0* for the second argument. Without error trapping, this causes your program to end abruptly with a system message. With error handling, control passes to *Computer2Handler* as soon as the function attempts to divide by *0*. The routine checks for error 11, and because error 11 occurred, it prints a message encouraging the user to enter a number other than *0* for the divisor. Type *?Computer2(1.79E308, 4, "multiplication")* and press Enter to generate an overflow error. The multiplication operation attempts to generate a result greater than Access can represent. Control again passes to *Computer2Handler* immediately after the attempted multiplication fails. After determining that the error code is not 11, the error trapping logic tests the error code against 6. This matches the error code and the function presents a message box explaining the source of the error.

The error handler section of the routine uses an *If...Then...ElseIf...Else* statement. The *Else* clause offers a way to catch errors that your code does not explicitly trap. When you initiate your application, you might not know what the likely errors are. In this case, just use an *If...Then...Else* statement without any *ElseIf* clauses. Your *Else* clause presents error numbers along with their descriptions as they occur during testing. You can then use this information to develop explicit traps for certain kinds of errors along with any remedies that are available. As you test your application, it might offer additional opportunities to enhance your collection of *ElseIf* clauses in the error handler.

The final line in the error handler section is a *Resume* statement. This *Resume* statement transfers control to a line that exits the procedure. You can also use separate *Resume* statements for each type of error trap. This approach makes sense when your application requires you to take different actions after each kind of error trap.

The error handler will not trap some types of errors. For example, it will not trap an error if a user misspells an operation—as in *multiplcation* instead of *multiplication*. An operational error of this sort passes through the *Select Case* statement without stopping to perform any arithmetic, and the program logic then encounters the *Exit Function*. You need a way to trap this error and tell the user what to do. The solution is to detect the problem with a *Case Else* clause in the *Select Case* statement. Then you raise a custom error that tells the user what to do. Because the error trapping logic is robust, you need only alter the *Select Case* statement. The following excerpt from the modified code shows the new version with just two additional lines of code:

```
Select Case Operation
    Case "Addition"
        Computer2 = dblNumber1 + dblNumber2
    Case "Subtraction"
        Computer2 = dblNumber1 - dblNumber2
    Case "Multiplication"
        Computer2 = dblNumber1 * dblNumber2
    Case "Division"
        Computer2 = dblNumber1 / dblNumber2
    Case Else
        Err.Raise 1, , "Wrong operation."
End Select
```

The line after *Case Else* shows the syntax for raising a custom error code. It turns out that error number 1 does not receive assignment from either VBA, DAO, or ADO. Therefore, our application can use the number 1 for a custom error code. When the *Case Else* clause catches the misspelled operation, it raises the custom error, and this passes control to the *Computer2Handler* statement. The *Else* clause in that block of statements detects error code 1, and it issues a message box with the error message and our custom error description, *"Wrong operation."* After reviewing how to do error trapping with a form, we will return to the topic of which custom error codes to use.

The code behind the form in Figures 1-18 through 1-20 on page 39 uses nested *For Each...Next* statements to process responses to a form. Recall that the procedure for the command button's click event looped through all the controls on the form to find the two text boxes. It did this to avoid an error that would occur if it applied the *IsNull* function to a control, such as a label or a command button, which did not support this function.

An alternative design is to let the error happen, trap it, and recover from the problem. Using the *IsNull* function with an inappropriate control generates error number 438. The new version of the *cmdSubmit_Click* event procedure appears below.

```
Private Sub cmdSubmit_Click()
On Error GoTo SubmitErrorTrap
'Check for valid entries.
    For Each ctl In Screen.ActiveForm.Controls
        If IsNull(ctl.Value) Then
            MsgBox "Please enter information " _
                & "in both input boxes.", _
                vbInformation, _
                "Programming Microsoft Access 2000"
            MarkFieldsToEdit
            Exit For
        End If
SubmitNextCtl:
    Next ctl

SubmitExit:
    Exit Sub

SubmitErrorTrap:
    If Err.Number = 438 Then
        Resume SubmitNextCtl
    Else
        MsgBox Err.Number & ": " & Err.Description, vbInformation, _
            " Programming Microsoft Access 2000"
        Resume SubmitExit
    End If
End Sub
```

Notice that the error trapping logic actually lengthens the code, although it does allow the removal of one of the two *For Each…Next* statements. The new error trapping logic is considerably more robust. The nested *For* loops avoid just one type of error—number 438. This new alternative can potentially process any kind of error that occurs. In addition, it has two different ways of responding to errors. Notice that error 438 results in control passing back to the *Next* statement in the remaining *For* loop. This enables the program to keep processing additional controls for which the *IsNull* function is appropriate. Any other type of error causes the event procedure to terminate after it displays the unexpected error number and description in a message box.

Raising Errors

The *Err* object's *Raise* method is robust, but it requires that error handling be enabled. Adding error-handling routines can lengthen your code. If you have a small procedure with little opportunity for errors and you are an inexperienced developer, you might want to use a simpler way of returning an error code.

The following procedure does this with the *CVErr* function. This method is not as robust as a full error handling approach because it traps just a single type of error. Because there is no error handler, your whole application can crash if a run-time error does occur. On the other hand, the *CVErr* function is quick and easy to use. It cannot result in conflicts with built-in error codes because it does not return error codes via the same route. You must weigh for yourself the merit of the *CVErr* function in cases that require an error code return.

```
Public Function Computer1(dblNumber1, dblNumber2, _
    Operation As String)
    Select Case Operation
        Case "Addition"
            Computer1 = dblNumber1 + dblNumber2
        Case "Subtraction"
            Computer1 = dblNumber1 - dblNumber2
        Case "Multiplication"
            Computer1 = dblNumber1 * dblNumber2
        Case "Division"
            Computer1 = dblNumber1 / dblNumber2
        Case Else
            Computer1 = CVErr(2002)
    End Select
End Function
```

This function traps the error of a misspelled or unsupported operation. The *Select Case* statement isolates these problems with its *Case Else* clause. When a user types in a faulty operation, the function returns a Variant data type of subtype Error containing error number 2002.

This version of the procedure is much leaner than the *Computer2* procedure shown earlier in this chapter. However, *Computer2* explicitly traps for division by 0 and overflow even while it returns other kinds of errors. The much shorter *Computer1* catches the single problem of the misspelled or unsupported operation.

While the *CVErr* function does not have to worry about error number conflicts with VBA and Access, the following pair of procedures dramatically simplifies the task of finding error codes that are free for your custom use. The first function, *VBADAOUsedErrorList*, lists the error codes in a range of numbers that are used by VBA and DAO. You specify the starting and ending numbers when you call the procedure. The numbers missing from the output are available for use as custom error codes. The second procedure also lets you specify a starting number, and an ending number for the range over which to search for error codes. This procedure, however, prints to the Immediate window the error numbers not reserved by either VBA or DAO. Many of the unique ADO error numbers are large negative numbers.

```
Sub VBADAOUsedErrorList(intStart, intEnd)
Dim intErrorCode As Long, strAccessError As String
    For intErrorCode = intStart To intEnd
        strAccessError = AccessError(intErrorCode)
        If strAccessError <> "" Then
            If strAccessError <> _
                "Application-defined or object-defined error" Then
                Debug.Print intErrorCode, strAccessError
            End If
        End If
    Next intErrorCode
End Sub


Sub VBADAOUnUsedErrorList(intStart, intEnd)
Dim intErrorCode As Long, strAccessError As String
    For intErrorCode = intStart To intEnd
        strAccessError = AccessError(intErrorCode)
        If strAccessError = "" Or strAccessError = _
            "Application-defined or object-defined error" Then
            Debug.Print intErrorCode, strAccessError
        End If
    Next intErrorCode
End Sub
```

MACROS

Macros are not part of VBA, but they do offer an easy way to automate your Access applications. One big attraction of macros is that you do not have to remember their syntax ; Access makes it easy to select a macro action from a drop-down list box. On the other hand, with macros the debugging techniques are not nearly as rich as with VBA. Another disadvantage is that macros are stored in their own macro container, not behind forms. Over time, this can lead to maintenance problems. Also, Access macros are different from the macros in Excel, Word, and PowerPoint. In fact, macros are becoming an obsolete technology.

If you have been using an earlier version of Access, you have probably had some hands-on experience with macros. In earlier releases of Access, macros were the only way to create special startup options and custom menus. You can now manage menus using the VBA *CommandBars* collection object. In addition, you can use a Startup dialog box for controlling various aspects of starting an Access application, such as displaying a form when the startup process concludes, specifying whether users can make changes to menus and toolbars, and specifying whether to display the Database window.

Designing Macros

To work with macros, you have to know how to use the macros user interface and you need a basic familiarity with macro actions. Figure 1-28 shows the Macro window with the Northwind database loaded.

Each Access macro consists of one or more rows in the Macro window. Each row specifies an action (such as moving the focus to a control), an optional condition for the action, and an optional comment. The Action Arguments area at the bottom of the window (visible when you select an action) allows you to specify the options for each action and displays help for the selected item. In addition, the first row of each macro specifies the macro's name. (Choose Macro Names from the Access View menu if you can't see the macro names.)

Many macro actions have options that you can select with a simple click. For example, the second row of the Preview macro in Figure 1-28 on the next page (the row with the right-pointing triangle in the first column) displays a message box. In the Action Arguments area of the window, you can select the arguments for a message box from drop-down list boxes. For example, you can use the Type drop-down list box to select the icon that is displayed in the message box.

In the early days, this point-and-click selection feature gave macros a definite usability advantage over VBA code. Now, VBA has IntelliSense. Macros are still fairly easy to use—you still enjoy the ease of selecting arguments—but you do not have a flexible interface in which you can simultaneously view the code (including arguments) for multiple macro lines.

The most important column in the Macro window is the Action column. You do not have to type actions into this column; you can simply click any row in the column for a full menu of macro actions. In the Condition column just to the left of the Action column, you can specify criteria that conditionally control the execution of the action on a line.

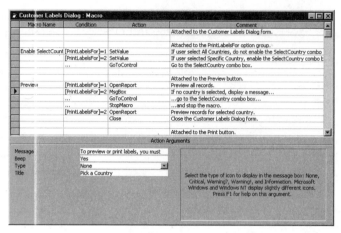

Figure 1-28. *The main user interface elements of the Macro window.*

You can store multiple macros in a single macro object. This is an efficient way to store multiple macros that share some common function. Use the Macro Name column to assign names to the individual macros within a macro object. When you assign a macro to an action for a control on a form or a report, you specify the macro using a two-part name. The first part is the name of the macro object; the second part is the macro's name, as shown in the Macro Name column. (Use a period to separate the parts of the name, as in *MyMacros.DisplayHelp*.)

Access features a built-in conversion procedure for translating macros to VBA code. You invoke the conversion features slightly differently depending on whether your application calls its macros from a form or from the Database window. From a form or report, choose Macro from the Tools menu and then choose Convert Form's Macros To Visual Basic or Convert Report's Macros To Visual Basic. To convert a macro from the Database window, select it on the Macro page. Choose File-Save As, and in the Save As dialog box, select Module from the As drop-down list box.

VBA vs. Macros

VBA keeps getting dramatically better with each new release, while macros have remained basically unchanged. This is the major reason for switching to VBA from macros, but there are several other reasons as well:

■ VBA's built-in error trapping and other flexible debugging can dramatically reduce the life cycle cost of ownership by reducing maintenance costs.

■ VBA offers many advanced processing features, such as looping options, great Internet functionality, and OLE DB links to external data sources.

■ VBA custom form and report classes simplify code reuse.

■ VBA enables you to view concurrently the arguments for all lines— not just one line.

■ You can tap into the Windows API from VBA.

Chapter 2

Data Access Models

Microsoft Access 2000 supports two data access models: the traditional Data Access Objects (DAO) and ActiveX Data Objects (ADO). DAO targets the Jet database engine to enable quick and easy database programming. Access 2000 is the first version of Access to also support ADO for manipulating Jet databases. Instead of being based on a single database engine, ADO uses a common programming model to deliver access to universal data. It relies on OLE DB providers for low-level links to data sources. OLE DB technologies will eventually make their ODBC predecessors obsolete, much as ADO will replace DAO. Therefore, if you invest in learning ADO now, you will get on the fast track to adopting future improvements in data access with upcoming versions of Access and you'll be able to use more and different kinds of data sources.

This chapter reviews the DAO and ADO data access models, with the primary emphasis on ADO as a programming model. The brief DAO coverage introduces core development concepts and provides a historical perspective on data access within Access. Since DAO will not play a critical role in any subsequent chapters, this chapter will cover using Jet and remote databases. For information on DAO code, see the Access online documentation and Microsoft's Support Online (support.microsoft.com/support/), a site that documents typical problems and their associated workarounds. Many of the articles include code samples.

This chapter will focus primarily on the ADO object models for Jet in Access and the ADODB and ADOX libraries. Extensive programming examples will show you how to accomplish typical database tasks. Other chapters in this book will build on the information in this chapter and will cover additional ADO topics, such as database replication, remote database access, and multi-user security.

DAO OVERVIEW

Access 2000 includes the 3.6 version of the DAO library, a maintenance upgrade to the 3.5 version that shipped with Access 97. (The basic architecture and functionality is very similar between versions.) DAO relies on a workspace object model for types of data access. The workspace object can contain session, security, and transaction information. (A workspace object defines how your application interacts with data.)

There are two types of workspaces: Microsoft Jet workspaces and ODBCDirect workspaces.

Jet Workspaces

Jet workspaces are for Jet, Jet-connected ODBC, and installable ISAM data sources. Jet-connected ODBC data sources let you link to remote data sources in a familiar DAO environment. Unfortunately, this type of connection requires the full DAO model, and it loads Jet even when no data access is required. Installable ISAM data sources come in a variety of formats, such as Paradox and Lotus 1-2-3.

Traditional Jet workspaces offer a set of advantages, which include the following:

- Updating data in recordset objects

- Joining tables from different data sources into a common recordset

- Creating tables based on familiar DAO methods instead of SQL Data Definition Language (DDL) conventions

- Binding data to forms and reports

Jet workspaces include *Groups* and *Users* collection objects, while ODBCDirect workspaces do not because remote database sources such as Microsoft SQL Server can manage their own security.

ODBCDirect Workspaces

ODBCDirect is a relatively new DAO technology that was introduced with Microsoft Office 97 and DAO 3.5. Because the security-related DAO objects are not used with remote ODBC data sources, and because other DAO objects work best with locally connected data sources, Microsoft created the ODBCDirect object model, which is available from a separate type of workspace. The ODBCDirect workspace offers fast, direct access to remote ODBC data sources (such as SQL Server) and can bypass Jet. You still get the richness of an object model without having to rely exclusively on SQL commands, as with SQL pass-through queries.

Some of the chief benefits of ODBCDirect workspaces are as follows:

- Use of remote data sources without loading the Jet engine

- Asynchronous queries

- Better access to remote database functionality, including cursors and stored procedures

- Batch updating of remote sources from a local cache

- Returning multiple result sets from a single query

ODBCDirect workspaces have a richer cursor library than Jet workspaces, and they support dynamic as well as update batch cursors, which are not available in Jet workspaces. The dynamic cursor lets a session view changes made to a database by other users without having to requery the data source. The batch update cursor permits asynchronous updates to a remote data source. This improves performance by removing the need for holding locks on records.

> **NOTE** Cursors define the type and location of access to a data source. Several data source properties can go into defining a cursor. For example, cursors can be updatable or not. They can permit forward-only movement or bidirectional navigation. Cursors can automatically update to reflect edits and other database modifications or they can require an explicit refresh operation to show the most recent version of a database. You can designate a cursor that works on a remote database server or on a local workstation.

You can enjoy the best of both workspaces by having multiple workspaces of both types open at the same time. Using concurrent, multiple workspaces, you can benefit from the simplicity of bound forms with data that originates in an ODBCDirect workspace. You simply use the returning records in a Jet workspace.

Objects Common to Jet and ODBCDirect Workspaces

Within both types of workspaces, DAO objects generally follow a hierarchical organization. Figure 2-1 shows the hierarchy of DAO collections and objects in Jet workspaces, and Figure 2-2 shows the hierarchy of DAO collections and objects in ODBCDirect workspaces.

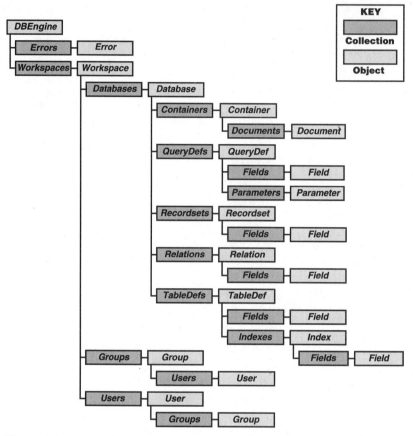

Figure 2-1. *DAO collections and objects for Jet workspaces.*

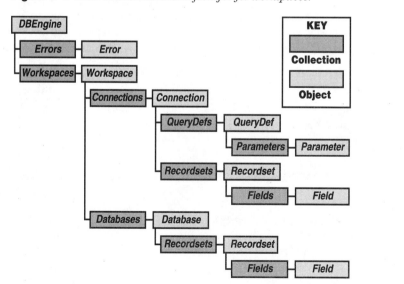

Figure 2-2. *DAO collections and objects for ODBCDirect workspaces.*

The *DBEngine* object

The top-level DAO object for both workspaces is *DBEngine*. You use its *CreateWorkspace* method to open a session. An optional *Type* argument for the method lets you designate either a Jet workspace or an ODBCDirect workspace. You can also set the *DefaultType* property of the *DBEngine* object so that either type of workspace opens in the absence of a specific *CreateWorkspace Type* setting. The Jet workspace type is the native default. Any setting for the *CreateWorkspace Type* argument overrides either a native or an explicitly set *DefaultType* property.

The *DBEngine* properties and methods available to both workspace types provide a core set of DAO functions. You can use *DBEngine* to both create and manage databases.

The *CreateDatabase* method creates new workspaces, and you can use arguments for this method to set a database's sort order and encryption status. You can also set the version format for a database to programmatically create databases compatible with prior versions of Access. The *OpenDatabase* method opens an existing database in a workspace object. After you create a database, you can apply the *Compact* and *Repair* methods to manage the database.

DAO enables transaction processing through *DBEngine* with three methods: *BeginTrans*, *CommitTrans*, and *Rollback*. A transaction is a set of operations that occur in all-or-none fashion. If any link in a chain of database operations fails, you can roll back all the operations. For example, if a bank transfers money from a checking to a savings account, both the debit to checking and the credit to savings must be successful in order for the books to balance. If either part fails, the bank's code should roll back both parts. Transactions can also speed up database processing by batching sets of disk writes. You can nest transactions up to five levels deep.

Some of the properties and methods available depend on the type of workspace used. However, no matter which workspace you use, *DBEngine* contains the *Errors* and *Workspaces* collections.

The *Errors* collection

You use the *Errors* collection to process data access errors. The *Errors* collection contains one or more error numbers and descriptions from the last failed statement. Multiple errors from a single failure are common with ODBC data sources because different ODBC layers can each report an error for the same failure, such as a remote database source that is not operational.

The *Errors* collection, like other DAO collections, is zero-based. Its *Count* property denotes the number of errors in a collection, and the individual errors have item numbers of 0 through *Count* −1. The last entry in the *Errors* collection corresponds to the Microsoft Visual Basic for Applications (VBA) *Err* object.

As you debug your applications, you might find it helpful to enumerate the *Errors* collection to simplify your search for the source of an error or the solution to an error.

The *Workspaces* collection

You use the properties and methods of the *Workspaces* collection to reference individual workspace sessions. Because the *Workspaces* collection is always available, Access can maintain multiple sessions concurrently and your applications can open and manage any combination of Jet and ODBCDirect workspaces. While these sessions do not persist beyond a logon session, they can exist for a whole session. You can use the *CreateWorkspace* method's *Name* argument to uniquely reference individual workspaces within a collection using one of these formats:

■ DBEngine.Workspaces (0)

■ DBEngine.Workspaces("Name")

■ DBEngine.Workspaces![Name]

All DAO objects have a similar referencing syntax to these examples. The first two styles listed above match ADO conventions. You should adopt one of these whenever possible to enhance your migration skills when you start coding in ADO.

Workspace objects share several important methods with the *DBEngine* object, such as *CreateDatabase*, *OpenDatabase*, and *BeginTrans*. Other methods, such as *CreateUser* and *CreateGroup*, are unique to the *Workspace* object. These two methods help manage user-level security within a workspace.

The *Databases* collection

Within any workspace, you can programmatically open multiple databases. Using DAO with VBA offers a distinct advantage over the user interface that enables the opening of a single database at a time. You use variable names to reference database objects to speed access. This same approach enhances speed for many DAO objects.

The *Name* property of an individual database in a Jet workspace is the path to the database file. You reference the database for the current project in your VBA code with the *CurrentDb* function. Access also supports the alternative syntax of *DBEngine (0) (0)* to reference the current database. The *CurrentDb* syntax creates another instance of the current project's database, but the *DBEngine* syntax refers to the open copy of the current database. You can open database objects on nonJet data sources, such as ISAM databases (for example, dBASE or Microsoft FoxPro). While it is also possible to use an ODBC data source in this way, you generally get better performance by using an ODBCDirect workspace (as explained in the section beginning on page 76).

The *Recordsets* collection

A *Recordset* object represents the records in a table or those resulting from a row-returning query. You create new recordsets using the *OpenRecordset* method. You can invoke this method from several objects, including both databases and *TableDef* objects, to create a recordset. Other objects that have an *OpenRecordset* method include *QueryDef* objects and even other recordsets. This method adds a new recordset to the *Recordsets* collection. You can create five types of recordsets, as shown in the following table.

RECORDSET OBJECTS

Type	*Description*
Table	This type refers to a record in a table, such as one you create using the *CreateTableDef* method. It always refers to a single Jet table. You can update the field values as well as add and delete records. There is no corresponding ODBC cursor.
Dynaset	This type is a dynamic collection of records that can result from one or more tables. Selected fields might be updatable, so you can add, delete, and modify records. You use a field's *DataUpdatable* property to determine whether a field is updatable. In a multi-user database, you can view selected changes made by other users. This recordset type corresponds to the ODBC keyset cursor.
Snapshot	With this type, you can examine records based on one or more tables, but you cannot change the underlying records. Once you load a snapshot into memory, it does not reflect any further modifications to the underlying tables. This recordset type corresponds to the ODBC static cursor.
Forward-only	This type is identical to the snapshot-type recordset, except that you can scroll forward only. This type corresponds to an ODBC forward-only cursor.
Dynamic	This type represents a query result based on one or more underlying tables. Users can update the recordset by adding, deleting, and modifying records. This type also shows changes made by other users in a multi-user environment. It is available only in ODBCDirect workspaces and corresponds to the ODBC dynamic cursor.

The *OpenRecordset* method   The *OpenRecordset* method requires a source argument that specifies the source of the resulting recordset. As mentioned, this is typically a table name, a query name, or a SQL statement. You can also specify the recordset type; if you don't, DAO returns a table, dynaset, or forward-only type, depending on the source.

An options argument lets you specify any of several recordset character-istics, such as prohibiting users from reading or writing to the recordset. A fi-nal argument lets you set the *LockEdits* property for a recordset. This property indicates the type of locking that is in effect when an application revises, adds, or deletes records from a recordset. With Jet workspaces, your settings for this final argument are likely to be read-only, pessimistic locks, and optimistic locks. With a read-only setting, no recordset revisions are possible. With pessimistic locks, invoking the *Edit* method locks the page containing the record. With optimistic locks, other users can revise the record until your application invokes the *Update* method. This can yield a faster-performing recordset, but it can also lead to conflicting updates.

Recordset methods   You can modify the records in a recordset using the *Edit, AddNew, Update*, and *Delete* methods. You use the *Edit* and *Update* meth-ods together to revise the values in a recordset. The *Edit* method opens a record for editing, and the *Update* method commits the new values to the recordset's underlying tables. The *AddNew* and *Update* methods operate as a team. You signal that your code will be adding a record by invoking the *AddNew* method. You save the new record with the *Update* method. The *Delete* method removes the current record from a recordset. After you delete a record, that record re-mains current until you navigate to a new record. The *Delete* method does not require the *Update* method.

You can use a set of *Move* methods to navigate a recordset once you add it to the *Recordsets* collection. The *MoveNext* and *MovePrevious* methods navi-gate forward and backward one record. If you are already at the first record and your application invokes the *MovePrevious* method, DAO returns a BOF marker from the recordset. You can use this marker to flag a movement beyond the first record. Similarly, DAO returns an EOF marker when an application invokes the *MoveNext* method from the last record. Any attempt to move beyond either the BOF or EOF markers generates a run-time error. The *Move* method lets you specify a fixed number of rows to move. You can also designate a starting position other than the current record. The *MoveFirst* and *MoveLast* methods move directly to the first and last record in a recordset, respectively. With very large recordsets, there might be a significant pause until you reach the last record in a recordset.

Another set of methods navigates to a new record that meets specified criteria. These methods are *FindFirst, FindLast, FindNext*, and *FindPrevious*. You designate the criteria for a *Find* method with the same syntax as the WHERE clause in a SQL statement. If no records meet the specified criteria, these meth-ods set the recordset's *NoMatch* property to True. Otherwise, they simply move to the record that meets the criteria. Both *FindNext* and *FindPrevious* move from the current record. *FindFirst* and *FindLast* search from the first or last records, respectively. When you work with *TableDef* objects, the *Seek* method can yield faster results than the *Find* methods. In general, you get better search performance using SQL statement searches in *OpenRecordset* methods. With *Find*, *Move*, and *Seek* methods, it is often desirable to set a recordset's *Index* property so that you can put the records in the precise order designated by the index fields.

Jet Workspace Objects

Database objects in Jet workspaces hold and can activate selected elements of a database schema. For example, you can open recordsets for manipulation or you can run action queries that update, append, or delete records. Database methods also let you create and manage replicas. The five hierarchical collections for a database are listed below. The *Database* object has methods for adding new elements to all of these collections.

- TableDefs
- Recordsets
- QueryDefs
- Relations
- Containers

The *TableDefs* collection

The *TableDefs* collection accesses the individual *TableDef* objects within a database. *TableDef* objects contain *Fields* and *Indexes* collections, so you can define a table using a *TableDef* object. You use *CreateField* and *CreateIndex* methods to compose the definition of a table. When you use the *CreateField* method, you first specify your field by designating its name, type, and size. Then you invoke the *Append* method to add your new field to the *Fields* collection for a *TableDef* object. If a collection already contains a field with the name you designate as an argument, your code generates a trappable run-time error. You can use this to manage your *TableDef* object by, for example, removing the old field with the *Delete* method.

When you create indexes, you invoke the *CreateIndex* method and append one or more fields to the index. Then you append the new index to the *Indexes* collection for the *TableDef* object. If an index already exists with the name you specify, a run-time error occurs. You can use these errors to manage the process of indexing a *TableDef* object.

The *TableDef* object can also manage links to tables in ISAM and ODBC data sources. Your code requires the *Connect* and *SourceTableName* properties and the *CreateTableDef* methods for this activity. You invoke the *CreateTableDef* method to set a reference in a variable to the linked table. Then you set the *Connect* and *SourceTableName* properties for the variable. The *Connect* property specifies the data source type, such as dBase 5.0 or Paradox 5.*x*, and the path to the specific data source that you want to link. The *SourceTableName* property is the table name that you link. After setting these properties for the variable referencing the linked table, you complete the process by appending the *TableDef* object to the *TableDefs* collection.

The *QueryDefs* collection

The *QueryDefs* collection stores the individual *QueryDef* objects in a database. A *QueryDef* object is a SQL statement that typically returns a row set or performs an action, such as updating, adding, or deleting records in a recordset. When the SQL statement for a *QueryDef* object returns rows, it can have a *Fields* collection of individual fields. If your SQL statement accepts arguments that specify its criteria at run time, a *QueryDef* object can have a *Parameters* collection. When the *QueryDef* object runs, you can specify these parameters programmatically or at run time by means of a dialog box.

You can create new *QueryDef* objects using the *CreateQueryDef* method for either the *Database* object in the Jet workspace or the *Database* or *Connection* object in an ODBCDirect workspace. If you name the *QueryDef* object a non-zero-length string, DAO automatically enters it in the *QueryDefs* collection and saves the *QueryDef* object to disk for permanent storage along with the database. Use the *Delete* method to remove an item from the *QueryDefs* collection. Any *Querydef* object created with a *Name* property equal to a zero-length string is temporary. DAO does not persist these. Temporary *QueryDef* objects are convenient when your applications need to create *QueryDef* objects dynamically.

Two methods allow you to activate a *QueryDef* object. The *OpenRecordset* method returns the rows in a *QueryDef* object with a SELECT statement, while the *Execute* method runs an action query. The *dbFailOnError* option can allow your application to determine whether a *QueryDef* object fails to perform its designated action for all records that meet its criteria. As long as a *QueryDef* object is syntactically correct, it does not generate an error—even if it fails to perform its action. The *dbFailOnError* option rolls back any changes if the *QueryDef* object cannot perform all the changes. This option also generates a run-time error to help you perform any associated processing, such as providing feedback to a user.

The *Relations* collection

You use the *Relations* collection and its individual relations to define links between tables programmatically. The *CreateRelation* method for the *Database* object can initially specify relations; it lets an application define one-to-one or one-to-many relations between any pair of tables. This method can also designate referential integrity as well as cascading deletes and updates. (See Chapter 4 for an in-depth discussion of these terms.) You define relations between tables based on common fields in both tables. The *Relation* object has a *Fields* collection to support this function. The *Relations* collection and individual *Relations* objects are unique to the Jet workspaces. They are unavailable in ODBCDirect workspaces because remote database engines typically maintain their own relations between tables.

The *Containers* collection

The *Containers* collection defines a set of container objects for database documents. Some of the container objects follow from the Database window: *Forms*, *Reports*, *Scripts for Macros*, and *Modules*. These are all Access objects, not Jet database objects. Other container objects are Jet-based, including *Databases*, *Tables*, and *Relationships*. The *Tables* container object includes information about both tables and queries. There is an additional container object for saved relationship layout information.

Container objects hold documents, which consist of all saved elements of a type, such as forms or relationships. These documents provide administrative, not content, information about the objects in a container object. Selected properties for documents include the date created and the date last updated as well as the owner, user, and permissions. Jet uses the information in documents to manage security for Access objects as well as its own native tables and queries.

It is important to understand that the documents in container objects are different from the elements in a collection. Documents consist of all saved objects—whether or not they are open. Collections are groups of objects that are open. If an object is not open, it is not part of a collection. However, it can belong to a container object. Also, documents hold administrative information about objects, but elements in a collection have information about the content, layout, and subelements of the objects of a collection.

The *Users* and *Groups* collections each have their matching objects. These collections and objects complement the container documents to help Jet manage user-level security. Documents have permissions. Users belong to groups. Document permissions describe levels of access by users and groups. Chapter 10 includes detailed coverage of user-level security, including users, groups, and permissions.

ODBCDirect Workspace Objects

By comparing Figure 2-2 with Figure 2-1 (on page 68), you can see that the ODBCDirect model is much more parsimonious because ODBCDirect workspaces hand over to remote database servers some of the functions that Jet manages. For example, remote database servers manage their own security, so *Users* and *Groups* collections aren't needed. There is also no *TableDefs* collection because remote database servers manage their own tables. The story is similar for relations.

The two workspace models are different in other ways. The ODBCDirect model has a new *Connections* collection with its corresponding objects. Also, in the ODBCDirect model the role of the *Database* object is different, and *QueryDef* objects do not have a *Fields* collection. You can derive a *Recordset* object from a *QueryDef* object via the *OpenRecordset* method.

Although both workspaces have a *Database* object, it behaves somewhat differently in the ODBCDirect workspace than it does in the Jet workspace. In the ODBCDirect workspace, that object has a *Connect* property that returns a reference to a *Connection*. The *Connection* object has a *Database* property that returns a reference to a *Database* object. In DAO models, *Connection* and *Database* objects are different ways of referencing the same thing. These properties simplify migration from Jet workspace models to ODBCDirect workspaces and back again.

The *Connections* collection

The *Connections* collection of a workspace and its objects are critical when you work with remote databases. In ODBCDirect workspaces, you use the *OpenConnection* method to establish a connection to a remote database. You need as many as four arguments, three of which are optional. The one required argument is the name. Naming a connection adds it to the *Connections* collection. The other three arguments define the nature of the connection. Since these are optional arguments, you can designate them when you create the connection or later. However, you must define a connection before you can use it to extract data or otherwise work with the data in a remote data source. One key remaining argument is the *Connect* argument that sets the *Connect* property of the *Connection* object. You use the *Connect* argument to specify the connection string. It starts with *ODBC* and a semicolon followed by other connection information needed to link to the remote data source. This can include a DSN and a database name and is also likely to include a user ID and corresponding password. You delimit each type of information with a semicolon. Your application can examine and reset the connection string through the *Connect* property of a *Connection* object.

A second optional *OpenConnection* parameter controls two distinct types of behavior: how a connection reacts to incomplete connection string information and how to open a connection asynchronously. In the case of incomplete connection string information, you can let the connection fail and generate a run-time error or you can trap the error and prompt for complete information. You can also use this parameter to designate that a connection is to open asynchronously. The application can open a connection and then go on to other tasks. Your Access application can serve the local user by opening forms or even interacting with the user. At the same time, the remote database server processes the request for a new connection. With the *Connection* object's *StillExecuting* property, your application can poll the connection to determine when it is available for use.

The *Connection* object has five methods:

- *OpenRecordset* This method returns a set of rows from a remote data source. It has more features in an ODBCDirect workspace than in a Jet workspace. Perhaps the most profound difference is that, when using this method in an ODBCDirect workspace, you can specify more than one SQL statement so that a single *OpenRecordset* statement can provide multiple recordsets for local use.

- *Close* This method closes an open connection.

- *CreateQueryDef* This method also has additional features in an ODBCDirect workspace. Perhaps the most obvious is that *QueryDef* objects do not have fields. If you want to view the rows returned by a row-returning *QueryDef* object, you invoke the *OpenRecordset* method for the object. All *QueryDef* objects in ODBCDirect workspaces are temporary. In the ODBCDirect object model, you cannot create stored procedures in a remote data source. *QueryDef* objects can belong only to *Connection* objects. There is no *CreateQueryDef* method for *Database* objects in an ODBCDirect workspace, as there is in a Jet workspace. You can open a *Recordset* object from a *Database* object in either kind of workspace.

- *Execute* This method runs action, parameter, and select queries. You designate the *dbRunAsync* constant to specify that a *QueryDef* object should run asynchronously. Just as for the *OpenConnection* method, users can perform other tasks simultaneously as the *QueryDef* object runs. The *StillExecuting* property enables an application to check on the completion status of the *QueryDef* object.

■ *Cancel* This method terminates an asynchronous query. It returns a run-time error if you invoke it without specifying asynchronous operation. You free the resources consumed by a *QueryDef* object by applying the *Close* method or by setting the *QueryDef* object reference to Nothing.

Batch updating

One of the more powerful innovations in ODBCDirect workspaces is batch updating, which enables an application to download a set of records, perform updates locally, and then update the original as a single batch instead of one record at a time. Batch updating has obvious concurrency advantages over single-record locking. Because of the potential for conflicts, it is best used when a database is unlikely to be changed by multiple users. However, some features for handling collisions are built into batch processing. For example, a *BatchCollisions* property returns bookmarks that point at collisions in a recordset after you upload the recordset. You can also force a remote database to match your update or accept the value in the remote data source. Three *Field* properties let you examine the original value before downloading, the updated value in the local recordset version, and the new field value in the remote data source.

There are five steps to implementing batch updating in an ODBCDirect workspace:

1. Set the *DefaultCursorDriver* property for the workspace to *dbUseClientBatchCursor*.

2. Create a *Connection* object or a *Database* object.

3. Invoke the *OpenRecordset* method for the object from step 2 with a *dbOptimisticBatch* setting for the *LockEdits* argument.

4. Edit the fields locally as needed.

5. Invoke the *Update* method for the recordset from the third step with a *dbUpdateBatch* setting for the type argument. If you have no collisions, you are done. If there are collisions, you need additional logic to reconcile them.

ADO OVERVIEW

Access 2000 supports ADO version 2.1, which includes three ADO data access models: the ADODB library, the ADOX library, and the JRO library. By segmenting data access into three libraries, Access offers a smaller footprint for applications that do not require all three. Another major component of the

Access 2000 data access strategy is reliance on OLE DB providers, which work with ADO to offer access to traditional data sources as well as new ones, such as e-mail directories. This vastly expands the power of database programming.

The ADODB library is a small, lightweight library that contains core objects and offers the basics for making connections, issuing commands, and retrieving recordsets, and it also enables recordset navigation. You can use it to perform basic maintenance tasks, such as modifying, adding, and deleting records. The nonhierarchical design of this library makes it easy for beginners.

The ADOX library supports data definition language and security issues. It offers objects that put you in touch with a database's overall schema. For example, it lets you create tables and relations. The model includes support for referential integrity and cascading updates and deletes, and it offers procedures and views as well as *Users* and *Groups* collections for user-level database security.

The JRO library enables Jet database replication. Access 2000 supports database replication with both Jet and SQL Server databases. Chapter 11 covers database replication in depth.

One major advantage that ADO offers is an event model. ODBCDirect permits asynchronous operations, but ADO provides events. This frees an application from polling an object and checking its *StillExecuting* property. Instead, you can simply create event handlers to respond to events whenever they happen. (Subsequent chapters will explain how to design event handlers.)

OLE DB providers help make ADO powerful. They offer a new way to access remote data that embraces and extends ODBC, and they provide access to both relational databases and nontraditional data sources with a consistent ADO interface. Access 2000 ships with a variety of OLE DB providers, including ones for Jet, SQL Server, Oracle, general ODBC data sources, and such nontraditional sources as Microsoft Active Directory Service and Microsoft Index Server. You can expect more of these providers over time.

Before you can use any of the ADO libraries, you must create a reference to at least one of them. You do this from the Visual Basic Editor (VBE) window using the Tools-References command. Figure 2-3 on the following page shows the References dialog box with all three libraries selected. While it might be more convenient to select all three, you can conserve resources by selecting just the libraries that you need. Experiment with the selections for your applications and the machines that they run on to determine what makes sense for your environment. If you have a production application that runs on many different types of machines, you should conserve resources for other application requirements.

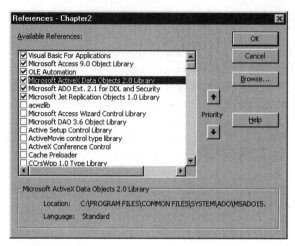

Figure 2-3. *You use the References dialog box to add ADO libraries to an application.*

The ADODB Library

The ADODB object library has seven main objects. Four of these objects have collections. The *Connection* object appears at the top of the hierarchy, but you can create connections implicitly using other objects. The *Connection, Command, Recordset,* and *Field* objects have *Properties* collections.

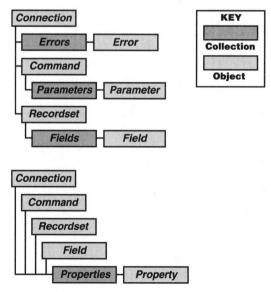

Figure 2-4. *The ADODB object library.*

The *Connection* object

The *Connection* object establishes a link to a database. You always use a *Connection* object either implicitly or explicitly when you work with a database. When you explicitly create one, you can efficiently manage one or more connections and reassign the roles that they serve in an application. By implicitly creating one you can shorten your code. Each new object that you create with an implicit connection consumes more resources. If your application has only one or two objects that each requires its own connection, implicit connections might serve your needs best. ADO lets you choose how to create and manage connections as you see fit.

Unlike DAO, ADO is a general data access language, so not all of its properties and methods are appropriate for the Jet engine. There is, however, a special OLE DB provider for Jet 4, which is the latest version of Jet that ships with Access 2000. Since *Connection* objects depend critically on provider specifications, the ability to set a *Connection* parameter that references the Jet 4 provider is valuable. This custom provider allows ADO to reflect many of the special strengths that Jet offers. When you refer to a database in another file, you might want to include a *Data Source* parameter, which points to the physical location of a database when it is not in the current project.

The following simple code sample opens the familiar Northwind database. Notice that a *Dim* statement declares and creates a reference to *cnnNorthwind* as a *Connection* object. The use of the *Open* method on *cnnNorthwind* makes the database available to the rest of the procedure. Notice that the *Provider* and *Data Source* parameters appear within a single pair of double quotes. The *Provider* parameter points to the Jet 4 OLE DB provider and the *Data Source* parameter points to the physical location of the Northwind database.

```
Sub OpenMyDB()
Dim cnnNorthwind As New Connection
Dim rsCustomers As Recordset

'Create the connection.
    cnnNorthwind.Open "Provider=Microsoft.Jet.OLEDB.4.0;" & _
        "Data Source=C:\Program Files\Microsoft Office\Office\" & _
        "Samples\Northwind.mdb;"

'Create recordset reference and set its properties.
    Set rsCustomers = New ADODB.Recordset
    rsCustomers.CursorType = adOpenKeyset
    rsCustomers.LockType = adLockOptimistic
```

(continued)

```
'Open recordset and print a test record.
    rsCustomers.Open "Customers", cnnNorthwind, , , adCmdTable
    Debug.Print rsCustomers.Fields(0).Value, rsCustomers.Fields(1).Value
    rsCustomers.Close
    cnnNorthwind.Close


End Sub
```

After creating a reference to the connection, the code creates a *Recordset* object. It sets a reference to the object variable denoting the recordset, and then it assigns values to a couple of properties for the recordset. The last block of code opens the recordset and prints a couple of fields from the first record. The *Open* method for a *Recordset* object can reference a connection to a database and some source of records in the database. The code above selects all of the records from the *Customers* table in the Northwind database. The *Open* method initially makes the first record available to an application.

The final two lines in the last block of code close the recordset and then the connection. Closing a connection makes all objects that reference it, such as a *Recordset* object, inoperable. Any attempt to set properties or invoke methods for a recordset that references a closed connection generates a run-time error. For this reason, implicitly creating a connection might be a better choice because the object has use of the connection for its lifetime.

The following code also opens a recordset based on the *Customers* table in the Northwind database and prints the first record. However, it uses fewer lines of code and the code is less complicated because it implicitly creates a connection and accepts more default settings.

```
Sub OpenFast()
Dim rsCustomers As Recordset
    Set rsCustomers = New ADODB.Recordset

'Less code, but potentially greater resource consumption
    rsCustomers.Open "customers", "Provider=Microsoft.Jet.OLEDB.4.0;" & _
        "Data Source=C:\Program Files\Microsoft Office\Office\" & _
        "Samples\Northwind.mdb;"
    Debug.Print rsCustomers.Fields(0), rsCustomers.Fields(1)
    rsCustomers.Close


End Sub
```

Since there is no explicit connection, the *OpenFast* procedure does not need to declare a connection object (and therefore doesn't have to open one or close one). As you can see, the *Open* method for a recordset object can include the essential connection information of a provider and a data source. The code above has only one other parameter—the source for the recordset, which is the *Customers* table. The *Open* method relies on the default *CursorType* and *LockType* settings, which are, respectively, forward-only and read-only. These settings provide for very fast operations, but they do not offer a lot of functionality. Nevertheless, if they suit your needs and let you divert your attention to other aspects of application development, they might be the best choice.

The *Mode* property   By default, the *Connection* object's *Open* method creates a database for shared access. However, you can set the *Connection* object's *Mode* property to any of seven other settings that grant various degrees of restricted access to a database. These mode settings pertain to all the recordsets and commands that assign a connection to their *ActiveConnection* property. The following code shows the impact of the read-only mode setting on the ability to update a recordset.

```
Sub OpenLookOnly()
Dim cnn1 As New Connection
Dim rsCustomers As Recordset
'    cnn1.Mode = adModeRead
    cnn1.Open "Provider=Microsoft.Jet.OLEDB.4.0;" & _
        "Data Source=C:\Program Files\Microsoft Office\Office\" & _
        "Samples\Northwind.mdb;"
    Set rsCustomers = New ADODB.Recordset
    rsCustomers.Open "Customers", cnn1, adOpenKeyset, _
        adLockPessimistic
'An adModeRead setting for cnn1.Mode causes an error in this procedure.
'Remove the comment from the cnn1.Mode line to see an error here.
    rsCustomers.Fields("CustomerID") = "xxxxx"
    rsCustomers.Update
    Debug.Print rsCustomers.Fields("CustomerID")
    rsCustomers.Close

End Sub
```

The *OpenLookOnly* procedure declares a new *Connection* object in its first line. The third line, if uncommented, sets the connection's *Mode* property to *adModeRead* for read-only access. Two more lines into the procedure, an *Open* method makes the *rsCustomers* recordset available. The next pair of lines attempts to update the value of the *CustomerID* field for the first record. If you remove the comment in the third line these updates will cause an error because you can't update a read-only database.

The following table describes the eight constants that you can use to set a connection's *Mode* property. You can use these constants to control the type of editing that one or more users can do through a connection to a database.

CONSTANTS USED TO SET THE
CONNECTION OBJECT'S *MODE* PROPERTY

Constant	*Value*	*Behavior*
adModeUnknown	0	Permissions not set or determined
adModeRead	1	Read-only permission
adModeWrite	2	Write-only permission
adModeReadWrite	3	Read/write permission
adModeShareDenyRead	4	Prevents others from opening record source with read permissions
adModeShareDenyWrite	8	Prevents others from opening record source with write permissions
adModeShareExclusive	12	Prevents others from opening the connection
adModeShareDenyNone	16	Shared access (default)

The *OpenSchema* method   The *Connection* object's *OpenSchema* method lets an application browse the objects in the collections available through a connection without enumerating the elements in a list. The output from the *OpenSchema* method can contain information about tables, views, procedures, indexes, and more. The specific details depend on how a given OLE DB provider implements the general capabilities of the method. The following code uses the *OpenSchema* method with the Jet 4 provider to list the views available through a connection.

```
Public Sub OpenSchemaX()
Dim cnn1 As New ADODB.Connection
Dim rstSchema As ADODB.Recordset

    cnn1.Open "Provider=Microsoft.Jet.OLEDB.4.0;" & _
        "Data Source=C:\Program Files\Microsoft Office\Office\" & _
        "Samples\Northwind.mdb;"

    Set rstSchema = cnn1.OpenSchema(adSchemaTables)

'Print just views; other selection criteria include
'TABLE, ACCESS TABLE, and SYSTEM TABLE.
    Do Until rstSchema.EOF
        If rstSchema.Fields("TABLE_TYPE") = "VIEW" Then
```

```
            Debug.Print "View name: " & _
                RstSchema.Fields("TABLE_NAME") & vbCr
        End If
        rstSchema.MoveNext
    Loop
    rstSchema.Close
    cnn1.Close

End Sub
```

The procedure starts by declaring a connection and a recordset. The recordset holds the output from the *OpenSchema* method. The argument for the *OpenSchema* method indicates that elements of the Tables domain for the database schema will make entries in the records. However, the *OpenSchema* method tracks several types of tables, including views, normal user tables, special system tables, another table of Access objects, and linked tables. The code above prints the output from the method just for views.

The *Recordset* object

A recordset is a programmatic construct for working with records. You can base your records on a table or a view in the current project or on another file, a SQL statement, or a command that returns rows. What you can do with a recordset depends on its OLE DB provider and on native data source attributes.

While you can extract recordsets using other objects, such as connections and commands, the *Recordset* object's rich mix of properties and methods make it a natural choice for doing much of your row-set processing. You can use recordsets to perform multiple actions against a set of rows: You can navigate between rows; print all or some of their contents; add, revise, and delete records; find records; and filter records to select one or any subset from a full recordset. Recordsets have historically been nonpersistent objects—they normally exist just for the time that they are open in a program. The 2.10 version of ADO that ships with Access 2000 offers persistent recordsets, which you can save to disk and then open again later.

The *ActiveConnection* property A recordset's *ActiveConnection* property lets your application tap an open connection to support a recordset. You can set this property any time after setting the object for the recordset. Its use simplifies your *Open* method statement for the recordset by removing the need to include the connection information. When you preset the property, you do not even need to reference an existing connection in the *Open* method statement.

The *Open* method The recordset's *Open* method is one common route for making a recordset available in a procedure. The source argument is the most critical one for this method. It designates the data source on which the method patterns the object that it opens. Typical options for the source argument include a table, a SQL statement, a saved recordset file, or a stored procedure. You use the *Open* method's *Options* argument to designate the source type when you open a recordset.

The cursor type   The cursor type is among the most basic features of a recordset. It determines how you can navigate through the recordset and the types of locks that you can impose on it. ADO supports four cursor types:

- *Dynamic*   This type of cursor lets users view changes to a data source made by other users. It enables recordset maintenance functions such as adding, changing, and deleting records, and it permits bidirectional navigation around a database without relying on bookmarks.

- *Keyset*   This cursor has most of the properties of a dynamic cursor, except you do not have ready access to changes by other users of a data source. One way to view changes made by others is to invoke a recordset's *Requery* method.

- *Static*   This cursor is a snapshot of a recordset at a point in time. It allows bidirectional navigation. Changes to the database by other users are not visible. Microsoft Internet Explorer 4 and later supports this type as its most flexible client-side cursor.

- *Forward-only*   Sometimes called the fire hydrant cursor, this type goes in one direction and can speed up cursor performance. This is the default ADO cursor type. If you need another type of cursor, you must set the *CursorType* property before opening the recordset.

    NOTE   The cursor type setting interacts with lock type settings. If you designate a forward-only cursor type with a lock type other than read-only (*adLockReadOnly*), ADO overrides your cursor type setting. For example, ADO automatically converts a forward-only cursor type to a keyset cursor type if you designate optimistic locking.

The *LockType* property   The *LockType* property partially interacts with the cursor type because it controls how users can manipulate a recordset. One lock type setting (*adLockReadOnly*) specifically matches forward-only cursors. This is the default lock type. The following table describes the four possible settings for the *LockType* property. The *adLockBatchOptimistic* setting is specifically for remote databases, such as SQL Server or Oracle, as opposed to a local Jet database. This topic will receive more attention in Chapter 12.

CONSTANTS USED TO SET THE
CONNECTION OBJECT'S *LOCKTYPE* PROPERTY

Constant	Value	Behavior
adLockReadOnly	1	Read-only access (default)
adLockPessimistic	2	Locks a record as soon as a user chooses to start editing it
adLockOptimistic	3	Locks a record only when a user chooses to commit edits back to the database
adLockBatchOptimistic	4	Allows edits to a batch of records before an attempt to update a remote database from the local batch of records

NOTE   You can determine whether the recordset you are using provides a particular type of functionality by using the *Supports* method. You simply put the constant that represents that functionality in parentheses when you invoke *Supports*. A return value of *True* indicates that the recordset provides that functionality. The online *Supports* documentation describes the names of the constants. Search the Object Browser for *CursorOptionEnum* to see a list of constants for which *Supports* returns *True* or *False*.

Recordset navigation   Four methods enable recordset navigation by changing the current record position:

- *MoveFirst*   This method changes the current record position to the first record in a recordset. The order of records depends on the current index, or, if there is no index, on the order of entry. This method functions with all cursor types. Its use with forward-only cursors can force a reexecution of the command that generated the recordset.

- *MoveLast*   This method establishes the last record in a recordset as the current record position. It requires a cursor type that supports backward movement or at least movement based on bookmarks. Using the method with a forward-only cursor generates a run-time error.

- *MoveNext*   This method relocates the current record position one record forward (in the direction of the recordset's final record). If the current record position is the last record, the recordset's *EOF* property is set to *True*. If this method is called when the recordset's *EOF* property is already *True*, a run-time error results.

■ *MovePrevious* This method sends the current record position one record backward. If the current record position is the first record, the recordset's *BOF* property is set to *True*. If this method is called when the recordset's *BOF* property is already *True*, a run-time error results. This method also generates a run-time error if you use it with a forward-only cursor type.

The *Move* method works differently than the other four recordset navigation methods because it can move the current record position a variable number of records in either direction. You use a positive argument to indicate moves toward the last record and a negative argument to identify moves toward the first record. If a move will extend beyond the first or last record, the *Move* method sets the recordset's *BOF* or *EOF* property to *True*. If that property is already *True*, the *Move* method generates a run-time error. Movement is relative to the current record unless you specify a *Start* parameter that can enable movement from the first or last record.

You can enhance the *Move* method's performance in a couple of ways by using it with a recordset's *CacheSize* property set to greater than the default value, which is 1. *CacheSize* settings cause ADO to store a fixed number of records in the local workstation's memory. Since it is much faster to retrieve records from memory than from a provider's data store, you can speed record navigation with *Move* by using a larger *CacheSize*. With a forward-only cursor and a larger *CacheSize*, you can actually enable backward as well as forward scrolling. If your cache setting is equal to the number of records in a recordset, you can scroll the full extent of the recordset in both directions. The *CacheSize* property does not enable backward scrolling with the *MovePrevious* method. (You can use the *Move* method with a negative argument.)

The *Find* method The recordset's *Find* method searches for the first record that matches a specified selection criterion. While this method bears a striking similarity to a collection of *Find* methods in earlier versions of Access, the Access 2000 version has a different syntax and behavior. Rather than attempt to map the similarities and differences, you should simply learn the syntax and behavior of the new version.

The new *Find* method takes as many as four arguments. The first argument is required and is the criterion for the search. Its syntax follows that of SQL statement WHERE clauses. If you do not specify any other arguments, the method searches from the current record through the last record to find a record that matches the criterion. Once the method finds a match, you must move off that record to find a new match in the recordset. If there is no match, the method sets the recordset's *EOF* property to *True*. See the online help for a description of the remaining three optional arguments.

The *Sort* property A recordset *Sort* property can affect the results of both the *Find* and *Move* methods. This property designates one or more fields that can determine the order in which rows display. The *Sort* property setting allows the designation of an ascending or descending order for any field. The default is ascending order. The *Sort* property settings do not physically rearrange the rows—they merely determine the order in which a recordset makes its rows available.

The *Filtered* property The *Filtered* property for a recordset defines a new recordset that is a filtered version of the original recordset. While this property has specialized applications for database synchronization and batch updating a remote data source, it can also be a simple alternative to defining a new recordset based on a SQL statement. If you already have a recordset and you need only a subset for another purpose, this property can serve admirably.

The *AddNew* method The *AddNew* method adds new records to a recordset. After you invoke the method, you set the values for the fields in a new row that you want to add. Then you either move off the record using a *Move* method or you call the *Update* method while still on the row. (You can modify the values in a field using a similar pair of techniques. You update fields by assigning them new values, and then you move off the record. Alternatively, you can remain on an edited record as long as you call the *Update* method. You can delete a record by simply navigating to it and then calling the *Delete* method. The deleted record remains current until you move away from it.)

Printing field values The following simple procedure opens a data source and then successively prints out the rows of the database. A loop passes through all the records and prints the first two fields of each record.

```
Sub EasyLoop()
Dim rsCustomers As Recordset

    Set rsCustomers = New ADODB.Recordset
    rsCustomers.Open "customers", & _
        "Provider=Microsoft.Jet.OLEDB.4.0;" & _
        "Data Source=C:\Program Files\Microsoft Office\Office\" & _
        "Samples\Northwind.mdb;"

'Loop through recordset.
    Do Until rsCustomers.EOF
        Debug.Print rsCustomers.Fields(0), rsCustomers.Fields(1)
        rsCustomers.MoveNext
    Loop

    rsCustomers.Close

End Sub
```

One weakness of the first *EasyLoop* procedure is that it prints only the values of the fields you specifically request. The *EasyLoop2* procedure below circumvents this difficulty. No matter how many fields are in the data source for a recordset, the procedure automatically prints all of them.

```
Sub EasyLoop2()
Dim rsCustomers As Recordset
Dim fldMyField As Field
Dim strForRow As String

    Set rsCustomers = New ADODB.Recordset

    rsCustomers.Open "customers", & _
        "Provider=Microsoft.Jet.OLEDB.4.0;" & _
        "Data Source=C:\Program Files\Microsoft Office\Office\" & _
        "Samples\Northwind.mdb;"

'Loop through recordset and fields with rows.
    Do Until rsCustomers.EOF
        strForRow = ""
        For Each fldMyField In rsCustomers.Fields
            strForRow = strForRow & fldMyField & "; "
        Next fldMyField
        Debug.Print strForRow
        rsCustomers.MoveNext
    Loop

    rsCustomers.Close


End Sub
```

The first several and last several lines in each procedure are identical. The *EasyLoop2* procedure nests a *For* loop inside a *Do* loop. This inner *For* loop enumerates the fields in a row and builds a string with all the field values on each row. (The string is cleared at the top of the loop to start the process over again for another row.)

Looping is an easy way to perform an operation on the rows and columns within a recordset. However, it is not the most efficient way to retrieve the field values of a recordset. The *NoEasyLoop* procedure below uses the *GetString* method to retrieve and print all the fields on all rows of a recordset in one step. The *GetString* method returns a recordset as a string. It can take up to five arguments; the code uses three of those arguments. You designate the *adClipString* constant as the first argument—this is your only choice. It specifies the format for representing the recordset as a string. The second argument specifies the number of recordset rows to return. This code returns five rows. Leaving this argument blank enables the method to return all the rows in the recordset. The third argument designates a semicolon delimiter for the columns within a row. The default column delimiter is a tab. The fourth and fifth arguments, neither of which appears below, specify a column delimiter and an expression to represent null values. The default values for these arguments are a carriage return and a zero-length string.

```
Sub NoEasyLoop()
Dim rsCustomers As Recordset

    Set rsCustomers = New ADODB.Recordset

    rsCustomers.Open "customers", _
        "Provider=Microsoft.Jet.OLEDB.4.0;" & _
        "Data Source=C:\Program Files\Microsoft Office\Office\" & _
        "Samples\Northwind.mdb;"

'Print records without a loop.
    Debug.Print rsCustomers.GetString(adClipString, 5, "; ")

    rsCustomers.Close

End Sub
```

The *GetString* method replaces a pair of nested loops. If the defaults are acceptable, you can use the method without any arguments. This makes for a simple way to extract values from a recordset. Although nested loops are the intuitive way to retrieve values from a recordset, the *GetString* method can achieve a similar result in a single line.

Adding a record   The following code tackles a new task—adding a new record to a data source.

```
Sub AddARecord()
Dim rsMyTable As Recordset

'Set your cursor so that it is not read-only to delete.
    Set rsMyTable = New ADODB.Recordset
    rsMyTable.ActiveConnection = CurrentProject.Connection
    rsMyTable.Open "MyTable", , adOpenKeyset, adLockOptimistic, _
        adCmdTable

'Invoke the AddNew method.
    rsMyTable.AddNew
    rsMyTable.Fields("Column1").Value = 16
    rsMyTable.Fields("Column2").Value = 17
    rsMyTable.Fields("Column3").Value = 18
    rsMyTable.Update

End Sub
```

While *EasyLoop*, *EasyLoop2*, and *NoEasyLoop* all accept the *Open* method's default cursor type and lock type settings, the *AddARecord* procedure does not. Recall that the defaults are a forward-only cursor and a read-only lock type. These settings are acceptable for merely printing the contents of a recordset. However, you need a cursor and a lock type that permit updates to a recordset when your task requires adding, editing, or deleting records. The *adOpenKeyset* and *adLockOptimistic* arguments to *Open* allow you to add new rows to a recordset. Also, notice that the *ActiveConnection* setting in the code above does not reference the Northwind sample project. It instead references the connection for the current project. When you need to reference a data source in the current project, use this syntax. The connection statement also explicitly designates a table in the current project as the data source for the recordset. There are several alternative sources, including the text for a SQL statement, a stored procedure, an external file saved in a special format, and more.

To use the *AddNew* method to add a record, you call the method, issue assignment statements to populate the new record with values, and then invoke the *Update* method. The call to *Update* is not strictly mandatory; you can simply move off the new, current record. For example, you can invoke *MoveFirst* or another method to navigate to a new record.

Editing or deleting a record　The following code edits or deletes a record. It does not use the *Edit* and *Update* methods to save the edited records. Instead, it moves off the record. If it is impractical to move off the record or if your application needs to commit the changes before moving, use the recordset's *Update* method instead.

```
Sub DeleteOrUpdateARecord()
Dim rsMyTable As Recordset

'Use a non-read-only lock type to be able to delete records.
    Set rsMyTable = New ADODB.Recordset
    rsMyTable.ActiveConnection = CurrentProject.Connection
    rsMyTable.Open "MyTable", , adOpenKeyset, adLockOptimistic, _
        adCmdTable

'Loop through recordset.
    Do Until rsMyTable.EOF
        If rsMyTable.Fields("Column1") = 16 Then
            rsMyTable.Fields("Column1") = 88
            rsMyTable.Delete
        End If
        rsMyTable.MoveNext
    Loop

    rsMyTable.Close

End Sub
```

A loop such as the one in the *DeleteOrUpdateARecord* procedure can help you select records for deleting or editing. The procedure examines each *Column1* field value in a recordset, searching for one with a value of 16. When it finds one, it deletes the row. Notice that the loop contains a comment line. To switch from a delete routine to an updating routine, you simply transfer the comment mark from the assignment line to the *Delete* method line.

Finding records Another common use for a recordset is to find one or more records that meet specified criteria. Access 2000 offers several approaches to this task. With earlier versions of Access, many developers used one or more variations of the *Find* method. As mentioned earlier, Access 2000 offers a single *Find* method that works somewhat differently from the earlier *Find* methods. If you liked the earlier *Find* methods, you can use the new *Find* method with its similar functionality.

The following code shows a simple application of the *Find* method that searches for a record with a customer ID that begins with the letter *D*. When it finds a record matching its criteria, the method relocates the current record to that location. The code prints the *CustomerID* and *ContactName* fields to confirm exactly which record matches the criteria.

```
Sub FindAMatch()
Dim rsCustomers As Recordset

    Set rsCustomers = New ADODB.Recordset
    rsCustomers.ActiveConnection = _
        "Provider=Microsoft.Jet.OLEDB.4.0;" & _
        "Data Source=C:\Program Files\Microsoft Office\Office\" & _
        "Samples\Northwind.mdb;"
    rsCustomers.Open "Customers", , adOpenKeyset, adLockPessimistic, _
        adCmdTable
    rsCustomers.Find ("CustomerID Like 'D*'")
    Debug.Print rsCustomers.Fields("CustomerID"), _
        rsCustomers.Fields("ContactName")

End Sub
```

One drawback to this approach is that it searches for a single match to the criteria, and then stops immediately after finding it. The code below discovers all the records that match the criteria statement. This simple application reveals more of the flexibility of the *Find* method.

```
Sub FindAMatch2()
Dim rsCustomers As Recordset

    Set rsCustomers = New ADODB.Recordset
    rsCustomers.ActiveConnection = & _
        "Provider=Microsoft.Jet.OLEDB.4.0;" & _
```

(continued)

```
                      "Data Source=C:\Program Files\Microsoft Office\Office\" & _
                      "Samples\Northwind.mdb;"
             rsCustomers.Open "Customers", , adOpenKeyset, _adLockPessimistic,
                 adCmdTable
             Do
                 rsCustomers.Find ("CustomerID Like 'D*'")
                 If rsCustomers.EOF Then
                     Exit Sub
                 End If
                 Debug.Print rsCustomers.Fields("CustomerID")
                 rsCustomers.MoveNext
             Loop

End Sub
```

The trick to finding all the records that match the search criteria is to embed the *Find* method in a *Do* loop. When the *Find* method sets the recordset's *EOF* property to *True*, there are no additional matching records. In this case, the code executes an *Exit Sub* statement to end the subroutine. As long as *Find* keeps discovering new matches, the procedure prints the customer IDs in the Immediate window. After printing a matching record, the procedure advances the current record by one. Without this, the *Find* method would repeatedly return the same record.

The *Find* method goes through a recordset sequentially and discloses matches one at a time. It does not create another version of the recordset that contains all the records that match the criteria. When you need a new or alternate recordset containing just the matches, your application needs a different approach. The recordset *Filter* property might be the answer. This property lets you designate a simple criterion for a field, and it returns a filtered version of the original recordset with only those records that match the criterion. By setting the *Filter* property equal to any of a series of constants, you can achieve special effects for database replication or for updating a remote data source. One filter constant, *adFilterNone*, removes the filter setting from a recordset and restores the original values.

Filtering records   The two following procedures filter a recordset based on the *Customers* table in the Northwind database. The *FilterRecordset* procedure manages the overall use of the *Filter* property, prints the result set, clears the filter, and then prints the result set again. The *FilterRecordset* procedure relies on the *FilterLikeField* function to manage the setting of the *Filter* property based on parameters passed to it by the *FilterRecordset* procedure.

```
Sub FilterRecordset()
Dim rsCustomers As Recordset

'Create recordset variable.
```

```
    Set rsCustomers = New ADODB.Recordset
    rsCustomers.ActiveConnection = & _
        "Provider=Microsoft.Jet.OLEDB.4.0;" & _
        "Data Source=C:\Program Files\Microsoft Office\Office\" & _
        "Samples\Northwind.mdb;"

'Open recordset.
    rsCustomers.Open "Customers", , , , adCmdTable

'Filter recordset.
    Set rsCustomers = _
        FilterLikeField(rsCustomers, "CustomerID", "D*")
    Debug.Print rsCustomers.GetString

'Restore recordset.
    rsCustomers.Filter = adFilterNone
    Debug.Print rsCustomers.GetString

    rsCustomers.Close

End Sub


Function FilterLikeField(rstTemp As ADODB.Recordset, _
    strField As String, strFilter As String) As ADODB.Recordset

'Set a filter on the specified Recordset object and then
'open a new Recordset object.
    rstTemp.Filter = strField & " LIKE '" & strFilter & "'"
    Set FilterLikeField = rstTemp

End Function
```

The *FilterRecordset* procedure starts by creating and opening the *rsCustomers* recordset. Next, it applies a filter by calling the *FilterLikeField* function, which takes three arguments and returns a filtered recordset based on them. *FilterRecordset* assigns the filtered return set to *rsCustomers* and prints it to confirm the result.

The arguments to *FilterLikeField* include *rsCustomers*, a field name on which to filter records, and a filter criterion value, which can include any legitimate expression for the Like operator used by *FilterLikeField*. *FilterRecordset* passes *D** to find just the records that have a *CustomerID* beginning with the letter *D*. The *Filter* property does not restrict you to filtering with the Like operator. Other acceptable operators include <, >, <=, >=, <>, and =. You can also include And and Or operators in your criteria expressions to combine two or more criteria expressions based on the other legitimate operators.

The *Filter* property does restrict your criteria expressions to those of the form *FieldName-Operator-Value*. However, some *Filter* constants enable special uses of the property. The *FilterRecordset* procedure uses the *adFilterNone* property to restore a recordset by removing its filters.

Using SQL to create a recordset   You should know one final thing about recordsets: how to generate recordsets based on SQL statements. SQL statements are often nothing more than "SELECT * FROM TABLENAME", but you can tap the full functionality of SQL to generate recordsets. You can even use complex multitable SELECT statements with computed fields that use either inner or outer joins and that constrain or organize return sets with WHERE, GROUP BY, and ORDER BY clauses. One easy way to create a custom recordset based on SQL statements is by using WHERE clauses. You can selectively extract records from an existing source using expressions that are more complicated than when you use the *Filter* property.

The following code uses an *Open* method with a SQL statement. When you base a recordset on a SQL statement instead of an existing table, you pass your SQL statement and use the optional *adCmdTable* argument instead of *adCmdText*. That's all there is to it. You can then use the recordset to construct any simpler recordset based on an individual table. More complicated SQL statements do not alter how you declare or use the recordset with ADO.

```
Sub SQLRecordset()
Dim rsCustomers As Recordset
'Create recordset variable.
    Set rsCustomers = New ADODB.Recordset
    rsCustomers.ActiveConnection = & _
        "Provider=Microsoft.Jet.OLEDB.4.0;" & _
        "Data Source=C:\Program Files\Microsoft Office\Office\" & _
        "Samples\Northwind.mdb;"

'Open the recordset.
    rsCustomers.Open "SELECT * FROM Customers", , adOpenForwardOnly, _
        adLockReadOnly, adCmdText
    Debug.Print rsCustomers.GetString

    rsCustomers.Close

End Sub
```

The *Field* object

A field is a column of data containing entries with the same data type. In the ADODB library, the *Fields* collection belongs exclusively to recordsets, and its members are *Field* objects. *Field* objects have properties and methods for storing and retrieving data.

Recordsets use a *Field* object's *Value* property to display the contents of a column in the current record. When you change the record, this value can change to reflect the contents of the new record. Many of the other *Field* properties contain metadata—data about the data in a record. The *Name* property is a handle by which your applications can reference a field. The *DefinedSize* property characterizes the maximum size of a field (in characters for Text fields). The *ActualSize* property is the actual length (in bytes) of the contents of a *Field* object's value. The *Attributes* property contains an array of information features about a field. It can indicate whether a field's value is updatable or whether it can contain Nulls.

> **NOTE** The *DefinedSize* and *ActualSize* properties use different measurements for Text fields. *DefinedSize* is the maximum number of characters in the field and *ActualSize* is the number of bytes in the field. Since Text fields with Jet 4 represent characters with 2 bytes each, their *ActualSize* value can be as much as twice the *DefinedSize* value. For numeric fields, and Text fields in databases that represent characters with 1 byte (for example, a Jet 3.51 database), this difference does not exist.

The *Field* methods *GetChunk* and *AppendChunk* facilitate processing of large text or binary data fields in smaller chunks that more conveniently fit into memory. You use the *GetChunk* method to bring into memory a portion of a large field. The *Size* argument specifies the number of bytes to retrieve in one invocation of the *GetChunk* method. Each uninterrupted, successive invocation of the method starts reading new data from where the previous one finished. The *AppendChunk* method lets you construct a large text or binary data field in chunks from memory. Like the *GetChunk* method, it writes new data into a field from where the previous *AppendChunk* method finished. To use either method correctly, a *Field* object's *adFldLong* bit in the *Attributes* property must be set to *True*.

The *Name* and *Value* properties   The following procedure shows common uses for the *Name* and *Value* properties. It lists all the field names with their corresponding values. This procedure creates its single-record recordset based on a SQL statement.

```
Sub FieldNameValue()
Dim cnn1 As ADODB.Connection
Dim rsCustomers As ADODB.Recordset
Dim fldLoop As ADODB.Field

'Open connection and recordset.
    strCnn = "Provider=Microsoft.Jet.OLEDB.4.0;" & _
        "Data Source=C:\Program Files\Microsoft Office" & _
```

(continued)

```
                "\Office\Samples\Northwind.mdb;"
        Set cnn1 = New ADODB.Connection
        cnn1.Open strCnn
        Set rsCustomers = New ADODB.Recordset
        rsCustomers.ActiveConnection = cnn1
        rsCustomers.Open "SELECT * FROM Customers " & _
            "WHERE CustomerID='BONAP'", , , , adCmdText

    'Report field names and values for record.
        For Each fldLoop In rsCustomers.Fields
            Debug.Print fldLoop.Name, fldLoop.Value
        Next fldLoop

    End Sub
```

The procedure begins by opening a connection and then creating a recordset on the connection. The SQL statement extracts the record for the customer with a *CustomerID* field equal to *BONAP*. The *Do* loop that follows the creation of the recordset loops through the recordset's fields. Printing the *Name* property along with the *Value* property helps readability.

The *Type* property   A *Field* object's *Type* property indicates the kind of data it can contain. This property returns one of the data type constants in the *DataTypeEnum* values range. You can view these options in the Object Browser for the ADODB library. Figure 2-5 shows these constants in the Object Browser screen. By selecting the type for a field, you can determine legitimate values for its *Value* property.

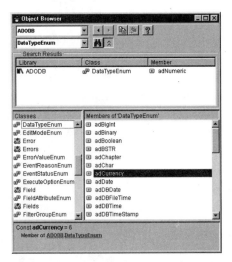

Figure 2-5. *The Object Browser showing a selection of data type constants.*

Printing field data types   The following two procedures work together to
process data type constants with ADO. The *FieldNameType* procedure opens
a recordset based on the *Orders* table in the Northwind database. This table has
a reasonable variety of data types, so it makes a nice case study for examining
data types. After opening a recordset, the procedure loops through the fields
in the recordset and prints each *Field* object's name and type. The *FieldType*
function translates the numeric constant's value to a string that represents the
constant. The *adCurrency* constant has a value of 6. The *FieldType* function
decodes the value 6 to the string *"adCurrency"*. The *FieldNameType* procedure
then prints each field's name and data type constant name.

```
Sub FieldNameType()
Dim cnn1 As ADODB.Connection
Dim rsOrders As ADODB.Recordset
Dim fldLoop As ADODB.Field

'Open connection and recordset.
    strCnn = "Provider=Microsoft.Jet.OLEDB.4.0;" & _
        "Data Source=C:\Program Files\Microsoft Office" & _
        "\Office\Samples\Northwind.mdb;"
    Set cnn1 = New ADODB.Connection
    cnn1.Open strCnn
    Set rsOrders = New ADODB.Recordset
    rsOrders.ActiveConnection = cnn1
    rsOrders.Open "orders", , , , adCmdTable

'Report field names and types for record.
    For Each fldLoop In rsOrders.Fields
        Debug.Print " Name: " & fldLoop.Name & vbCr & _
            " Type: " & FieldType(fldLoop.Type) & vbCr
    Next fldLoop

End Sub


Public Function FieldType(intType As Integer) As String
    Select Case intType
        Case adVarWChar
            FieldType = "adVarWChar"
        Case adCurrency
            FieldType = "adCurrency"
        Case adInteger
            FieldType = "adInteger"
        Case adDate
            FieldType = "adDate"
    End Select

End Function
```

Figure 2-6 shows an excerpt from the output from *FieldNameType*. This excerpt includes at least one field from each of the data types decoded in the *FieldType* function. You can easily run *FieldNameType* and *FieldType* against recordsets based on other data sources than the *Orders* table. You might encounter another data type besides the four in the list. In this case, the *Type* field in the report will be blank. You can fix this problem by determining the value of the field. You do this by putting a breakpoint on the *Debug.Print* statement inside the *Do* loop in the *FieldNameType* procedure. You examine the value of *fldloop.Type* for a field whose type doesn't display and then match that constant value against the constant names in the Object Browser for *DataTypeEnum*. (See Figure 2-5 on page 98.) Finally, you amend the *Select Case* statement in the *FieldType* procedure to decode the new constant.

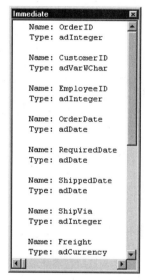

Figure 2-6. *An excerpt from the output for the* FieldNameType *procedure.*

Finding the longest field entry   The *FieldSizes* procedure below applies the *ActualSize* property to find the longest entry in the *CompanyName* field of the *Shippers* table in the Northwind database. The procedure begins by creating a connection to the Northwind database, and then it opens a recordset based on the *Shippers* table. The second portion of the routine finds the longest shipper's name and displays a message box showing the number of characters in the name and the name itself.

```
Sub FieldSizes()
Dim cnn1 As ADODB.Connection
Dim rsShippers As ADODB.Recordset
Dim fldLoop As ADODB.Field
```

```
Dim intMaxChars As Integer, strMsg As String
Dim strName As String
'Open connection and recordset.
    strCnn = "Provider=Microsoft.Jet.OLEDB.4.0;" & _
        "Data Source=C:\Program Files\Microsoft Office" & _
        "\Office\Samples\Northwind.mdb;"
    Set cnn1 = New ADODB.Connection
    cnn1.Open strCnn
    Set rsShippers = New ADODB.Recordset
    rsShippers.ActiveConnection = cnn1
    rsShippers.Open "SELECT * FROM Shippers" _
        , , , , adCmdText

'Find longest shipper's name.
    intMaxChars = 0
    Do Until rsShippers.EOF
        If rsShippers!CompanyName.ActualSize / 2 _
            > intMaxChars Then
            intMaxChars _
                = rsShippers!CompanyName.ActualSize / 2
            strName = rsShippers.Fields("CompanyName")
        End If
        rsShippers.MoveNext
    Loop
    strMsg = "The longest shipper's name is '" & _
        strName  & "' (" & intMaxChars & " characters)."
    MsgBox strMsg, vbInformation, "Programming Microsoft Access 2000"

    rsShippers.Close

End Sub
```

The *intMaxChars* variable tracks the longest field length. The second portion of *FieldSizes* initializes the variable to 0 before opening a loop that goes through all of the records in the recordset. It is not strictly necessary to set *intMaxChars* to 0 because VBA does that automatically. However, doing so helps to make the procedure self-documenting. Any shipper's name containing more characters than the current value of *intMaxChars* is the longest name up to that point. When the procedure finds such a name, it updates *intMaxChars* and saves the name. Notice that the procedure uses two different syntax conventions for referencing a field. Several statements use a bang character (!), an older Access notation. In this notation, the bang character separates the recordset name and the name of the field. The newer and more common way is to reference the field using the *Fields* collection. You can use the numerical index if you know it, or you can include the field name in quotes.

Command and *Parameter* objects

Within the ADODB library, *Command* objects deliver three major benefits:

- They can perform a select query to return a set of rows from a data source.

- They execute a parameter query so that you can input run-time search criteria.

- They support action queries against a data source to perform such operations as the updating, deleting, and adding of records.

The *Command* object can serve additional roles with other libraries, as discussed in later sections.

You must designate a *Connection* object on which to run a command. You can either implicitly create a *Connection* object when you specify a command or explicitly assign an existing *Connection* object to a command. These are the same options as for recordsets.

The *CommandTimeout* property determines how long ADO waits for the execution of a command to conclude. This property takes a Long value that specifies the maximum wait time in seconds. Its default value is 30. If the timeout interval elapses before the *Command* object completes execution, ADO cancels the command and returns an error. The *Connection* object also supports a *CommandTimeout* property. It has the same name, but it is independent of the *Command* object's *CommandTimeout* property. The *Command* object's *CommandTimeout* property does not inherit the setting of the *Connection* object's *CommandTimeout* property.

The *CommandType* property   There are actually several different types of *Command* objects. The *CommandType* property sets the type of *Command* object. You can base your command on a SQL statement, a table, or a stored procedure, as shown in the following table. One main reason for resorting to a *CommandType* property setting is to enable the creation of a *Command* object based on a SQL statement. Changing the *CommandType* constant from its default setting can speed up the operation of a command. Therefore, if you know the source, you should set this constant.

The *CommandText* property   To write a SQL statement for the command to execute, you use the *Command* object's *CommandText* setting. You can also set this property to the name of a stored procedure. When you run a SQL statement, you can use the *Prepared* property to indicate that the statement is to be compiled and stored on the database server. This slows the first execution of the command but speeds up subsequent executions. You assign *True* to the *Prepared* property to invoke compilation of a SQL statement.

COMMANDTYPE CONSTANTS

Constant	Value	Behavior
adCmdText	1	Lets you run a command based on a SQL statement, a stored procedure, or even a table. Usually, you reserve this setting for a SQL statement.
adCmdTable	2	Bases the return set on a previously designed table. Returns all columns from a table based on an internally generated SQL statement.
adCmdStoredProc	4	Runs a command based on text for a stored procedure.
adCmdUnknown	8	There is no specification of the type of command text. This is the default.
adCmdFile	256	Evaluates a command based on the filename for a persistent recordset.
adCmdTableDirect	512	Evaluates a command as a table name. Returns all columns in a table without any intermediate SQL code.

The *Execute* method   The *Execute* method for a *Command* object invokes the code behind the *Command* object (a query, a SQL statement, or a stored procedure). You can specify up to three arguments for the *Execute* method. The first argument allows the *Command* object to tell the procedure invoking it how many records it has affected. The second argument can be a *Variant* array with parameters to drive the command. The third argument tells ADO how to evaluate the source. It can be any of the constant names listed in the table above.

The *CreateParameter* method   The *Command* object's *CreateParameter* method creates a new parameter for a command. After creating the parameter, you can use the *Append* method to add the parameter to the *Parameters* collection for a command. Before running a parameter query, you also have to assign a value to the parameter.

Creating a recordset with a select query   One of the most straightforward tasks you can perform with a *Command* object is to create a recordset based on a select query. The *Command* object runs the select query and represents its return set. Your code can then open a *Recordset* object based on the return set from the *Command* object. The *SelectCommand* procedure below accomplishes this. It has two parts: One part creates the *Command* object and a connection for it to relate to a database, and the second part processes a recordset based on the return set from the *Command* object.

```
Sub SelectCommand()
Dim cmd1 As Command
Dim rs1 As Recordset, str1 As String
Dim fldLoop As ADODB.Field

'Define and execute command.

    Set cmd1 = New ADODB.Command

    With cmd1
        .ActiveConnection = CurrentProject.Connection
        .CommandText = "SELECT MyTable.* FROM MyTable"
        .CommandType = adCmdText
        .Execute
    End With

'Open and print recordset.
    Set rs1 = New ADODB.Recordset
    rs1.Open cmd1

    Do Until rs1.EOF
        str1 = ""
        For Each fldLoop In rs1.Fields
            str1 = str1 & fldLoop.Value & Chr(9)
        Next fldLoop
        Debug.Print str1
        rs1.MoveNext
    Loop

End Sub
```

The first part declares *cmd1* as a *Command* object and then sets three critical properties of the object. Every command must have an *ActiveConnection* property in order to run against a database. The *Command* object relies on a SQL statement to represent its select query. You can substitute a saved query. An *Execute* statement runs the select query. After the *Execute* method runs, *cmd1* contains a reference to a recordset.

The second part of the procedure opens a *Recordset* object based on *cmd1* and prints the return set with tab delimiters (*Chr(9)*) in the Immediate window. The procedure can handle any number of columns in any number of rows.

Creating a recordset with a parameter query The following code is an example of a parameter query. This code also has a two-part design. The parameter query in the first part has some extra ADO code lines and a different SQL statement syntax than that of the previous select query. The second part that prints the return set is the same as the previous select query.

```
Sub ParameterQCommand()
Dim cmd1 As Command
Dim rs1 As Recordset, str1 As String
Dim fldLoop As ADODB.Field
Dim prm1 As ADODB.Parameter, int1 As Integer

'Create and define command.
    Set cmd1 = New ADODB.Command

    With cmd1
        .ActiveConnection = CurrentProject.Connection
        .CommandText = "Parameters [Lowest] Long;" & _
            "SELECT Column1, Column2, Column3 " & _
            "FROM MyTable " & _
            "WHERE Column1>=[Lowest]"
        .CommandType = adCmdText
    End With

'Create and define parameter.
    Set prm1 = cmd1.CreateParameter("[Lowest]", _
        adInteger, adParamInput)
    cmd1.Parameters.Append prm1
    int1 = Trim(InputBox("Lowest value?", _
        "Programming Microsoft Access 2000"))
    prm1.Value = int1

'Run parameter query.
    cmd1.Execute

'Open recordset on cmd1 and print it out.
    Set rs1 = New ADODB.Recordset
    rs1.Open cmd1

    Do Until rs1.EOF
        str1 = ""
        For Each fldLoop In rs1.Fields
            str1 = str1 & fldLoop.Value & Chr(9)
        Next fldLoop
        Debug.Print str1
        rs1.MoveNext
    Loop

End Sub
```

The SQL statement syntax uses a new *Parameters* declaration line that specifies the parameter's name and data type. The WHERE clause should also reference one or more parameters so that the parameters can affect the return set. These SQL syntax statement adjustments are not by themselves sufficient to make the parameter query work—you must add the parameter and append it to the command using ADO code.

You invoke the *CreateParameter* method to add the parameter. The code above uses three arguments with the *CreateParameter* method. The first one names the parameter, the second designates a data type for the parameter, and the third declares a direction for the parameter. The *adParamInput* constant is actually the default that declares the parameter an input to the query. Other constants let you designate output, input/output, and return value parameters. After creating a parameter, you must append it to the *Parameters* collection for the command.

After writing the code to add a parameter, you must assign a value to the parameter to make the parameter query command function properly: The code above uses an *InputBox* function to gather input from a user. The procedure then invokes the *Command* object's *Execute* method to generate a return set.

Deleting records   You can use the *Command* object to delete, update, and add records to a data source. *Command* objects offer a programmatic means of maintaining a data source. The *DeleteARecord* and *DeleteAllRecords* procedures below prune records from a data source. You designate the data source and the criteria for selecting records using the SQL DELETE statement. The SQL view in the Access query window lets you graphically design a query and then copy the code to the *CommandText* property of a command. You typically want to edit the SQL code from the Access query designer to remove extra parentheses. If your query operates on a single table, you can remove the table prefix before field names. As you can see, the difference between the two delete queries is simply the syntax of the SQL statement.

```
Sub DeleteARecord()
Dim cmd1 As ADODB.Command

    Set cmd1 = New ADODB.Command

    With cmd1
        .ActiveConnection = CurrentProject.Connection
        .CommandText = "DELETE MyTable.Column1 FROM " & _
            "MyTable WHERE (((MyTable.Column1)=13));"
        .CommandType = adCmdText
        .Execute
    End With

End Sub


Sub DeleteAllRecords()
Dim cmd1 As ADODB.Command
```

```
    Set cmd1 = New ADODB.Command

With cmd1
    .ActiveConnection = CurrentProject.Connection
    .CommandText = "DELETE MyTable.* FROM MyTable"
    .CommandType = adCmdText
    .Execute
End With

End Sub
```

Inserting records   When you develop an application, you might want the ability to delete all the records from a table and then reset its contents. The *InsertRecords* procedure below uses the *Command* object to stock a table with values. You can use this procedure in conjunction with the *DeleteAllRecords* procedure to refresh a table with a small base set of records.

```
Sub InsertRecords()
Dim cmd1 As ADODB.Command

    Set cmd1 = New Command

    With cmd1
        .ActiveConnection = CurrentProject.Connection
        .CommandText = "INSERT INTO MyTable(Column1, " & _
            "Column2, Column3) VALUES (1,2,'3')"
        .CommandType = adCmdText
        .Execute
        .CommandText = "INSERT INTO MyTable(Column1, " & _
            "Column2, Column3) VALUES (4,5,'6')"
        .CommandType = adCmdText
        .Execute
        .CommandText = "INSERT INTO MyTable(Column1, " & _
            "Column2, Column3) VALUES (7,8,'9')"
        .CommandType = adCmdText
        .Execute
        .CommandText = "INSERT INTO MyTable(Column1, " & _
            "Column2, Column3) VALUES (10,11,'12')"
        .CommandType = adCmdText
        .Execute
        .CommandText = "INSERT INTO MyTable(Column1, " & _
            "Column2, Column3) VALUES (13,14,'15')"
        .CommandType = adCmdText
        .Execute
        .CommandText = "INSERT INTO MyTable(Column1, " & _
            "Column2, Column3) VALUES (16,17,'18')"
```

(continued)

```
                    .CommandType = adCmdText
                    .Execute
            End With

    End Sub
```

The *InsertRecords* procedure has general and specific elements. The general elements do not depend on the design of a particular table. In the code above, the specific elements tailor the general elements for the *MyTable* table. Figure 2-7 shows *MyTable* in Design view. It has three columns, named *Column1*, *Column2*, and *Column3*. The first two columns have Long Integer data types, and the third column has a Text data type. (When you add records to a table, you must consider the field data types.)

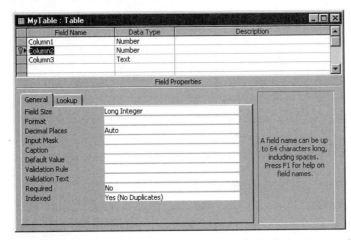

Figure 2-7. *The Design view of the table to which the* InsertRecords *procedure adds records.*

The general elements of the *InsertRecords* procedure are shared with other applications of the *Command* object. You create a reference to the *Command* object and set its connection property. For each row that you need to add to a record, three lines are required: the *CommandText* property setting, which indicates what the command will do; the *CommandType* property setting, which designates the format of the instruction; and the *Execute* method, which launches the addition of the new record. You can repeat these three lines for each row added to the data source. If you specify an updatable dynaset as the target, these steps can concurrently add records to two or more tables at the same time.

The syntax of the *CommandText* SQL statement has three features. (This syntax is not available from the SQL view of the Access query designer.) First, it uses the INSERT INTO keyword, which is followed by the name of the data source to which you want to add records. Second, it takes the optional step of listing the field names for which it submits values. If you do not take this step, your values in the third step will append in sequential order, which can be a problem if the data source design changes over time. Third, the VALUES keyword appears before the field values for the new record.

Updating record values The *OddToEven* and *EvenToOdd* procedures below update data source values of *Column1* using the *Command* object. Figure 2-8 shows a fresh view of the table immediately after the *DeleteAllRecords* and *InsertRecords* procedures run. Notice that in Figure 2-8 the *Column1* values alternate between odd and even: If the value in *Column1* is odd, the value in *Column2* is even. The procedures use this information to manage the contents of the table.

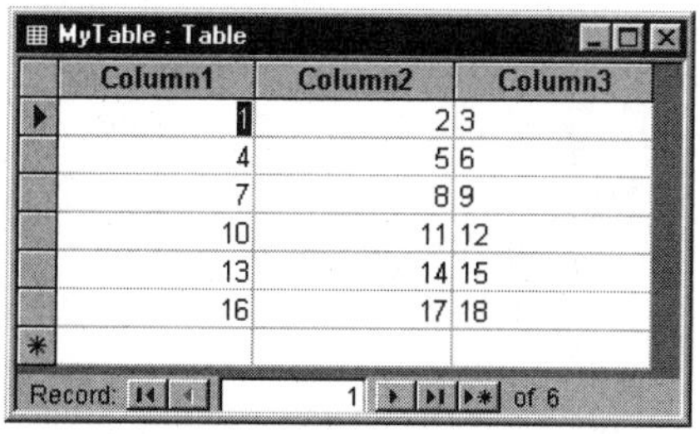
MyTable : Table

Column1	Column2	Column3
1	2	3
4	5	6
7	8	9
10	11	12
13	14	15
16	17	18

Record: 1 of 6

Figure 2-8. *A Datasheet view of the table that the* OddToEven *and* EvenToOdd *procedures update.*

```
Sub OddToEven()
Dim cmdO2E As ADODB.Command
Dim intRowsChanged As Integer

    Set cmdO2E = New ADODB.Command

    With cmdO2E
        .ActiveConnection = CurrentProject.Connection
        .CommandText = "UPDATE MyTable SET Column1 = " & _
            "Column1+1 WHERE ((-1*(Column1 Mod 2))=True)"
        .CommandType = adCmdText
        .Execute intRowsChanged
        Debug.Print intRowsChanged & " rows were affected."
    End With

End Sub


Sub EvenToOdd()
Dim cmdE2O As ADODB.Command
```

(continued)

```
    Set cmdE20 = New ADODB.Command

With cmdE20
    .ActiveConnection = CurrentProject.Connection
    .CommandText = "UPDATE MyTable SET Column1 = " & _
        "Column1-1 WHERE ((-1*(Column2 Mod 2))=False)"
    .CommandType = adCmdText
    .Execute
End With

End Sub
```

The overall design of these procedures should be familiar by now. The most significant difference between these examples and earlier ones is in the syntax of the SQL statement for the *CommandText* property. In this case, you can easily derive that general syntax from the Access query designer. The WHERE clause in the *OddToEven* procedure selects records whose Column1 value is odd. The UPDATE part of the syntax adds 1 to the value to convert the value from an odd to an even number. The *Execute* method uses one of its built-in arguments to return the number of rows that a command changes. A simple *Print* method sends this value to the Immediate window for viewing.

The *EvenToOdd* procedure examines the entry in *Column2* to determine whether it should subtract 1 from the value in *Column1*. When the entry in *Column2* is not odd, the SQL statement operates on the value in *Column1*. This restores the entries in *Column1* to their initial values if *EvenToOdd* runs immediately after the *OddToEven* procedure runs.

The *Errors* collection

The *Errors* collection lets you trap some, but not all, errors that occur in an ADO application. It also returns errors from an OLE DB provider. A single error condition can return multiple errors, each of which causes a new *Error* object to be placed in the *Errors* collection. Some errors cause a program termination; others do not. A new failure automatically clears the *Errors* collection for the entry of errors associated with it. Some ADO errors enter the *Err* object rather than *Errors* collection, but you might want to use the latter collection as well. The *Errors* collection is most appropriate for handling connection-based errors returned from a remote database through its OLE DB provider.

The *Error* objects in the *Errors* collection have five properties that help you gather more information so that you can respond to them with program logic. The *Number* and *Description* properties parallel those for the *Err* object. These properties complement one another. The *Number* property returns a unique number that identifies an error, and the *Description* property returns a brief string that describes the error. The *NativeError* property offers a provider-specific error code. If you often work with a particular provider, this property might provide useful information about how to resolve an error. The *Source* property names the object or application that originated the error. The *SQLState* property can contain SQL statement syntax error messages originating from the database server to which you submit your request.

The *OpenLookOnlyErrors* procedure below is an adaptation of an earlier procedure that reveals the impact of the *Connection* object's *Mode* property. A read-only setting for this property causes an error to be generated when you attempt to update a database. Interestingly, this error does not become part of the *Errors* collection. You can trap the error and respond to it using the *Err* object. The last member of the *Errors* collection also appears in the *Err* object. The error-trapping logic at the end of the procedure avoids printing two lines with an identical number and description.

```
Sub OpenLookOnlyErrors()
Dim cnn1 As New Connection
Dim rsCustomers As Recordset
Dim errLoop As Error, intInErrors As Integer
On Error GoTo LookOnlyTrap

    cnn1.Mode = adModeRead
    cnn1.Open "Provider=Microsoft.Jet.OLEDB.4.0;" & _
        "Data Source=C:\Program Files\Microsoft Office\Office\" & _
        "Samples\Northwind.mdb;"
'Spell Northwind incorrectly to generate trappable error.
'    cnn1.Open "Provider=Microsoft.Jet.OLEDB.4.0;" & _
        "Data Source=C:\Program Files\Microsoft Office\Office\" & _
        "Samples\Northwinds.mdb;"
'No Errrors element for faulty provider spelling
'    cnn1.Open "Provider=Microsoft.Jets.OLEDB.4.0;" & _
        "Data Source=C:\Program Files\Microsoft Office\Office\" & _
        "Samples\Northwind.mdb;"

    Set rsCustomers = New ADODB.Recordset
    rsCustomers.ActiveConnection = cnn1
'Spell rsCustomers incorrectly to make a 424 non-tappable error.
'Spell cnn1 as cnn to make 3001 non-trappable error.
'    rsCustomer.ActiveConnection = cnn1
'Spell table name as "Customer" to make -2147217900 trappable error.
    rsCustomers.Open "Customers"
'adModeRead setting for cnn1.Mode causes an error (3251) here.
'Comment out cnn1.Mode line to enable updates.
    rsCustomers.Fields("CustomerID") = "xxxxx"
    rsCustomers.Update
    Debug.Print rsCustomers.Fields("CustomerID")
    rsCustomers.Close
```

(continued)

```
LookOnlyTrap:
    intInErrors = 0
    For Each errLoop In cnn1.Errors
        Debug.Print errLoop.Number, errLoop.Description
        intInErrors = intInErrors + 1
    Next errLoop
    If intInErrors = 0 Then
        Debug.Print Err.Number, Err.Description
    End If

End Sub
```

The *OpenLookOnlyErrors* procedure creates several different types of errors and attempts to write to a read-only connection. Figure 2-9 shows the VBE Code and Immediate windows for these errors. The messages with large, negative error codes are from the *Errors* collection. The remaining errors are ADO errors that report through the *Err* object. Only two of the errors have the large negative numbers characteristic of the *Errors* collection. The remaining errors are ADO errors that are available through the *Err* object. One error within the connection string (error number 3706) still did not report through the *Errors* collection. This, plus the fact that the last member of the *Errors* collection appears in the *Err* object, points to usefulness of error trapping with the *Err* object. This same design works for VBA errors.

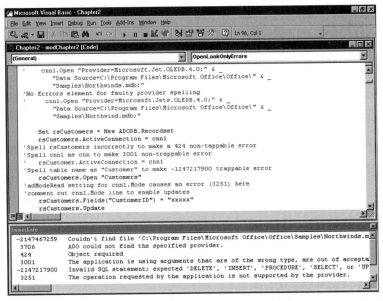

Figure 2-9. *The VBE Code and Immediate windows showing error codes from typical kinds of errors.*

NOTE You can insert an *Option Explicit* statement in the general declarations area of a module to eliminate the possibility of certain errors, such
as references to objects that do not exist.

The *LoopToUsingErrors* procedure below offers some alternative approaches to error processing with the *Err* object. The procedure generates one
error and includes a comment that details the modifications to the code that are
necessary to create another error. It also responds specifically to two errors and
includes a general error handling routine for all others:

- In the case of a 3251 error, the procedure changes the lock type so
  that the recordset is updatable. This error occurs because the lock
  type is wrong. To fix the problem, the error-processing code closes
  the old recordset, resets the *LockType* property, and reopens the
  recordset object.

- With a 424 error, the procedure does not try to fix the error but alerts
  the user to the potential cause of the problem. This error occurs when
  a method is invoked or a property is set against a variable not
  declared as an object. For example, a typographical error can cause
  this problem.

- If the error does not have a 3251 or 424 error number, the routine
  prints out the number and description properties for the *Err* object.

```
Sub LoopToUsingErrors()
On Error GoTo DErrorsTrap
Dim cnn1 As Connection
Dim rsMyTable As Recordset

    Set cnn1 = New ADODB.Connection
    cnn1.Open "Provider=Microsoft.Jet.OLEDB.4.0;" & _
        "Data Source=C:\Program Files\Microsoft Office\Office\" & _
        "Samples\Northwind.mdb;"

    Set rsMyTable = New ADODB.Recordset

'Open recordset with defaults.
OpenRSMyTable:
    rsMyTable.Open "MyTable", cnn1

'Loop through recordset.
    Do Until rsMyTable.EOF
'Make 424 error by using next instead of preceding line.
'    Do Until rsMyTables.EOF
    If rsMyTable.Fields(0) = 4 Then
```

(continued)

```
'This line makes 3251 error because recordset is read-only.
        rsMyTable.Fields(0) = 88
    Else
        Debug.Print rsMyTable.Fields(0), rsMyTable.Fields(1)
    End If
    rsMyTable.MoveNext
    Loop

    rsMyTable.Close

ErrorsExit:
    Exit Sub

DErrorsTrap:
    If Err.Number = 3251 Then
        MsgBox "OLEDB Provider does not support operation. " & _
            "Find another way to get the job done or get a new " & _
            "OLEDB Provider. Error happened in LoopToDeleteErrors."
        Debug.Print rsMyTable.LockType
        rsMyTable.Close
        rsMyTable.LockType = adLockOptimistic
        Resume OpenRSMyTable
    ElseIf Err.Number = 424 Then
        MsgBox "The code tried to do something requiring an " & _
            "object, such as set a property or invoke a method, " & _
            "but the code did not have an object. Check spelling."
    Else
        MsgBox "Check Immediate window for error # and desc."
            Debug.Print Err.Number, Err.Description
    End If
    Resume ErrorsExit

End Sub
```

The ADOX Library

The ADOX library supports schema and security tasks. You use this library to manage objects and thereby modify the architecture of your application's database design. With the exception of the *Catalog* object, all objects have matching collections. You use these collections to add and organize new objects in a catalog. Selected objects, such as tables, indexes, keys, and columns, have *Properties* collections. You use these to manage the behavior of the objects within an application. You manage the *Users* and *Groups* collections to control permissions for other ADOX objects, such as tables, views, and procedures. Figure 2-10 shows an overview of the ADOX library.

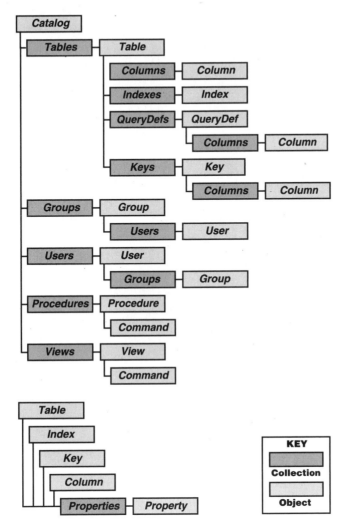

Figure 2-10. *The ADOX object library.*

The ADOX library is an extension of the ADODB library. The Jet ADO provider fully supports ADOX. Other database providers can selectively implement its features, and you can use the two libraries together to build applications. For example, you can build *Command* objects with the ADODB library and then save them as procedures with the ADOX library. Or you can search for the availability of a table before basing a recordset on it. If the table does not exist, you can add it and populate it with values. The ability of the ADOX library to define new data structures makes it an alternative to SQL DDL.

The *Catalog* object

The *Catalog* object is the highest-level container in the ADOX library. Its members define the schema and security model for a database. Its *ActiveConnection* property defines the connection to which the catalog belongs. The *Connection* object is the database. The *Catalog* object is the database's container for tables, views, procedures, users, and groups within a connection or database. The *Name* property for a catalog is read-only. You designate it when you declare the catalog. You use the *Catalog* object's *Create* method to assign a connection and source to a catalog so that you can concurrently open a new database and gain access to its catalog.

The following code examples show the *Catalog* object in three typical contexts. The *CatCon* procedure opens the Northwind database and gives the current application programmatic access to the structure of the database. Notice that you need a *Connection* object for the catalog so that ADO knows which catalog to make available. You assign the *Connection* object to the catalog using its *ActiveConnection* property. Once ADO knows which database to reference with a catalog, you have programmatic access to the contents of the catalog. You control access using database and user-level security techniques.

```
Sub CatCon()
Dim cnn1 As New Connection
Dim cat1 As New Catalog

'Open the catalog of another database.
    cnn1.Open "Provider=Microsoft.Jet.OLEDB.4.0;" & _
        "Data Source=C:\Program Files\Microsoft Office\Office\" & _
        "Samples\Northwind.mdb;"
    Set cat1.ActiveConnection = cnn1
    Debug.Print cat1.Tables(0).Name

End Sub



Sub CatCon2()
Dim cnn1 As New Connection
Dim cat1 As New Catalog
Dim proc1 As Procedure

'Open the catalog of this database.
'Print a range of selected collection information.
    Set cnn1 = CurrentProject.Connection
    Set cat1.ActiveConnection = cnn1
    Debug.Print cat1.Tables(1).Name
    Debug.Print cat1.Views(0).Name
    Debug.Print cat1.Procedures(0).Name
    Debug.Print cat1.Users(0).Name
```

```
    Debug.Print cat1.Groups(0).Name

End Sub


Sub CatCon3()
Dim cat1 As New ADOX.Catalog

'Open the catalog to a new database.
    cat1.Create "Provider=Microsoft.Jet.OLEDB.4.0;" & _
        "Data Source=c:\My Documents\NewDB.mdb"
    Debug.Print cat1.Tables(0).Name

End Sub
```

CatCon2 lists a member from each collection within the *Catalog* object of
the current database. While you can reference a table's contents with an ADODB
library reference, you must use an ADOX reference to loop through the *Columns*
collection of a table. Only the ADOX library has *Tables* and *Columns* collections.

> **NOTE** You must impose a logon requirement before you can list the
> members of the *Users* and *Groups* collections. Any attempt to print them
> without logging on can generate a run-time error. You can impose a logon
> requirement by setting a password for the Admin user.

CatCon3 creates a new database and exposes its catalog in one step. Notice
that you apply the *Create* method to the *Catalog* object. The method takes a
connection string as an argument. If the file specified in the connection string
already exists, *CatCon3* generates a run-time error. When the file runs successfully, it prints out one of the system table names because no user files are available just after the creation of a database.

You can use the *Catalog* object to enumerate the members of any of the
collections within it. The following procedure enumerates the members of the
Views collection, which corresponds to the set of all row-returning queries that
do not rely on parameters that have Jet databases. When you use a SQL Server
database, views are explicitly available from the Access 2000 database container.

```
Sub ListViews()
Dim cnn1 As New Connection
Dim cat1 As New Catalog
Dim view1 As View

    cnn1.Open "Provider=Microsoft.Jet.OLEDB.4.0;" & _
        "Data Source=C:\Program Files\Microsoft Office\Office\" & _
        "Samples\Northwind.mdb;"
    Set cat1.ActiveConnection = cnn1
```

(continued)

```
For Each view1 In cat1.Views
    Debug.Print view1.Name
Next view1

End Sub
```

The *Views* collection is available from the catalog for a connection. To enumerate the views, you must declare one view that your code will use to reference each member of the *Views* collection as it loops through the collection. Printing the *Name* property of each view provides an inventory of the *View* objects in a catalog.

The *Table* object

The *Table* object is a member of the *Tables* collection, which is a member of the *Catalog* object. Each *Table* object has a *Name* property and a *Type* property. A *Table* object can be a standard table within the current database or a linked table based on ODBC and non-ODBC data sources. It can even be a view. The *Type* property values also include two system table types—Jet system tables and the Access system table.

Type *values for the* Table *object*	*Description*
ACCESS TABLE	An Access system table
LINK	A linked table from a non-ODBC data source
PASS-THROUGH	A linked table through an ODBC data source
SYSTEM TABLE	A Jet system table
TABLE	A table developed by or for your application
VIEW	A table from a row-returning, nonparameterized query

A *Table* object in the ADOX library can contain up to three collections: *Columns*, *Indexes*, and *Keys*.

The *Column* object

The *Columns* collection is for tables, keys, and indexes. A *Column* object is roughly comparable to a *Field* object in the ADODB library. For a table, a column represents a set of data referring to a specific characteristic of the entity represented by the table. The *Column* object has several properties:

- *Name* This property is the name of the column.

- *Type* This property indicates the data type of a column within the table. All the data within a column is of the same type.

■ *Attributes*   The *Attributes* property describes the characteristics of a column. The two column characteristics are whether the column can contain nulls and whether it has a fixed length.

■ *DefinedSize*   This property designates the maximum size of an entry in the column.

■ *Precision* and *NumericScale*   These properties are used exclusively for numeric fields, such as integers, currency, and floating point numbers. *Precision* represents the maximum total number of digits used to convey the value of a column. *NumericScale* designates how many digits to the right of the decimal point are available to express a value.

When a *Column* object is an index, other properties, such as *SortOrder* and *RelatedColumn*, are also available.

NOTE   The *NumericScale* property can yield confusing results. For example, *Currency* values have four places to the right of the decimal point, but their *NumericScale* property equals 0 because Access stores Currency data types as scaled integers. When you modify the *Scale* setting of a column that uses a Decimal data type in a table's Design view, the column's *NumericScale* property adjusts accordingly.

The *Index* object

The *Index* object sets indexes for a table. It has five properties: *Clustered*, *IndexNulls*, *Name*, *PrimaryKey*, and *Unique*. With the exception of the *Name* property, all are read-only after you append the index. The *Name* property is the name of the index. Three other properties are Boolean and indicate, respectively, whether the index is clustered (an index is said to be *clustered* when the physical order of rows matches the indexed order of rows), unique, or a primary key.

The *IndexNulls* property can assume any of three different values. Setting it to *adIndexNullsDisallow* causes the *Index* construction to fail if there is a Null in the index for the column. Assigning the *adIndexNullsIsIgnore* constant to *IndexNulls* allows the construction of the index if there is a Null in the index, but sets the *Ignore Nulls* property (on the Indexes window in the user interface) to *Yes*. Using the *adIndexNullsIsIgnoreAny* also constructs the index when the index contains a null, but it sets the *Ignore Nulls* property to *No*.

The *Key* object

The *Key* object embodies the behavior of foreign keys in its properties. Of course, the *Name* property is the name of the key. The *RelatedTable* property designates the table to which a foreign key points. The *DeleteRule* and *UpdateRule* properties determine what happens when a primary key is deleted or updated. The *Type* property is the type of the key and has three options: *adKeyForeign* for foreign keys, *adKeyUnique* for unique keys, and *adKeyPrimary* for primary keys.

Enumerating tables   One of the easiest ways to start working with tables is to enumerate them. The *ListTables* procedure below shows how to list the tables in the Northwind database. The declarations instantiate *cat1* as a *Catalog* object and *tbl1* as a *Table* object. Next, the procedure assigns the Northwind database and the Jet 4 provider to the *ActiveConnection* property for the catalog. The following loop identifies the longest table name in the catalog. The final segment prints the table names to the Immediate window. A string formula appends blanks to table names so they all occupy a fixed number of characters. The code appends the table type.

```
Sub ListTables()
Dim cat1 As New ADOX.Catalog
Dim tbl1 As ADOX.Table
Dim intMaxLength As Integer

'Specify active connection for the Catalog object.
    cat1.ActiveConnection = "Provider=Microsoft.Jet.OLEDB.4.0;" & _
        "Data Source=C:\Program Files\Microsoft Office\Office\" & _
        "Samples\Northwind.mdb;"

'Find longest table name.
    intMaxLength = 0
    For Each tbl1 In cat1.Tables
        If Len(tbl1.Name) > intMaxLength Then intMaxLength = _
            Len(tbl1.Name)
    Next tbl1

'Print table names to Immediate window.
    intMaxLength = intMaxLength + 2
    For Each tbl1 In cat1.Tables
        strName = tbl1.Name
        strFiller = String(intMaxLength - Len(tbl1.Name), " ")
        Debug.Print strName & strFiller & tbl1.Type
    Next tbl1

End Sub
```

Figure 2-11 shows output from the *ListTables* procedure. Notice that it appears as two columns, each showing a table's name. Next to the name is the *Type* property for the table. Recall that the *Table* object includes six types. Four of these appear in the figure.

```
Immediate
Categories                        TABLE
Category Sales for 1995           VIEW
Current Product List              VIEW
Customers                         TABLE
Employees                         TABLE
MSysAccessObjects                 ACCESS TABLE
MSysACEs                          SYSTEM TABLE
MSysObjects                       SYSTEM TABLE
MSysQueries                       SYSTEM TABLE
MSysRelationships                 SYSTEM TABLE
MyTable                           TABLE
Order Details                     TABLE
Order Details Extended            VIEW
Order Subtotals                   VIEW
Orders                            TABLE
Product Sales for 1995            VIEW
Products                          TABLE
Products Above Average Price      VIEW
qryForSource                      VIEW
Quarterly Orders                  VIEW
Sales by Category                 VIEW
Shippers                          TABLE
Suppliers                         TABLE
Ten Most Expensive Products       VIEW
```

Figure 2-11. *The output from the* ListTables *procedure.*

Enumerating fields The *ListTableTypeColumns* and *ColumnType* procedures below are more elaborate samples that dig into table hierarchy and properties. Once *ListTableTypeColumns* finds a *Table* object with its *Table* property set to TABLE, it lists the column names and types of the columns within that table. These appear below the table's name and its column count. Each column name is next to its *ColumnType* constant. Figure 2-12 shows an excerpt from the listing. The sample is considered rich because it manipulates several types of *Table* objects and multiple properties, and the objects and properties are at different points on the ADOX object model hierarchy.

```
Immediate
Categories                          4
      CategoryID          adInteger
      CategoryName        adWChar
      Description         adLongVarWChar
      Picture             adLongVarBinary
Customers                          11
      Address             adWChar
      City                adWChar
      CompanyName         adWChar
      ContactName         adWChar
      ContactTitle        adWChar
      Country             adWChar
      CustomerID          adWChar
      Fax                 adWChar
      Phone               adWChar
      PostalCode          adWChar
      Region              adWChar
Employees                          17
      Address             adWChar
      BirthDate           adDate
      City                adWChar
      Country             adWChar
      EmployeeID          adInteger
      Extension           adWChar
      FirstName           adWChar
      HireDate            adDate
      HomePhone           adWChar
      LastName            adWChar
      Notes               adLongVarWChar
```

Figure 2-12. *The output from the* ListTableTypeColumns *and* ColumnType *procedures.*

```
Sub ListTableTypeColumns()
Dim cat1 As New ADOX.Catalog
Dim tbl1 As ADOX.Table
Dim col1 As ADOX.Column

    cat1.ActiveConnection = "Provider=Microsoft.Jet.OLEDB.4.0;" & _
        "Data Source=C:\Program Files\Microsoft Office\" & _
        "Office\Samples\Northwind.mdb;"

    For Each tbl1 In cat1.Tables
        If tbl1.Type = "TABLE" Then
            strName = tbl1.Name
            strFiller = String(30 - Len(tbl1.Name), " ")
            Debug.Print strName & strFiller & tbl1.Columns.Count
            For Each col1 In tbl1.Columns
                strFiller = String(20 - Len(col1.Name), " ")
                Debug.Print String(5, " ") & col1.Name & _
                strFiller & ColumnType(col1.Type)
            Next col1
        End If
    Next tbl1

End Sub


Public Function ColumnType(intType As Integer) As String

    Select Case intType
        Case adVarWChar
            ColumnType = "adVarWChar"
        Case adCurrency
            ColumnType = "adCurrency"
        Case adInteger
            ColumnType = "adInteger"
        Case adDate
            ColumnType = "adDate"
        Case adWChar
            ColumnType = "adWChar"
        Case adLongVarWChar
            ColumnType = "adLongVarWChar"
        Case adLongVarBinary
            ColumnType = "adLongVarBinary"
        Case adBoolean
            ColumnType = "adBoolean"
        Case adSmallInt
            ColumnType = "adSmallInt"
```

```
      Case Else
          ColumnType = CStr(intType)
   End Select

End Function
```

The declarations include a catalog, a table, and a column from the ADOX library. The catalog's declaration instantiates its object, but the other two are used as item references in collections. Immediately after the declarations, the procedure assigns a connection string to the *ActiveConnection* property of the *Catalog* object.

A pair of nested *For* loops search through the tables and their columns. The outer loop seeks tables whose *Table* property is set to TABLE. When it finds one, it prints the name and column count for that table. The inner *For* loop enumerates the columns of the table and handles the formatting of the output. The loop calls the *ColumnType* function, which returns a character string that represents the constant designating the column's *Type* property. It is a very robust function, so you can adapt it for your own conversion tasks. If it encounters a type that it does not recognize, it converts the type's value to a string. This helps you to go back into the function and add the new decode specification.

Creating tables   The ADOX library is especially important because you can programmatically create tables along with their indexes and keys.

If you are comfortable adding tables in Design view, you only have to learn a little more to do it programmatically. You define the table and then append it to the catalog's *Tables* collection. Defining a table involves a similar kind of logic. You first declare a table object variable, and then you append columns to the object variable. When you append the columns, your code can assign data types and other column properties. After you finish defining a table, you might want to populate it with data. Earlier in the chapter, you saw two approaches to tackling this issue (using SQL code and the recordset's *AddNew* method.) We'll examine this topic in greater detail in Chapter 3.

Adding an index   The *AddIndex* procedure on the next page demonstrates how to programmatically add an index to a table. As when you create a table, you use the *Append* method twice. First, you append one or more columns of data to your index. These columns define the index. Next, you set the *Name* property of the *Index* object. You can also set several other properties. The comment lines in the procedure below give instructions on how to set several optional properties and describe the impact of assigning values to the properties. After completing the specification of your index, you invoke the *Append* method again. This time, however, you use it to add the new index to the table's *Indexes* collection. This completes the task—unless there are run-time errors!

```
Sub AddIndex()
Dim cat1 As New ADOX.Catalog
Dim tbl1 As New ADOX.Table
Dim idx1 As New ADOX.Index

    cat1.ActiveConnection = CurrentProject.Connection

    Set tbl1 = cat1.Tables("MyTable")

    idx1.Name = "MyFirstIndex"
    idx1.Columns.Append ("Column1")

'Rules and syntax for setting IndexNulls property
'Does not create index if field contains Nulls; yields error.
'    idx1.IndexNulls = adIndexNullsDisallow
'Sets Ignore Nulls index property to Yes -- creates index.
'    idx1.IndexNulls = adIndexNullsIgnore
'Sets Ignore Nulls index property to No -- creates index.
'    idx1.IndexNulls = adIndexNullsIgnoreAny

'If you want to set the PrimaryKey property
'    idx1.PrimaryKey = True
'you must also set the Unique property for the
'primaryKey property to take effect and avoid an error.
'    idx1.Unique = True

    tbl1.Indexes.Append idx1

End Sub
```

PKErrorCatcher, shown below, performs error trapping when you create a new primary key in a table. The same general error trapping approach works for other indexes and foreign keys. The error trap explicitly handles two types of errors and includes a more general trap for other errors.

```
Sub PKErrorCatcher()
On Error GoTo PKErrorCatcherTrap

Dim cat1 As New ADOX.Catalog
Dim tbl1 As New ADOX.Table
Dim idx1 As New ADOX.Index
Dim iNumber As Integer

    cat1.ActiveConnection = CurrentProject.Connection
```

```
    Set tbl1 = cat1.Tables("MyTable")

PKErrorCatcherTry:
    With idx1
        .Name = "MyPrimaryKey"
        .PrimaryKey = True
        .Unique = True
        .IndexNulls = adIndexNullsDisallow
    End With

    idx1.Columns.Append "Column2"
    tbl1.Indexes.Append idx1

    Set cat1 = Nothing

PKErrorCatcherExit:
    Exit Sub

PKErrorCatcherTrap:
    If Err.Number = -2147217856 Then
        MsgBox "Table currently in use."
    ElseIf Err.Number = -2147467259 Then
        For Each idx1 In tbl1.Indexes
            If idx1.PrimaryKey = True Then
                tbl1.Indexes.Delete (iNumber)
                Resume PKErrorCatcherTry
            End If
            iNumber = iNumber + 1
        Next idx1
    Else
        MsgBox "Error #" & Err.Number & ": " & Err.Description
End If
    Resume PKErrorCatcherExit

End Sub
```

The procedure starts by declaring new *Catalog*, *Table*, and *Index* objects. (A primary key is just an index with its *Unique* and *PrimaryKey* properties set to *True*.) The main portion of *PKErrorCatcher* sets the necessary properties, appends a column to the index, and then appends the index to the table. At least two conditions can cause these simple instructions to fail at run time. First, the table might be open. ADO assigns error number −2147217856 to this condition. When the error trap detects this error number, it displays a message telling the user that the table is currently in use. Second, the attempt to append a new primary key can fail if a primary key is already defined for the table. The procedure deletes the old obsolete primary key and then tries to create the primary key a second time. Since there is no longer a primary key, the routine cannot fail again for that reason.

Setting *autoincrement* field values   Access 2000 is the first version of Access that lets developers set the start and step value of *autoincrement* columns. You can programmatically set the start and step value of *autoincrement* columns by creating the table using Jet 4 SQL statements. You use the CREATE TABLE command to create the overall table, and you use the IDENTITY data type in Jet SQL for the *autoincrement* field. The IDENTITY data type has start and step values that let you specify the initial value for the *autoincrement* field, as well as how much it increases with each new record. The following *SetStartAndStep* procedure taps this new technology.

```
Sub SetStartAndStep()
Dim cnn1 As Connection
Dim cmd1 As Command
Dim tbl1 As New Table

    Set cnn1 = CurrentProject.Connection
    Set cmd1 = New ADODB.Command

    With cmd1
        .ActiveConnection = cnn1
'First create a table with two columns.
'Make one column an Identity column.
'Set its start value first, and its step value second.
        .CommandType = adCmdText
        .CommandText = "CREATE TABLE Contacts (ContactID " & _
            "IDENTITY(2,4),ContactName Char)"
        .Execute
'After creating the table with the autoincrement/identity
'column you should add data.
        .CommandText = "INSERT INTO Contacts(ContactName) " & _
            "Values ('Kevin Mineweaser')"
        .CommandType = adCmdText
        .Execute
        .CommandText = "INSERT INTO Contacts(ContactName) " & _
            "Values ('Mike Gilbert')"
        .CommandType = adCmdText
        .Execute
        .CommandText = "INSERT INTO Contacts(ContactName) " & _
            "Values ('Neil Charney')"
        .CommandType = adCmdText
        .Execute
    End With

End Sub
```

The code begins by creating a table. Although this procedure does not have an error-trapping routine, you should either make sure that such a table does not already exist or include an error trap to delete the table if it does exist. Within the CREATE TABLE statement, you specify the IDENTITY data type. You set the *autoincrement* field's first argument to the initial value and its second argument equal to the step. The code indicates that contacts will start with a value of 2 and increase by 4 for each new entry. Figure 2-13 shows the output from running the *SetStartAndStep* procedure. Notice that the *ContactID* field starts at 2 and increments in steps of 4. These are the settings for the IDENTITY data type specified in the procedure.

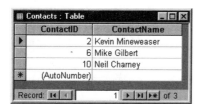

Figure 2-13. *The output from the* SetStartAndStep *procedure.*

The *View* object

A *View* object is a row-returning query without any parameters that your application persists. When your application saves the other types of queries, it stores them as members of the *Procedures* collection. You can manipulate the *Views* collection members using the *Command* object and the *Views* and *Tables* collections. *View* objects have two critical properties for the purposes of this discussion: the *Name* property is the name of the view, and the *Command* property lets you get at the SQL statement underlying the view.

In this section, we'll construct a view using the *MakeAView* procedure and edit the SQL statement underlying an existing view using the *ChangeAView* procedure. Both the *MakeAView* and *ChangeAView* procedures tap the *ViewAView* procedure. The code prints three fields from either view to the Immediate window. You'll also learn how to delete a view.

Creating a view   The *MakeAView* procedure on the next page adds a new view by creating a *Command* object that represents the view and appends the *Command* object to the *Views* collection. *MakeAView* needs a connection to a database. The *cnn1 Connection* object opens a link to the Northwind database. Then the application's code sets the *ActiveConnection* property of the *Command* object in the sample, *cmd1*, to *cnn1*. Next, and critically, the code sets the *CommandText* property of *cmd1*. The *CommandText* property holds the SQL statement that sets the view. The SQL statement in *MakeAView* constructs the view to reveal employee first and last names followed by their phone extensions. The code sets the *ActiveConnection* property of *cat1*, a *Catalog* object, to the Northwind database. An *Append* command names *cmd1 AllEmployees* and adds it to the Northwind catalog. Finally, *MakeAView* calls *ViewAView* to print the contents of the view to the Immediate window.

```
Sub MakeAView()

Dim cnn1 As New ADODB.Connection
Dim cmd1 As New ADODB.Command
Dim cat1 As New ADOX.Catalog


'Open the connection.
    cnn1.Open "Provider=Microsoft.Jet.OLEDB.4.0;" & _
        "Data Source=C:\Program Files\Microsoft Office\Office\" & _
        "Samples\Northwind.mdb;"

'Create the command representing the view.
'Remember to delete it first.
    Set cmd1.ActiveConnection = cnn1
    cmd1.CommandText = "SELECT FirstName, LastName, " & _
        "Extension FROM Employees"

'Open the catalog.
    Set cat1.ActiveConnection = cnn1

'Create the new view.
    cat1.Views.Append "AllEmployees", cmd1

'Show the view.
    ViewAView


End Sub
```

Printing a view   The *ViewAView* procedure below prints the *AllEmployees* view. *ViewAView* starts by making a connection to the Northwind database, and then opens the *rst1 Recordset* object based on the *AllEmployees* view. Once the recordset is open and pointing to the right data source, the procedure takes a loop through the records to determine the longest name. Since the recordset is relatively small, there is not much of a penalty for making this extra pass. The maximum length for a name is convenient because it suggests a starting point for printing the extension after the name. This step allows the extension numbers to left align irrespective of the length of the names. Before starting the next loop through the names, *ViewAView* moves back to the recordset. Then, it moves through the names a second time. This time it constructs a string with the help of information gathered in the first loop.

```
Sub ViewAView()
Dim cnn1 As New ADODB.Connection
Dim rst1 As New ADODB.Recordset
Dim intMaxLength As Integer, Length As Integer

'Open the connection.
    cnn1.Open "Provider=Microsoft.Jet.OLEDB.4.0;" & _
        "Data Source=C:\Program Files\Microsoft Office\" & _
        "Office\Samples\Northwind.mdb;"

'Find the longest name.
    rst1.Open "AllEmployees", cnn1
    Do Until rst1.EOF
        Length = Len(rst1.Fields("FirstName")) + _
        Len(rst1.Fields("LastName"))
        If Length > intMaxLength Then intMaxLength = _
            Length
        rst1.MoveNext
    Loop

'Print first name, last name, and third field.
    rst1.MoveFirst
    Do Until rst1.EOF
        strFiller = (intMaxLength + 2) - _
            (Len(rst1.Fields("FirstName")) + _
            Len(rst1.Fields("LastName")))
        Debug.Print rst1.Fields("FirstName") & " " & _
        rst1.Fields("LastName") & String(strFiller, " ") & _
        rst1.Fields(2)
        rst1.MoveNext
    Loop

End Sub
```

Modifying a view   The *ChangeAView* procedure below alters the SQL statement behind a view. You can use this simple approach to add new fields, replace old ones, or even change the whole design of the view, such as by adding sorting and filtering. The procedure modifies the view to show the *HomePhone* field instead of the *Extension* field.

```
Sub ChangeAView()
Dim cnn1 As New ADODB.Connection
Dim cat1 As New ADOX.Catalog
Dim cmd1 As New ADODB.Command
```

(continued)

```
'Open the connection.
    cnn1.Open "Provider=Microsoft.Jet.OLEDB.4.0;" & _
        "Data Source=C:\Program Files\Microsoft Office\" & _
        "Office\Samples\Northwind.mdb;"

'Open the catalog.
    Set cat1.ActiveConnection = cnn1

'Update the view.
    cmd1.CommandText = "SELECT FirstName, LastName, " & _
        "HomePhone FROM Employees"
    cat1.Views("AllEmployees").Command = cmd1

'Show view.
    ViewAView

End Sub
```

The trick to editing the SQL statement behind a view is to open the associated *Command* object and edit its *CommandText* property. To do this, you must point the *ActiveConnection* property of a *Catalog* object (see *cat1* in the code above) to the database containing the view you want to edit—in this case, the Northwind database. Then you assign the SQL statement for the view you want to the *CommandText* property of a new *Command* object. Next, you assign that new *Command* object to the view that you want to change. The assignment automatically saves the new SQL statement over the old one.

Deleting a view The *DeleteAView* procedure below deletes one view. It is almost too simple to include, but you will be glad to have it if you want to run *MakeAView* more than once because ADO doesn't let you append one view over another of the same name. Therefore, you must first delete the last created view in order to rerun *MakeAView*. To delete a view, you first set the *ActiveConnection* of a *Catalog* object to point at the database that has the view you want to delete. Then you invoke the *Delete* method for the *Views* collection while you reference the specific member you want expunged from the schema.

```
Sub DeleteAView()

Dim cat1 As New ADOX.Catalog

'Open the catalog.
    cat1.ActiveConnection = "Provider=Microsoft.Jet.OLEDB.4.0;" & _
        "Data Source=C:\Program Files\Microsoft Office\Office\" & _
        "Samples\Northwind.mdb;"
```

```
'Delete the procedure.
    cat1.Views.Delete ("AllEmployees")

End Sub
```

The *Procedure* object

A procedure is a parameterized row-returning query or an action query that adds, deletes, or updates records. We'll discuss parameterized queries in this section; see Chapter 4 for more complete coverage of queries, including procedures that persist action queries.

Procedures and views are similar: Both can persist *Command* objects. Views represent nonparameterized row-returning queries, and procedures represent the remaining query types. If you enumerate the *Procedure* objects within a catalog, the enumeration will include the set of all views. However, procedures do not appear in an enumeration of *View* objects. The syntax for enumerating either is similar.

Procedure objects have two critical properties for this discussion: *Name* and *Command*. The *Name* property is the name of the procedure. The *Command* property makes accessible the properties of the *Command* object behind the procedure. The *CommandText* property is particularly useful because it sets or returns the SQL statement for the *Command* object. You can use this property to modify the SQL statement in the command behind a procedure or to view the object's SQL statement. Examining the object's SQL statement can acquaint you with the parameters that you need to set in order to run a procedure.

Enumerating views and procedures The *ListMyProcs* procedure below actually displays both the *Views* and *Procedures* collections. The first *For* loop enumerates only members of the *Views* collection. The second loop enumerates members of the *Procedures* collection and lists both procedures and views. The second loop also displays the SQL statement for each query that it enumerates.

```
Sub ListMyProcs()
Dim cnn1 As New Connection
Dim cat1 As New Catalog
Dim proc1 As Procedure
Dim view1 As View

'Set database connection for catalog.
    cnn1.Open "Provider=Microsoft.Jet.OLEDB.4.0;" & _
        "Data Source=C:\Program Files\Microsoft Office" & _
        "\Office\Samples\Northwind.mdb;"
    Set cat1.ActiveConnection = cnn1
```

(continued)

```
'Enumerate views -- notice this returns just
'nonparameterized row-returning queries.
    For Each view1 In cat1.Views
        Debug.Print "View name: " & view1.Name
    Next view1

'Enumerate views -- this returns views
'and procedures.
    For Each proc1 In cat1.Procedures
        Debug.Print "Procedure name: " & proc1.Name
        Debug.Print "SQL: " & proc1.Command.CommandText
    Next proc1
End Sub
```

Views and procedures let you persist commands. You simply append the *Command* object to the appropriate collection. The following code saves a parameter query as a stored procedure. This query uses the *MyTable* table (which appears in several of the preceding procedure examples), and it is available on the companion CD along with the samples to manipulate it. Design and Datasheet views of *MyTable* appear in Figures 2-7 and 2-8.

```
Sub SaveParmeterQuery()
On Error GoTo SavePQTrap
Dim cmd1 As Command
Dim cnn1 As New Connection
Dim cat1 As New adox.Catalog

'Create connection.
    Set cnn1 = CurrentProject.Connection

'Create and define command.
    Set cmd1 = New ADODB.Command

    With cmd1
        .ActiveConnection = cnn1
        .CommandText = "Parameters [Lowest] Long;" & _
            "SELECT Column1, Column2, Column3 " & _
            "FROM MyTable " & _
            "Where Column1>=[Lowest]"
        .CommandType = adCmdText
    End With

'Open the catalog.
Set cat1.ActiveConnection = cnn1

'Create the new procedure based on parameter query.
cat1.Procedures.Append "spLowestRow", cmd1
```

```
SavePQExit:
    Exit Sub

SavePQTrap:
    If Err.Number = -2147217816 Then
'If err.number = -214... query already exists
        deleteProcedure("spLowestRow")
        Resume
    Else
        Debug.Print Err.Number, Err.Description
    End If

End Sub

Sub deleteProcedure(procName as String)
Dim cnn1 As New Connection
Dim cat1 As New adox.Catalog

'Open the catalog.
    Set cnn1 = CurrentProject.Connection
    Set cat1.ActiveConnection = cnn1

'Delete existing procedure.
    cat1.Procedures.Delete (procName)

End Sub
```

The procedure constructs a parameter query and saves it as a stored procedure. Its query prompts for the lowest value to appear in the first column. Notice that you can set the *CommandText* and *CommandType* properties for the query. The SQL statement includes a declaration for the parameter. After creating the *Command* object for a stored procedure, you use the *Append* method of the *Procedures* collection to persist the *Command* object as a stored procedure. If you run *SaveParameterQuery* more than once, the second attempt to save spLowestRow generates a run-time error. *SaveParameterQuery* traps for this error and deletes the old copy if it already exists. The procedure that deletes the stored procedure accepts an argument for the name of the procedure to delete. The *ParameterQCommand* procedure, shown earlier, performs the same task as the stored procedure, *spLowestRow*. Since ADO runs stored procedures as compiled objects, they run faster than when you construct a *Command* object each time you want to execute a SQL statement.

Creating and running stored procedures   The following pair of procedures prepares and runs a stored procedure. The first procedure creates a stored procedure that looks up the extension number for employees in the Northwind database; the second procedure invokes the stored procedure.

```
Sub procLookupNumber()
Dim cnn1 As New ADODB.Connection
Dim cmd1 As New ADODB.Command
Dim prm1 As ADODB.Parameter
Dim cat1 As New ADOX.Catalog

'Open the connection.
    cnn1.Open "Provider=Microsoft.Jet.OLEDB.4.0;" & _
        "Data Source=C:\Program Files\Microsoft Office" & _
        "\Office\Samples\Northwind.mdb;"

'Create the parameterized command.
    Set cmd1.ActiveConnection = cnn1
    cmd1.CommandText = "SELECT FirstName, LastName, Extension " & _
        "FROM Employees WHERE LastName = [LName]"
    Set prm1 = cmd1.CreateParameter("[LName]", adWChar, adParamInput, 20)
    cmd1.Parameters.Append prm1

'Open the catalog.
    Set cat1.ActiveConnection = cnn1

'Create the new procedure based on parameter query.
    cat1.Procedures.Append "spEmployeeExtension", cmd1

End Sub


Sub RunLookUpProc()
Dim cnn1 As New Connection
Dim cat1 As New Catalog
Dim rst1 As New Recordset
Dim cmd1 As New Command
Dim prm1 As Parameter
Dim typedName As String

'Create and assign a connection for the catalog.
    cnn1.Open "Provider=Microsoft.Jet.OLEDB.4.0;" & _
        "Data Source=C:\Program Files\Microsoft Office" & _
        "\Office\Samples\Northwind.mdb;"
    Set cat1.ActiveConnection = cnn1

'Set the Command and parameter object references.
    Set cmd1 = cat1.Procedures("spEmployeeExtension").Command
    Set prm1 = cmd1.CreateParameter("[LName]", adWChar, adParamInput, 20)
    cmd1.Parameters.Append prm1

'Gather the parameter value from the user and assign it.
    typedName = InputBox("Last name for extension?", _
        "Programming Microsoft Access 2000")
    prm1.Value = typedName
```

```
'Execute the parameter query and show first match.
   cmd1.Execute
   rst1.Open cmd1
   MsgBox "The extension for " & rst1.Fields(0) & _
       " " & rst1("LastName") & " is " & rst1.Fields(2), _
       vbInformation, "Programming Microsoft Access 2000"
```

End Sub

The *procLookupNumber* procedure creates a persistent parameter query as a stored procedure. This query looks up a telephone number extension for an employee based on the employee's last name. The procedure defines the *Command* object and its associated parameter, *[LName]*. The *adWChar* constant designates the parameter as a fixed-width text string. The *adParamInput* constant designates this parameter for input only, and the trailing number denotes that the parameter can contain up to 20 characters. After defining both the *Command* and its associated parameter, the procedure sets the catalog connection to the Northwind database and appends the *Command* object to the *Procedures* collection with the name *spEmployeeExtension*.

If you run *procLookupNumber* more than once, it will fail when it tries to write *spEmployeeExtension* over itself. Add error trapping to detect this situation. Then create a delete routine. You will need to edit the one used in the previous sample since it deletes procedures in the current project, and this sample needs to delete procedures in the Northwind database.

The *RunLookUpProc* procedure runs the stored procedure created by the *procLookupNumber* procedure. This short procedure does four things:

- It creates a connection to the database with the stored procedure.

- It designates object variables that point at the stored procedure and its parameter. The code uses a *Command* object to refer to the stored procedure.

- It displays a dialog box in which the user must indicate the last name of the employee's extension. The code assigns the return value from the dialog box to the command's parameter.

- It executes the command and opens a recordset based on the command's return set. It displays the first row from the return set in a dialog box. The code uses both naming conventions for selecting one member from the *Fields* collection in a recordset. You can use either its ordinal position or its *Name* property.

Chapter 3

Designing Tables

Many businesses that use databases do not appreciate the importance of table design—they tend to focus on forms and reports, which are more visible to users. But the design and content of tables and the relationships among tables can significantly affect the services that custom database solutions can provide. Table design can also affect the speed of a custom solution as well as how easily new services can be added to the system.

This chapter starts by briefly examining general table design considerations, such as how to split information into logical groupings so that it can be stored in various tables. Next, it explores how to create tables with Microsoft Access 2000 manually and by using the Access wizards. You'll also learn about indexes, primary keys, and how to form relationships among tables.

This chapter also shows you how to dynamically create and populate tables in Access, which allows you to create powerful, feature-rich custom database solutions. The companion CD includes many ActiveX Data Objects (ADO) samples that dynamically create and populate an Access table. These samples build on the introductory ADO coverage in Chapter 2. One set of samples even shows how to combine ADO and the easy-to-use *DoCmd* object to dynamically interact with Indexed Sequential Access Method (ISAM) and open database connectivity (ODBC) data sources.

RELATIONAL DATABASES AND TABLES

Tables are among the most fundamental building blocks of a relational database. The Northwind sample database that ships with Access includes several tables that track important information about a fictitious business. The *Customers* table tracks information about customers, such as company and contact name.

The *Products* table tracks product-related data, such as product name, units on hand, and unit price.

Each table in a database should contain information that is appropriate for only one specific type of entity. For example, a typical school contains students, teachers, and classes (among other things). Students enroll in the classes; teachers lead the classes. A database application for the school might contain a table for students, a table for classes, and a table for teachers. The *Teachers* table should contain information about teachers, but not about students or classes. Likewise, the *Classes* table should not contain the addresses, social security numbers, and telephone numbers of teachers.

Database tables have a structure similar to that of spreadsheets. The *rows*, or *records*, in a table represent unique instances of the entities stored in the table. For example, a *Customers* table includes a single row for each customer, and a *Products* table has a single row for each product. (There is no significance to the order of rows; you can arrange them in any order without changing the meaning of the information in a table.)

Each *field* (column) in a table holds a specific type of information. For example, each customer in the Northwind database has a name, an address, a phone number, and so on, and this information is stored in the fields of the *Customers* table.

Many database tables include one or more fields that uniquely identify each row in the table. Such a unique identification is known as a *primary key*. The primary key of the *Customers* table in the Northwind database is the *CustomerID* field.

Normalization

Normalization involves applying a set of design rules to database tables. Normalization offers at least four benefits:

- *It eliminates redundant information.* Many unnormalized databases require that the same contact information be entered on multiple forms. Eliminating this redundancy reduces the likelihood of data entry errors that can corrupt the database. It can also simplify database maintenance because a value is stored and therefore deleted and updated in just one place.

- *It reduces the size of a database.* Because each type of information is stored in just one location, your database does not have to save multiple copies of the same information. Normalization also minimizes the number of columns in a table, which minimizes the overall size of the database.

■ *It simplifies searches.* Database professionals who understand normalization rules will instantly know how to navigate a database's tables to find the information that they seek. Casual database users will find the table design logical because each table describes a single entity and all of its properties are columns in that table.

■ *It simplifies querying.* A table column holds a single type of data, such as first name or last name, but not both names. By storing last names in a separate column, a database can readily provide a list of all rows with a specific last name. With an unnormalized database that stores first names and last names in the same column, a query must extract the last name before selecting on a specific value for it.

There are three popular normalization rules—typically called First Normal Form, Second Normal Form, and Third Normal Form—as well as a variety of special rules.

First Normal Form

First Normal Form states that every field in a table should contain a single in-divisible item. The *Order Details* table in the Northwind database illustrates this rule. Figure 3-1 shows an excerpt from the table that displays three orders. Each column contains a single type of data. The second column contains just product names—not product names and prices. Also, there is just one instance of a product in each row.

Order ID	Product	Unit Price	Quantity	Discount
10248	Queso Cabrales	$14.00	12	0%
10248	Singaporean Hokkien Fried Mee	$9.80	10	0%
10248	Mozzarella di Giovanni	$34.80	5	0%
10249	Tofu	$18.60	9	0%
10249	Manjimup Dried Apples	$42.40	40	0%
10250	Jack's New England Clam Chowder	$7.70	10	0%
10250	Manjimup Dried Apples	$42.40	35	15%
10250	Louisiana Fiery Hot Pepper Sauce	$16.80	15	15%

Record: 1 of 2155

Figure 3-1. *An excerpt from the* Order Details *table illustrating the first normalization rule. The elements in each column, or field, are of a single type, and for any row the elements in a column are indivisible.*

Database tables that fail to comply with First Normal Form generally do so in two ways. First, they put more than one item in a single field. (Notice that the table in Figure 3-1 contains just one item per field.) An example is a table that stores a first name and a last name in a single field. This complicates ex-traction of information. A second way that First Normal Form is often violated is that a table has a field for each product in an order, which requires multiple unit price, quantity, and discount fields, further violating First Normal Form. This design increases the size of a table, and many of the values for some columns are likely to be empty.

Tables that comply with First Normal Form are likely to be organized around logical entities, which makes it easy to find information, and they are likely to have a primary key, which ensures that each row in a table is unique. Recall that database tables represent instances of entities. In the table shown in Figure 3-1, each row is one item from a customer order. The primary key for the table is a compound key based on the *OrderID* and *ProductID* numbers because each item from a customer order can be identified by a unique combination of the customer order number and the product's ID.

Second Normal Form

Second Normal Form specifies a required relationship among the columns in a row. To comply with Second Normal Form, a table must comply with First Normal Form, plus all values within a row must contain information about the specific entity represented by that row. Also, no two fields can be dependent on one another. One common violation of this rule is placing fields for two distinct entities in a single table.

The Northwind *Order Details* table complies with Second Normal Form. The quantity field is clearly appropriate for each item. Unit price and discount can change independently for each item, and placing unit price and discount in the table enables an application to easily track those items for each order.

The Northwind database has the unit price in both the *Order Details* and *Products* tables. This might appear to violate Second Normal Form. However, this design enables an administrator to update item prices without affecting the prices of items already ordered. Individual orders can use the price and discount schedule in the *Products* table as a guideline rather than as a rigid rule for all transactions.

Third Normal Form

Third Normal Form specifies that all the fields in each row must be unique and not dependent on one another. For example, this rule permits only one date field per row. If the *Orders* table contains an order date field, it must not also contain fields for order day, week, or month. (The application can derive the month of an order from the order date.) The *Orders* table does have several fields that contain Date/Time values, but these refer to the time of the initial order, the date by which a customer requires an order, the date an order ships, and so forth.

Following the rules

While it is wise to follow normalization rules, you might sometimes have reason to selectively comply with them—for example, to avoid having too many tables. A postal code field along with dependent geographic code fields can stand alone as a separate table. When you know the postal code for an address, you also know its country, state or province, and city. Therefore, you do not have to store both the postal code and the city in the same table.

Setting up multiple tables to store postal code, city, geographic region, and country information might not be practical for some small and medium-sized database projects. Even for a large database project, such a design requires the joining of the main *Contacts* table with multiple tables on each occasion that requires contact information. This can seriously degrade performance—especially if there are many such instances requiring the joining of multiple tables.

Relationships Between Tables

When you create tables for an application, you should also consider the relationships between them. These relationships give a relational database much of its power. There are three types of relationships between tables: one-to-one, one-to-many, and many-to-many.

One-to-one relationships

In a one-to-one relationship, each record in one table corresponds to a single record in a second table. This relationship is not very common, but it can offer several benefits. First, you can put the fields from both tables into a single, combined table. One reason for using two tables is that each field is a property of a separate entity, such as owner operators and their trucks. Each operator can operate just one truck at a time, but the fields for the operator and truck tables refer to different entities.

A one-to-one relationship can also reduce the time needed to open a large table by placing some of the table's columns in a second, separate table. This approach makes particular sense when a table has some fields that are used infrequently. Finally, a one-to-one relationship can support security. Access applies user-level security at the table level. Therefore, if a subset of the fields in a table requires security, placing them in a separate table lets your application restrict access to certain fields. Your application can link the restricted table back to the main table via a one-to-one relationship so that people with proper permissions can edit, delete, and add new records to those fields.

One-to-many relationships

A one-to-many relationship, in which a row from one table corresponds to one or more rows from a second table, is more common. This kind of relationship can form the basis for a many-to-many relationship as well. The *Customers* and *Orders* tables from the Northwind database have a one-to-many relationship. Any customer can have one or more orders, but each order belongs to exactly one customer. Figure 3-2 on the following page shows the Design view of the

Orders table. Its primary key is *OrderID*. Each *OrderID* value can appear in just one row. The table also includes a field, *CustomerID*, which links to the *Customers* table. (The *CustomerID* field is the primary key of the *Customers* table. A field that serves as a link to another table is known as a *foreign key*.) *CustomerID* values can appear multiple times in the *Orders* table. In fact, a customer ID appears once for each order that the customer makes. This foreign key links the "many" side of a relationship back to its "one" side.

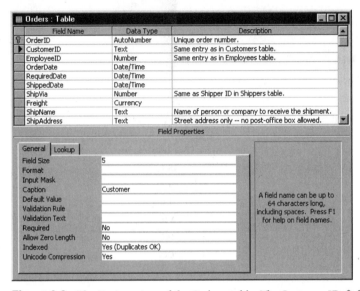

Figure 3-2. *The Design view of the* Orders *table. The* CustomerID *field serves as a foreign key for the one-to-many relationship with the* Customers *table.*

Many-to-many relationships

The many-to-many relationship exists only indirectly; it builds on two one-to-many relationships. The *Orders* and *Products* tables are in a many-to-many relationship. Any order can have many products in it. Similarly, a single product can appear in many different orders.

I imported four tables—*CustomersNW*, *OrdersNW*, *Order DetailsNW*, and *ProductsNW*—from the Northwind database to this chapter's sample database. Figure 3-3 shows the relationships among these tables in the Relationships window. The *CustomersNW* table is in a one-to-many relationship with the *OrdersNW* table, the *OrdersNW* table is in a one-to-many relationship with the *Order DetailsNW* table, and the *ProductsNW* table is in a one-to-many relationship with the *Order DetailsNW* table. The *Order DetailsNW* table acts as a "junction box" that links the *OrdersNW* and *ProductsNW* tables in a many-to-many relationship.

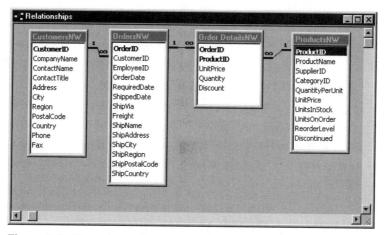

Figure 3-3. *The Relationships window view of the many-to-many relationship between the* OrdersNW *and the* ProductsNW *tables.*

All many-to-many relationships have a "junction box" design, in which a third table, the junction box, serves as a link between the two named tables in the relationship. This design helps to maintain the efficiency of the database because the junction box can have a large number of rows but you can define it to contain just a few columns. As with all normalized tables, you should restrict the columns to those that characterize its entities. This rule is especially important with junction box tables because they can contain such a relatively large number of rows.

Referential integrity

You can make your databases more robust by incorporating *referential integrity* and cascading updates and deletes. The rules of referential integrity ensure that relationships between tables are valid. These rules also prevent you from accidentally changing related data. (For example, you don't want to delete a customer if that customer has one or more unpaid orders.)

Referential integrity does not permit the addition of a row to the many side of a relationship with a foreign key value that does not match the values on the one side of the relationship. You can, however, enter a missing, or Null, foreign key value that does not match any primary key value on the one side of a relationship.

Referential integrity also helps to avoid orphan records—records in a table on the many side of a relationship that don't have matching records on the one side. It does this by blocking the deletion of records on the one side that still have matching records on the many side. (For example, you typically wouldn't want to remove the sales associated with an employee if that employee leaves the company.) In some cases, orphan records can undermine the validity of results that you obtain from a database. At the very least, they can bloat a database with unnecessary and unusable records.

At times, you'll want changes to occur on both sides of a relationship. In these situations, the cascading delete and cascading update features of referential integrity are useful. These features are not automatic; you have to explicitly invoke them. With the cascading delete feature enabled, deleting any record on the one side of a relationship removes all matching records from the many side of the relationship. Cascading updates works the same way for primary key modifications. If you change a primary key value on the one side of a relationship, it cascades to the many side. All matching foreign key values update automatically.

CREATING TABLES WITH WIZARDS

Access wizards simplify many database tasks, such as building and maintaining tables. Access offers more than 20 database wizards, such as the Contact Management wizard, Time And Billing wizard, Service Call Management wizard, and Video Collection Management wizard. All of these create whole applications, including the table design. The Table wizard automatically builds individual tables and even adds primary keys to a table and links one table to another table for you. The Field Builder helps you maintain tables by simplifying the addition of fields.

Database Wizards

You can view the available database wizards when you start Access 2000 by selecting the Access Database Wizards, Pages, And Projects option in the Microsoft Access dialog box and then clicking OK. When the New dialog box appears, click on the Databases tab and then double-click the icon for the wizard that you want to start. (You can also open the New dialog box by choosing New from the File menu.)

The basic functionality of a wizard-generated database is perfect for novices because it contains forms, tables, reports, and even some sample data. You can examine the database design and use it as a model for your own custom applications. More advanced developers can edit the basic design by adding their own tables, queries, forms, reports, and modules.

The Table Wizard

The Table wizard focuses exclusively on table design. You can open it from the Tables item in the *Objects* collection in the Database window. Double-click the Create Table By Using Wizard icon to open the initial Table Wizard dialog box.

This wizard offers a collection of prebuilt business and personal designs. The business table designs include *Contacts*, *Customers*, *Employees*, *Products*, *Orders*, *Invoices*, and *Events* tables. The personal designs are very complete and can also serve some small business functions. The designs include *Recipes*, *Plants*, *Exercise Log*, *Books*, *Video Collection*, and *Recordings* tables. The wizard does not populate a table with starter values, but it does suggest links to other tables that are already in the database design. It will even automatically construct these relationships.

After selecting a prebuilt table design, you can populate your custom version of it with fields from a list box. The initial Table Wizard dialog box offers a set of buttons for transferring field names between the Sample Fields list box and the Fields In My New Table list box. Figure 3-4 shows an *Invoices* table in the process of construction. Several sample fields have been transferred to the Fields In My New Table list box. At this point, you can click Next three times to construct an *Invoices* table. The defaults create a primary key for you, link your new table to any table already in the database that links to it naturally, and let you enter data directly into the table. When you click the final Finish button after accepting all the defaults, the table opens in Datasheet view so you can populate it with values. You can override any of the defaults before clicking Finish in the final dialog box.

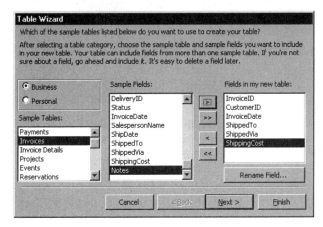

Figure 3-4. *Creating an* Invoices *table in the initial Table Wizard dialog box.*

The automatic detection of links to other tables is particularly helpful if you are just starting to learn about relational databases. Figure 3-5 on the following page shows the third Table Wizard dialog box for the creation of an *Invoice Details* table. This table can include an *InvoiceID* field that acts as a foreign key to the *Invoices* table. If the wizard detects the *Invoices* table, it automatically relates the two tables. While you can override the link or create other links not suggested by the wizard, the safe thing for new developers to do is to accept the default recommendations.

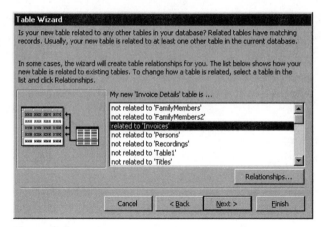

Figure 3-5. *A Table Wizard dialog box showing the detection of an automatic link between the* Invoice Details *table and the previously created* Invoices *table.*

The Field Builder

After you use a wizard to construct a table, you might want to add another field to the table. This apparently simple task can be more difficult than it initially appears, especially if the field needs to link with fields in other tables. This is because it is easier to create a new field with a different data type than it is to create a field in another table. When you try to relate similarly named fields from different tables whose data types are not identical, the attempt will fail without explanation. One solution to this problem is to use the Field Builder when you add new fields to tables.

You open the Field Builder by right-clicking on a blank row in a table's Design view and choosing Build from the shortcut menu. The Field Builder dialog box has two list boxes: one for selecting a table type, such as *Invoices* or *Invoice Details*, and one for selecting a field from that table type. When you highlight different table types, the entries change in the Sample Fields list box. Find the field that you want to add, and click OK to add it to the table. This ensures that your new fields will have data types that are consistent with the fields added using the Table wizard.

CREATING TABLES MANUALLY

To create a table manually, you double-click the Create Table In Design View icon in the Database window to open a blank Table window in Design view. From here, you can add fields, a primary key, and an index. (Primary keys are indexes with special property settings.)

To add a field, type the field's name in a blank Field Name column in the Design view window. Field names follow normal Visual Basic for Applications

(VBA) naming conventions. They can be up to 64 characters long, and the characters can be letters, numbers, spaces, and special characters—except the period, the exclamation mark, square brackets, and the grave accent character (`). Also, you cannot start a field name with a space or a control character (ASCII values 0 through 31). While you can include internal spaces in field names, they must be bracketed in expressions and queries.

Data Types

In the Data Type column, you can specify a data type for the field. A drop-down list box offers 10 options: Text, Memo, Number, Date/Time, Currency, AutoNumber, Yes/No, OLE Object, Hyperlink, and Lookup wizard. (Data types are commonly used to identify the information a field contains. A Text field contains a Text data type, an AutoNumber field contains an AutoNumber data type, and so on.) You can use options within many of these data types to further refine your data type specifications. For example, the Number data type has seven subtypes. You can specify one of these by selecting Number for the data type and then making a selection from the Field Size drop-down list box on the General page at the bottom left of the Table window.

AutoNumber fields

AutoNumber field types frequently serve as the primary key for a table. Access automatically assigns a new value to the field when you add a record to the table. This field is not manually updateable, so its values are ideal for uniquely marking a row within a table.

Access automatically sets the value of AutoNumber field types. To cause an AutoNumber field to increment sequentially, select Increment (the default value) from the New Values drop-down list box on the General page at the bottom left of the Table window. To indicate that an AutoNumber field should have a randomly assigned value, select Random from the New Values drop-down list box.

You can use the General and Lookup pages to select other properties that affect the field, such as whether the user must enter a value into the field or whether the field has a default value. Field properties set at the table level propagate through to forms and reports. Table field properties can also simplify the code written for forms and reports. Maintaining data properties at the table level also means that properties are changed in a single place rather than within each form and report that uses a field.

Access 2000 is the first version of Access to enable programmatic control over the initial value and step size of AutoNumber field types. (Chapter 2 initially explored this capability.) You can use the ALTER TABLE and ALTER COLUMN keywords in Jet SQL to update the next start and step values for an AutoNumber field. Recall from Chapter 2 that an AutoNumber field in Jet SQL has an IDENTITY data type. The *start* and *step* properties of this data type let you programmatically modify the next AutoNumber value and the step size for subsequent values.

Text fields

You use Text fields to hold string entries that contain up to 255 characters. The Text data type can store items such as contact information and numerical values that do not require computation (for example, social security numbers, telephone numbers, and parts numbers). You can also use Text fields in a table to persist computed string values. You can index primary keys for fast sorts and retrieval based on last name or another Text field type.

Lookup fields

A lookup field shows a meaningful value that corresponds to the value stored in the field. (For example, a database might use unique numbers to represent products. A lookup field can display a product's actual name instead of the number used to represent the product.) This type of field (also known as a *key column*) lets you store an index value in the table but display a meaningful text value when the table is in Datasheet view. A lookup field can link to values in another table or query or to a custom list of values maintained by the table for the lookup field. After you add a lookup field that references values in another table, you cannot delete the field until you delete the relationship to the other field using the Relationships window. When you delete the relationship, Access reminds you that the field is still part of a relationship and asks you to confirm the deletion. Choose Yes at this point to remove the lookup field from the table.

You create a lookup field using the Lookup wizard. Select Lookup Wizard from the Data Type drop-down list box for a table in Design view. The wizard's initial dialog box asks whether your lookup values will come from another table or from a custom list of values. You'll usually click Next to use lookup values from another table.

If you want to use lookup values from another table, in the second wizard dialog box you can select the table or query that contains the values displayed by the lookup field. In the third dialog box, you select the field or fields that contain the values displayed by your lookup field. (Generally, you'll select a text field that is a primary key.)

The fourth dialog box allows you to set the width of the column (or columns) used to display the lookup list in Datasheet view. The lookup list can display the lookup field's value and one list item for each field that you selected in the related table. (You'll usually want to hide the key column.) The final dialog box lets you assign a caption to the lookup field.

Figure 3-6 shows the second, third, and fourth dialog boxes that were used to create the *TitleID* field of the *Persons* table in the Chapter 3 database file on the companion CD.

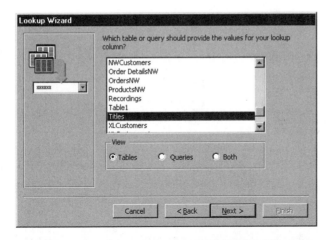

Figure 3-6. *The second, third, and fourth dialog boxes of the Lookup wizard.*

The *Persons* table in Design view shows *TitleID* as a number field—not a lookup field or a Text field. (See Figure 3-7.) The data type of a lookup field depends on the key column's data type. Even if you hide the key column, its data type determines the data type for the lookup field.

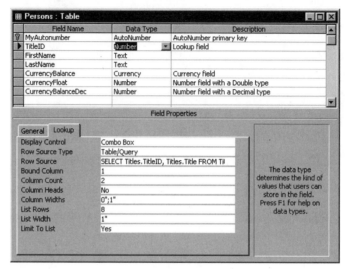

Figure 3-7. *The Design view of the* Persons *table with the lookup field created in Figure 3–6.*

The Lookup page in the table's Design view contains the SQL statement used by the lookup field. Access prepares this automatically as you make your selections in the Lookup wizard.

Number fields

Number fields are different from Text fields because they can assume a variety of subtypes, ranging from a single byte (Byte subtype) to 16 bytes (Replication ID subtype). The other data subtypes between these extremes include Integer, Long Integer, Single, Double, and Decimal. With the exception of the Byte and Replication ID subtypes, all of these data types are covered in Chapter 2 in the "Data Types" section.

The Byte subtype is similar to the Boolean variable data type. Both types can store Boolean values, but the Byte subtype requires just 1 byte of storage while the Boolean data type requires 2 bytes. The Replication ID data type is not available as a variable data type. Its primary use is in replication, but it serves as a unique identifier. Its length and method of creation make it a more secure way to ensure uniqueness than an AutoNumber field.

The Decimal subtype facilitates the elimination of rounding errors while still accommodating large numbers using *Precision* and *Scale* properties. These properties control the number of digits on either side of the decimal point. *Precision*, which represents the total number of digits that can be stored in the field, can range from 1 through 28. *Scale*, which indicates the number of digits to the right of the decimal that can be stored in the field, can range from 0 through the value in the *Precision* property. Because of the *Scale* property, the Decimal data subtype can store more digits after the decimal point without rounding errors than other Number data subtypes can.

Figure 3-8 shows the *Persons* table in Datasheet view. The *CurrencyBalance* field uses the Currency data type, *CurrencyFloat* uses the Number data type with the Double subtype, and *CurrencyBalanceDec* uses the Number data type with the Decimal subtype. The *CurrencyBalanceDec* field has a *Scale* property setting of 6, which indicates that the field can store six digits to the right of the decimal point. This is more digits than the Currency data type can precisely represent—its limit is four digits after the decimal. The Double data subtype can represent a number with four, five, or six places after the decimal, but it does not perform this task with integer precision. The first row in *Persons* displays the value 1.0001 in Currency, Double, and Decimal data formats. The second row expresses 1.00001 in the same three formats. Notice that in Datasheet view the Currency format initially shows 1.00001 as 1.0000 since it is limited to four places after the decimal. The Double and Decimal representations appear identical.

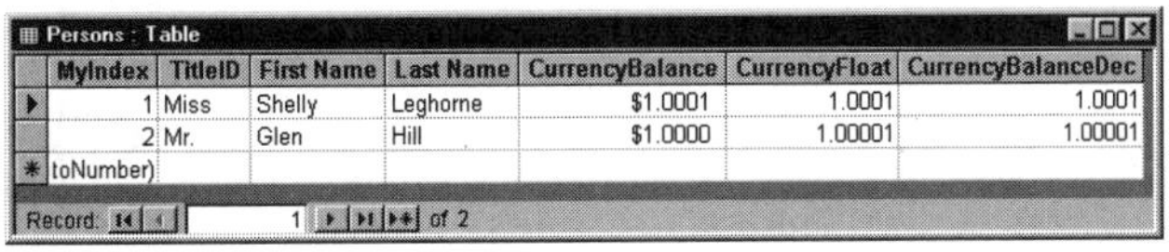

MyIndex	TitleID	First Name	Last Name	CurrencyBalance	CurrencyFloat	CurrencyBalanceDec
1	Miss	Shelly	Leghorne	$1.0001	1.0001	1.0001
2	Mr.	Glen	Hill	$1.0000	1.00001	1.00001
(toNumber)						

Record: ◄◄ ◄ 1 ► ►► ►► of 2

Figure 3-8. *The Datasheet view of the* Persons *table with numeric values in Currency, Double, and Decimal data formats.*

The *DecimalArithmetic* procedure below further shows the differences between these formats. It calculates the difference of each number stored in the respective fields from 1. The procedure opens a recordset based on the *Persons* table and then subtracts 1 from each of the three number fields in the first row and prints the results to the Immediate window. Then it moves to the second row and repeats the process.

```
Sub DecimalArithmetic()
Dim cnn1 As New ADODB.Connection
Dim rst1 As Recordset
Dim intCounter As Long, sumD As Variant
Dim sumC As Variant, sumF As Variant
```

(continued)

```
'Open and set recordset.
    Set rst1 = New ADODB.Recordset
    rst1.ActiveConnection = CurrentProject.Connection
    rst1.CursorType = adOpenKeyset
    rst1.LockType = adLockOptimistic
    rst1.Open "Persons", , , , adCmdTable

    Debug.Print "Decimal arithmetic: " & rst1.Fields(6) - 1
    Debug.Print "Floating arithmetic: " & rst1.Fields(5) - 1
    Debug.Print "Currency arithmetic: " & rst1.Fields(4) - 1
    rst1.MoveNext
    Debug.Print
    Debug.Print "Decimal arithmetic: " & rst1.Fields(6) - 1
    Debug.Print "Floating arithmetic: " & rst1.Fields(5) - 1
    Debug.Print "Currency arithmetic: " & rst1.Fields(4) - 1

End Sub
```

Figure 3-9 shows the results of calling the procedure. The Currency and Decimal formats yield the same result, 0.0001. The Double format cannot obtain this precise result; it yields .000099999999999989. For many purposes, this result is indistinguishable from the Currency and Decimal results. Nevertheless, when you need a precise outcome, it is not sufficient. When the same operation is performed on the second row, which contains the value 1.00001, the Decimal format is the only format that returns a precise result. These computations illustrate the special role that the Decimal data subtype can play. You should use it when you require precision that is not available with the Currency or Double data formats.

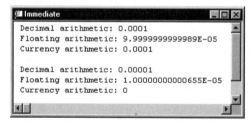

Figure 3-9. *The output from calling the* DecimalArithmetic *procedure.*

Memo, OLE Object, Date/Time, and Yes/No fields

Other data types included the Memo data type, which holds very large text data strings that can exceed the 255-character limit of the Text data type. A single Memo data type can grow to 64 KB. You can access and write back its contents in 64-KB blocks using the *GetChunk* and *AppendChunk* methods.

Jet 4 supports indexing the first 255 characters of a Memo field. This is particularly useful for Hyperlink data types that depend on the Memo data type.

OLE Object is another large data type. It works with objects in their binary format, such as a Microsoft Excel workbook or a Microsoft Word document.

Date/Time data types can represent either dates or times. Date values are stored to the left of the decimal point; time values are stored to the right of the decimal point. (See Chapter 2 for code samples that manipulate values of Date/Time fields.)

The Yes/No data type is the smallest. It is always in one of two states—either Yes/No, True/False, or On/Off. It occupies a single byte of storage.

Validating Data

To design tables for a robust database, you must ensure that only valid data gets into your database. Access 2000 offers several features to help you do this.

Required and *Allow Zero Length* properties

Sometimes a record is not valid unless it has an entry for a particular field, such as a primary key or a foreign key field. Setting the *Required* property for a foreign key to *Yes* guarantees that users cannot enter a record on the many side of a relationship without matching at least one record on the relationship's other side.

When the *Required* property of a field is set to *Yes*, Access does not accept a record with a Null value for the field. Depending on a field's setting for *Allow Zero Length*, you might be able to enter a zero-length string (""). Access differentiates between a field that has not been assigned a value (Null) and a field that has no value (zero-length strings for Text fields).

The *Input Mask* property

An input mask is a template that prompts the user about the type and format of data a field requires. Like other field properties, the *Input Mask* property propagates through to the use of the field in forms and reports.

You can use standard input masks or create your own custom input masks. Figure 3-10 on the following page shows the Input Mask wizard displaying a selection of input masks for a Date/Time field. You can enter values in the Try It text box to see how the mask will work in a real data entry situation.

The wizard controls both the input to a field and the display of the field's data unless you also specify the *Format* property for a field. When an application sets a field's *Format* property, that property controls the display of the field's data. The *Format* property does not affect the display of a value until an application saves the value to the database.

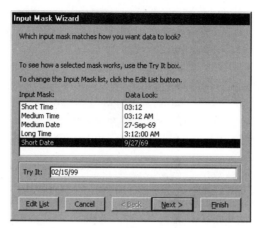

Figure 3-10. *The Input Mask wizard with a selection of input masks for Date/ Time fields.*

Validation Rule and *Validation Text* **properties**

You use the *Validation Rule* and *Validation Text* properties to ensure that the user enters valid information. You use the *Validation Rule* property to set criteria for valid entries in a field. (If a field should accept only numbers greater than 1, for example, you set *Validation Rule* to *>1*.) You can use the *Validation Text* property to specify feedback that users see when they try to enter a value outside the range designated by the *Validation Rule*.

You can also specify validation rules for the table as a whole. To do so, open the table in Design view and click the Properties button on the Table Design toolbar. Then use the *Validation Rule* and *Validation Text* properties to specify a validation rule for the entire table and a feedback message for a violation of the rule. With the table's validation rule, you can specify criteria that extend beyond a single field.

If you require multiple sets of rules, you can include them in your validation rule expression using *And* clauses. (If a field should accept only numbers greater than 1 and less than 10, for example, you set *Validation Rule* to *>1 And <10*.) Click the Build button next to the *Validation Rule* property box to open the Expression Builder. You can use the built-in Access functions for validation of table fields, but custom functions are not permitted in table or field validation expressions. The Expression Builder works equally well for creating overall table validation as well as field validation expressions.

Creating Indexes

Indexes determine how tables perform and how they relate to one another. Indexes generally speed up sort, find, and selection operations on a field.

Although applications can experience a performance penalty for data entry when indexes are used (because indexes require assignment with each new record), their benefits far outweigh their drawbacks.

Indexes also support referential integrity. At least one of the linking fields in a relationship must be a primary key or a unique index.

Figure 3-11 shows the *Orders* table in Design view with its main window and Indexes window open. The Indexes button on the Table Design toolbar toggles the visibility of the Indexes window.

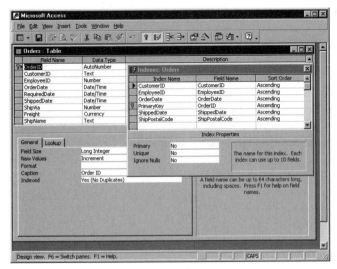

Figure 3-11. *The main and Indexes windows for the* Orders *table in Design view.*

The Indexes window in Figure 3-11 also includes a row with a key on it. Just as in the main window, this row marks the primary key. The Indexes window selects the CustomerID index. This index depends on the *CustomerID* field, which is a foreign key in the *Orders* table. The CustomerID index links the *Customers* and *Orders* tables in a one-to-many relationship. It is not the primary key in the *Orders* table. Therefore, it can duplicate across records. Notice additionally that some indexes, such as OrderDate and ShipPostalCode, are not keys to other tables. One reason to create an index is to speed the operations performed on the table's data, such as selecting by date or sorting by postal code.

> **NOTE** One way to ensure that you get the property settings for a foreign key correct is to copy the field to the Windows Clipboard on the one side of the relationship. Then you can paste it into the Design view of the table on the many side of the relationship. This avoids the need to set the foreign key properties manually.

You create an index by typing a name in the Index Name column of the Indexes window. Then, use the drop-down box to select a field for the index. Select the sort order for the field. Your choices are ascending or descending. If there is another field that belongs to the index, select its name and sort order in the immediately following row. You can add more fields to the index in the same fashion. Each additional field for the index should appear immediately below the preceding one. Only the first field in an index should have an entry for the Index Name column. All immediately succeeding rows with a blank Index Name column belong to the same index. Every entry in the Index Name column starts a new index.

You can set the three index properties independently. However, setting *Primary* to *Yes* automatically converts *Unique* to *Yes* and *Ignore Nulls* to *No*. A primary key has to be unique for every record. You cannot create a primary key on a field or fields with Null values. There can only be one primary key per table. A table can have multiple fields with unique indexes that ignore Nulls. Any index, except a primary key, can ignore Nulls. This lets you define an index on the non-Null values in a field. Choosing to ignore Nulls can save storage requirements for an index.

Figure 3-12 presents the main and Indexes windows for the Design view of the *Order Details* table. Notice that the main window shows the selection of the *ProductID* field. Its caption is *Product*. This is the second of the two fields that define the primary key. The other field is *OrderID*. Both fields are Number fields with a Long Integer data subtype. Neither field is an AutoNumber field. Rather they are foreign keys based on the AutoNumber fields in the *Orders* and *Products* tables. Both primary key components are foreign keys. Together they uniquely identify each row in the *Order Details* table. Junction box tables always behave this way.

The Indexes window in Figure 3-12 further identifies the primary key. Notice that the *Order Details* table also maintains separate indexes based on the *OrderID* and *ProductID* fields. These indexes maintain links with the *Orders* and *Products* tables. The referential integrity links between *Order Details* and *Products* draw on these indexes.

You can manually create and manage referential integrity relations between tables from the Relationships window. First, add the tables to the window if they are not there already. Right-click in the window, choose Show Table, and add as many tables as necessary. Second, join the tables by the common fields over which the tables link. Do this by dragging one or more fields from one table to the other. Drag from the one side to the many side of a relationship. Third, select the join line. Fourth, right-click the line and choose Edit Relationship. Fifth, check the Enforce Referential Integrity check box. Make any other necessary design changes to the relationship. This can include selecting the check boxes for cascading updates and cascading deletes. You can also click Join Types to choose either of two other join types besides the standard one that includes rows from both tables only when the join fields in both tables are equal. The other two options include either all the records from the one side or all the records from the many side of the relationship.

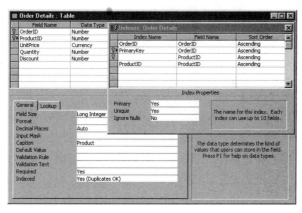

Figure 3-12. *The main and Indexes windows for the Northwind* Order Details *table in Design view.*

Figure 3-13 on the following page reveals the Edit Relationships dialog boxes that define referential integrity relations between the *Order Details* table and either the *Orders* or the *Products* tables. Notice that Access automatically interprets both relationships as one-to-many. The relationship between the *Orders* and *Order Details* tables specifies cascading deletes. This allows the deletion of an order and all its line items with a single operation. Without this specification, the application would have to use two delete queries—one for each table. The relationship between the *Products* and the *Order Details* tables does not include cascading deletes. In this case, there is no automatic deletion of order line items when it becomes necessary to remove a product from the *Products* table. The business model may call for a special effort to purchase the product for the existing orders in the pipeline.

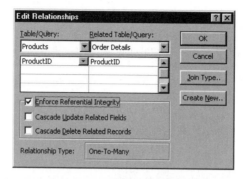

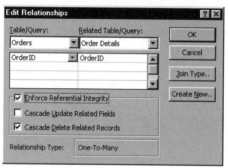

Figure 3-13. *Two Edit Relationships dialog boxes depicting the referential integrity relationships between the Northwind* Products *and* Order Details *tables (above) and the* Orders *and* Order Details *tables (below).*

CREATING AND MANAGING TABLES PROGRAMMATICALLY

Sometimes—perhaps even most of the time—you will create tables manually. However, on occasion you might find it convenient to create a table dynamically, such as when you need to persist intermediate results for reuse in a subsequent operation. Access 2000 lets you do this using ADO techniques as well as the more traditional Data Access Objects (DAO) techniques. This section describes how to create and manage tables using ADO techniques. Once you learn this approach, you'll be able to take advantage of upcoming innovations in Microsoft data access technology.

After creating a table programmatically, you will often want to populate it with data. Even if you do not create a table programmatically, populating it with data programmatically has appeal. You can use many different data sources for populating an Access table. This section explores using another Access table, an Excel table (as an example of an ISAM data source), and an ODBC data source. You'll also learn how to populate an Access table using OLE database

(OLE DB) providers and the native Access *DoCmd* object, which makes it easy to link to remote data sources. Unlike using OLE DB, using *DoCmd* makes the linked data source available from the Database window.

Creating a Table

To add tables dynamically, all you need is ADO—the ADOX library, to be specific. Just as when you manually create a table in a database, when you create a table dynamically you must name it, add columns to it, and append it to the *Tables* collection.

The *MakeLocalTable* procedure below creates a table dynamically. It starts by declaring the *Catalog* object and the *Table* object. The *Catalog* object is a container for the database schema, including the *Tables* collection. Next, the procedure instantiates the *Catalog* and *Table* objects. It names the new table *FamilyMembers2* and assigns four columns to it using four *Append* methods nested inside a *With...End* statement. Each *Append* method includes a column name, a constant specifying a data type, and a length argument, if appropriate. The three Text fields (those created by specifying the *adVarWChar* data type) each have a field size specification. The procedure ends by appending the completed table to the catalog's *Tables* collection and closing the *Catalog* object.

```
Sub MakeLocalTable()
Dim cat1 As ADOX.Catalog
Dim tbl1 As ADOX.Table

'Reference objects for table
    Set cat1 = New Catalog
    cat1.ActiveConnection = CurrentProject.Connection
    Set tbl1 = New Table

'Name table and append columns.
    With tbl1
        .Name = "FamilyMembers2"
        .Columns.Append "FamID", adInteger
        .Columns.Append "Fname", adVarWChar, 20
        .Columns.Append "Lname", adVarWChar, 25
        .Columns.Append "Relation", adVarWChar, 30
    End With

'Append new table to Tables collection
'and free catalog resource.
    cat1.Tables.Append tbl1
    Set cat1 = Nothing

End Sub
```

The following table lists the data type and subtypes represented by the ADOX library's *DataTypeEnum* class constants.

COLUMN TYPE CONSTANTS AND THEIR MANUAL DATA TYPE EQUIVALENTS

Constant	Value	Manual Data Type
adBoolean	11	Yes/No
adCurrency	6	Currency
adDate	7	Date/Time
adDecimal	14	Number—Decimal
adDouble	5	Number—Double
adGuid	72	Number—Replication ID
adInteger	3	AutoNumber
adInteger	3	Number—Long Integer
adLongVarBinary	205	OLE Object
adLongVarWChar	203	Hyperlink
adLongVarWChar	203	Memo
adSingle	4	Number—Single
adSmallInt	2	Number—Integer
adUnSignedTinyInt	17	Number—Byte
adWChar	130	Text

The table shows a couple of interesting points. First, the Hyperlink data type is equivalent to the Memo data type from a programming perspective. Second, there is no distinct data type for AutoNumber fields in the ADOX library. If your code checks the *Type* property of an AutoNumber field, you get the value *adInteger*. This value does not reflect the dynamic nature of the AutoNumber data type. Jet 4, however, does have a distinct data type, Identity, that corresponds to the AutoNumber data type. (See Chapter 2 for more on using this data type.) Also, the "Creating Tables Manually" section earlier in this chapter mentions more keywords for programmatically managing AutoNumber fields.

Avoiding replacing a table

When you add a table to a database manually, it is easy to check whether a table name already exists. If you inadvertently try to save a table with the name of an existing table in the database, Access warns you and asks if you want to overwrite the existing table. When you create a table programmatically, however, Access VBA halts with a run-time error when a procedure attempts to create a new table that has the name of an existing table. Therefore, you need error trapping to handle this situation. There are at least a couple of approaches to this task. The one that makes the most sense depends on the frequency with which you will be creating new tables.

The *MakeLocalTableErrCatcher* procedure below uses a classic error trapping approach. First, it enables a custom error handling routine so that the program can manage errors. The *On Error* statement at the beginning of the procedure accomplishes this. Next, it attempts to create and append the same *FamilyMembers2* table as in the *MakeLocalTable* procedure. If the table already exists in the catalog, the Access VBA generates an error (-2147217857) and transfers control to the *TableErrCatcher* error handling routine. The error trapping logic checks for the "already exists" error. If it detects that error, it deletes the existing table and returns control to the line that caused the error. This allows the program to save the new table and exit the procedure normally. If another error causes a visit to the error handling routine, the routine prints the error's number and description to the Immediate window before gracefully exiting the procedure. The procedure never ends abnormally with a system message.

```
Sub MakeLocalTableErrCatcher()
On Error GoTo TableErrCatcher
Dim cat1 As ADOX.Catalog
Dim tbl1 As ADOX.Table

'Reference objects for table
    Set cat1 = New Catalog
    cat1.ActiveConnection = CurrentProject.Connection
    Set tbl1 = New Table

'Name table and append columns.
    With tbl1
        .Name = "FamilyMembers2"
        .Columns.Append "FamID", adInteger
        .Columns.Append "Fname", adVarWChar, 20
        .Columns.Append "Lname", adVarWChar, 25
        .Columns.Append "Relation", adVarWChar, 30
    End With

'Append new table to Tables collection
'and free catalog resource.
    cat1.Tables.Append tbl1
    Set cat1 = Nothing

'Exit the procedure.
TableErrExit:
    Exit Sub
```

(continued)

```
        TableErrCatcher:
'Trap "table already exits" error.
'Delete table and resume.
    If Err.Number = -2147217857 Then
        cat1.Tables.Delete "FamilyMembers2"
        Resume
    End If
'Print details for other errors and exit.
    Debug.Print Err.Number, Err.Description
    Resume TableErrExit

End Sub
```

Replacing a table

If the database application regularly creates the *FamilyMembers2* table, the procedure can generate the "already exists" error nearly every time it runs. In this situation, your procedure will run faster if you try to delete the existing table before appending the new one. This generally avoids the need to process an error. You still need an error handler for when the table does not already exist or when another condition generates an error. The following procedure writes the error handler when you unconditionally delete a table with the same name as the one that you are about to append to the database.

```
Sub MakeLocalTableErrCatcher2()
On Error GoTo TableErrCatcher
Dim cat1 As ADOX.Catalog
Dim tbl1 As ADOX.Table

'Reference objects for table
    Set cat1 = New Catalog
    cat1.ActiveConnection = CurrentProject.Connection
    Set tbl1 = New Table

'Name table and append columns.
    With tbl1
        .Name = "FamilyMembers2"
        .Columns.Append "FamID", adInteger
        .Columns.Append "Fname", adVarWChar, 20
        .Columns.Append "Lname", adVarWChar, 25
        .Columns.Append "Relation", adVarWChar, 30
    End With

'Delete the old table (if it is there).
'Append the new one, and free the resource.
    cat1.Tables.Delete "FamilyMembers2"
    cat1.Tables.Append tbl1
    Set cat1 = Nothing
```

```
'Exit the procedure.
TableErrExit:
    Exit Sub

TableErrCatcher:
'Trap "object not in collection" error.
'Resume at next line.
    If Err.Number = 3265 Then
        Resume Next
    End If
'Print details for other errors and exit.
    Debug.Print Err.Number, Err.Description
    Resume TableErrExit

End Sub
```

The 3265 error mentioned in *MakeLocalTableErrCatcher2*'s error handling routine results when you attempt to delete an object that is not in the collection. *MakeLocalTableErrCatcher2* simply traps the error and resumes after the line that caused it. Any other error causes the program to end gracefully with the only trace being the error number and description in the Immediate window.

Working with Indexes

You can also add primary keys, indexes, and relationships programmatically. You can define primary keys and indexes across a single field or multiple fields.

Creating a primary key

Adding a primary key or an index to a table is similar to adding a new table to a catalog. First, you create a context to which to add the index, including a catalog and a table. Second, you define the index properties. These can differ between indexes and primary keys. Third, you append a column to the index and then append the new index to the table. If an error occurs, for example if the index already exists, you must respond appropriately. The *AddPK* procedure below dynamically creates a primary key.

```
Sub AddPK()
Dim cat1 As New ADOX.Catalog
Dim tbl1 As New ADOX.Table
Dim pk1 As New ADOX.Index

'Create a context for the new primary key.
    cat1.ActiveConnection = CurrentProject.Connection
    Set tbl1 = cat1.Tables("FamilyMembers2")
```

(continued)

```
'Set the primary key properties.
   With pk1
       .Name = "MyPrimaryKey"
       .PrimaryKey = True
       .Unique = True
       .IndexNulls = adIndexNullsDisallow
   End With

'Append column to index and index to table.
   pk1.Columns.Append "FamID"
   tbl1.Indexes.Append pk1

'Free resources.
   Set cat1 = Nothing

End Sub
```

The procedure begins by declaring and instantiating *Catalog*, *Table*, and *Index* objects. (You need all three objects to create a primary key.) Notice that there is no explicit object for a primary key. Next, the procedure sets the context for defining the new primary key. It sets the *ActiveConnection* property of the *Catalog* object to point the catalog at a specific database. Then it sets the table reference to a table within that database. This reference is the table to which your procedure will add the new primary key.

Next, the procedure sets four index properties. The first is the name of the primary key. It appears as an entry in the Index Name column in the table's Indexes window. The remaining three properties differentiate the primary key from a simple index. You should always set these properties as they appear in the *AddPK* procedure when you create a primary key.

The procedure then invokes two *Append* methods. The first one appends the *FamID* column from the *FamilyMembers2* table to the index. The second one appends the index to the table. Finally, the procedure sets the *Catalog* object to *Nothing*, thereby freeing the resources used to create the primary key.

It is often desirable to have an AutoNumber, Long Integer, or Text field as a primary key. These can be faster than a multiple field primary key. However, at times a multiple field index makes sense in terms of uniquely defining records and in terms of how you will use the data from the table. When a multiple key index is appropriate, you simply append more than one column to the index before you append the index to the table.

In the preceding example, you can replace the line

```
pk1.Columns.Append "FamID"
```

with the lines

```
pk1.Columns.Append "Lname"
pk1.Columns.Append "Fname"
pk1.Columns.Append "Relation"
```

These lines define a primary key on three fields instead of just one. The *AddPK* procedure generates a primary key based on a single field; the top Indexes window in Figure 3-14 shows the result of calling *AddPK*. The bottom Indexes window shows the result of calling *AddPK3*, which is identical to *AddPK* except for the code replacement shown above. (Both procedures are in the database for Chapter 3 on the companion CD.) Because you can have only one primary key at a time, you must manually remove the primary key between calling the *AddPK* and *AddPK3* procedures.

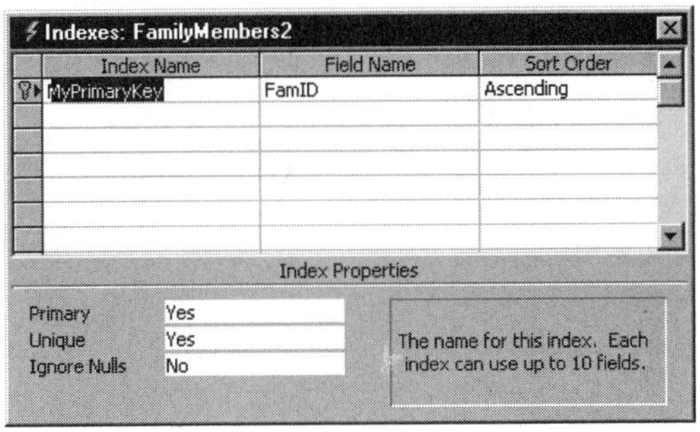

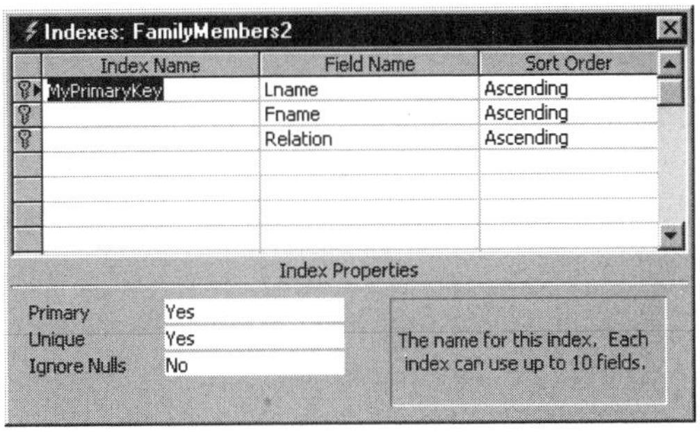

Figure 3-14. *The Indexes windows after running the* AddPK *and* AddPK3 *procedures.*

The *AddPK* and *AddPK3* procedures can fail for any of several reasons. Two errors that the following *AddPKErr* procedure traps are an already existing primary key (-2147467259) and the table already being open (-2147217856). (As stated above, you cannot add a new primary key if one already exists; also, you cannot even modify the index structure if the table is open.)

```
Sub AddPKErr()
On Error GoTo PKErr
Dim cat1 As New ADOX.Catalog
Dim tbl1 As New ADOX.Table
Dim pk1 As New ADOX.Index
Dim iNumber As Integer

'Create a context for the new primary key.
    cat1.ActiveConnection = CurrentProject.Connection
    Set tbl1 = cat1.Tables("FamilyMembers2")

'Set the primary key properties.
'The label (SetPKvariable) gives the procedure a
'recovery point from a previously existing primary key.
SetPKvariable:
    With pk1
        .Name = "MyPrimaryKey"
        .PrimaryKey = True
        .Unique = True
        .IndexNulls = adIndexNullsDisallow
    End With

'Append column to index and index to table.
    pk1.Columns.Append "FamID"
    tbl1.Indexes.Append pk1

'Exit procedure.
PKErrExit:
    Set cat1 = Nothing
    Exit Sub

PKErr:
'Checks for table already in use
    If Err.Number = -2147217856 Then
        MsgBox "FamilyMembers2 currently in use.  This" & _
            " operation requires the table to be closed."
'Checks for primary key already exists
    ElseIf Err.Number = -2147467259 Then
        For Each pk1 In tbl1.Indexes
            If pk1.PrimaryKey = True Then
                tbl1.Indexes.Delete (iNumber)
                Resume SetPKvariable
            End If
            iNumber = iNumber + 1
        Next pk1
'Traps for other errors
    Else
        MsgBox "Open Immediate window for Bug report"
```

```
      Debug.Print Err.Number; Err.Description
      Resume PKErrExit
   End If

End Sub
```

With a few exceptions for error trapping, the *AddPKErr* procedure follows the logic of the *AddPK* procedure in its main segment. *AddPKErr* first enables an error handling routine with an *On Error* statement. The declaration area includes a new *Dim* statement for an Integer variable. The error trapping logic uses this variable as an index in the loop that iterates through the Indexes collection of the table.

The error trapping logic in *AddPKErr* starts at the *PKErr* label. An *If...Then* statement initially tests for whether the table is open. If it is, the routine displays a message box that explains the problem and offers a solution before gracefully exiting. The *ElseIf* clause detects the existence of a primary key. In this case, the routine enumerates the indexes in the table until it detects the one with its *PrimaryKey* attribute set to *True*. Then it deletes that index and returns control to the initial step for defining a new primary key. This is necessary since the error wipes out the previous settings. If the table is not open and no primary key exists, the routine writes the error number and its description to the Immediate window before exiting the procedure. A message box tells the user to view the Immediate window for the cause of the error.

Creating an index

Adding a simple index to a table is not much different from adding a primary key. The major difference is that you do not set the *PrimaryKey* property to *True*. (It is *False* by default.) The *AddIdx* procedure below has a design similar to that of *AddPK*. Aside from not setting the primary key property, the major difference is that it explicitly assigns a sort order for the index. By instructing the table to sort on the *FamID* column values in descending order, the procedure makes the table show the most recent records first (assuming that records with a higher *FamID* value are added after earlier ones). When assigning the sort order, you must specify which number column it applies to. The numbering for columns is zero-based.

```
Sub AddIdx()
Dim cat1 As New ADOX.Catalog
Dim tbl1 As New ADOX.Table
Dim idx1 As New ADOX.Index

'Create a context for the new index.
    cat1.ActiveConnection = CurrentProject.Connection
    Set tbl1 = cat1.Tables("FamilyMembers2")
```

(continued)

```
'Set the index properties.
    With idx1
        .Name = "LastIsFirst"
        .Unique = True
        .IndexNulls = adIndexNullsDisallow
    End With

'Append column to index and set its sort order.
'Append new index to table.
    idx1.Columns.Append "FamID"
    idx1.Columns(0).SortOrder = adSortDescending
    tbl1.Indexes.Append idx1

'Free resources.
    Set cat1 = Nothing

End Sub
```

Dynamically Populating a Table

After you design a table and set its indexes, you populate it with values using one of two approaches. When the data for the table resides in another table, you can define recordsets on the data source table and the new table. Then you simply navigate through both recordsets in synchrony as you copy records to the new table using the *AddNew* method. (This approach loops through a recordset, so it is not appropriate for very large tables.) A second approach is to use SQL to insert values into the new table based on the values of the original table. This approach does not rely on recordsets or the *AddNew* method, but it does need at least one *Command* object.

Using recordsets

The first approach, illustrated in the following procedure, requires a *Connection* object and a *Catalog* object in addition to a pair of recordsets. The *Catalog* object and the two recordsets share a common *Connection* object. Because so many objects share a common connection, it makes sense to declare a *Connection* object and invoke it for each of the other objects that need it.

```
Sub AddValues()
Dim cnn1 As ADODB.Connection
Dim cat1 As New ADOX.Catalog
Dim rst1 As New ADODB.Recordset
Dim rst2 As New ADODB.Recordset

'Set context for populating new table (FamilyMembers2).
'Empty values from FamilyMembers2 before running.
    Set cnn1 = CurrentProject.Connection
    Set cat1.ActiveConnection = cnn1
```

```
        Set rst1.ActiveConnection = cnn1
'       Set rst2.ActiveConnection = cnn1

'Open recordsets based on new and original tables.
     rst1.Open "FamilyMembers2", , adOpenKeyset, _
        adLockOptimistic, adCmdTable
     rst2.Open "FamilyMembers", cnn1, adOpenForwardOnly, _
        adLockReadOnly, adCmdTable

'Loop through recordsets to copy from original to new table.
     With rst1
        Do Until rst2.EOF
           .AddNew
              .Fields(0) = rst2.Fields(0)
              .Fields(1) = rst2.Fields(1)
              .Fields(2) = rst2.Fields(2)
              .Fields(3) = rst2.Fields(3)
'          .Update
           .MoveNext
           rst2.MoveNext
        Loop
     End With

End Sub
```

After declaring objects and assigning the connection to the other objects that will use it, the procedure opens recordsets on the table with the source records, *FamilyMembers*, and the new table, *FamilyMembers2*.

The code above shows two approaches to assigning a connection to a recordset. You can assign a connection to a recordset's *ActiveConnection* property—*AddValue* uses this technique for *rst1*. Or you can reference a *Connection* object in the *Open* method for a recordset—the *Open* method for *rst2* uses this technique. You can use either approach with both recordsets. The *AddValues* procedure comments out a line that reveals how to set *rst2's ActiveConnection* property with an assignment. If you use that technique for *rst2*, you can remove the reference to *cnn1* in the *Open* method for *rst2*.

The *Do...Loop* statement that iterates through the records in *rst2* occurs inside of a *With...End* statement that references *rst1*. (Because there are so many references to *rst1* in the loop, this statement makes the code faster and much easier to read.) Within the loop, an *AddNew* method enables the assignment of the current record in *rst2* to *rst1*. The use of the *Update* method to complete the operation of the *AddNew* method is optional. (The sample shows it commented out of the procedure.) After adding the current record in *rst2* to *rst1*, the procedure advances one record in *rst2*. There is no need to advance in *rst1* since each iteration of the loop simply adds a new record to the end of *rst1*. The *Do* loop continues until it encounters an end-of-file (EOF) for *rst2*.

Saving a recordset

After populating a recordset and its underlying table with values (and maybe even updating them), you can save a copy of the recordset using the new recordset *Save* method and its persistent file type, which uses a compact binary format. Access 2000 offers several ways to save and retrieve recordsets with this new format and a corresponding provider. The following procedures save a recordset, by using a client cursor, and then open it.

```
Sub SaveRST()
On Error GoTo SaveRSTErr
Dim rst1 As New ADODB.Recordset

'Open client cursor and recordset.
    rst1.CursorLocation = adUseClient
    rst1.Open "FamilyMembers2", CurrentProject.Connection, _
        adOpenStatic, adLockBatchOptimistic

    rst1.Save "c:\FamilyMembers3.adtg", adPersistADTG

SaveRSTExit:
    Exit Sub

SaveRSTErr:
'Trap file already exists error
    If Err.Number = -2147286960 Then
        Kill "c:\FamilyMembers3.adtg"
        Resume
    End If
'Exit for other errors.
    MsgBox "View Immediate window for error diagnostics.", _
        vbCritical, "Programming Microsoft Access 2000"
    Resume SaveRSTExit

End Sub


Sub OpenSavedRST()
Dim rst1 As New ADODB.Recordset

'Open saved recordset file.
    rst1.Open "c:\FamilyMembers3.adtg", "Provider=MSPersist"

'Print selected info to confirm retrieval.
    Debug.Print rst1.Fields(0).Name & " = " & _
        rst1.Fields(0).Value

End Sub
```

The main part of the *SaveRST* procedure opens a client cursor and then places a recordset in it. Then it invokes the recordset's *Save* method. Persisting a recordset to a file is no more complicated than that. The ADTG (Advanced Data TableGram) file is minimal (just 1 KB on my system). This represents substantial savings over storing the recordset as a table in a database file.

If you regularly save a recordset after updates, the *Save* method will fail unless you delete the old filename or use a new name. Alternatively, you can trap the error, delete the old file version, and then invoke the *Save* method again. The error handling routine in *SaveRST* illustrates this technique.

You can open a saved recordset with just two lines of code, as demonstrated by *OpenSavedRST*. The first line declares and instantiates a *Recordset* object. The second line invokes the *Open* method for the recordset. Its source is the file saved by the *SaveRST* procedure, and its connection argument references the persistence provider that ships with Access 2000. A third line prints a field from the recordset to confirm that the information in the file is correct.

Using SQL

To many developers, looping through a recordset one record at a time has the appeal of being concrete. It is easy to envision moving from one record to the next in *rst2* and adding individual records to *rst1*. However, it is more efficient to use SQL code to perform the same task. In addition, the SQL approach requires just a single *Command* object from the ADODB library. The looping approach relies on several objects from both the ADODB and ADOX libraries. If you are uncomfortable with writing SQL, you can use the Access visual query designer to get a first draft of the correct SQL syntax for a task, such as inserting records from one table into another. The following *AddValuesSQL* procedure demonstrates how compact the SQL approach can be. (In fact, if your application does not need to know how many records it adds, the SQL approach can be even shorter.)

```
Sub AddValuesSQL()
Dim cmd1 As ADODB.Command
Dim intRowsAdded As Integer
Dim str1

'Instantiate cmd1.
    Set cmd1 = New ADODB.Command

'Set the connection and text for cmd1
'before executing it.
    With cmd1
```

(continued)

```
        .ActiveConnection = CurrentProject.Connection
        .CommandText = "INSERT INTO FamilyMembers2 " & _
            "SELECT FamilyMembers.* " & _
            "FROM FamilyMembers;"
        .CommandType = adCmdText
        .Execute intRowsAdded
    End With

'Report how many records cmd1 added.
    str1 = intRowsAdded & " rows were added to the table."
    MsgBox str1, vbInformation, "Programming Microsoft Access 2000"

End Sub
```

The procedure begins by declaring and instantiating a *Command* object. It uses a *With...End* statement to simplify setting the object's properties and invoking its methods. The *With...End* code block begins by setting the *Command* object's *ActiveConnection* and *CommandText* properties. (The command text is always a SQL statement with this approach.) The block then sets the *CommandType* property to *adCmdText* to optimize performance. (Failing to set the *CommandType* property forces Access to resolve the type of *Command* object before it can process the command.) Finally, the block calls the *Execute* method with an optional argument, *intRowsAdded*. When the call to *Execute* returns, *intRowsAdded* contains the number of records the SQL statement affected. A subsequent message box statement uses *intRowsAdded* to report to the user the number of records that were added to the new table.

Working with Data in Other Formats

In Chapter 2, you learned how to use the Jet 4 OLE DB provider to open the Northwind database from an application. You can use this technique to access the data in one Access database from any other Access database. The technique even works for data stored in other formats for which an OLE DB provider exists. Even when an OLE DB provider is not available, you can link to another database via DAO and access its information with all the ease of use and power of any linked data source.

You can use the Jet 4 provider to open an Excel data source. Figure 3-15 shows a simple worksheet in an Excel workbook, named Customers.xls. Sheet1 contains a Customers range (see the Name Box) with information about customer ID, company name, contact name, and payment terms. The following procedure opens a range in an Excel 2000 workbook with Access 2000.

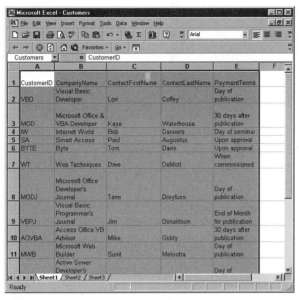

Figure 3-15. *Access can easily work with the information in this Excel spreadsheet.*

```
Sub OpenPrintXLDataSource()
Dim cnn1 As New ADODB.Connection
Dim rst1 As Recordset

'Open and set recordset.
    cnn1.Open "Provider=Microsoft.Jet.OLEDB.4.0;" & _
        "Data Source=C:\Programming Access\Chap03\Customers.xls;" & _
        "Extended Properties=Excel 8.0;"
    Set rst1 = New ADODB.Recordset
    rst1.CursorType = adOpenKeyset
    rst1.LockType = adLockOptimistic
    rst1.Open "customers", cnn1, , , adCmdTable

'Open recordset and print a test record.
    Do Until rst1.EOF
        Debug.Print rst1.Fields(0).Value, rst1.Fields(1).Value
        rst1.MoveNext
    Loop

End Sub
```

OpenPrintXLDataSource uses a *Connection* object to open an Excel workbook. The *Open* method for the *cnn1* object creates a connection to the worksheet file. The provider in this call is the same one used for Jet 4 files, the Extended Properties argument specifies a format compatible with Excel 2000 files, and the

Data Source argument points to an Excel workbook in the My Documents folder of the C drive. The next four lines in the procedure create and open a reference to a recordset defined on the Customers range in the Customers.xls file. The *Do* loop at the end of the procedure prints the first two fields in the recordset to the Immediate window.

After you open a recordset for an Excel data source, you can do anything that Access permits you to do with a record source, such as update field values. The difference is that your application updates values in a range on the Excel worksheet rather than those in an Access table. The *OpenPrintXLDataSource* example clearly demonstrates the power of ADO and OLEDB providers within an Access application.

Using the MSDASQL provider

Access 2000 works with other OLEDB providers, such as MSDASQL, which works for all ODBC data sources. Although there is a special provider for Microsoft SQL Server, the following procedure uses the general OLEDB ODBC provider to illustrate how you can use the provider with any ODBC data source. Since this provider always references an ODBC data source, you can use it in coordination with a DSN. The procedure shows the MSDASQL provider referencing the SQL Server Pubs database to print the author social security number, first name, and last name.

```
Sub GetODBCThroughOLEDB()
Dim cnn1 As New ADODB.Connection
Dim rst1 As ADODB.Recordset

'Open ODBC sources with msdaSQL provider and DSN reference.
    cnn1.Open "Provider=MSDASQL;DSN=Pubs;"
    Set rst1 = New ADODB.Recordset
    rst1.CursorType = adOpenKeyset
    rst1.LockType = adLockOptimistic
    rst1.Open "authors", cnn1, , , adCmdTable

'Open recordset and print a test record.
    Do Until rst1.EOF
        Debug.Print rst1.Fields(0).Value, _
            rst1.Fields(2), rst1.Fields(1).Value
        rst1.MoveNext
    Loop
End Sub
```

The *GetODBCThroughOLEDB* procedure starts by opening a connection to the SQL Server Pubs database and invokes the object's *Open* method. The provider argument specifies the MSDASQL provider, and the DSN argument contains the connection information and acts as a Data Source argument for the Jet 4 provider. The *Open* method can specify the connection string information, which eliminates the need to reference the DSN. The following statement shows how to open the SQL Server Pubs database without denoting a DSN:

```
cnn1.Open "Provider=MSDASQL;DRIVER=SQL Server;" & _
    "SERVER=CAB2200;DATABASE=Pubs;uid=sa;pwd=;"
```

The SQL Server name is CAB2200. Notice that the connection string also contains user ID and password arguments. The connection string is specific to the database to which you connect.

The next four lines of the procedure open a recordset on the *Authors* table in the SQL Server Pubs database. The syntax of the *Open* method is identical to the one used to open a range on an Excel worksheet. This symmetry of form between two such diverse sources illustrates the power of ADO with OLE DB providers. The final *Do* loop iterates through the records to print the social security number, first name, and last name for each author. Since the *Value* property is the default for the *Recordset* object's *Fields* collection, you don't need to specify it. (Notice that the second argument to the *Debug.Print* method does not explicitly reference the *Value* property of the *Fields* collection.) The overall design of the *GetODBCThroughOLEDB* procedure shows that Access 2000 can link to a SQL Server database as easily as it can to an Excel workbook.

The *TransferDatabase* and *TransferSpreadsheet* methods of the *DoCmd* object are an easy and robust way to link to data in another application; they do not even depend on a reference to the DAO library. These methods expose their sources through the Database window, while the OLE DB provider offers an exclusively programmatic interface to its data sources. Whether exposure through the Database window is a benefit to you will depend on your application and the preferences of its users.

Using the *TransferDatabase* or *TransferSpreadsheet* method

The *TransferDatabase* and *TransferSpreadsheet* methods follow from macro actions that enable importing, linking, and exporting. The *TransferSpreadsheet* method supports a wide array of Lotus and Excel formats. The *TransferDatabase* method supports ODBC data sources, such as SQL Server and Oracle, as well as ISAM data sources, such as Paradox, dBase, Microsoft FoxPro, and Jet. *TransferSpreadsheet* and *TransferDatabase* tap into the ISAM and ODBC drivers that ship with Access. Good sources of documentation on these methods include the Access online documentation and a Macro window open in Design view with drop-down boxes offering options for selected arguments.

The *linkXLCustomers* procedure on the following page shows the syntax for the *TransferSpreadsheet* method. You can compare this technique with the functionality of an OLE DB provider. This sample links to the Customers range in the Customers.xls workbook. (Customers.xls is included in this book's companion CD.) It specifies an Excel 97 file format, but also supports Excel 5, Excel 4, and Excel 3. *TransferSpreadsheet* also supports Lotus formats, such as WK1, WK3, and WK4. The *DoCmd* object creates a linked table named *XLCustomers* in the Database window. The next-to-last argument to *TransferSpreadsheet* (−1) indicates that the Excel range has field names in the first row.

```
Sub linkXLCustomers()
Dim cnn1 As New ADODB.Connection
Dim rst1 As ADODB.Recordset

'Use DoCmd to programmatically make the link.
    DoCmd.TransferSpreadsheet acLink, acSpreadsheetTypeExcel97, _
        "XLCustomers", "C:\Programming Access\Chap03\Customers.xls", _
        -1, "Customers"

'Open and set recordset.
    Set rst1 = New ADODB.Recordset
    rst1.ActiveConnection = CurrentProject.Connection
    rst1.CursorType = adOpenKeyset
    rst1.LockType = adLockOptimistic
    rst1.Open "XLCustomers", , , , adCmdTable

'Open recordset and print a test record.
    Do Until rst1.EOF
        Debug.Print rst1.Fields(0).Value, rst1.Fields(2)
        rst1.MoveNext
    Loop

End Sub
```

After the *TransferSpreadsheet* method executes, your application can use its return set similarly to one from an OLE DB provider. First, you open a recordset on the linked table. Then you programmatically manipulate the recordset to serve the requirements of your application. (*linkXLCustomers* merely prints several fields for each row.)

The *TransferDatabase* method offers a wider range of data access options than the *TransferSpreadsheet* command. These include its historical ISAM drivers and ODBC drivers. Since most databases support ODBC access, this method can interface with nearly any relational database management system (RDBMS) data source. Furthermore, the *TransferDatabase* method has a similar syntax to the *TransferSpreadsheet* method, which makes it easy to use.

The following *linkODBCAuthors* procedure uses the *TransferSpreadsheet* method to link to the *Authors* table in the SQL Server Pubs database. *linkODBCAuthors* forms a link to the *Authors* table under the name *dboAuthors* in the current database. If *dboAuthors* is already in the current database, the method silently retains the original copy and makes another copy, naming it *dboAuthors1*.

```
Sub linkODBCAuthors()
Dim cnn1 As New ADODB.Connection
Dim rst1 As ADODB.Recordset

'Use DoCmd to programmatically make the link.
    DoCmd.TransferDatabase acLink, "ODBC Database", _
        "ODBC;DSN=Pubs;UID=sa;PWD=;DATABASE=pubs", _
        acTable, "Authors", "dboAuthors"

'Open and set recordset.
    Set rst1 = New ADODB.Recordset
    rst1.ActiveConnection = CurrentProject.Connection
    rst1.CursorType = adOpenKeyset
    rst1.LockType = adLockOptimistic
    rst1.Open "dboAuthors", , , , adCmdTable

'Open recordset and print a test record.
    Do Until rst1.EOF
        Debug.Print rst1.Fields(0).Value, rst1.Fields(2)
        rst1.MoveNext
    Loop

End Sub
```

The first argument to *TransferSpreadsheet* specifies the transfer type to the data source; the *acLink* argument creates a linked table in the Database window. The next two arguments specify the type of database and its name. (*linkODBCAuthors* specifies an ODBC data source. In fact, this sample uses the popular SQL Server Pubs database.) The final arguments designate the type of database object on which you want to base your source, its name in the remote source (*Authors*), and its name in your application (*dboAuthors*). The remainder of *linkODBCAuthors* performs the same actions as the other samples in this section.

Chapter 4

Manipulating Data Using Queries

Queries are the workhorses of database applications. You can apply them to achieve many different kinds of objectives. Queries allow you to manipulate the data in database tables. You can use them to specify the content for forms and reports. Queries can also designate the data source for a web page.

One major reason why queries are so potent is that there are so many different varieties of them. Chapter 2 illustrated how to design row-returning and bulk operation queries with ActiveX Data Objects (ADO). You can optionally achieve these and other query functions with Structured Query Language (SQL). Developers frequently use SQL to manipulate a table by extracting selected rows or columns, but these are not the only options for manipulating a data source. The classic bulk operations include appending and deleting table rows as well as updating fields. You can also use SQL to build new queries.

This chapter explores queries within Access 2000 at multiple levels.

■   First, it gives a general overview of the different types of queries. What are they? What can you do with them? How do they complement one another?

- Second, the chapter describes manual techniques for building queries. The review of manual techniques serves multiple purposes. It reinforces the general discussion of query types with the steps to generate each kind.

- Third, the chapter explores how action queries automate a task. Developers can use Microsoft Visual Basic for Applications (VBA) to programmatically apply simple row-returning queries and action queries.

- The fourth approach the chapter takes to queries is a programmatic one that builds on SQL. The discussion in this chapter complements the ADO-centric discussion of views and stored procedures from Chapter 2.

- The final approach to queries deals with processing remote databases. Access 2000 is much more adept at working with remote data sources than earlier versions. Learning how to use queries to easily tap into remote data sources can dramatically enhance your solutions and your value as a developer.

A REVIEW OF QUERY TYPES

While you may think of queries as tools for extracting information from one or more databases, there is a phenomenal amount of diversity in how they can accomplish this task. In addition, queries can perform other kinds of functions—especially if you include the data definition features of SQL and linking to remote data sources. This section surveys many query options that Access 2000 supports. This review of queries will equip you with the information you need to make an optimal choice about which type of query to use in a given situation.

Select Queries

Select queries let you create a subset of the information in one or more database tables. Developers have a rich array of options including selecting and processing data in any of several different ways. Use these options to determine the column and field values in the return set from a query. Select queries make good record sources for forms, reports, and web pages. Therefore, mastering the basics of select queries will enhance your work with these other application development components.

A query that selects a subset of the fields from a table is one of the most basic select queries. This type of query is convenient when you want to display just a few columns from a table that has many columns. Extracting some but not all the columns in a table can speed the operation of the query. Since Access computes a select query each times it runs, you will always deliver the most recent data to a user. When an application should not expose the most current data in a table, consider using criteria to restrict the row values that a query returns. Alternatively, you can use another type of query to create a new temporary table that contains a subset of the columns at a specific moment in time.

Setting criteria

Whether or not a select query chooses a subset from a data source, it can restrict the rows in the return set. You can specify which rows a query returns by setting its criteria. Use the Criteria row in the query design grid to set criteria. Programmatic options for setting criteria include the WHERE and HAVING clauses of a SQL statement. The WHERE clause applies to individual records in the record source for a query, but the HAVING clause can restrict return sets based on the values of a GROUP BY clause.

Select queries can return row sets that match a particular value or range of values. When using a table of geographic data, a select query can specify a zip code to return the corresponding city and state. If the records in a data source contain a Date/Time field, such as an order or invoice date, then you can select those on a specific date. You can also use comparison operators, such as greater than (>), less than (<), or not equal to (<>), to select a range of rows. You can match to a particular string value or to a range of values by using wild card parameters. Use special wildcard characters in criteria to designate a range of string values. For example, the criteria S*l matches *Sal* and *Saul*, because the * character matches any number of intervening characters. In contrast, the ? character matches just one missing character. Therefore, the criterion S?l matches *Sal*, but not *Saul*.

Using aggregate functions

Developers can use aggregate functions with SQL to summarize the records in a data source. Typical SQL aggregate functions count, sum, or average the records in a data source for a select query. You can additionally use aggregate functions to compute the variability of a record source with functions such as *StDev* or *VarP*. You can even compute the minimum or the maximum of a set of values in a field with aggregate functions.

Select queries can also apply SQL aggregate functions in combination with GROUP BY clauses. This enables a query to compute aggregate data for grouped records within a data source. Using aggregate functions along with a GROUP BY clause, an application can return the number of line items per order in a select query.

Using joins

You can base select queries on a single table, two or more tables, another query, or any combination of tables and select queries. When you select from more than one table, your application will typically link the tables on several common fields. If your database links tables via referential integrity settings, Access will automatically detect this and join them when you bring them together as the record source for a query. Access also detects common fields in other situations, allowing you to retain, modify, or replace automatically detected relationships between tables.

The default way to join tables is by combining all the records between two tables that have a matching value on a field. Joining the Northwind *Orders* and *Orders Details* tables in a simple select query can return all the line items for each order. In this situation, you only want line items that match orders. It is possible for related tables to have field values without matching entries in a joined table (for example, you can receive data from a legacy database that does not enforce referential integrity). Your application can detect unmatched records by forcing all the records for one of two joined tables into a return set. Then, all those combined records with a value from one table but a missing join field from the other table will point to unmatched records.

The result of any pair of joined recordsets can join with another table or query. If you are facile at SQL, you can tap several tables and queries with complex join relationships in a single SQL statement to develop a return set. Those learning SQL may find it safer to build queries graphically in the query design grid between pairs of tables or other queries. When database designers take this preliminary step, they can verify the result of joining two tables before combining the return set with another table or query.

Updating source data

One common outcome from a select query is a dynaset. (A dynaset is a recordset that stores primary keys instead of actual data.) A select query permits an application to modify the fields in records behind the query. Sometimes the fields behind a select query are not updateable. For select queries built on a single table or on two tables in a one-to-one relationship, you can always update the underlying records (unless another user locks them). Tables in a one-to-many relationship are usually updateable.

View the status bar of the Datasheet view for a query to determine if a field is updateable. If the field is not updateable and you need to be able to change it, consider directly accessing the table containing the field or redesigning the query to make it updateable.

Saving queries

When a query is particularly complex, it can be useful to save it and then refer to it in other queries. An example of this may involve a select query that joins two or more other queries and then applies SQL aggregate functions to generate data summaries. Save a complex query and reference it in other queries to help avoid syntax errors. Sometimes when you combine one or more queries to form another, your query logic can become too complex for a database engine to compute. In this situation, save one or more or your input queries as temporary tables. Then, use these tables as surrogates for the queries. Recompute the temporary tables whenever the input data to the original tables changes.

Action Queries

Instead of returning a set of rows like a select query, action queries perform a task against one or more tables. Action queries make it easy to start automating an application. You can design action queries graphically, yet they perform the essential functions of adding, deleting, and updating records. Because action queries use SQL to perform tasks, they can be used as sophisticated table commands for manipulating records. Experienced Access developers are probably wondering about the fourth Access action query—namely, the make-table query. This action query enables data definition as well as data manipulation. The make-table query is the sole focus of the section "Make Table Queries" on page 218.

Append queries

Append queries enable a developer to add records to one table based on those in a second table. Use the append query when your application acquires records from an exogenous source, such as a table from another computer. The source table must be in, or at least linked to, the current database. The destination table can be in the current database or in another database file. The field names in the two tables can differ, but you must have matching data types to append values from a field in one table to a matching field in another. The source table does not require all the fields to be in the destination table.

Several situations can generate errors with append queries. You should not generally attempt to append values for an AutoNumber field since these fields populate automatically. If you attempt to add a record with a duplicate primary key, your application will generate a key violation error. Access will not let you append records if their addition violates the table's validity or referential integrity rules.

Delete queries

Delete queries enable an application to automate the removal of records from a table. Use criteria to designate which records to delete. You can delete two or more records by using a single delete query. When your database schema specifies cascading deletes, a delete query will delete matching records from both the one side and the many side of a one-to-many relationship.

If you need to delete records from just the one side of the relationship, eliminate cascading deletes from the referential integrity settings. If you have to eliminate all the records on the many side of a one-to-many relationship with referential integrity, turn off the relationship. Then, execute the delete query. Finally, restore the referential integrity settings.

Update queries

The update action query does not operate on whole records, as do the delete and append queries. Instead, this action query revises values in selected fields. Designate particular rows by setting criteria. You can use this type of query to compute new prices when items increase by a constant percent. If prices increase for just one category of product, denote that product category in the criteria settings.

Other Types of Queries

A number of special queries further extend the usefulness of queries. These queries typically, but not always, extend or complement select and action queries.

Parameter queries

Parameter queries are a special type of query that can return rows or perform actions. At run time, a parameter query can prompt the user for input that controls how it performs. You can prompt for one or more inputs by using different data type specifications. You tell the parameter query what to do by inputting values to its prompts or by setting its parameters with VBA code before executing the query to control the return set or action that it performs. This allows the designation of a customer ID value at run time to determine the customer about which a select query returns information.

As an alternative to a parameter query, your application can reference a SQL string for a select or action query with string variables. Before executing the SQL statement in an ADO command, assign the string variables specific values. This can provide more flexible results than a parameter query since you can actually alter whole clauses in the SQL statement for a query. For certain cases, parameter queries offset these benefits with data typing and built-in prompts for values. In addition, parameter queries eliminate the need to refine string concatenation statements as you refine your query's SQL statement.

Union queries

The union query is a type of SQL query. The union query is especially interesting because of its novel behavior (it places tables one behind the other instead of side by side). Union queries bring together the fields from two or more tables. Instead of joining the records from tables in a side-by-side fashion, union queries append the records from one table directly after another. You must construct union queries by using SQL statements. You cannot design them graphically in the query design grid. Input the SQL for the union query directly into the query's SQL view. This sets union queries apart from all other queries discussed so far because you can create any of them graphically. With union queries, you gain the full power of the SQL language for such capabilities as specifying criteria and designating sort orders.

Crosstab queries

Crosstab queries accept a table or query as a data source and return sums, averages, or counts for one field based on two other categorical fields. This type of query requires a field that your application can count, sum, or average. In addition to specifying a field in which to present aggregate results, developers must designate row and column category fields. These must have discrete values that can serve as categories for reporting aggregation results. Access supports the creation of crosstab queries with a wizard and with Jet SQL. In addition, you can manually tweak a crosstab query design in its Design and Datasheet views.

Subqueries

A SQL subquery is a SQL SELECT statement nested inside another select or action query. Use the nested SELECT statement as an expression in a criterion for a field. The nested SELECT statement returns a value that, in turn, can act as a criterion for another query. Although you must write the subquery in SQL, you can nest the SQL in the query design grid. Furthermore, you can use another query to confirm that you properly designed your nested statement. Use the nested SQL statement just like any other criterion to specify a value or range of values for a return set.

Data Definition Operations

The SQL Data Definition Language (DDL) enables developers to create tables with SQL statements. The make-table query uses DDL to automate the creation of tables. One big attraction of make-table queries is that you can design them graphically. It is common to launch the design of a make-table query as a standard select query. After refining the select query to return precisely what you seek, convert the query type to a make-table.

Use SQL DDL to manually design tables with SQL statements. If you are comfortable with SQL this is a powerful and fast way to design tables. SQL DDL is an alternative to ADO. There are selected tasks, such as setting the step value and initial value for the AutoNumber data type or turning Unicode compression on and off, that Jet SQL exclusively provides. Of course, one major use for SQL statements by Access developers is to set the *CommandText* property of an ADO Command object. If your *CommandType* property is *adCmdText*, you must use a SQL statement to set the *CommandText* property. Invoke the *Execute* method for the command to launch the SQL statement.

Working with Remote Data Sources

When working with remote data sources, such as a Microsoft SQL Server or Oracle database, there are special rules for working with the data source and for optimizing your query performance. Four basic routes to remote data include attached tables, SQL pass-through queries, ODBCDirect, and OLE DB.

With Access 2000, you will mostly avoid access via ODBCDirect. Learning and using ADO with OLE DB providers is preferable since ADO/OLE DB is part of the Microsoft Universal Data Access strategy. ODBCDirect is on the way to becoming an obsolete technology that OLE DB will replace.

SQL pass-through queries specify queries based on a remote database engine's native SQL syntax. This type of query allows you to work directly with tables on the remote server instead of linking them. Since you can achieve the same result by using ADO with a more transferable syntax, pass-through queries are also obsolete.

Working with linked tables can enable your application to have cached access to the records in a remote data source. While this may slow the opening of an application, it can speed queries that have linked data sources, especially when the data are not changing frequently.

As you design your queries for remote data sources, it is important to plan your queries so that they perform as much of the query as possible on the computer running the remote database engine, which is generally vastly more powerful than a typical desktop computer. In addition, you reduce network traffic when you run the query on the server and pass just a small subset of data across the network. Tips for optimizing queries with remote data sources include the following:

- Restricting SQL aggregate functions to just those supported by the remote database engine (typically these are *COUNT, SUM, MIN, MAX,* and *AVG*)

- Setting the *adLockBatchOptimistic* lock type and invoking the *UpdateBatch* method to optimize working with a remote data source on a disconnected basis

- Avoiding the use of custom functions since they require local processing

- Using criteria that specify a fixed range, such as *Between 100 And 1000* vs. open-ended criteria, such as *>100*

- Following general rules for query optimization, such as sort, search, and join on indexed fields, and using wildcard parameters with LIKE operators only at the end of a string search criterion

NOTE SQL Server uses % instead of * for wildcard searches with the LIKE operator. If your query runs on a SQL Server database engine, including the new Microsoft Data Engine, be sure and use the new, alternative wildcard symbol in your queries.

DESIGNING QUERIES MANUALLY

Custom applications can build queries programmatically or use prebuilt queries as record sources. Just as with tables, it is likely that you will sometimes build queries manually and sometimes construct them programmatically. A good knowledge of manual query design principles serves as a foundation for learning how to design and run queries programmatically.

This section explores building queries with wizards and reviews using the query Design view. While the wizards are easy to use, they substantially constrain your design options relative to manually building queries on the query design grid in Design view. The review of techniques for using the query design grid covers adding tables, selecting rows, and designating criteria. You will also discover how to construct parameter queries, union queries, and subqueries.

Using the Wizards

The Access query wizards provide a fast and easy way to create queries. This section describes each of the four query wizards.

The Simple Query wizard

The redesign of the Database window in Access 2000 makes accessing the Simple Query wizard somewhat unique. Select Queries in the Database window and double-click the Create Query By Using Wizard icon to open the Simple Query wizard. You can also reach the Simple Query wizard via the more traditional route by selecting Queries and clicking the New button on the Database window toolbar.

The Simple Query wizard enables three kinds of query design. All of its features target beginning developers. However, even you, as an experienced developer, will find you can develop queries just as fast as with the query design grid. The major disadvantage of the Simple Query wizard is that it does not permit the full range of query designs that you can achieve via the query design grid or SQL. Developers who are unfamiliar with SQL and joining rules will find its graphical interface attractive.

> **NOTE** There are no query wizards for the new Microsoft Access Project (this type of project has an .adp file type as opposed to the traditional .mdb database file type). In addition, the query Design view layout is different for .mdb and .adp files. See the last section in this chapter for an initial consideration of query design with Access Projects. See Chapter 12 for in-depth coverage of working with remote databases and the Microsoft Data Engine.

The most basic way to build a query with the Simple Query wizard, shown in Figure 4-1, is to base it on a single table or query. Use the wizard this way to delimit the fields that a query returns. Even this simple application of the wizard adds value since restricting the return set improves query performance.

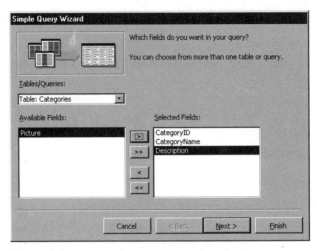

Figure 4-1. *The Simple Query wizard on the way to creating a query based on a subset of the fields in the Northwind* Categories *table.*

The real power of the Simple Query wizard comes in its ability to join two or more tables without requiring a query designer to actually create joins between tables. This lets the designer focus on the fields needed in the query and the tables from which they must come without spending any time at all focusing on the proper query design. The wizard is smart enough to generate correct results.

Figure 4-2 shows the Simple Query wizard on the way to developing a query that joins two tables in the Northwind database. All you need to do is select a table and then select fields within the table and move them from the Available Fields list box to the Selected Fields list box. The bottom window shows an excerpt of the result set of joining the *CategoryName* field from the *Categories* table and the *ProductName* field from the *Products* table.

The query in Figure 4-2 joins the *Categories* and *Products* tables on their common *CategoryID* field. However, at no point do you have to specify this. The Simple Query wizard automatically detects the shared field and joins the two tables on it. The wizard automatically assumes an equi-join that includes only records with matching *CategoryID* field values in both tables. If a record in one table had a *CategoryID* value that was not present in a record in the other table, the Simple Query wizard would ignore the record. If your application requires records excluded by an equi-join, then you can edit the query design from the wizard, design the query in Design view, or use SQL statements to construct the query.

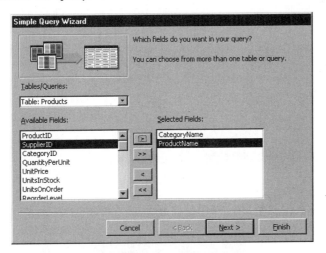

Figure 4-2. *The Simple Query Wizard dialog box and the resulting query's Datasheet view.*

The query in Figure 4-2 joins the *Categories* and *Products* tables on their common *CategoryID* field. However, at no point do you have to specify this. The Simple Query wizard automatically detects the shared field and joins the two tables on it. The wizard automatically assumes an equi-join that includes only records with matching *CategoryID* field values in both tables. If a record in one table had a *CategoryID* value that was not present in a record in the other table, the Simple Query wizard would ignore the record. If your application requires records excluded by an equi-join, then you can edit the query design from the wizard, design the query in Design view, or use SQL statements to construct the query.

You can also design queries that perform some aggregations with the Simple Query wizard. The wizard automatically detects when an aggregation is possible and does as much as possible to help the query designer. It presents a dialog box like the top one in Figure 4-3 only when numerical aggregations are possible. You can still decline the aggregation route by selecting the Detail option in the second step of the wizard. If you choose the Summary option, then you should also click the Summary Options button to specify which fields to aggregate and which functions to use for the aggregation. The wizard only presents legitimate options. The wizard does occasionally prepare an extra summary field. If this happens, just delete the field in the query design grid.

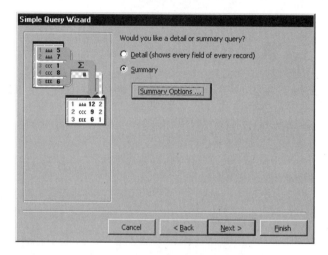

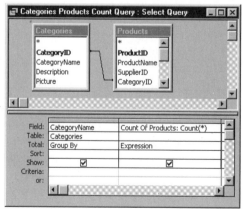

Figure 4-3. *The second step in the Simple Query Wizard dialog box allows you to designate the computation of aggregates in a query.*

The two bottom windows in Figure 4-3 show the Design and Datasheet views of the query. Notice that the query counts the products in each category. The bottom left window shows the query design grid that computes the result. However, the Simple Query wizard removes the need to know where to place the aggregate function and what selections to make in the Total row. (You need to click the Totals toolbar button to make the Total row appear in the query design grid when designing a query manually.) The wizard relieves you of all this detail.

The Find Duplicates Query wizard

A pair of query wizards helps create queries that perform common tasks. The Find Duplicates Query wizard searches a recordset to determine whether there are two or more records with the same values. It returns the duplicate values for all records with common values for fields specified by the search criteria.

One common reason for wanting to find duplicates is to eliminate the extra copies of records from a record source. However, you cannot convert the resulting query to a delete query since it will remove the original records along with their duplicates. The Access 2000 online help describes a procedure for automatically removing duplicates based on the result from the Find Duplicates Query wizard. To discover the procedure, type "automatically delete duplicates" as the search criterion for the Office Assistant.

Open the specific instructions by choosing the prompt reading "Automatically delete duplicate records from a table".

Our sample for this wizard uses the *FamilyMembers* table (see the top window in Figure 4-4 on the following page). The Find Duplicates Query Wizard dialog box in the middle of Figure 4-4 contains a pair of list boxes for choosing fields on which to search for duplicate values. As with the Simple Query wizard, you move fields from the Available Fields list box into the Duplicate-Value Fields list box. In the sample, I chose the *Lname* field on which to search for duplicates. As the top window in Figure 4-4 shows, all the records in *FamilyMembers* are duplicates of one of the two values for this field. Step 3 of the wizard enables you to designate other fields that will show in the return set. The sample chooses all the remaining fields.

The bottom window in Figure 4-4 highlights one of the strengths of Access wizards, which is that they simplify complex tasks. The bottom window also shows the query design grid layout created by the wizard. Notice that it contains a SQL subquery. The subquery statement includes an aggregate function as well as GROUP BY and HAVING clauses. It is this subquery in the criterion row of the design grid that detects duplicate values in the source recordset. You can fine-tune the resulting query design by adding or removing fields, including new or replacement source fields, or even by using additional criteria to eliminate some duplicates.

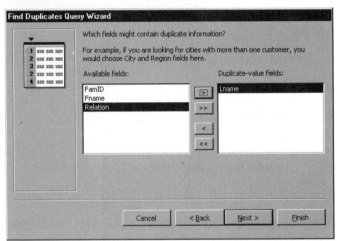

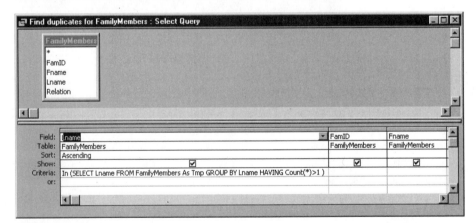

Figure 4-4. *The Find Duplicates Query wizard. The top window shows the input record source. The middle dialog box shows the selection of a field on which to search for duplicate values. The bottom window shows the resulting query in Design view.*

The Find Unmatched Query wizard

The Find Unmatched Query wizard is another feature that supports a common database management chore. This wizard returns records in one table that do not have a match in a corresponding table. It is particularly convenient for managing tables that do not have referential integrity, but that are in a one-to-many relationship. In this situation, you can inadvertently, or purposefully, remove the one or the many side of a relationship. When either the one or the many side is without a match in its corresponding table, the Find Unmatched Query wizard will discover it. You will typically want to remove these records from a record source. Happily, all you have to do is convert the automatically created query to a delete query.

The query in Figure 4-5 checks the *FamilyNames* table and the *FamilyMembers* table for unmatched records. The comparison takes place on the *Lname* field in both tables. The query joins the two tables by forcing all the records from the *FamilyNames* table into the query, as shown by the directional arrow from the *FamilyNames* table to the *FamilyMembers* table. Then, the query searches for null record values for the *Lname* field in the *FamilyMembers* table. If the record value for *Lname* in the *FamilyMembers* side of the return set is null, the *FamilyNames* side of the return set has no match in the *FamilyMembers* table. The proper design of this query requires an understanding of left joins and null values. Studying the design of queries such as this one and queries that return duplicate values can help to sharpen your query design skills if you do not routinely write queries like these.

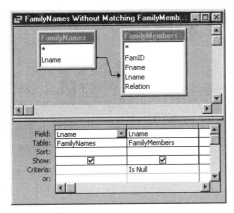

Figure 4-5. *The Find Unmatched Query wizard and its resulting query. The second record source is the* FamilyMembers *table. The match criterion is the* Lname *field.*

The Crosstab Query wizard

Decision support analysts sometimes find that crosstab queries yield insights about objects and processes. Figure 4-6 shows an input table to the Crosstab Query wizard and resulting return set. I refined the return set's display in both its Design and Datasheet views.

The crosstab query in the bottom datasheet counts *FamID* by *Relation* and *Lname* fields from the top datasheet. The tweak I made in Design view adjusts the order for *Relation* from ascending to descending. In Datasheet view, I dragged the column labeled *Total Of FamID* from the second column to the last column. Otherwise, the layout was automatic. There was no need to enter field names and keywords in the query design grid. Nor did I have to write SQL code.

FamilyMembers : Table

	FamID	Fname	Lname	Relation
▶	1	Rick	Dobson	Me
	2	Virginia	Dobson	wife
	3	Glen	Hill	son
	4	Tony	Hill	son
	5	Shelly	Hill	daughter-in-law
*				

Record: ◄◄ ◄ | 1 | ► ►► ►* of 5

FamilyMembers_Crosstab : Crosstab Query

	Relation	Dobson	Hill	Total Of FamID
▶	wife	1		1
	son		2	2
	Me	1		1
	daughter-in-law		1	1

Record: ◄◄ ◄ | 1 | ► ►► ►* of 4

Figure 4-6. *A query created by the Access 2000 Crosstab Query wizard. The top datasheet shows the input for the query return set that appears in the bottom datasheet.*

Two newer technologies for analysis emerge as challenges to the crosstab queries. First, a pivot table can compute basic crosstab results from a record source, but it can additionally enable the dynamic manipulation of the data after the computation of the crosstab. This permits decision analysts to interact dynamically with their analysis results. Access enables pivot table analysis through its forms and Data Access Pages, but Microsoft Excel is the primary vehicle for performing pivot table analysis within Office. Second, online analytical processing database (OLAP) technology enables dynamic data analysis against potentially very large data sources. This technology requires a remote database server, such as SQL Server 7, and an OLAP consumer for the data. Within the traditional Microsoft Office 2000 components, Excel 2000 is the designated resource for that role.

Using Design View

While wizards enable query design with little or no knowledge of query syntax and design issues, they do not offer great variability relative to the total scope of what queries can accomplish. As is frequently the case with wizards, the design of the query wizards is sometimes more complicated than absolutely necessary to accomplish some tasks. This can complicate minor changes to a query. If you initially design a query yourself, then you are likely to recall the logic and be able to modify it easily later.

Adding tables and queries

You can create your own custom queries by adding tables or other queries to the query design grid. Taking this route will generally remove the requirement that you write SQL code to create and edit your queries. Open the query design grid by double-clicking the Create Query In Design View option in the Database window's Queries objects group. Next, add one or more tables, queries, or a combination of tables and queries to the top of the design grid. Select a table or query and click Add to move a table or query from the Show Table dialog box to the top of the design grid.

After adding a table to the top of the Design view, you need to select fields that will be part of the query in the bottom grid. There are at least three ways to add fields to the query. First, drag and drop them from the record source's field list box to the Field row in the bottom grid. If you drag and drop a field on the left top edge of an already occupied column, Access automatically moves the remaining columns to the right. Second, you can double-click an entry in the field list. This copies the field to the first vacant column in the grid. Third, you can choose a field from the drop-down box in each column's Field row. If you have more than one record source in the top of the grid, then the Field row's drop-down list enumerates fields grouped by record source.

You can use any of the three techniques with a single table to specify a few columns from a table with many columns. Figure 4-7 on the next page shows the Design and Datasheet views of a query based on the sample's *Products* table. This query specifies three fields from the *Products* table.

The Sort row in the *ProductName* column of Figure 4-7 is set to Ascending. This row contains a drop-down list with three options: Ascending, Descending, and (Not Sorted). If you choose the last option, the cell appears blank in the grid and the column's data is not sorted when the query is displayed in Datasheet view. Choosing Ascending for the *ProductName* column causes the records to appear in alphabetical order based on *ProductName*. If the Sort row for *ProductName* is blank, the datasheet in the bottom window of Figure 4-7 would appear sorted on the table's primary key, *ProductID*.

Figure 4-7. *The top window shows the query design for a manually created query based on the* Products *table. The bottom window is the resulting datasheet.*

It is easy to add more than one record source to a query's design. You can choose an input record source from tables and other queries. It is highly desirable to join record sources (if Access does not automatically join them based on the relationships denoted in the Relationships window). Failing to join the tables will cause the resulting datasheet to show the Cartesian product of the two tables. This will often be a table with an excessively large number of rows.

Figure 4-8 shows the *Products* and *Order Details* tables joined on the *ProductID* field. You can create a default join like this by dragging a field from one table and dropping it on the matching field in another table. This creates a datasheet with one row for each matching field in both tables. If a record appears in just one table, it does not show in the query's datasheet. There are two other types of joins. One adds all the rows from the *Products* table on the left. The other adds all the rows from the *Order Details* table on the right. You can choose either of these join types by right-clicking the join line and then choosing the desired join type.

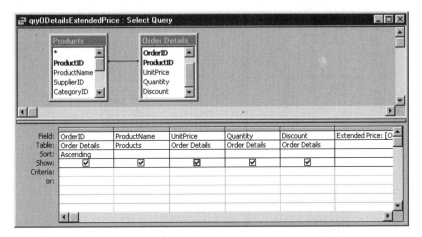

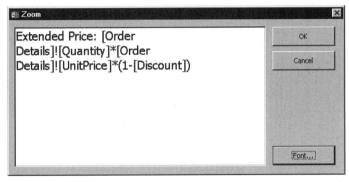

Figure 4-8. *The top window shows the query design for a manually created query based on both the* Products *and* Order Details *tables. The bottom window displays a Zoom dialog box that shows the formula for the calculated field in the query.*

The Table row in Figure 4-8 shows four of the columns belonging to the *Order Details* table. Another column, *ProductName*, belongs to the *Products* table. The query design's last field does not show completely in the top window of the figure.

Referencing subdatasheets

One of the innovations introduced with Access 2000 is the ability to reference hierarchically one table or query from within another query. In a sense, it is as if one parent query has a child table or query.

Figure 4-9 on the following page displays a subdatasheet within a query datasheet. The parent query is named *qryCategories*. Notice the + in the query's first column. Clicking any of these, such as the one for the Meat/Poultry category, opens a child datasheet and transforms the + to a -. This +/- sign acts like a toggle switch for opening and closing the subdatasheet linked to any row in the parent query. The child subdatasheet in the figure displays the product fields for one row in its parent's datasheet. More generally, the child subdatasheet references another query or a table linked to the current row. You can concurrently open multiple child subdatasheets. In fact, a query property lets you leave all the child datasheets open by default.

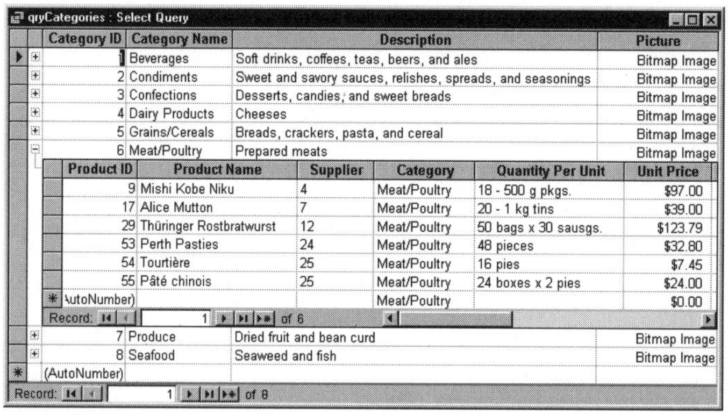

Figure 4-9. *A parent query,* qryCategories, *displays its subdatasheet for the* Meat/Poultry *category.*

Five new query properties control the behavior and appearance of subdatasheets. The *Subdatasheet Name* property points at a table or query with the child data. To access this and the other four properties, open the Query Properties dialog box in the query's Design view. The five new properties are at the bottom of the dialog box. The *Subdatasheet Name* property box contains a drop-down box that simplifies selecting another query or table as the record source for the subdatasheet. For the query in Figure 4-9, *Subdatasheet Name* is the table *MyProducts*. Enter field names for the *Link Child Fields* and *Link Master Fields* properties to synchronize the parent query with its child query or table. As with a main/sub form, the field names do not have to be the same, but they must have the same data type. The *Subdatasheet Height* property controls the height of the subdatasheet within the parent's Datasheet view. Finally, the *Subdatasheet Expanded* property takes values of *Yes* or *No*. The Query Properties dialog box offers a drop-down list for entering either value.

Access 2000 also supports subdatasheets for parent datasheets based on tables as well as queries. However, slightly different mechanisms support subdatasheets for parent queries vs. parent tables. With a parent table, you can designate the relationship between a parent table and its child table or query in the Relationships window. If you do elect to use the Table Properties dialog box, you must open the table in Design view. Then, you must explicitly open the Table Properties dialog box by right-clicking in the top part of the grid and choosing Properties. This makes the same five properties as for queries available for setting relationships between a parent table and its subdatasheet.

Using calculated fields

You can create a calculated field that derives its value from one or more fields in a query. Use simple arithmetic and string operators, built-in functions, or custom functions to express computed fields.

Calculated fields are not directly updateable. This is because Access stores just the expression in a SQL statement, rather than the result for the calculation. You can revise calculated fields by altering the inputs to the expression for the calculation. Although calculated fields are not updateable, your applications can aggregate them across records.

Specifying fields as expressions in a query has several benefits. First, since an expression can display data without actually storing data, using an expression for a field allows a query to show a result without consuming storage space. Second, expressions recompute automatically. This enables them to reflect the most recent data without any special action on the part of a database administrator. Third, there is a rich diversity of ways to include expressions as fields. Learning these ways will heighten your overall understanding of Access.

Arithmetic operators   Figure 4-8 (on page 197) shows a calculated field to compute an extended price. The expression for the extended price relies on simple arithmetic operators, such as multiplication and subtraction, to develop its calculated field. Notice that the Table row for the calculated field in the top window of Figure 4-8 is blank. This signifies that the field does not consume any storage space. The calculated field in Figure 4-8 uses the field label to represent a meaningful label for the field in Datasheet view.

Built-in functions   Figure 4-10 on the following page shows a calculated field that relies on built-in functions. Since the expression builds a string, it can use the *Left$* function. This saves memory over the more generic *Left* function that returns a string in a variant data type.

The expression in Figure 4-10 concatenates three distinct strings. First, it retrieves the first letter of a family member's first name with the *Left$* function. Second, it appends the string ". " to add a period and a space after the first letter of a person's name. The expression closes by appending the family member's last name. This calculated field still has the default field label, but the query's Datasheet view shows the column with a different header that is more descriptive. The top right dialog box in Figure 4-10 shows that you can achieve this result by assigning a value to the field's caption. Any entry in the caption property box overrides a field expression as the column heading.

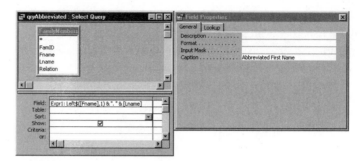

Figure 4-10. *Three windows reveal the syntax and label conventions for adding a string expression to a query to define its sole field. The bottom window displays the return set from the query.*

You can ease the process of using built-in functions and referring to table, query, and form values by using the Expression Builder. If you find it necessary to refine the expression after adding it with the Expression Builder or manually, use the Zoom dialog box. You can do this by right-clicking in the Field row and choosing Zoom. This opens the Zoom dialog box with your expression. Edit the expression as necessary before clicking OK to close the Zoom dialog box and enter your edited expression into the query. The bottom window in Figure 4-8 (on page 197) is a Zoom box that displays a calculated field from a query.

Custom functions   In addition to using operators and built-in functions, you can develop your own custom functions to return field values. Figure 4-11 shows a query that links to the *dbo_titles* table in the SQL Server Pubs database.

This query lists the *title* and *pubdate* fields for each record. In addition, it includes a calculated field that calls the custom function *daysto2K*. The expression passes the *pubdate* field value to the function. The *daysto2K* function appears below. By comparing the function name below with the query design in Figure 4-11, you can see that function references in a query are case insensitive.

```
Public Function DaysTo2K(InDate As Date) As Integer

    DaysTo2K = DateDiff("d", InDate, #1/1/2000#)

End Function
```

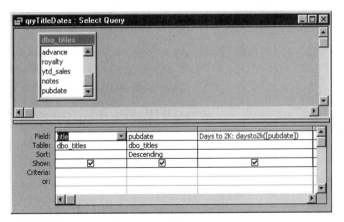

Figure 4-11. *This query uses a custom function to compute the difference between a field in the query and January 1, 2000*

The function accepts the *pubdate* field value as an argument and returns an integer data type to the query. This enables automatic right alignment. (Failing to specify an integer return causes the function to return a variant to the query, which results in left alignment.) The custom function has a single line. It applies the built-in *DateDiff* function to compute the difference in days between the *pubdate* field value and January 1, 2000.

There is a potential downside to applying custom functions in expressions for query fields—particularly with large, remote databases. Your application must pause while a potentially large table moves over the wire from the remote server to your local workstation. In addition, you lose the power of computing your query on the remote server computer. In situations where you absolutely require a custom function, construct a query that extracts the fewest number of records from the remote server and performs all other functions on the remote server. Then, apply your custom function to the small return set from the server. These objections to custom functions are not pertinent to the sample in Figure 4-11 because the *dbo_titles* table is very small. Custom functions work well with Jet databases of any size.

Aggregate SQL functions   You can compute a value without using expressions. One way to accomplish this is by clicking the Totals button—the button with a sigma (Σ)—on the Query Design toolbar. Then, drag one or more fields to the query design grid and choose Group By in the Total row. You must have at least one field with a numeric value whose Total row is not set to Group By. You can designate a calculated field as the numeric field. Choose Expression in the Total row. Insert an aggregate SQL function around your calculated field to report a count, sum, or average of the calculated field for each unique combination of fields whose Total row is set to Group By in the record source.

Figure 4-12 shows a query design that sums the extended price by *OrderID*. The query computes the extended price for each line item before summing and grouping them by *OrderID*. The *Group By* keyword appears in the Total row of the *OrderID* column. The *Sum* function around the Extended Price expression indicates that the query will compute the sum of the extended price for each order.

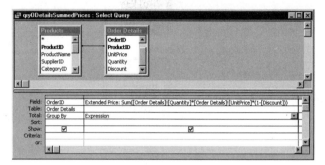

Figure 4-12. *The expression for the calculated field in this query computes the extended price for each line item in every order. The* Group By *keyword in the Total row forces the aggregate function in the expression to compute the sum of values across line items for each order.*

Computing a value from more than one query   Statistical results are most interesting when they compare two or more bits of information. While it is useful to know the amount of each order, you may want to know whether the price of each order is above or below the average and by how much. Access does not permit you to compute this kind of outcome in a single query. My sample for this problem requires three queries, and one of these contains a Cartesian product of the other two queries. The first query is the one shown in Figure 4-12. The second is a query that computes the average price across all orders. This query involves a simple *AVG* aggregate function on the extended price for the query in Figure 4-12. The top window of Figure 4-13 illustrates the Cartesian product of the query that sums extended prices by order (*qryODetailsSummed-Prices*) and the query that computes the average extended price across orders (*qryODAvgPrices*). Recall that the way to compute a Cartesian product is to include both queries in the Design view without joining them. The bottom window of Figure 4-13 shows the percent change between each order's total and the average across all orders. If the sum is greater than the average, the percent is positive—otherwise, it is negative.

The formula that computes the average percent change does not show in Figure 4-13. The expression is merely the ratio of two numbers. The numerator is the difference between the order's extended price and the average across all orders. The denominator is the average extended price across all orders. This calculated field has its format property set to *Percent* with 0 places after the decimal.

```
% Delta from Avg: ([Extended Price]-[Avg of Extended Price])/
    [Avg of Extended Price]
```

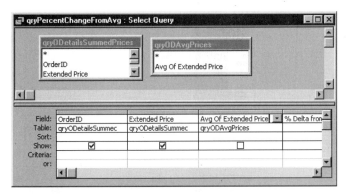

Figure 4-13. *The top window shows a query that computes a Cartesian product between two queries. The expression in the calculated field computes the percent change between the summed extended price per order and the average extended price across all orders.*

Working with criteria

Criteria can have a critical impact on the behavior of queries. By specifying criteria with expressions and constants, you can designate which records a query will return. Criteria cause the inclusion or exclusion of records in a select query's return set. The samples in this section highlight simple queries that have one condition. Once you learn how to create these, you can readily extend the knowledge to create compound condition criteria that combine two or more individual criterion conditions with either And or Or operators.

Using a single criterion   Figure 4-5 (on page 193) illustrates a simple criterion that uses the key phrase *Is Null*. Use the *Is Null* phrase to detect an empty field value in a query. The query's design joins the *FamilyNames* and *FamilyMembers* tables on the *Lname* field. The join type includes all the names from the *FamilyNames* table whether or not they match a *Lname* value in the *FamilyMembers* table. In the *FamilyNames* table, the *Lname* field has one of four values. These are Dobson, Hill, Simmons, and Edelstein. The *Lname* field in the *FamilyMembers* table has values of Dobson and Hill. Therefore, the query returns both Simmons and Edelstein since these two names are in *FamilyNames* but not in *FamilyMembers*. Changing the *Is Null* phrase to *Is Not Null* causes the return set to change to Dobson and Hill.

Figure 4-14 illustrates a query design that includes only those records in the *FamilyMembers* table with *Lname* field values that contain a lower case *s* in the fourth position. The *InStr* function is one of the many powerful built-in operators in Access. It compares one string vs. another in any of several ways. The fourth parameter sets the search type; 0 specifies a binary search. The *InStr* function returns a number that is the position of the first occurrence of the second string within the first string. For the expression in Figure 4-14, *InStr* finds the string *s* at position 4 in the name Dobson. Therefore, setting the criterion to *4* selects records whose *Lname* field contains an *s* at position 4.

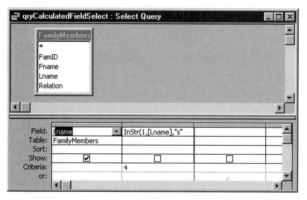

Figure 4-14. *This query returns the records in the* FamilyMembers *table whose* Lname *field contains an* s *at position 4.*

If you add more names to the *FamilyMembers* table whose *Lname* field contains an *s* at position 4, the query will return those records as well. For example, adding a new record with an *Lname* value of Samson will cause the query to return Samson along with Dobson.

Notice that the result of the expression in Figure 4-14 does not show in the query's return set because its Show box is unchecked.

Using multiple criteria The query in Figure 4-15 creates a series of sentences. The query dynamically constructs the sentences from the values in fields, but it also excludes the record whose *Relation* value is *me*. (The sentences in the query's return set describe the relation of each family member to me (the person). Therefore, the record whose *Relation* value is *me* should not be in the query.) This query uses two expressions. One specifies a criterion for including records; the other is a string expression that constructs the sentences using selected field values.

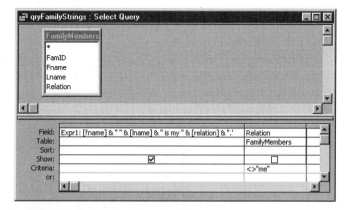

Figure 4-15. *A query that dynamically constructs sentences.*

Using a compound criterion After creating and testing individual criteria for specific fields, you may find it necessary to create compound criteria that combine two or more criteria for specific fields. There are two basic strategies to accomplish this. First, you can combine criteria with an And operator. This design technique causes a query to return rows for records that meet all its criteria concurrently. Second, you can combine multiple criteria with an Or operator. With the Or operator, a query returns rows for records that meet any of its criteria.

Happily, the Access query design grid insulates you from the syntax details of constructing SQL statements. When using the And operator, place all your criteria on a single row of the design grid. If you want to see all customers in a particular city that have ordered more than a minimum sales amount, you might start with a query that sums sales by customer from any city. Then, in a second query that references the first, you might use compound And criteria: one criterion to designate the particular city about which you seek information and a second criterion to set a lower limit so that the query only returns customers with more than a minimum sales amount. Since the task calls for an And operator, both criteria will reside on the same row of the query design grid.

After finding all the customers that meet the criteria in a particular city, you might decide to drill down into the buying patterns of your customers within a city. To develop data on this topic, you might start with a query that joins the *Orders* and *Order Details* tables. Your query design grid can include separate pairs of criteria on multiple rows. Placing criteria on different rows within the query design grid combines them with Or logic. The criteria on each row will have a city and customer. The city will be the same for all rows, but the customer criterion will be unique for each row. To group sales alphabetically by customer click the Sort row for the *Customer* field and choose Ascending.

SPECIAL SELECT QUERIES

Much of the query design discussion to this point has focused on the basic elements of design for select queries. This subsection presents three extensions to select queries that significantly enhance the flexibility and adaptability of your applications. First, you will learn about parameter queries. Many developers relish parameter queries because they make applications interactive. Others like them because of their exceptional ease of use. Second, union queries allow you to form data in ways that joining just cannot accomplish. When you need to concatenate two or more recordsets with common fields, union queries may be your most efficient tool. Union queries, unfortunately, require a working knowledge of SQL. The last section in this chapter includes some review of SQL syntax and many samples demonstrating the application of the language. Third, subqueries are the tool of choice when you require intelligent criteria that adapt to the values in your database. This technique for creating dynamic criteria that change along with the entries in your database will often benefit from a medium to advanced knowledge of SQL.

Parameter Queries

Parameter queries get their name because they require the input of a parameter at run time before they can complete. When you create a parameter query in Design View, you can designate the prompt for the input parameter in the Criteria row. Use the prompt in the criterion statement as a variable that the user will set at run time. The user interface also enables you to declare a data type for each input parameter. Chapter 2 demonstrates how to code a parameter query in ADO. This section describes how to manage the same task through the user interface.

Figure 4-16 shows a parameter query design along with its built-in prompt dialog box. Notice that the prompt in the criteria statement for the *UnitPrice* field is enclosed within brackets. The preceding less than (<) symbol is used to set an upper limit for the return set's *UnitPrice* field values. If the user enters *35* to the parameter query prompt and clicks OK, the query responds with a list of all the products that have a price less than 35 dollars. The bottom window in Figure 14-6 displays the first several products satisfying the criteria as well as the total number of records meeting the criterion (56).

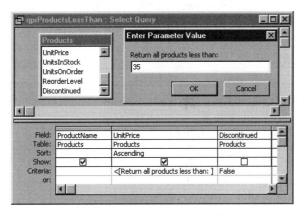

Figure 4-16. *A parameter query and its return set.*

The users of your applications will not typically run parameter queries from a query's Design view as was done in Figure 4-16. Figure 4-17 on the next page shows how the query looks when run from the database container. This particular query returns the customers in the UK, Germany, and France whose orders exceed the value specified by the user. It is this ability for users to control the return set that makes parameter queries highly interactive and dynamic.

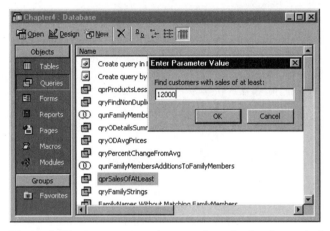

Figure 4-17. *A parameter query run from the database window.*

Figure 4-18 shows the previous query in Design view. This query has two criteria. The first uses the *In* keyword to select customers that have headquarters in the UK, France , or Germany. This eliminates the need to specify three separate rows with a different country name in each row. The prompt in the *Extended Price* column follows a great than (>) symbol. Therefore, the query returns all records that have an extended price greater than the amount specified by the user.

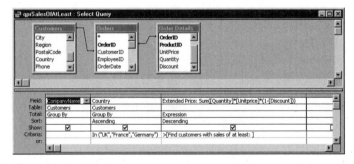

Figure 4-18. *The Design view of the query in Figure 4-17.*

The query in Figure 4-18 accomplishes other tasks as well. It computes and sums extended price by company and sorts its return set alphabetically by country and in descending extended price order. Its sorting design causes the biggest customers to appear at the top of the customer list for each country.

Union Queries

Union queries are unique from several perspectives. First, they dramatically simplify the task of concatenating two or more recordsets. (Recall that joining two recordsets brings them together in a side-by-side rather than one-after-the-other fashion.) Second, you can only define union queries with SQL. The only two views for union queries are Datasheet and SQL views; they have no Design view at all. Third, you cannot directly update the field values in a union query's Datasheet view. Many select queries, which appear identical to union queries in Datasheet view, are dynasets, which let a user revise the tables behind a recordset. If you must edit the data resulting from a union query, you should use a make-table query to construct a copy that you can edit. This will still not change the original inputs to the union query, but it will at least allow changes to the copy of the resulting data.

Figure 4-19 shows a very simple union query that combines the *FamilyMembers* and *AdditionsToFamilyMembers* tables. If you feel uncomfortable about developing with SQL, you can always keep your union queries this simple for the basic design. Make the first statement a simple SELECT statement that lists the field names and the record source for the fields in the FROM clause. Your references to all remaining record sources must start with UNION SELECT, but you still list the field names and the record source. It is possible to do more advanced operations, but that is not essential. You can always combine the record sources just this simply and reserve more sophisticated manipulation of the combined record sources to another select query that relies on the union query output. You can perform these more sophisticated operations in Design view.

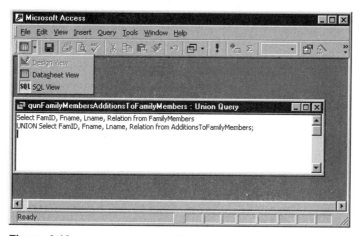

Figure 4-19. *A union query in SQL view.*

Notice from the SELECT and UNION SELECT statements that I am concatenating tables with the same field data types. This is a requirement for union queries. The tables, or at least the fields that you combine, need to have the same number, order, and types of columns. While you cannot update the source from the Datasheet view, the query recomputes each time you open it with the most recent data from its inputs. Notice that Access disables the Design view icon for the union query. You cannot examine a union query in Design view. You must design or edit it in SQL view, and you examine the impact of your SQL statements in Datasheet view.

Figure 4-20 reveals the operation of the union query in Figure 4-19. The *FamilyMembers* and *AdditionsToFamilyMembers* tables are on the left in Figure 4-20; the output of the union query is the datasheet on the right. As you can see from the sequencing of the *FamID* field, the query creates a new datasheet that appends the two rows in *AdditionsToFamilyMembers* table to the *FamilyMembers* table.

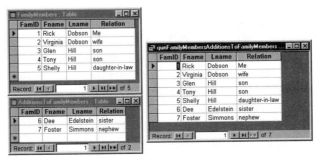

Figure 4-20. *The two datasheets on the left are the inputs to the union query in Figure 4-19. The datasheet on the right is the output of the union query.*

Subqueries

A subquery is a select query inside of another query. The subquery must always be a SELECT statement, but you can use it inside of any other query, such as a select or an action query. There are a few extra keywords that can moderate the behavior of the standard SQL SELECT keyword in a subquery. Because the SELECT statement returns values, the subquery represents an important option for building dynamic criteria in queries that use them.

The embedded SELECT statement on the Criteria row for the *Lname* column in the bottom window in Figure 4-4 (on page 192) is a subquery.

Figure 4-21 shows a query that returns the nonduplicated *Lname* values returned by a union query named *qunFamilyMembersAdditionsMoreAdditions*. The union query concatenates three separate record sources. The lower left window in Figure 4-21 is the return set from the union query. Notice that there is only one nonduplicated *Lname* value, namely Edelstein. The lower right window is the return set from the select query.

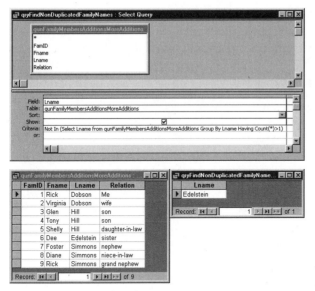

Figure 4-21. *The top window is a query that finds non-duplicated field values in a record source. The bottom left and right windows are the input and output datasheets from the query.*

The top window in Figure 4-21 is the subquery design for finding non-duplicated *Lname* values. Notice that it is similar to the query in Figure 4-4 (on page 192). Aside from the fact that it searches a different record source, its sole distinction is that the subquery starts with *Not In* instead of *In*. The expression containing *Not In* returns nonduplicated names while the one with *In* returns duplicated names.

> **NOTE** While you can combine the return sets from queries like those in Figures 4-4 and 4-21 to return all distinct names, Access offers more direct graphical and expression-based routes to the same result. More consideration of the expression-based approach appears later in this chapter. The graphical approach involves setting the *Unique Values* property of a query to *Yes*.

ACTION QUERIES

Access offers four action queries that you can use by means of the user interface as well as programmatically. These are update, append, delete, and make-table queries. As an intermediate level developer, you'll find that action queries are very interesting since they provide a quick and relatively easy way to build "action" into your Access applications.

An earlier section in this chapter reviewed action query functionality without focusing on how to implement them. This section describes how to incorporate action queries into your custom applications. The query design grid has special extensions that support the unique functionality of each action query type. This section illustrates these queries as it reveals how to design and use them.

Update Queries

Use update queries to revise field values in the record source for a query. You begin creating an update query just as you would a select query. After double-clicking the Create Query In Design View option in the Database window, add one or more record sources to the query with the Show Table dialog box. Although the dialog box's name is Show Table, you can add one or more tables or queries. You will typically want to join all tables and queries that you include in your update query design after closing the Show Table dialog box. (You can manually remove any undesired record sources by selecting them and pressing the Delete key on the keyboard.)

In order to create an action query, you must choose its type. Do this by choosing Update Query from the Query Type button on the Query Design toolbar. The button's face will then display the update query icon (a pencil followed by an exclamation mark). Notice this adds an Update To row on the query design grid, and it removes the Sort and Show rows. Next, add one or more fields to the Field row of the query design grid. You should include the field that you plan to update. Other fields can be in the query for identification purposes or to help specify criteria for determining which records to update.

After selecting the fields for your update query, enter a value or expression in one cell of the Update To row. The entry in this cell determines the new, replacement values. If there are no criteria, running the query revises all records in the query's record source. Including one or more criteria restricts the update action to just rows satisfying the criteria.

Once you run an update query, you cannot undo the changes with just the click of a single key. You must either restore the whole table from a backup copy or run one or more other update queries to restore the original values. The View button on the Design view toolbar lets you examine which records a query will alter without actually performing the update. When you have the proper records selected, you can click the Run button to run the query. This opens a message box announcing how many records the query will update. You can cancel the update action at this point by clicking No. If you click Yes, the update will proceed. If the field is not updateable, Access issues a message box to that effect instead.

Access will present an additional message box if you attempt to run the update query from outside of Design view. You can decline the option to change field values or you can proceed. If you proceed, the next dialog box is like the first one in the Design view. It indicates how many records will change and gives you a second and final chance to alter the records.

Update queries can revise many fields in their record sources. You can always update the fields in a record source so long as you have permission to revise the data source and it is available. Data from a one-to-many relationship is often, but not always, updateable. For example, you cannot revise the primary key if cascading updates are not enabled. Calculated fields and values in crosstab queries are similarly not updateable. If a field is calculated, action queries cannot revise its values. The online help offers detailed descriptions of fields that can and cannot be updated.

The top window in Figure 4-22 shows the query design grid for a basic update query that revises two field values in the *FamilyMembers* table. This query changes the value of the *Relation* field to *spouse* if the prior field value is *me* or *wife*. The bottom two windows in Figure 4-22 show two additional update queries that restore the original values of the record source. These queries indicate one approach to structuring update queries so that you can restore initial values. Notice that it takes two queries to undo what the first query did. Also, observe that the criteria are compound in all three cases. The compound criteria help to better target the records to update.

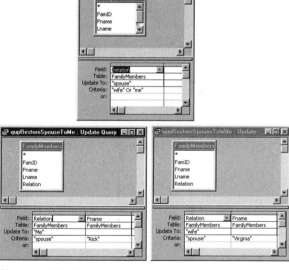

Figure 4-22. *Three update queries.*

Running the restore queries has a couple of problems. First, you have to run both of them. Second, Access asks you to confirm that you want to run each query (it asks twice if you're running them from the Database window). If you were making many kinds of updates, it would be useful to automate the process to save time and improve accuracy. The following subprocedure performs the update. All the user has to do is invoke it.

```
Sub RestoreMeAndWife()
    DoCmd.SetWarnings False
    DoCmd.OpenQuery "qupRestoreSpouseToMe"
    DoCmd.OpenQuery "qupRestoreSpouseToWife"
    DoCmd.SetWarnings True
End Sub
```

The code uses four lines to run two update queries. The *SetWarnings* method disables the warning dialog boxes. The *OpenQuery* method is used twice to invoke the two queries. The last line re-enables warning dialog boxes.

Append Queries

Append queries add new records from a source recordset to a target recordset. The target recordset can be either a single table or the tables behind an updateable select query. The source recordset can be a table or select query with fields that match at least some of those in the target recordset. The source recordset must reside in the current database. The target recordset can reside in any Access database file.

An append query does not have to add records that contain every field in the target, but it must at least include one required field. If the target table has a primary key, be sure that the values for the primary key are unique in both recordsets. The append query will fail to add records with nonunique primary key values.

You begin designing an append query by adding the source recordset to the query's Design view. Next, add fields from the source to the Field row of the query design grid. Then, open the Query Type button on the toolbar and choose Append Query to display the Append dialog box. This dialog box simplifies the task of designating another table in the current database as the target. You can also indicate that you want to add records to a table in another Access database file by selecting the Another Database radio button and entering the path and file name for the other database. After selecting a database, the Table Name drop-down list box lists the tables in that file. Specify a target recordset by selecting a table name from that list box. If you want to add records to a select query, you must manually code the action query (see Chapter 2 for samples that accomplish this task using ADO and SQL).

After choosing a target record source, Access revises its query design grid to include an Append To row. It also automatically matches as many fields as it recognizes in the target recordset to those in source recordset. You can override the automatic selections. For those fields that Access does not match, you can insert a matching field (for example, one with a different name, but the same data type). Click in the Append To row of a column and choose the corresponding field name from the drop-down list of target recordset field names.

The top window in Figure 4-23 is an append query in Design view that has fields already added to the Field and Append To rows and the Append dialog box open. This append query adds records from the *AdditionsToFamilyMembers* table to the *FamilyMembers* table. After closing the Append dialog box, click the Run button to run the query. As with any other action query, click the View button on the toolbar to show the records the query will affect without running the query.

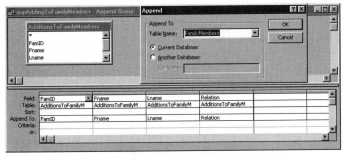

Figure 4-23. *The top window is an append query that individually lists all the fields to add to the target record source. The bottom window is an append query that uses the asterisk to designate all the fields from both the target and source recordsets.*

The bottom window in Figure 4-23 shows a variation of the append query in the top window. The bottom query copies all the fields from the *MoreAdditionsToFamilyMembers* table to the *FamilyMembers* table. I dragged the asterisk from the source recordset field list to the Field row in the query design grid. Similarly, I chose the asterisk from the drop-down list in the Append To row. Both queries append all the existing fields from the source to the target record source. However, the bottom one is more flexible. This is because it automatically includes any new fields that you will add to both tables. When you explicitly list the fields, you are limited to those fields until you manually revise the entries in the Field and Append To rows.

NOTE In some cases, Access may not immediately redraw the display of a table after it completes an append query. Therefore, the query can actually update the target recordset without the display reflecting the changes. You can rectify this problem by changing the target recordset's display to Design view and back again to Datasheet view. (Shift+F9 also redraws the display for a recordset.)

Delete Queries

Delete queries permanently remove records from a target recordset. For that reason, you should be exceptionally careful when using delete action queries. Always use the View button to verify the records that you will be removing before invoking the query. Delete queries can also delete records in other recordsets besides the target. This is true when your target is on the one side of a one-to-many relationship with cascading deletes selected. In this situation, deleting a record on the one side removes matching records on the many side as well.

You should generally protect your data sources when using action queries, but this is especially true with delete queries because of their ability to permanently remove large sets of records from a record source. Consider maintaining a backup copy of your record source so that you can automatically restore it in the case of inadvertent activation of a delete query. Another strategy for delete queries is to make them hidden in the Database window, which will reduce the chance of a user accidentally invoking a delete query. (You can still programmatically invoke action queries that you elect to hide.) Hidden database objects are not displayed unless you choose to reveal them by choosing Options from the Tools menu and selecting Hidden Objects on the View page of the Options dialog box.

> **NOTE** To hide an action query, right-click on it in the Database window and choose Properties from the shortcut menu. Select the Hidden check box on the Property sheet and click OK. (You might need to unselect the Hidden Objects check box on the View page of the Options dialog box as well.)

You begin designing a delete query by double-clicking the Create Query In Design view option in the Database window. From the Show Table dialog box, add the record source from which you want to delete records. Specify rows that you want to delete by dragging fields from a field list to the Field row in the query design grid. Insert entries in the design grid's Criteria row to specify target records for deletion. If you want the delete query to remove all records from the target source, place an asterisk (or any field name) in the Field row and do not insert any criteria. You must have at least one entry in a Field row for the delete query to operate.

Figure 4-24 shows the design of a pair of delete queries. The top query deletes all the records from the *FamilyMembers* table; it has no Criteria row entries. If you knew the *FamID* values for the specific records that you want to delete you could insert them in the Criteria rows before invoking the query.

If you do not know what rows to delete at design time, you can create the delete query as a parameter query. The bottom window in Figure 4-24 shows this type of query. The prompt is the parameter query prompt that appears at run time. A user can then input a *FamID* value to delete all records that contain a *FamID* value greater than or equal to the specified value.

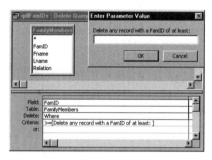

Figure 4-24. *Two delete queries.*

The following procedure pulls together some information about both delete and append queries. The procedure optionally deletes or restores all the records in the *FamilyMembers* table. When the procedure ends, the table is open and available for viewing. If you hide the *qdlAllFamilyMembers* and *qapRestoreAllFamilyMembers* queries, your only way to invoke them will be through code, as shown here.

```
Sub ActionQueryDemo()
Dim varYesNo

'Prompt to delete all records.
    varYesNo = MsgBox("Do you want to remove all records?", _
        vbYesNo, "Programming Microsoft Access 2000")

'If answer is yes, remove them all.
    If varYesNo = vbYes Then
        DoCmd.SetWarnings False
        DoCmd.OpenQuery "qdlAllFamilyMembers"
        DoCmd.SetWarnings True
    End If
```

(continued)

```
'Prompt to restore all records.
    varYesNo = MsgBox("Do you want to restore all records?", _
        vbYesNo, "Programming Microsoft Access 2000")

'If answer is yes, restore them all.
    If varYesNo = vbYes Then
        DoCmd.SetWarnings False
        DoCmd.OpenQuery "qapRestoreAllFamilyMembers"
        DoCmd.SetWarnings True
    End If

'Closing and opening table redraws it
'while making the table available for viewing.
DoCmd.Close acTable, "FamilyMembers"
DoCmd.OpenTable "FamilyMembers"

End Sub
```

The procedure starts with a *MsgBox* function that asks the user whether he or she wants to remove all records from the *FamilyMembers* table. If the user clicks Yes, the procedure invokes the *qdlAllFamilyMembers* query that appears at the top of Figure 4-24. (Notice that *ActionQueryDemo* contains a pair of statements that turn warning dialog boxes off and then on.) Next, the procedure prompts to find out whether it should restore all the records in *FamilyMembers*. If the user clicks Yes, the code invokes the *qapRestoreAllFamilyMembers* query to add records from a backup copy of the table back into *FamilyMembers*.

Before exiting, the procedure closes and then opens the *FamilyMembers* table, which ensures that the table will show the most recent modification, and leaves the table open in Access for easy viewing.

Make-Table Queries

Make-table queries, unlike the other three action queries, do not change, add to, or delete an original data source. The sole purpose of a make-table query is to create an Access table based on a record source. Any combination of data that you can link in a select query can qualify as a valid record source from which to make a table.

Several common application scenarios call out for make-table queries. First, you can use a make-table query to make backup copies of critical tables. This is particularly true just before it is time to delete records from the active system's data store. Second, a make-table query can preserve the state of a table or a joined set of tables at a fixed point in time. Third, you can make a copy of data in one database file for the purposes of another database application. While it is always possible to link (and you can get fresher data by linking), you can achieve faster performance with a table in a file than with a linked table from another file. Fourth, queries can become too complex for Access to process or their processing can take an excessive amount of time. In these situations, re-place the offending complex query with a table generated by a make-table query. This will circumvent the too complex error message and will result in better performance.

Since a make-table query is at its core an action query, it is substantially easier to create a table with a make-table query than with ADO, SQL, or DAO. You begin creating a make-table query by opening a blank query in Design view, adding other tables and queries as resources for the new table, joining inputs as necessary, and choosing Make-Table Query from the Query Type button list. Next, drag the fields that you want in your new table to the Field row of the query design grid. Click the Run button to create the new table. If a table al-ready exists with the name for the target table, Access asks whether you want to delete the old version before creating a new one.

Figure 4-25 shows a simple make-table query that makes a backup copy of the *FamilyMembers* table. The Make Table dialog box appears when you run a make-table query. You can use the dialog box to specify a table name within the current database file or the path and filename of another database. Then, you can use the Table Name drop-down list box to select a table to copy.

The sample in Figure 4-25 targets the *FamilyMembersCopy* table in the current database as the destination for the database. The Field row entry in the query design grid specifies that all the fields in the *FamilyMembers* table con-tribute to the new table. There are no criteria for including or excluding rows from the source recordset.

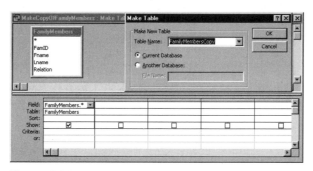

Figure 4-25. *A simple make-table query.*

PROGRAMMING QUERIES WITH SQL AND ADO

SQL is a widely accepted language for manipulating relational data. Most re-mote relational database manager engines rely on SQL, and just about every query you create in Design view can also be created programmatically using SQL. With a working knowledge of generic SQL (often called SQL-92), you can design more efficient query statements for your queries in the natural language of those database engines.

The following sections will explore common uses for SQL in Access applications. First, we'll examine the SQL SELECT statements. Then we'll look at data definition functions. SQL statements that implement data definition functions can build directly on the SELECT statement syntax and add a new class of functionality. Finally, we'll review SQL techniques for generating and running views and stored procedures.

SELECT Statements

A SQL SELECT statement returns a set of rows from one or more database tables. You can use related clauses such as WHERE and ORDER BY to dramatically extend how the SELECT statement selects and displays rows in its return set. SQL aggregate functions offer additional options for managing the return set.

A basic SELECT statement designates one or more columns from a record source. It has this general format:

```
SELECT FieldList FROM RecordSource
```

Field lists

You select a subset of the fields in a record source by specifying a comma-separated list for the *FieldList* column. You select all the fields in the record source by using an asterisk. If one or more of the fields in *FieldList* have the same name but are in different tables, you must precede the field names with their table name and a period. If the table name contains one or more blanks, you must embed the table name in brackets.

Joins

To specify how two tables relate to one another as record sources for a SELECT statement's return set, you use *joins*. The SELECT statement's FROM clause specifies any joins for combining two or more tables. A join must at least specify on which columns to combine tables and how to determine a match between the tables. (You nest joins within one another to specify relationships between more than two tables.) Typical join types are inner joins, which select matching records from each of two tables; left joins, which include all records from the first table and only matching records from the second table; and right joins, which include all records from the second table and only matching records from the first table.

WHERE clauses

You use the SELECT statement's WHERE clause to specify criteria for selecting rows from a record source. Unlike the FROM clause, the WHERE clause is optional. You use it only to restrict the records in a return set.

LIKE operators

You use the optional LIKE operator to find values in fields that match a specified pattern. This operator supports pattern matching across the Jet and SQL Server database engines, but you must use caution because wildcard characters vary between the Jet file-server engine and many client/server engines. For example, Microsoft SQL Server uses % and ^ as wildcard characters instead of the * and ? characters that Jet uses.

ORDER BY clauses

You use the optional ORDER BY clause with the SELECT statement to return a recordset in an order other than by primary key. You list the first field on which you want to sort immediately after the ORDER BY keyword. The default sort order is ascending (ASC), but you can specify a descending order (DESC). If you want to sort on more than one field, you delimit the field name and sort order pairs with commas.

GROUP BY and HAVING clauses

The optional GROUP BY and HAVING clauses complement one another. They work with SQL aggregate functions such as *COUNT* and *SUM*. The GROUP BY clause specifies fields over which to compute aggregates. The HAVING clause is similar to the WHERE clause; it restricts the recordset returned by the GROUP BY clause to records that match given criteria.

DISTINCT keywords

One way to limit the number of records that a SELECT statement returns is with the DISTINCT keyword, which eliminates duplicate data in the selected fields. You place the DISTINCT keyword between the SELECT keyword and the field list. The general format for this keyword is:

```
Select Distinct FieldList from RecordSource
```

Using the *Command* object to execute SQL

You use the ADODB *Command* object to execute a SQL command against a data source by following this procedure:

1. Set the *Command* object's *CommandText* property to the SQL statement you want to execute.

2. Set the object's *CommandType* property to *adCmdText* to optimize performance.

3. Invoke the *Command* object's *Execute* method to generate the SQL return set.

4. Open a *Recordset* object based on the *Command* object so that you can manipulate the SQL return set in your application.

The following code uses a *Command* object to execute a simple SQL statement:

```
Sub MySelect()
Dim cnn1 As New ADODB.Connection
Dim cmd1 As ADODB.Command
Dim rst1 As ADODB.Recordset

'Create the connection to another database.
    cnn1.Open "Provider=Microsoft.Jet.OLEDB.4.0;" & _
    "Data Source=C:\Program Files\Microsoft Office\Office\" & _
    "Samples\Northwind.mdb;"

'Define and execute command to select all ProductID field
'values from a single table.
    Set cmd1 = New ADODB.Command
    With cmd1
        .ActiveConnection = cnn1
        .CommandText = "Select ProductID from [Order Details]"
        .CommandType = adCmdText
        .Execute
    End With

'Assign the return set to a recordset.
    Set rst1 = New ADODB.Recordset
    rst1.CursorType = adOpenStatic
    rst1.LockType = adLockReadOnly
    rst1.Open cmd1
    Debug.Print rst1.RecordCount

End Sub
```

MySelect prints the number of records in the return set (2155) to the Immediate window. The return set from the SQL statement includes each record in the *Order Details* table. By default, the SELECT statement selects all the records in the underlying record source, and *MySelect*'s SQL statement contains no restrictions on the records to return.

Example using INNER JOIN

The following SELECT statement illustrates a number of new features. First, it shows the syntax for an inner join between the *Order Details* and the *Products* tables. Second, it enumerates the rows in the return set and prints them to the Immediate window.

```
Sub MySelect3()
Dim cnn1 As New ADODB.Connection
Dim cmd1 As ADODB.Command
Dim rst1 As ADODB.Recordset, int1 As Integer
```

```
'Create the connection to another database.
    cnn1.Open "Provider=Microsoft.Jet.OLEDB.4.0;" & _
    "Data Source=C:\Program Files\Microsoft Office\Office\" & _
    "Samples\Northwind.mdb;"

'Define and execute command to select distinct ProductName field
'values from a pair of joined tables.
    Set cmd1 = New ADODB.Command
    With cmd1
        .ActiveConnection = cnn1
        .CommandText = "Select Distinct ProductName from " & _
            "[Order Details] Inner Join Products on " & _
            "[Order Details].ProductID = Products.ProductID"
        .CommandType = adCmdText
        .Execute
    End With

'Assign the return set to a recordset
'and print the results to the Immediate window.
    Set rst1 = New ADODB.Recordset
    rst1.CursorType = adOpenStatic
    rst1.LockType = adLockReadOnly
    rst1.Open cmd1
    Debug.Print rst1.RecordCount
    For int1 = 1 To rst1.RecordCount
        Debug.Print rst1("ProductName")
        rst1.MoveNext
    Next int1

End Sub
```

MySelect3's SELECT statement draws on fields from two tables—not just one, as in the preceding sample. The statement performs an inner join on the *Products* table and the *Order Details* table to match the *ProductID* fields from both tables. Because the SQL statement uses the DISTINCT keyword, no duplicate *ProductName* field values are returned. Finally, the inner join enables the procedure to print the descriptive product name that corresponds to each product ID code.

Example using *SUM* and ORDER BY

The following procedure uses the SQL aggregate function *SUM* and the joining and sorting options. It computes the sum of the extended price for each product in the *Order Details* table. The return set for the statement orders the outcome by how much revenue the products generate (from most to least).

```
Sub MySelect4()
Dim cnn1 As New ADODB.Connection
```

(continued)

```
Dim cmd1 As ADODB.Command
Dim rst1 As ADODB.Recordset, int1 As Integer

'Create the connection to another database.
    cnn1.Open "Provider=Microsoft.Jet.OLEDB.4.0;" & _
    "Data Source=C:\Program Files\Microsoft Office\Office\" & _
    "Samples\Northwind.mdb;"

'Define and execute command to select distinct ProductName field
'values from a pair of joined tables; compute extended price.
    Set cmd1 = New ADODB.Command
    With cmd1
        .ActiveConnection = cnn1
        .CommandText = "Select Distinct Products.ProductName, " & _
            "Sum([Order Details].[UnitPrice]*" & _
            "[Order Details].[Quantity]*" & _
            "(1-[Order Details].[Discount])) As [Extended Price] " & _
            "From Products Inner Join [Order Details] On " & _
            "Products.ProductID = [Order Details].ProductID " & _
            "Group By Products.ProductName " & _
            "Order By Sum([Order Details].[UnitPrice]*" & _
            "[Order Details].[Quantity]*" & _
            "(1-[Order Details].[Discount])) Desc"
        .CommandType = adCmdText
        .Execute
    End With

'Assign Select statement return set to a recordset
'and print the results to the Immediate window.
    Set rst1 = New ADODB.Recordset
    rst1.CursorType = adOpenKeyset
    rst1.Open cmd1
    Debug.Print rst1.RecordCount
    For int1 = 1 To rst1.RecordCount
        Debug.Print rst1("ProductName"), _
            rst1.Fields("Extended Price")
        rst1.MoveNext
    Next int1

End Sub
```

MySelect4 creates a calculated field in code. The procedure uses the *SUM* function with a GROUP BY clause to calculate the revenue generated by each product. Without the GROUP BY clause, the code would create the calculated field for each row in the original table but would not provide summary results by group. (It would calculate the total revenue of all products instead of the total revenue of each individual product.)

The ORDER BY clause controls the sort order of the return set. Although you could write this code more succinctly (it duplicates the code that computes the extended price), as written it is easy to understand and is similar to code produced by the query design grid.

Data Definition Functions

There are several ways to approach data definition with SQL statements. This section examines how to create a table with make-table queries. Make-table queries are action queries that create a new table based on the result set of an existing query. This is a data definition function.

This section also demonstrates how to modify autoincrement fields with the ALTER TABLE and ALTER COLUMN SQL keywords. Jet 4 SQL introduces a new identity field data type to facilitate this objective. Jet 4 supports setting step and start values for these counter fields. (You can reset them at any time.) The sample procedures in this section are complete by themselves, but they are even more valuable if you examine them in light of the discussion in Chapter 3. ALTER TABLE and ALTER COLUMN are part of a whole set of keywords (for example, CREATE TABLE, CREATE INDEX, and DROP) that directly support data definition functions through SQL.

SELECT...INTO

The syntax for a make-table query in SQL is as follows:

```
SELECT FieldList INTO NewTableName FROM RecordSource
```

If you create a new table in a database file other than the current one, add an IN clause after the INTO clause and before the FROM clause. You use the IN clause to designate the path and filename of the database that will hold the output from the SELECT...INTO statement.

RecordSource can consist of one table, one query, or several of either, and it should contain all the fields that you want in your new table. The SELECT...INTO statement copies the design of the specified fields and their data to the new table. You cannot create any new fields with the SELECT...INTO statement. You can easily prototype this type of query by creating it in Design view and then switching to SQL view and copying the SQL statement into a procedure that uses an ADO object. With this approach, you don't have to design the SQL statement.

The following procedure uses a simple SELECT...INTO statement. It backs up the *FamilyMembers* table in the current database to a new table named *FMBackup*.

```
Sub MyMakeTable()
Dim cnn1 As ADODB.Connection
```

(continued)

```
'Reference connection.
    Set cnn1 = CurrentProject.Connection

'Execute SQL for maketable query.
    cnn1.Execute "SELECT FamilyMembers.* INTO " & _
        "FMBackup FROM FamilyMembers"

'This procedure fails if FMBackup already exists.

End Sub
```

Unfortunately, there is generally more to creating and running a SELECT...INTO statement than these two ADO statements. For example, this procedure can fail if the *FMBackup* table already exists. It can also fail if another user opens either table. These and other complications demand error trapping. The following sample illustrates how you might start error processing for an application that uses a procedure with a SELECT...INTO statement.

```
Sub MyMakeTable2()
On Error GoTo Make2Err:
Dim cnn1 As ADODB.Connection

'Reference connection.
    Set cnn1 = CurrentProject.Connection

'Test for unanticipated errors.
'    Err.Raise 1

'Execute SQL for make-table query.
    cnn1.Execute "SELECT FamilyMembers.* INTO " & _
        "FMBackup FROM FamilyMembers"

Make2Exit:
'Close the connection and set it equal to nothing
'and exit the sub.
    cnn1.Close
    Set cnn1 = Nothing
    Exit Sub

Make2Err:
'Trap for table already exists.
    If Err.Number = -2147217900 Then
        cnn1.Execute "Drop Table FMBackup"
        Resume
    Else
        MsgBox "The program generated an unanticipated " & _
            "error. Its number and description are " & _
```

```
            Err.Number & ": " & Err.Description, vbCritical, _
            "Programming Microsoft Access 2000"
    End If
Resume Make2Exit

End Sub
```

This procedure accomplishes the same task as the original procedure, but it does not fail if the *FMBackup* table already exists. The error handler recognizes this type of failure and deletes the existing table before executing the command again. If another error occurs, the application presents the essential information in a message box so that the user can inform the developer of the problem.

The procedure includes one more error-trapping feature. Immediately after setting the connection, the code can call the *Raise* method of the *Err* object. (The feature is commented out, but I removed the comment to evaluate the performance of my error trapping.) This use of the *Err* object creates an artificial error that helps indicate how the procedure should be designed to respond to unanticipated errors.

The sample also closes the connection and sets the *Connection* object to *Nothing*. These two actions have similar and complementary purposes. When you close a connection, the resources used for the connection become available to the rest of the system. The object remains in memory, however, and its properties are still intact. Later, you can open the same *Connection* object with its former property settings or new ones. You must set an object equal to *Nothing* to remove it from memory.

Using ALTER TABLE and ALTER COLUMN to reset *Autoincrement* fields

Many Access developers will be thrilled by the new control that they gain over Counter data types that serve as identity fields for records. Chapter 3 already showed how to set the start and step values for a counter field. While this is impressive, you have more complete control over these fields than just the initial setting of values. The following procedure resets the start and step values of the Counter data type.

```
Sub ResetCounter(intStart, intStep)
Dim cnn1 As ADODB.Connection
Dim strSQL

'Reference connection and execute SQL for view.
    Set cnn1 = CurrentProject.Connection

'Create SQL string that references passed arguments.
    strSQL = "ALTER TABLE FamilyMemberNames " & _
```

(continued)

```
          "ALTER COLUMN FamID Identity " & _
          "(" & intStart & "," & intStep & ")"

'Execute the SQL statement to update the counter.
    cnn1.Execute strSQL

End Sub
```

The *ResetCounter* procedure above demonstrates how to make a SQL command dynamic by appending arguments to a SQL statement. This process is analogous to passing values to a parameter query. The *ResetCounter* procedure alters the *FamID* field in the *FamilyMemberNames* table and takes two arguments. The first one is the new counter field value for the next record added to the table; the second is the step size for subsequent new records. You can run the procedure by typing in the Immediate window a line similar to the following:

```
ResetCounter 2,2
```

These two arguments force the next record added to the table to have a *FamID* field value of *2*; each additional record will have a *FamID* field value that is larger by a step value of *2*. Be careful how you set the start and step counter values because you can create key violations (such as duplicate values) that deny users the right to enter new records into a table. Happily, Access 2000 lets you survey the existing counter field values programmatically. You can therefore construct code that guarantees that this problem will not occur, as shown in the next procedure.

The heart of *ResetCounter* is the SQL statement. As you can see, it has three critical elements. The ALTER TABLE keywords change the design of the specified table. The ALTER COLUMN keywords change the design of the specified field. The IDENTITY keyword updates the counter field with arguments that specify the start and step values for the field.

The following procedure, *SetResetCounter*, is long but not very complicated. It uses a method of manipulating counter field values that avoids key violations. Figure 4-26 shows the table just after the last successful run of *SetResetCounter*. Notice that the first record has a *FamID* value of *2*, and the *FamID* value of the following record is increased by a step value of *2*. The third record, with a *FamID* value of *8*, is out of line with the preceding step value. In addition, subsequent records increase the *FamID* field by a step value of *4* with each new record. The change in start and step values for the Counter field results from calling *ResetCounter*. A text string in *MyMemoField* marks the change in these values.

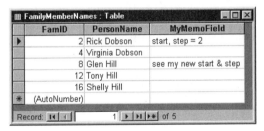

Figure 4-26. *The* FamilyMemberNames *table after the* SetResetCounter
procedure executes.

```
Sub SetResetCounter()
Dim cnn1 As New ADODB.Connection
Dim cmd1 As ADODB.Command
Dim rst1 As ADODB.Recordset, rst2 As New ADODB.Recordset
Dim int1 As Integer

'Reference connection.
    Set cnn1 = CurrentProject.Connection

'Clear FamilyMemberNames table and reset table counter.
    DoCmd.SetWarnings False
    DoCmd.OpenQuery "qd1AllFamilyMemberNames"
    DoCmd.SetWarnings True
    ResetCounter 2, 2

'Add a couple of records to the FamilyMemberNames
'table from the FamilyMembers table with the
'initial start and step values.
    Set rst1 = New ADODB.Recordset
    rst1.Open "FamilyMemberNames", cnn1, adOpenKeyset, _
        adLockOptimistic, adCmdTable
    rst2.Open "FamilyMembers", cnn1, adOpenForwardOnly, _
        adLockReadOnly, adCmdTable
    For int1 = 1 To 2
        rst1.AddNew
            rst1(1) = rst2(1) & " " & rst2(2)
            If int1 = 1 Then
                rst1("MyMemoField") = "start, step = 2"
            End If
            rst2.MoveNext
        rst1.Update
    Next int1
    rst1.Close
```

(continued)

```
'Define and execute command to select all FamID field values
'with highest FamID value first --> last counter value.
    Set cmd1 = New ADODB.Command
    With cmd1
        .ActiveConnection = cnn1
        .CommandText = "Select FamID from FamilyMemberNames " & _
            "Order By FamID Desc"
        .CommandType = adCmdText
        .Execute
    End With

'Save last counter value, and use it to
'reset start and step to new values.
    Set rst1 = New ADODB.Recordset
    rst1.CursorType = adOpenForwardOnly
    rst1.LockType = adLockReadOnly
    rst1.Open cmd1
    int1 = rst1(0)
    rst1.Close
    ResetCounter int1 + int1, int1

'Add remaining records from the FamilyMembers table
'to the FamilyMemberNames table with the
'new start and step values.
    rst1.Open "FamilyMemberNames", cnn1, adOpenKeyset, _
        adLockOptimistic, adCmdTable
'   rst1(2) = "see my new start & step"
    int1 = 3
    Do Until rst2.EOF
        rst1.AddNew
            rst1(1) = rst2(1) & " " & rst2(2)
            If int1 = 3 Then
                rst1("MyMemoField") = _
                    "see my new start & step"
            End If
            rst2.MoveNext
            int1 = int1 + 1
        rst1.Update
    Loop

End Sub
```

SetResetCounter has six parts separated by comments. The first part establishes a connection to the current database. The second part runs a delete query that removes all the rows from the *FamilyMemberNames* table, enables system warnings by calling the *SetWarnings* method, and then resets the start and step values of the counter for the *FamilyMemberNames* table by calling the *ResetCounter* procedure.

The third part uses a *For...Next* loop to copy the first two records of the *FamilyMembers* table to the *FamilyMemberNames* table. The Jet database engine automatically assigns *FamID* values for these two records using the start and step values set by the preceding part.

The fourth part uses a *Command* object on the *FamilyMemberNames* table to find the largest value of the *FamID* field. When the command executes, it sorts the table's records in descending *FamID* order, which places the largest *FamID* field—the table's primary key—at the top of the return set. Knowing this value lets your application set a new start value for additional records that does not duplicate the primary key value of any other records in the table.

The fifth part opens a recordset on the command's return set and stores the value of the *FamID* field of the recordset's first record. This part then invokes the *ResetCounter* procedure to set a new start value that is twice as large as the highest *FamID* value and a new step size equal to the highest *FamID* field value.

The final part adds the remaining records of the *FamilyMembers* table to the *FamilyMemberNames* table. To reinforce the flexible control over counter primary key fields, the *Memo* column contains a message indicating how the *SetRetCounter* procedure freely manipulates the counter field.

Views and Stored Procedures

Views and stored procedures, previously available only in high-end database managers, are available in Access 2000. Access 2000 implements views, which do not support parameters, as stored queries that return rows. Access 2000 offers stored procedures as both saved action queries and parameter queries that work as either action or select queries. As you'll see, you can achieve the functionality of a parameter query by passing string constants to a procedure that merges the passed values into a SQL statement and then executes the statement.

Views

The SQL CREATE VIEW statement creates a view by adding a stored select query to the Database window under the *Queries* object category. (In an Access .adp project, your views are saved under the *Views* object category of the Database window.) The process for creating a stored select query with CREATE VIEW is more direct than with ADO, which requires that you first construct a *Command* object and then append it to the *Views* collection.

The following procedure demonstrates the syntax and operation of SQL CREATE VIEW statements in ADO code.

```
Sub CreateView()
Dim cnn1 As ADODB.Connection
```

(continued)

```
'Reference connection.
    Set cnn1 = CurrentProject.Connection

'Execute SQL for view.
    cnn1.Execute "Create View CategoryView as " & _
        "SELECT * From Categories"
    RefreshDatabaseWindow

'This simple routine fails if CategoryView already exists.

End Sub
```

The procedure invokes the *Execute* method of the connection and passes it a SQL CREATE VIEW statement. The name of the select query immediately follows the CREATE VIEW keywords, and is followed by the AS keyword and the SQL SELECT statement. The SELECT statement can be any standard SELECT statement. Finally, the procedure calls *RefreshDatabaseWindow* to update the Database window so that a user can view the new query without having to manually refresh the window.

One deficiency of *CreateView* is that it fails if the view it attempts to create already exists. You can, of course, manually remove the old query. However, your code can also automatically delete the old query. The following two procedures illustrate one approach to this problem:

```
Sub CreateReplaceView(ViewName As String)
Dim cnn1 As ADODB.Connection
Dim cat1 As ADOX.Catalog
Dim vew1 As ADOX.View

'Reference objects for view
    Set cnn1 = CurrentProject.Connection
    Set cat1 = New Catalog
    cat1.ActiveConnection = cnn1

'Enumerate views.
    For Each vew1 In cat1.Views
'Delete named view and replace it with a new version.
        If vew1.Name = ViewName Then
            cat1.Views.Delete ViewName
            CreateCustomView ViewName
            Exit Sub
        End If
    Next vew1

'If the view is not there, create from scratch.
    CreateCustomView ViewName
    RefreshDatabaseWindow

End Sub
```

```
Sub CreateCustomView(MyViewName)
Dim cnn1 As ADODB.Connection, strSQL

'Reference connection and execute SQL for view.
    Set cnn1 = CurrentProject.Connection

'Create SQL string for view.
    strSQL = "Create View " & MyViewName & _
        " as Select * From Categories"

'Create the custom view.
    cnn1.Execute strSQL
    RefreshDatabaseWindow

End Sub
```

The *CreateReplaceView* procedure does not directly execute the CREATE VIEW statement; it leaves that task to the second procedure, *CreateCustomView*. *CreateReplaceView* enumerates the views to assess whether it is necessary to delete the old view before attempting to create a new one with the same name. Then it calls *CreateCustomView* and passes the name of the view to create. *CreateCustomView* is identical in design to the previous sample, except it uses string concatenation with the passed argument and a string constant to devise a SQL statement for the connection's *Execute* method.

You create a new view by typing in the Immediate window a simple one-line command similar to the following:

```
CreateReplaceView "NameOfView"
```

You must enclose the name of the view in quotes. You can easily revise *CreateCustomView* to allow a dynamic SELECT statement.

Instead of iterating through the elements in the *Views* collection, you can simply attempt to create a new view and trap the error that occurs when a view with that name already exists. The error number for a duplicate view is -2147467259. Trap for this number and delete the old view before reexecuting the CREATE VIEW statement. The *FieldedView* procedure on this book's companion CD illustrates this approach.

Stored procedures

A stored procedure simplifies the reuse of SQL code. Stored procedures perform bulk operations, such as delete, update, or append queries, and they accept run-time parameters for both bulk operations and row-returning queries.

You use the SQL CREATE PROC statement to create a stored procedure. This statement has the same general syntax as the CREATE VIEW statement. You follow CREATE PROC with the name of your stored procedure and the AS keyword, which serves a marker for the beginning of the SQL code that defines the behavior of the stored procedure. You can design your action queries in the

Access query Design view, copy the SQL code in SQL view, and then paste it in after the AS keyword.

Stored procedures do not appear in the Database window. However, they exist as items in the *Procedures* collection of the *Catalog* object. Your code can reference individual procedures through this hierarchical object schema. For example, if your application generates a stored procedure that deletes records, it exists in the *Procedures* collection (along with the action queries in a project).

The following procedure illustrates the syntax for applying the CREATE PROC statement. It invokes the *Connection* object's *Execute* method and passes a SQL statement as a string. The CREATE PROC statement attempts to create a query named *DeleteThese*. The query deletes all records in the *FamilyMemberNames* table with a *FamID* value of *10* or greater. Without any special measure, the procedure fails if *DeleteThese* already exists. To make it possible to run the procedure, even when it exists already, the code resumes from the next line in the event of an error.

```
Sub CreateProcToDelete()
On Error Resume Next
Dim cnn1 As ADODB.Connection
Dim cat1 As Catalog
Dim proc1 As Procedure
Dim cmd1 As Command

'Reference connection.
    Set cnn1 = CurrentProject.Connection
    Set cat1 = New Catalog
    cat1.ActiveConnection = cnn1
    Set cmd1 = New Command
    cmd1.ActiveConnection = cnn1

'Execute SQL to make the procedure.
    cnn1.Execute "Create Procedure DeleteThese As " & _
        "Delete From FamilyMemberNames Where FamID>=10"

'Enumerate Procedures collection members.
'For DeleteThese procedure, set command properties
'and execute it.
    For Each proc1 In cat1.Procedures
        If proc1.Name = "DeleteThese" Then
            cmd1.CommandText = proc1.Name
            cmd1.CommandType = adCmdStoredProc
            cmd1.Execute
        End If
    Next proc1

End Sub
```

The *CreateProcToDelete* procedure commences with a series of declarations and assignments to support the logic for creating and then running the procedure. The *Connection* object's *Execute* method makes the procedure by running a SQL statement. At this point an error will occur if the procedure already exists. The *Execute* method actually adds the *DeleteThese* procedure to the *Procedures* collection in the connection's catalog.

Because procedures reside in a collection, you can enumerate the collection's members with a *For...Each* loop. The sample uses such a loop to locate *DeleteThese*. When it finds the procedure, it assigns the procedure's *Name* property to the *CommandText* property of a *Command* object. Then, it sets the *Command* object's *CommandType* property to *adCmdStoredProc*. These two assignments generate the SQL string *Execute DeleteThese*. Invoking the *Execute* method for the *Command* object launches the procedure in Jet and removes the records from the *FamilyMemberNames* table.

You can make the preceding sample more flexible and smarter in a couple of ways. First, a more elaborate error trap can specifically isolate an error resulting from the procedure from other types of errors. Second, you can make the procedure accept parameters for the *FamID* field. The following sample uses the CREATE PROC statement to define a parameter query that deletes all records in the *FamilyMemberNames* table with a *FamID* value greater than or equal to a specific value designated at run time. The code reminds you of the steps for setting a command parameter value. Recall that you have to create the parameter, append it to the *Parameters* collection, and then assign a value to it. The sample also traps for the error that results when you attempt to create a procedure that has the same name as an existing procedure.

```
Sub CreateProcToDelete2()
On Error GoTo Delete2Err
Dim cnn1 As ADODB.Connection
Dim cmd1 As ADODB.Command
Dim prm1 As Parameter

'Reference connection.
    Set cnn1 = CurrentProject.Connection

'Test for unanticipated errors.
'    Err.Raise 1

'Execute SQL to make the procedure.
    cnn1.Execute "Create Proc DeleteThese " & _
        "(Parameter1 Long) As " & _
        "Delete From FamilyMemberNames " & _
        "Where FamID>=Parameter1"
```

(continued)

```
'Assign SQL from procedure to command.
    Set cmd1 = New ADODB.Command
    With cmd1
        .ActiveConnection = cnn1
        .CommandText = "DeleteThese"
        .CommandType = adCmdStoredProc
    End With

'Set the procedure's parameter.
    Set prm1 = cmd1.CreateParameter("Parameter1", _
        adInteger)
    cmd1.Parameters.Append prm1
    prm1.Value = 10

'Invoke the procedure's SQL statement in the command.
    cmd1.Execute

Delete2Exit:
    Exit Sub

Delete2Err:
    If Err.Number = -2147217900 Then
'Trap for procedure already exists.
        cnn1.Execute "Drop Proc DeleteThese"
        Resume
    Else
        MsgBox "The program generated an unanticipated " & _
            "error.  Its number and description are " & _
            Err.Number & ": " & Err.Description, vbCritical, _
            "Programming Microsoft Access 2000"
    End If
    Resume Delete2Exit
End Sub
```

When you specify a parameter in a CREATE PROC statement, include the parameter designation after the procedure name but before the AS keyword. You can declare its name and data type in parentheses, as shown above. You refer to the parameter again in the WHERE clause to restrict the behavior of the procedure. This syntax is the same as for parameter queries that you create in Design view.

Notice that you do not actually have to loop through the *Procedures* collection to invoke a specific procedure. You can reference its name so long as you specify *adCmdStoredProc* as the value for the command's *CommandType* property. The sample assigns the constant *10* to the parameter (*Parameter1*) for consistency with the prior sample, but you could use an *InputBox* function statement or a form to collect a value for the parameter.

This sample also includes basic error trapping for the situation in which a procedure of the same name already exists (error number -2147217900). *CreateProcToDelete2* simply drops the old procedure when the error occurs by invoking the SQL DROP PROC statement. The syntax of the DROP PROC statement is "Drop Proc *ProcedureName*".

QUERYING REMOTE DATA SOURCES

So far, the samples in this chapter have referenced local data sources or data in another Access file. Access 2000 makes it easy to work with remote data sources as well, such as Microsoft SQL Server or Oracle. This section will briefly explore this topic. You'll find a more in-depth treatment in Chapter 12.

Querying Linked ODBC Sources

You can query a linked ODBC source just as you query a linked Access data source from another file. Figure 4-27 shows the Database window with three linked tables from the Pubs database that ships with SQL Server. Follow these steps to link to a table in a remote database:

1. Choose Get External Data from the Access File menu and then click Link Tables.

2. In the Link dialog box, select ODBC Databases from the Files Of Type drop-down list.

3. Select a DSN from the Machine Data Source. (You can create a new DSN if the one you need is not available.)

4. Complete the link by selecting a table and clicking OK.

Since nearly every remote data source supports ODBC, this way of working with remote data provides universal access with a familiar Access front end.

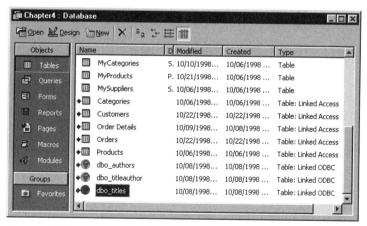

Figure 4-27. *This Database window shows three linked tables—*dbo_authors, dbo_titleauthor, *and* dbo_titles. *You can use ODBC drivers to link to tables from any data source with an ODBC driver.*

Figure 4-28 shows, in its top window, the three linked tables from Figure 4-27 in an Access 2000 query Design view. After you link to a remote table, you can treat it as if it were a local table. Because tables in remote databases can be very large, some special considerations apply when you design queries for them. The first section in this chapter highlights some techniques to consider. The size of the tables and the type of physical connection to the remote data source will help determine the best query designs. The bottom window in Figure 4-28 shows the query from the top window in Datasheet view.

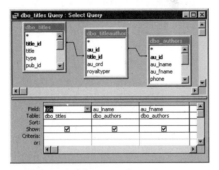

Figure 4-28. *A simple query that relies on three tables from a remote data source. Notice in the top window that you can build queries to linked remote tables as if they were local tables. The bottom window shows the query in Datasheet view.*

Querying in Access Data Projects

Access 2000 introduces a new project type called the Access Project, which bypasses the Jet database engine as it links directly to SQL Server 6.5 or 7.0 and the Microsoft Data Engine. The Microsoft Data Engine is the new version of SQL Server for the Windows 9*x* environment. In this environment, you can form a direct link to a remote database and work with it as if it were a local database.

The top window in Figure 4-29 shows the Database window of an Access Project. Notice that it looks like the Database window of an .mdb database, but its data source is the Pubs database. (You can change the database to which the Database window links by choosing Connection from the File menu.)

The bottom window in Figure 4-29 is the Data Link Properties dialog box for the project. The server for this project is cab22000, the name of a connected SQL Server 7.0 database server. To establish a working connection to a server, you must specify the logon information. This example uses Microsoft Windows NT integrated security. After the connection is established, you can open any database on the server that your logon status permits. Click Test Connection to verify the validity of the link to a specific database.

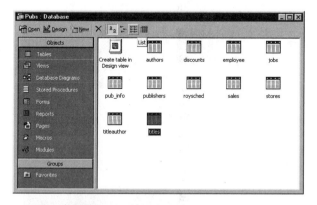

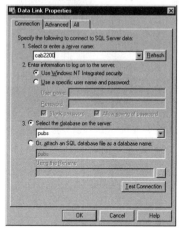

Figure 4-29. *The top window is the Database window for an Access Project; the bottom window is the project's Data Link Properties dialog box.*

Figure 4-30 on the next page shows the Design view of a query in an Access Project. Its query design grid resembles the one for an .mdb database, but it is part of the Microsoft Da Vinci visual database design tools. You can right-click to add tables or other queries as record sources for a new query design, and you can drag and drop fields between tables to build relationships. While there is no explicit SQL view, you can toggle the visibility of a SQL pane in Design view using a button on the Database toolbar. The first button on this toolbar still lets you toggle back and forth between the Design view and Datasheet view. The query design grid orientation changes from vertical to horizontal, but the layout is similar. You build views by entering constants and expressions in the criteria cells to the right of the field names in the design grid.

Figure 4-30. *The query Design view for an Access Project. Notice that it displays the SQL for a query in a separate pane rather than in a separate view.*

Programmatic Querying of Remote Databases

Many developers prefer to work directly with a programmatic interface rather than a graphical user interface. Access 2000 offers tighter compatibility between queries for local and remote data sources at the programmatic level than at the graphical user interface level because you can use ADO and SQL for both local and remote data sources. The biggest difference between local and remote data access is that for remote data access you must specify the OLE DB parameters for the OLE DB provider with the data that you want to query. You might also encounter SQL dialect issues when you migrate your applications from one remote data source to another because each remote database engine can require slightly different logon parameters and can use unique SQL extensions to accommodate its special features.

To connect to a Microsoft SQL Server data source, you use a special OLE DB driver called SQLOLEDB, which is optimized for Microsoft SQL Server, instead of the generic ODBC driver, MSDASQL, which is for working with ODBC databases. The MSDASQL driver predates SQLOLEDB, but it remains a good general-purpose OLE DB driver for situations in which there might not be a specific OLE DB driver. The parameters for these two drivers are slightly different. (Chapter 3 shows how to set the parameters for MSDASQL.)

The following sample shows how straightforward it is to programmatically query a remote SQL Server 7 data source. Notice that the procedure uses the SQLOLEDB driver. The query is against the Pubs database on the cab2200 server. After opening the connection based on the SQLOLEDB driver and its parameter settings, the procedure creates a *Command* object and sets its *CommandText* and *CommandType* properties. Then it executes the command, assigns the return set to a *Recordset* object, and prints the return set.

```
Sub SQLOleDBQuery()
Dim cnn1 As ADODB.Connection
Dim cmd1 As ADODB.Command
Dim rst1 As ADODB.Recordset

'Establish a connection to the database.
'Specify the server (cab2200) as the data source and
'catalog as the database.
    Set cnn1 = New ADODB.Connection
    With cnn1
        .Provider = "sqloledb"
        .ConnectionString = "data source=cab2200;" & _
            "user id = sa;initial catalog=pubs"
        .Open
    End With

'Set up a command object.
    Set cmd1 = New ADODB.Command
    With cmd1
        .ActiveConnection = cnn1
        .CommandText = "SELECT titles.title, " & _
            "authors.au_lname, authors.au_fname " & _
            "FROM titles INNER JOIN (authors INNER JOIN " & _
            "titleauthor ON authors.au_id = " & _
            "titleauthor.au_id) ON " & _
            "titles.title_id = titleauthor.title_id"
        .CommandType = adCmdText
    End With

'Open and print a recordset based on the executed
'query statement.
    Set rst1 = cmd1.Execute
    Debug.Print rst1.GetString

End Sub
```

This query yields results identical to those of the queries in Figures 4-28 and 4-30. I took the SQL in this sample directly from the SQL view of the query in Figure 4-28. Notice that it is similar but not identical in arrangement to the SQL in Figure 4-30 for the Access Project. However, you can substitute the SQL from Figure 4-30 into the above procedure without changing the return set. This confirms that the .mdb programmatic approach and the Access Project query approach can yield equivalent results despite some stylistic differences in the SQL representations for selected cases.

Chapter 5

Building User Interfaces with Forms

Applications use forms, along with reports, to present data. Forms are also a means of accepting and responding to user input. Because database application users interact with an application almost entirely through forms, form design and behavior are very important.

This chapter begins by explaining how to create an exciting first impression by using a form called a splash screen. It then explores how to make forms (particularly data-bound forms) interact with data. You'll also learn about conditional formatting and performing lookup operations with forms. Finally, you'll learn how to programmatically reference forms and toggle their visibility, as well as how to work with form class modules.

NOTE Microsoft Access 2000 offers two types of forms: UserForms, which are also available in other Office applications, and a custom type of form that is an updated version of the form in prior Access versions. UserForms do not integrate as tightly into the Access development environment as Access forms do. For example, UserForms do not bind to Access tables and queries. In addition, the Access form wizards and control wizards do not work with UserForms. For these reasons, this chapter will deal with Access forms only. You can learn more about UserForms from the online help system.

SPLASH SCREEN FORMS

One easy way to get started with forms is by creating a splash screen. A splash screen is a form that appears before another, more interactive form appears. Splash screens often state what an application does or who created it. You can easily control how long this form stays visible. Figure 5-1 shows a sample splash screen from the companion CD, which you can adapt to your own purposes.

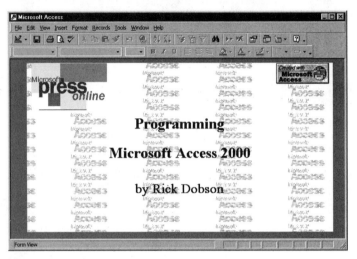

Figure 5-1. *A sample splash screen.*

Creating a Splash Screen

You can start by creating a tiled background. You do so by setting two form properties while the form is open in Design view. First, you set the form's *Picture* property (on the Format page of the Property sheet) to the path and filename for the image. You can use a bitmap in .bmp, .ico, .dib, .wmf, or .emf format. Access can also use other graphic file formats for which you have filters installed. (Rerun the Setup program if you need to install additional filters.) Images that contain gray or other muted colors work best for backgrounds because they make your foreground images and text look more prominent. Second, you change the form's *Picture Tiling* property to *Yes*. (It is *No* by default.)

Next, you can add a foreground image by choosing Picture from the Insert menu. You can also add an Image control to the form. Either method opens the Insert Picture dialog box, where you can select an image to add. Clicking OK automatically sets the image's *Picture* property. Access lets you programmatically set the *Picture* property with Microsoft Visual Basic for Applications (VBA) so you can construct the look of a form dynamically in response to user input (such as a text box entry) or environmental factors (such as a user's security ID). You can position and size the image and use the special effects created by various *Size Mode* property settings. The property accepts three values: *Clip*, *Stretch*, and *Zoom*.

You complete the splash screen by adding one or more Label controls. You can use VBA to set properties for the Label controls at run time. This lets you dynamically format a splash screen's text.

You can set a splash screen to open automatically by choosing Startup from the Tools menu and selecting the splash screen's form name in the Display Form/Page drop-down list in the Startup dialog box. You can also hide the Database window when an application opens by deselecting the Display Database Window check box in the Startup dialog box. Click OK to save your choices.

Controlling Display Duration

The following pair of event procedures displays a splash screen for 10 seconds. (To get to the VBA behind a form, right-click on the form, choose Build Event from the shortcut menu, and then select Code Builder in the Choose Builder dialog box and click OK.) The *Form_Open* event procedure sets the form's *TimerInterval* property value to *10000* (10 seconds; the interval is in milliseconds). The *Form_Timer* event procedure closes the form. Notice that *Form_Open* uses the *Me* keyword to denote the form. You could replace "frmSplashTimer" with *Me.Name* in *Form_Timer*; the *Me* naming convention is more robust because it lets you change a form's name without revising the code.

```
Private Sub Form_Open(Cancel As Integer)
    Me.TimerInterval = 10000

End Sub


Private Sub Form_Timer()
    DoCmd.Close acForm, "frmSplashTimer"

End Sub
```

SWITCHBOARD FORMS

Switchboard forms are a common way to facilitate navigation in an application. It is common for switchboard forms to contain several command buttons that users can click to open another form. This section offers two approaches to using switchboard forms: one based on hyperlinks and the other based on VBA procedures.

Navigating with Hyperlinks

Hyperlink navigation is particularly easy to create because you do not have to write any code (although you can manage hyperlinks with VBA). Hyperlinks can act as shortcuts to database objects in an application, documents on your hard drive, files on a network, or World Wide Web pages on the Internet or pages on an intranet. Access lets you use hyperlinks with labels, buttons, and images.

You can set and edit hyperlink properties from a form's Design view or programmatically using VBA. Using the manual procedures for setting and editing hyperlinks is not only easier but can yield faster-loading forms because forms with hyperlinks created in Design view do not require that a module contain VBA code. To deliver this benefit, a form must have its *Has Module* property set to *No*.

> NOTE The Hyperlink data type lets an Access application launch hyperlinks from table or query fields. While Hyperlink fields are in many ways like the hyperlink properties, you use them differently. See Chapter 13 for coverage of using hyperlinks for Web development.

Figure 5-2 shows four forms that use a simple navigation system. The main switchboard form on the left transfers focus to one of the other three forms when the user clicks a hyperlink on the main form. Once another form has the focus, the user can return the focus to the switchboard by clicking the hyperlink to the main form.

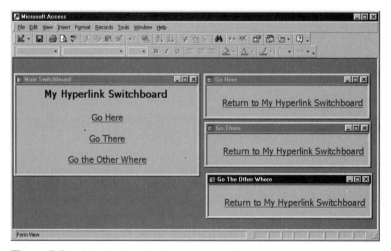

Figure 5-2. *A simple hyperlink navigation system.*

You can easily introduce more than two tiers into a navigation system. Typically, each child form can return focus to its parent form. Main forms often include a way to exit the application or exit Access.

To create a hyperlink using the Label control, follow these steps:

1. Click the Build button next to the *Hyperlink Address* property or the *Hyperlink SubAddress* property on the label's property sheet.

2. In the Insert Hyperlink dialog box, select the type of object to link to from the Link To list.

3. Enter the information for the type of object.

4. Click OK.

> **NOTE** By default, unfollowed hyperlinks in an Access session are blue and followed hyperlinks are maroon. You can change these colors by choosing Options from the Tools menu, clicking on the General tab, and then clicking Web Options. Use the two list boxes in the Web Options dialog box to set the colors.

Figure 5-3 shows the Insert Hyperlink dialog box for the label on the *frmGoHere* form in this chapter's sample database. The hyperlink simply transfers focus back to the switchboard form.

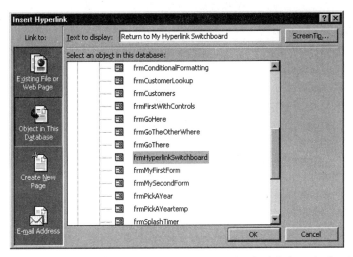

Figure 5-3. *The Insert Hyperlink dialog box for the label on the* frmGoHere *form.*

Navigating with Code

Another common way to implement switchboard navigation is with VBA code behind command button click events. This approach offers richer exposure to Access functionality than hyperlink-based navigation because you can mix navigation functions with other events, such as the closing of a form. (With a hyperlink, one form can open another, but returning to a switchboard leaves the child form open; VBA-based navigation lets an application programmatically close the child form when a user returns to the main form.) An event procedure also gives you greater control over multiple database objects. Hyperlink-based navigation merely transfers focus to another object, such as a form.

Figure 5-4 shows a pair of forms that use the VBA approach to navigation. This sample relies on button click events. When the user clicks one of the switchboard buttons, the code for the button's click event opens the target form and closes the main switchboard. Clicking the Return To Main button on the target form closes the form and opens the main switchboard form. (The sample uses command buttons, but you can use any other type of control that lets a user generate events.)

Figure 5-4. *These forms use code behind button click events to perform navigation.*

The following pair of event procedures shows the code for the click events of the two buttons in Figure 5-4. The first procedure switches control from the main switchboard form to the second form. It also closes the main form. The second procedure transfers control back to the main switchboard and then closes the second form. I used the Command Button wizard to create a first draft of each procedure; I then added a line of code to each procedure to close the appropriate form.

```
Private Sub cmdGoHere_Click()
On Error GoTo Err_cmdGoHere_Click

Dim stDocName As String

    stDocName = "frmButtonGoHere"
    DoCmd.OpenForm stDocName
    DoCmd.Close acForm, "frmButtonSwitchboard"

Exit_cmdGoHere_Click:
    Exit Sub
```

```
Err_cmdGoHere_Click:
    MsgBox Err.Description
    Resume Exit_cmdGoHere_Click

End Sub


Private Sub cmdReturnToMain_Click()
On Error GoTo Err_cmdReturnToMain_Click

Dim stDocName As String
Dim stLinkCriteria As String

stDocName = "frmButtonSwitchboard"
DoCmd.OpenForm stDocName
stDocName = "frmButtonGoHere"
DoCmd.Close acForm, stDocName, acSaveNo

Exit_cmdReturnToMain_Click:
    Exit Sub

Err_cmdReturnToMain_Click:
    MsgBox Err.Description
    Resume Exit_cmdReturnToMain_Click

End Sub
```

LINKING FORMS TO DATA

Access has always let you bind forms to data simply and easily. This is one major reason why it is a rapid application development environment.

Using the AutoForm Wizard

To bind a form to data, you can use the AutoForm wizard. Select a table or query in the database window and click the New Object: AutoForm button on the Database toolbar. The wizard opens a new form that binds directly to the selected data source. Figure 5-5 on the following page shows a sample form based on the *Order Details* table in this chapter's sample database. You could use this form for browsing, editing, adding, and deleting records in the *Order Details* table.

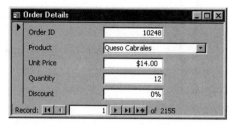

Figure 5-5. *A form created by the AutoForm wizard.*

Because the data source for the form's *Product* field is a lookup field in the underlying *Order Details* table, the *Product* field automatically appears as a combo box that displays product names instead of the underlying *ProductID* values. All of this functionality was provided automatically by the wizard.

Conditional Formatting

Access 2000 lets you conditionally format the data displayed by a text box or combo box control without programming. You can selectively apply formatting to form controls for both bound and calculated fields.

Figure 5-6 shows three instances of the same form. I used conditional formatting to control the appearance of the *Discount* and *Extended Price* fields. The *Discount* field in the top form is disabled. The middle form highlights the value in the *Extended Price* field using bold and italic formatting. The bottom form enables the *Discount* field and highlights the value in the *Extended Price* field.

The *Extended Price* field is calculated; it does not derive its value directly from an underlying table. An expression in the text box's *Control Source* property setting ([UnitPrice]*[Quantity]*(1-[Discount])) computes the value when the user moves to a new record or updates the *UnitPrice*, *Quantity*, or *Discount* fields of the current record. (The terms in brackets reference controls, not field names for the underlying data source.)

> NOTE Beginners sometimes give fields and controls the same name. This practice can be confusing and lead to errors. (The AutoForm wizard is also guilty of this practice.) Consider adding prefixes to control names to distinguish them from their underlying field names. For example, a good name for a text box control that is bound to a field named *UnitPrice* is *txtUnitPrice*.

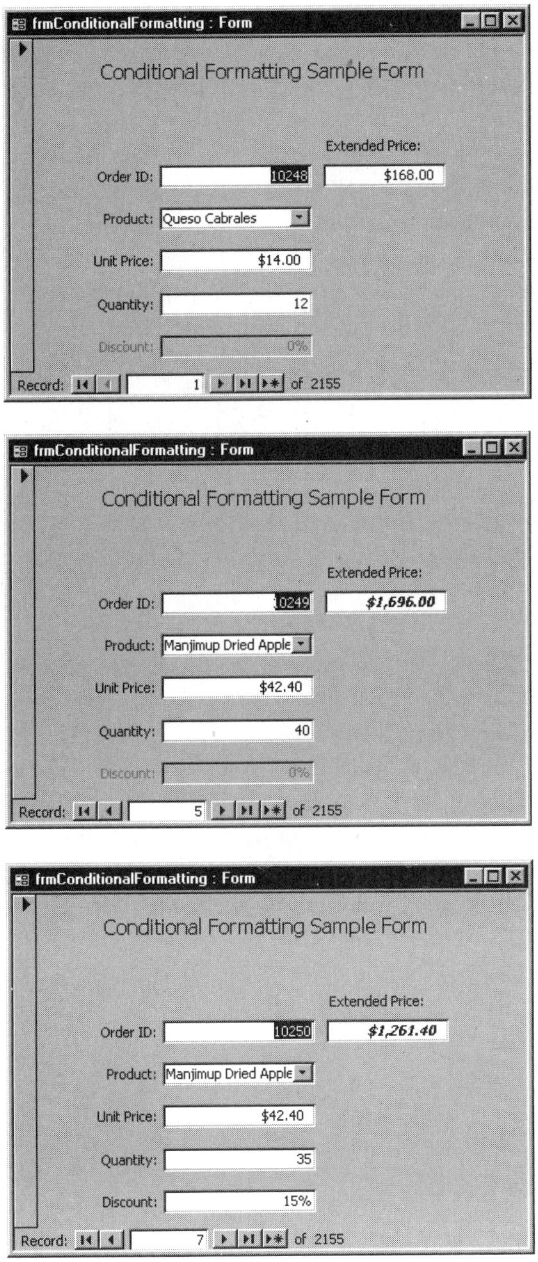

Figure 5-6. *Conditional formatting controls the appearance of the* Extended Price *and* Discount *fields on this form.*

To apply conditional formatting to a control, select the control and choose Conditional Formatting from the Format menu to open the Conditional Formatting dialog box, shown in Figure 5-7. Every control with conditional formatting has at least two formats—a default format and a special format when a specified condition is true. You can format based on a control's field value, its expression value, or when it gets the focus. When you work with the field value for a control, you can select from a list of comparison operators, such as equal to (=), greater than (>), and less than (<). The condition for the *Discount* field in Figure 5-7 is *Field value is equal to 0*. The formatting option for this condition disables the control when the discount is 0.

Figure 5-7. *The Conditional Formatting dialog box.*

If you apply conditional formatting to a calculated field, such as *Extended Price*, you must write an expression using standard VBA operators. The condition for the *Extended Price* field is *Expression is text4.value>500*. (*Text4* is the control that displays the calculated value.) When the field is greater than 500, bold and italic formatting highlight the text box contents.

You can easily apply another condition and special format to a control by clicking the Add button in the Conditional Formatting dialog box and specifying the new condition and its formatting information.

Subforms

A *subform*, one of the most popular ways of displaying data in Access, is a form embedded within a main form. The main form holds general information about an object (such as an order or a patient name). One or more hierarchically related details (such as order line items or patient visits) appear in one or more subforms on the main form. At least one common field must tie the record source of the main form and each subform together. The common field enables the subform to show only records that match the current record in the main form. When the user moves to a new record on the main form, the subform displays a new set of records that tie uniquely to the new record in the main form.

Figure 5-8 shows a main form, *MyOrders*, which contains an embedded *MyOrderDetails* subform. The *MyOrders* form links the *MyOrders* query and the

MyOrderDetails query based on a shared *OrderID* field. (These queries and their underlying tables are from the Northwind database.) When I created the main form and the subform, I did not create a relationship between the two queries in the Relationships window or by using subdatasheets. (See Chapter 4 for a discussion of subdatasheets.)

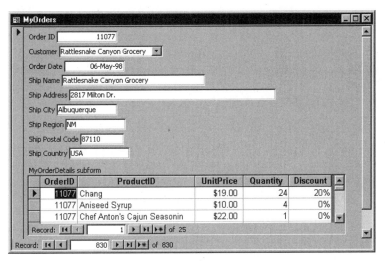

Figure 5-8. *A form that contains a subform.*

To create a subform, open the main form in Design view, make sure that the Control Wizards button on the Toolbox is depressed, and then drag a table, query, or form from the Database window and drop it on the main form. The subform appears as a control on the main form. To synchronize the main form and the subform, you must designate at least one common field. Select the subform container and set its *Link Child* and *Link Master* properties to the common field. For the *MyOrders* and *MyOrderDetails* queries, the common field is *OrderID*.

A main form can have multiple subforms. The only requirement is that the record source for each subform share at least one common field with the record source for the main form. For example, if the main form in Figure 5-8 contained an *EmployeeID* field, the form could have a second subform based on the *Employees* table.

If you define relationships between tables and queries in the Relationships window or by using the properties of a subdatasheet, you can create a main form with an embedded subform as easily as you create a simple bound form. In the Database window, select the table or query on which the main form will be based, and then click the New Object: AutoForm button. The AutoForm wizard will build a main form with an embedded subform. The subform uses the information in the Relationships windows or the subdatasheet. You can manually drag other tables, queries, or forms to the main form in Design view to create additional subforms.

LOOKING UP AND DISPLAYING DATA

A lookup form is similar to a parameter query with a custom front end; the form simply collects input that drives a query. When you use forms and VBA, you can be flexible in how you gather input as well as in the type of information that you can return to users.

Creating a Lookup Form

The easiest way to implement a form that looks up information is to have the user type the lookup information in a text box and click a button to start the search. The text box should be unbound because it doesn't enter information into the database; it simply gathers search information from the user. A query uses the value specified in the text box to find the matching information.

Figure 5-9 shows a form that opens the *qprHistoryfromTextBox* query when the user types a customer ID in the text box and clicks Look It Up. The query finds the total quantity ordered of each product bought by that customer.

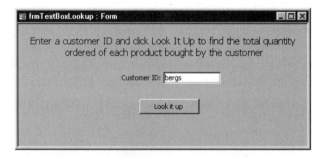

Figure 5-9. *A form that performs a simple lookup operation.*

Figure 5-10 shows the *qprHistoryfromTextBox* query in Design view. Notice that it is a simple query that sums the *Quantity* field of the *Order Details* table for each product the customer ordered. (The WHERE clause in the last column limits the query to rows in which the *CustomerID* field matches the value in the form's text box.)

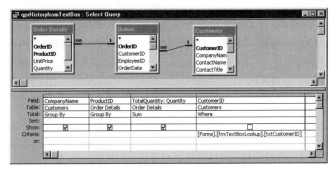

Figure 5-10. *The* qprHistoryfromTextBox *query in Design view.*

The final element is a short VBA event procedure that fires when the user clicks Look It Up. The procedure has a single line that opens the query *qprHistoryfromTextBox*:

```
Private Sub cmdLookup_Click()
    DoCmd.OpenQuery "qprHistoryfromTextBox"
End Sub
```

Using a combo box for user input

The form shown in Figure 5-11 has a better design than the one in Figure 5-9. Instead of forcing the user to guess the customer ID, it lets the user select the customer from a combo box. A procedure for the combo box's *After Update* event opens the *qprHistoryfromComboBox* query that uses the customer selected by the user, so the command button is unnecessary.

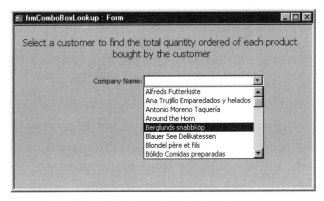

Figure 5-11. *A better design for a lookup form.*

NOTE Combo box lookup forms can become prohibitively slow as the number of lookup items becomes large. In this situation, you have at least two choices. First, you can revert to the text box lookup form described above. Second, you can create a tiered system in which users make choices that restrict the range of items that a combo box makes available.

To give any combo box control over this functionality, follow these steps:

1. Set the control's *Row Source Type* property to *Table/Query* (the default).

2. Set the control's *Row Source* property to a SQL string that returns the fields you want. (The SQL string for the sample is SELECT CUSTOMERID, COMPANYNAME FROM CUSTOMERS.)

3. Set the control's *Column Count* property to *2*.

4. Specify the column widths, separated by a semicolon. (The first value should always be *0*.)

If you prefer, the Combo Box wizard can create the control for you. Simply ensure that the Control Wizards button on the Toolbox is depressed, and then add the combo box to the form.

Displaying results in a message box

The preceding samples suffer from two weaknesses. First, they pass values to and expose values from queries. This means that users can inadvertently damage the query's design. Second, a user can also modify the data underlying a query.

The sample lookup form at the top of Figure 5-12 remedies both of these deficiencies by using VBA and ActiveX Data Objects (ADO). The input form has the same look and feel as the form in Figure 5-11. While the return sets of the queries opened by both forms are identical, they are displayed in different ways. The sample in Figure 5-12 displays its return set in message boxes rather than in a query window in Datasheet view. (The sample uses as many message boxes as necessary to display its return set.) This protects the underlying data from inadvertent damage by a user.

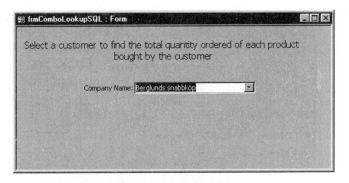

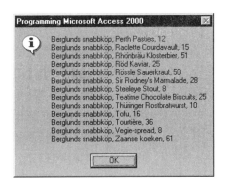

Figure 5-12. *The form at the top displays its result set in message boxes so that users can view the result set but not alter its underlying data.*

The following procedure fires on the *After Update* event of the combo box in Figure 5-12. It executes a command based on a query to develop a return set. It then assigns the return set from the command to a recordset and displays the recordset using one or more message boxes.

```
Private Sub cboLookup_AfterUpdate()
Dim ctl1 As Control
Dim cmd1 As Command
Dim rst1 As Recordset, str1 As String

'Set reference to ComboBox control.
Set ctl1 = Me.Controls("cboLookup")

'Create and define command.
'Use ComboBox value in SQL string for command.
    Set cmd1 = New ADODB.Command
    With cmd1
        .ActiveConnection = CurrentProject.Connection
        .CommandText = "Select Customers.CompanyName, " & _
            "Products.ProductName, " & _
            "Sum([Order Details].Quantity) As TotalQuantity " & _
            "From Products Inner Join ((Customers Inner Join Orders " & _
            "ON Customers.CustomerID = Orders.CustomerID) " & _
            "Inner Join [Order Details] ON " & _
            "Orders.OrderID = [Order Details].OrderID) " & _
            "ON Products.ProductID = [Order Details].ProductID " & _
            "Where Customers.CustomerID = '" & ctl1.Value & "'" & _
            "GROUP BY Customers.CompanyName, Products.ProductName;"
        .CommandType = adCmdText
        .Execute
    End With

'Create recordset based on return set from SQL string.
    Set rst1 = New ADODB.Recordset
    rst1.Open cmd1, , adOpenKeyset, adLockOptimistic

'Loop through return set to display in message box(es)
'in blocks of 925 characters or less.
    Do Until rst1.EOF
        str1 = str1 & rst1.Fields(0) & ", " & _
            rst1.Fields(1) & ", " & rst1.Fields(2)
        str1 = str1 & vbCrLf
        If Len(str1) > 925 Then
            str1 = str1 & vbCrLf & "Click OK to see more " & _
                "in another message box"
```

```
        MsgBox str1, vbInformation, _
            "Programming Microsoft Access 2000"
            str1 = ""
        End If
        rst1.MoveNext
    Loop
    MsgBox str1, vbInformation, _
        "Programming Microsoft Access 2000"

End Sub
```

I could not use the SQL code from a query window in Design view in this procedure because the SQL string for *Command* objects does not support lookup fields. Therefore, I added the *Products* table to the query design so that I could report each product's name in the return set instead of just a product ID from the *Order Details* table. Adding this extra table further complicated the join logic for the query. (See Chapter 4 for an introduction to the SQL statement syntax.)

A *Do* loop steps through the recordset sequentially and writes its contents to a string. At the end of each record, it inserts a carriage return and a linefeed. If the string length exceeds 925 characters, the procedure inserts a blank line and an instruction to view the continuation of the sales history for the customer in the next message block. A message box can hold just over 1000 characters. (The *testmsgbox* procedure in this chapter's sample database helps you determine the maximum number of characters that a message box can hold; each of the top 19 lines has two nonprinting characters.) Limiting additions to the current message box to 925 characters allows the message box to be filled without truncating any characters.

Dynamically Displaying Information

You can display data, such as a record, in a form, and you can even design a form so that users can view the record but not edit it. Figure 5-13 on the following page shows a pair of forms that work together to let the user view a customer's record. The user selects a customer in the *frmCustomerLookup* form and clicks Show Customer In Form to open the *Customers* form, which displays the customer's record. (The *Allow Edits*, *Allow Deletions*, and *Allow Additions* properties of the *Customers* form are set to *No*, which prevents the user from changing the data.) The user can then click the Return To Customer Lookup Form button to transfer control back to the initial lookup form. The user can also launch another lookup or exit the application from this form.

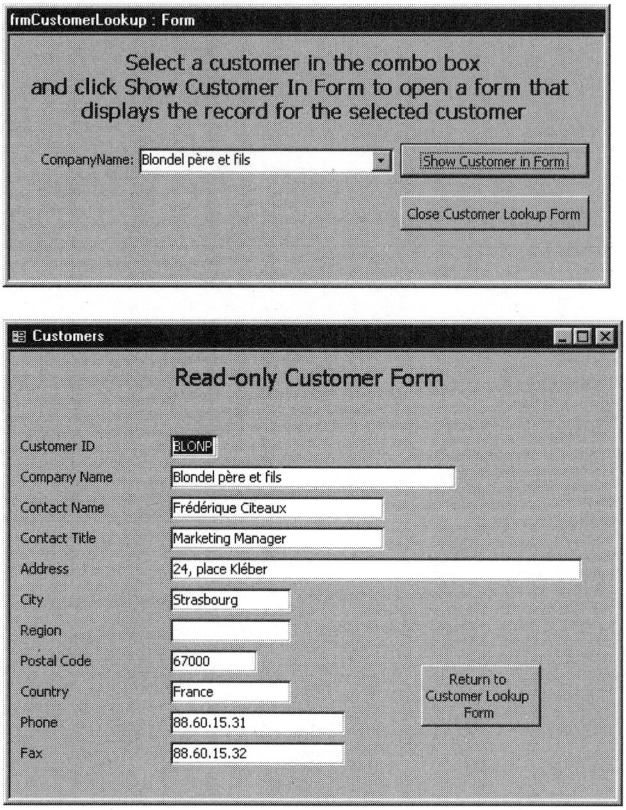

Figure 5-13. *These forms let the user select and view a customer's record.*

The following elegant and simple event procedure is the code behind the Show Customer In Form button.

```
Private Sub cmdShowCustomer_Click()
On Error GoTo ShowCustomerTrap
Dim strValue As String, strMsg As String

    strValue = Me.Combo2.Value
    DoCmd.OpenForm "frmCustomers", acNormal, , _
        "CustomerID = '" & strValue & "'"

ShowCustomerTrapExit:
    Exit Sub

ShowCustomerTrap:
    If Err.Number = 94 Then
        MsgBox "Select a customer in the combo box " & _
            "before attempting to open the Customer form.", _
            vbExclamation, "Programming Microsoft Access 2000"
```

```
        Else
            strMsg = "Error number: " & Err.Number & "caused " & _
                "failure. Its description is:" & vbCrLf & _
                Err.Description
            MsgBox strMsg, vbExclamation, _
                "Programming Microsoft Access 2000"
        End If
        Resume ShowCustomerTrapExit

End Sub
```

Charting a Subset of Data

The Microsoft Graph 2000 *Chart* object makes it easy to create professional looking charts. The object, which sits in an unbound object control on a form, can be bound to Access tables and queries, and you can choose from a wide selection of graph types and formatting options. (Double-click the object on a form in Design view to expose the custom menu for the object. When you finish using the *Chart* object menu, click on the form outside the object to restore the normal Access form Design menu.)

Creating a chart using the Chart wizard

You can add a *Chart* object manually, but using the Chart wizard is easier. Simply follow these steps:

1. Click the *Forms* object in the Database window and then click New.
2. Select Chart Wizard and the table or query on which your chart will be based, and then click OK.
3. Select the fields that will be on your chart datasheet and then click Next.
4. Select the chart type and click Next.
5. Drag and drop the desired field buttons to the chart and click Next.
6. Select Modify The Design Of The Form Or The Chart and click Finish.

You can add aggregation and formatting functions by modifying the SQL string in the *Row Source* property for the unbound object control containing the *Chart* object. (The wizard creates this statement for you.)

Using code to display the chart

Figure 5-14 on the following page shows two forms that let the user chart sales for a selected month. The top form lets the user select any year in the *Orders* table. The combo box's *After Update* event opens the bottom form, which uses the Microsoft Graph 2000 *Chart* object to display total sales quantity by month for the specified year.

In Figure 5-14, the chart is based on a query that retrieves all orders from the specified year. The query translates each order date to the first of its month.

(The underlying data remains unchanged.) This makes it simple to aggregate sales quantity by month, which in turn makes it easy to chart sales quantity by month. (The Chart wizard automatically sums sales quantity by month for a record source such as this.)

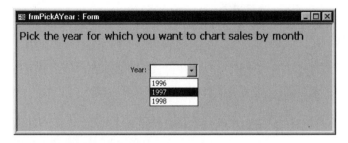

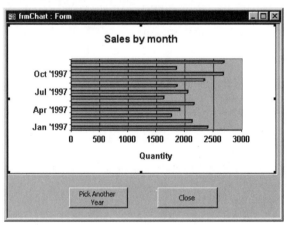

Figure 5-14. *These forms let the user see monthly order data for a selected year.*

The following three event procedures control the interaction between the two forms. The *cboPickAYear_AfterUpdate* procedure loads the charting form and minimizes the form in which the user selects a year. (You must minimize instead of close this form because the query for the chart determines what year the user selected using the combo box on the first form.)

```
Private Sub cboPickAYear_AfterUpdate()
    DoCmd.Minimize
    DoCmd.OpenForm "frmChart"

End Sub



Private Sub cmdClose_Click()
    DoCmd.Close acForm, "frmPickAYear"
    DoCmd.Close

End Sub
```

```
Private Sub cmdPickAYear_Click()
    DoCmd.OpenForm "frmPickAYear"
    DoCmd.Close acForm, "frmChart"

End Sub
```

MANIPULATING FORMS WITH VBA

This section describes some techniques for automating the use of forms. In particular, it illustrates how to enumerate forms and controls, techniques for programmatically hiding and showing forms, and methods for listing the form in another project.

Enumerating Forms and Controls

The *AllForms* collection, which belongs to the *CurrentProject* object, contains an item for each form in a project. An application can enumerate the *AccessObject* objects in the *AllForms* collection to find all the forms in a project. The *AccessObject* object's *Name* and *IsLoaded* properties are particularly convenient: The *Name* property represents the name of each form in a project, and the *IsLoaded* property indicates whether the form is open.

The following procedure uses the *Count* property of the *AllForms* collection to determine how many forms are in the current project. Then it prints the name and loaded status of each form in the project. (The *AllForms* collection is indexed beginning with *0*; therefore, the *For* loop runs from *0* to one less than the total number of forms in the project.)

```
Sub ListAllForms()
Dim int1 As Integer

'Print the number of forms in the project.
    Debug.Print CurrentProject.AllForms.Count
    Debug.Print

'Enumerate each form in the project.
    For int1 = 0 To CurrentProject.AllForms.Count - 1
        Debug.Print CurrentProject.AllForms.Item(int1).Name
        Debug.Print CurrentProject.AllForms.Item(int1).IsLoaded
        Debug.Print
    Next int1

End Sub
```

The *Forms* collection contains the set of all open forms in a project, and the *Controls* collection contains the set of controls on a form. Your applications can use these collections to find a specific form and an individual control on that form.

The following procedure enumerates all open forms in a project. For each open form, it lists the form's controls by name and type. The *Control* object's *ControlType* property indicates the type of control. You can use the *TypeOf* keyword in a similar way.

```
Sub ListControlsOnOpenForms()
Dim frm1 As Form, ctl1 As Control

'Enumerate all open forms.
    For Each frm1 In Forms
        Debug.Print frm1.Name

'Enumerate each control on a specific open form.
        For Each ctl1 In frm1.Controls
            Debug.Print "     " & ctl1.Name & _
                ", " & _
                IIf(ctl1.ControlType = 100, "label", "not label")
        Next ctl1
    Next frm1

End Sub
```

Notice that the procedure decodes the value of the *ControlType* property. When this value is *100*, the control is a label. In a practical decoding exercise, you are more likely to use a *Select Case* statement instead of the *Immediate If* function in the preceding sample. The *Immediate If* function, however, works adequately for decoding a single value. (You can use the Object Browser to find the *ControlType* values.)

Hiding and Showing Forms

You can use VBA and the *AllForms* collection along with some other objects to make forms invisible in the Database window. If you also make the form invisible in your application, the user might think that you removed the form. Hidden forms can still expose values for use by the other objects in an application.

The following pair of procedures hide and unhide an Access form:

```
Sub HideAForm(frmName As String)

'Close form if it is open so that it can be hidden.
    If CurrentProject.AllForms(frmName).IsLoaded = True Then
        DoCmd.Close acForm, frmName
    End If

'Set form's Hidden property and do not show hidden
'objects in Database window.
```

```
        Application.SetHiddenAttribute acForm, frmName, True
        Application.SetOption "Show Hidden Objects", False

End Sub


Sub UnhideAForm(frmName As String)

'If form is hidden, set form's hidden property to False
'and open form.
    If Application.GetHiddenAttribute(acForm, frmName) = True Then
        Application.SetHiddenAttribute acForm, frmName, False
        DoCmd.OpenForm frmName
    End If

End Sub
```

The *SetHiddenAtrribute* method sets or clears the Hidden attribute from the Database window for database objects, such as forms, reports, and queries. This method takes two arguments, an *AccessObject* object and a Boolean argument that indicates whether the object is to be hidden. Calling this method with an object and the value *True* is the same as setting the object's *Hidden* property in the Database window.

By itself, *SetHiddenAtrribute* just grays the object; users can still select and use it. To make hidden objects invisible to the user, choose Options from the Tools menu, click Hidden Objects, and then click OK.

Before invoking *SetHiddenAttribute*, you should check the *AccessObject* object's *IsLoaded* property. If the object is loaded, you should close it before attempting to invoke *SetHiddenAttribute*; calling the method with an open object generates an error.

Enumerating Forms in Another Project

VBA does not restrict you to working with database objects in the current project. For example, you can test for the existence of forms in another instance of an Access application. One essential step in this process is to compare the *Name* property of *AllForms* members to the name of the target form. There is also a new trick to learn: You open a new instance of an Access *Application* form with the target database in it, and then you use the current project of that instance as the source for your *AllForms* collection. This subtle refinement lets you process database objects in another database file.

The following two procedures implement this with VBA. *FormToLookFor* sets the database path to the other database file and gathers the name of the target form. The second procedure, *FormExistsInDB*, searches for a target form.

You call the second form from the first one.

```
Sub FormToLookFor()
Dim strDB As String
Dim strFormName As String

'Search for forms in the Northwind database.
    strDB = "C:\Program Files\Microsoft " & _
        "Office\Office\Samples\Northwind.mdb"
'Get the name of the form to search for from the user.
    strFormName = InputBox("Enter the name of the form to search for: ", _
        "Programming Microsoft Access 2000")

'Call FormExistsInDB to check whether the form exists.
    FormExistsInDB strDB, strFormName

End Sub


Sub FormExistsInDB(strDB As String, strFormName As String)
Dim appAccess As Access.Application, int1 As Integer

'Return reference to Microsoft Access Application.
    Set appAccess = New Access.Application

'Open a database in the other application.
    appAccess.OpenCurrentDatabase strDB

'Check whether the form exists.
    For int1 = 0 To (appAccess.CurrentProject.AllForms.Count - 1)
        If (appAccess.CurrentProject.AllForms.Item(int1).Name = _
            strFormName) Then
            MsgBox "Form " & strFormName & " exists in the.", _
                & strDB & " database.", _
                vbInformation, "Programming Microsoft Access 2000"
            GoTo FormExistsExit
        End If
    Next int1

'Report that form does not exist.
    MsgBox "Form " & strFormName & " does not exist in the.", _
        & strDB & " database."

'Close other Access application.
FormExistsExit:
    appAccess.CloseCurrentDatabase
    Set appAccess = Nothing

End Sub
```

The first procedure sets *strDB* equal to a typical path for the Northwind database. If you have your copy of Northwind elsewhere, you should update this path. An *InputBox* function prompts the user to input the name of the form to search for, and then the first procedure calls the second procedure.

The second procedure sets and opens a reference for the new instance of the Access application, and then enters a loop that checks whether any of the forms in the new database match the target form name. The procedure reports whether it found the target form and frees its resources before returning.

USING FORM CLASSES

Any Access 2000 form with a module behind it is a form class; you can create new instances of the class with the *New* keyword just as you do with any generic Access class. One advantage of form classes is that they have all the standard form properties and methods as well as your custom additions.

Viewing Form Class Properties and Methods

You can view the properties and methods of form classes using the Object Browser. You select the Project's name in the Project/Library drop-down list box and select a form class name to see its properties and methods.

The Object Browser in Figure 5-15 displays a subset of the members in the *Form_frmButtonSwitchboard* class. Recall that this form navigates to any of three other forms via event procedures. The event procedures are class methods, such as *cmdGoHere_click*. The buttons, such as *cmdGoHere*, are class properties.

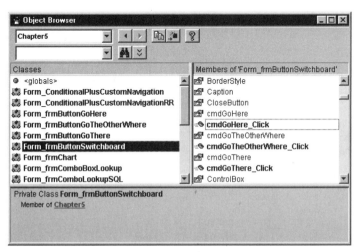

Figure 5-15. *Methods and properties of a form class.*

Manipulating Form Classes

The following procedure references class modules in Access 2000. It has several code segments that manipulate the basic form class in progressively more sophisticated ways. Working with form classes and their instances resembles working with a cookie cutter and cookies. The cutter is the form class, and the cookies are instances of it. Changes to a cookie do not impact the cutter. On the other hand, changes to the cutter impact all cookies after the change.

```
Sub testformclass()
Dim frm1 As Form

'First code segment
'Saves reference to instance of a form class in frm1.
'Can reference with either class or reference name.
    Set frm1 = Form_frmCustomers
    frm1.Caption = "foo"
    MsgBox Form_frmCustomers.Caption
    MsgBox frm1.Caption
    DoCmd.Close acForm, frm1.Name

'Second code segment
'Programmatically alters and opens default form instance.
'Does not set reference to instance.
'Clears instance by setting Visible to False.
    Form_frmCustomers.Caption = "foo"
    Form_frmCustomers.Visible = True
    MsgBox Form_frmCustomers.Caption
    If MsgBox("Do you want to close form instance?", vbYesNo, _
        "Programming Microsoft Access 2000") = vbYes Then
        Form_frmCustomers.Visible = False
    End If

'Third code segment
'Open form in Design view to modify class properties.
'Open in Form view to see impact of Design view change.
    DoCmd.OpenForm "frmCustomers", acDesign
    Forms("frmCustomers").Caption = "foo"
    MsgBox Form_frmCustomers.Caption
    DoCmd.Close acForm, "frmCustomers", acSaveYes
    Form_frmCustomers.Visible = True
    MsgBox Form_frmCustomers.Caption

'Fourth code segment
'Restore class caption property.
    DoCmd.OpenForm "frmCustomers", acDesign
    Set frm1 = Form_frmCustomers
    frm1.Caption = "Customers"
    DoCmd.Close acForm, frm1.Name, acSaveYes
```

```
    Form_frmCustomers.Visible = True
    MsgBox Form_frmCustomers.Caption

End Sub
```

The first code segment assigns a form class to a reference. It creates an instance of the *Form_frmCustomers* class and assigns it to *frm1*. You can manipulate the instance using either the class or the reference name; the identical results from the two message boxes confirm this. Changing the instance of a form class does not alter the class itself.

You do not need references to designate or modify the properties of form class instances. The second segment accomplishes the same task as the initial one without creating a pointer to the form class. This segment also includes a prompt to ask the user whether he or she wants to close the form instance. (An instance survives for the life of the procedure that creates it unless your code terminates it sooner.)

The third code segment opens a form in Design view and manipulates its properties. Unlike when you programmatically modify the properties of a form in Form view, changes to properties in Design view are persistent after you save the form. The last two lines of the third segment open an instance of the form class in Form view. For the first time in the procedure, the form opens with the caption "foo".

The fourth code segment restores the form class's caption to its original value of "Customers".

References to Form Class Instances

The form class sample below drills down further into form classes. You can easily test the behavior of this procedure by using the *frmFirstWithControls* form, which includes a button that launches the *testformclass2* procedure. *testformclass2* processes multiple instances of a form class.

```
Sub testformclass2()
On Error GoTo testclass2Trap
Dim frm1 As Form
Dim frm2 As New Form_frmCustomers
Dim int1 As Integer

'Show caption of frm2 before editing the property.
    MsgBox "Frm2 default caption is " & frm2.Caption, _
        vbInformation, "Programming Microsoft Access 2000"

'Set frm1 as a reference to frmCustomers class.
    Set frm1 = Form_frmCustomers
    frm1.Caption = "Caption from frm1 instance"
```

(continued)

```
'Reset caption for frm2 instance.
    frm2.Caption = "Caption from frm2 instance"

'Show the captions of the class instances referenced by
'frm1 and frm2.
    frm1.SetFocus
    frm2.SetFocus
    MsgBox frm1.Caption, vbInformation, _
        "Programming Microsoft Access 2000"
    MsgBox frm2.Caption, vbInformation, _
        "Programming Microsoft Access 2000"

'Close form instances by their references.
    frm1.SetFocus
    DoCmd.Close
    frm2.SetFocus
    DoCmd.Close

testclass2Exit:
    Exit Sub

testclass2Trap:
    If Err.Number = 2467 Then
'Trap attempt to print caption for closed form.
        MsgBox "Cannot print caption of closed form", _
            vbInformation, "Programming Microsoft Access 2000"
        Resume Next
    Else
        Debug.Print Err.Number, Err.Description
        Resume testclass2Exit
    End If

End Sub
```

It is convenient to use references to form class instances when you deal with more than one instance. The sample above uses the references *frm1* and *frm2*. After declaring *frm1* as a general form class, the code assigns a reference to an instance of the *Form_frmCustomers* class to it. The *frm2* declaration statement points it at an instance of the same form class. Therefore, *frm1* and *frm2* are two separate instances of the identical form class.

The second *Dim* statement creates an instance based on a form class using the *New* keyword. (You must refer to a form class with the *Form_* prefix when using the *New* keyword to create an instance.) After creating the references, you can invoke standard form properties and methods for the objects to which the variables refer. For example, the procedure resets the *Caption* property of *frm2* and then assigns the focus first to *frm1* and then to *frm2*. This opens both forms with one behind the other on the Access screen.

You can close a form instance by giving it the focus and then invoking the *DoCmd* object's *Close* method.

Chapter 6

Creating Reports

Your understanding of forms from the previous chapter will serve you well as you consider how to use reports in your applications. Although reports do not support interactive controls, you can populate reports with controls that display data, such as text boxes and check boxes. Reports can also contain bound and unbound graphic images and ActiveX controls for special displays, such as charts. The report charting capability in Microsoft Access 2000 behaves much like the one for forms.

This chapter explores some pragmatic design and display issues for reports. It also covers programming for dynamic content in a report as well as the enumeration and manipulation of reports and their controls. The chapter presents a case study of a Microsoft FrontPage guestbook that addresses the typical small business and departmental needs that Access often serves. Two more sections demonstrate report design issues. Another short section explores presenting Access reports via its snapshot file format. This format makes it easy to share Access reports through email and over the web even on workstations that do not have Access installed. The chapter closes with three sections that demonstrate specific programmatic issues. The first two deal with dynamic content on a report. The final section explores the programmatic manipulation of reports and their controls. This last section illustrates techniques for processing different types of *AccessObject* objects, such as members of the *AllReports* and *AllForms* collections.

HOW TO CREATE A REPORT

You can manually create a report in three ways:

■ Using the AutoReport wizard. This one-click technique is attractive because of its simplicity.

■ Using other wizards. The Report wizard saves you time, and the Label and Chart wizards help you tackle specialized design issues.

■ Using Design view. Creating a report manually in Design view offers maximum layout, formatting, sorting, and grouping flexibility.

Using the AutoReport Wizard

The AutoReport wizard available from the Database window toolbar is a columnar report. Text and numeric fields appear in text boxes, Yes/No data types appear in check boxes, and OLE Object data types (such as .bmp images) appear in bound object frames. The records display one after the other in a streaming format from the first to the last record.

You can also select a tabular style report in the New Report dialog box. Advanced and intermediate developers will find this a fast, convenient way to generate a subreport.

Using Other Wizards

Access offers a general Report wizard as well as specialized wizards for labels and charts. You should use wizards liberally for reports and other kinds of database objects. They can speed up your development efforts and lead to standardization that makes maintenance easier.

The Report wizard lets you specify your report much like the Simple Query wizard lets you design a query. (See Chapter 4.) It saves you from having to design a query as a preliminary step for your reports. The wizard also simplifies setting sorting, grouping, and formatting options for your custom reports. The Label and Chart wizards perform specialized functions. The FrontPage guestbook case study later in this chapter illustrates output from the Label wizard. The Chart wizard for reports works like the one for forms. Figure 6-1 shows a chart report in Print Preview mode. (To refresh your understanding of the Microsoft Graph 2000 *Chart* object, see the discussion in Chapter 5 about picking a subset of data to chart.)

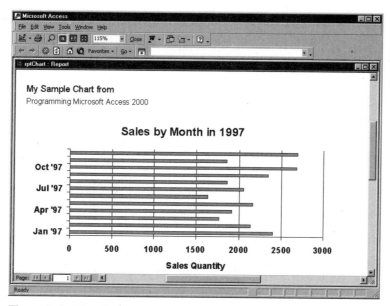

Figure 6-1. *This chart was prepared using the Chart wizard for reports.*

Creating a Report Manually in Design View

You can create a report manually by double-clicking the Create Report In Design View option in the Database window. (First select Reports from the *Objects* collection.) This opens a blank form whose base properties reflect the entry in the Report Template text box on the Forms/Reports page of the Options dialog box. (You open this dialog box with the Tools–Options command.) The default is Normal, which displays a plain white page with no colors or special fonts for labels. If you have a report with property settings that you want to use as a template for all other reports in an Access project, you can enter the name of that report in the Report Template text box. The settings of that report will be the default settings for all new reports. Existing reports will remain unchanged. You can use the template to determine the number of sections that initially show on a report as well as the default settings for report section properties and their controls.

NOTE   You use the Form Template entry for forms much like you use the Report Template entry for reports.

After opening a new report instance based on a template, you can populate it with controls to build your report. It is important to understand that

Access reports are banded. In the Normal template, for example, a Detail band appears between a pair of Page bands. Any contents in the top and bottom bands appear at the top and bottom of each report page. The Detail band repeats once for each record on a page. It derives successive values from the report's record source.

Another standard pair of bands that can surround a Detail section in a report are the Report Header and Report Footer bands. These bands appear just once at the beginning and end of each report. Use the View menu to turn on and off display of the Report and Page bands around the central Detail band.

You can resize any report section by dragging its boundaries. For example, to cause the Report Footer band not to occupy any space while you still have a Report Header section, drag the Report Footer band's lower bound so that it is flush with its top bound.

The report in Figure 6-1 contains a Page Header band and a Detail band. The Page Header section contains two headlines: *My Sample Chart from* and *Programming MS Access 2000*. The unbound object frame displays from the report's Detail band. Since the frame control is not bound to a record source, it occurs only once.

Report controls

Access reports typically contain a mix of text boxes and labels. The text boxes reflect the values of fields in the underlying record source, while the labels identify the names of the text boxes and other controls. Other controls that typically display field values in a report include check boxes and bound object frames. The frames are appropriate for holding graphic images in a table. You use image controls to hold unbound images that are not field values in a table.

A main report can also serve as a host for one or more subreports, which appear as controls on the main report. The Sales By Category report in the Northwind database (shown in Figure 6-2) contains a subreport that lists sales by product. The main report presents the same data graphically. The subreport appears as a table on the left. The chart uses the ActiveX Microsoft Graph 2000 *Chart* object in an unbound frame. The subreport and chart both appear in the CategoryName Header band, which causes the subreport and chart to select the products for the category name appearing in the band's header for each page. Any single report can have multiple nested group bands, such as regions within countries or product groups within company divisions.

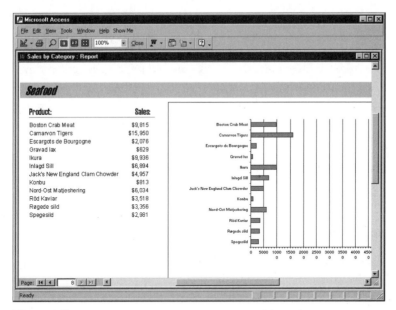

Figure 6-2. *A subreport and a chart on a page of the Sales By Category report. The products change within each category heading.*

Code behind reports

Custom applications usually require manual reports with formatting tailored to the specific content. While Access offers a wide array of programmatic options, you'll typically use only a small number of them:

- Automatically printing or previewing a report by invoking the *DoCmd OpenReport* method or hyperlinking to the report. (See the section titled "Switchboard Forms" in Chapter 5 for samples that you can adapt for reports.)

- Making a report dynamic. You can update one or more properties for a *Report* object. For example, you can change the record source property for a report and the caption for a label in the report.

- Enumerating the *AllReports* collection members to determine whether a report exists and is open.

- Creating multiple instances of reports. (Reports with modules are class modules.)

Intermediate and advanced developers often work with report events, which you can use to dynamically control the content and formatting of a report. Use custom *Open, Activate, Close,* and *Deactivate* form events instead of the *Initialize* event and the *Terminate* event for each new instance of the class module associated with a report. When you print or preview a report, the *Format* and *Print* events occur for successive sections of the report. The *Format* and *Print* events are useful for dynamically altering content and formatting. When you set the *Keep Together* property to *True*, this can cause the *Retreat* event to occur selectively. Report sections split bands into matching but distinct elements. For example, the Report Header section is the first section when it is present, and the Report Footer is the last section when you have a Report band.

CASE STUDY: A FRONTPAGE GUESTBOOK

Using FrontPage, you can easily create a guestbook that collects visitor information (such as name and contact information) in an HTML-formatted web page. This approach requires no knowledge of databases or open database connectivity (ODBC) connections. Site visitors see a professional-looking form in which they can enter contact information, and FrontPage users have a simple way to create and view the guestbook. This approach works well as long as the site does not attract a high volume of visitors.

If visitor volume swells, you can transfer the complete set of contact information to a database file. Even if a site switches to depositing the data directly into a database, you still have the problem of recovering the initial HTML-formatted information. This case study illustrates one approach to recovering legacy text data and demonstrates how to generate mailing labels and form letters with the converted information.

Importing Data

You can use the Text Import wizard to copy the raw guestbook file into an Access table. Figure 6-3 shows excerpts displaying two records from the raw HTML-formatted file (for Karl Doe1 and Boban Doe2). Notice the huge number of HTML tags. The internal FrontPage browser uses these tags to format the guestbook display, but the tags make it impossible to directly import the data into an Access table for the preparation of mailing labels. All the contact information appears in one long column. Some rows contain contact data, but other rows hold descriptive labels or serve general formatting purposes. Relational database processing conventions dictate a separate row for each guestbook registrant. This requires spreading the information that appears for one registrant in a single column across several columns.

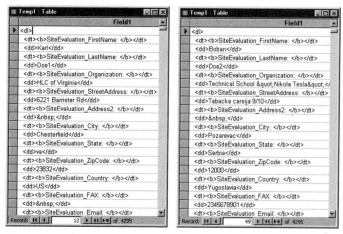

Figure 6-3. *Excerpts from a FrontPage guestbook file imported into an Access table.*

Whether or not you encounter this precise data conversion requirement, Access development typically requires the processing of a text stream. Large businesses often must convert legacy departmental data to a relational database format using a similar process. The rich array of string processing functions and Microsoft Visual Basic for Applications (VBA) in Access help you automate this kind of task.

Converting the Data Structure

The goal of this string processing effort is to transform the data in a table similar to the *Temp1* table in Figure 6-3 into a more traditional contact table layout, such as that of the table shown in Figure 6-4. The strategy defines two recordsets—one for the source table and one for the destination table. The procedure moves down the rows of the source table to extract the contact information and store the parsed data in variables. After parsing all the essential data for a contact, it adds the parsed data as a new row to the destination table. Because different contact fields have unique requirements, the parsing rules sometimes vary between fields. Rules can also vary because the raw data for a field represents unique problems not present for other fields.

The following excerpt from the procedure transforms the data from the format of the data in the table in Figure 6-3 to the format of the data in the table in Figure 6-4 (on the next page). The complete version is on the book's companion CD. This abbreviated version shows the conversion code for the first three fields represented by the variables *strFname*, *strLname*, and *strCname*. While the listing is lengthy and the complete version is even longer, converting data is a critical first step for Access database projects. If you don't successfully address this critical issue, your Access project might not start.

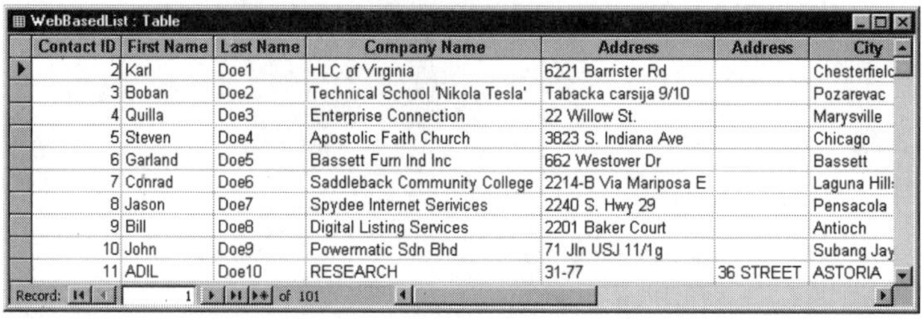

WebBasedList : Table

Contact ID	First Name	Last Name	Company Name	Address	Address	City
2	Karl	Doe1	HLC of Virginia	6221 Barrister Rd		Chesterfielc
3	Boban	Doe2	Technical School 'Nikola Tesla'	Tabacka carsija 9/10		Pozarevac
4	Quilla	Doe3	Enterprise Connection	22 Willow St.		Marysville
5	Steven	Doe4	Apostolic Faith Church	3823 S. Indiana Ave		Chicago
6	Garland	Doe5	Bassett Furn Ind Inc	662 Westover Dr		Bassett
7	Conrad	Doe6	Saddleback Community College	2214-B Via Mariposa E		Laguna Hill:
8	Jason	Doe7	Spydee Internet Serivices	2240 S. Hwy 29		Pensacola
9	Bill	Doe8	Digital Listing Services	2201 Baker Court		Antioch
10	John	Doe9	Powermatic Sdn Bhd	71 Jln USJ 11/1g		Subang Jay
11	ADIL	Doe10	RESEARCH	31-77	36 STREET	ASTORIA

Record: 1 of 101

Figure 6-4. *Converted contact data from a FrontPage guestbook file in HTML format. The conversion removes HTML tags and places each contact record on a separate row.*

```
Sub getfp()
Dim cnn1 As New ADODB.Connection
Dim rst1 As ADODB.Recordset
Dim strFname As String, strLname As String
Dim strCname As String, strSt1 As String
Dim strSt2 As String, strCity As String
Dim strSt As String, strPostal As String
Dim strCountry As String, blSkip As Boolean
Dim rst2 As New Recordset

'Open two recordsets and set references to them.
    cnn1 = CurrentProject.Connection
    Set rst1 = New Recordset
    rst1.ActiveConnection = CurrentProject.Connection
    rst1.CursorType = adOpenKeyset
    rst1.LockType = adLockOptimistic
'Raw contact information is in table temp1.
    rst1.Open "temp1"
    rst2.ActiveConnection = CurrentProject.Connection
    rst2.CursorType = adOpenKeyset
    rst2.LockType = adLockOptimistic
'The application stores parsed contact info in the WebBasedList table.
    rst2.Open "WebBasedList"

'Start a loop through the recordset of raw contact information.
    Do Until rst1.EOF
        blSkip = False

'Start a new contact record when you find
'a label named "SiteEvaluation_FirstName:".
        If InStr(1, rst1.Fields(1), _
            "SiteEvaluation_FirstName:") <> 0 Then
            rst1.MoveNext
```

```
            If rst1.Fields(1) <> "  <dd> </dd>" Then
'The length of the first name field is the number of
'characters between ">" and "<" delimiters.
            intFirst = InStr(1, rst1.Fields(1), ">") + 1
            intLen = InStr(6, rst1.Fields(1), "<") - intFirst
            strFname = Mid(rst1.Fields(1), intFirst, intLen)

'Move two records to process last name field.
            rst1.Move 2
        Else
'If the first name is blank, set a Boolean flag
'to skip the whole record.
            blSkip = True
        End If


'Process last name field.
        intFirst = InStr(1, rst1.Fields(1), ">") + 1
        intLen = InStr(6, rst1.Fields(1), "<") - intFirst
        strLname = Mid(rst1.Fields(1), intFirst, intLen)

'Process company name field.
        rst1.Move 2
        If rst1.Fields(1) <> "  <dd> </dd>" Then
            intFirst = InStr(1, rst1.Fields(1), ">") + 1
            intLen = InStr(6, rst1.Fields(1), "<") - intFirst
'If there is a leading blank in the company name field,
'see if you can find the name after the blank.
            If InStr(2, rst1.Fields(1), " ") <> 0 Then
                intLen = InStr(6, rst1.Fields(1), " ") _
                    - intFirst
            End If
'The parsing rule for the company name field converts with the new
'VBA Replace function html's &quot; into a single apostrophy.
            strCname = Replace(Mid(rst1.Fields(1), _
                intFirst, intLen), "&quot;", "'")
        Else
'Set company name to zero-length string if there is no
'entry for the field.
            strCname = ""
        End If
.
.
.
'If Boolean skip flag is False, copy converted contact information
'to rst2, which is reference for WebBasedList table.
        If blSkip = False Then
```

(continued)

```
            With rst2
                .AddNew
                    .Fields("FirstName") = strFname
                    .Fields("LastName") = strLname
                    .Fields("CompanyName") = strCname
                    .Fields("Address1") = strSt1
                    .Fields("Address2") = strSt2
                    .Fields("City") = strCity
                    .Fields("StateOrProvince") = strSt
                    .Fields("PostalCode") = strPostal
                    .Fields("Country") = strCountry
                .Update
            End With
        End If
    End If

'Move to next record in temp1 table and start search
'for a record including label for first name.
        rst1.MoveNext
    Loop
End Sub
```

Each of the three converted fields relies on slightly different parsing logic. There is more consistency in the remaining fields. Nevertheless, several significant distinctions in parsing rules between alternative fields remain. You can read the comments and study the code to gain insights about VBA functions useful for string processing. After conversion, the code checks to make sure that any field conversion did not set the skip flag to *True*. A *False* value for the skip flag enables the procedure to add a new record to the relational contact table in the format shown in Figure 6-4. The procedure then moves on to a new record in the source table (the copy of the FrontPage guestbook). When the original source table returns its end of file (EOF) as *True*, the outer *Do* loop ends and the procedure halts.

Creating Mailing Labels

Figure 6-5 shows the Design view of a mailing label report and an excerpt from the Preview display of the mailing labels. These draw on the contact information shown in Figure 6-4.

Access ships with a graphical mailing label wizard that can accommodate multiple label sizes for laser and tractor-feed printers from many manufacturers, including Avery, EXPE, Herma, and Zweckform. The wizard also lets you define new form sizes. It removes the need to write string-processing expressions for the construction of labels. The top window in Figure 6-5 shows the label fields expanded longer than they would otherwise appear so you can see the complete expressions within them. The wizard automatically sizes the text boxes containing its string expressions so that the labels fit on the form.

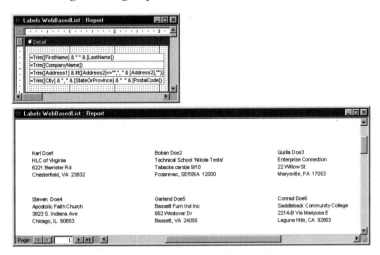

Figure 6-5. *The top window shows a mailing label report in Design view. The bottom window shows an excerpt of the labels in Preview mode.*

Creating a Form Letter

Another typical use for a table of contacts is for use in a form letter. Using a mix of controls, string constants and variables, and custom VBA functions, you can create a form letter such as the one depicted in Figure 6-6 on the following page, which features several noteworthy Access report features:

- A logo heads the letter.

- The return address information appears in a different font than the body of the letter.

- The letter's date spells the month's name.

- The outgoing address and salutation change for each record.

- The letter's final paragraph also changes for each record.

- The letter's closing appears with a signature.

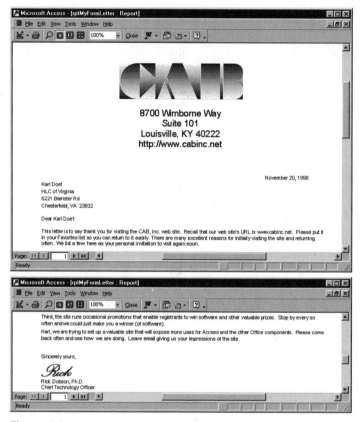

Figure 6-6. *Excerpts from a form letter.*

While it was never a programmatic challenge to convert a month number to a month name (such as converting 1 to January), Microsoft has simplified this task further with Access 2000 and VBA 6. The text box showing the date reveals the innovation and one way to use it. It contains the following string expression:

```
=ThisMonthName() & " " & Day(Date()) &  ", " & Year(Date())
```

The expression contains a pair of nested built-in functions for the day and the year, but a custom function (*ThisMonthName*) returns the month's name. Below is a custom VBA 6 function, *MonthName*, that convert's a month's number to its matching name. This function relieves you from having to code a *Select Case* statement in a function procedure or invoke a *Choose* function to make a month name appear in a report.

```
Public Function ThisMonthName()
    ThisMonthName = MonthName(Month(Date))
End Function
```

You might wonder why you couldn't apply the *MonthName* function directly to the text box within the report. Doing so would generate an error because *MonthName* is not an Access function. You have to call it in a procedure and then return the result to an Access object such as a text box on a form.

Figure 6-7 presents the Design view of the form letter report showing a mix of label and text box controls. If the body of the letter includes no customization for each record, a simple label can display all the text. However, since the last paragraph starts with the contact's first name, the report needs a way to recover the *FirstName* field value. A string expression inside a text box is an easy way to accomplish this. The bottom portion mixes the field value with the string constant. You can tell that you have to experiment with the placement of the text box relative to the preceding label control. To have the text flow nicely in Preview mode, you must overlap the controls in Design view. Proper alignment can require some trial and error.

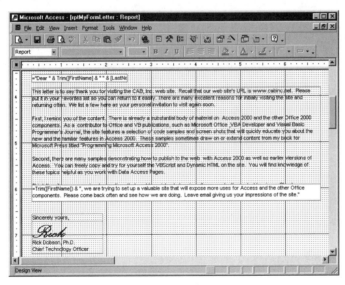

Figure 6-7. *The bottom portion of the letter in Figure 6-6 in Design view.*

Note the use of a script font with a label control to simulate a signature. This is a viable option when you don't need an actual signature—for example, for large mailings such as form letters.

SORTING, GROUPING, AND CALCULATING

One of the major benefits of Design view is that it facilitates grouping and sorting records for display in a report. Two factors underlie this capability: the report bands and the Sorting And Grouping dialog box. The grouping capability simplifies computation of subtotals by group, and it also calculates grand totals.

Figure 6-8 presents a simple report that demonstrates basic sorting, grouping, and calculating functionality for a report. This two-page report shows the report title at the top of the first page only. The label control for the report's title is thus in the Report Header section. In contrast, the two column headings appear in the Page Header section because these headings appear at the top of the columns on both pages. The Detail section contains a pair of text boxes bound to fields in the report's record source. On the report, these text boxes repeat once for each record in the underlying record source. The sort order of these rows can be independent of the order of records in the underlying record source. This capability improves the overall usability of a record sources for multiple reports.

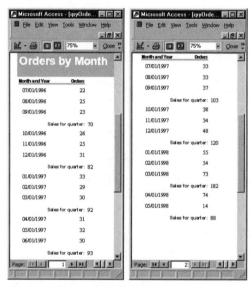

Figure 6-8. *A report that shows grouping by date.*

The rows in Figure 6-8 are grouped by quarter. You use the Grouping And Sorting dialog box in Design view to select one or more fields on which to group rows. Grouping on a field adds Report Header and Report Footer sections to a report for each new group. This built-in grouping capability automatically adapts to the field data type on which a report groups. For date fields, Access supports grouping by year, quarter, month, week, day, hour, and minute. AutoNumber, Currency, and Number fields enable you to group rows by a custom range. You can group product unit prices in $5 intervals for one report and in $10 intervals for another. You can also group Text fields based on their leading characters. This permits you to create a directory-style report that groups all products beginning with *A* followed by those beginning with *B*, and so on.

The built-in grouping capabilities support the calculation of subtotals. Notice that the report in Figure 6-8 summarizes sales orders by month and by quarter. You use an aggregate function, such as *SUM*, in a group footer section to compute a calculation for the items in a group. Other aggregate functions that can add value to a report include *AVG*, *COUNT*, *MAX*, and *MIN*. The aggregate function for the subtotal in Figure 6-8 appears in the text box in the Date Footer section. The Control Source expression for the text box is

```
=Sum([CountOfOrderID])
```

The argument for this function points at an underlying field for a control in the Detail section. Using *txtCountOfOrderID* as the argument to point directly at the text box control generates an error.

> **NOTE** Rules for calculating subtotals differ from other calculated fields on a report. With a standard calculated field, such as one to compute an extended price for an order, you can refer to the individual control values on the current record. Your expressions can also reference the underlying fields for controls. When you compute subtotals, you must reference the underlying field value.

CREATING MULTICOLUMN REPORTS

The samples presented so far in this chapter do not present classic database reports that display multiple columns from one or more underlying tables. You can create this kind of report in at least two ways: using the Report wizard and using manual layout techniques.

Using the Report Wizard

The Report wizard, which has an interface similar to the Simple Query wizard, lets you create a multicolumn report. Figure 6-9 shows a report prepared using the Report wizard. As you can see, the wizard provides a lot of computations. The report's underlying record source counts sales quantity and sums extended price by product for each customer. The report also sums the order quantities and prices by customer and overall customers. It then uses these results to compute the percent of total sales and extended price for each customer. It also sums the number of records for each customer and prints a one-line message with the customer's name and its record count.

The Report wizard can add a flurry of formatting touches as well. Figure 6-9 shows one set of choices. Using spacing and horizontal lines, the layout distinguishes the report's title from the rest of the report. You can also choose from several different field layouts. The layout in the figure places the grouping variable—*CompanyName*—on the far left of report pages. Note that that this layout required no code.

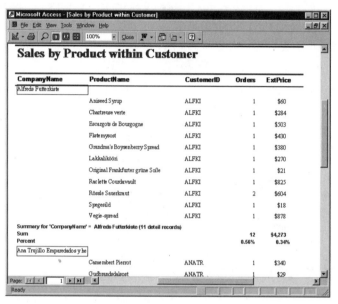

Figure 6-9. *This excerpt from a report shows some of the Report wizard's calculations and formatting options.*

Creating a Custom Report

When you need a special arrangement of controls on a report as well as unique computations, you must lay out the report manually. Figure 6-10 shows excerpts from a custom report whose functionality is similar to the report in Figure 6-9. This custom report has simpler formatting to make it easier to follow. The top window shows the sales by product for a customer along with the sums for order quantities and extended price and the percentages of the grand total for both items. The bottom window shows the continuation of the report for the second customer. The Page Footer section shows the date of the report, the current report page, and the total number of pages.

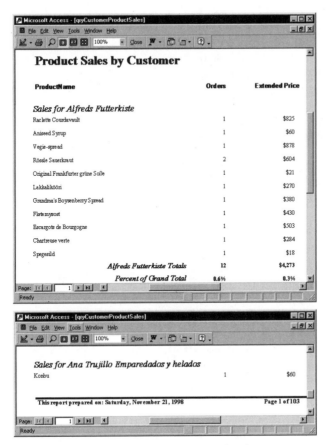

Figure 6-10. *Excerpts from a custom multicolumn report.*

Figure 6-11 (on the next page) shows the Design view of the report in Figure 6-10. Nearly all the controls on the report are labels or text boxes. You should generally assign string constants to labels and set their caption property to the string constant. The text in the Report Header section is in a label.

Controls that display numeric fields or string expressions are always text boxes. The first string expression appears in the CompanyName Header section. It is a concatenation of a string constant and the *CompanyName* field in the report's record source. The Detail section appears next. Its three text boxes each reference a field. Since these controls do not combine the field into an expression, there is no need for a leading equal sign (=) or for placing the field name in brackets.

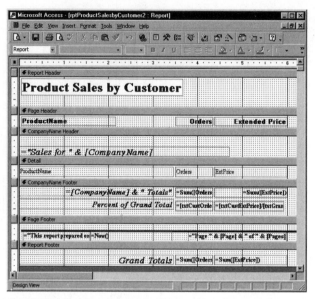

Figure 6-11. *The report in Figure 6-10 in Design view.*

The four right-hand controls in the CompanyName Footer section contain expressions for computing the sum of sales orders and extended price for each customer, along with each customer's percentage of the total sales quantity and extended price. The following table shows the control names and their expressions. The expressions for the percentages rely on two controls that appear in the Report Footer sections, *txtGrandOrders* and *txtGrandExtPrice*. These controls compute the total sales quantity and extended price across all customers.

EXPRESSIONS FOR SUMS AND PERCENTAGES IN FIGURE 6-11

Control	Expression
txtCustOrders	Sum([Orders])
txtCustExtPrice	Sum([ExtPrice])
txtOrdersPercent	=[txtCustOrders]/[txtGrandOrders]
txtExtPricePercent	=[txtCustExtPrice]/[txtGrandExtPrice]
txtGrandOrders	=Sum([Orders])
txtGrandExtPrice	=Sum([ExtPrice])

The sums for individual customers and the grand total refer directly to the underlying field values, *Orders* and *ExtPrice*. The percentage calculations for individual customers refer to control names that, in turn, depend on field values.

NOTE By default, Access gives a text box control the same name as the field to which it binds. To avoid confusion, you can give the controls different names. For example, if a field name is *Orders*, you can change the name of a text box control that references it to *txtOrders*. This makes it easy for you to read expressions and determine whether they reference a field value or a control.

Notice in Figure 6-10 that the date of a report prints at the bottom of a page, but there is a leading string constant. If you want to apply a format, such as the Long Date format, you must isolate the *Now* function in a text box by itself. Figure 6-11 shows two concatenated text boxes containing the leading text string and the trailing formatted value of the *Now* function.

The right side of the report shown in Figure 6-11 uses two keywords, *Page* and *Pages*, that identify the current report page and the total number of pages in the report. (These keywords do not appear in the figure.) Notice that you can include these keywords in string expressions.

DISTRIBUTING REPORTS USING SNAPSHOTS

You can make Access reports available to others via the World Wide Web or e-mail using snapshot files. The workstation viewing a snapshot of an Access report requires a Snapshot viewer, which is available for free as a standalone application, and an ActiveX control for use in a web browser. The viewer allows a much wider audience, such as those without Access and those not connected to your LAN, to use your reports. While the Netscape browser does not support ActiveX controls, it can download snapshot files over an http connection. Netscape users can then use the standalone version of the Snapshot viewer with the saved file on their local hard drive.

Creating a Snapshot

You can create a snapshot for a report by selecting the report in the Database window and choosing File-Export. This enters your report name as the name of the snapshot file in the Export Report dialog box. (See Figure 6-12.) In the Save As Type drop-down list box, select Snapshot Format. In the Save In drop-down list box, designate a location for your snapshot file. Figure 6-12 saves the report from Figure 6-9 to a virtual directory (namely, CAB_Office_2000) on an intranet. Clicking Save in the dialog box in Figure 6-12 on the following page opens a progress dialog box and opens the file after saving it in the Snapshot viewer (which ships with Access 2000). The file resides on the server and has an .snp extension.

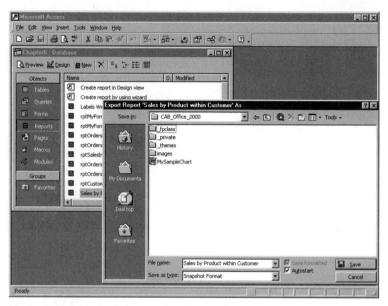

Figure 6-12. *Creating a snapshot file manually.*

Viewing a Snapshot

A workstation running Microsoft Internet Explorer 3 and later with the viewer installed can open the snapshot file. Figure 6-13 shows the report in Internet Explorer 4. The viewer appears to be inside the browser, but it actually takes over the browser. Special navigator controls on a bar at the bottom of the ActiveX control enable navigation around the pages of a report. The same navigator bar also includes a button for printing (because the control disables the native browser printing functionality).

Notice the close correspondence between the browser image in Figure 6-13 and the original report image in Figure 6-9. This level of correspondence does not occur when you export to the HTML Documents format. In addition, exporting to HTML does not provide the built-in navigation functionality that the Snapshot viewer control offers.

The Snapshot viewer control lets you embed an Access report on a web page along with other content. The following HTML excerpt shows the body of a web page with H3 and H4 tags before the object reference to the Snapshot viewer control. The text blocks preceding the control explain how to download the viewer if the report does not appear, and they offer a hyperlink to a site from which a user can download the browser. The instructions also explain how to view the report in Netscape Navigator. You typically want to update the *SnapshotPath Param* value setting to the URL for the snapshot file that you want to show.

```
<body>
<H3>Snapshot Sample page</H3>
<H4>If you have an IE 3+ browser but cannot see the report below,
 download and install the
 <a href="http://www.microsoft.com/accessdev/prodinfo/snapdl.htm">
 Microsoft Access Snapshot viewer</a>. Then
 refresh the page. Netscape users will not even see the report
 container in their browsers, but they can open the report
 outside their browser using the same snapshot viewer mentioned
 above. Netscape users can download the snapshot file from
 a web server over http protocol to their workstation.</H4>
<OBJECT ID="SnapshotViewer" WIDTH=640 HEIGHT=480
CLASSID="CLSID:F0E42D60-368C-11D0-AD81-00A0C90DC8D9">
    <PARAM NAME="_ExtentX" VALUE="16722">
    <PARAM NAME="_ExtentY" VALUE="11774">
    <PARAM NAME="_Version" VALUE="65536">
    <PARAM NAME="SnapshotPath"
    VALUE="http://cab2200/cab_office_2000/MySampleChart.snp">
    <PARAM NAME="Zoom" VALUE="0">
    <PARAM NAME="AllowContextMenu" VALUE="-1">
    <PARAM NAME="ShowNavigationButtons" VALUE="-1">
</OBJECT>
</body>
```

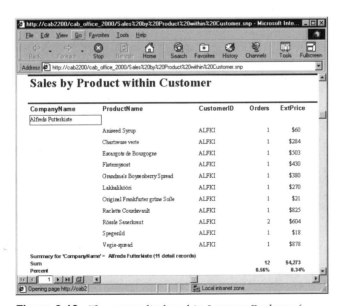

Figure 6-13. *The report displayed in Internet Explorer 4.*

Other Uses for Snapshots

Snapshot files based on Access reports have many other uses as well. For example, you can electronically mail a snapshot file as an attachment by right-clicking on the report in the Database window and choosing Send To and then Mail Recipient from the shortcut menu. Remember to include a link in your message to the download site for the Snapshot viewer. This will enable recipients who do not have the viewer to install it.

You can also use the *DoCmd OutputTo* and *SendObject* methods to automate conversion and copying of snapshot files to an intranet web server site or to e-mail recipients. This chapter's final section includes a sample that programmatically e-mails multiple files to one or more recipients. The following statement publishes a report from the Northwind database to a local site on my intranet:

```
DoCmd.OutputTo acOutputReport, "Alphabetical List of Products", _
    "Snapshot Format", _
    "\\cab2200\c\inetpub\cab_office_2000\mysnapshot.snp", True
```

MAKING A REPORT DYNAMIC

Three report section events—*Format, Retreat,* and *Print*—let you build dynamic formatting and content into a report. Other report events that can help you build smart reports include *Page, NoData, Close,* and *Open.* These events can also help you manage the application's behavior before, during, and after the opening of a form. You can use combinations of report events to create report formatting and special effects.

You use the *Open* event to programmatically set properties for reports and their controls. This is the first event for a report. If your application can have more than one report open at the same time, you can use the *Activate* and *Deactivate* events to monitor the flow of focus into and away from a report. Use the *Close* event to perform special actions just before a report closes, such as opening a form or presenting a message box.

You use the *NoData* event to detect a report that has no data in its record source. This event occurs after Access formats a report for printing. Your application can use it to cancel a report that is about to print with no data. You can also program event procedures that prompt a user to make data available by entering records or by going to another record source for the report.

Formatting and Adding Content

The following samples format and add content to a report dynamically using the *Print* and *Format* events. Figure 6-14 shows a report that uses the *Print* event for three sections to add red rectangles around the Report Header section and the Page Footer section. Note the different thicknesses of the rectangle borders. The Detail section shows an oval around all monthly order totals greater than or equal to 30.

While the Report Header *Print* event occurs a single time per report and the Page Footer *Print* event occurs just once per page, the Detail section *Print* event occurs once for each row on a page. This means that the page in Figure 6-14 has 16 Detail section *Print* events. With each event, your application can examine control values for the current record. This means that you can selectively display ovals around some monthly order totals.

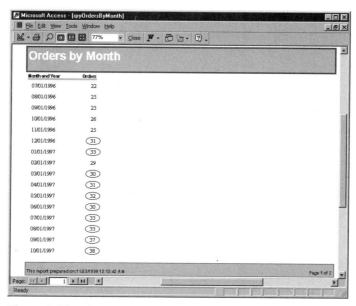

Figure 6-14. *The* Print *event in this report draws rectangles around the Report Header and Page Footer sections. Another event selectively draws ovals around the monthly orders totals in the report.*

The following three event procedures are the code behind the report in Figure 6-14. Your applications can apply the *Line* method (as in the Report Header and Page Footer event procedures) to draw a rectangle around the report section. Four *Single* variables accept the top, left, width, and height values of the section. A *Long* variable accepts the color number for the rectangle (red in the sample). Just before invoking the *Line* method to draw the rectangle, the *ReportHeader_Print* procedure sets the line width to 25 pixels. Two pairs of coordinates denote points for the *Line* method. The value in *lngColor* specifies the line's color. The *Line* method's closing argument, *B*, instructs the method to draw a rectangle, or box, using the two coordinates as diagonally opposite end points.

```
Private Sub ReportHeader_Print(Cancel As Integer, _
    PrintCount As Integer)
Dim sngTop As Single, sngLeft As Single
Dim sngWidth As Single, sngHeight As Single
Dim lngColor as Long

'Set top, left, width, & height.
    sngTop = Me.ScaleTop
    sngLeft = Me.ScaleLeft
    sngWidth = Me.ScaleWidth
    sngHeight = Me.ScaleHeight

'Set color.
    lngColor = RGB(255, 0, 0)

'Draw line as a box.
 Me.DrawWidth = 25
    Me.Line (sngTop, sngLeft)-(sngWidth, sngHeight), lngColor, B

End Sub


Private Sub PageFooterSection_Print(Cancel As Integer, _
    PrintCount As Integer)
Dim sngTop As Single, sngLeft As Single
Dim sngWidth As Single, sngHeight As Single
Dim lngColor as Long

'Set top, left, width, & height.
    sngTop = Me.ScaleTop
    sngLeft = Me.ScaleLeft
    sngWidth = Me.ScaleWidth
    sngHeight = Me.ScaleHeight

'Set color.
    lngColor = RGB(255, 0, 0)

'Draw line as a box.
    Me.Line (sngTop, sngLeft)-(sngWidth, sngHeight), lngColor, B

End Sub


Private Sub Detail_Print(Cancel As Integer, PrintCount As Integer)
Dim sngHCtr As Single, sngVCtr As Single
Dim sngRadius As Single
```

```
'Position and size circle.
    sngHCtr = (Me.ScaleWidth / 2) - 3670
    sngVCtr = (Me.ScaleHeight / 2) - 20
    sngRadius = Me.ScaleHeight / 1.5

'Conditionally draw circle; last argument sets aspect ratio.
    If Me.CountOfOrderID.Value >= 30 Then
        Me.Circle (sngHCtr, sngVCtr), sngRadius, , , , 0.5
    End If

End Sub
```

The only difference between the *ReportHeader_Print* and *PageFooter_Print* procedures is the line setting the width of the rectangle's border. The Report Header section uses a width of 25 pixels, but the Page Footer section draws a rectangle with the default width of 1 pixel. Both procedures draw a rectangle on a layer in front of the standard report layer. You can tell this because the red border from the *Line* method appears over the background shading for the report title.

The Detail section event procedure relies on the *Circle* method to draw an oval around the order totals for each row in the Detail section. You must empirically determine horizontal and vertical centers as well as the radius of your circle. You use an aspect ratio argument in the *Circle* method to transform a circle to a long or narrow oval. Like the *Line* method, the *Circle* method draws its output on a layer in front of the standard report layer. Embedding the *Circle* method in an *If...Then* statement allows the procedure to draw the oval conditionally around some but not all *Orders* field values.

Summing Page Values

If your report requires the sum of the entries on a report page, you must program these page sums using event procedures because Access offers no built-in way to accomplish this task. The book's sample for this task uses a text box with its *Running Sum* property set to *Over All*. This causes the text box to sum its *Control Source* field over the whole report. Figure 6-15 on the next page shows the first and second pages of a report with the extra column for computing the running sum. The far right column appears for tutorial purposes, but in practice you set the *Visible* property for the control with the running sum to *False*.

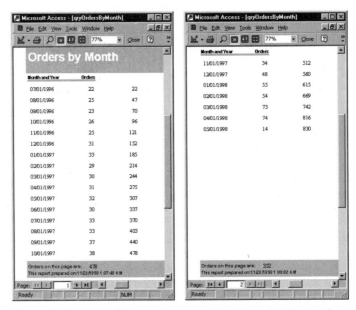

Figure 6-15. *This report uses two event procedures and a text box in the Detail section with its* Running Sum *property set to* Over All *to compute the sum of the orders on a page.*

You can compute page sums with as few as two event procedures (shown below). The *PageFooterSection_Format* event procedure only requires two lines. First it copies the value for the control with the running sum (*pagesum*) set to *lngCurrentRSum*. Then it sets another text box in the Page Footer section (*txtpagesum*) to the difference between *lngCurrentRSum* and *lngLastRSum*. The value of *lngLastRSum* is initially *0*. After every page finishes formatting, a procedure firing with the report's *Page* event copies the current value of *lngCurrentRSum* into *lngLastRSum*, so the difference between *lngLastRSum* and *lngCurrentRSum* in the *Report_Page* event procedure is the page sum for the current page.

```
Public lngLastRSum As Long, lngCurrentRSum As Long
Public lngPageRSum As Long


Private Sub PageFooterSection_Format _
    (Cancel As Integer, FormatCount As Integer)
    lngCurrentRSum = Me.pagesum
    Me.txtpagesum = lngCurrentRSum - lngLastRSum


End Sub
```

```
Private Sub Report_Page()
    lngLastRSum = lngCurrentRSum

End Sub
```

Notice that the *PageFooterSection_Format* event procedure in the sample computes and displays page sums by writing a value into a text box within the Page Footer section. *Print* event procedures do not enable this kind of manipulation because the *Print* event fires after the report is already formatted. The *Format* event fires as your application is formatting the report.

DYNAMICALLY UPDATING A REPORT

You can use VBA to add a new record source property to a report. While your application causes a report's content to change, you can update the report's title to reflect the new content. If you present the results of a parameter-like query in a report, you can also use many formatting options for the result.

Figure 6-16 shows a form and a report. Users can manipulate the form to change the content for the report. The form includes a text box, an option group of five check boxes, and a command button. After entering a number in the text box and selecting a comparison, the user can click the command button to open the report on the right in Design view. This view is necessary to add a new record source property and to reset the *Caption* property for the label that displays the report's title. After programmatically updating the two report properties, the application opens the results in Preview mode to display the results of the new record source. The instructions below the title explain how to close the form.

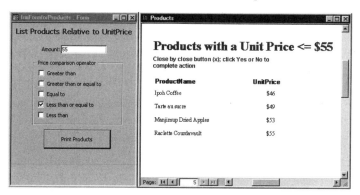

Figure 6-16. *In the form on the left, users can designate a record source and a corresponding title for the report on the right.*

The *cmdPrintThem_Click* event procedure (shown below) for the command button performs three tasks. First, it constructs a SQL string based on selections made in the form. The procedure successively adds clauses to a starter statement that lists product name and unit price from the *Products* table. It initially appends a WHERE clause to the core statement based on the selected check box and the quantity entered in the text box. After adding the WHERE clause, the procedure appends an ORDER BY clause that sorts the return set from the SQL string by unit price. If a user selects the greater than (>) or the greater than or equal to (>=) operator, the procedure specifies a descending sort order. Otherwise, the return set sorts by unit price in the default ascending order.

The second component of the *cmdPrintThem_Click* procedure programmatically revises the record source and caption for a label on a report. After opening the report in Design view, it executes a *With...End With* statement based on the report. To eliminate screen clutter, the second component invokes the *Echo* method with an argument of *False*. This suppresses screen updates until the next statement invokes the *Echo* method with an argument of *True*. Inside the *With...End With* block, the procedure sets the report's *RecordSource* property to the SQL string in the first part of the procedure. Then it changes the caption for the label that displays the report's title. A string expression that draws on the option group value and the amount in the text box facilitates this task.

The third component performs two functions. It opens the report in Preview mode so that users can see it. Then the final command restores the *Echo* function, which displays the report. This technique of turning off and then restoring the *Echo* effect leads to crisp screen transitions.

```
Private Sub cmdPrintThem_Click()
Dim strSQL As String, strOperator As String
Dim strWhere As String

'Set up SQL statement for report record source.
    strSQL = "Select ProductName, UnitPrice " & _
        "from Products"
    strOperator = Choose(optRule, ">", ">=", "=", "<=", "<")
    strWhere = "Where UnitPrice" & strOperator & txtAmount
    strSQL = strSQL & " " & strWhere & " Order By UnitPrice"
    If optRule <= 2 Then
        strSQL = strSQL & " Desc"
    End If

'The commented debug.print statement is convenient for debugging
'your SQL statement; remove the comment when you change the
'SQL statement construction.
'    Debug.Print strSQL
```

```
'Open report in Design view to set the report's record source
'and its label's caption.
    DoCmd.Echo False
    DoCmd.OpenReport "rptProductsfromForm", acViewDesign
    With Reports("rptProductsfromForm")
        .Visible = False
        .RecordSource = strSQL
        .Controls("lblTitle").Caption = _
        "Products with a Unit Price " & strOperator & " $" & txtAmount
    End With

'Now show the form to the user.
    DoCmd.OpenReport "rptProductsfromForm", acViewPreview
    DoCmd.Echo True

End Sub
```

MANIPULATING REPORTS AND REPORT CONTROLS PROGRAMMATICALLY

Access offers two levels of entry to reports, forms, and other important database objects. In Chapter 5, you learned about the *AllForms* collection. Access also has an *AllReports* collection—as well as *AllTables*, *AllQueries*, *AllMacros*, *AllViews*, *AllModules*, *AllStoredProcedures*, *AllDataAccessPages*, and *AllDataDiagrams* collections. A member of any of these collections is an *AccessObject* object (a new type of object in Access 2000). You can refer to an *AllReports* member by one of three conventions:

```
AllReports (0)
AllReports ("name")
AllReports![name]
```

Enumerating Reports

Your code can enumerate *AccessObject* objects in any of the *All* collections to determine whether objects are in a database connection. It does not matter whether the object is open or closed. You can also determine whether an object is loaded. When an *AccessObject* object is loaded or open, your application can work with a parallel collection space. Such collections are all the open reports, forms, and so forth in an Access database. Members of the *Reports* collection are individual reports that are open in an application. These open *Report* objects expose all the properties available through VBA instead of the much more restricted set in the *AllReports* collection. You can use the *Name* property in *AllReports* and *Reports* to move between the two parallel collections.

By using the *IsLoaded* property in the *AllReports* collection, you can verify whether you need to open a report before attempting to manipulate its properties and methods.

The *ListAllReports* procedure below enumerates the members of the *AllReports* collection while listing their name and loaded status. The *AllReports* collection members belong to either the *CurrentProject* or the *CodeProject*, which are members of the *Application* object. You must reference one of these to expose the *AllReports* members. Therefore, the *ListAllReports* procedure starts by setting a reference to the *CurrentProject* member of the *Application* object. You need this reference to reach the members of the *AllReports* collection. Notice that the *For…Each* loop passes through each *AccessObject* object (*obj1*) in *AllReports*, but the path to *AllReports* starts with the reference to *Application.CurrentProject*.

```
Sub ListAllReports()
Dim obj1 As AccessObject, app1 As Object

'Create a reference to the current project instance.
    Set app1 = Application.CurrentProject

'List each report in the application and
'describe as loaded or not.
    For Each obj1 In app1.AllReports
        If obj1.IsLoaded = True Then
            Debug.Print obj1.Name & " is loaded."
        Else
            Debug.Print obj1.Name & " is not loaded."
        End If
    Next obj1

End Sub
```

The *AllReports* and *AllForms* collections are directly analogous to one another. You are not restricted to examining *AccessObject* members in the active project. The *ListAllFormsElsewhere* and *ListAllReportsElsewhere* procedures below show how to program both collections when they point at another project. Notice the similarity of the code between collections as well as between the current project and another project.

The *ListAllFormsElsewhere* procedure below prints the total number and the names of individual members in the *AllForms* collection for Chapter5.mdb. This file is on the book's companion CD. The procedure assumes that you load the file from the CD and store it in your My Documents folder. It enumerates *AccessObject* members in another database file.

```
Sub ListAllFormsElsewhere()
Dim appAccess1 As Access.Application
Dim obj1 As AccessObject

'Create a reference to another database file.
    Set appAccess1 = New Access.Application
    appAccess1.OpenCurrentDatabase "c:\Programming Access\" & _
        "Chap05\Chapter5.mdb"

'Print the total number of forms in the database.
    Debug.Print appAccess1.CurrentProject.AllForms.Count
    For Each obj1 In appAccess1.CurrentProject.AllForms
        Debug.Print obj1.Name
    Next obj1

End Sub
```

The *ListAllReportsElsewhere* procedure below follows the same general design as the preceding one, although it deals with the *AllReports* collection instead of the *AllForms* collection and uses the Northwind.mdb database instead of Chapter 5.mdb. The layout is nearly identical except for the use of string variables to define the database name. This change is strictly for convenience and generality—nothing in Access or VBA mandates the use of strings.

```
Sub ListAllReportsElsewhere()
Dim appAccess1 As Access.Application
Dim obj1 As AccessObject
Dim srtPath As String, strFile As String, strDBName As String

'Create a reference to another database file.
    Set appAccess1 = New Access.Application
    strPath = "c:\Program Files\Microsoft Office\Office\Samples\"
    strFile = "Northwind.mdb"
    strDBName = strPath & strFile
    appAccess1.OpenCurrentDatabase strDBName

'Print the total number of reports in the database.
    Debug.Print appAccess1.CurrentProject.AllReports.Count
    For Each obj1 In appAccess1.CurrentProject.AllReports
        Debug.Print obj1.Name
    Next obj1
End Sub
```

Modifying Report Control Properties

Your application code can use the *AllReports* collection as a pathway to individual open reports and the controls on them. Once you pass through the pathway, your application can read and modify the properties of individual open reports. The *ControlsInReports* procedure drills down from the *AllReports* collection members to the text box and label properties on individual open reports.

```
Sub ControlsInReports()
Dim obj1 As AccessObject, ctl1 As Control

    For Each obj1 In CurrentProject.AllReports
        If obj1.IsLoaded = True Then
            For Each ctl1 In Reports(obj1.Name)
                If ctl1.ControlType = 100 Then
                    Debug.Print ctl1.Name, ctl1.Caption
                ElseIf ctl1.ControlType = 109 Then
                    Debug.Print ctl1.Name, ctl1.Value
                Else
                    Debug.Print ctl1.Name & " is not a" & _
                        " label or a text box."
                End If
            Next ctl1
        End If
    Next obj1

End Sub
```

The *ControlsInReports* procedure starts with a *For...Each* loop that iterates through the members of the *AllReports* collection. If a member is open, as indicated by a value of *True* for its *IsLoaded* property, the code enters a nested *For...Each* loop to enumerate the controls on that report. You can use the *ControlType* property to determine a control's type. It is important to know the type because it determines the properties that the control exposes. For example, a label control displays its *Caption* property, but a text box uses a *Value* property to depict what it shows. You can use the Object Browser in VBE to view the numeric codes of other control types that you want to edit or examine.

Mailing Snapshots

The sample on the facing page enumerates reports to determine whether they are marked for mailing as snapshot files. The sample relies on two procedures. First, the *SendSnapShots* procedure enumerates the members of the *AllReports* collection. Since the code checks whether the report's *Tag* property is "mail it", the report must be open. The *Tag* property is not available through the *AllReports* collection—it is only available through the *Reports* collection. The *SendSnapshots* procedure checks the *IsLoaded* status of each *AllReports* member. If the report is loaded, the procedure calls the *CheckMailItTag* procedure. If *IsLoaded* has a value of *False,* the procedure opens the report before calling the second procedure. The sample does not call the *Echo* method with a *False* parameter, so a user can easily get feedback as the second procedure runs. This is particularly appropriate for long reports for which it can take a while for the snapshot file to be created and mailed.

```
Sub SendSnapShots()
Dim obj1 As AccessObject, app1 As Object

'Create a reference to the current project instance.
    Set app1 = Application.CurrentProject

'Enumerate each member in AllReports to verify if loaded.
'If not loaded, open before calling CheckMailItTag.
    For Each obj1 In app1.AllReports
        If obj1.IsLoaded = True Then
            CheckMailItTag obj1.Name
        Else
            DoCmd.OpenReport obj1.Name, acViewPreview
            CheckMailItTag obj1.Name
            DoCmd.Close acReport, obj1.Name, acSaveNo
        End If
    Next obj1

End Sub



Sub CheckMailItTag(obj1name)
Dim rep1 As Report

'Set reference to Reports member corresponding
'to AllReports member.
    Set rep1 = Reports(obj1name)

'If Tag property says "mail it"
'create a snapshot file and mail it.
    If rep1.Tag = "mail it" Then
        DoCmd.SendObject acOutputReport, obj1name, _
        acFormatSNP, "virginia@cabinc.net", , , _
        "Snapshot Report", "Here is the report.", False
    End If

End Sub
```

The *CheckMailItTag* procedure accepts the report name passed to it by *SendSnapShots*. It uses this name to create a reference to the *Reports* collection member with the same name. Then it checks the *Tag* property of the report to determine whether it equals "mail it". If so, the procedure invokes *DoCmd's* *SendObject* method to create a snapshot file and send it to an e-mail address (in this case, virginia@cabinc.net). You can replace the string constant for the address with any single address or series of addresses that your application requires. It is important that the argument after the message body be *False*. With the default value of *True*, your procedure will halt with the message open and wait for the user to edit the message. Setting the value to *False* enables the procedure to loop through all the reports without any operator intervention.

Chapter 7

Class, Form, and Report Modules

To program Microsoft Access efficiently, you must manage your programmatic resources so that they are easy to use and reuse. The value of code grows in proportion to how much use you can get from it.

Class modules package code for easy reuse. The class module acts as a container that exposes the code and selected variables inside it in a way that is familiar to Microsoft Visual Basic for Applications (VBA) developers. Basically, you invoke class procedures and assign values to variables with the same syntax used for the properties and methods of built-in Access objects. To use the code in a class module, you do not have to know anything about how it works. Also, since class modules expose properties, methods, and events like other objects do, even beginning VBA developers can use them.

This chapter first introduces standalone class modules and form and report class modules. Then it demonstrates simple ways to build classes into your Access applications and to develop custom properties and methods. Next comes a case study that uses three forms, a few custom *Property Get* and *Property Let* functions, and a couple of techniques based on ActiveX Data Objects (ADO) to start building an application. The section after the case study shows the syntax for programming events into your custom classes and introduces the *WithEvents* keyword.

The focus then shifts to the containers for class, form, and report modules as we look at the All collections that are new to Access 2000. Just as there are *AllForms* and *AllReports* collections, there is an *AllModules* collection. (In fact, there are ten All collections altogether.) The chapter wraps up by explaining how to combine the *AllModules* collection with the *Modules* collection to manage code in an application.

MODULE TYPES

There are three basic kinds of modules:

■ *Standard modules.* These hold subprocedures and function procedures that you want to make available throughout a database file. Standard modules can also contain variables defined with a Public declaration that you want to make available to procedures in other modules.

■ *Standalone class modules.* These let you create custom objects. You can define properties, methods, and events for these objects, and you can use the *New* keyword to create instances of the form objects.

■ *Class modules for forms and reports (often called form and report modules).* Forms and reports by default all have modules behind them (their *HasModule* property is set to *True* by default). You can use the *Me* keyword when referring to the modules behind forms and reports.

CLASS MODULES

Standalone class modules differ from form and report class modules in several ways.

First, standalone class modules do not have a built-in user interface, as form and report class modules do. This makes standalone class modules more suited to tasks that do not require an interface, such as performing calculations, looking up data, or modifying a database. When form or report modules require computationally intensive tasks, they can call a standalone class module.

Second, standalone class modules offer *Initialize* and *Terminate* events that enable operations that need to take place at the opening and closing of a class instance. Report and form modules do not have these events, but you can perform similar functions with the *Load* and *Close* events.

Third, you must use the *New* keyword to create instances of standalone class modules. Report and form class modules also let you create instances with the *DoCmd OpenForm* and *OpenReport* methods as well as by referencing the report or form class module's properties or methods. For example, *Form_MyForm.SetFocus* opens the *MyForm* form.

You can create a standalone class module from the Insert menu in VBE. (The same menu offers commands for building a standard module or a procedure.) After creating a class module shell, you can populate it with procedures and declarations, which equip it with custom properties and methods.

Custom Property Functions and Custom Methods

Special property functions make it easier to develop any combination of read-only, write-only, and read/write properties for your classes. If your application permits, you can define properties by simply declaring a public variable. When a class module defines a property with a public variable, it is always a read/write property. The ability to declare custom properties lets you extend the basic Access functionality for forms and reports. In addition, these property functions allow you to create powerful standalone classes.

Your applications can also build custom methods into classes. You can use subprocedures or function procedures to accomplish this. By selectively exposing variables and procedures with the *Public* keyword, you can narrowly define what methods and properties they expose. This lets your applications define interfaces to your class objects that perform in very specific ways.

Instantiating Classes

The public methods and procedures support programmatic access by procedures outside the class. You must first instantiate the class in a host procedure within another module, using the *New* keyword. (You use the same keyword to instantiate objects from other classes, such as ADO *Connection* and *Recordset* objects. In fact, your applications can instantiate multiple copies of a custom class at the same time—just like the ADO classes.) After instantiating a class, the code in your host procedure manipulates the instance of the class, not the class itself. You can change a property in one instance of a form, but when you instantiate a second instance of the form it appears with the default property setting.

Custom Classes and Events

Although VBA in Access lets you build custom classes with their own properties and methods, you cannot build custom events within those classes. You can, however, design a class that hooks onto a built-in class or type library that you attach. For example, you can build a class module that launches VBA code in response to the *ItemAdded* and *ItemRemoved* events of the *References* collection. This collection tracks links to external type libraries and ActiveX controls. After referencing a library, such as the Microsoft ActiveX Data Objects 2.1 Library, you can build custom events around the ADO events for the *Connection* and *Recordset* objects. These events can enable asynchronous data access that lets your application respond to users even while it remains ready to respond to a completed connection or the availability of a fetched set of records.

You use the *WithEvents* keyword within a *Public* declaration to point to an object reference that monitors and reports events within an ActiveX control. This keyword is valid only in class modules. You can define multiple variables within a module with the *WithEvents* keyword, but you cannot create arrays with it. Also, a declaration cannot contain both the *WithEvents* and *New* keywords.

CUSTOM PROPERTIES AND METHODS

When you use class modules, you inevitably work with two separate modules. The class module exposes properties and methods and propagates events. A second module references the class module; it assigns and reads property values as well as invokes methods. This module can initiate actions that fire events, and these, in turn, can invoke any associated event procedures in the class module.

Exposing a Property with a Public Variable

The following sample shows two listings. The first is from the *MyTestClass* module. It is a class module, and it starts with a couple of variable declarations—one for this sample and one for the next sample. The procedure named *EP* computes the extended price from three arguments passed to it: units, price, and discount. The procedure saves the result of its expression in the variable name *ExtendedPrice*. A declaration in the module's general area defines *ExtendedPrice* as a public variable. This enables a host procedure in another module that works with an instance of the *MyTestClass* object to read the variable's value.

```
FROM MyTestClass module (a class module)
Public ExtendedPrice As Currency
Private MyComputedPrice As Currency

Public Sub EP(units As Long, price As Currency, _
    discount As Single)

'Compute with result in public variable.
    ExtendedPrice = units * price * (1 - discount)

End Sub


FROM Module1 (a standard module)
Sub ComputeExtendedPrice()
'Create new instance of class module.
Dim MyPriceComputer As New MyTestClass
```

```
'Invoke EP method for class, and
'print Extended Price property.
    MyPriceComputer.EP 5, 5, 0.02
    Debug.Print MyPriceComputer.ExtendedPrice
End Sub
```

The host procedure, *ComputeExtendedPrice*, resides in a standard module named *Module1*. This procedure instantiates an object based on the class defined by *MyTestClass*. Next, it invokes the *EP* method for the object. Finally, it prints the *ExtendedPrice* property for the object.

While this sample is very basic, it demonstrates several important points about using class modules:

- Class modules are a good choice for computing critical business expressions. You will generally use class modules for encapsulating a more sophisticated computation than the one for extended price.

- The second procedure, which is in the standard module, starts by referencing the class module, *MyTestClass*. The *New* keyword instantiates an object based on the class. In the sample, the variable named *MyPriceComputer* references the class.

- You can use the object reference for the instance of the class to invoke methods and set or read property values. You reference the class's *EP* method with the standard dot notation. You list arguments after the method's name and you reference properties with the same basic notation.

- Creating a property for a class can be as simple as declaring a *Public* variable in the class module.

Exposing a Property with a Property Function

The first of the following listings shows a different approach to the same task. It relies on a property defined with a *Property Get* function. The *ep2* method is nearly identical to the *EP* method in the preceding sample. The only difference is that *ep2* deposits the result of its expression into a private variable, *ComputedPrice*. (See the private variable declaration in the preceding sample.) All by itself, this means that instances of the class cannot expose the expression's result. You use a *Property Get* function to expose a private variable. Since there is no other property function defined for *ComputedPrice*, the property is read-only. If there were a *Property Let* function with the same name, the property would be read/write. Using read-only properties can help to secure the values of your properties—or at least the ways to set them.

```
FROM MyTestClass module (a class module)
Public Sub ep2(units As Long, price As Currency, _
    discount As Single)

'Compute with result in private variable; expose
'result through Property Get function.
    MyComputedPrice = units * price * (1 - discount)

End Sub


Property Get ComputedPrice()

'This is how to return a read-only property.
    ComputedPrice = MyComputedPrice

End Property


FROM Module1 (a standard module)
Sub GetComputedPrice()
Dim MyPriceComputer As New MyTestClass

'Using a value defined by a property looks the same
'as one defined with a public variable.
    MyPriceComputer.ep2 5, 5, 0.02
    Debug.Print MyPriceComputer.ComputedPrice
End Sub
```

Public Variables vs. Property Functions

The syntax for invoking the method and printing the property value is identical in the two samples, although the property is exposed differently. This confirms that properties work in the same way whether you define them with a public declaration or one or more property functions. Public variables might be a simpler way to implement properties in class modules, but property functions are a more flexible way to expose them. You use a *Property Get* function by itself for a read-only variable, and you use a *Property Let* function by itself for a write-only property. You use both types of property functions for a read/write property. If your property references an object instead of a scalar variable, you can use a *Property Set* function instead of a *Property Let* function. You use the *Property Get* function to return object property values whether you are working with a scalar variable or an object.

Class Modules and Data Sources

Class modules are good for encapsulating any kind of code. They have special values that are useful for when you want to a make a data source available for updating or viewing, but you need to secure the data source from accidental or inadvertent damage by users.

Updating data with a SQL string

The following sample uses a class module to update the *UnitsInStock* field for the *Products* table based on a *ProductID* field and the quantity ordered. A procedure with two lines passes two arguments to a subprocedure in a class module. This sample uses a different class module from the two samples for calculating extended price (*MyTestClass2* instead of *MyTestClass*). In practice, you divide your functions and declarations into homogeneous collections of method procedures and properties representing distinct object classes. The *OrderIt* variable represents the *MyTestClass2* module. Within the module is a function named *PO1*. It takes two arguments, one for the *ProductID* and one for the units ordered.

```
Sub MyOrder()
Dim OrderIt As New MyTestClass

    OrderIt.PO1 1, 10

End Sub
```

The next procedure, *PO1*, updates the Products database. Specifically, it decreases *UnitsInStock* by the number of units ordered. This procedure resides in the class module (*MyTestClass2*). Note the procedure's design: it uses a *Command* object with a SQL string that defines the update query. Although the procedure accepts two arguments, it does not apply a parameter query. Instead, it uses the passed arguments as variables in the string expression defining the SQL string. This design leads to a very compact procedure that is relatively easy to read.

```
'A method for updating a table
Public Sub PO1(ProductID, units)
Dim cmd1 As Command
Dim strSQL As String

'Assign the command reference and connection.
    Set cmd1 = New ADODB.Command
    cmd1.ActiveConnection = CurrentProject.Connection
```

(continued)

```
'Define the SQL string; notice
'the insertion of passed arguments.
    strSQL = "UPDATE Products " & _
        "SET UnitsInStock = " & _
        "UnitsInStock-" & units & " " & _
        "WHERE ProductID=" & ProductID

'Assign the SQL string to the command and run it.
    cmd1.CommandText = strSQL
    cmd1.CommandType = adCmdText
    cmd1.Execute

End Sub
```

Updating data with a parameter query

Many developers prefer a more traditional approach that relies on a parameter query. The *PO2* procedure below uses a parameter query to perform with a SQL string the task accomplished by *PO1*. A parameter query lets you declare data types with traditional VBA conventions. Notice that the ADO constant *adInteger* represents a long data type, and the constant *adSmallInt* designates an integer data type. You must create the parameters with the *CreateParameter* method in the same order in which you declare them in the *Parameters* clause of the query statement. Failing to do so will generate a run-time error.

NOTE Look up the *Type* property of the ADO *Parameter* object in the Access 2000 online Help to see the complete selection of data types for variable declarations.

```
Public Sub PO2(ProductID As Long, units As Integer)
Dim cmd1 As Command
Dim strSQL As String
Dim prm1 As ADODB.Parameter, prm2 As ADODB.Parameter

'Assign the command reference and connection.
    Set cmd1 = New ADODB.Command
    cmd1.ActiveConnection = CurrentProject.Connection

'Write out SQL statement with parameters & assign to cmd1.
    strSQL = "Parameters PID Long,Quantity Integer;" & _
        "UPDATE Products " & _
        "SET UnitsInStock = " & _
        "UnitsInStock-Quantity " & _
        "WHERE ProductID=PID;"
    cmd1.CommandText = strSQL
    cmd1.CommandType = adCmdText
```

```
'Declare parameters; must have same order as declaration.
   Set prm1 = cmd1.CreateParameter("PID", adSmallInt, _
      adParamInput)
   prm1.Value = ProductID
   cmd1.Parameters.Append prm1
   Set prm2 = cmd1.CreateParameter("Quantity", adInteger, _
      adParamInput)
   prm2.Value = units
   cmd1.Parameters.Append prm2

'Run update query.
   cmd1.Execute

End Sub
```

There are four main components to the parameter query design of the update task:

- The procedure makes variable declarations and assigns references.

- It specifies the SQL string for the update query and assigns that string to a command property.

- It creates and assigns values to the parameters declared in the second step.

- It runs the command to update the database.

CASE STUDY: CODING A LOGIN INTERFACE

This case study shows one approach to coding a login interface with Access. It uses both standalone class modules and form class modules. The login process and the class module contents use coding techniques that are applicable to any task requiring the use of data with unbound forms.

To highlight the role of class modules and to keep the process transparent, the sample does not use built-in Access security. Instead, it relies on a pair of tables and three forms. The *Passwords* table has just two fields: *EmployeeID* and *Password*. The *Employees* table, which is imported directly from the Northwind database, contains *EmployeeID* as a primary key along with other business, personal, and contact information about employees. The three forms refer to the contents of these tables to manage the login process.

> **NOTE** The case study excludes error trapping, which any operational system should have. Error trapping is especially important if the system is dependent on user input. After you learn the basics of class modules from this chapter, you might want to review the information in Chapter 1 about error-trapping logic.

The First Login Form

Figure 7-1 shows the first form, along with two message boxes that it can generate. A user enters values into both text boxes on the form and clicks Let Me In. If the password matches the saved one for the *EmployeeID* field, the application presents a welcome message box. If it does not match the stored password for an employee ID, the user can try again or change the password.

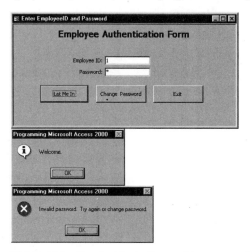

Figure 7-1. *The first login form with two possible reply messages.*

The password mask

In addition to the code behind the form and the class module invoked by the form, you should closely examine the Password text box. It has a password mask that displays an asterisk for each character entered in the box. You assign this mask to a text box from the Data page of its Properties dialog box. Click the Build button next to the *Input Mask* property to open a dialog box that lets you select it.

The code behind the form

The module behind the form, shown below, contains three event procedures—one for each button. The Exit button merely closes the form. The Change Password button opens a second form and copies the value of a field from the current form into it. The procedure that opens the *frmWhoAmI* form also moves the focus to an empty text box. Then it closes the current form.

The Let Me In button invokes a standalone class module (*MyTestClass3*). Notice that the procedure passes the contents of its two text boxes to the *cpw* method procedure in the class module. This module looks up the password for the employee ID and determines whether it matches the password on the form.

The class replies with one of the two possible messages. (See Figure 7-1.) The class module simplifies the code in the event procedure. This points to another benefit of class modules—they facilitate team development. Advanced developers can write more involved procedures in class modules, and beginning developers can perform basic development tasks and simply reference class modules to incorporate advanced ones.

```
Private Sub cmdExit_Click()
    DoCmd.Close
End Sub


Private Sub cmdNewPassword_Click()

    DoCmd.openform "frmWhoAmI"
    Forms("frmWhoAmI").txtEmpID = Me.txtEmpID
    Forms("frmWhoAmI").txtHireDate.SetFocus
    DoCmd.Close acForm, "frmInputPassword"

End Sub


Private Sub cmdLetMeIn_Click()
Dim PWT As New MyTestClass3

    PWT.cpw Me.txtEmpID, Me.txtPassword

End Sub
```

Invoking the class module

The *cpw* procedure in *MyTestClass3*, shown on the next page, uses a parameter query to look up the password for an employee ID in the *Passwords* table. One of the two arguments passed to the procedure is the employee ID. The procedure sets its parameter equal to the value of this argument. After executing the *Command* object with a select query, the procedure assigns the return set to a *Recordset* object. Since the *EmployeeID* field in the *Passwords* table is a primary key, the select query always returns a single record.

The *cpw* procedure closes by comparing the password returned by the query with password typed on the form as the condition of an *If...Then* statement. If there is a match, the procedure welcomes the user into the application. In practice, you open another form or some other database object to which you are restricting access with password security. If there is no match, the procedure asks the user to resubmit the password or change the password.

```
Sub cpw(empid As Long, pw As String)
Dim cmd1 As Command
Dim strSQL As String
Dim prm1 As ADODB.Parameter
Dim rst1 As ADODB.Recordset

'Assign the command reference and connection.
    Set cmd1 = New ADODB.Command
    cmd1.ActiveConnection = CurrentProject.Connection

'Write out SQL statement with parameters & assign to cmd1.
    strSQL = "Parameters Secret Long;" & _
        "Select EmployeeID, Password from Passwords " & _
        "Where EmployeeID=Secret"
    cmd1.CommandText = strSQL
    cmd1.CommandType = adCmdText

    Set prm1 = cmd1.CreateParameter("Secret", adInteger, adParamInput)
    prm1.Value = empid
    cmd1.Parameters.Append prm1

'A handy line for catching SQL syntax errors
'    Debug.Print cmd1.CommandText

    cmd1.Execute

    Set rst1 = New ADODB.Recordset
    rst1.Open cmd1
    If rst1.Fields("Password") = pw Then
        MsgBox "Welcome on in.", vbInformation, _
            "Programming Microsoft Access 2000"
    Else
        MsgBox "Invalid password.  Try again or " & _
            "change password.", vbCritical, _
            "Programming Microsoft Access 2000"
    End If

End Sub
```

The Second Login Form

Figure 7-2 shows the form that appears when a user opts to change the password for the employee ID. This form merely asks users to confirm their identity. The system requires this confirmation before it permits users to change a password. The form has two text boxes. Under normal circumstances, the first text box is always filled by the form that loads it. (See the *cmdNewPassword_Click* procedure above.) All users do is enter their hire date and click Submit. The main point here is to use a field whose value is known only by the employee. Use one or more other fields if you have better alternatives available.

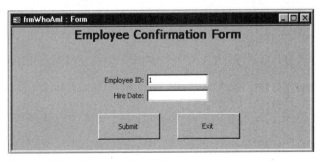

Figure 7-2. *The second login form, which asks users to confirm their identity.*

The code behind the form

The form launches a query when a user clicks the Submit button. A form class module processes the query and matches the return set result to the user input. The event procedure behind the Submit button has a *Dim* statement that instantiates a copy of the *MyTestClass3* module with a reference to *ProcessMe*. A second line invokes the *WhoAmI* method for the class, as shown below.

```
Private Sub cmdSubmit_Click()
Dim ProcessMe As New MyTestClass3

    ProcessMe.WhoAmI CLng(txtEmpID), _
        CDate(txtHireDate)


End Sub
```

Invoking the form class module

The lookup procedure for the second form appears below. It uses a parameter query to perform the lookup of a hire date for an employee ID. By strongly typing the variables (notice the *CLng* and *CDate* functions in *cmdSubmit_Click*) before going into the class module, you can take advantage of the data typing option in a *Parameters* declaration as well as the data typing in the table. Without this data typing, Access must do internal transformations to the variant data type. The basic design for the lookup and return messages follows that for the password lookup. If the hire date on the form matches the one in the *Employees* table, the procedure opens the third form.

```
Sub WhoAmI(empid As Long, hd As Date)
Dim cmd1 As Command
Dim strSQL As String
Dim prm1 As ADODB.Parameter
Dim rst1 As ADODB.Recordset
```

(continued)

```
'Assign the command reference and connection.
    Set cmd1 = New ADODB.Command
    cmd1.ActiveConnection = CurrentProject.Connection

'Write out SQL statement with parameters & assign to cmd1.
    strSQL = "Parameters InEID Long;" & _
        "Select EmployeeID, HireDate From Employees " & _
        "Where EmployeeID=InEID"
    cmd1.CommandText = strSQL
    cmd1.CommandType = adCmdText

    Set prm1 = cmd1.CreateParameter("InEID", adInteger, adParamInput)
    prm1.Value = empid
    cmd1.Parameters.Append prm1

'A handy line for catching SQL syntax errors
    Debug.Print cmd1.CommandText

'Execute command.
    cmd1.Execute

'Check Input vs. Table HireDate.
    Set rst1 = New ADODB.Recordset
    rst1.Open cmd1
    If rst1("HireDate") = hd Then
        DoCmd.openform "frmChangePassword"
        Forms("frmChangePassword").txtEmpID = Forms("frmWhoAmI").txtEmpID
        DoCmd.Close acForm, "frmWhoAmI"
    Else
        MsgBox "HireDate not valid for EmployeeID.  Try " & _
            "again or Quit.", vbCritical, _
            "Programming Microsoft Access 2000"
    End If

End Sub
```

The Third Login Form

Figure 7-3 shows the final form, which appears when a user clicks the Submit button on the second form after entering the correct hire date. The form has three text boxes. One is for the employee ID. (This box fills in automatically under normal circumstances.) The second text box is for a new password and a third text box is for confirming the password. If those text boxes do not match, the system alerts the user. If the user clicks the Submit button without entries in all three boxes, another reminder message appears. Finally, if the form satisfies these two requirements, the class module referenced by the form updates the password for an employee ID in the *Passwords* table.

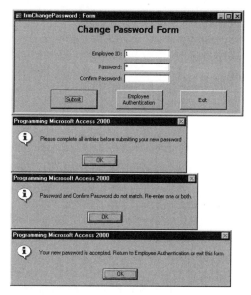

Figure 7-3. *The third form, which lets users update their password.*

The code behind the form

The module behind this form is the most interesting one in the case study. The module does data validation instead of passing the data off to a class module. The procedure still invokes a class module for the SQL statement that updates the password for an employee.

This split of data validation from database updates shows another way to apply class modules—by performing sensitive tasks using a class module. This standardizes the tasks and ensures proper performance. Other application elements that do not require standardization are candidates for customization by end-user departments.

Using *Property Get* and *Property Let* functions   This particular data validation logic relies on a pair of *Property Let* and *Property Get* functions. The *AfterUpdate* event for each of the three text boxes invokes the *Property Let* function, which updates the value of the *AllFilled* variable to *True* or *False*. (It's *True* if all the boxes are filled with legitimate values; it's *False* otherwise.)

A *Property Get* function reflects the status of all three text boxes with the form's *filledCheck* property. The *cmdSubmit_Click* procedure checks this single value to determine whether all three boxes are checked. If the value is *False*, the procedure displays a message reminding the user to complete all boxes. Otherwise, the click event procedure tests whether the password and confirm password text boxes match. If they do not, another message reminds the user to make them match. Finally, when a user clears these two obstacles, the procedure invokes the *NewPS* method of the local instance of the *MyTestClass3* module.

```
Private AllFilled As Boolean
Private Sub txtConfirm_AfterUpdate()
    Me.filledCheck = txtConfirm

End Sub


Private Sub txtEmpID_AfterUpdate()
    Me.filledCheck = txtEmpID

End Sub


Private Sub txtPassword_AfterUpdate()
    Me.filledCheck = txtPassword

End Sub


Public Property Let filledCheck(vntNewValu)
    If (IsNull(txtEmpID) Or txtEmpID = "") Or _
        (IsNull(txtPassword) Or txtPassword = "") Or _
        (IsNull(txtConfirm) Or txtConfirm = "") Then
        AllFilled = False
    Else
        AllFilled = True
    End If

End Property


Public Property Get filledCheck()
    filledCheck = AllFilled

End Property


Private Sub cmdSubmit_Click()
Dim UpdatePW As New MyTestClass3

    If Me.filledCheck = False Then
        MsgBox "Please complete all entries before " & _
            "submitting your new password.", vbInformation, _
            "Programming Microsoft Access 2000"
```

```
    ElseIf txtPassword <> txtConfirm Then
        MsgBox "Password and Confirm Password do not " & _
            "match.  Re-enter one or both.", vbInformation, _
            "Programming Microsoft Access 2000"
    Else
        UpdatePW.NewPW txtEmpID, txtPassword
    End If

End Sub


Private Sub cmdLogin_Click()
    DoCmd.openform "frmInputPassword"
    Forms("frmInputPassword").txtEmpID = txtEmpID
    Forms("frmInputPassword").txtPassword = txtPassword
    DoCmd.Close acForm, "frmChangePassword"
End Sub


Private Sub cmdExit_Click()
    DoCmd.Close

End Sub
```

Transferring values to another form   Two remaining procedures complete the functionality of the module behind the third form. A click event procedure behind the Employee Authentication button takes a user back to the first form and fills in the employee ID and password text boxes with their values from the third form. This feature relieves the user from having to reenter this data just after confirming it, but going back to the first form offers a single point of entry into the application. This simplifies maintenance in the long run. The form's Exit button simply closes the form.

Invoking the class module

The class module invoked by the module behind the third form uses a string expression to compute the SQL statement that a *Command* object uses to update an employee's password. This is one way to represent a string (such as the password value) inside another string (the overall SQL statement). Notice the multiple double apostrophes both before and after the new password value. These are escape codes for representing a double apostrophe inside another pair of double apostrophes. Aside from this VBA requirement for nesting one string inside another string, the code is easy to read. A message block statement at the procedure's close confirms the password change and advises the user how to proceed.

```
Sub NewPW(eid As Long, NuPassword As String)
Dim cmd1 As Command
Dim strSQL As String

'Assign the command reference and connection.
    Set cmd1 = New ADODB.Command
    cmd1.ActiveConnection = CurrentProject.Connection

'Define the SQL string; notice
'the insertion of passed arguments.
    strSQL = "UPDATE Passwords " & _
        "SET Passwords.Password = """ & NuPassword & """ " & _
        "WHERE EmployeeID=" & eid & ";"
    Debug.Print strSQL

'Assign the SQL string to the command and run it.
    cmd1.CommandText = strSQL
    cmd1.CommandType = adCmdText
    cmd1.Execute

'Confirmation message
    MsgBox "Your new password is accepted.  " & _
        "Return to Employee Authentication or " & _
        "Exit this form.", vbInformation, _
        "Programming Microsoft Access"

End Sub
```

PROGRAMMING EVENTS
INTO CUSTOM CLASSES

You can use VBA in Access to create classes for instantiating objects, but VBA objects cannot initiate their own events. However, you can build classes around type libraries and ActiveX controls that propagate their events to a host environment. For objects that propagate events, your VBA application can wrap code around events that occur within the class. When a host procedure for an instance of a class launches a method that causes the firing of a propagating event from inside the class, the event procedure works its way to the host for the class module. (See Figure 7-4.)

The *References* collection relates hierarchically to the *Application* object. You invoke the *AddFromFile* and *Remove* methods to enable an application to programmatically add and delete references to type libraries. These library files contain standard descriptions of exposed objects, methods, properties, and events. Recall that the ADODB object model is dependent on a library. You can add references to it and other libraries manually or programmatically.

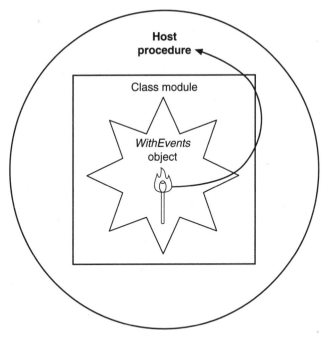

Figure 7-4. *The* WithEvents *keyword propagates an object's event procedures to the object's host when an event fires.*

Chapter 2 explains how to add references manually to the three ADO libraries. The following section will explain how to add references programmatically to any library or ActiveX control. You can issue a confirmation message when your application finishes adding or removing a reference.

Two Built-In Class Events

Class modules have two built-in events: *Initialize* and *Terminate*. The *Initialize* event occurs when you create a new instance of a class module. You create a shell for the *Initialize* event procedure by selecting Class from the class's Object box and Initialize from the Procedure box. You can do anything necessary in an *Initialize* event procedure to prepare your class instance for use.

In the *Terminate* event procedure, you should clean up after your current application. This can be as simple as setting an object reference to *Nothing*. The *Initialize* and *Terminate* events occur just once at the beginning and end of the life of a class instance. Therefore, they are not particularly handy for generating interactive or dynamic behavior at any times other than the birth and death of the instance of a class.

Using the *WithEvents* Keyword to Trap Propagated Events

The following class module uses the *WithEvents* keyword to trap events propagated by the *References* collection. The *References* collection has a separate item for each checked item in the References dialog box. The *ItemAdded* and *ItemRemoved* events occur only when your code adds or removes references. If a user manually modifies the *References* collection, these events do not fire.

```
Option Compare Database
'Declare object variable to represent References collection.
Public WithEvents evtReferences As References

'When instance of class is created, initialize evtReferences
'variable.
Private Sub Class_Initialize()
    Set evtReferences = Application.References

End Sub



'When instance is removed, set evtReferences to Nothing.
Private Sub Class_Terminate()
    Set evtReferences = Nothing

End Sub



'Display message when reference is added.
Private Sub evtReferences_ItemAdded(ByVal Reference As _
        Access.Reference)
    MsgBox "Reference to " & Reference.Name & " added.", _
        vbInformation, "Programming Microsoft Access 2000"

End Sub



'Display message when reference is removed.
Private Sub evtReferences_ItemRemoved(ByVal Reference As _
        Access.Reference)
    MsgBox "Reference to " & Reference.Name & " removed.", _
        vbInformation, "Programming Microsoft Access 2000"

End Sub
```

Starting and ending a *WithEvents* reference

You use the *WithEvents* keyword in combination with a class that propagates events. The *Public* statement in the class module above declares a reference (*evtReferences*) to the *References* collection in the Access application object. The *WithEvents* keyword within the statement enables the class module to trap events propagated by the *References* collection. The *Class_Initialize* event procedure sets a reference. Recall that you cannot use the *New* keyword for a reference that you declare with *WithEvents*.

Wrapping code around captured events

Two event procedures in the class module, *ItemAdded* and *ItemRemoved*, invoke message block statements. These show messages naming the reference that a method adds or removes. The event procedures show the syntax for wrapping custom code around objects that propagate events. In this case, the object is the *References* collection. The event procedures merely write out the name of the library being added to or removed from the *References* collection.

Standard Modules Cause Events

As with any class module, you need one or more procedures in a standard module to instantiate the class (see the sample below) and to invoke methods, assign property values, or read property values. In the declarations area of the module hosting the class, you include a *Dim* or *Public* statement with the *New* keyword and the class name. This instantiates the class and sets an object reference (*objRefEvents* in the sample).

Standard module syntax for events

If the instance of the class propagates events from an embedded object, you should use a *Public* statement with the *WithEvents* keyword. This statement exposes the events to other modules referencing the class. When you invoke the methods from the underlying class, you must traverse the local object reference (*objRefEvents*), the reference within the class module exposing the events (*evtReferences*), and then a specific method name, such as *AddFromFile* or *Remove*. Unlike a normal reference to a class module, this one points to a method for the source object in the *WithEvents* declaration.

```
'Create new instance of RefEvents class.
Dim objRefEvents As New RefEvents

Sub InvokeAddReference()

'Pass file name and path of type library to AddReference procedure.
```

(continued)

```
    AddReference _
        "C:\Program Files\Common Files\System\ado\msjro.dll"

End Sub


Sub InvokeRemoveReference()

'Pass name of existing reference. (Use internal name from File
'Properties list; same name appears when adding reference.)
    RemoveReference "JRO"

End Sub


Sub AddReference(strFileName As String)

    objRefEvents.evtReferences.AddFromFile (strFileName)

End Sub


Sub RemoveReference(strRefName As String)

    objRefEvents.evtReferences.Remove _
        objRefEvents.evtReferences(strRefName)

End Sub
```

The sample above adds a reference to the library holding the JRO model. (This model enables Jet replication via ADO.) You run the *InvokeAddReference* procedure to create the reference. The procedure calls a procedure, *AddReference*, with the syntax for adding an item to the *References* collection via the *RefEvents* class module. The library holding the JRO model is a dynamic link library (DLL) that typically resides in the ADO folder of the System folder in the Common Files directory of the Program Files directory. Launching the *InvokeRemoveReference* procedure eliminates the JRO item from the *References* collection. The JRO designation is the *Name* property for the item in the *References* collection.

> **NOTE** To discover the arguments for the *AddFromFile* and *Remove* methods, you add references manually. Then you enumerate the items in the *References* collection with a *For...Each* statement while listing their *Name* and *FullPath* properties. You use these property values to uniquely identify arguments for the *AddFromFile* and *Remove* methods.

Extending the application

You can easily adapt the *RefEvents* class by using the *AddReference* and *RemoveReference* procedures to accommodate a broader and more flexible selection process. For example, your application can derive the input to the *AddReference* procedure from a collection of type libraries, executables, ActiveX controls, and even database files. A combo box can offer users a list of references to add or remove. Alternatively, your procedure can make a selection from a list based on other factors, such as what a user is trying to accomplish.

USING THE ALL COLLECTIONS

If you are the type of developer who likes to track your objects in a database project (most of us find this essential), you'll be happy to know that there is an *AllModules* collection, which is a counterpart to the *AllForms* and *AllReports* collections you learned about in Chapters 5 and 6. The members of the All collections are not database objects, such as forms, reports, and modules, but *AccessObject* objects that contain a minimal amount of detail about most types of saved objects in a database.

AccessObject Properties

You can quickly enumerate the *AccessObject* objects in any All collection. Since *AccessObject* objects point at saved objects, you cannot add or delete members. You perform these tasks through the open collections they point to.

When you encounter an *AccessObject* object that your application needs more detail on, you can use the *IsLoaded* and *Name* properties to examine the properties of the object the *AccessObject* object points to. These open object collections have a fuller set of properties and methods that are not available with the All collections.

AccessObject objects have a *Type* property that describes the type of *AccessObject* rather than the type of database object. The *Type* property value of any *AllModules* member is *5*. This distinguishes an *AccessObject* member in the *AllModules* collection from one in the *AllForms* collection with a *Type* property value of *2*. In either case, you cannot determine whether you are dealing with a class module or a form class module by simply examining the *AccessObject* member of the All collection. You must examine the *Type* property of a *Module* object and the *HasModule* property of a *Form* object.

The All Collections

There are seven All collections besides the *AllModules*, *AllForms*, and *AllReports* collections. This set of ten collections (see Figure 7-5 on the next page) divides naturally into two sets of five each. The *AllForms*, *AllReports*, *AllMacros*, *AllModules*, and *AllDataAccessPages* collections are members of the *CurrentProject* and *CodeProject* objects in the Access *Application* object. The

AllTables, AllQueries, AllViews, AllStoredProcedures, and *AllDatabaseDiagrams* collections are members of the *CurrentData* and *CodeData* objects in the Access Application object. When you designate *AccessObject* objects in any of the ten All collections, you must set a reference that points at the appropriate antecedent object. Failing to do so will generate an error.

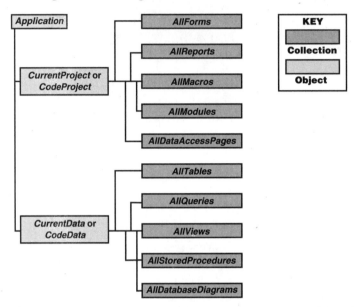

Figure 7-5. *The ten All collections and their hierarchical relationship to* Project *and* Data *objects.*

The *AllQueries, AllViews, AllStoredProcedures*, and *AllDatabaseDiagrams* collections have restricted availability by Access file type. Recall that Access projects can be in a traditional .mdb file or in the new Access 2000 .adp file. (Chapter 4 touched on the .adp file type, and Chapter 12 will discuss it further.) The *AllQueries* collection is available in .mdb files but not .adp files. In contrast, you can tap the *AllViews, AllStoredProcedures*, and *AllDatabaseDiagrams* collections from .adp files but not from .mdb files. Your applications can still reference views and stored procedures in .mdb files by using the ADOX object library.

> **NOTE** You might wonder why Access 2000 permits *Views* and *Procedures* collections in .mdb files but does not offer *AllViews* and *AllStoredProcedures* in .mdb files. These two All collections were not exposed in .mdb files because of the need to satisfy higher priority requirements. Look for *AllViews* and *AllStoredProcedures* collections with .mdb files in future releases of, or updates to, Access.

Enumerating the All Collection Members

The following three procedures show the high degree of similarity in programming different All collections. The first procedure performs a simple enumeration of all the modules in the current project. Notice that it initially declares *obj1* as an *AccessObject* type because it accepts the identity of elements in the *AllModules* collection, which contains *AccessObject* objects. Also note that the enumeration loop passes through the *AllModules* collection but the code reaches this collection through the *Application* and *CurrentProject* objects.

```
Sub EnumerateAllModules()
Dim obj1 As AccessObject
    For Each obj1 In Application.CurrentProject.AllModules
        Debug.Print obj1.Name & vbTab & obj1.Type & _
            vbTab & obj1.IsLoaded
    Next obj1

End Sub


Sub EnumerateAllForms()
Dim obj1 As AccessObject
    For Each obj1 In Application.CurrentProject.AllForms
        Debug.Print obj1.Name & vbTab & obj1.Type & _
            vbTab & obj1.IsLoaded
    Next obj1

End Sub


Sub EnumerateAllTables()
Dim obj1 As AccessObject
    For Each obj1 In Application.CurrentData.AllTables
        Debug.Print obj1.Name & vbTab & obj1.Type & _
            vbTab & obj1.IsLoaded
    Next obj1

End Sub
```

The *EnumerateAllForms* and *EnumerateAllTables* procedures have the same structure as the *EnumerateAllModules* procedure. You should note some significant differences in content, however. First, the specific *AccessObject* collection changes from *AllModules* to *AllForms* in one procedure and *AllTables* in the other procedure. Second, the path to the *AllTables* collection passes through the *CurrentData* object rather than the *CurrentProject* object. If we were to switch the *AllTables* collection to either an *AllViews* or an *AllStoredProcedures* collection, the code would work in an .adp file but not in an .mdb file.

Adapting to .mdb and .adp File Types

Using the *ProjectType* property of the *CurrentProject* object, you can detect whether you are working with an .adp or an .mdb file. This lets you write single procedures that adapt to their environment. The following sample prints the names of all the views and stored procedures in an .adp file, but it switches to printing all the queries in an .mdb file. As you can see, the only trick required is to test for the value of the *ProjectType* property. The *AccessObject Type* property adds values by distinctly differentiating objects for views with a type value of 7 from objects pointing at stored procedures, whose type value is 9.

```
Sub EnumerateAllViews2()
Dim obj1 As AccessObject, dbs1 As Object
    Set dbs1 = Application.CurrentData
    If Application.CurrentProject.ProjectType = acADP Then
        For Each obj1 In dbs1.AllViews
            Debug.Print obj1.Name & vbTab & obj1.Type & _
                vbTab & obj1.IsLoaded
        Next obj1
        For Each obj1 In dbs1.AllStoredProcedures
            Debug.Print obj1.Name & vbTab & obj1.Type & _
                vbTab & obj1.IsLoaded
        Next obj1
    Else
        For Each obj1 In dbs1.AllQueries
            Debug.Print obj1.Name & vbTab & obj1.Type & _
                vbTab & obj1.IsLoaded
        Next obj1
    End If

End Sub
```

Using *AllForms* and *AllModules*

The sample on the next page uses the All collections and the corresponding collections of open modules and forms to develop a list of all the modules (by type) and the class modules for forms in a project. Since the property for denoting standard class modules is different from the one for class modules for forms, the code requires different expressions to test for standard class modules vs. class modules for forms.

Recall that modules have a *Type* property but forms have a *HasModule* property. The code must iterate through the members of the *AllModules* and *AllForms* collections because some, or even all, modules and forms can be closed. You check the *IsLoaded* status of the *AccessObject* objects in *AllModules* and *AllForms* to determine whether you need to open a module or form before

assessing its module type, or to determine whether a form has a class module.
The procedure recloses forms and modules after it examines them.

```
Sub ListAllModulesByTypeAndClassForms()
Dim obj1 As AccessObject, dbs1 As Object
Dim mod1 As Module, frm1 As Form

    Set dbs1 = Application.CurrentProject

'Search for open AccessObject objects in AllModules collection.
'Open and reclose those that are not open.

    For Each obj1 In dbs1.AllModules
        If obj1.IsLoaded = True Then
            ListTypeOfModule obj1.Name
        Else
            DoCmd.OpenModule obj1.Name
            ListTypeOfModule obj1.Name
            DoCmd.Close acModule, obj1.Name
        End If
    Next obj1

'Search for open AccessObject objects in AllForms collection.
'Open and reclose those that are not open.

    For Each obj1 In dbs1.AllForms
        If obj1.IsLoaded Then
            DoesFormHaveModule obj1.Name
        Else
            DoCmd.openform obj1.Name
            DoesFormHaveModule obj1.Name
            DoCmd.Close acForm, obj1.Name
        End If
    Next obj1

End Sub


Sub ListTypeOfModule(modname)
Dim strType As String

'Decode module Type value.
    If Modules(modname).Type = 0 Then
        strType = "Standard Module"
    Else
        strType = "Class Module"
    End If
```

(continued)

```
'Print module name and type.
    Debug.Print Modules(modname).Name & vbTab & strType

End Sub


Sub DoesFormHaveModule(frmname)

'Only print form name if it has a module.
    If Forms(frmname).HasModule = True Then
        Debug.Print frmname & vbTab & "Form Class Module"
    End If

End Sub
```

PROGRAMMATICALLY EDITING MODULES

Since you can perform so many different tasks with standard modules, standalone class modules, and class modules for forms, your applications are likely to have many of these modules. This will eventually create a need for maintenance. One common maintenance requirement is the insertion or deletion of one or more lines of code in a set of modules. This section shows how to add a line to and remove a line from all the standard and standalone class modules, and then it shows the same for form class modules. Because the code for standard and standalone class modules is stored differently from the code for class modules for forms, the steps are slightly different.

Editing Approaches

The *Module* object offers an array of methods and properties that can help you programmatically edit modules. The samples in this section use the *InsertLines*, *Find*, and *DeleteLines* methods. These methods process both standard and class modules, including standalone class modules and report and form class modules. These are a subset of the methods and properties that support programmatically managing module content.

You use the *InsertLines* method with a *Module* object to insert one or more lines into the module. Module line numbers start with *1* and extend through the *CountOfLines* property value for the module. The method takes a line number and a string argument. If you need to insert multiple lines into a module, add *vbCrLf* constants into the string expression representing the method's string argument. When you insert lines with this method, it moves down the remaining lines in the module.

The *Find* method searches for a text string in a module. It returns a value of *True* if it finds the search text, and it returns *False* otherwise. If you know precisely where some text is, you can specify a starting line and column and an ending line and column. If you do not know where some search text resides in a module, leave the text position arguments blank and the function will return the values of the search text in the module. You can also designate pattern searches and case-restrictive searches.

The *DeleteLines* method removes one or more lines of text from a module. The method takes two arguments: a start line and the total number of lines to remove from a module. You can use the *DeleteLines* method in combination with the *Find* method. You use the *Find* method to search for text in a module. You can then base the invocation of the *DeleteLines* method on the return value from the *Find* method.

Inserting Text into Modules

The procedures below combine the *AllModules* and *Modules* collections to edit the text in a collection of modules. Specifically, they insert a comment line at the beginning of each module, proclaiming it a standard module or a class module. The *EnumerateAllModulestoInsert* procedure loops through the members of the *AllModules* collection and calls the other procedure, which actually updates the target modules. Since the *InsertIntoModules* procedure requires an open module, the first procedure opens the module if it is not already open. Then, when the second procedure returns control to the first one, it closes the module again to restore its initial state.

```
Sub EnumerateAllModulestoInsert()
Dim obj1 As AccessObject

'Loop through AllModules members.
'If module is open, call sub to insert lines;
'else open module first, then close afterwards.
    For Each obj1 In Application.CurrentProject.AllModules
        If obj1.IsLoaded = True Then
            InsertIntoModules obj1.Name
        Else
            DoCmd.OpenModule obj1.Name
            InsertIntoModules obj1.Name
            DoCmd.Close acModule, obj1.Name, acSaveYes
        End If
    Next obj1

End Sub
```

(continued)

```
Sub InsertIntoModules(modname)
Dim strType As String, mod1 As Module

    Set mod1 = Modules(modname)

'Detect module type to determine which
'string to insert.
    If mod1.Type = 0 Then
        strType = "'Standard Module"
    Else
        strType = "'Class Module"
    End If
    mod1.InsertLines 1, strType
    Set mod1 = Nothing

End Sub
```

The *InsertIntoModules* procedure accepts a single argument—the name of the module to edit. It performs no iteration because the first procedure calls it once for each member in the *AllModules* collection. The procedure begins by setting a reference to the module named in the passed argument. Then it determines the type of module to which the reference points and sets a string variable to a comment naming the module type. After determining the text to insert, the procedure invokes the *InsertLines* method for the referenced module.

Deleting Text from Modules

The following two procedures delete a line from a procedure. In fact, they remove the line added by the preceding pair of procedures. The design of these next two procedures is flexible enough so that you can easily extend them to accommodate the deletion of multiple selected lines from any set of modules.

The procedures follow the same general logic as the preceding pair, with one major difference: this pair uses the *Find* and *DeleteLines* methods to remove text instead of the *InsertLines* method. The *Find* method is often critical when you prepare to use the *DeleteLines* method because the *Find* method lets your code determine whether some text is there before it deletes any content. In this instance, the *Find* method looks for the word *Module* in the first 40 characters of the first line. The *DeletefromModules* procedure invokes the *DeleteLines* method to delete one line starting with the first line in the module. The *DeleteLines* method removes lines unconditionally. However, you can manually invoke the *Undo Delete* function to restore removed text.

```
Sub EnumerateAllModulestoDelete()
Dim obj1 As AccessObject, dbs As Object
Dim mod1 As Module, frm1 As Form
```

```
'Loop through AllModules members.
'If module is open, call sub to delete line;
'else open module first, then close afterwards.
    For Each obj1 In Application.CurrentProject.AllModules
        If obj1.IsLoaded = True Then
            DeletefromModules obj1.Name
        Else
            DoCmd.OpenModule obj1.Name
            DeletefromModules obj1.Name
            DoCmd.Close acModule, obj1.Name
        End If
    Next obj1

End Sub


Sub DeletefromModules(modname)
Dim mod1 As Module

    Set mod1 = Modules(modname)

'Delete first line if first 40 characters
'contain "Module".
    If mod1.Find("Module", 1, 1, 1, 40) = True Then
        mod1.DeleteLines 1, 1
    End If
    Set mod1 = Nothing

End Sub
```

Inserting Text into Form Class Modules

The following two procedures insert a line at the beginning of each form class module with the comment that it is a class module. Instead of looping through the *AllModules* collection, the first procedure loops through the *AllForms* collection. For each member of the *AllForms* collection, it calls the *InsertIntoForms* procedure.

This second procedure assesses whether the passed form name is a class module. If it is, the procedure sets a reference to the module behind the form. This step exposes that module. The procedure closes by inserting the comment line into the module and setting the reference to *Nothing* to free its resources.

```
Sub EnumerateAllFormsToInsert()
Dim obj1 As AccessObject
```

(continued)

```
'Loop through AllForms members;
'if form is loaded invoke module to insert line,
'else open form first and then close afterwards.
    For Each obj1 In Application.CurrentProject.AllForms
        If obj1.IsLoaded Then
            InsertIntoForms obj1.Name
        Else
            DoCmd.openform obj1.Name
            InsertIntoForms obj1.Name
            DoCmd.Close acForm, obj1.Name, acSaveYes
        End If
    Next obj1

End Sub


Sub InsertIntoForms(frmname)
Dim mod1 As Module, strType As String

'If Form has module, set reference to it
'and insert line into the module.
'Free reference resource when done.
    If Forms(frmname).HasModule = True Then
        Set mod1 = Forms(frmname).Module
        strType = "'Form Class Module"
        mod1.InsertLines 1, strType
        Set mod1 = Nothing
    End If

End Sub
```

Deleting Text from Form Class Modules

The two procedures below remove the *Class Module* comment line from the first line of modules behind forms. As you can see, this pair's design mimics critical elements from the preceding pairs of procedures for inserting and deleting lines. This pair iterates through the *AllForms* collection, like the pair that added a comment line to the beginning of all form class modules in a project.

However, the second procedure in this pair uses the *Find* and *DeleteLines* methods to remove the first line in a module if it contains the word *Module* in the first 40 characters of its first line. This resembles the procedure for deleting lines from the *Modules* collection.

```
Sub EnumerateAllFormstoDelete()
Dim obj1 As AccessObject
```

```
'Loop through AllForms members;
'if form is loaded invoke module to remove line,
'else open form first and then close afterwards.
    For Each obj1 In Application.CurrentProject.AllForms
        If obj1.IsLoaded Then
            DeletefromForms obj1.Name
        Else
            DoCmd.openform obj1.Name
            DeletefromForms obj1.Name
            DoCmd.Close acForm, obj1.Name, acSaveYes
        End If
    Next obj1

End Sub


Sub DeletefromForms(frmname)
Dim mod1 As Module, strType As String

'If form has module, then check contents of first line
'for "Module", and delete the first line if it is present.
'Free module reference resource when done.
    If Forms(frmname).HasModule = True Then
        Set mod1 = Forms(frmname).Module
        If mod1.Find("Module", 1, 1, 1, 40) = True Then
            mod1.DeleteLines 1, 1
        End If
        Set mod1 = Nothing
    End If
End Sub
```

Chapter 8

Microsoft Office Objects

As part of Microsoft Office 2000, Microsoft Access 2000 shares a select group of objects with the other Office applications. These objects let you carry out such tasks as searching for files, manipulating the Office Assistant help feature, modifying standard menus and toolbars, and developing custom menus and toolbars. In addition, your knowledge of how to program these objects in Access will transfer to the other Office applications—Microsoft Excel, Microsoft Word, and even Microsoft FrontPage. Most of the objects work in all of the Office applications.

This chapter starts with an overview of Office objects and then focuses on three specific objects: *FileSearch*, which you use to programmatically manage file searches; *Assistant*, which provides a programmatic interface to the Office feature called the Office Assistant; and *CommandBars*, which you use to create custom menus and toolbars.

USING THE SHARED OFFICE OBJECTS

The shared Office objects, listed in the table on the following page, provide support in several important areas of functionality. Some of these object models are not available in all Office components. The table describes the models, mentions when they have restricted availability across Office components, and highlights where you can find further information about them in this book. To get online help and work with any of these objects, you must reference the Microsoft

Office 9 Object Library. You can do this through the Tools menu in the Microsoft Visual Basic Editor (VBE) or programmatically (as this chapter will show later).

SHARED OFFICE OBJECTS

Object	Description	Comment
CommandBar	You can use this object and its collections to create and modify toolbars, menu bars, and shortcut menus. You can make design-time changes manually and with VBA code. You can make run-time changes exclusively with VBA code.	See further discussion and samples in this chapter.
Assistant	You use this object to support custom help requirements for the Office Assistant and Office Assistant balloon. Various properties and methods let you control the type and animation of the Assistant as well as the content and behavior of the balloon.	See further discussion and samples in this chapter.
FileSearch	You use this object to represent the functionality of the Open dialog box.	See further discussion and samples in this chapter.
COMAddin	This is a representation of a COM add-in in Access and other Office host applications.	See the Microsoft Office 2000 Programmer's Guide.
LanguageSettings	This object lets you programmatically return information about language installation, user interface, and help settings.	Tracks locale identifier information when deploying Office internationally.
AnswerWizard	You use this object to programmatically manipulate the Answer wizard.	Includes properties and methods for manipulating files returned by the Answer wizard.
DocumentProperty	This object represents a built-in or custom property of an Office document. There are up to 28 built-in properties, which include such document attributes as title, author, comments, last print date, last save time, and total editing time. This object also supports custom document properties.	For Word documents, Excel workbooks, and Microsoft PowerPoint presentations only.

Object	Description	Comment
HTMLProject	This object is a top-level project in the Microsoft Script Editor. You use the *HTMLProjectItem* collection to track HTML documents within a project.	For Word documents, Excel workbooks, and PowerPoint presentations only.
Script	This object represents a block of script in the Script Editor.	For Word documents, Excel workbooks, and PowerPoint presentations only.
WebPageFont	This object represents the default font when a document is saved as a web page.	For Word documents, Excel workbooks, and PowerPoint presentations only.

ACCESS DATABASE PROPERTIES

Access does not have a shared *DocumentProperty* object as Word, Excel, and PowerPoint do, but it makes much of the same kind of information available using three *Documents* objects: *MSysDB*, *SummaryInfo*, and *UserDefined*. These are available exclusively through Data Access Object's (DAO's) Database Container. You can't use them with Microsoft ActiveX Data Objects (ADO). The *SummaryInfo* object contains all properties on the Summary tab of the Database Properties dialog box. The *UserDefined* object contains all properties on the Custom tab of that dialog box. The *MSysDB* object contains all the properties defined under Tools-Startup in a database.

The following sample enumerates the properties collection of each DAO Database Container object:

```
Sub enumDBProps()
Dim db As Database, p As DAO.Property

'Set reference to current database.
    Set db = CurrentDb

'Print heading for results.
    Debug.Print "User defined properties"
    Debug.Print "======================="
```
(continued)

Access Database Properties *continued*

```
'Iterate through UserDefined database properties.
    For Each p In db.Containers!Databases. _
        Documents!UserDefined.Properties
        Debug.Print p.Name, p.Value
    Next

'Print heading for results.
    Debug.Print
    Debug.Print "Summary Properties"
    Debug.Print "=================="

'Iterate through SummaryInfo database properties.
    For Each p In db.Containers!Databases. _
        Documents!SummaryInfo.Properties
        Debug.Print p.Name, p.Value
    Next

'Print heading for results.
    Debug.Print
    Debug.Print "MSysDB Properties"
    Debug.Print "================="

'Iterate through MSysDB database properties.
    For Each p In db.Containers!Databases. _
        Documents!MSysDB.Properties
        Debug.Print p.Name, p.Value
    Next

End Sub
```

THE *FILESEARCH* OBJECT

You use the *FileSearch* object model (shown in Figure 8-1) to integrate file searches into your applications. You can search the hard drives of a computer and any drives on LAN-linked computers. This object exposes the functionality of the Open and the Find dialog boxes. As Figure 8-1 shows, the *FoundFiles* object and *PropertyTests* collection are hierarchically dependent on *FileSearch*.

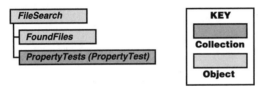

Figure 8-1. *The* FileSearch *object is one of the shared Office objects.*

There are two basic ways to specify a file search, and each approach corresponds to options in the Open dialog box:

■ You can designate a single criterion (a filename or pattern, a file type, or a path).

■ You can designate multiple search criteria programmatically using the *PropertyTests* collection.

With the second approach, you specify arguments that serve as input to the Open dialog box. You can use this dialog box to specify multiple search criteria and rules for concatenating them, such as And and Or operators. Use *FoundFiles* to enumerate the return set from either approach.

The *FileSearch* object has two methods: *NewSearch* and *Execute*. The *NewSearch* method resets all *FileSearch* properties to their default values. You can then edit the properties that require special values for a particular file search. If you do not invoke *NewSearch* at the beginning of a search specification, your new search inherits its property settings from the previous search.

You invoke the *Execute* method to launch a file search after you specify it. This method can take several arguments that control the arrangement of filenames in the *FoundFiles* object and that control whether to update the file index before conducting a new search. The return value from this method is the number of filenames that match the search specification.

Conducting a Basic File Search

Many *FileSearch* properties permit flexible search specifications. The simple code sample on the next page specifies a search and retrieves its return set. It creates an instance of the *FileSearch* object by using the *FileSearch* property of the *Application* object. Then it restores all *FileSearch* property settings to their default values by invoking the *NewSearch* method. Next, it assigns the *LookIn* and *FileName* properties, which specify where to look and what to look for. The test machine for this search includes a series of .mdb files with names such as Chapter1 and Chapter2. The *SearchSubFolders* property accepts a Boolean value that indicates whether to restrict the search to the current folder or extend it to subfolders of the *LookIn* property setting.

```
Sub FileSearch1()
'Search in My Documents folder and its subfolders
'for Chapter*.mdb.
With Application.FileSearch
'Start a new search.
    .NewSearch
'Set search criteria.
    .LookIn = "C:\My Documents"
    .FileName = "Chapter*.mdb"
    .SearchSubFolders = True
End With

With Application.FileSearch
'Execute the Search.
    If .Execute() > 0 Then
        MsgBox "There were " & .FoundFiles.Count & _
            " file(s) found."
'Display names of all found files.
        For i = 1 To .FoundFiles.Count
            MsgBox .FoundFiles(i)
        Next i
    Else
'If no files found, say so.
        MsgBox "There were no files found."
    End If
End With

End Sub
```

After creating the specification for the search, the procedure invokes the *Execute* method for the *FileSearch* object. This method has a return value that indicates the number of files that meet the search criteria. If the value is *0*, the criteria yield no matching filenames and the procedure issues a message indicating that no files were found. If the criteria yield one or more matching files, the procedure displays the *Count* property of the *FoundFiles* object before presenting each name in *FoundFiles*.

Sorting the Return Set

The following sample sorts the return set from a search by file size. The first two parameters for the *Execute* method designate the sort criterion and order, respectively. The constant names for the first parameter indicate the variable on which to sort the returned filenames. These constants are: *msoSortByFileName*, *msoSortByFileType*, *msoSortByLastModified*, and *msoSortBySize*. The *Execute* method's second parameter specifies either ascending or descending order. The sample designates a search sorted by file size in descending order. This differs from the previous sample, which returned results in the default ascending order based on filename.

```
Sub FileSearch2()
Dim sngMB As Single

'Search in My Documents folder and its subfolders
'for Chapter*.mdb.
With Application.FileSearch
'Start a new search.
    .NewSearch
'Set search criteria.
    .LookIn = "C:\My Documents"
    .FileName = "Chapter*.mdb"
    .SearchSubFolders = True
End With

With Application.FileSearch
'Return found files in descending order by file size.
    If .Execute(msoSortBySize, msoSortOrderDescending) > 0 Then
        MsgBox "There were " & .FoundFiles.Count & _
            " file(s) found."
        For i = 1 To .FoundFiles.Count
'Compute file size in MB and display with filename.
            sngMB = FileLen(.FoundFiles(i)) / (1024 ^ 2)
            MsgBox .FoundFiles(i) & vbCrLf & vbTab & _
                "Filesize (MB): " & Round(CDec(sngMB), 3)
        Next i
    Else
'If no files found, say so.
        MsgBox "There were no files found."
    End If
End With

End Sub
```

The message box that displays the return set shows the file sizes and filenames. You pass the *FoundFiles* object to the *FileLen* function to determine the size of a file. The file sizes are rounded to the nearest 1/1000 of a MB.

> **NOTE** The Visual Basic for Applications (VBA) *Round* function is new in VBA 6. To derive consistent results with this function, you should first pass its argument to the *CDec* function. The sample above uses this syntax. (See Chapter 1 for information on the *CDec* function.)

Searching Based on File Contents

Even with a simple search, such as the two previous samples, you can selectively search for specific text in the document or its *DocumentProperty* object. The sample below does this. You use the *FileSearch* object's *TextOrProperty* property to target a text string in the file's body or its *Properties* collection. Notice that you can specify folders on remote computers using the Uniform Naming Convention (UNC). (*cab233**c**cab* points to the cab folder in the share named c of a computer named cab233.)

```
Sub FileSearch3()
Dim sngStart As Double, sngEnd As Double
Dim i As Integer
'Search in cab folder on linked computer
'for files containing CAB.
With Application.FileSearch
'Start a new search.
    .NewSearch
'Set search criteria.
    .LookIn = "\\cab233\d\cab\"
    .SearchSubFolders = False
'When searching for text consider
'restricting the files you search.
'*.* takes 300 seconds, but
'msoFileTypeWordDocuments takes 22 seconds.
'    .FileName = "*.*"
    .FileType = msoFileTypeWordDocuments
    .TextOrProperty = "CAB"
End With

With Application.FileSearch
'Execute the search.
    sngStart = Now
    If .Execute() > 0 Then
        sngEnd = Now
        Debug.Print DateDiff("s", sngStart, sngEnd)
        MsgBox "There were " & .FoundFiles.Count & _
            " file(s) found."
'Display names of all found files.
        For i = 1 To .FoundFiles.Count
            MsgBox .FoundFiles(i)
        Next i
```

```
    Else
'If no files found, say so.
        MsgBox "There were no files found."
    End If
End With

End Sub
```

Some file searches can be lengthy. By specifying a restrictive *FileSearch* property, you can dramatically improve the performance of the *Execute* method. For example, the sample above finds all Word documents in a folder that contain a specific string. By using the *msoFileTypeWordDocuments* constant for the *FileType* property, the sample restricts the search to just Word document files. You might be tempted to specify *.* for the *FileName* property and then filter the returned results, but this would seriously impair performance. For the sample files in the cab folder on the cab233 computer, the difference is 22 seconds for the *msoFileType* constant vs. 300 seconds for the *.* *FileName* specification. (Notice that it takes just three lines to time the operation—one line before the *Execute* and two more immediately after it.)

Specifying Multiple Search Criteria

The advanced search format lets you specify multiple search criteria for your return set in the *FoundFiles* object. You use the *Add* method two or more times to specify multiple criteria for the *PropertyTests* collection. Your individual criterion specifications must include *Name* and *Condition* settings.

The *Add* method can specify a *Connector* setting as well as one or two *Value* settings. The *Add* method's *Condition* setting determines whether a criterion requires *Value* settings. You view the members of the *MsoCondition* class to see all the available options. (Figure 8-2 on the next page shows an excerpt.) Your *Connector* settings can take one of two values to specify how to combine a criterion with other criteria. This setting enables And or Or operators for merging a criterion with other search criteria. You use Or to treat the criterion separately, and you use And to combine the designated criterion with others. And is the default setting. The *Condition*, *Value*, and *Connector* settings together offer the same functionality as the Find dialog box.

You can enumerate *PropertyTests* members using a *For...Each* loop. Each member constitutes a unique search criterion. The *Name* property identifies the criterion as you enumerate them.

Figure 8-2. *You use the members of the* msoCondition *enumeration group to specify conditions for advanced criteria in the* PropertyTests *collection of the* FileSearch *object.*

The last *FileSearch* sample, shown below, has three segments. The first segment specifies the criteria after setting a reference to a *FileSearch* object. The sample targets all database files between two dates. It shows the correct syntax for invoking the *Add* method for the *PropertyTests* collection. The first criterion designates a database type. The second criterion denotes files last modified between January 1, 1996, and June 30, 1999. The *msoConnectorOr* setting indicates that files must meet both criteria separately to be in the return set. You need not specify a *Connector* property for the second criterion because it adopts the default *msoConnectorAnd* value. Before displaying the return set, the procedure enumerates the *PropertyTests* members in its second segment. The final segment displays the return set.

```
Sub Search4()
Dim fs As FileSearch, mystring As String
Dim i As Integer

    Set fs = Application.FileSearch

'Set lookin and subfolder properties.
    With fs
        .NewSearch
        .LookIn = "c:\My Documents"
        .SearchSubFolders = False
    End With
```

```
'Set a pair of property conditions.
    With fs.PropertyTests
        .Add name:="Files of Type", _
            Condition:=msoConditionFileTypeDatabases, _
            Connector:=msoConnectorOr
        .Add name:="Last Modified", _
            Condition:=msoConditionAnytimeBetween, _
            Value:="1/1/1996", SecondValue:="6/30/1999"
    End With

'Display property tests.
    For i = 1 To fs.PropertyTests.Count
        With Application.FileSearch.PropertyTests(i)
        mystring = "This is the search criteria: " _
            & " The name is: " & .name & ". The condition is: " _
            & .Condition
        If .Value <> "" Then
            mystring = mystring & ". The value is: " & .Value
            If .SecondValue <> "" Then
                mystring = mystring _
                    & ". The second value is: " _
                    & .SecondValue & ", and the connector is" _
                    & .Connector
            End If
        End If
        MsgBox mystring

        End With
    Next i

'Display return set from property tests.
    With fs
'Execute the search.
        If .Execute() > 0 Then
            MsgBox "There were " & .FoundFiles.Count & _
                " file(s) found."
'Display names of all found files.
            For i = 1 To .FoundFiles.Count
                MsgBox .FoundFiles(i)
            Next i
        Else
'If no files found, say so.
            MsgBox "There were no files found."
        End If
    End With

End Sub
```

THE *ASSISTANT* OBJECT

The Office Assistant is a friendly help feature in Office. Although developers and power users might not like the Assistant, it is appealing to typical users. The Assistant is relatively easy to program, so you can easily give your custom Office applications the same look and feel as the standard Office applications.

The *Assistant* object model is shown in Figure 8-3. The top-level *Assistant* object can appear on the screen with or without its hierarchically dependent *Balloon* object. Because the Assistant can use a wide range of characters and animations, it can be entertaining and informative without explanatory text. If you want to include explanatory text, you can program *Balloon* objects to appear with the Assistant. Balloons can include explanatory text or even serve as a simple data entry device. You use the *BalloonCheckBox* and the *BalloonLabel* collections with button controls to make your assistants interactive.

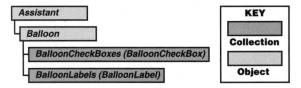

Figure 8-3. *You use the* Assistant *object to present an assistant, animate it, and display a balloon.*

Assistants

Assistants can add value to an application by conveying visually the various actions that your application is performing. You can further distinguish your custom application by consistently using a specific assistant or by regularly using different assistants but in highly differentiated circumstances. For example, use The Genius assistant representation for help pertaining to computations, but use the F1 robot when offering help about computer system topics. Your development team can adopt a rule to always invoke the working animation for any task that takes more than a couple of seconds.

Showing and animating an assistant

You can easily control the display and animation of an assistant by using the three short procedures shown here: *AssistantIdleOn*, *AssistantNotVisible*, and *AssistantSearchOn*. The *AssistantIdleOn* procedure contains a single line that sets the *Assistant* object's *Visible* property to *True*. Since *msoAnimationIdle* is the default animation type (the animation character is idle), the line that sets the *Animation* property is not needed and is commented out. In addition, this basic animation is part of the core Access library, so you can invoke it without referencing the Microsoft Office 9 Object Library. You can also run the *AssistantNotVisible* procedure without referencing the Office Object Library.

```
Sub AssistantIdleOn()
'Setting animation for idle is optional.
'    Assistant.Animation = msoAnimationIdle
    Assistant.Visible = True

End Sub


Sub AssistantNotVisible()
        Assistant.Visible = False

End Sub


Sub AssistantSearchOn()
        If Assistant.Visible = False Then Assistant.Visible = True
    Assistant.Animation = msoAnimationSearching

End Sub
```

To change the animation character's behavior to something other than idle, your procedure must set the object's *Animation* property as well as its *Visible* property. The *AssistantSearchOn* procedure causes an *Assistant* object to display its searching animation. Unlike many of the other animations, the searching animation repeats until you assign a new *Animation* setting. In addition, your project must have a reference to the Office Object Library for the searching animation to appear. (You can set this manually using the Tools menu in VBE.)

Automatically referencing the Office Object Library

One disadvantage of the *AssistantSearchOn* procedure is that it assumes a reference to the Office Object Library. If there is none, the procedure fails silently. The assistant appears, but it shows an idle, instead of a searching, animation. One way to handle this problem is to verify whether there is a reference to the Office Object Library and to add one automatically if necessary. Your application can then confidently invoke any animation, or indeed any other property of another shared Office object. The *AssistantSearchOn2* and *ReferenceOffice* procedures on the next page show this solution.

```
Sub AssistantSearchOn2()
    ReferenceOffice
    AssistantSearchOn

End Sub

Sub ReferenceOffice()
Dim ref1 As Reference
Dim blnOffice9In As Boolean, mso9Library As String

'Enumerate members of References collection to determine
'whether Office Object Library is already referenced.
    blnOffice9In = False
    For Each ref1 In References
        If ref1.name = "Office" Then
            blnOffice9In = True
        End If
    Next ref1

'If Office Object Library reference is missing, reference it.
    If blnOffice9In = False Then
        mso9Library = _
            "C:\program files\Microsoft Office\Office\mso9.dll"
        Application.References.AddFromFile mso9Library
    End If

End Sub
```

AssistantSearchOn2 is nearly identical to the original procedure for invoking a searching animation. It actually calls *AssistantSearchOn*, but it calls *ReferenceOffice* first. *ReferenceOffice* ensures that the current project has a reference to the Office Object Library. It starts by enumerating all the members of the *References* collection to determine whether any of them have a *Name* property of Office. If yes, then the procedure sets a Boolean variable to *True*. Otherwise, *blnOffice9In* retains its default setting of *False*. The second segment of *ReferenceOffice* creates a reference to the Office Object Library if the Boolean variable is *False*. Having ensured that the Office Object Library is referenced, *AssistantSearchOn2* can invoke the *AssistantSeachOn* procedure to finish activating the animation.

Displaying a searching animation

You can use the *Assistant* object to complement the *FileSearch* object. I already noted that some searches can take a while. In these situations, it is useful to present some kind of cue on the screen to show that your application is doing something. The Assistant's searching animation serves this purpose well.

The following procedure searches the entire C drive for .mdb files and returns a count of the files. By displaying the searching animation just before launching the search and restoring the idle animation just after the search, the Assistant informs the user that the search is in progress and then informs the user that it's completed. It uses two procedure calls—one just before invoking the *Execute* method and the other just after. Since the *FileSearch* and *Assistant* objects depend on the Office Object Library, the procedure calls *ReferenceOffice* as its first step. If a reference to the Office Object Library does not exist, the procedure creates one. Without this precaution, the procedure would fail if a user inadvertently canceled a reference to the Office Object Library.

```
Sub FileSearchAct()
'Reference the Office Object Library before using
'either the FileSearch or the Assistant objects.
    ReferenceOffice

'Search on C drive and its subfolders
'for *.mdb.
    With Application.FileSearch
'Start a new search.
        .NewSearch
'Set search criteria.
        .LookIn = "C:\"
        .SearchSubFolders = True
        .FileName = "*.mdb"
    End With

    With Application.FileSearch
'Execute the search.
'Turn searching assistant on first.
        AssistantSearchOn
        If .Execute() > 0 Then
            AssistantIdleOn
            MsgBox "There were " & .FoundFiles.Count & _
                " file(s) found."
        Else
'If no files found, say so.
            MsgBox "There were no files found."
        End If
    End With

End Sub
```

Selecting animation types

The Office Object Library contains over 30 different animation types. Figure 8-4 shows an Object Browser view that enumerates a subset of the animation types. Most animations, such as *msoAnimationSendingMail* and *msoAnimationPrinting*, go through a single cycle and return to idle. Other animations, such as *msoAnimationSearching* and *msoAnimationThinking*, repeat until you invoke an alternative animation. Because of IntelliSense, you do not have to recall the constant names for referring to animations. You can often simply select one from a list.

Figure 8-4. *The* msoAnimationType *member of the Office Object Library contains the more than 30 animation constants.*

Selecting Assistant characters

Eight Assistant characters ship with Office 2000, but Microsoft might add more in the future. You present an Assistant character by setting its *FileName* property to the name of that file. The following table lists the Assistant character names and their corresponding files.

Assistant Character	Filename
Clippit	Clippit.acs
Links	OffCat.acs
Rocky	Rocky.acs
Office Logo	Logo.acs

Assistant Character	Filename
The Dot	Dot.acs
Mother Nature	MNature.acs
The Genius	Genius.acs
F1	F1.acs

Previewing Assistant animations

Figure 8-5 shows a form in which the assistants act out their animations. The same animation can appear differently from one occurrence to the next. For example, there are at least three different versions of the goodbye animation for the F1 robot. The form offers seven animation types for each of three assistants. You can use the form to preview animations by making a selection from the Animation option group and then clicking an assistant command button. Analyzing the form's code will show you how to incorporate animations and change assistants in your applications.

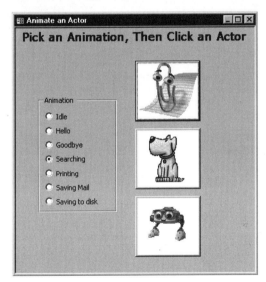

Figure 8-5. *You can use this form to preview the assistant animations.*

Figure 8-6 on the next page shows a selection of Assistant types and animations that you can preview using the form in Figure 8-5. At the top left, F1, the robot, executes the goodbye animation by burning to oblivion. Clippit rolls up a piece of paper and uses it to portray its searching animation. When Rocky performs the saving to disk animation, it holds up the disk before moving it to a collar pocket for safekeeping. F1 turns into a printer for the printing animation.

F1 - goodbye

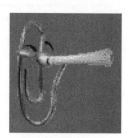

Clippit - searching

Rocky - saving to disk

F1 - printing

Figure 8-6. *A selection of animations performed by three different assistants. These were generated with the form shown in Figure 8-5.*

The following listing shows the code behind the form in Figure 8-5. The declaration area at the top of the module contains the design-time settings for the command buttons showing the Assistant types, and the buttons for different animation types in the option group. Notice that the buttons store the filename corresponding to the assistant on their face in their *Tag* property. Each button also has a simple event procedure for its click event. The buttons in the option group each have a value denoting an *msoAnimationType* constant. You use the Object Browser, shown in Figure 8-4, to determine the numerical value that matches a constant name. (For example, *msoAnimationSendingMail* equals 25.) As the form loads, it sets a series of properties to ensure that the assistant is ready when the user selects a button in the option group and clicks a command button.

```
Option Compare Database
'
'Design-time Command button settings
'    Name: cmdClippit , cmdRocky, cmdF1
'    Picture: c:\My Documents\My Pictures\clippit.bmp,
'        or rocky.bmp, or F1.bmp
```

```
'      Picture Type: Embedded
'      Tag: clippit.acs, or rocky.acs, or F1.acs
'      On Click: [Event Procedure]
'
'Design-time Option button settings
'      Idle button's Option Value = 1
'      Hello button's Option Value = 2
'      Goodbye button's Option Value = 3
'      Searching button's Option Value = 13
'      Printing button's Option Value = 18
'      Saving Mail button's Option Value = 25
'      Saving to disk button's Option Value = 112


Private Sub Form_Load()

    With Assistant
        .On = True
        .Sounds = True
        .Visible = True
    End With

End Sub



Private Sub cmdClippit_Click()
    AnimateActor Me.Controls("cmdClippit").Tag

End Sub



Private Sub cmdRocky_Click()
    AnimateActor Me.Controls("cmdRocky").Tag

End Sub



Private Sub cmdF1_Click()
    AnimateActor Me.Controls("cmdF1").Tag

End Sub


Sub AnimateActor(Fname As String)
```

(continued)

```
With Assistant
    .FileName = Fname
    .Animation = _
        Me.Controls("optAnimation")
    .Visible = True
End With
```

```
End Sub
```

The command buttons are central to the process. When you click a command button, the event procedure passes its tag value to the *AnimateActor* procedure. This procedure uses its passed argument to set the assistant's *FileName* property. Next, it sets the assistant's *Visible* property to *True* and sets its *Animation* property to the option group's value. The option group's value is, in turn, a function of the button that you clicked. The control has a default value of *1*, in case the user does not make a selection.

Balloons

You can use balloons to present text or graphics as well as to gather feedback from users. You can present balloons as modal, modeless, or autodown dialog boxes. The balloon's *Mode* property controls the type of balloon. The *msoModeAutoDown* setting closes the balloon if the user clicks anywhere on the screen. The modeless (*msoModeModeless*) and modal (*msoModeModal*) settings are more common. The modeless setting keeps a balloon open while users work outside of it. The modal setting forces a response before allowing any other behavior to occur. The default value for the *Mode* property is *msoModeModal*.

You use the *NewBalloon* property for the *Assistant* object to create a *Balloon* object. Balloons have heading, text, label, check box, and button areas. You can populate these areas using corresponding property settings or hierarchical objects such as *BalloonCheckBoxes* and *BalloonLabels*. You assign text to the check boxes and labels using their *Text* property. You can further customize the content of a balloon using its *Icon* property. Six icons convey various types of message features, such as alerts, questions, information, and tips.

Balloon graphics

The following procedure presents a balloon with a heading, text, and icon. It also uses the default button (OK). Escape formatting strings in the *Heading* property's text mark the beginning (*{ul 1}*) and end (*{ul 0}*) of underlined text in the heading area. (The escape formatting strings can also be used to designate underlined text in the text area.) The *Text* property setting includes a bitmap image in the text area. Notice that you can wrap text around an image. The *Icon* property setting marks the balloon's content as information. Finally, the *Show* method opens the Assistant and its associated balloon. Figure 8-7 shows the Assistant and balloon that appear after you run the *balloonTextImageIcon* procedure.

```
Sub balloonTextImageIcon()

    With Assistant.NewBalloon
        .Heading = "This is what {ul 1}F1{ul 0} looks like" & _
            " in a balloon text area"
        .Text = " Some text before it " & _
            "{bmp ""C:\My Documents\My Pictures\F1.bmp""}" & _
            "and more after it."
        .Icon = msoIconAlertInfo
        .Show
    End With

End Sub
```

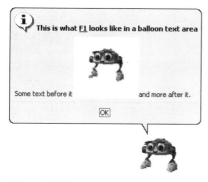

Figure 8-7. *You can include graphics in your balloons, and you can define the content using* Icon *property settings (such as the* AlertInfo *icon setting used for this balloon).*

Balloon labels

The two procedures on the next page prepare a balloon with labels and no buttons. The *setLabelCount* procedure passes an argument to the *balloonHeadTextLabel* routine. For valid arguments from 1 through 5, the called procedure presents an assistant with a balloon that contains as many labels as the value passed to it. Each label appears with a simple text string declaring the label number. Buttons in the balloon are not necessary with this design because clicking a label closes the balloon. The *Show* method opens the balloon and passes the value of the clicked label to the integer variable, *i*. A message box displays the number of the label the user clicked to close the balloon.

```
Sub setLabelCount()
    balloonHeadTextLabel 5
End Sub

Sub balloonHeadTextLabel(LabelCount As Integer)
On Error GoTo LabelTrap
Dim b1 As balloon, i As Integer

'Check for 0 or negative label count.
    If LabelCount <= 0 Then
        Err.Raise 9
    End If

    Set b1 = Assistant.NewBalloon

'Create balloon with specified number of labels.
    With b1
        .Heading = "This is my heading"
        .Text = "Select one of these things:"
        For i = 1 To LabelCount
            .Labels(i).Text = "Label " & i
        Next i
        .Button = msoButtonSetNone
        i = .Show
    End With

'Confirm label that user clicked.
    MsgBox i, vbInformation, "Programming Microsoft Access 2000"

LabelExit:
    Exit Sub

LabelTrap:
    If Err.Number = 9 Then
        MsgBox "Number of labels more than 5 or less than " & _
            "1. Retry with another number.", vbInformation, _
            "Programming Microsoft Access 2000"
    Else
        Debug.Print Err.Number
        MsgBox "Unanticipated error. Error number = " & _
            Err.Number & vbCrLf & "Error Description: " & _
            Err.Description, vbInformation, _
            "Programming Microsoft Access 2000"
    End If
    Resume LabelExit

End Sub
```

Built-in and custom error-trapping logic detects illegitimate arguments for the number of labels. If the passed argument is greater than 5, the *For...Next* loop that assigns label values fails on the attempt to assign text to the sixth label. This error (error number 9) results because balloons can show up to five labels only. Zero and negative arguments to the procedure do not generate the same error, but they also do not populate the balloon with labels. Therefore, the *balloonHeadTextLabel* procedure traps these values with an *If...Then* statement and raises a custom error with a number of 9. The procedure's trap for the error instructs the user to enter only values from 1 through 5.

Collecting user input with balloons

The *BalloonCheckBoxes* collection lets you present a suite of options and collect user responses. You are again limited to five controls—in this case, the controls are check boxes. Unlike label controls, check box controls do not close a balloon after they are selected. Therefore, if you specify a balloon with check boxes, you must assign a button set that can close the balloon.

The two procedures below offer a general framework for displaying check box controls in a balloon. They do not include error trapping, but in practice, you should include error logic like that in the preceding sample. The *setCheckCount* procedure passes an argument in the range of 1 through 5 to indicate how many check boxes to include. The second procedure starts by setting a reference, *b1*, to a new balloon. It assigns the *Balloon* object's *Button* property to *msoButtonSetOkCancel* to include OK and Cancel buttons. This offers two routes to closing the balloon. After setting values for the heading and text in the balloon, it assigns text to each text box. The return value from the *Show* method in this case indicates which button the user clicked.

```
Sub setCheckCount()

    balloonHeadTextCheck 5

End Sub


Sub balloonHeadTextCheck(CheckCount As Integer)
Dim b1 As balloon, i As Integer
Dim strChecks As String, iChecks As Integer

'Set reference to the balloon.
    Set b1 = Assistant.NewBalloon

'Assign text to check box controls.
    With b1
```

(continued)

```
            .Button = msoButtonSetOkCancel
            .Heading = "Here's the Heading"
            .Text = "This is some text in the balloon."
            For i = 1 To CheckCount
                .Checkboxes(i).Text = "Check box # " & i
            Next
            i = .Show
        End With

'Did user click Cancel button?
        If i = msoBalloonButtonCancel Then
            MsgBox "You cancelled the balloon.", vbInformation, _
                "Programming Microsoft Access 2000"
            Exit Sub
        End If

'Record individual boxes checked and count of
'all checked boxes.
        For i = 1 To CheckCount
            If b1.Checkboxes(i).Checked = True Then
                If strCheck = "" Then
                    strCheck = CStr(i)
                Else
                    strCheck = strCheck & ", " & CStr(i)
                End If
                iChecks = iChecks + 1
            End If
        Next i

'Present a message box with the results.
        If iChecks = 0 Then
            MsgBox "No boxes checked.", vbInformation, _
                "Programming Microsoft Access 2000"
        ElseIf iChecks = 1 Then
            MsgBox "You checked box " & strCheck & ".", _
                vbInformation, "Programming Microsoft Access 2000"
        Else
            MsgBox "You checked " & iChecks & " boxes. " & _
                "These were boxes: " & strCheck & ".", _
                vbInformation, "Programming Microsoft Access 2000"
        End If

End Sub
```

The remainder of the *balloonHeadTextCheck* procedure processes the reply to the balloon. First, the procedure checks the return value from the *Show* method. If this value equals the *msoBalloonButtonCancel* constant, the user clicked the Cancel button. After displaying a message announcing this, the procedure simply exits.

Since the only way to close the balloon is by clicking OK or Cancel, the user must have clicked OK if he or she did not click Cancel. The next block of code performs two tasks: It develops a text string indicating boxes with a check, and then it counts the number of boxes with checks. The last block of code in the procedure uses the string and count to prepare a message box statement that no boxes were checked, only one box was checked, or several boxes were checked.

Modeless balloons

The sample below processes modeless balloons, which stay open while the user does something in another part of the application. All the samples so far have dealt with modal balloons. One feature tailored for working with modeless balloons is the *Callback* property. You set this property to the name of another procedure that will do something with the response to the balloon. The *Callback* procedure for a modeless balloon must contain three parameters in a set sequence. The first parameter includes a variable that represents the balloon reference. The second one includes a variable to pass along the control a user clicked. The third one uses a long variable that identifies the *Private* property of the balloon invoking the callback procedure. It is especially important with a modeless balloon that you designate a control for closing it. If you do not offer the user such a control, the balloon might stay open indefinitely.

The procedure below presents a balloon with four labels. Notice that the balloon's *Mode* property is *msoModeModeless*. This setting requires a *Callback* property setting. Without one, the procedure will generate an error. Notice that one of the labels explicitly denotes a close option. You can also represent a close option using a *Button* property setting. Clicking a label does not automatically close the balloon; it invokes the *Callback* procedure named *answerHelp*. This procedure appears in Figure 8-8 on the following page.

```
Sub modalCallbackDemo()
Dim bl As balloon

    Set bl = Assistant.NewBalloon

    With bl
        .Heading = "Balloon to Call for Help with a Process"
        .Text = "Give me more info about:"
        .Labels(1).Text = "Printing"
        .Labels(2).Text = "Saving as mail"
        .Labels(3).Text = "Saving to disk"
```

(continued)

```
        .Labels(4).Text = "Close"
        .Button = msoButtonSetNone
        .Mode = msoModeModeless
        .Callback = "answerHelp"
        .Show
    End With

End Sub
```

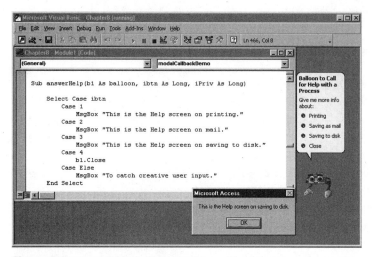

Figure 8-8. *A modeless balloon and its callback routine.*

The *answerHelp* procedure presents a message box whose content is determined by the label that was clicked in the balloon. The *Select Case* statement that processes the reply reads the label clicked from the second parameter passed to the callback procedure. After the user closes the message box, the balloon remains open. Generally, users can navigate around a form while a modeless balloon presents help on how to respond to a field on the form. If the user clicks the fourth button, the procedure uses the reference to the balloon, *b1*, to invoke the *Close* method.

THE *COMMANDBAR* OBJECT

The *CommandBar* object model (shown in Figure 8-9) is very rich—it includes both built-in and custom command bars. *Command bar* is a generic term that refers to a menu bar, a toolbar, or a popup menu bar. *CommandBar* controls enable users to interface with command bars and interact with an application. The three broad classes of *CommandBar* controls are *CommandBarButton*, *CommandBarComboBox*, and *CommandBarPopup* objects.

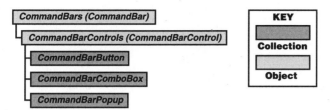

Figure 8-9. *You use the* CommandBar *object model to customize built-in command bars and create custom command bars.*

Enumerating Command Bar Elements

Enumerating command bar elements is critical to working with command bars. Enumeration is a vehicle for learning the hierarchy of the *CommandBar* object. The knowledge that you gain through the following samples will help you when you modify built-in command bars and develop custom ones.

The following short procedure gives a count of command bars in an application. If there are no custom command bars, the procedure reports a count of the built-in command bars, 140. The number would be higher if an application had custom command bars.

```
Sub countCommandBars()

    MsgBox "There are " & CommandBars.Count & _
        " bars in the CommandBars collection."

End Sub
```

There are three types of command bars. The Office Object Library includes the *msoBarType* constants to reference these as *msoBarTypeNormal*, *msoBarTypeMenuBar*, and *msoBarTypePopup*. You can also distinguish between built-in and custom command bars. The following procedure gives the count by type of command bar for each built-in toolbar.

```
Sub builtinCommandBarCount()
Dim cbr1 As CommandBar
Dim iMbars As Integer, iTbars As Integer
Dim iPbars As Integer, ibuiltin As Integer

    For Each cbr1 In CommandBars
        If cbr1.BuiltIn Then
            ibuiltin = ibuiltin + 1
            If cbr1.Type = msoBarTypeMenuBar Then
                iMbars = iMbars + 1
            ElseIf cbr1.Type = msoBarTypeNormal Then
                iTbars = iTbars + 1
```

(continued)

```
            Else
                  iPbars = iPbars + 1
            End If
        End If
    Next
    MsgBox "There are " & ibuiltin & " command bars. " & _
        IMBars & "is a menu bar, " & iTbars & " are toolbars, and " & _
        iPbars & " are popup bars."

End Sub
```

Listing visible command bars

Since there are 140 built-in command bars, you probably will not want to enumerate all of them very often. However, subsets of them can be important to an application. For example, your application might want to know which command bars are visible. The following *enumerateVisibleCommandBars* procedure writes a line to the Immediate window for each visible command bar. The lines display three properties for each command bar— the command bar name, type, and count of controls. A pair of nested *Immediate If* functions decode the *Type* property. Rather than enumerate the controls on command bars to develop a count, the procedure simply reports the command bar's *Count* property.

```
Sub enumerateVisibleCommandBars()
Dim cbr1 As CommandBar

    For Each cbr1 In CommandBars
        If cbr1.Visible = True Then
            Debug.Print cbr1.name, _
                (IIf(cbr1.Type = msoBarTypeNormal, _
                "toolbar", _
                IIf(cbr1.Type = msoBarTypeMenuBar, _
                "menu bar", "popup bar"))), _
                cbr1.Controls.Count
        End If
    Next cbr1

End Sub
```

It is relatively easy to extend the above code to enumerate the individual controls on each visible command bar. Command bars have a *Controls* collection, and the elements of this collection are *CommandBarControl* objects. The following procedure applies a *CommandBar* object and a *CommandBarControl* object while listing the captions for the controls on all visible command bars.

```
Sub enumerateControlCaptions()
Dim cbr1 As CommandBar
Dim ctl1 As CommandBarControl
```

```
    For Each cbr1 In CommandBars
        If cbr1.Visible = True Then
            Debug.Print "Command bar name: " & cbr1.name & _
                " and control count: "; cbr1.Controls.Count
                For Each ctl1 In cbr1.Controls
                    Debug.Print cbr1.name, ctl1.Caption
                Next ctl1
        End If
    Next cbr1

End Sub
```

Listing menu commands

Finally, you might need to list the individual commands on a menu. This involves treating the menu as a command bar so that the commands expose themselves as controls. You can determine the name for a command bar representing a menu using the *enumerateControlCaptions* procedure (or a variation of it). The following pair of procedures loop through the controls on a menu. The first procedure passes a command bar name to the second procedure, which loops through the controls for that command bar.

```
Sub listCommands()
        enumerateCommandsOnMenu ("Help")

End Sub


Sub enumerateCommandsOnMenu(menuName)
Dim cbr1 As CommandBar
Dim ctl1 As CommandBarControl

'Set a reference to a command bar.
    Set cbr1 = CommandBars(menuName)

'Loop through the controls for that command bar.
    For Each ctl1 In cbr1.Controls
        Debug.Print ctl1.Caption
    Next ctl1

End Sub
```

Manipulating Built-In Command Bars

You can modify built-in command bars in several ways. The following sections explore some of these.

Disabling and reenabling command bars and their controls

You can disable and restore entire command bars. The following two procedures disable the built-in menu bar (called Menu Bar) and then reenable it. To make this command bar inoperable on a form, you simply set its *Enable* property to *False* within a form event procedure. Your applications can condition the disabling of a command bar on various factors, such as a user ID.

```
Sub disableMenuBar()
Dim cbr1 As CommandBar

    For Each cbr1 In CommandBars
        If cbr1.name = "Menu Bar" Then
            cbr1.Enabled = False
        End If
    Next cbr1

End Sub


Sub enableMenuBar()
Dim cbr1 As CommandBar

    For Each cbr1 In CommandBars
        If cbr1.name = "Menu Bar" Then
            cbr1.Enabled = True
        End If
    Next cbr1

End Sub
```

You can also disable individual commands on a menu bar or toolbar. The first procedure in the following pair disables the View command on the Menu Bar menu bar and the Form View toolbar. This helps to secure a form's design by removing two familiar routes for switching from Form view to Design view. In addition to disabling the View control, the first procedure protects the change by setting the command bar's *Protection* property to *msoBarNoCustomize*. This setting grays the Reset button in the Customize dialog box for the Menu Bar and Form View command bars. The second procedure reenables the commands on both command bars.

```
Sub disableViewMenuAndControl()
Dim ctl1 As CommandBarControl

'Disable and protect View Menu.
    Set ctl1 = CommandBars("Menu Bar").Controls("View")
```

```
    ctl1.Enabled = False
    CommandBars("Menu Bar").Protection = msoBarNoCustomize

'Disable and protect View Control.
    Set ctl1 = CommandBars("Form View").Controls("View")
    ctl1.Enabled = False
    CommandBars("Form View").Protection = msoBarNoCustomize

End Sub



Sub enableViewMenuAndControl()
Dim ctl1 As CommandBarControl

'Enable View Menu.
    Set ctl1 = CommandBars("Menu Bar").Controls("View")
    ctl1.Enabled = True

'Enable View Control.
    Set ctl1 = CommandBars("Form View").Controls("View")
    ctl1.Enabled = True

End Sub
```

Making invisible command bars visible

Another simple but powerful manipulation you can carry out is exposing a built-in menu that does not normally show. The following procedure displays the name, type, and number of controls on each visible command bar. If the Web toolbar is not visible, the procedure resets its *Visible* property and leaves a record of it in the Immediate window by printing its name, type, and control count. You can make the Web toolbar disappear by resetting its *Visible* property to *False*.

```
Sub showWebBar()
Dim cbr1 As CommandBar

    For Each cbr1 In CommandBars
        If cbr1.Visible = True Then
            Debug.Print cbr1.name, cbr1.Type, cbr1.Controls.Count
        ElseIf cbr1.name = "Web" Then
            cbr1.Visible = True
            Debug.Print cbr1.name, cbr1.Type, cbr1.Controls.Count
        End If
    Next cbr1

End Sub
```

Adding commands to built-in command bars

Besides manipulating built-in members of the *CommandBars* collection, you can add custom commands to any built-in toolbar. One simple way to do this is to add a *CommandBarButton* object. You must know the precise name of a command bar to add a new button to it with the *Add* method. (Recall that you can run the *enumerateControlCaptions* procedure to list the command bar names.) After adding the button, you set properties for the new *CommandBarButton* object so that it points at a custom procedure or function.

The *newMenuItem* procedure and three related procedures below add new menu items. The *newMenuItem* procedure adds *CommandBarButton* objects to the end of a Tools command bar. The three related procedures let users specify whether the Assistant appears as Clippit, Rocky, or F1. The new *CommandBarButton* objects lets users invoke the procedures that control which assistant to display.

```
Sub newMenuItem()
Dim newItem As CommandBarButton

'Set reference to new control on the Tools command bar.
    Set newItem = CommandBars("Tools").Controls. _
        Add(Type:=msoControlButton)
'Start new group with command to invoke showClippit.
    With newItem
        .BeginGroup = True
        .Caption = "Show Clippit"
        .OnAction = "showClippit"
    End With

'Set reference to new control on the Tools command bar.
    Set newItem = CommandBars("Tools").Controls. _
        Add(Type:=msoControlButton)
'Assign command to invoke showRocky.
    With newItem
        .Caption = "Show Rocky"
        .OnAction = "showRocky"
    End With

'Set reference to new control on the Tools command bar.
    Set newItem = CommandBars("Tools").Controls. _
        Add(Type:=msoControlButton)
'Assign command to invoke showRocky.
    With newItem
        .Caption = "Show F1"
        .OnAction = "showF1"
    End With

End Sub
```

```
Sub showRocky()

    With Assistant
        .Visible = True
        .FileName = "Rocky.acs"
        .On = True
    End With

End Sub


Sub showClippit()

    With Assistant
        .Visible = True
        .FileName = "Clippit.acs"
        .On = True
    End With

End Sub


Sub showF1()

    With Assistant
        .Visible = True
        .FileName = "F1.acs"
        .On = True
    End With

End Sub
```

You use the *Add* method for the *Controls* collection of a command bar to insert a new control on a built-in menu. This method takes several arguments, including a *Type* parameter. In addition to the button control (*msoControlButton*) in the sample, you can specify a simple text box (*msoConrolEdit*), a combo box (*msoControlComboBox*), and more. By default, the *Add* method inserts your new control at the end of a command bar, but you can override this feature so that the control appears elsewhere on the command bar. Another parameter, *ID*, facilitates the addition of built-in commands from other menus to your custom command bar.

After adding a control to a built-in command bar, you can tie it to a custom function using the *OnAction* property. You set the property's value equal to the name of a procedure you want your new control to invoke. The control's *Caption* property offers an easy way to label the new control. You can use the

CopyFace and *PasteFace* methods to mark your custom controls. When the *BeginGroup* property is set to *True*, a control appears on a command bar with a divider line before it. The sample sets this property to *True* for the first of the three custom controls, but it leaves it at the default value of *False* for the remaining two controls.

Restoring command bars

As you refine custom applications, you will sometimes want to remove custom controls on built-in menus. You can do this using the *Reset* method. The following procedure clears any custom controls on the Tools command bar.

```
Sub removeMenuItem()
    CommandBars("Tools").Reset

End Sub
```

Creating Custom Command Bars

Creating a custom command bar involves at least three steps:

1. Adding a new command bar to your application. It will be blank when your code initially inserts it.

2. Positioning controls on the command bar. This is similar to placing controls on a built-in command bar.

3. Setting the *Visible* property of the command bar to *True* when you want to show it. You can also let users expose your custom command bar using standard features (such as the Customize dialog box).

The following two procedures add a custom command bar with a single button control to make Rocky appear. The *newCommandBarAndButton* procedure passes off the first two steps of creating command bars to the procedure *addShowAssistantsAndRocky*. Placing these steps in a separate procedure has advantages for a subsequent sample. The *addShowAssistantsAndRocky* procedure names the new custom command bar Show Assistants. Next, the procedure adds a custom control. When you specify controls for custom command bars, you must assign a value to the *Style* property as well as the other property values that you set with built-in command bars. Failing to do so in the procedure *addShowAssistantsAndRocky* can cause the button on the command bar to appear blank.

```
Sub newCommandBarAndButton()
On Error GoTo CBarBtnTrap
Dim cbr1 As CommandBar
Dim cbr1btn1 As CommandBarButton
Dim cbr1Name As String
```

```
'Add command bar to show Rocky.
    addShowAssistantsAndRocky

'Make CommandBar visible.
    Set cbr1 = CommandBars("Show Assistants")
    cbr1.Visible = True

CBarBtnExit:
    Exit Sub

CBarBtnTrap:
    Debug.Print Err.Number; Err.Description
    Resume CBarBtnExit
End Sub


Sub addShowAssistantsAndRocky()
Dim cbr1 As CommandBar
Dim cbr1btn1 As CommandBarButton

'Add a command bar named Show Assistants.
    Set cbr1 = CommandBars.Add("Show Assistants", _
        msoBarTop, , True)

'Add a button control to the command bar.
    Set cbr1btn1 = cbr1.Controls _
        .Add(msoControlButton, , , , True)
'Set button properties.
    With cbr1btn1
        .Caption = "Show Rocky"
        .BeginGroup = True
        .OnAction = "showRocky"
        .Style = msoButtonCaption
    End With

End Sub
```

After the *newCommandBarAndButton* procedure regains control, it sets the control's *Visible* property to *True*. Without this step, the only way a user can view the new custom command bar is by explicitly showing it (for instance, by right-clicking a command bar and selecting the name of the command bar you want to show). The error-trapping logic in the *newCommandBarAndButton* procedure allows the application to invoke the procedure even when the command bar is already present. Without the error-trapping logic, the *addShowAssistantsAndRocky* procedure generates a fatal error when it tries to add a command bar that already exists. Since this error is not critical (after all, the command bar is there already), it is reasonable to ignore it.

Modifying Custom Command Bars

The following three procedures add new controls to an existing custom command bar. They also reveal another approach to handling the problem of an existing command bar. The *addCbrBtns* procedure inserts another pair of buttons on the Show Assistants command bar created in the previous sample. If that command bar does not already exist, this procedure is smart enough to run the *addShowAssistantsAndRocky* procedure. *addCbrBtns* conditionally calls the procedure that creates the Show Assistants command bar based on the return value of the *doesCbrExist* function procedure. This function procedure checks for the existence of a command bar. Whether or not the Show Assistants command bar exists, the initial *If...Then...Else* statement sets a reference to it. The rest of the procedure adds two more buttons to the command bar. *addCbrBtns* closes by making the command bar visible if it is not already visible.

```
Sub moreButtons()
    addCbrBtns "Show Assistants"

End Sub



Sub addCbrBtns(cbrName As String)
Dim cbr1 As CommandBar
Dim cbr1btn1 As CommandBarButton

'Optionally create Show Assistants command bar.
'Reference it with a variable.
    If Not doesCbrExist(cbrName) Then
        addShowAssistantsAndRocky
        Set cbr1 = CommandBars(cbrName)
    Else
        Set cbr1 = CommandBars(cbrName)
    End If

'Add a new button to Show Assistants command bar.
    Set cbr1btn1 = cbr1.Controls _
        .Add(msoControlButton, , , , True)
'Set properties for button to show Clippit.
    With cbr1btn1
        .Caption = "Show Clippit"
```

```
        .OnAction = "showClippit"
        .Style = msoButtonCaption
    End With

'Add a new button to Show Assistants command bar.
    Set cbr1btn1 = cbr1.Controls _
        .Add(msoControlButton, , , , True)
'Set properties for button to show F1.
    With cbr1btn1
        .Caption = "Show F1"
        .OnAction = "showF1"
        .Style = msoButtonCaption
    End With

'Make the Show Assistants command bar visible.
    If Not cbr1.Visible = True Then cbr1.Visible = True

End Sub


Function doesCbrExist(cbrName As String) As Boolean
Dim cbr1 As CommandBar

    doesCbrExist = False
    For Each cbr1 In CommandBars
        If cbr1.name = cbrName Then
            doesCbrExist = True
        End If
    Next cbr1

End Function
```

Creating Popup Command Bars

The first sample procedure on the following page enables a combo box control on a custom command bar and makes the command bar a popup menu bar. Figure 8-10 (on the next page) shows the behavior of the popup menu bar on a form. You click anywhere on the form to bring up a custom command bar with a single control. This control is a combo box with entries for selecting the Clippit, Rocky, or F1 assistant. The process starts with a click event for the form's Detail section. The next three procedures code the sample depicted in Figure 8-10.

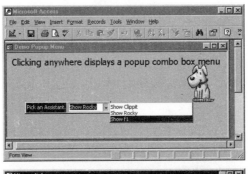

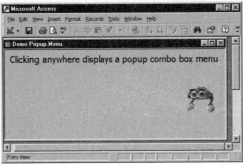

Figure 8-10. *A custom popup menu bar with a combo box control. You click anywhere on the form to open the custom menu bar.*

```
Private Sub Detail_Click()
    ShowAndProcessComboBox

End Sub



Sub showAndProcessComboBox()
Dim cbr1 As CommandBar

'Call from Click Event in form.

    If doesCbrExist("Custom1") Then
        CommandBars("Custom1").ShowPopup
    Else
        createAndShowPopUpMenu
    End If

End Sub



Sub createAndShowPopUpMenu()
Dim cbr1 As CommandBar
```

```
'Add command bar named Custom1.
    Set cbr1 = CommandBars _
        .Add(name:="Custom1", Position:=msoBarPopup, Temporary:=True)

    With cbr1
        .Controls.Add Type:=msoControlComboBox
        With .Controls(1)
            .Style = msoComboLabel
            .Caption = "Pick an Assistant."
            .AddItem "Show Clippit"
            .AddItem "Show Rocky"
            .AddItem "Show F1"
            .OnAction = "processComboBoxChoice"
        End With
    End With

    cbr1.ShowPopup

End Sub


Sub processComboBoxChoice()
Dim caseValue As Integer

'Decode selected item and implement corresponding method.
    Select Case _
        CommandBars("custom1").Controls(1).ListIndex
        Case 1
            showClippit
        Case 2
            showRocky
        Case 3
            showF1
    End Select

End Sub
```

The first procedure is the event procedure behind the form. It calls *showAndProcessComboBox*, a procedure that resides in a standard module. This procedure determines whether the Custom1 command bar already exists. If the command bar exists, the procedure invokes the *ShowPopup* method to display the command bar as a popup menu bar. Otherwise, it creates the Custom1 command bar with a call to *createAndShowPopUpMenu*. As the name of this third procedure implies, it creates the custom command bar just before displaying it as a popup menu bar.

The *createAndShowPopUpMenu* procedure is compact, but it uses interesting techniques. First, it uses nested *With...End* statements. The outer one adds a new member to the *CommandBars* collection, and the inner one adds a control to that member. The property assignments within the inner *With...End* statement specify a combo box style for the control, define the elements in the combo box list, and denote a procedure, *processComboBoxChoice*, that fires after a selection from the combo box. This final procedure uses a *Select Case* statement based on the selected element from the combo box list to invoke one of three custom procedures that display an assistant.

Deleting Custom Command Bars

If you build custom command bars, you will eventually need to remove one or more of them within an application. The following sample does this by looping through all the command bars to find the custom ones—those with a *Built-in* property of *False*. When the procedure finds a custom command bar, it asks the user whether to delete the command bar. If the user replies Yes, it deletes that command bar and adds one to the count of deleted command bars. In any event, the procedure adds one to a variable that tallies custom command bars.

```
Sub deleteCustomCbr()
Dim cbr1 As CommandBar, delFlag As Boolean
Dim delBars As Integer, cusBars As Integer

'Not necessary to initialize delFlag, delBars, or
'cusBars because their default values (False and 0)
'are OK.

'Conditionally delete custom menu bars.
    For Each cbr1 In CommandBars
        If (cbr1.BuiltIn = False) Then
            If MsgBox("Are you sure that you want to " & _
                "delete the " & cbr1.name & " command bar?", _
                vbYesNo, "Programming Microsoft Access 2000") = _
                vbYes Then
                cbr1.Delete
                delFlag = True
                delBars = delBars + 1
            End If
            cusBars = cusBars + 1
        End If
    Next cbr1
```

```
'Report outcome of command bar enumeration.
    If Not delFlag Then
        If cusBars > 0 Then
            MsgBox "No custom command bars deleted " & _
                "out of a total of " & cusBars & ".", _
                vbInformation, "Programming Microsoft Access 2000"
        Else
            MsgBox "No custom command bars.", vbInformation, _
                "Programming Microsoft Access 2000"
        End If
    Else
        MsgBox delBars & " custom command bar(s) deleted.", _
            vbInformation, "Programming Microsoft Access 2000"
    End If

End Sub
```

The *deleteCustomCbr* procedure closes by presenting one of three possible statements based on the number of deletions and the number of custom command bars. A pair of nested *If…Then…Else* statements handles the routing to the correct message box statement. If there are no deletions but there is at least one custom command bar, the statement displays a message reporting that no custom command bars were deleted and displaying the total number of custom command bars. If there are no deletions and no custom command bars, the procedure presents a message to that effect. Finally, if the procedure deleted any command bars, the message box reports that number.

Chapter 9

Integrating Access with Other Office Applications

Microsoft Access initially gained immense popularity as a component of the Microsoft Office suite. The Access user interface shares many elements with the user interfaces of the other Office applications, and it is relatively easy to transfer data between Access and the rest of Office. In addition, you can integrate Access with the other Office components in custom applications, allowing you to provide the strengths of a database package in the familiar and friendly environment of word processors and spreadsheets.

This chapter explains how to programmatically integrate Access 2000 with the other Office applications using built-in Access features:

■   Your applications can tap installable ISAM drivers through the *Connection* object to work with the data in a Microsoft Excel spreadsheet. A *Connection* object based on an ISAM driver can serve as a two-way data-sharing channel between Access and Excel.

■ You can tap Access data sources programmatically with the Microsoft Word mail merge capability to facilitate creation of mailing labels, form letters, and product catalogs.

■ Using automation, your applications can simultaneously exploit the object models from two or more Office applications. For example, an application can export names and addresses from an Access data store to a Microsoft Outlook Contacts folder. Similarly, you can populate values to tables in a Word document from an Access data source.

The samples in this chapter focus on Access, Outlook, and Word, but the general principles extend to other Office applications as well as third-party packages that expose their object models through automation and that enable manipulation using Microsoft Visual Basic for Applications (VBA).

LINKING ACCESS TO OTHER OFFICE APPLICATIONS

This section introduces three techniques (using installable ISAM drivers, the *OpenDataSource* method of the *MailMerge* object, and automation) for making Access work with other Office applications. Subsequent sections will apply these techniques in practical contexts.

Installable ISAM Drivers

You use the familiar Microsoft ActiveX Data Objects (ADO) *Connection* object to link to other data sources through installable ISAM drivers. These data sources can include non-Jet, non–open database connectivity (ODBC) data sources such as Excel, dBASE, and Paradox. In this section, we'll use the Excel ISAM driver for linking to Excel workbooks from Access. Similar techniques apply to ISAM drivers for dBASE, Paradox, Lotus 1-2-3, text, and HTML files, but each driver has its unique features and restrictions. You can learn more by examining the *Connect* property summary in the online help.

> **NOTE** Installable ISAM support continues to change with user requirements and technology developments. ISAM support for Microsoft FoxPro databases was discontinued with Access 2000 in favor of the Microsoft ODBC FoxPro driver. The traditional ISAM drivers still work for dBASE and Paradox data in version 5 and earlier. If you need read/write access to other versions, you must independently acquire the Borland Database Engine through Inprise.

When you use an ISAM driver, your connection string has three arguments, each of which must terminate with a semicolon. First, you designate a provider. When you use an installable ISAM driver, start your connection string with a reference to the Jet 4 provider. Follow this with a specification that points at the file for the data source. In the case of Excel, this includes the drive, path, and filename. In certain other cases, you can designate just the drive and the path. You designate this final parameter by setting the extended properties parameter equal to the name of the ISAM driver. There are specific drivers for different versions of Excel and for the other types of data sources you can link to. You reference an Excel 2000 workbook using the string *"Excel 8.0"* followed by a semicolon.

The following simple sample uses an ISAM driver to link to an Excel 2000 workbook in an Access 2000 application. The *Dim* statement declares and creates a new *Connection* object. The next statement opens the connection by pointing it at an Excel workbook through the Excel 8 ISAM driver. After creating the connection to the data source, your application must specify a range of cells in the workbook. This sample assigns the *customers* range within the file to a recordset named *rst1*. Access uses this link to work with the data in the workbook. The sample concludes by printing the first two columns of the first row from the range in the Excel workbook to the Immediate window in Access.

```
Sub connect2XLPrintFromFirst()
Dim cnn1 As New ADODB.Connection, rst1 As ADODB.Recordset

'Make connection to Excel source.
    cnn1.Open "Provider=Microsoft.Jet.OLEDB.4.0;" & _
        "Data Source=C:\Programming Access\Chap09\customers.xls;" & _
        "Extended Properties=Excel 8.0;"

'Open read-only recordset based on Excel source.
    Set rst1 = New ADODB.Recordset
    rst1.CursorType = adOpenForwardOnly
    rst1.LockType = adLockReadOnly
    rst1.Open "customers", cnn1, , , adCmdTable

'Print selected fields from first record.
    Debug.Print rst1.Fields(0).Value, rst1.Fields(1).Value

'Close connection to source.
    cnn1.Close

End Sub
```

When you work with an ISAM driver, the Excel data source (or even Excel itself) need not be open. Your application also doesn't require a reference to the Excel object model. Despite the Excel ISAM driver's minimal requirements, you can use it to both read and update Excel data sources.

The *OpenDataSource* Method

You can use the *OpenDataSource* method of the *MailMerge* object to link to an Access data source from within a Word application. You use Access—or more specifically, Jet—as a data store for mail merge applications that create mailing labels, form letters, product catalogs, and so on. While Access can do some of this through its *Report* object, Word is a more natural environment for composing content. It also has excellent text formatting tools and WYSIWYG features that the Access *Report* object does not have. You can tap these resources with Word-based VBA procedures as well as through automation from within Access.

When you reference an Access data source using the *OpenDataSource* method, you must first reference a Word document file and the Word *MailMerge* object. You specify two parameters for the method with Access: the *Name* parameter, which indicates the drive, path, and filename for the Access data source; and the *Connection* parameter, which designates either a Table or Query data source type and the name of the Access database object. Your Word document must have either bookmarks or mail merge fields that point to the fields in the Jet database. You invoke the *Execute* method for the *MailMerge* object to launch a merge that pulls data from a designated data source, such as an Access table, into a Word document.

You can filter values that appear in a Word mail merge document in several ways. For example, you can use the *OpenDataSource* method's *SQLStatement* parameter to specify which records to extract from a data source. When you do this with a Jet data source, you reference Access through an ODBC driver and specify *constr* as the *Connection* setting. You use SQL statement syntax to filter records from an Access table or query.

A second approach to filtering is with a special query within Access. The *OpenDataSource* method's *Connect* parameter merely references that query. You use the *FirstRecord* and *LastRecord* properties of the *DataSource* object to specify the first and last records to appear in a merged Word document. The *DataSource* object points to a target specified by the *OpenDataSource* method.

Automation

Using automation, you can enable one application to control another. The Microsoft Component Object Model (COM) defines the protocol for this capability. The controlling application interacts with the controlled application by manipulating its exposed properties and methods and responding to its events. To do this, it must have a reference to the other application's object library and must create an instance of the application. (See Chapters 7 and 8 for information on how to create and manage references programmatically.) The controlling application invokes methods and assigns property values through that instance of the controlled application.

Figure 9-1 shows a References dialog box from an Access application with references to Excel, Outlook, and Word as well as the Office library with the shared object models. In a sense, automation makes all the Office component object models shared. Access can expose its object model as an automation server, and it can tap the object models of other applications by acting as an automation client.

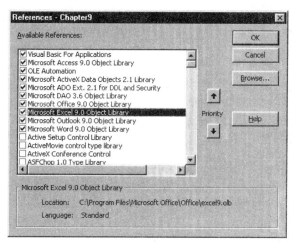

Figure 9-1. *A References dialog box in Access showing references to Excel, Outlook, and Word.*

CreateObject vs. GetObject

You use the *CreateObject* and *GetObject* functions to generate instances of other applications. You use *GetObject* to determine whether an instance of an application is already open. If it is, you can create a reference to it. If a user is not actively working with the instance, this might be acceptable. If the automation server application is not already open or if you prefer not to use an open instance, you can use the *CreateObject* function to create a new instance of an application. You can also use *GetObject* to open an instance of an application with a particular file open in it.

The following two procedures create an instance of Excel from an Access application. The second procedure, *isAppThere*, uses late binding to test for an instance of any Office application. An *objApp* variable with a generic object specification can represent any Office application (or even another COM object). The first procedure, *xlThere*, uses early binding. The *xlApp* variable can represent only an Excel *Application* object. You cannot replace *Excel.Application* in either the *CreateObject* or *GetObject* functions with another Office *Application* object, such as *Word.Application*. However, you can create another entire procedure—for example, one named *wordThere*—that includes a variable declared as a *Word.Application* object type. This new procedure can reference the generic *isAppThere* procedure in the same way that *xlThere* does.

```
Sub xlThere()
Dim xlApp As Excel.Application

    If isAppThere("Excel.Application") = False Then
'If no, create a new instance.
        Set xlApp = CreateObject("Excel.Application")
        xlApp.Visible = True
    Else
'Otherwise, reference the existing instance.
        Set xlApp = GetObject(, "Excel.Application")
    End If

'If user wants instance closed, close app
'and set reference to Nothing.
    If MsgBox("Close XL ?", vbYesNo, _
        "Programming Microsoft Access 2000") = vbYes Then
        xlApp.Quit
        Set xlApp = Nothing
    End If

End Sub


Function isAppThere(appName) As Boolean
On Error Resume Next
Dim objApp As Object

isAppThere = True

Set objApp = GetObject(, appName)
    If Err.Number <> 0 Then isAppThere = False

End Function
```

Automation does not normally make an Office application visible when it opens it. If you want an application to show, you must normally set its *Visible* property to *True*. Different applications expose different objects for you to automate. Excel exposes objects such as *Application*, *Workbook*, and *Worksheet*. The latter two, of course, are not available with other Office applications.

Closing an automation reference

The *xlThere* procedure conditionally disposes of a reference to another Office application. First, you close or quit the application. (Excel supports a *Quit* method.) Then you set the reference to *Nothing*. Both steps are required to retrieve the resources consumed by the automation reference.

WORKING WITH EXCEL FROM ACCESS

The first two samples below demonstrate some capabilities that the Excel installable ISAM can add to an application. The third sample shows a simple but powerful way to use automation. Instead of directly manipulating detailed elements of the object model of an automation server, the procedure launches a procedure within the automation server. The procedure, in turn, updates the spreadsheet file, but at the time and in the manner that an Access application determines.

Working with Values from Excel Worksheets

All three samples work with the Excel workbook depicted in Figure 9-2. The file is MyGas.xls. The first four columns of Sheet1 contain manually entered data, and the next four columns contain expressions based on the first four. The formula bar shows the expression for entries in the MPG column. The data resides in a range named *gas*. The Define Name dialog box shows the extent of the range in Sheet1.

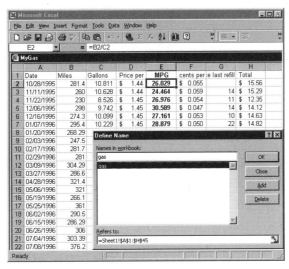

Figure 9-2. *An Excel spreadsheet with a named range,* gas, *extending over cells A1 through H45.*

The first sample reads the entries from Excel, performs some calculations in Access, and prints the results to the Immediate window. After establishing a connection to the Excel data source, your application can programmatically treat the data source just like an internal Access table. For example, you can enumerate records in the table or compute values based on the entries in the record source. The sample prints to the Immediate window the existing entries in the Excel worksheet alongside the results of expressions computed in Excel. This, incidentally, confirms that Access computations can generate results identical to those in Excel. This capability can reduce the amount of data that your application must read from a computationally intensive spreadsheet.

```
Sub openXLComputePrint()
Dim cnn1 As New ADODB.Connection
Dim rst1 As ADODB.Recordset
Dim computedMPG As Double, computedTotal As Currency

'Make connection to Excel source.
    cnn1.Open "Provider=Microsoft.Jet.OLEDB.4.0;" & _
        "Data Source=C:\Programming Access\Chap09\mygas.xls;" & _
        "Extended Properties=Excel 8.0;"

'Open read-only recordset based on Excel source.
'Recall default is read-only.
    Set rst1 = New ADODB.Recordset
    rst1.Open "gas", cnn1, , , adCmdTable

'Enumerate records and compute with field values.
    Do Until rst1.EOF
        computedMPG = rst1.Fields("Miles") / _
            rst1.Fields("Gallons")
        computedTotal = rst1.Fields("Gallons") * _
            rst1.Fields("Price per Gallon")
        Debug.Print rst1.Fields("Date"), _
            rst1.Fields("Miles"), _
            rst1.Fields("Gallons"), _
            rst1.Fields("Price per Gallon"), _
            rst1.Fields("MPG"), computedMPG, _
            rst1.Fields("Total"), computedTotal
        rst1.MoveNext
    Loop

'Close connection to source.
    cnn1.Close

End Sub
```

The subprocedure declares and creates a new *Connection* object, and then it opens the *Connection* object. This is critical when you work with an ISAM driver because this is how you manage your link to the data source outside of Access. The connection string points the object at the Excel file MyGas.xls. (Its data is excerpted in Figure 9-2.) You must conclude the connection string with an *Extended Properties* specification that points at the ISAM driver that your application uses. The sample uses one (*Excel 8.0*) that works with Excel 2000 and Excel 97 workbook files.

The *Recordset* reference that follows is another critical and relatively standard component of ISAM applications. By defining a recordset on the connection, your application gains the ability to read from and write to the remote data source. If your Access Application links to the Excel data source, you use the *Recordset* object's *AddNew* and *Update* methods to add new rows to a worksheet from Access. The recordset specification must also designate which portion of the workbook to link. If you reference the gas range, the recordset can use the built-in range for the worksheet. The syntax for referencing an external Excel table is identical to that for referencing an internal Access table.

> **NOTE**   If your application must write to or revise an Excel data source from Access, be sure to define a cursor that supports this functionality (for example, pass the *adOpenKeyset* constant for the cursor type and the *adLockOptimistic* constant for the lock type). Unlike DAO, the default ADO cursor does not support updating.

The next major element of the procedure is a *Do* loop that enumerates all the records in the gas range. The first two lines in the loop evaluate expressions for two computed values. The *computedMPG* and *computedTotal* variables compare Access to Excel arithmetic as they confirm your ability to manipulate data read from an Excel data source. The next seven lines within the *Do* loop print to the Immediate window Excel table field values along with the two computed variables for each row. You navigate through an Excel table exactly as you do an internal table. Of course, you must invoke a *MoveNext* method within the loop to progress through the spreadsheet rows.

Figure 9-3 on the next page shows the five rightmost columns of the output from the preceding sample. The first two columns show identical results for MPG from Excel (the first column) and Access (the second column). The same is true for the total gas bill for each gas fill-up. This confirms that the double and currency data types from Access can duplicate results from Excel.

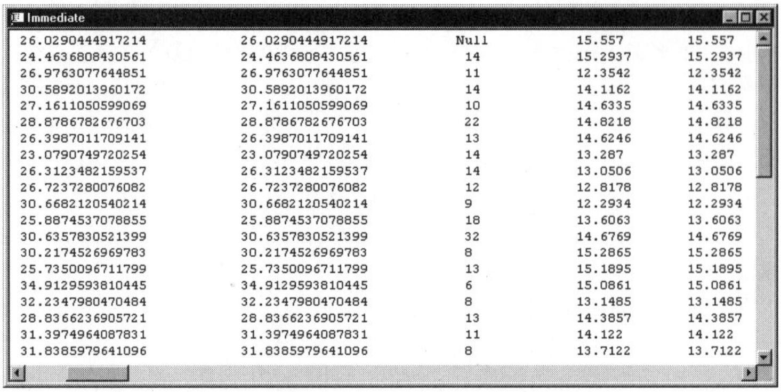

26.0290444917214	26.0290444917214	Null	15.557	15.557
24.4636808430561	24.4636808430561	14	15.2937	15.2937
26.9763077644851	26.9763077644851	11	12.3542	12.3542
30.5892013960172	30.5892013960172	14	14.1162	14.1162
27.1611050599069	27.1611050599069	10	14.6335	14.6335
28.8786782676703	28.8786782676703	22	14.8218	14.8218
26.3987011709141	26.3987011709141	13	14.6246	14.6246
23.0790749720254	23.0790749720254	14	13.287	13.287
26.3123482159537	26.3123482159537	14	13.0506	13.0506
26.7237280076082	26.7237280076082	12	12.8178	12.8178
30.6682120540214	30.6682120540214	9	12.2934	12.2934
25.8874537078855	25.8874537078855	18	13.6063	13.6063
30.6357830521399	30.6357830521399	32	14.6769	14.6769
30.2174526969783	30.2174526969783	8	15.2865	15.2865
25.7350096711799	25.7350096711799	13	15.1895	15.1895
34.9129593810445	34.9129593810445	6	15.0861	15.0861
32.2347980470484	32.2347980470484	8	13.1485	13.1485
28.8366236905721	28.8366236905721	13	14.3857	14.3857
31.3974964087831	31.3974964087831	11	14.122	14.122
31.8385979641096	31.8385979641096	8	13.7122	13.7122

Figure 9-3. *An excerpt from the output of the* openXLComputePrint *procedure. Notice the identical computational results from Access and Excel.*

Dynamically Creating Access Tables Based on Excel Worksheets

The preceding sample exposes the values in a spreadsheet through a recordset. If your application must regularly work with the data in a spreadsheet, you can improve performance by copying the spreadsheet values to a local table within Access. In addition, an application can reduce its demand for connection resources by copying spreadsheet values to local tables when it requires simultaneous access to several different spreadsheet ranges. The following sample programmatically creates a table that has an index for a spreadsheet range and then populates the table with values from the range. Incidentally, the sample uses the new Identity data type to specify the start and step values for the table's index field (*MyID*).

```
Sub createTableFromXL()
On Error GoTo createTableTrap
Dim cnn1 As ADODB.Connection
Dim cnn2 As New ADODB.Connection
Dim rst1 As ADODB.Recordset
Dim rst2 As ADODB.Recordset
Dim cat1 As ADOX.Catalog
Dim tbl1 As ADOX.Table
Dim pk1 As ADOX.Index

'Set catalog and table objects.
    set cnn1 = CurrentProject.Connection
    Set cat1 = New ADOX.Catalog
    cat1.ActiveConnection = cnn1
    Set tbl1 = New ADOX.Table
```

```
'Define table named gas and append it
'to the Tables collection.
    With tbl1
        .Name = "gas"
        .Columns.Append "Date", adDate
        .Columns.Append "Miles", adDouble
        .Columns.Append "Gallons", adDouble
        .Columns.Append "PricePerGallon", adCurrency
    End With
    cat1.Tables.Append tbl1

    strSQL = "ALTER TABLE Gas ADD COLUMN MyID Identity(2,2)"
    cnn1.Execute strSQL

    Set pk1 = New ADOX.Index
    With pk1
        .Name = "MyPrimaryKey"
        .PrimaryKey = True
        .Unique = True
        .IndexNulls = adIndexNullsDisallow
    End With
    pk1.Columns.Append "MyID"
    tbl1.Indexes.Append pk1

'Make connection to Excel source.
    cnn2.Open "Provider=Microsoft.Jet.OLEDB.4.0;" & _
        "Data Source=C:\Programming Access\Chap09\mygas.xls;" & _
        "Extended Properties=Excel 8.0;"

'Open read-only recordset based on Excel source.
'Recall default is read-only.
    Set rst1 = New ADODB.Recordset
    rst1.Open "gas", cnn2, , , adCmdTable


'Open read-write recordset based on local table
'named gas.
    Set rst2 = New ADODB.Recordset
    rst2.ActiveConnection = cnn1
    rst2.CursorType = adOpenKeyset
    rst2.LockType = adLockOptimistic
    rst2.Open "gas"

    Do Until rst1.EOF
        With rst2
            .AddNew
```

(continued)

```
                .Fields("Date") = rst1.Fields("Date")
                .Fields("Miles") = rst1.Fields("Miles")
                .Fields("Gallons") = rst1.Fields("Gallons")
                .Fields("PricePerGallon") = _
                    rst1.Fields("Price Per Gallon")
                .Update
            End With
            rst1.MoveNext
        Loop

createTableExit:
    Exit Sub

createTableTrap:
    If Err.Number = -2147217857 Then
        cat1.Tables.Delete "gas"
        Resume
    Else
        Debug.Print Err.Number; Err.Description
        Resume createTableExit
    End If

End Sub
```

The procedure above is lengthy because it performs several discrete but related functions. To create a local table with Excel spreadsheet values, the sample needs a pair of *Connection* and *Recordset* objects. These objects provide simultaneous connectivity to the spreadsheet and the local table so that the procedure can copy a row from one data source to the other. To define a local table programmatically within Access, the code declares *Catalog*, *Table*, and *Index* objects.

Before copying the data from Excel, the procedure prepares a local table to accept them. It starts by assigning the connection for the current project to the *cnn1* reference. Since *cnn1* refers to the native project connection, there is no need to include the *New* keyword in its declaration. On the other hand, the procedure does create new instances of the *Catalog* and *Table* objects (and their declarations reflect this by the inclusion of *New*). It then uses ADO code to define and append fields for holding spreadsheet values. However, it reverts to SQL code for specifying the start and step values for the index. This capability depends completely on built-in Jet engine functionality. Therefore, the SQL code is specific to the Jet database engine. After completing the definition of the index and appending it to the table, the procedure opens a connection to the spreadsheet. (This sample uses the same spreadsheet as the preceding one.)

Any attempt to redefine an existing table generates error number –2147217857. The procedure deletes the old table and resumes adding the new table. In a full-scale application, you might want to archive the old table.

The procedure prepares for copying values by creating two *Recordset* objects—one for the spreadsheet and one for the local table. The code uses the default cursor for the spreadsheet because it just reads values sequentially from it, but it uses an *adOpenKeyset* cursor type for the link to the local table so that it can add records. Since Access can exactly duplicate the computations of Excel, there is no need to copy computed fields. This keeps your table's field values independent of one another so that your table is normalized.

Running Excel Procedures from an Access Procedure

In the following procedure, *runXL*, Access uses the *GetObject* function to create an instance of the Excel *Application* object that contains the *MyGas* workbook shown in Figure 9-2 on page 387. It sets the *Visible* property of the *Application* and *Window* objects to *True*. Then it invokes the *Application* object's *Run* method for the *computeOnGas* procedure in the ThisWorkbook folder of the MyGas.xls file. After the *computeOnGas* procedure from the Excel file returns control to Access, the *runXL* procedure invokes the *Save* method for the ActiveWorkbook in Excel. This commits the changes to storage and avoids a prompt asking whether to do that when the next line invokes the *Quit* method. If you want to close Excel without saving the changes and without a prompt that asks whether to save them, you set the workbook's *Saved* property to *True* before invoking the *Quit* method. (See the commented line for the correct syntax.) You retrieve the automation resources by setting the automation object reference to *Nothing*.

```
Sub runXL()
Dim myXLWrkBk As Excel.Workbook

'Open connection to XL workbook and make visible.
    Set myXLWrkBk = GetObject("c:\Programming Access\Chap09\MyGas.xls")
    myXLWrkBk.Application.Visible = True
    myXLWrkBk.Application.Windows("MyGas.xls").Visible = True

'Run procedure in ThisWorkBook folder.
    myXLWrkBk.Application.Run "ThisWorkBook.computeOnGas"

'Close automation object.
'Either invoke the Save method or set the Saved
'property to True to avoid a prompt about saving changes.
    myXLWrkBk.Application.ActiveWorkbook.Save
'    myXLWrkBk.Application.ActiveWorkbook.Saved = True
    myXLWrkBk.Application.Quit
    Set myXLWrkBk = Nothing

End Sub
```

Figure 9-4 shows the worksheet after *computeOnGas* runs. Notice that it computes summary information two rows below the table's last row, and it adds a new column that displays the miles traveled per day between refills. The procedure also resizes the columns so that they fit their widest entry.

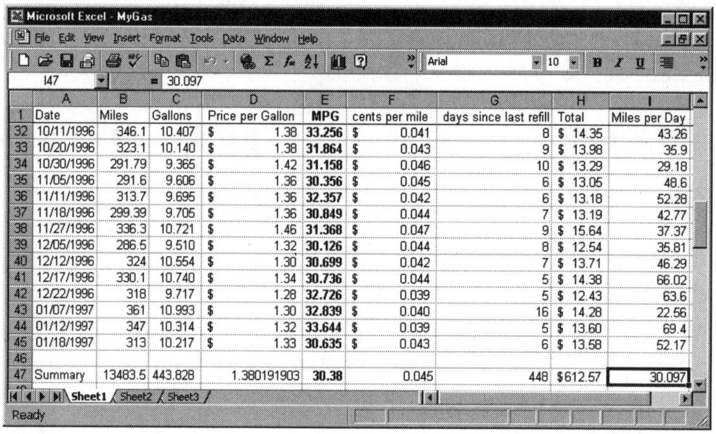

	A	B	C	D	E	F	G	H	I
1	Date	Miles	Gallons	Price per Gallon	**MPG**	cents per mile	days since last refill	Total	Miles per Day
32	10/11/1996	346.1	10.407	$ 1.38	**33.256**	$ 0.041	8	$ 14.35	43.26
33	10/20/1996	323.1	10.140	$ 1.38	**31.864**	$ 0.043	9	$ 13.98	35.9
34	10/30/1996	291.79	9.365	$ 1.42	**31.158**	$ 0.046	10	$ 13.29	29.18
35	11/05/1996	291.6	9.606	$ 1.36	**30.356**	$ 0.045	6	$ 13.05	48.6
36	11/11/1996	313.7	9.695	$ 1.36	**32.357**	$ 0.042	6	$ 13.18	52.28
37	11/18/1996	299.39	9.705	$ 1.36	**30.849**	$ 0.044	7	$ 13.19	42.77
38	11/27/1996	336.3	10.721	$ 1.46	**31.368**	$ 0.047	9	$ 15.64	37.37
39	12/05/1996	286.5	9.510	$ 1.32	**30.126**	$ 0.044	8	$ 12.54	35.81
40	12/12/1996	324	10.554	$ 1.30	**30.699**	$ 0.042	7	$ 13.71	46.29
41	12/17/1996	330.1	10.740	$ 1.34	**30.736**	$ 0.044	5	$ 14.38	66.02
42	12/22/1996	318	9.717	$ 1.28	**32.726**	$ 0.039	5	$ 12.43	63.6
43	01/07/1997	361	10.993	$ 1.30	**32.839**	$ 0.040	16	$ 14.28	22.56
44	01/12/1997	347	10.314	$ 1.32	**33.644**	$ 0.039	5	$ 13.60	69.4
45	01/18/1997	313	10.217	$ 1.33	**30.635**	$ 0.043	6	$ 13.58	52.17
46									
47	Summary	13483.5	443.828	1.380191903	**30.38**	0.045	448	$612.57	30.097

Figure 9-4. *An excerpt from the output of the* computeOnGas *procedure. Notice the new column of data and the resized columns.*

The *computeOnGas* procedure involves nothing more than standard VBA, but it uses objects, properties, and methods that are unique to Excel. When you perform automation, you inevitably require some knowledge of at least one other object model—namely the object model for the Office application that you are automating. One advantage of using the *Run* method, as in the *runXL* procedure, is that it lets individual developers specialize in particular object models. When a developer wants to use a standard function in an unfamiliar application, he or she can copy a procedure designed by another developer. Even without detailed knowledge of an application, a developer can invoke the *Run* method for the copied procedure.

```
Sub computeOnGas()
Dim mySheet As Worksheet
Dim iRow As Integer, lastRow As Integer
Dim sumDays As Long

'Set reference to first worksheet.
    Set mySheet = Worksheets(1)
    lastRow = Range("gas").Rows.Count

'Assign column heading.
    mySheet.Cells(1, 9) = "Miles per Day"
```

```
'Compute miles per day.
    For iRow = 3 To lastRow
        mySheet.Cells(iRow, 9) = _
            Format(Range("gas").Cells(iRow, 2) / _
            Range("gas").Cells(iRow, 7), _
            "0.##")
        sumDays = sumDays + mySheet.Cells(iRow, 7)
    Next iRow

'Compute summary statistics.
    mySheet.Cells(Range("gas").Rows.Count + 2, 1).Select
    ActiveCell.Formula = "Summary"
'Compute total miles.
    ActiveCell.Offset(0, 1).Activate
    ActiveCell.Formula = "=Sum(b2:b" & lastRow & ")" & ""
'Compute total gallons.
    ActiveCell.Offset(0, 1).Activate
    ActiveCell.Formula = "=Sum(c2:c" & lastRow & ")" & ""
'Compute total gas dollars.
    ActiveCell.Offset(0, 5).Activate
    ActiveCell.Formula = "=Sum(h2:h" & lastRow & ")" & ""
'Compute days since last refill.
    ActiveCell.Offset(0, -1).Activate
    ActiveCell.Formula = "=Sum(g3:g" & lastRow & ")" & ""
'Compute price per gallon.
    mySheet.Cells(Range("gas").Rows.Count + 2, 4).Select
    ActiveCell.Formula = "=H" & (lastRow + 2) & "/C" & (lastRow + 2)
'Compute miles per gallon.
    ActiveCell.Offset(0, 1).Activate
    ActiveCell = Format(mySheet.Cells(lastRow + 2, 2) / _
        mySheet.Cells(lastRow + 2, 3), "0.###")
    ActiveCell.Font.Bold = True
'Compute cents per mile.
    ActiveCell.Offset(0, 1).Activate
    ActiveCell = Format(mySheet.Cells(lastRow + 2, 8) / _
        mySheet.Cells(lastRow + 2, 2), "0.###")
'Compute miles per day.
    ActiveCell.Offset(0, 3).Activate
    temp = mySheet.Cells(lastRow + 2, 2)
    temp2 = sumDays
    ActiveCell = Format(mySheet.Cells(lastRow + 2, 2) /
 sumDays, "0.###")

'Resize columns to show values.
    Worksheets("Sheet1").Columns("a:I").AutoFit

End Sub
```

WORKING WITH OUTLOOK FROM ACCESS

Outlook comes with a standard set of folders, including folders for its calendar, contacts, deleted items, drafts, e-mail inbox, journal, notes, e-mail outbox, sent e-mail, and tasks. Users can also add custom folders and can nest folders within one another. Users work with items within their folders—adding, deleting, viewing, and performing other functions.

The initial version of Outlook shipped with programmatic support only through Microsoft VB Script. Outlook 2000 adds programmatic control with VBA. Outlook 2000 supports scripting with either VBA or VB Script. For compatibility with the rest of the book, this section focuses on scripting Outlook from Access using VBA. In addition, all the samples use the Contacts folder to provide a familiar context.

You can establish a reference to an instance of Outlook in Access with the *CreateObject* function. Before you can reference a particular folder, you typically must apply the *GetNameSpace* method to the *Application* object. The *NameSpace* object is an abstract root object that exists between the *Application* object and individual folders. The method takes a single argument, which must be *MAPI* for the current release. You apply the *GetDefaultFolder* method to the *NameSpace* object to get the default folder of a certain type. You use a constant to designate which default folder your application will manipulate. The Contacts folder constant is *olFolderContacts*.

Enumerating Items in the Contacts Folder

The following procedure manipulates the Contacts folder to enumerate all its items. You can set up a sample Contacts folder with a few entries to evaluate this and subsequent samples. The book's companion CD also includes some sample contact information for populating a Contacts folder.

```
Sub listContacts()
Dim myOlApp As Outlook.Application
Dim myNameSpace As NameSpace
Dim myContacts As Items
Dim myItem As ContactItem

'Create an instance of Outlook.
'Reference its MAPI Namespace.
'Reference MAPI's Contact folder.

    Set myOlApp = CreateObject("Outlook.Application")
    Set myNameSpace = myOlApp.GetNamespace("MAPI")
    Set myContacts = _
        myNameSpace.GetDefaultFolder(olFolderContacts).Items
```

```
'Enumerate items in Contact folder and
'print selected fields.
   For Each myItem In myContacts
       Debug.Print myItem.FirstName, myItem.LastName, _
          myItem.Email1Address
   Next

End Sub
```

The procedure starts by declaring four variables: one for the Outlook application, one for its *NameSpace* object, one for the collection of items in the Contacts folder, and one for enumerating those items. It takes three *Set* statements to expose the items in the Contacts folder. The last of these uses the *GetDefaultFolder* method to return the Contacts folder, and it uses the *Items* property to access the individual items. The enumeration takes place with a *For...Each* loop. The items in the Contact folder have a series of properties that identify information about contacts. The sample uses three of these properties to print the first name, last name, and first e-mail address for each entry in the Contacts folder.

Adding an Item to the Contacts Folder

You can also build Access-based solutions that manipulate the contents of the Contacts folder. The first of the next three procedures, *addOneContact*, inserts a new contact into the folder. It uses string constants to define the first name, last name, and e-mail address for a contact, but you can easily modify the procedure to pass these as arguments. The next two procedures, *removeOneEmail* and *deleteAContact*, do just that. The *removeOneEmail* procedure passes an e-mail address to the *deleteAContact* procedure, finds a contact item with a matching e-mail address, and then deletes it.

```
Sub addOneContact()
Dim myOlApp As Outlook.Application
Dim myItem As ContactItem

'Create an instance of Outlook.
    Set myOlApp = CreateObject("Outlook.Application")

'Create an item for the folder.
'Populate the item with values.
'Save the item.
    Set myItem = myOlApp.CreateItem(olContactItem)
```

(continued)

```
        With myItem
            .FirstName = "foo"
            .LastName = "bar"
            .EmailAddress = "foobar@yourcompany.com"
            .Save
        End With

End Sub


Sub removeOneEmail()
    deleteAContact ("foobar@yourcompany.com")

End Sub


Sub deleteAContact(strEmail)
Dim myOlApp As Outlook.Application
Dim myNameSpace As NameSpace
Dim myContacts As Items
Dim myItem As ContactItem

'Create an instance of Outlook.
'Reference its MAPI Namespace.
'Reference MAPI's Contact folder.
    Set myOlApp = CreateObject("Outlook.Application")
    Set myNameSpace = myOlApp.GetNamespace("MAPI")
    Set myContacts = _
        myNameSpace.GetDefaultFolder(olFolderContacts).Items

'Enumerate to search for item to delete.
    For Each myItem In myContacts
        If myItem.EmailAddress = strEmail Then
            myItem.Delete
            Exit Sub
        End If
    Next

'No entry found
    MsgBox "No entry found with email of " & strEmail, vbCritical, _
        "Programming Microsoft Access 2000"

End Sub
```

The procedure requires just two objects—the Outlook *Application* object and a *ContactItem* object to represent an item in the Contacts folder. The procedure creates a reference to the *Application* object with the *CreateObject* function. This reference supports the *CreateItem* method, which creates an empty instance of an item for any specified folder. You designate the type of folder for the item using a constant that you pass to the *CreateItem* method. You can choose from more than 140 properties to specify the characteristics of a contact. The sample assigns string constants for the *FirstName*, *LastName*, and *Email1Address* properties. (Yes, each contact can have more than one e-mail address.) Then it invokes the *Save* method to store the new entry in the Contacts folder.

Deleting an Item from the Contacts Folder

The *deleteAContact* procedure (shown on the facing page) accepts a string argument that is the value of the *Email1Address* property of the contact item to delete. The procedure enumerates members of the Contacts folder until it finds one with an *Email1Address* property that matches the passed argument. When it finds a match, it removes the item by invoking the *Delete* method and exits the procedure to eliminate further searching. If the procedure enumerates the entire contents of the Contacts folder without discovering a match, control passes to a message box statement, which reports that no entries match the e-mail address passed to it.

Adding Multiple Items to the Contacts Folder

One common task performed with a database manager such as Access is adding multiple contact items to the Contacts folder. These contacts can come from any source, such as the Contacts folder on another computer, addresses entered over the Internet, or even an old Access contact file. The *addContacts* procedure below uses one approach to updating an Outlook Contacts folder with the contact information in an Access table.

```
Sub addContacts()
Dim myOlApp As Outlook.Application
Dim myItem As ContactItem
Dim rst1 As New Recordset

'Open the Contacts folder in Outlook.
    Set myOlApp = CreateObject("Outlook.Application")

'Open the table with the new contacts.
    With rst1
        .ActiveConnection = CurrentProject.Connection
        .Open "oe4pab"
    End With

'Create a ContactItem for adding contacts and
'loop through the table records to add them to the folder.
```

(continued)

```
            AssistantWorkingOn
            Do Until rst1.EOF
                Set myItem = myOlApp.CreateItem(olContactItem)
                With myItem
                    .FirstName = IIf(IsNull(rst1.Fields(0)), _
                    "", rst1.Fields(0))
                    .LastName = rst1.Fields(1)
                    .Email1Address = rst1.Fields(2)
                    .Save
                End With
                rst1.MoveNext
            Loop
            AssistantIdleOn

        End Sub
```

The procedure sets a reference to the Outlook application and then opens a recordset based on the *oe4pab* table. This is the local table in the Access Tables folder. The table contains just 34 entries, but the procedure can accommodate a much longer list of addresses. For this reason, the procedure calls another procedure that turns on the Assistant with a working animation and leaves it on until Access and Outlook finish updating the Outlook Contacts folder with the entries in the *oe4pab* table. (Chapter 8 describes how to design procedures to control Assistant animation. You can find the procedures for Assistant animation in the Chap08 directory on the companion CD.) In between the two calls to turn Assistant animation on and off, a *Do* loop iterates through all the records in the *oe4pab* table. The loop creates a new *ContactItem* object on each pass, and then it assigns the records for that pass to the item and saves the item.

Deleting Multiple Items from the Contacts Folder

The following procedure, *removeEmails*, is an adaptation of the *deleteAContact* procedure shown earlier. It deletes multiple records from a Contacts folder. It removes one item at a time by successively calling *deleteAContact* with different e-mail addresses. The sample uses the addresses in the *oe4pab* table as the source for the arguments. This procedure offers two advantages: it is easy to write and it reuses the *deleteAContact* procedure.

```
Sub removeEmails()
Dim rst1 As New Recordset

'Open the table with the new contacts.
    With rst1
        .ActiveConnection = CurrentProject.Connection
        .Open "oe4pab"
    End With
```

```
'Loop through the table records to add them to the folder.
    AssistantWorkingOn
    Do Until rst1.EOF
        deleteAContact (rst1.Fields(2))
        rst1.MoveNext
    Loop
    AssistantIdleOn

End Sub
```

While this procedure can get the job done, it has at least two deficiencies.
First, it searches through the Contacts folder for each item that it wants to remove. This gets increasingly costly as the number of items to delete grows, the
number of items in the Contacts folder grows, or both. Second, if there is no
match for an item, it pauses with a message box that requires the user to click
a button to proceed. If there are numerous entries in the list of items to delete
that are already missing from the Contacts folder, having to click a button for each
item not present in the folder can become tedious. One solution to these weaknesses is to replace the call to *deleteAContact* with a call to *deleteAContact2*,
shown below.

```
Sub deleteAContact2(strEmail)
On Error GoTo delete2Trap
Dim myOlApp As Outlook.Application
Dim myNameSpace As NameSpace
Dim myContacts As Items
Dim myItem As ContactItem
Dim strFilter As String

'Create an instance of Outlook.
'Reference its MAPI Namespace.
'Reference MAPI's Contact folder.
    Set myOlApp = CreateObject("Outlook.Application")
    Set myNameSpace = myOlApp.GetNamespace("MAPI")
    Set myContacts = _
        myNameSpace.GetDefaultFolder(olFolderContacts).Items

'Find target item and remove it.
    strFilter = "[Email1Address] = """ & strEmail & """"
    Set myItem = myContacts.Find(strFilter)
    myItem.Delete

delete2Exit:
    Exit Sub
```

(continued)

```
delete2Trap:
    If Err.Number = 91 Then
'If item is not there, just keep on going.
        Resume Next
    Else
'Otherwise, pause with a message box.
        MsgBox Err.Number & ": " & vblfcr & _
            Err.Description, vbCritical, _
            "Programming Microsoft Access 2000"
        Resume Next
    End If

End Sub
```

This procedure expedites the search for an item to delete by using the *Find* method. It constructs a criterion for the *Find* method based on the e-mail address passed to it. After finding an item with a matching e-mail address, it applies the *Delete* method to that item. Using *Find* saves a noticeable amount of time even with a short list of items such as those in the *oe4pab* table, but its speed advantage grows with longer lists of e-mail addresses or with Contact folders that have many items. The procedure also traps failures of the *Find* method to return an item. This happens when there is no matching item in the Contacts folder for an e-mail address. In this situation, *deleteAContact2* silently returns control to the calling routine so that it can search again for a new e-mail address. There is no need for operator intervention.

WORKING WITH WORD FROM ACCESS

The first sample in this section demonstrates how to build, design, and populate a table in Word based on data in an Access table. It uses automation to control Word from Access, and it even includes a simple Access form for invoking the automation procedure. The second and third samples tackle two mail merge tasks programmatically: generating mailing labels and generating a form letter.

The form letter sample here accomplishes the same thing as the form letter sample in Chapter 6. You can compare the two approaches to see which best fits your needs. In general, the philosophy behind having multiple components is that you should use each to do what it does best. The sample in this chapter enables Access to store data and Word to generate form letters for printing. If you find it easy to work with the Word object model and the *MailMerge* object, this approach might work best for you. If you prefer to concentrate on becoming expert in Access by itself, the approach in Chapter 6 might be preferable.

Automating Word from Access

The following automation sample transfers contents from a recordset based on a table in Access to a table in Word. When you have references to multiple object models with similar terms, you should include a prefix before the object data type designation in its declaration: you should use *Word.Table* instead of *Table,* for example. This tells the VBA interpreter which kind of *Table* object you want. Recall that Access can also declare a *Table* object from the ADOX library. Also, note that the *Range* object in Word behaves differently from than the one in Excel. VBA and IntelliSense let you build cross-application solutions, but they do not relieve you of the chore of learning the object models for individual applications.

```
Sub fromAccessToWordTable()
Dim myWDApp As Word.Application
Dim myRange As Word.Range, myTable As Word.Table
Dim acell As Word.Cell, emailCol As Integer
Dim rst1 As New Recordset, irow As Integer

'Open the table with the new contacts.
    With rst1
        .ActiveConnection = CurrentProject.Connection
        .Open "oe4pab", , adOpenKeyset, adLockOptimistic, adCmdTable
    End With

'Create a Word application instance and turn on
'the Assistant's working animation.
    AssistantWorkingOn
    Set myWDApp = CreateObject("Word.Application")

'Add a document to the application and a table to the document.
'Specify rows to equal one more than e-mail address
'table in Access.
    myWDApp.Documents.Add
    Set myRange = myWDApp.ActiveDocument.Range(0, 0)
    myWDApp.ActiveDocument.Tables.Add Range:=myRange, _
        NumRows:=rst1.RecordCount + 1, NumColumns:=3

'Insert column headings for table.
    With myWDApp.ActiveDocument.Tables(1).Rows(1)
        .Cells(1).Range.Text = rst1.Fields(0).Name
        .Cells(2).Range.Text = rst1.Fields(1).Name
        .Cells(3).Range.Text = rst1.Fields(2).Name
    End With
```

(continued)

```
'Insert first name, last name, and e-mail from Access table.
'Insert contact info in the second through the last row.
    For irow = 2 To myWDApp.ActiveDocument.Tables(1).Rows.Count
    emailCol = 0
        For Each acell In _
            myWDApp.ActiveDocument.Tables(1).Rows(irow).Cells
            acell.Range.Text = IIf(IsNull(rst1.Fields(emailCol)), _
                "", rst1.Fields(emailCol))
            emailCol = emailCol + 1
        Next acell
    rst1.MoveNext
    Next irow

'Format table to fit content, turn on idle animation, and
'make Word visible so user can see table in Word.
    myWDApp.ActiveDocument.Tables(1).AutoFitBehavior wdAutoFitContent
    AssistantIdleOn
    myWDApp.Visible = True

End Sub
```

The procedure starts by opening a recordset object based on a table in Access—the familiar *oe4pab* that you saw in the Outlook samples. Since the application uses the *RecordCount* property, you should avoid using a forward-only cursor. The sample uses the *adOpenKeyset* constant for the cursor type specification. After opening the recordset, the application turns on the working animation for the Assistant and runs the *CreateObject* function to create a fresh instance of Word.

The procedure then constructs the table in Word. It adds a new document and then adds a table to the document's top left corner. The parameters of the *Add* method for the *Table* object specify that the table will have one more row than there are rows in the Access table. This allows one row of column headers plus all the data in the *oe4pab* table. Before starting to work with the recordset values, the procedure writes the column headers in the first row. These are the field names for the table in Access.

A pair of nested *For* loops navigate through the cells in the table. The outer loop progresses sequentially through the rows. The inner one marches across the columns within a row. Notice that Word has a *Cells* collection for the columns within the row of a table. The inner loop navigates to individual cells within the Word table. The reference to a cell starts with the automation object, *myWDApp*, and then hierarchically moves to the *ActiveDocument* object, the first table on the document, and the row in the table. After identifying a cell within a row to process, an *IIf* function based on the recordset values computes a value for the *Text* property of the cell.

After iterating through all of the table's cells, the procedure closes by performing three steps. First, it reformats the columns' widths so they are wide enough to display column values without wrapping. Second, it assigns an idle animation to the Assistant. This essentially turns off the working animation that starts just before the Word *Application* object launches. Finally, the procedure sets the *Application* object's *Visible* property to *True*. This changes the focus from Access to Word.

Figure 9-5 shows a form in Access that lets users start the procedure by clicking a button. The figure shows the form just after a user clicks the button. You can see a still shot of the Assistant with its working animation. When the Assistant comes to rest, the focus shifts from the Access form to the Word document with the table created by the *fromAccessToWordTable* procedure.

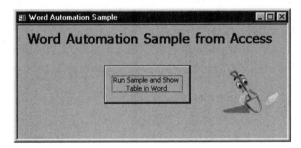

Figure 9-5. *This form invokes the* fromAccessToWordTable *procedure. When the Assistant stops its working animation, the focus shifts to the table in Word.*

Producing Mailing Labels

The built-in Word mail merge feature can draw on an Access database table or query as a record source for generating mailing labels. While you can programmatically lay out the mail merge fields or bookmarks to support the placement of Access data on Word documents, it is often much simpler to lay them out manually where you want data inserted on a document. In addition, you can use built-in wizards to help with the layout of controls for forms with multiple labels per page.

Figure 9-6 on the next page shows an excerpt from the mlabels.doc file. The mail merge fields were positioned with the built-in Mail Merge wizard that you can invoke from the Tools menu. After laying out the controls, you can programmatically control the printing of labels based on Access tables or queries through the *MailMerge* object.

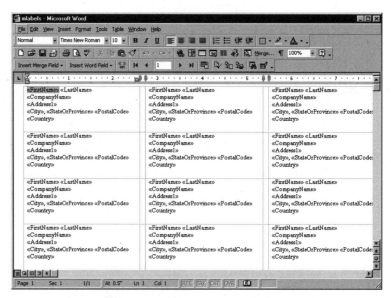

Figure 9-6. *An excerpt from a Word document for printing mailing labels on Avery 5260 laser forms.*

The following Word procedure is designed to run from the ThisDocument folder of the Normal template. It starts by opening the mlabels.doc file that contains the mail merge fields depicted in Figure 9-6. Then it sets a reference, *myDoc*, to a document based on the file. The mlabels.doc file actually contains no code of its own.

```
Sub printPreviewLabels()
Dim myDoc As Document

'Set reference to the document.
    Documents.Open FileName:="mlabels.doc"
    Set myDoc = Documents("mLabels")

'Reference the data source in Access.
    myDoc.MailMerge.OpenDataSource Name:= _
        "C:\Programming Access\Chap09\Chapter9.mdb", _
        Connection:="TABLE WebBasedList"

'Send the labels to a new document.
    With myDoc.MailMerge
        .Destination = wdSendToNewDocument
        .Execute Pause:=True
    End With
```

```
'Either Print Preview or Print labels.
    If MsgBox("Do you want to preview before printing?", _
        vbYesNo, "Programming Microsoft Access 2000") = vbYes Then
        ActiveDocument.PrintPreview
    Else
        ActiveDocument.PrintOut
    End If

End Sub
```

The key to performing any mail merge with data from Access is to invoke the *OpenDataSource* method for the *MailMerge* object within a document, such as the document that the *myDoc* reference points to. You often must assign two arguments, *Name* and *Connection*. You point the *Name* argument at the Access source file containing the data for the mail merge. The *printPreviewLables* procedure references Chapter9.mdb, the file for this chapter on the companion CD. You use the *Connection* argument to designate a type of database object and its name. Your code can designate either a *Table* or a *Query*. The sample points to a table named *WebBasedList*.

You can use the Word *MailMerge* object to write over the template with the mail merge fields or create a new document with the merged data. You use the *MailMerge* object's *Destination* property to designate your choice. The sample uses the constant to create a new document for the merged data. After setting all the *MailMerge* properties that you want, you apply the *Execute* method to the *MailMerge* object. This merges the Access data into a Word document that creates your mailing labels. The sample presents a message box asking whether to print or preview the labels. After you no longer need the document with the merged fields and the one controlling the layout of the fields in a document, you can close both of them manually or with another program.

You can easily invoke a procedure such as *printPreviewLabels* from within Access. The procedure below does this in just three lines. This sample runs from a standard module in an Access file.

```
Sub runMLabels()
Dim myWDApp As Word.Application

'Open connection to Word and make Word visible.
    Set myWDApp = CreateObject("Word.Application")
    myWDApp.Application.Visible = True

'Run mailing label procedure.
    myWDApp.Application.Run "printPreviewLabels"

End Sub
```

Producing Form Letters

The procedure on the facing page for producing form letters is essentially the same as the one for mailing labels except that the layout of mail merge fields is more straightforward. This is because you typically have just one occurrence of a record per page instead of multiple records on a page. Figure 9-7 shows the layout of a form letter in Word that is identical to the one in Chapter 6. It is easy to include a mail merge field within the body of a letter. The figure shows this in its bottom panel.

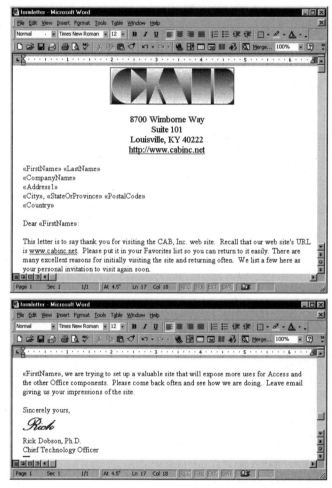

Figure 9-7. *Excerpts from a Word document for printing form letters.*

Do not use the full Mail Merge wizard if you plan to programmatically control the printing of labels. The code that it generates has many extra parameters and is designed explicitly for use with the wizard, not necessarily with custom applications. The sample below and the one in the previous section are designed for use from the ThisDocument folder of the Normal template. They are good starting points for your own custom form letter or mailing label applications. However, you should start the Mail Merge wizard to add the Mail Merge toolbar to the window of a document. Once you have the toolbar exposed, you can freely insert mail merge fields anywhere in a document.

The following procedure works with the document depicted in Figure 9-7, which shows excerpts from the top and bottom of the formletter.doc file. The procedure opens this file. The use of the *OpenDataSource* method is the same for both a form letter and mailing labels. This sample, however, designates values for the *FirstRecord* and *LastRecord* properties of the *DataSource* object. The *OpenDataSource* method specifies parameters pointing at the data source that the *DataSource* object represents. Setting the *FirstRecord* and *LastRecord* properties establishes a range of records for which to print form letters. This sample works with the default sort order for the records in the data source.

```
Sub printPreviewLetters()
Dim myDoc As Document

'Load file and set a reference to it.
    Documents.Open FileName:="formletter.doc"
    Set myDoc = Documents("FormLetter")

'Reference the data source in Access.
    myDoc.MailMerge.OpenDataSource Name:= _
        "C:\Programming Access\Chap09\Chapter9.mdb", _
        Connection:="TABLE WebBasedList"

'Send the labels to a new document.
    With myDoc.MailMerge
        .Destination = wdSendToNewDocument
        With .DataSource
            .FirstRecord = 5
            .LastRecord = 9
        End With
        .Execute Pause:=True
    End With

'Either Print Preview or Print labels.
    If MsgBox("Do you want to preview before printing?", _
        vbYesNo, "Programming Microsoft Access 2000") = vbYes Then
        ActiveDocument.PrintPreview
```

(continued)

```
        Else
            ActiveDocument.PrintOut
        End If

End Sub
```

You can invoke the procedure from within Access by invoking the *Run* method for the Word *Application* object, as shown in the following procedure. This takes just three lines. While the *runFormletters* and *runLabels* procedures are procedures for a standard module in Access, you can place either or both of them behind an Access form and invoke them from command buttons. If your code designates a query in the *OpenDataSource Connection* parameter, you can modify the query before invoking the Word mail merge operation to further enhance your control of the mail merge.

```
Sub runFormLetters()
Dim myWDApp As Word.Application

'Open connection to Word and make Word visible.
    Set myWDApp = CreateObject("Word.Application")
    myWDApp.Application.Visible = True

'Run form letter procedure.
    myWDApp.Application.Run "printPreviewLetters"

End Sub
```

Chapter 10

Working with Multi-User Databases

Much of the rest of this book covers building Microsoft Access applications for groups of users. This chapter discusses some core multi-user issues: sharing files and controlling security. In reviewing file sharing, this chapter explicitly examines techniques and issues for sharing forms and recordsets. Subsequent chapters explore technologies for sharing Access databases, such as database replication, using Microsoft SQL Server, and using Access databases over the World Wide Web. This chapter assumes that you have a working knowledge of basic multi-user and security issues and focuses on new programmatic developments. For example, it includes samples that compare the new row-level locking with the more traditional page-level locking for recordset manipulation and samples that show how to control security programmatically with the new ADODB and ADOX libraries. The chapter closes with a sample demonstrating transactions in a multi-user environment.

SHARING FILES

The first step in sharing an Access application is to make the default open mode shared. You can accomplish this using the Advanced tab of the Options dialog box. This tab also offers other options that facilitate sharing. The *SetOption* and *GetOptions* methods of the Access *Application* object enable your applications to set and read these settings

You place Access multi-user files in shared file directory folders. Since Access with the Jet engine is a file server as opposed to a client/server database, you should minimize the file size that travels over the physical network connection. One way to do this is to split an application into two files. You save the data tables in an Access file on the shared directory folder and distribute another Access file to individual users for use on their local workstations. The distributed file links back to the data tables in the shared folders. This design speeds performance and reduces network traffic. You can generally improve performance by including more content in the distributed file, such as data that changes infrequently. You can use automated procedures to update locally stored data at specific times, such as when an application opens or a user clicks a button.

> **NOTE** You can use the Database Splitter wizard to divide one Access file into two. (Choose Database Utilities from the Tools menu.) One file contains tables, and the other file holds queries, forms, reports, macros, modules, and shortcuts to data access pages (data access pages are new with Access 2000). You place the first file in a shared folder on the network and link the other file to it. You distribute the second file to individual users for use on their workstations.

You can set user-level security settings that let a user open a file exclusively (so others cannot use it). A user needs exclusive use of a database to make database modifications, such as adding new modules or revising existing ones. The *Connection Control* property and the User List feature are used to obtain exclusive access to a database in a multi-user environment.

The *Connection Control* Property

The new *Connection Control* property facilitates programmatic control of database accessibility. You can set the *Connection Control* property for an ActiveX Data Objects (ADO) *Connection* object to make it impossible for new users to open a database and to prohibit existing users from reconnecting to it after they close the file. The *Connection Control* property allows you to obtain exclusive access to the database in order to store new modules and make other application design changes once the last current user disconnects from the database.

The following two procedures change the setting of the *Connection Control* property. You use the *Properties* collection of the *Connection* object to set the property. A property setting of *1* sets the feature so that it closes down passively when users disconnect from the application file. A value of *2* enables other users to resume connecting to the database file. This feature is handy for developers who need to evaluate their changes after saving them in the file.

```
Sub closeDBConnection()
Dim cnn1 As ADODB.Connection

    Set cnn1 = CurrentProject.Connection
    cnn1.Properties("Jet OLEDB:Connection Control") = 1

End Sub



Sub openDBConnection()
Dim cnn1 As ADODB.Connection

    Set cnn1 = CurrentProject.Connection
    cnn1.Properties("Jet OLEDB:Connection Control") = 2

End Sub
```

The User List

The User List, introduced with Jet 4, is a set of user data stored in the lock file for an .mdb file. This information is available exclusively through the Jet provider, but you can only gain access to the information through ADO. (If your database resides on a read-only file share, this feature is not available because Jet does not create lock files for read-only shares.) You invoke the *OpenSchema* method for a *Connection* object to return a recordset with four fields of information for each recent user. The method extracts data from the lock file for an .mbd file. The four fields in the recordset are

- *computer_name*   The name of the computer the user connects from.

- *login_name*   The login user-level security name.

- *connected*   Indicates that a user is currently connected. (User IDs sometimes remain in the lock database after a user disconnects from a Jet database.)

- *suspected_state*   Indicates that a connection to the database has terminated abnormally.

The following procedure invokes the User List. You reference the User List using a Globally Unique ID (GUID) that points at the control for returning the recordset of active users. The sample returns *computer_name* and *login_name* for all active users. When this list has a count of 1, a developer can save changes to modules in a database. In addition, a developer can use the list to determine who to contact to gain exclusive control of a database.

```
Sub listActiveUsers()
Dim cnn1 As ADODB.Connection, rst1 As New ADODB.Recordset

'Set the connection for the current project and invoke the
'OpenSchema method to return the current list of users.
    Set cnn1 = CurrentProject.Connection
    Set rst1 = cnn1.OpenSchema(adSchemaProviderSpecific, , _
        "{947bb102-5d43-11d1-bdbf-00c04fb92675}")

'Print a heading for the User List recordset
'and enumerate list members.
    Debug.Print "Machine Name     " & "User Name"
    Debug.Print "============" & "      ========="
    Do Until rst1.EOF
        Debug.Print rst1.Fields("computer_name") & _
            rst1.Fields("login_name")
        rst1.MoveNext
    Loop

End Sub
```

SHARING FORMS

Even without any code, Access forms allow multiple users to edit, add, and delete records in a database. However, you can enhance this capability in a multi-user environment using modules behind forms.

A simple AutoForm based on a table or other recordset source can work in a multi-user environment. Two or more users can open such a form and then page through records. They can also modify the form's bound recordset in all the ways that Access permits. You can program Access to change the defaults for how and when one user can view the changes made by another. The database file for this chapter includes five forms (WebBasedList, WebBasedList1, WebBasedList2, WebBasedList3, and WebBasedList4) that reflect varying types of programmatic control.

Locking Records Manually

You'll find form-sharing controls on the Advanced tab of the Tools-Options dialog box. The Edited Record option button imposes pessimistic page-level locking. With pessimistic page-level locking, Access locks the page (or pages) containing a record as soon as a form opens the record for editing. Any other records on the same page(s) also lock. The Open Databases With Record-Level Locking check box applies optimistic locking to just the current record. Other records on the same page remain unlocked. This new record-level locking feature was requested by many developers to reduce the chance of concurrency conflicts in a multi-user environment. Microsoft added this feature to counter-act the impact of expanding its page size from 2 KB to 4 KB (which was necessary to accommodate Unicode format for character-based, as opposed to numeric, fields).

Refreshing Field Values

The default refresh interval on the Advanced tab specifies the maximum number of seconds before an updated field value on one form appears to other users. Users can manually refresh a field by choosing the Refresh command from the Records menu or by simply moving the cursor over the field. If the cursor is inactive on a form, a relatively long time might elapse before a change appears to another user who is looking at the same record.

The WebBasedList form shows the behavior of the current lock and re-fresh settings for an Access form in a multi-user environment. If you open two different copies of the form and change the same record from two different computers (or two different Access sessions on the same computer), you can see the locking behavior and update refresh intervals.

The WebBasedList1 form improves on the no-module WebBasedList form using two short event procedures, shown below. The *Form_Open* event procedure sets the refresh interval option setting to 2 seconds. The *Form_Close* event procedure restores the default interval to 60 seconds. Note that the procedures use the *SetOption* method for the Access *Application* object.

```
Private Sub Form_Open(Cancel As Integer)
    Application.SetOption "Refresh Interval (Sec)", 2
End Sub


Private Sub Form_Close()
    Application.SetOption "Refresh Interval (Sec)", 60
End Sub
```

When two sessions open the WebBasedList1 form, simple data updates appear to propagate from one session to the next much more quickly than with the WebBasedList form. The shorter refresh interval does not reflect any reordering, adding, or deleting of records between sessions, but it reflects updates very quickly with a light resource consumption requirement.

The simple update that the *Form_Open* procedure achieves can dramatically affect the apparent responsiveness of a multi-user Access application. In fact, this setting has no impact in single-user operation. Its sole purpose is to influence when changes by other users are reflected on forms (and on datasheets).

Custom refresh and requery controls

The WebBasedList2 form includes a Refresh button that invokes the *Refresh* method for the form. The code behind the button's click event is simply *Me.Refresh*. The *Refresh* method functions just like the timeout for a refresh interval. Again, users do not see revised sorts, added records, or deleted records, but they instantly see changes to records made by other users. While users can achieve similar results by moving the cursor over a field, the button is named Refresh so users immediately know what it does.

The *Refresh* method is fast, but it does not update a form to reflect a new record, and it shows a deleted record with a deleted marker. You invoke a form's *Requery* method to reflect the look of a recordset after one or more other users adds and deletes records. In the default mode, the *Refresh* method leaves the current record active, but the *Requery* method selects the first record after its operation. If you want to return to your previous position (which will likely be different from the first record), you must add logic to navigate back to it. If any users alter sort criteria, such as primary key or sort key values, the *Requery* method reflects these changes but the *Refresh* method does not update the record order. The *Requery* method works in both single-user and multi-user environments. (The *Refresh* method has no effect in single-user applications.)

The following two procedures add a Requery button to the Refresh button in the WebBasedList2 form. The *cmdRequery_Click* procedure has three parts. First, it saves the current primary key value to help relocate the record after the *Requery* method repositions the recordset point to the form's first record. Second, it applies the *Requery* method. Third, it sets the focus to the primary key field (*ContactID*) and invokes the *DoCmd FindRecord* command. This repositions the form from the first record to the record that was current before the application of the *Requery* method. If another user deleted that record, the form repositions the display to the first record. You can use more elaborate logic to position the current record elsewhere.

```
Private Sub cmdRefresh_Click()
    Me.Refresh
End Sub


Private Sub cmdRequery_Click()
Dim pkBefore As Long

'Save primary key value before requery.
    pkBefore = Me.ContactID.Value

'Apply requery method.
    Me.Requery

'Attempt to find primary key value before requery.
    Me.ContactID.SetFocus
    DoCmd.FindRecord pkBefore

End Sub
```

Locking Records Programmatically

Record locking means locking record values so other users cannot edit them. Access 2000 offers record locking for the first time, instead of only page locking. You control when to apply locks using the locking options on the Advanced tab of the Options dialog box. You can also programmatically assign values to the *RecordLocks* property for a form to determine whether it locks records optimistically or pessimistically at the page level or table level. The *RecordLocks* property can assume one of three values. The default value of *0* specifies optimistic page locking. A value of *2* specifies pessimistic page locking. A value of *1* exclusively locks the whole table.

The Advanced tab also offers a new check box for record-level locking instead of page-level locking. It is selected by default. This setting lets two users simultaneously update two different records on the same page, using forms. Row-level locking is not available for memo data types or on index pages. Access does not generally support naming users with conflict locks. You can programmatically set row-level locking with the *SetOption* method for the Access *Application* object. The *GetOption* method offers a mechanism for returning row-vs.-page lock settings.

The *Form_Open* and *Form_Close* procedures on the next page manipulate different styles of page locking and record-vs.-page locking. The *Form_Open* event offers form users the option of locking pages optimistically or pessimistically. If a user chooses either option, the procedure assigns a value of *False* to the row-level locking setting. If a user does not choose either page-locking option, the procedure assigns a value of *True* to the row-level locking setting. These *True/False* values correspond to a selected or deselected check box on the Advanced tab for record-level locking.

```
Private Sub Form_Open(Cancel As Integer)

'Present a series of message boxes to let a user set the
'page-locking style and record-level locking for a form.
    If MsgBox("Optimistic page locking?", vbYesNo, _
        "Programming MS Access") = vbYes Then
        Me.RecordLocks = 0
        Application.SetOption "Use row-level locking", False
    ElseIf MsgBox("Pessimistic Page locking?", vbYesNo, _
        "Programming MS Access") = vbYes Then
        Me.RecordLocks = 2
        Application.SetOption "Use Row Level Locking", False
    Else
        MsgBox "Setting new row-level locking.", _
            vbInformation, "Programming MS Access"
        Application.SetOption "Use row-level locking", True
    End If

'Handy for confirming selected states
    Debug.Print Me.RecordLocks
    Debug.Print Application.GetOption("Use row-level locking")

End Sub


Private Sub Form_Close()

'Restore default locking.
    Me.RecordLocks = 2
    Application.SetOption "Use row-level locking", True

End Sub
```

NOTE The first user to set locking options in a multi-user session controls locking for all other users in that session. When testing procedures assign values to different locking options, you should exit and restart Access between tests to initialize new locking options.

Not all of the *RecordLocks* settings have corresponding options on the Advanced tab. The two print statements at the bottom of the *Form_Open* event procedure reflect the current settings for the style and type of page locking as well whether your system is using row-level instead of page-level locking.

Access 2000 has an optional feature for changing multiple page-level locks to a single lock for the whole table. As the number of locks per table increases, Access can automatically replace the individual record locks with a single lock per table. This automatic lock promotion can dramatically lower the cost of lock management while offering the flexibility of record locks when locks are sparse. You can select this feature by turning off default row-level locking and using the *SetOption* method for the *Application* object. You must also assign a value to the new *PagesLockedToTableLock* registry entry. A default value of *0* disables automatic lock promotion. Values greater than *0* indicate the minimum number of locks per table before Jet attempts to replace individual record locks with a single table lock. A value of *100* means that Jet will attempt to replace page locks with a single table lock on the application of the 101st lock per table, 201st lock per table, and so on. The attempts succeed only if Jet can get exclusive access to the table (because placing a lock on a table locks out all users except the one with the lock). Jet performs data manipulation much more rapidly when it has exclusive access to the table. This feature also removes the need for the developer to determine in advance when to apply exclusive table locks.

SHARING RECORDSETS

For recordsets and SQL statements, Jet uses smart defaults to determine which page and record locking settings to use. With ADO code that relies on cursors, Jet defaults to record-level locking. With SQL statements that can easily affect thousands of rows, Jet switches to page-level locking as the default. This, in turn, lets your application benefit from lock promotion (if lock promotion is enabled).

When you use row-level locking with recordsets, you achieve concurrency and performance enhancements only if you explicitly wrap recordset maintenance tasks in transactions. You use the *BeginTrans*, *CommitTrans*, and *Rollback* methods (discussed later in this chapter) to wrap each record operation. Without this precaution, locks accumulate until they reach the value of the *FlushTransactionTimeout* registry setting.

When you use record-level locking, you should carefully consider the data types for fields and record lengths to control database file size growth. Record-level locking writes rows rather than pages; rows that extend across a page boundary must be moved to a new page. Using fixed-length data types, you can determine the precise length of records; you cannot do this with the variable-length character fields for Access tables. (However, Jet SQL's data definition language includes a CHAR data type that lets you determine the length of string data type fields. This, in turn, can help to control record size bloat caused by records that do not fit entirely within one page.)

Row-Level Locking

The following procedure illustrates row locking in a multi-user application. It simulates a two-user application by running two connections against the same data file. The application also requires a second file named TestRowLock.mdb. Run the procedure in step mode to see how the row locking succeeds and fails under different circumstances.

```
Sub RowLockingPessimistic()

'Use TestRowLocking.mdb to run this demo of
'row locking; DO NOT HAVE TESTROWLOCK.MDB OPEN
'WHEN RUNNING THE DEMO.

Dim cnn1 As New ADODB.Connection
Dim cnn2 As New ADODB.Connection
Dim rs As New ADODB.Recordset
Dim rs2 As New ADODB.Recordset
Dim j As Integer

On Error GoTo ErrHandler

'Open two connections against the same database,
'both using row locking mode;
'Jet OLEDB:Database Locking Mode info -
'0 is "page mode",
'1 is "row mode"

'Open first connection to TestRowLocking.mdb.
cnn1.Open "Provider=Microsoft.Jet.OLEDB.4.0;Data " & _
    "Source=c:\Programming Access\Chap10\TestRowLocking.mdb;" & _
    "Jet OLEDB:Database Locking Mode=1;"

'Open second connection to TestRowLocking.mdb.
cnn2.Open "Provider=Microsoft.Jet.OLEDB.4.0;" & _
    "Data Source=c:\Programming Access\Chap10\TestRowLocking.mdb;" & _
    "Jet OLEDB:Database Locking Mode=1;"

'Open a recordset in the first connection and
'begin editing the first row.
rs.Open "TestRowLocking", cnn1, adOpenKeyset, _
    adLockPessimistic, adCmdTableDirect

'Edit first field value.
Debug.Print rs.Fields("col1")
rs.Fields("col1") = 2
'rs2.Update; putting an update here would
'close the record lock
Debug.Print rs.Fields("col1")
```

```
'Open a recordset in the second connection.
rs2:Open "TestRowLocking", cnn2, adOpenKeyset, _
    adLockPessimistic, adCmdTableDirect

'Attempt to edit the first row; even in row locking,
'since we are in the pessimistic
'locking mode, this will fail.
Debug.Print rs2.Fields("col1")
rs2.Fields("col1") = 3
Debug.Print rs2.Fields("col1")

'Move to another row in the same page.
rs2.MoveNext

'Attempt to edit the next row; this works under
'the row locking mode because the lock only applies
'to a single row, not the whole page.
Debug.Print rs2.Fields("col1")
'Should not fail (row locking)
rs2.Fields("col1") = 4 Debug.Print rs2.Fields("col1")

'Update recordsets.
rs.Update
rs2.Update
'Close connections and exit.
cnn1.Close
cnn2.Close
Set cnn1 = Nothing
Set cnn2 = Nothing

Exit Sub

ErrHandler:
For j = 0 To cnn1.Errors.Count - 1
    Debug.Print "Errors from cnn1 connection"
    Debug.Print "Conn Err Num : "; cnn1.Errors(j).Number
    Debug.Print "Conn Err Desc: "; cnn1.Errors(j).Description
Next j

For j = 0 To cnn2.Errors.Count - 1
    Debug.Print "Errors from cnn2 connection"
    Debug.Print "Conn Err Num : "; cnn2.Errors(j).Number
    Debug.Print "Conn Err Desc: "; cnn2.Errors(j).Description
Next j

Resume Next

End Sub
```

Notice that the second connection's attempt to write to the first record in TestRowLocking.mdb fails because the first connection still has the first record open. This attempt can succeed if the first connection unlocks the record (by, for instance, running a *rs.Update* statement). The second connection's attempt to write to the second record succeeds immediately since there are no locks on that record. The error-handling logic displays the entries from the Jet connection's *Errors* collection.

Page-Level Locking

The following is an excerpt from a similarly designed procedure that uses page locking instead of record locking. Notice that the Database Locking Mode value, which was *1* in the preceding sample, is *0* in this one. These values denote, respectively, row-level and page-level tracking. Both attempts by the second connection to update records fail because the first connection has a lock open and all the records for this short table fit on a single page.

```
'Open first connection to TestRowLocking.mdb.
cnn1.Open "Provider=Microsoft.Jet.OLEDB.4.0;Data " & _
    "Source=c:\Programming Access\Chap10\TestRowLocking.mdb;" & _
    "Jet OLEDB:Database Locking Mode=0;"

'Open second connection to TestRowLocking.mdb.
cnn2.Open "Provider=Microsoft.Jet.OLEDB.4.0;" & _
    "Data Source=c:\Programming Access\Chap10\TestRowLocking.mdb;" & _
    "Jet OLEDB:Database Locking Mode=0;"

'Open a recordset in the first connection and
'begin editing the first row.
rs.Open "TestRowLocking", cnn1, adOpenKeyset, _
    adLockPessimistic, adCmdTableDirect

'Edit first field value.
Debug.Print rs.Fields("col1")
rs.Fields("col1") = 2
Debug.Print rs.Fields("col1")

'Open a recordset in the second connection.
rs2.Open "TestRowLocking", cnn2, adOpenKeyset, _
    adLockPessimistic, adCmdTableDirect

'Attempt to edit the first row; because of
'pessimistic page locking mode setting, this fails.
Debug.Print rs2.Fields("col1")
rs2.Fields("col1") = 3
Debug.Print rs2.Fields("col1")
```

```
'Move to another row in the same page.
rs2.MoveNext

'Attempt to edit the next row; this fails too because
'the next row is on the same page.
Debug.Print rs2.Fields("col1")
 rs2.Fields("col1") = 4
Debug.Print rs2.Fields("col1")

'Update recordsets.
rs.Update
rs2.Update
```

SECURITY

Access offers a rich array of security features to support the needs of different types of Access applications. Most multi-user Access applications can benefit from user-level security, which lets developers designate groups of users. But some applications have more specialized needs. The following section offers a brief overview of security techniques other than user-level security. Subsequent sections cover programmatic approaches to managing user-level security using ADO.

Alternatives to User-Level Security

One of the strengths of Access is its ability to serve different audiences. Some applications are code-intensive, so you need to secure your investment in source code. Other applications serve small workgroups with limited technical capabilities but still require minimum levels of security to restrict access to data. Still other applications benefit from a custom user interface that restricts functionality simply by exposing a restricted set of commands.

Using a custom interface

Sometimes you can adequately secure an application by simply replacing the standard Access interface with a custom one. Choose Startup from the Tools menu to open a dialog box that lets you specify a custom application title and icon, a custom startup form, and custom menus to replace the standard Access ones. This dialog box also lets you suppress the Database window and the status bar. You can also manipulate the features of the Startup dialog box programmatically. If this type of manipulation is suitable for your security needs, consider augmenting it with the *Show* and *Hide* methods, the *Visible* property, and the *Hidden* property for objects in the Database window. (See earlier chapters for techniques on creating custom features: Chapter 8 describes how to program the *CommandBars* object model to build your own custom menus as well as adapt built-in ones, and Chapter 5 shows how to build a custom startup form.)

Setting a database password

You can require users to enter a password to gain unrestricted access to all Access data and database objects. Passwords are easy to administer compared to user-level security. Password security is appropriate if you have a group whose members need equal access to all elements of a database file but not everyone in the office is a member of that group.

You cannot use a password-protected file as a member in a replica set because Jet database replication cannot synchronize with a password-protected file. (See Chapter 11 for details.) You should also be careful about linking to database files with password protection because anyone who can access the file that links the protected file has unrestricted access to the protected file. Furthermore, Access stores an encrypted version of the password along with other information about the linked file. Finally, if someone changes the password for a linked file, Access prompts for the new password the next time another database file links to it.

To assign and remove a database password, you need exclusive access to the file. Take the following steps:

1. Open a file by choosing Open Exclusive from the Open button in the Open dialog box to assign a password to a file.

2. Choose Security-Set Database Password from the Tools menu.

3. In the Set Database Password dialog box, enter your password of choice in the Password and Verify text boxes and then click OK. The next time a user opens the file, the application will ask for the password.

4. After opening a database exclusively, choose Tools-Security-Unset Database Password. Remove the password by typing the password in the Unset Database Password dialog box. This removes the initial prompt for a password before a database is made available.

Setting a module password

Access 2000 uses password security for modules instead of user-level security. This new approach makes Access consistent with the other Office 2000 components. It applies to all standard and standalone class modules as well as the modules behind forms and reports.

You set password security once for all the modules in a VBA project from the Visual Basic Editor (VBE). Choose the Properties command for the project from the Tools menu to open the Project Properties dialog box. The Protection tab (shown in Figure 10-1) offers the Lock Project For Viewing check box and text boxes for entering and confirming a password for the module. Assigning a password for viewing modules in a project does not prevent your code from running as if it were not protected. If you assign a password but do not select the Lock Project For Viewing check box, anyone can edit the code but the Project Properties dialog box will be protected. You remove password security from the modules in a project by clearing all entries on the Protection tab.

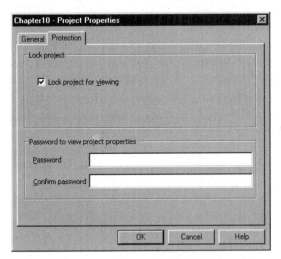

Figure 10-1. *You use the Protection tab of the Project Properties dialog box to set password security for the modules in a project.*

After securing your modules with a password, you must enter the password once per session before you can view, edit, or add new code. You can secure forms and reports with both user-level security and module password security. User-level security applies to designing and using forms and reports. You can require a user to have Modify Design permission to add controls to forms. That user will also need the password for modules in a project in order to write event procedures for the control. Conversely, knowing the password for the modules in a project does not enable a user to add controls to or remove controls from a form. Also, Modify Design permission does not allow a user to change the *HasModule* property of forms and reports to *No*; the user must first enter the password for the modules in a project.

Using .mde files

An .mde file totally secures the code for an Access database file. When you convert an .mdb file to an .mde file, Access compiles all your modules, removes editable code, and compacts the destination database while preserving the original .mdb file. The size of your database will shrink because of the removal of editable code. Also, since the conversion optimizes memory usage, your code will run faster.

To convert an .mdb file to an .mde file, you must have exclusive access to the file (see the earlier section titled "Setting a Database Password"). Choose Database Utilities from the Tools menu and then choose Make MDE File. After saving your converted file, be sure to save your original file. The only way to edit or add to the code in a database file is to modify the original file and then convert it to an .mde file.

An .mde file has some restrictions:

■ You cannot modify or add forms, reports, or modules.

■ You cannot import or export forms, reports, or modules to a standard .mdb file. You can, however, freely import and export tables, queries, macros, and shortcuts for data access pages with other database files.

■ You cannot add, delete, or change references to other object libraries or databases.

■ You cannot dynamically change code because .mde files contain no editable code. (See Chapter 7 for a sample illustrating this restriction.)

■ You cannot convert any existing member of a replica set to an .mde file, but an .mde file can participate in a replica set.

■ An .mde file can reference another database file only if that file is also an .mde file. You must start converting .mdb files (or .mda add-in files) that are referenced before you convert the .mdb file that references them. The new reference must point at the new .mde file.

Programmatically Controlling User-Level Security

With user-level security, you can define a workgroup composed of user accounts and group accounts. You can programmatically create user and group accounts as well as assign permissions to those accounts. The new ADOX model supports this functionality through its *Catalog* object as well as its *Users* and *Groups* collection objects. Figure 10-2 shows the hierarchy: groups can belong to users, and users can belong to groups; users and groups both belong to the *Catalog* object.

Figure 10-2. *The relationship of the* User *and* Group *objects to the* Catalog *object.*

You can assign permissions to users, groups, or both. It is generally most efficient to assign permissions to groups. You clear all default permissions from existing individual user accounts and then assign users to all appropriate groups. With this type of user-level design, you can administer permissions by assigning users to groups and assigning permissions to groups because users inherit all permissions from the groups to which they belong. By restricting permission assignments to groups, this design provides a single focal point for managing permissions.

The upcoming samples show how to code typical user-level administration tasks. Because they are meant to highlight basic security management procedures, only a couple of the samples demonstrate error-trapping logic.

Connecting to a secure database

The following procedure connects to a secure database file. The connection string includes four phrases. The first phrase designates the *Provider* property for the procedure's *Connection* object. It specifies the Jet 4 OLE DB provider. The second phrase assigns the system database property for the connection. This is the name and path to the workgroup information file (systemdemo.mdw in the Office folder; you must manually copy the file to the Office folder). The third phrase specifies the data source, which in this case is the secure database file, UserLevel.mdb. The fourth phrase denotes user ID and password values for logging into the secure database. In this sample, the procedure logs on as the Admin user. Unless you change the default settings, this user has special administrative permissions.

```
'Turn logon procedure on before running this procedure.
'Assign password of "password" to Admin user account.

Sub openUserLevel()
Dim cnn1 As New ADODB.Connection
Dim rst1 As New ADODB.Recordset

'Open connection to target user-level secured data
'source; specify path for workgroup information
'file; designate logon ID and password.
    cnn1.Provider = "Microsoft.Jet.OLEDB.4.0"
    cnn1.Properties("Jet OLEDB:System database") = _
        "C:\Program Files\Microsoft Office\" & _
        "Office\systemdemo.mdw"
    cnn1.Open "Data Source=C:\Programming Access\Chap10\UserLevel.mdb;" & _
        "User Id=Admin;Password=password;"
```

(continued)

```
'Print first field from first record to confirm connection.
    rst1.Open "WebBasedList", cnn1, , , adCmdTable
    Debug.Print rst1.Fields(0)

    cnn1.Close

End Sub
```

The two lines following the comment open a recordset based on the connection and print the first field's value from the first record. This simply confirms the operation of the sample. The table, *WebBasedList*, is the same one used in the earlier multi-user sample.

For the *OpenUserLevel* procedure to work, you must invoke the logon procedure. This involves giving the Admin user a password. The procedure also requires a workgroup information file. In this case, its name must be systemdemo.mdw, and you must save it in the path indicated by the procedure. The companion CD includes both the secure database file and the workgroup information file for easy testing of the procedure.

Adding and deleting users

When you develop and manage a custom application with user-level security, you are likely to add and delete users. Before you can add users, you must log on as a member of the Admins group, such as Admin. You can use the *Append* method of the *Users* collection to add users to a catalog or group. You must specify a name for the new user, and you can designate a password. ADO lets you assign a password later using the *ChangePassword* method for the *User* object. Unfortunately, you cannot assign a PID. ADO picks one randomly.

The following two procedures show one approach to invoking the *Append* method to add a new user to an application. The *callMakeUser* procedure launches the *makeUser* procedure as it passes along two arguments. The first argument designates a new user's name. The second argument sends a password. In the sample, the string *"password"* is the value of the password argument.

```
'Make sure NewUser account does not exist prior to running
'this procedure; for example, run callDeleteUser first.

Sub callMakeUser()
    makeUser "NewUser", "password"

End Sub


Sub makeUser(usrName As String, secureWord As String)
Dim cat1 As New ADOX.Catalog
```

```
    cat1.ActiveConnection = _
        "Provider=Microsoft.Jet.OLEDB.4.0;" & _
        "Data Source=C:\Programming Access\Chap10\UserLevel.mdb;" & _
        "Jet OLEDB:System database=C:\Program Files\" & _
        "Microsoft Office\Office\systemdemo.mdw;" & _
        "User Id=Admin;Password=password;"

    cat1.Users.Append usrName, secureWord

End Sub
```

The *makeUser* procedure specifies a target for the new group using the *Catalog* object's *ActiveConnection* setting. Note that it designates a user ID with the authority to make a new user, and it points to a workgroup information file. The *Append* method in *makeUser* adds a new member to the *Catalog* object. Therefore, this new user is not yet a member of any groups. You can also add a member to a *Group* object so that the user has immediate membership in that group. One of the following samples uses this technique.

The next two procedures remove a user from the catalog for a database. The *Delete* method for the *Users* collection has the same syntax as the *Delete* method for the *Tables*, *Procedures*, and *Views* collection objects. The first procedure, *callDeleteUser*, passes a single argument—the user name—to the second procedure, *deleteUser*. The second procedure removes the user from the catalog and concurrently removes the user from any groups as well.

```
'Make sure NewUser account exists prior to running this
'procedure; for example, run callMakeUser.

Sub callDeleteUser()
    deleteUser "NewUser"

End Sub


Sub deleteUser(usrName As String)
Dim cat1 As New ADOX.Catalog

    cat1.ActiveConnection = _
        "Provider=Microsoft.Jet.OLEDB.4.0;" & _
        "Data Source=C:\Programming Access\Chap10\UserLevel.mdb;" & _
        "Jet OLEDB:System database=C:\Program Files\" & _
        "Microsoft Office\Office\systemdemo.mdw;" & _
        "User Id=Admin;Password=password;"

    cat1.Users.Delete usrName

End Sub
```

You must log on to a database as a member of the Admins group to delete a user. The *Delete* method does not require a password. All that the second procedure needs is a string argument naming the user to delete.

Assigning groups to users

One common technique for administering permissions is to assign groups to users and manage permissions for groups. Users derive all their permissions implicitly through their group memberships. The samples in this section add and remove group memberships from a user account. Both samples use the built-in Users group, but the same techniques work for custom groups.

The following two procedures add a group to a user account called NewUser. Make sure the user account exists before running the procedure. The first procedure, *callAddGroupToUser*, passes a user name and a group name to the second procedure, *AddGroupToUser*, which uses the *Append* method to add the *Group* object to the *Groups* collection for the user. The sample passes arguments to the second procedure that tell it to add the Users group to the NewUser user.

```
Sub callAddGroupToUser()
    AddGroupToUser "NewUser", "Users"
End Sub


Sub AddGroupToUser(usrName As String, grpName As String)
On Error GoTo AddTrap
Dim cat1 As New ADOX.Catalog
Const acctNameAlreadyExist = -2147467259

    cat1.ActiveConnection = _
        "Provider=Microsoft.Jet.OLEDB.4.0;" & _
        "Data Source=C:\Programming Access\Chap10\UserLevel.mdb;" & _
        "Jet OLEDB:System database=C:\Program Files\" & _
        "Microsoft Office\Office\systemdemo.mdw;" & _
        "User Id=Admin;Password=password;"

    cat1.Groups.Append grpName
    cat1.Users(usrName).Groups.Append grpName

AddExit:
    Exit Sub
```

```
AddTrap:
    If Err.Number = acctNameAlreadyExist Then
        Resume Next
    Else
        Debug.Print Err.Number; Err.Description
    End If

End Sub
```

The second procedure invokes the *Append* method in an attempt to create a group with the name of the second argument passed to it. This procedure works for groups whether or not they already exist. Since Users is a built-in group account, it will always exist. If a group with the name of the second argument does not already exist, the *Append* method succeeds; otherwise, the procedure falls into an error trap with error number –2147467259 and moves on to the next statement. Then, the procedure appends the group to the *Groups* collection for the *NewUser* object. Again, if the group is already in the *Groups* collection for the user, the procedure progresses to the next statement.

The next two procedures remove a group from a user's *Groups* collection. The first procedure, *callRemoveUserFromGroup*, passes user and group name parameters to the second procedure, *removeUserFromGroup*, which does the work. Since there is no error checking in this sample, make sure the group belongs to the user. You can do this by running the preceding sample.

```
'Make sure the group account exist for the user
'prior to running this procedure; for example,
'run callAddGroupToUser.

Sub callRemoveUserFromGroup()
    removeUserFromGroup "NewUser", "Users"
End Sub


Sub removeUserFromGroup(usrName As String, grpName As String)
Dim cat1 As New ADOX.Catalog

    cat1.ActiveConnection = _
        "Provider=Microsoft.Jet.OLEDB.4.0;" & _
        "Data Source=C:\Programming Access\Chap10\UserLevel.mdb;" & _
        "Jet OLEDB:System database=C:\Program Files\" & _
        "Microsoft Office\Office\systemdemo.mdw;" & _
        "User Id=Admin;Password=password;"

    cat1.Users(usrName).Groups.Delete grpName

End Sub
```

You invoke the *Delete* method to remove a group from the *Groups* collection for a *User* object. Notice the hierarchical specification for an individual user. After identifying a user, the syntax requires the designation of the *Groups* collection and, finally, the *Delete* method. The syntax designates the group name as a parameter for the *Delete* method.

Creating, deleting, and tracking groups in a catalog

When you develop custom user-level solutions, you'll probably want to create custom groups with names that are meaningful to your clients and whose permissions fit the special requirements of your custom application. The four upcoming samples do the following: create a custom group, delete a custom group, prepare a report itemizing all the groups in a catalog and the groups associated with each user account, and toggle the membership of a group in the *Users* collection, respectively.

The two procedures below add a group named *MySecretGroup1*. After referencing a database file with a user ID sufficient to make the addition, the procedure invokes the *Append* method of the *Groups* collection. You must specify a container for the *Groups* collection. When you add a new group to the project's *Users* collection, the container is a *Catalog* object. When you assign a group to the *Groups* collection of a *User* object, you must specify the user as the root object for the *Groups* collection.

```
'Make sure MySecretGroup1 does not exist before running
'this procedure; for example, run callDeleteGroup.

Sub callMakeGroup()
    makeGroup "MySecretGroup1"

End Sub


Sub makeGroup(grpName As String)
Dim cat1 As New ADOX.Catalog

    cat1.ActiveConnection = _
        "Provider=Microsoft.Jet.OLEDB.4.0;" & _
        "Data Source=C:\Programming Access\Chap10\UserLevel.mdb;" & _
        "Jet OLEDB:System database=C:\Program Files\" & _
        "Microsoft Office\Office\systemdemo.mdw;" & _
        "User Id=Admin;Password=password;"

    cat1.Groups.Append grpName

End Sub
```

The two procedures below remove a group from a catalog. You must make sure that the group already exists in the catalog before running the procedures. You can do this by running the preceding sample. In fact, the sample below removes the group added in the preceding sample.

```
'Make sure MySecretGroup1 exists prior to running this
'procedure; for example, run callMakeGroup.

Sub callDeleteGroup()
    deleteGroup "MySecretGroup1"

End Sub


Sub deleteGroup(grpName As String)
Dim cat1 As New ADOX.Catalog

    cat1.ActiveConnection = _
        "Provider=Microsoft.Jet.OLEDB.4.0;" & _
        "Data Source=C:\Programming Access\Chap10\UserLevel.mdb;" & _
        "Jet OLEDB:System database=C:\Program Files\" & _
        "Microsoft Office\Office\systemdemo.mdw;" & _
        "User Id=Admin;Password=password;"

    cat1.Groups.Delete grpName

End Sub
```

The syntax for deleting a group very closely parallels that for adding a group. It invokes the *Delete* method of the catalog's *Groups* collection. You pass the method one parameter—the name of the group to delete.

As you add and delete groups and users and reassign groups to users, you can easily create a custom report that tracks the group memberships for the *Catalog* and individual *User* objects. The procedure below itemizes the groups in a *Catalog* object that points at a specific database. Then it itemizes the *Groups* collection members for each user in the catalog's *Users* collection.

```
Sub listGroupsInCat()
Dim cat1 As New ADOX.Catalog
Dim grp1 As New ADOX.Group, usr1 As New ADOX.User

cat1.ActiveConnection = _
    "Provider=Microsoft.Jet.OLEDB.4.0;" & _
    "Data Source=C:\Programming Access\Chap10\UserLevel.mdb;" & _
    "Jet OLEDB:System database=C:\Program Files\Microsoft Office\" & _
    "Office\systemdemo.mdw;" & _
    "User Id=Admin;Password=password;"
```

(continued)

```
'Groups in overall Catalog
    Debug.Print cat1.Groups.Count & " groups are in the catalog"
    For Each grp1 In cat1.Groups
        Debug.Print String(3, " ") & "* " & grp1.Name
    Next grp1
    Debug.Print

'Groups in each user
    For Each usr1 In cat1.Users
        If usr1.Name <> "Creator" And usr1.Name <> "Engine" Then
            Debug.Print String(5, " ") & usr1.Groups.Count & _
                " groups are in  " & usr1.Name
            For Each grp1 In cat1.Users(usr1.Name).Groups
                Debug.Print String(8, " ") & "* " & grp1.Name
            Next grp1
            Debug.Print
        End If
    Next usr1

End Sub
```

At the head of each listing of *Groups* collection members, the procedure reports the number of members in the collection by referencing the *Counts* property for the collection. Notice in Figure 10-2 on page 426 that this varies by user. The Admin user belongs to the built-in Admins and Users groups. The NewUser user belongs to a single group, Users. You can use the preceding samples to create and delete users, groups, and user membership in groups.

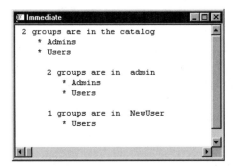

Figure 10-3. *A group membership report from the* listGroupsInCat *procedure.*

The following procedure shows one possible application of the *listGroups InCat* procedure above. The *toggleNewUserInAdminsGroup* procedure does what its name implies. It toggles the membership of the *NewUser* object in the Admins group. It also documents the current status of the *NewUser* object in the Admins group by calling the *listGroupsInCat* procedure.

```
Sub toggleNewUserInAdminsGroup()
On Error GoTo ToggleTrap
Dim cat1 As New ADOX.Catalog
Const notInCollection = 3265

cat1.ActiveConnection = _
    "Provider=Microsoft.Jet.OLEDB.4.0;" & _
    "Data Source=C:\Programming Access\Chap10\UserLevel.mdb;" & _
    "Jet OLEDB:System database=C:\Program Files\Microsoft Office\" & _
    "Office\systemdemo.mdw;" & _
    "User Id=Admin;Password=password;"

cat1.Users("NewUser").Groups.Delete ("Admins")

ToggleExit:
    listGroupsInCat
    Exit Sub

ToggleTrap:
    If Err.Number = notInCollection Then
        cat1.Users("NewUser").Groups.Append "Admins"
    Else
        Debug.Print Err.Number; Err.Description
    End If
    Resume Next

End Sub
```

Notice that the toggling procedure relies on error trapping. After connecting to the target database and working group information file through the *cat1* object reference, the procedure attempts to delete *Admins* from the *Groups* collection of *NewUser*. If it is successful, the procedure closes by calling *listGroupsInCat* and exiting. Otherwise, an error occurs. If the error occurs because the group is not in the user's *Groups* collection, the procedure adds *Admins* to the *NewUser Groups* collection. Then it closes by resuming as if no error occurred.

Setting permissions

You can use the *SetPermissions* method for *Group* and *User* objects to manage the permissions available to a security account. You invoke the *GetPermissions* method for these objects to return a Long value that specifies the types of permissions assigned to a group or to a user. Both methods offer a wide array of outcomes; they can assign and report various permissions for a number of database object types. In addition, you can use the *SetPermission* method to assign, revoke, and deny permissions as well as audit their use.

The two procedures below grant a group full permissions for any new table. Setting the permission for new tables has no impact for existing tables. Therefore, a group can have full permissions for all new tables and no permissions for existing tables.

```
'Make sure MySecretGroup1 exists before running procedure.

Sub callSetAllTablePermissionsForGroup()
    setAllTablePermissionsForGroup "MySecretGroup1"

End Sub


Sub setAllTablePermissionsForGroup(grpName As String)
Dim cat1 As New ADOX.Catalog
Dim grp1 As New ADOX.Group, usr1 As New ADOX.User

cat1.ActiveConnection = _
    "Provider=Microsoft.Jet.OLEDB.4.0;" & _
    "Data Source=C:\Programming Access\Chap10\UserLevel.mdb;" & _
    "Jet OLEDB:System database=C:\Program Files\Microsoft Office\" & _
    "Office\systemdemo.mdw;" & _
    "User Id=Admin;Password=password;"

cat1.Groups(grpName).SetPermissions Null, adPermObjTable, _
    adAccessSet, adRightFull

End Sub
```

The first procedure passes a group name, *MySecretGroup1*, to the second procedure. The second procedure invokes the *SetPermissions* method for the group member with that name. Therefore, you must make sure that the group exists before you run the procedure or add error-trapping logic. The method's first parameter has an explicit Null value. This parameter normally specifies the name of a database object, such as a table. A Null value indicates that you want to set permissions for any new database objects. The second parameter designates a *Table* object type. The third parameter serves as a verb; it indicates that the command will set a permission. Other constants indicate different actions, such as revoking permissions, that the method can launch. The fourth parameter grants the user full rights. The method and its parameters grant *MySecretGroup1* full rights for all new tables in the UserLevel.mdb database file with the systemdemo.mdw workgroup information file.

This basic design is flexible and can serve in many different situations. For example, to revoke all rights for new tables, you change the third parameter for the *SetPermissions* method from *adAccessSet* to *adAccessRevoke*. To set rights for an existing database object, you replace the Null for the first parameter with the database object's name.

Putting it all together

The following two procedures tap a cross-section of prior samples and show a new twist to the *SetPermissions* method. The first procedure calls the *makeGroup* procedure to create a new group in the systemdemo.mdw workgroup information file. Then it invokes the second procedure and passes along the new group's name as well as the name of a database object for which it wants to assign permissions. The last two lines in the first procedure create a new user named NewUser2 and add *MySecretGroup2* to its *Groups* collection. In this way, NewUser2 inherits the permissions assigned to *MySecretGroup2* by the second procedure.

```
Sub callSetRIDTablePermissionsForGroupTable()

'This procedure makes a group called MySecretGroup2 and
'assigns Read/Insert/Delete Permissions for
'WebBasedList table to MySecretGroup2.
'Then, it creates NewUser2 and assigns
'MySecretGroup2 to NewUser2.

'Before running this, delete MySecretGroup2 and
'NewUser2 from UserLevel.mdb if they exist.

makeGroup "MySecretGroup2"
setRIDTablePermissionsForGroupTable "MySecretGroup2", "WebBasedList"
makeUser "NewUser2"
AddGroupToUser "NewUser2", "MySecretGroup2"

End Sub


Sub setRIDTablePermissionsForGroupTable(grpName As String, tblName)
Dim cat1 As New ADOX.Catalog
Dim grp1 As New ADOX.Group, usr1 As New ADOX.User

cat1.ActiveConnection = _
    "Provider=Microsoft.Jet.OLEDB.4.0;" & _
    "Data Source=C:\Programming Access\Chap10\UserLevel.mdb;" & _
    "Jet OLEDB:System database=C:\Program Files\Microsoft Office\" & _
    "Office\systemdemo.mdw;" & _
    "User Id=Admin;Password=password;"

cat1.Groups(grpName).SetPermissions tblName, adPermObjTable, adAccessSet, _
    adRightRead Or adRightInsert Or adRightDelete

End Sub
```

The second procedure assigns read, insert, and delete permissions for the *WebBasedList* table in UserLevel.mdb to *MySecretGroup2*. This procedure is similar to the earlier sample that applied for rights to a specific database object, but this one concatenates three separate rights to get a combined set of permissions. Notice that the syntax uses an Or operator for concatenating rights.

TRANSACTIONS

You can use transactions to bundle two or more database operations so that either they all occur or none of them occur. Transactions are useful in two types of situations: when your application must perform a set of operations as a unit (such as a funds transfer between a savings account and a checking account); and when you have to speed up a set of database operations by wrapping them in a transaction (because writing to a temporary cache in memory is faster than writing to a disk for each element within the transaction group).

Three *Connection* object methods in ADO support transactions: *BeginTrans*, *CommitTrans*, and *Rollback*. *BeginTrans* opens a transaction level. Jet supports up to five nested transactions. Once you start a transaction, you can end it with either the *CommitTrans* method or the *Rollback* method. You use *CommitTrans* to complete the database operations. You invoke the *Rollback* method to end a transaction without performing the database operations launched since the last *BeginTrans* method.

The procedure below uses three transaction methods for the *Connection* object. It loops through the records in a database while looking for one of three criteria matches. Once it finds a match, the procedure writes *US* in a field that Access stores in a data cache rather than to the database file. The procedure invokes the *BeginTrans* method just before starting the *Do* loop. At the end of the loop, the procedure asks whether the user wants to commit the changes. If the user replies *yes*, the sample invokes the *CommitTrans* method to commit the changes to the database. If the user replies *no*, the procedure discards the changes by invoking the *Rollback* method.

```
Sub changeInTrans()
On Error GoTo changeTrap
Dim cnn1 As ADODB.Connection
Dim rst1 As New ADODB.Recordset
Dim iChanges As Long
Const conLockedByAnotherUser = -2147217887

'Open recordset based on WebBasedList in current project.
Set cnn1 = CurrentProject.Connection
rst1.Open "WebBasedList", cnn1, adOpenKeyset, _
    adLockPessimistic, adCmdTable
```

```
'Loop through all records to find those to update to US.
cnn1.BeginTrans
Do Until rst1.EOF
    If rst1.Fields("Country") = "" _
        Or IsNull(rst1.Fields("Country")) = True _
        Or rst1.Fields("Country") = "USA" Then
        rst1.Fields("Country") = "US"
        iChanges = iChanges + 1
    End If
rst1.MoveNext
Loop

'Commit all changes if user says so.
'Roll changes back otherwise.
If MsgBox("Are you sure that you want to update" & _
    " these " & iChanges & " records?", vbYesNo, _
    "Programming MS Access") = vbYes Then
    cnn1.CommitTrans
Else
    cnn1.RollbackTrans
End If
Exit Sub

changeExit:
    Exit Sub

changeTrap:
    If Err.Number = conLockedByAnotherUser Then
        MsgBox "Recordset not available for update.  " & _
            "Try again later.", vbCritical, _
            "Programming MS Access"
    Else
        Debug.Print Err.Number; Err.Description
    End If
    cnn1.RollbackTrans
    Resume changeExit

End Sub
```

The *changeInTrans* procedure also invokes the *Rollback* method if a run-time error occurs—such as when the database is locked by another user. In this situation, it is impossible to edit one or more records. With some databases, performing an operation on a subset of records can corrupt the whole database. If the procedure encounters an error for any reason, it rolls back any pending operations before exiting the procedure. Invoking the *Rollback* method maintains the integrity of the database file.

Chapter 11

Replicating Databases

A Microsoft Access application can present separate copies, or replicas, of databases to different groups of users while managing the replicas as a single database. This capability is particularly important for high-end Access applications with many users or with a few users who need exclusive database access while others read or update the database. Database replication also adds value to projects in which branch offices or mobile workers need to share parts of a database with a complete version at headquarters. Data can be shared without the need for a constantly open connection between two points.

Since Access 2000 is the third version of Access to offer database replication, this feature is mature and highly integrated. This chapter offers an overview of replication and introduces the new replication features in Access 2000. It also explains how to manage replication using the JRO 2.1 library. The code samples will benefit those who are just starting to program replication solutions and will help those who already know how to program replication with Data Access Objects (DAO) to make the transition to ActiveX Data Objects (ADO). The JRO discussion in this chapter also extends to areas that do not explicitly relate to replication.

HOW REPLICATION WORKS

Access lets you replicate multiple copies of a database over a LAN, WAN, intranet, extranet, or the Internet. Users can modify their individual copies as their needs dictate. The connection between copies can be inoperable for long periods. You can also require that changes to any copy be replicated in each other copy.

Access calls the collective set of copies a *replica set*. (You are not restricted to working with a single replica set.) Each copy in the set is a replica. One copy within a replica set must function as a *design master*. The design master differs from the other replicas in that it can transfer structural changes (such as new forms and reports) and data changes to other members of the replica set. (Other products that offer database replication support data exchange between replicas but do not offer the ability to propagate structural changes across a replica set.)

Database replication occurs between pairs of replicas. Changes propagate throughout a replica set as replicas synchronize with each other. Each replica in a pair can send its changes to the other. If these changes do not conflict, the replicas update themselves with the package of changes they receive from each other. If some changes conflict because both replicas change the same content, one change wins and the other loses. Access saves the losing change in a conflict table. You can use this table to manually resolve conflicts, or your application can apply automatic rules for processing the conflicts. Access has a built-in Conflict Resolution wizard; you can also build your own wizard to replace or supplement it.

Replication errors can occur when a change is valid in a local replica but is invalid in one or more other replicas within a set—for example, if you enter a record with the same primary key in two separate copies in a replica set. When you synchronize the two copies, the Jet database engine rejects the record with the duplicate primary key from the other replica. Other conditions can generate replication errors, such as the introduction of a field validation rule in one replica that creates invalid data in another replica.

Replicas can diverge from one another in one of two ways. First, they might need to complete a synchronization cycle in which all the replicas exchange data with one another. You can remedy this by completing the synchronizations among replica set members. Replicas can also diverge from one another because of replication conflicts and errors—even if they are completely synchronized.

You can replicate databases in five ways:

- Using the Briefcase icon
- Using the Replication command
- Using JRO (or DAO) programming
- Using the Replication Manager
- Using Internet synchronization

Using the Briefcase Icon

Using the Briefcase icon, end users can take a copy of a database off site and make updates to it. When they return it, they can synchronize the replica on a laptop with the one on their desktop computer or department computer. Developers can use Briefcase replication to place a design master on their laptop and build custom forms and reports. Later, they can synchronize the new database objects with the production version.

The Microsoft Briefcase icon is available on the Microsoft Windows desktop in Windows 9*x* and Microsoft Windows NT 4. (The Briefcase might not be installed on your Windows 9*x* computer. To install Briefcase, double-click the Add/Remove programs option in Control Panel. Click the Windows Setup tab of the Add/Remove Programs Properties dialog box, select Accessories, and click the Details button. Then, in the Accessories dialog box, select Briefcase, click OK, and follow the prompts.) Dragging an .mdb file from Windows Explorer to the Briefcase icon converts a database from a standard format to one equipped with special tables and fields that support replication. (With other Microsoft Office applications, the Briefcase merely makes copies of whole files without any synchronization between copies.) The Briefcase reconciler leaves the updated original as a design master at the source and places a replica in the Briefcase. You can alter this if you need a design master in the Briefcase.

> **NOTE** When the Briefcase reconciler creates a replica set, it asks whether you want a backup version of the original database. Unless you are sure that you won't need to return to the original, you should accept this option because the conversion adds many new tables and fields. There is no simple, automatic way to remove these with built-in Access tools. At least one third-party source (www.trigeminal.com) offers a utility that strips the replication system fields from user tables.

Using the Replication Command

You choose Tools-Replication to access the commands that make a database replicable, create more replicas, synchronize replicas, reconcile conflicts, and prototype test versions of a replication application. You can create a Prevent Deletes replica (a new feature) only through the Tools menu (although you can control it programmatically after you create it).

To reconcile replication conflicts and errors, you probably have to manually review individual exceptions that appear in the conflict tables. Even if you ultimately program custom reconciliation rules, you probably have to evaluate the rules manually before adopting them for production use.

Using JRO Programming

JRO programming is fundamentally an ADO approach because it relies on ADO connection objects. While ADO is a universal data access technology, the JRO extension functions exclusively with the Jet database engine. If you programmed custom replication solutions in Access 95 or Access 97, now is the time to transition from DAO to JRO programming.

The JRO model supports three general tasks:

- Creating and managing replica sets
- Compacting and encrypting databases
- Refreshing the memory cache to improve apparent performance

The three main objects in the JRO model are shown in Figure 11-1. The first is the *Jet Engine* object, which supports features specific to the Jet database engine, including compacting and encrypting databases and refreshing the memory cache.

Figure 11-1. *The JRO model.*

The second main object is the *Replica* object, which represents a copy of a database. *Replica* objects are the basic building block of a replica set. You can manage a replica set by manipulating the properties and methods of the *Replica* objects. Among the functions that you can administer are

- Making a database replicable
- Creating replicas from the design master and other replicas
- Synchronizing replicas
- Reading the replicability of individual objects
- Assigning a new design master
- Managing the retention period for replication history

The JRO model also includes properties for managing many new and revised features, such as visibility, replica type, and priority-based conflict resolution.

The third main object is the *Filter* object. You use this with partial replicas to restrict the contents of a database copy. You can base a filter on a table or a relationship. JRO has a *Filters* collection for all the filters in a replica. These collectively limit the data that can enter into a partial replica.

Using the Replication Manager

The Replication Manager, which ships with the Office Developer edition, helps you administer a replica set over a network, which can include LAN and WAN connections. In its initial release with Access 97, the Replication Manager supported Internet synchronization via FTP. The new Internet synchronization with Access 2000 has rendered this feature obsolete. However, you must still use the Replication Manager with the version of Internet synchronization in Access 2000.

You use the Replication Manager to make occasional connections to a network or for indirect synchronization, in which changes from one replica to another can go to a drop box if the receiving replica is not open. Later, when the receiving database opens, the Synchronizer agent that the Replication Manager controls passes along the updates. The Replication Manager also offers a graphical user interface for scheduling periodic updates. You must configure the Replication Manager for your server.

You can also use the Replication Manager to coordinate replicas across a WAN. It offers a graphical depiction of your replica set's topology. One common design is a star topology in which a hub replica exchanges data with a related set of spoke replicas that each connects with just the central replica. A fully connected topology links each replica directly with all other replicas. This allows for much faster transfer of data updates throughout the replica set at the expense of increased network traffic. Other typologies offer different design/performance tradeoffs.

Using Internet Synchronization

Using Internet synchronization, you can replicate databases across a World Wide Web (FTP or HTTP 1.1) connection. The connection can be across the Internet, an intranet, or an extranet, and the computers need not be connected all the time. Unlike the indirect synchronization supported by the Replication Manager, Internet synchronization does not require a Synchronizer agent running on the client computer. Furthermore, Internet synchronization can work with anonymous replicas. This is one of the replica *Visibility* property settings introduced with Access 2000. (See the white paper titled "Internet Synchronization with Microsoft Jet 4.0" at http://support.microsoft.com for details on setting up, administering, and testing an Internet synchronization system.)

As mentioned earlier, Internet synchronization with Access 2000 has made the Access 97 version obsolete. Four main enhancements differentiate Internet synchronization with Access 2000 from its predecessor:

- Support for replication over an HTTP 1.1 protocol connection (Support for Netscape servers is available via this protocol.)
- Performance enhancements relating to encryption
- Support for a new lightweight replica tailored for Web-based replication
- New registry keys to fine-tune synchronizer timeouts

When you select a web server with which to synchronize, Access can automatically determine whether to use HTTP or FTP. Besides permitting operation on Netscape servers, the HTTP protocol lets a replica synchronize from behind a properly configured proxy server to a synchronizer on the Internet. Access 2000 does not explicitly support the reverse configuration. If your originating replica is not encrypted, Internet synchronization does not automatically encrypt the updates that it sends to the synchronizing target replica. The initial version of Internet replication automatically encrypted all updates for transfer over the Web. The new, lightweight anonymous replicas can only replicate with their parent replica on a web server. You must manage that parent replica on the web server using the Replication Manager.

Replication Design Changes

When you make a database replicable by any of the means discussed above, you typically add a collection of system tables as well as a set of fields to each table. These tables and fields help manage the replication project. They can also add substantially to the size of a database. Beyond that, the special replication tables and fields consume resources that slightly lower the maximum number of custom tables per database, the maximum number of custom fields per table, and the number of bytes per record available for custom uses in your database application. Understanding these design changes will help you manage Access replication projects.

> **NOTE** To view most of the special replication fields and tables, choose Options from the Tools menu. Select the System Objects check box, and then click OK.

Replication system fields

Tables in a replication application typically gain four new fields: *s_GUID*, *s_Generation*, *s_Lineage*, and *s_Collineage*. The *s_GUID* field uniquely identifies each row in each table in the replica set. The same row in the same table in two different replicas will have different GUID (Globally Unique ID) values. Access constructs the 16-byte GUID strings to be globally unique.

When you design tables for a replication application, you can use an autogenerated GUID as the primary key for a database. If a GUID serves as the primary key field for a table, Access does not create the *s_GUID* field when you make a table replicable. Instead, it uses the primary key to serve the same purpose. To use a GUID as a primary key, select *Replication ID* as the *FieldSize* property for a field with Number or AutoNumber as the data type.

The *s_Generation* field tracks the generation of a change to a table. This field has a Long Integer data type. A value of *0* represents a new change that unconditionally requires replication. After initially propagating a change to another replica, Access updates the field value so it represents the highest generation of change. The replication process keeps track of the last generation sent to each replica from each replica. When a new exchange commences, Access resumes with the next highest generation of change from the last synchronization with a replica.

The *s_Lineage* field tracks the history of changes to each row in a table. The field has an OLE Object data type. The field specifies when a row is sent to another replica. It eliminates the possibility of repetitively sending the same changes to another replica.

The *s_Collineage* field, which has an OLE Object data type, supports column-level replication. This feature is new with Access 2000. Prior versions of Access used row-level replication. (The upcoming section titled "What's New in Access 2000 Replication" explores this further.) The *s_Collineage* field tracks information that enables the detection of changes at the column level during synchronization.

Each field with the Memo or OLE Object data type also receives a separate generation field. Since such fields can be especially large, they do not necessarily propagate from one replica to another when a field in a row changes value. These fields propagate between replicas only when they actually change value. Their individual generation fields track this for the replication process. A replicable version of the Northwind *Category* table has one special generation field for the category pictures, but the *Employees* table has two special generation fields—one each for the *Note* and *Photo* fields.

Replication system tables

A number of system tables support the behavior of a replica set, as shown in the table below. Some of these tables, such as *MSysTableGuids*, can be sparse and basic. *MSysTableGuids* stores GUIDs for each table name in a replica (excluding the replication system tables and the special hidden conflict tables). Some tables use the GUIDs denoted in *MSysTableGuids* to identify specific tables in a replica set. Other tables store information about historical or pending operations. The *MSysTombstone* table stores information on deleted records. The built-in replication logic uses this table to delete records in receiving replicas during synchronization.

REPLICATION SYSTEM TABLES

Table	Description
MSysConflicts	Tracks all conflicts. Replicated to all members of the replica set.
MSysExchangeLog	Tracks synchronization information between a replica and all other members in the replica set.
MSysGenHistory	Stores information about each generation of synchronization. Avoids resending old generations to active replica members and updating replicas restored from backup copies.
MSysOthersHistory	Stores information about generations of updates from other replica members.
MSysRepInfo	Contains a single record with details relevant to the whole replica set. Replicated across the members of the replica set.
MSysReplicas	Stores information about all replicas in a replica set.
MSysSchChange	Stores information about changes to the design master replica for dissemination to other replica set members.
MSysSchemaProb	Stores information about conflicts between replica set members. If there are no unresolved conflicts this table does not appear.
MSysSchedule	Used by the Local Synchronizer agent to manage timing of synchronizations with other replicas.
MSysSideTable	Contains detailed conflict information.
MSysTableGuids	Relates table names to GUIDs. Other replication system tables use these GUIDs.
MSysTombstone	Stores history of deleted records and supports delete updates throughout the replica set.
MSysTranspAddress	Stores information about synchronizers that manage replicas in a replica set.
MSysContents	Stores information about rows for partial replicas. Appears only in partial replicas.
MSysFilters	Stores information about filters for partial replicas. Appears only in partial replicas.

The *MSysConflicts* table references a set of nonsystem but hidden tables that store details about individual conflicts and errors for each table. The naming convention for these hidden tables is *UserTableName_Conflict*. For example, if there are one or more conflicts with the information between two replicas for the *Employees* tables, the replica that loses a conflict has a hidden table named *Employees_Conflict*. The rows of the tables document the losing record and contain a recommendation about how to proceed. When users resolve conflicts through the built-in logic, Access depends on and manages these tables. If you build custom conflict resolution logic, your custom solutions must also manage these tables. For example, after all the conflicts for a table are resolved, your application should remove the *UserTableName_Conflict* table. This removes the corresponding row from the *MSysConflicts* table.

The replication fields and tables place additional constraints on the design of your Access applications. For example, Access permits an upper limit of 255 fields per table. However, replications typically add four fields (*s_GUID*, *s_Generation*, *s_Lineage*, and *s_Collineage*) plus one additional field for each Memo and OLE Object field in a table. As you plan the fields for a table, you must leave room for the special replication fields. The same type of considerations applies to the maximum byte count per record. See the white paper titled "Database Replication in Microsoft Jet 4.0" at http://support.microsoft.com for guidance on these and other advanced replication design matters.

Backing up and restoring the original database

You must carefully consider whether you want to make a file replicable because there is no built-in feature for restoring your original database. For this reason, you might want to back up the database file before making it replicable.

If you know the names of the replication tables and fields, you can reconstruct a new nonreplicable database file with the current information from any replica within a replica set. You must append tables from the selected replica to the new database copy. You append only the user fields, not any of the special replication fields. You can import all the tables instead (except, of course, the special replication tables) and then run delete queries to remove the special replication fields. You add the relationships between tables and then import the other database objects.

WHAT'S NEW IN ACCESS 2000 REPLICATION

One of the most significant upgrades in Access 2000 is the introduction of the JRO model for programmatically controlling replication. Since some new features, such as the *Visibility* property, are not available with the traditional DAO programmatic interface—even in its latest upgrade (version 3.6)—you should definitely learn the new way of programming replication.

Jet–SQL Server Bidirectional Replication

Access 2000 offers bidirectional replication between Jet and Microsoft SQL Server replicas. This kind of transfer requires Jet 4 and SQL Server 7. Bidirectional transfer means that SQL Server can serve as a central repository for a disconnected set of Access applications. Mobile workers with Access applications can transfer updates to a central database and download the latest changes from a headquarters database. You need to start with a SQL Server replica or upsize an Access replica to SQL Server.

When you set up a Jet–SQL Server replica set, a SQL Server replica must be at the hub and Jet replicas can function at the spokes. The Jet replicas can exchange content bidirectionally with the SQL Server hub replica. However, Jet replicas cannot exchange content bidirectionally with other Jet replicas at the spokes. The SQL Server hub replica must always serve as an intermediary between Jet replicas at the spokes. Since SQL Server is just a database engine and not a full application development environment like Access, you cannot replicate Access-specific application objects, such as forms and reports, to the SQL Server hub. Nevertheless, this kind of design compensates by offering the other special advantages of SQL Server systems, such as client/server processing and multiprocessor scalability. (See "Implementing Merge Replication to Access Subscribers" in SQL Server Books Online for more details on the behavior of Jet–SQL Server replica sets.)

Column-Level Updates

One important way to improve the productivity of workers using a replicable database is to reduce the number of conflicts. Access 2000 introduces column-level updates to minimize collisions between two replicas. With prior Access versions, updates from two replicas collided if they changed the same record—even if they changed two different fields on the same record—because the lowest level of update tracking for replicas was the row. With Access 2000, you can create replicas that detect changes down to the level of individual fields. Therefore, one user can change a customer's fax number in one replica while another user changes the street address of the contact person for the same customer in another replica. When the two replicas synchronize, no conflicts result.

Column-level tracking is the default setting for all new replicas. If you prefer, you can choose the traditional row-level tracking. When you update a replicable database from an earlier version of Access, it retains row-level tracking. Since there is a performance and size penalty for column-level tracking, you should not use it if conflicts are highly unlikely. The column-level tracking feature works in conjunction with SQL Server replicas as well.

Replica Visibility Levels

Access 2000 introduces three degrees of visibility for replicas: global, local, and anonymous. You can control the visibility of a replica as a property in JRO. You cannot change the visibility of a replica after you create it.

Replicas with global visibility function like traditional Access replicas. They can replicate with any other replica, and they are visible throughout a replica set. Local and anonymous replicas have special roles that allow a reduction in their size relative to the traditional global replicas. Replicas created from local and anonymous replicas share their parent's visibility property setting, except that they have a unique *ReplicaId* property. You cannot create a design master replica from either a local or an anonymous replica.

Local replicas are visible only to their parent, and they exchange content exclusively with their parent. Either the parent or the local replica can initiate an exchange. In addition, the hub parent for a local replica can schedule recurring synchronizations with a local replica. Local replicas cannot exchange information directly with other replicas in a replica set. However, changes to a local replica can propagate from a local replica throughout a replica set by passing through the parent. Any conflicts between a local replica and its hub parent always result in the parent winning.

Anonymous replicas are for distribution across a Web-based (FTP or HTTP 1.1) connection. For successful synchronization of an anonymous client replica with a Web-based hub replica, the original anonymous replica must have as its source a global replica managed by the Replication Manager on the web server. You can distribute copies using any appropriate means (for example, over the Web or using a CD). Like the local replica, the anonymous replica can synchronize only with its parent, but the parent cannot schedule replications with its anonymous children replicas. Exchanges must always be initiated by the anonymous replica to its parent. If any conflicts occur during synchronization, the parent replica always wins.

Priority-Based Conflict Resolution

Access 2000 has a new default conflict resolution rule. The earlier releases of Access resolved conflicts between two replicas in favor of the replica that changed a record the most. If two replicas changed a record an equal number of times, the replica with the lowest *ReplicaId* property won. The new default conflict resolution scheme employs a variation of the 800-pound gorilla rule: The replica with the highest priority wins. Priority property settings for replicas can range from *0* through *100*. Again, if two replicas have an equal priority, the one with the lowest *ReplicaId* property wins. This new rule has the advantage of being consistent with the one in SQL Server 7 replication.

A replica's *Priority* property setting is read-only after you create it. By default, the initial replica for a database has a setting of *90*. Any global replica based on another replica has a priority that is 90 percent of the initial one. Anonymous and local replicas have their *Priority* property forced to *0*. Replicas copied via MS-DOS or the *CompactDatabase* method have a priority that matches the original. Converted databases have a priority of 90. Otherwise, you can assign a *Priority* property anywhere in the legitimate range when you initially make a database replicable. All subsequent global replicas must have a *Priority* value that is less than or equal to their parent (unless the person creating the replica is a member of the Admins group or is an owner of the database).

Miscellaneous Refinements

A set of miscellaneous adjustments rounds out the new replication functionality in Access 2000. A couple of them simplify such common tasks as restricting the behavior of a replica or reconciling synchronization errors. In another case, a design change can affect the optimal method of distributing application design changes.

The new Prevent Deletes replica (described earlier) prohibits users from deleting records. This feature is an easy way to ensure that inexperienced users cannot inadvertently delete important content. The replica can still have deletions propagated to it from another replica, such as one managed by a database administrator.

As mentioned previously, you can now process synchronization conflicts and errors with the same interface. The Conflict Resolution wizard presents both conflicts and errors. (See Figure 11-2.) This removes the need for separate processing of both with different interfaces. In addition, the wizard works with both Jet 4 and SQL Server 7 replication.

Deletions always have a higher priority than any change associated with a record in synchronization. This is true for all versions of Access, but with Access 2000, records losing to a delete add an entry to the conflict table for a user table. Prior versions simply ignored updates that lost to a delete.

Access 2000 introduces support for cascading through conflicting records. If the primary keys in two replicas conflict, one wins and the other loses. Records in other related tables also lose. When you fix the primary key in the losing replica, your fix in Access 2000 cascades through to the related records in other tables so they do not require individual adjustment. Earlier Access versions required independent fixes to the primary table and its related tables.

Access 2000 has a new storage format that can affect how you decide to distribute software changes for a replicated project. With prior releases, you could synchronize changes to individual Access objects, such as forms and reports. With Access 2000, Access objects such as forms, reports, modules and pages are either in a single binary large object or in the separate "project.adp" file. This new storage design forces the replication of all objects if it is necessary to update any object. If this solution is not attractive, you can make the Access project in the design master not replicable. Then you are free to distribute design changes by other means (for example, using a CD).

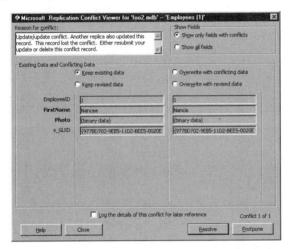

Figure 11-2. *The Conflict Resolution wizard's Replication Conflict Viewer, which displays both conflicts and errors.*

JRO DEVELOPMENT TECHNIQUES

This section presents JRO development techniques for working with replication, including making a database replicable, creating full and partial replicas, compacting databases, synchronizing databases, and documenting replica properties.

Making a Database Replicable

You use the *MakeReplicable* method of a *Replica* object to make a database replicable. This process results in the new replica becoming a design master with a global *Visibility* property setting. Converting a standard Access database to a replicable database adds the special fields and tables discussed previously. These additional fields and tables can increase the size of a database substantially, so you might want to make a backup copy of your database before making it replicable.

The syntax for the *MakeReplicable* method is

```
Replica.MakeReplicable ConnectionString, ColumnTracking
```

The connection string points at the database that you want to convert to a replicable format. You can set the *Replica* object's *ActiveConnection* property before invoking the *MakeReplicable* method. However, the connection string argument for the method overrides the *ActiveConnection* property for a replica. The *ColumnTracking* argument for the method is a Boolean variable. Its default value is *True*. Recall that this can potentially help to reduce synchronization conflicts. If conflicts are unlikely (for example, because all the editing will take place with one replica), you should consider setting the value to *False*. Synchronization conflict tracking then falls back to the traditional row-level tracking. This eliminates a performance hit associated with column-level tracking.

The following routines apply the *MakeReplicable* method to the Northwind database as the database performs backup and error-trapping functions. The *callMakeDesignMaster* procedure assigns values to its *path* and *replicaName* arguments before calling the *makeDesignMaster* procedure. The sample concatenates *path* and *replicaName* variables as it calls the second procedure. The second procedure invokes the *MakeReplicable* method for the values passed to it.

```
Sub callMakeDesignMaster()
    path = "C:\Program Files\Microsoft Office\" & _
        "Office\Samples\"
    replicaName = "Northwind.mdb"
'Set the second parameter to True to invoke
'column-level tracking of resolution conflicts.
    makeDesignMaster path & replicaName, True
End Sub


Sub makeDesignMaster(newReplica As String, _
    Optional ColumnTracking As Boolean)
On Error GoTo DMTrap
Dim repMaster As New JRO.Replica

'Offer to copy database for restoring it after
'making the database replicable.
    If MsgBox("Do you want to make a backup copy", _
        vbYesNo, "Programming Microsoft Access 2000") = vbYes Then
        Set fs = _
            CreateObject("Scripting.FileSystemObject")
        fs.Copyfile newReplica, "c:\My Documents\DMBackup.mdb"
    End If

'Optionally make the newReplica database replicable.
    If ColumnTracking = True Then
        repMaster.MakeReplicable newReplica
```

```
        Else
            repMaster.MakeReplicable newReplica, False
        End If

'Clear reference to Design master.
    Set repMaster = Nothing

DMExit:
    Exit Sub

DMTrap:
    If Err.Number = -2147467259 And _
        Left(Err.Description, 5) = "Could" Then
        MsgBox "Can not create replica because file does " & _
            "not exist. Fix path/file name and try again.", _
            vbCritical, "Programming Microsoft Access 2000"
        Resume DMExit
    ElseIf Err.Number = -2147467259 And _
        Left(Err.Description, 8) = "Database" Then
        MsgBox "Database is already replicable. Use the " & _
        "CreateReplica method to base a new replica " & _
        "on it.", vbCritical, "Programming Microsoft Access 2000"
        Resume DMExit
    ElseIf Err.Number = 53 Then
        MsgBox "Original file not found for backup copy. " & _
            "Correct file name and try again.", vbCritical, _
            "Programming Microsoft Access 2000"
        Resume DMExit
    Else
        Debug.Print Err.Number; Err.Description
    End If

End Sub
```

Before invoking the *MakeReplicable* method, the *makeDesignMaster* procedure asks whether the user wants to make a backup copy. If the user responds Yes, the procedure creates an instance of the *FileSystemObject*. Then it invokes the *Copyfile* method to back up the file. This makes it easy to return to a version of the database without the special replication fields and tables.

The *makeDesignMaster* procedure accepts up to two arguments. The first argument is the concatenation of *path* and *replicaName*. The design master for the new replica set is a file named by the value for *replicaName*. The second procedure optionally accepts a second argument. If present, this Boolean variable specifies whether to invoke column-level tracking of synchronization conflicts. The sample passes a value of *True*. The sample's design requires the user to specify *True* for the second argument to obtain column-level tracking. Failure to specify the second argument causes the Boolean variable to assume its default value of *False*. Since the *MakeReplicable* method creates replicas with column-level tracking by default, the procedure does not actually have to specify *True* to create a replica with this feature.

> **NOTE** There is no column-level tracking property. Therefore, you must manually track the status of this variable for all your replicas.

The procedure explicitly traps three distinct errors. One is for the operation of the *FileSystemObject*, and other two are from Jet. Notice that the replication component in Jet passes back the same *Err* number (–2147467259) for two distinctly different errors. Happily, these errors have different descriptions. The sample on the preceding page uses this feature to distinguish between the two. (A production system would use a longer description segment to identify the error type definitely or use a more advanced technique for parsing errors.)

> **NOTE** You can differentiate native errors from Jet errors without relying on the *Err Description* property. However, this property is potentially meaningful to more developers. The other technique involves enumerating the *Errors* collection of the *Connection* object. It returns distinct error numbers from the native database engine.

Creating Additional Full Replicas

You apply the *CreateReplica* method to a new instance of a *Replica* object to transform the instance into a new member of a replica set. Before invoking the method, you assign the *ActiveConnection* property for the new instance so that it points at the design master or another replica from the target replica set. This method fails if the *ActiveConnection* setting inadvertently denotes a database with a *ReplicaType* property of *jrRepTypeNotReplicable*. In general, this method returns a new replica of the same type and visibility as the model. However, since there should be only one design master, modeling a new replica on a design master returns another global replica subject to the parameters for the method. The general syntax for the application of the method is:

```
Replica.CreateReplica ReplicaName, Description, ReplicaType, _
    Visibility, Priority, Updatability
```

The *ReplicaName* parameter specifies the path and filename of the new replica. It can be up to 255 characters long. *Description* is an optional field that helps identify members in a replica set. The default *ReplicaType* value is *jrRepTypeFull* for a full replica. You can specify *jrRepTypePartial* instead. The *Visibility* parameter can have a value of *jrRepVisibilityGlobal* (the default), *jrRepVisibilityLocal*, or *jrRepVisibilityAnon*. If you do not specify a value for *Priority*, it uses its default rules; the maximum range is 0 through 100. A full replica has 90 percent of its parent's *Priority* value by default. The *Updatability* parameter can designate either a read-only replica (*jrRepUpdReadOnly*) or a read-write replica (*jrRepUpdFull*).

The following sample creates a replica based on the Northwind design master from the preceding sample. The *ActiveConnection* setting establishes this replica. The new replica is a full one with global visibility. The path for the replica is c:\My Documents\foo.mdb. In accordance with the parameter settings for the new replica, its description is "foo full replica".

```
Sub makeFullReplica()
Dim repMaster As New JRO.Replica

'Point repMaster at a design master mdb.
    repMaster.ActiveConnection = _
    "C:\Program Files\Microsoft Office\" & _
        "Office\Samples\Northwind.mdb"

'Make sure foo.mdb is deleted before running the next line.
    repMaster.CreateReplica "c:\My Documents\foo.mdb", _
        "foo full replica", jrRepTypeFull, _
        jrRepVisibilityGlobal, , jrRepUpdFull

End Sub
```

You need not create a backup in this case because the command creates a new replica that must be based on an existing replica. However, the procedure can fail if the replica already exists or if the model for the replica does not exist (that is, if the file is missing). These are simple error-trapping issues. The initial sample took one approach to this kind of task while creating a replica. You might want to assume that the new version makes any existing version with the same name obsolete. The second sample implements that logic by deleting the old replica, which eliminates the source of one error before it arises.

Creating Partial Replicas and Filters

A partial replica is a replica with less than all of the data for a full replica. Recall that this type of replica is useful for branch offices and mobile workers who need access to a subset of the data maintained at headquarters. Using partial replicas limits the amount of data that the users of a replica can view, and it reduces the amount of updating necessary to synchronize a replica.

After you make a blank partial replica with the *CreateReplica* method, you must populate the partial replica with data. Each partial replica has a *Filters* collection. Each *Filter* object within the *Filters* collection specifies a different slice of data that the partial replica contains. In order for a partial replica to contain data initially, you must specify one or more filters for it, append these to the replica's *Filters* collection, and then invoke the *PopulatePartial* method.

You can base a filter on the WHERE clause of a SQL statement (without the WHERE keyword) or on a relationship. You add and specify filters to a partial replica with the *Filters* collection's *Append* method. This method takes three arguments: The *TableName* property designates the table for which the filter specifies the content, the *FilterType* property denotes with a constant whether a SQL criteria statement (*jrFilterTypeTable*) or a relationship (*jrFilterType Relationship*) filters entries for the table, and the *FilterCriteria* property includes the relationship name or the WHERE phrase from a SQL statement that delimits the records for a table.

The *PopulatePartial* method for a replica clears all records in a partial replica and repopulates the replica based on its current filters. It does this by synchronizing the partial replica with a full replica. The method takes two arguments. The first one is an object variable that points to the partial replica to repopulate. The second is a string variable that designates the path and filename for the full replica with which the partial replica synchronizes. You should generally use the *PopulatePartial* method for a partial replica when you initialize the replica or change its filters. To use the *PopulatePartial* method with a partial replica, you must first open the replica with exclusive access because the method removes all records from the replica as the first step to repopulating the replica with records.

The following four procedures illustrate one approach to defining two partial replicas by using *Filter* collections and the *PopulatePartial* method. The *callMakePartialFilter* procedure calls *makePartialFilter* twice with two different sets of arguments. First, it launches the process to create a partial replica named "Partial of Northwind.mdb". Then it repeats the process for another replica named "Partial of foo.mdb".

```
Sub callMakePartialFilter()
    makePartialFilter "Partial of Northwind.mdb", _
        "Northwind.mdb", "C:\Program Files\" & _
        "Microsoft Office\Office\Samples\"
    makePartialFilter "Partial of foo.mdb", _
        "foo.mdb", "C:\My Documents\"
End Sub


Sub makePartialFilter(replicaName As String, _
    sourceName As String, path As String)
Dim rep As New JRO.Replica
Dim flt1 As JRO.Filter
```

```
'Delete old partial.
    strfile = path & replicaName
    deleteFile (strfile)

'Make partial.
    makePartial path, replicaName, sourceName

'Open connection to partial and append filter.
    rep.ActiveConnection = _
        "Provider=Microsoft.Jet.OLEDB.4.0;Data Source=" & _
        path & replicaName & ";Mode=Share Exclusive"
    rep.Filters.Append "Employees", jrFilterTypeTable, _
        "Title='Sales Representative'"
    rep.Filters.Append "Customers", jrFilterTypeTable, _
        "Country='Spain' AND City='Madrid'"

'Populate partial from source.
    rep.PopulatePartial path & sourceName

End Sub


Sub deleteFile(strfile)
On Error GoTo deleteTrap
Dim cnn1 As New ADODB.Connection

'Prepare to delete file.
    Set fs = _
        CreateObject("Scripting.FileSystemObject")
    fs.deleteFile strfile

deleteExit:
    Exit Sub

deleteTrap:
    If Err.Number = 70 Or Err.Number = 75 Then
        MsgBox "Partial is unavailable to system. " & _
            "Close it so that the system can create a " & _
            "new one.", vbCritical, "Programming Microsoft Access 2000"
    ElseIf Err.Number = 53 Then
        Resume Next
    Else
        Debug.Print Err.Number; Err.Description
    End If
    Resume deleteExit

End Sub
```

(continued)

```
Sub makePartial(path As String, replicaName As String, _
    sourceName As String)
Dim rep As New JRO.Replica

    rep.ActiveConnection = path & sourceName
    rep.CreateReplica path & replicaName, _
        replicaName, jrRepTypePartial, _
        jrRepVisibilityGlobal, , jrRepUpdFull

End Sub
```

The *makePartialFilter* procedure accepts arguments from the procedure *callMakePartialFilter* that specify the name of the partial replica to create and the full replica data source for the partial replica. The *makePartialFilter* procedure also defines and appends the *Filter* objects for a partial replica, and it invokes the *PopulatePartial* method to apply the filters.

The procedure first deletes the name of any existing partial replica with the same name and location as the one it wants to create. It does this by defining a string variable based on the *path* and *replicaName* variables it receives from the calling routine. Then it passes that new string variable to the *deleteFile* procedure. Barring an unanticipated error, *deleteFile* performs one of three tasks: It deletes the old file for the replica, it reminds a user to close a replica so that the application can delete it, or it ignores an error caused by the fact that the file does not exist (error number 53).

After attempting to delete the existing file, the procedure creates a new partial replica by calling the *makePartial* procedure. The call passes three arguments: *path*, *replicaName*, and *sourceName*. The *makePartial* procedure is nearly identical in design to the *makeFullReplica* procedure. Both invoke the *CreateReplica* method for a new instance of a *Replica* object. Aside from using variables to denote the path and filename, the key difference is that the *makePartial* procedure specifies *jrRepTypePartial* as the *ReplicaType* property while *makeFullReplica* uses *jrRepTypeFull* as its *ReplicaType* argument. Notice that *makePartial* specifies the new replica's name as the concatenation of the *path* and *replicaName* variables. The *ActiveConnection* property for the new replica instance specifies the full replica source for the partial replica. The procedure specifies this source as the concatenation of the *path* and *sourceName* variables. It requires that the full and new partial replica both reside in the same path. It is easy to remove this constraint; the chapter's final sample shows how to do this.

After the *makePartial* procedure returns control to the procedure *makePartialFilter*, the new partial replica exists but has no data, so *makePartialFilter* populates it with data. First, it sets the *ActiveConnection* of a replica instance to the new partial replica and it opens the replica in exclusive mode. Recall that this is necessary for the application of the *PopulatePartial* method. Next, it defines and appends a couple of *Filter* objects to the replica. The first filter extracts sales representatives from the *Employees* tables. The second filter extracts customers from Madrid, Spain. Finally, the *PopulatePartial* method synchronizes the full replica denoted by the concatenation of *path* and *sourceName* with the new partial replica. Only two tables receive records. (You can add filters to populate more tables in the partial replica.)

Synchronizing Replicas

The following two procedures synchronize replicas in typical replication scenarios. Both use basic ADO procedures. The *synchNorthwindFooToAdd* procedure adds a new record to the *Employees* table in the Northwind.mdb replica. This is the design master for a replica set that includes foo.mdb. The procedure then synchronizes Northwind with foo to propagate the new record to foo.mdb. The second procedure, *synchFooNorthwindToDelete*, deletes the new employee record from foo and then synchronizes foo with Northwind to remove the record from the Northwind replica as well.

```
Sub synchNorthwindFooToAdd()
Dim rep1 As JRO.Replica
Dim cnn1 As New ADODB.Connection
Dim rst1 As ADODB.Recordset

'Open connection to Northwind and
'set reference for Northwind as a replica.
    cnn1.Open "Provider=Microsoft.Jet.OLEDB.4.0;" & _
        "Data Source=c:\Program Files\Microsoft Office\" & _
        "Office\Samples\Northwind.mdb"
    Set rep1 = New JRO.Replica
    rep1.ActiveConnection = cnn1

'Add a new employee to Northwind.
    Set rst1 = New ADODB.Recordset
    rst1.Open "Employees", cnn1, adOpenKeyset, adLockOptimistic, _
        adCmdTable
    rst1.AddNew
        rst1.Fields("FirstName") = "Rick"
        rst1.Fields("LastName") = "Dobson"
        rst1.Fields("BirthDate") = Date - 1
'When it comes to learning about computers and my faith
'in the Lord, I am always newly born.
    rst1.Update
```

(continued)

```
'Synchronize Northwind with its full replica (foo.mdb).
    rep1.Synchronize "c:\My Documents\foo.mdb", _
        jrSyncTypeImpExp, jrSyncModeDirect

End Sub


Sub synchFooNorthwindToDelete()
Dim rep1 As JRO.Replica
Dim cnn1 As New ADODB.Connection, cmd1 As ADODB.Command

'Open connection to foo and
'set reference to foo as a replica.
    cnn1.Open "Provider=Microsoft.Jet.OLEDB.4.0;" & _
        "Data Source=c:\My Documents\foo.mdb"
    Set rep1 = New JRO.Replica
    rep1.ActiveConnection = cnn1

'Execute command to remove an employee from foo.mdb.
    Set cmd1 = New ADODB.Command
    With cmd1
        .ActiveConnection = cnn1
        .CommandText = "DELETE Employees.* FROM Employees" & _
            " WHERE LastName='Dobson'"
        .CommandType = adCmdText
        .Execute
    End With

'Synchronize foo with its design master (Northwind.mdb).
    rep1.Synchronize "c:\Program Files\Microsoft Office\" & _
        "Office\Samples\Northwind.mdb", jrSyncTypeImpExp, _
        jrSyncModeDirect

End Sub
```

The *synchNorthwindFooToAdd* procedure uses ADO to add a record to a table in one replica and then propagate that record to a corresponding table in another replica. It starts by declaring *Replica*, *Connection*, and *Recordset* objects. Then it opens a connection to the Northwind database and sets the *ActiveConnection* property of the replica with the connection. It creates an instance of a *Recordset* object on the same connection as the replica. Then it adds an employee named Rick Dobson. The procedure closes by applying the *Synchronize* method to the Northwind replica and naming foo as the replica with which to exchange updates. This final step passes the new employee record from Northwind to foo.

The *synchFooNorthwindToDelete* procedure removes the new record from foo. It also restores Northwind by synchronizing with it. This procedure uses a

Command object to drop an employee with a last name of Dobson from the *Employees* table in foo. After executing the command, it applies the *Synchronize* method to the foo replica to propagate the delete to Northwind.

Working with Prevent Deletes Replicas

A Prevent Deletes replica is easy to create, but you must create it from the user interface. Choose Tools-Replication-Create Replica and select the Prevent Deletes check box in the dialog box that opens. This type of replica allows an application to distribute a replica that does not support direct deletes to its contents. While you can achieve this result using Access security settings, it is a lot easier to just select the check box. While the user of a Prevent Deletes replica cannot directly delete records, the replica can accept delete updates from other replicas. One use for this type of replica is to enable an administrator to make sure that records are not deleted until they are properly archived.

The following three procedures manipulate Prevent Deletes replicas with ADO. *SynchAddToFoo2* adds a new employee to the foo2.mdb replica from the foo.mdb replica. The employee's name is Rick Dobson. The second procedure, *TryToDeleteFromFoo2*, attempts to delete the same record directly from the foo2.mdb replica. The error message in Figure 11-3 on the next page shows how Access responds to the Execute command in the procedure. If you need to restrict additions as well as deletions, you can set the *Updatability* argument in the *CreateReplica* method to *jrRepUpdReadOnly*. You do not need the user interface to do this. The third procedure, *synchFooFoo2ToDelete*, removes Rick Dobson from the foo.mdb replica and then propagates that deletion to the foo2.mdb replica. Although users cannot delete a record directly from a Prevent Deletes replica, an administrator can propagate a deletion using synchronization.

```
Sub SynchAddToFoo2()
Dim rep1 As JRO.Replica
Dim cnn1 As New ADODB.Connection
Dim rst1 As ADODB.Recordset

'Open connection to foo and
'set reference to foo as a replica.
    cnn1.Open "Provider=Microsoft.Jet.OLEDB.4.0;" & _
        "Data Source=c:\My Documents\foo.mdb"
    Set rep1 = New JRO.Replica
    rep1.ActiveConnection = cnn1

'Add a new employee to foo.
    Set rst1 = New ADODB.Recordset
    rst1.Open "Employees", cnn1, adOpenKeyset, adLockOptimistic, _
        adCmdTable
```

(continued)

```
        rst1.AddNew
            rst1.Fields("FirstName") = "Rick"
            rst1.Fields("LastName") = "Dobson"
            rst1.Fields("BirthDate") = Date - 1
        rst1.Update

'Synchronize foo with foo2.mdb.
        rep1.Synchronize "c:\My Documents\foo2.mdb", _
            jrSyncTypeImpExp, jrSyncModeDirect

End Sub


Sub TryToDeleteFromFoo2()
Dim rep As JRO.Replica
Dim cnn1 As New ADODB.Connection, cmd1 As ADODB.Command

'Open connection to foo2 and
'set a reference to it as a replica.
        cnn1.Open "Provider=Microsoft.Jet.OLEDB.4.0;" & _
            "Data Source=c:\My Documents\foo2.mdb"
        Set rep1 = New JRO.Replica
        rep1.ActiveConnection = cnn1

'Execute command to remove employee from foo2.mdb;
'it fails because Foo2 is a Prevent Deletes replica.
        Set cmd1 = New ADODB.Command
        With cmd1
            .ActiveConnection = cnn1
            .CommandText = "DELETE Employees.* FROM Employees" & _
                " WHERE LastName='Dobson'"
            .CommandType = adCmdText
            .Execute
        End With

End Sub


Sub synchFooFoo2ToDelete()
Dim rep1 As JRO.Replica
Dim cnn1 As New ADODB.Connection, cmd1 As ADODB.Command

'Open connection to foo and
'set reference to foo as a replica.
        cnn1.Open "Provider=Microsoft.Jet.OLEDB.4.0;" & _
            "Data Source=c:\My Documents\foo.mdb"
        Set rep1 = New JRO.Replica
        rep1.ActiveConnection = cnn1
```

```
'Execute command to remove an employee from foo.mdb.
    Set cmd1 = New ADODB.Command
    With cmd1
        .ActiveConnection = cnn1
        .CommandText = "DELETE Employees.* FROM Employees" & _
            " WHERE LastName='Dobson'"
        .CommandType = adCmdText
        .Execute
    End With

'Synchronize foo with its design master (Northwind.mdb).
    rep1.Synchronize "c:\My Documents\foo2.mdb", _
        jrSyncTypeImpExp, jrSyncModeDirect

End Sub
```

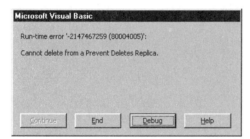

Figure 11-3. *A Prevent Deletes replica returns an error message like this one when you try to delete one of its records.*

Working with Replica Properties

By examining replica properties, you can understand the behavior of a replica set. For example, if you know a replica's type, you know whether it will share schema changes with other replicas. A replica's *Priority* property indicates which replica wins when two replicas conflict with one another. In general, the replica with the higher priority value wins. The three procedures on the following pages print replica properties and expose property values in the process.

Since there is no *Replicas* collection, you are likely to list sequentially a number of replicas when you want to process them—especially if the replicas belong to different replica sets. The *callPrintTypePriority* procedure sets *path* and *replicaName* variables for each replica it wants to examine, and then it calls two subroutines. One subroutine (*printReplicaType*) returns information about the type of replica, and the other (*printPriority*) returns the *Priority* property value for a replica. In addition to *path* and *replicaName*, the set of procedures exchanges values with an argument named *Exist*. This Boolean variable tracks whether a file exists in a path. If a file does not exist, it obviously has no priority value.

```
Sub callPrintTypePriority()
On Error GoTo TypeTrap
Dim repMaster As New JRO.Replica
Dim path As String, replicaName As String
Dim Exist As Boolean

'Assign Boolean for file existing.
    Exist = True

'Assign path and replica names, then
'call procedures for printing type and priority.
    path = "C:\Program Files\Microsoft Office\" & _
        "Office\Samples\"
    replicaName = "Northwind.mdb"
'If file does not exist, the next line catches it.
    repMaster.ActiveConnection = path & replicaName
    printReplicaType replicaName, repMaster.ReplicaType, Exist
    printPriority replicaName, path, Exist

    replicaName = "Copy of Northwind.mdb"
    repMaster.ActiveConnection = path & replicaName
    printReplicaType replicaName, repMaster.ReplicaType, Exist
    printPriority replicaName, path, Exist

    replicaName = "Northwind2.mdb"
    repMaster.ActiveConnection = path & replicaName
    printReplicaType replicaName, repMaster.ReplicaType, Exist
    printPriority replicaName, path, Exist

    path = "C:\My Documents\"
    replicaName = "foo.mdb"
    repMaster.ActiveConnection = path & replicaName
    printReplicaType replicaName, repMaster.ReplicaType, Exist
    printPriority replicaName, path, Exist

    path = "C:\Program Files\Microsoft Office\" & _
        "Office\Samples\"
    replicaName = "Partial of Northwind.mdb"
    repMaster.ActiveConnection = path & replicaName
    printReplicaType replicaName, repMaster.ReplicaType, Exist
    printPriority replicaName, path, Exist

    path = "C:\My Documents\"
    replicaName = "Partial of foo.mdb"
    repMaster.ActiveConnection = path & replicaName
    printReplicaType replicaName, repMaster.ReplicaType, Exist
    printPriority replicaName, path, Exist
```

```
        replicaName = "DMBackup.mdb"
        repMaster.ActiveConnection = path & replicaName
        printReplicaType replicaName, repMaster.ReplicaType, Exist
        printPriority replicaName, path, Exist

        path = "C:\My Documents\"
        replicaName = "foo2.mdb"
        repMaster.ActiveConnection = path & replicaName
        printReplicaType replicaName, repMaster.ReplicaType, Exist
        printPriority replicaName, path, Exist

TypeExit:
    Exit Sub


TypeTrap:
    If Err.Number = -2147467259 And _
        Left(Err.Description, 19) = _
        "Could not find file" Then
        Exist = False
        Resume Next
    Else
        Debug.Print Err.Number, Err.Description
        Resume TypeExit
    End If

End Sub



Sub printReplicaType(repName As String, _
    typeNumber As Integer, Exist As Boolean)

    If Exist Then
'Decode replica type enumeration constants or...
        Select Case typeNumber
            Case jrRepTypeNotReplicable
                Debug.Print repName & " is not replicable."
            Case jrRepTypeDesignMaster
                Debug.Print repName & " is a Design Master."
            Case jrRepTypeFull
                Debug.Print repName & " is a Full Replica."
            Case jrRepTypePartial
                Debug.Print repName & " is a Partial Replica."
        End Select
    Else
'print that file does not exist.
```

(continued)

```
            Debug.Print repName & " does not exist."
        End If

End Sub


Sub printPriority(replicaName As String, path As String, _
    Exist)
Dim repMasterP As New JRO.Replica

'Print priorty and reset Exist.
    If Exist = True Then
'Assign connection for replica.
        repMasterP.ActiveConnection = path & replicaName

        If repMasterP.ReplicaType <> jrRepTypeNotReplicable Then
'Print priority for replicas.
            Debug.Print "It's priority is " & repMasterP.Priority & "."
        Else
'Print message for no replica.
            Debug.Print "Therefore, it has no priority."
        End If
    Else
'Print message for file does not exist.
        Debug.Print "Therefore, it has no priority."
    End If
    Debug.Print

    Exist = True

End Sub
```

The *callPrintTypePriority* procedure uses error trapping to determine whether a file exists and to respond appropriately if it does not. When it tries to set the *ActiveConnection* property of a replica instance to a file that does not exist, the Jet replication component returns its standard *Err* number (−2147467259) with a descriptive phrase. The error trap checks for the phrase with the Jet replication *Err* number. If the error-trap logic determines that the file does not exist, the trap sets *Exist* to *False* and resumes. The two subroutines, *printReplicaType* and *printPriority*, interpret the *False* value for *Exist* and respond appropriately.

The *callPrintTypePriority* procedure sends the *ReplicaType* property value for a replica when it calls the *printReplicaType* procedure. The *printReplicaType* procedure checks the value of *Exist* before trying to decipher the value of the *ReplicaType* property. If *Exist* is *False*, the procedure simply prints a message to the Immediate window that the file does not exist. If *Exist* is *True*, a *Select Case* statement decodes the *ReplicaType* property.

> **NOTE** The *printReplicaType* procedure represents *ReplicaType* values with the JRO *ReplicaTypeEnum* constant names. You can view these with the Object Browser. Enter *ReplicaType* in the Search text box and click the Search button. Select from the return set the *ReplicaTypeEnum* class for the JRO library. (Be careful: The DAO library has a different *ReplicaTypeEnum* class.) This selection lists the constant names and their *ReplicaType* values.

The design of the *printPriority* procedure is slightly different from that of the *printReplicaType* procedure. The *printPriority* procedure creates a replica instance within it. Then it derives a property value for the replica. In addition to checking the value of the *Exist* function, it checks the *ReplicaType* property of the replica instance. If the property shows that the file is not replicable by returning a value of *jrRepTypeNotReplicable*, the procedure prints that there is no priority for the file. Otherwise, the procedure prints the value returned by the *Priority* property of its replica instance. Before returning control to the *callPrintTypePriority* procedure, *printPriority* resets the value of *Exist* to *True* for processing the next replica.

Compacting and Encrypting Replicas

The JRO library supports more than just replication. For example, you can compact and encrypt files and you can refresh the memory cache. The following two procedures make a backup of a replica by compacting it and encrypting the compacted copy. This approach is particularly appropriate when you send a file with sensitive information over the Internet. The sample compacts the Northwind.mdb file to Northwind2.mdb. You can optionally specify separate paths for Northwind and Northwind2.

```
Sub callCompactADB()
    compactADB "Northwind.mdb", "Northwind2.mdb", _
        "C:\Program Files\Microsoft Office\Office\Samples\"
End Sub

Sub compactADB(oName As String, cName As String, _
    opath As String, Optional cpath As String)
Dim je As New JRO.JetEngine
Dim strIn As String, strOut As String
```

(continued)

```
'Is optional path specified?
    If cpath = "" Then
        cpath = opath
    End If

    strIn = opath & oName
    strOut = cpath & cName

    deleteFile strOut

    je.CompactDatabase _
    "Provider=Microsoft.Jet.OLEDB.4.0;" & _
        "Data Source=" & strIn, _
    "Provider=Microsoft.Jet.OLEDB.4.0;" & _
        "Data Source=" & strOut & ";" & _
    "Jet OLEDB:Encrypt Database=True"

End Sub
```

Chapter 12

Building Solutions with MSDE and Access Projects

Microsoft Access 2000 introduces two innovations for working with Microsoft SQL Server databases. The first innovation is the Microsoft Data Engine (MSDE). MSDE permits local data storage in a SQL Server database format. MSDE databases can serve as the back end, just as SQL Server databases do, for solutions in .adp file types. By developing with MSDE, you can smooth the transition of your solutions from those serving local, department needs to those addressing the needs of entire enterprises with thousands of users. The second innovation is the new .adp file type. Microsoft calls applications developed with .adp files Access Projects. (The letters *adp* stand for Access Data Project.) Access Projects use traditional forms, reports, modules, and even macros but with a SQL Server database instead of a Jet database. The new database file type does not contain Microsoft Access tables or queries, but it makes available SQL Server tables, views, and stored procedures.

In this chapter, you'll learn how to install and manage MSDE and how to develop custom applications with Access Projects. You'll learn how to work with tables, views, stored procedures, reports, and forms. The code samples will illustrate how to automate your Access Project applications with ActiveX Data Objects (ADO) and Microsoft Visual Basic for Applications (VBA). (Chapters 3 and 4 cover OLE DB routes to other remote database formats besides SQL Server.)

THE MICROSOFT DATA ENGINE

You can use MSDE to build solutions on single-processor personal computers running Microsoft Windows 9x operating systems or Microsoft Windows NT systems. Solutions run on MSDE are appropriate for small workgroups, but you can readily transfer MSDE solutions to Microsoft SQL Server 7 so that your solutions can scale to multiprocessor clusters running the most advanced Windows operating systems. These advanced systems include Windows NT Server Enterprise Edition and higher-end Windows 2000 operating systems.

MSDE solutions are completely compatible with those developed for SQL Server 7. You can prototype a solution with MSDE and .adp files on your local computer, and then later you can transfer the database tables, views, and stored procedures to SQL Server for testing, refinement, and rollout. You can distribute to testers and users the original .adp files with their data link changed to point at the SQL Server database instead of your prototype MSDE-based system. Such applications are suited to serving enterprise, as opposed to departmental, needs.

MSDE vs. Jet

Jet-based Access solutions are basically easier to manage, more compatible with solutions built with prior Access versions, and consume fewer resources. MSDE-based Access solutions require that you have some familiarity with new data types, different rules for developing queries, and database administration techniques. In return, MSDE offers superior data recovery, built-in transaction logging, integrated Windows NT security, and the potential for huge database capacity (when you migrate to SQL Server 7). You can use the Access user interface to build forms and reports for solutions with either database engine. Because of the inherent client/server design of MSDE solutions, you must follow certain rules for using MSDE and the user interface. You can also program solutions with VBA and ADO for either database engine.

Both MSDE and Jet support declarative referential integrity, so you can graphically declare relations between tables. However, while Jet supports cascading updates and deletes at the engine level, with MSDE you must implement these features programmatically in SQL using triggers. You open a trigger template for a table by right-clicking on the table in the Database window and choosing Triggers. You then click New to open the template. (SQL Server Books Online includes syntax rules, samples, and general background on developing triggers.)

If you need only a full restore from a backup file, you choose Tools-Database Utilities-Restore in an Access Project. This is similar to maintaining backup copies of Jet database files and restoring them from copies. Only MSDE supports recovery to a point in time from a log file. You must program this type of restore with Transact-SQL, which Access 2000 online help supports. Online help includes sample scripts and syntax for recovering data in a table to a specific point in time from its log file.

> **NOTE** If you find yourself managing a collection of tasks that require Transact-SQL, you might want to obtain a full copy of SQL Server 7 (instead of the free MSDE package with the same core database engine code). The SQL Server Enterprise Manager provides a large collection of wizards and a graphical user interface that eliminates the need for Transact-SQL code for tasks such as backing up and restoring.

Jet database files are typically smaller than comparable MSDE-based solutions. The Northwind.mdb file ships at about 2 MB. This includes all the database tables, other database objects, and code. The MSDE-based version of Northwind includes a database (.mdf) file and an Access Project (.adp) file. These files total about 3.7 MB. MSDE solutions automatically maintain log files that help in the event of a recovery. However, Jet databases must pass their databases across a network in multi-user solutions. MSDE-based solutions perform all database processing at the server and pass their return sets across a network. This can reduce network traffic and speed performance. Both Jet and MSDE permit databases as large as 2 GB, but MSDE solutions can migrate easily to SQL Server 7 for support of databases in excess of 1 million terabytes (TB). SQL Server 7 scales up its performance as you run on computers with more processors, but Jet does not substantially escalate performance as you add processors.

> **NOTE** MSDE, unlike its older sibling SQL Server 7, is tuned for working with small workgroups.

Both Jet and MSDE have their place. MSDE is the ideal tool if you envision using SQL Server for future versions of your application. When MSDE runs on Windows NT systems, it can offer integrated operating system and database security, which can reduce your security administration burden. MSDE also offers point-in-time recovery. Jet is more appropriate for non–mission critical applications for which ease of development is an overriding consideration.

Jet solutions have smaller footprints and can be a better choice if you have memory or disk constraints. Because only a marginally updated Jet engine ships with Access 2000, it offers the highest compatibility with Access 97 and earlier versions.

Installing and Configuring MSDE

MSDE is an optional database engine for Access developers and users. You can install it by running SetupSQL.exe from your Office 2000 CDs. No special operating system preparation is necessary for installation on a Windows 9x system. Users of Windows NT 4 must perform two steps to prepare for MSDE installation. First, they must install Service Pack 3, and then they must run hotfix.exe from the Office 2000 CDs. Windows NT 4 with Service Pack 4 requires no special setup requirements.

After installing MSDE, you must start the engine before you can use it. For Windows 9x computers, you can perform this with the following steps:

1.	Choose Programs from the Start menu.

2.	Choose Msde and then choose Service Manager.

3.	From the Services drop-down list box, select MSSQLServer and then Click Start/Continue.

You can select the Auto-Start Service check box if you want MSDE to start automatically when the operating system starts. If you do not select this option, you must repeat the above steps whenever you use MSDE.

Windows NT users can launch MSDE just like any other Windows NT service. On the Control Panel, you double-click the Services icon and then choose MSDE Service. Click the Start button in the Services dialog box to launch the service. Then click Startup and select a Startup Type (Automatic, Manual, or Disabled).

After installation and startup, an icon representing SQL Server Service Manager appears on your Windows task bar. You can use this icon to start, pause, or stop MSDE. You can also use it to open Service Manager so you can perform the same functions for the Microsoft Distributed Transaction Coordinator and Microsoft SQL Server Agent.

It is normal to require a user to enter a user ID and a password before opening a file for a client/server database. MSDE lets you manage login security with individual and group accounts for specific databases or with integrated, pass-through security from Windows NT. The MSDE defaults are *sa* for the user ID and blank for the password. You can choose Tools-Security-Database Security to establish security accounts for individual databases. Windows 9*x* users can use MSDE security accounts only for individual databases. MSDE database roles are comparable to groups in Access. An individual can belong to two or more different roles, and individuals inherit the most permissive security of any role to which they belong.

When you run MSDE from Windows 9*x*, it supports TCP/IP and Multi-Protocol, but not Named Pipes. However, most clients attempt to connect to an MSDE server computer via Named Pipes by default. If you want a client computer to establish an alias for the MSDE server that connects via either TCP/IP or Multi-Protocol, choose the MSDE Client Network Utility command from the Msde menu off the Start button.

ACCESS PROJECTS

You can use Access Projects with MSDE or SQL Server to develop client/server applications almost as easily as you develop file server applications. The Access Project interface exposes nine basic application object types. Tables, views, stored procedures, and database diagrams are for the catalog of an MDSE or SQL Server database and are stored in the database file. Forms, reports, data access pages (for Web development), macros, and modules are stored in the .adp file. The Access Project coordinates with its client/server database via an OLE DB connection. These two parts—the database file, which is typically an .mdf file, and the .adp file—jointly comprise the client/server solution.

Connecting an Access Project to a Database

You can connect an .adp file to one of three database types:

- A SQL Server 7 database file on Windows 9*x* or Windows NT (Service Pack 4 or later)
- An MSDE file on Windows 9*x* or Windows NT
- SQL Server 6.5 on Windows NT (Service Pack 5 or later)

To monitor or reset the connection to the client/server database, choose Connection from the File menu. In the Data Link Properties dialog box (shown in Figure 12-1 on the next page), select a database server, type of security, and database name. Typically, the database server name is the name of the computer running the server.

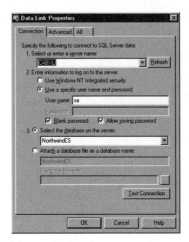

Figure 12-1. *The Data Link Properties dialog box.*

The figure shows a connection to an MSDE database running on a computer with the name CABXLI. Nothing in the dialog box clearly indicates that the database is an MSDE database instead of a SQL Server database. Since the CABXLI computer runs a Windows 9*x* operating system, it cannot run Windows NT integrated security. The Data Link Properties dialog box uses the default user-specific connectivity information. After the connection to the database server is established, the drop-down list box shows all the databases at the server. After you make these selections, the .adp file populates its table, views, stored procedures, and database diagram collections with objects. These settings persist between instances of an Access Project.

Learning from the NorthwindCS and Pubs Databases

Access 2000 ships with both file server and client/server versions of the Northwind sample application. The client/server version sets up as an Access Project. The Pubs database does not ship with Access 2000, but it has long been the standard SQL Server sample. If you use Access Projects with a SQL Server database manager, this sample will almost surely be available to you. You can open it in an Access Project. Many ADO and other database samples in the Access 2000 online help files specifically reference this database. Therefore, you can enhance your grasp of new database features in Access 2000 by becoming familiar with Pubs.

Using the NorthwindCS Project and database

The NorthwindCS.adp copies to your computer when you install Access Samples. This Access Project parallels much of the functionality and all of the data in the classic Northwind.mdb file. Access 2000 makes both available. To use

NorthwindCS, you must either have MSDE installed on your computer or have a connection to a SQL Server 7 database manager because the Northwind database files ship with both of these products.

The first time you run NorthwindCS.adp, a script detects whether you have MSDE on your computer. If you do, the script asks whether you want to load the NorthwindCS database. A positive reply causes the script to load the database and connect the NorthwindCS Project to it. Otherwise, you can attach the NorthwindCS Project to the Northwind database on a SQL Server database manager.

The NorthwindCS Project inserts a special Show Me item on its menu bar. If you choose this item, you see a dialog box (shown in Figure 12-2) that makes available the Access Project demonstration, which explains special Access Project features and SQL Server data types. While Jet and SQL Server data types correspond in some ways, they also differ significantly. For example, the Timestamp data type is unique to SQL Server. SQL Server can also represent Currency and Date/Time values differently than Jet. In addition, SQL Server has explicit Unicode and non-Unicode data types.

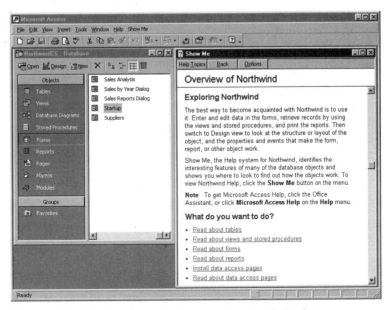

Figure 12-2. *The NorthwindCS Project's Show Me dialog box.*

Another critical difference between Access Projects and traditional .mdb files is in their use of views, stored procedures, and queries. The Show Me dialog box explains how views and stored procedures replace queries in custom applications. Recall that .mdb files enable views and stored procedures against the

Jet database engine, but the syntax rules for views in Jet and SQL Server differ. For example, .mdb files let you sort records in a view with the ORDER BY SQL term. Neither SQL Server nor MSDE permits ORDER BY in the SQL for a view. These client/server database managers reserve the ORDER BY phrase for stored procedures.

If the Show Me dialog box fails to address your needs completely, try the Access online help. Open the Office Assistant and ask for help on "Work with a Microsoft Access Project." You can get additional online help for Access Projects by opening an Access Project table in Design view and pressing F1. Close the Microsoft Access Help window before pressing F1 to enter another part of the help system with a lead heading of "Working with Access Project Components." This area of online help also includes details on Transact-SQL and SQL Server error messages. Finally, consider using SQL Server Books Online. (You need a computer with the full version of SQL Server 7 to tap this resource.)

Using Pubs with Access Projects

If you've ever worked with ODBCDirect or developed a custom remote database solution with Access, you've probably spent some time with the Pubs database. You can build on and expand that knowledge with Access Projects. Recall that you need a copy of SQL Server to work with Pubs. You can run the database in either SQL Server 7 or 6.5 with an Access Project.

To work with Pubs from an Access Project, you need an .adp file that points to Pubs. If a disconnected .adp file is not already available, you can create one by creating a new Access Project and then dropping its database. Then open the Data Link Properties dialog box and point the disconnected Access Project at the Pubs database.

To create a new .adp file, start Access and choose to create a new database selecting the Access Database Wizards, Pages, And Projects option. This opens the New dialog box. (Alternatively, you can click New on the Database toolbar.) Click on the General tab and then double-click Project (New Database). In the File Name text box, type a name for your new .adp file. Then click Create. This launches the Microsoft SQL Server Database wizard (shown in Figure 12-3), which contains the name of the local server (CABXLI in this example) and a suggested name for the database based on your filename entry. You must enter the user account information (an appropriate user ID and password—*sa* and blank usually work). Click Next and then Finish to complete the process. Once the Access

Project is available, disconnect it from its data source by dropping its database: Choose Tools-Database Utilities-Drop-SQL Database. Finally, open the Data Link Properties dialog box for the disconnected Access Project. Enter information that points to the project file at the Pubs database on your SQL Server.

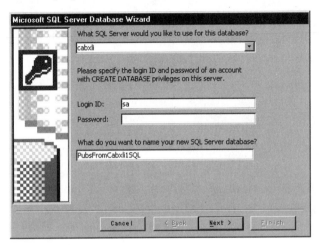

Figure 12-3. *The opening screen of the Microsoft SQL Server Database wizard.*

NOTE If all you want is a disconnected .adp file (so you can point it at Pubs or some other existing database), you can abbreviate the process. Press the Esc key when you see the opening screen of the Microsoft SQL Server Database wizard. Then open the Data Link Properties dialog box for the resulting disconnected .adp file and point it at the database you want to work with.

After you create an Access Project linking to the Pubs database, you can mine the database for interesting samples of SQL Server technology that will let you refine your own tools. Figure 12-4 on the next page shows the four stored procedures in Pubs with the *byroyalty* procedure open. This sample returns the author IDs for any authors with a royalty percentage agreement that matches the one input in response to the parameter query. The *Mybyroyalty* stored procedure is an extension of the initial one that returns the authors' first name, last name, and phone number.

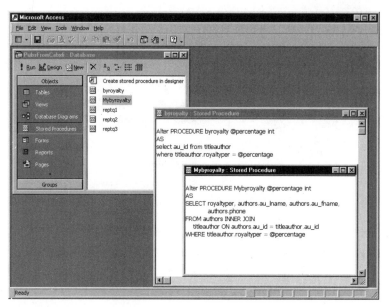

Figure 12-4. *The stored procedures in the Pubs database.*

Recovering SQL Server databases

SQL Server is an industrial-strength database, but it is possible to damage its system so that you lose the ability to work with your data. For example, a media failure can corrupt the master database file. With very severe damage, you might not be able to start SQL Server, so you have to uninstall SQL Server or MSDE. You can choose MSDE-Uninstall from the Start menu or the Control Panel to remove the faulty installation. This removes all system databases, such as the master database, but it leaves any user databases, such as NorthwindCS.

As you begin working with MSDE or SQL Server, you might repeatedly install your client/server database manager to gain familiarity with the process. After reinstalling SQL Server or MSDE, copy over your new master with a recent backup of the master database or rebuild your master so that it recognizes your previously existing databases. Either action will permit you to connect with your previously existing user databases.

Keeping a current copy of the master database is a good idea because it can simplify connecting a fresh installation of SQL Server with your previously existing databases. Back up your master database after creating or deleting new user databases or login accounts. Adding a new user to a database does not modify the master because security information, such as user accounts, go into the database file.

Rebuilding the master involves renaming your old user database files and creating placeholder databases with the same names as your previously existing databases. Create new Access Projects for every database file that you need to recover. As you create a new Access Project, edit the name in its Microsoft SQL Server Database wizard dialog boxes to one of the database files you want in your new master. After you build a new Access Project for each database file you want to recover, copy the renamed old user database files over the newly created ones. This updates your master so that it knows about the user database files from a prior installation, and it copies each old file to a name that the new master knows.

DATABASE DIAGRAMS AND TABLES

A database diagram is a collection of database objects, much like tables, views, and stored procedures are. Access 2000 stores them with the SQL Server or MSDE database file as opposed to the Access Project. While an individual database diagram can resemble the display that appears in the Relationships window of a classic .mdb Access file, client/server database diagrams are much more flexible and offer more granular control over the design of a database. For example, you can initiate the design of new tables from a database diagram window.

Using Database Diagrams to Map Relationships

Figure 12-5 shows the database diagram for the NorthwindCS database. As with the Relationships window in traditional Access files for Jet databases, it depicts the tables in the database design and the relationships among them. You can fine-tune the relationship between two tables by clicking the line that connects them and choosing Properties from the shortcut menu. The diagram in Figure 12-5 shows the relationship between the *Products* and *Categories* tables selected.

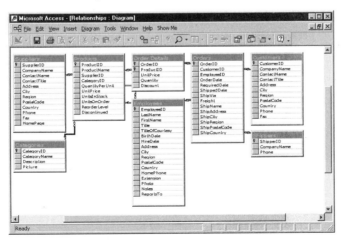

Figure 12-5. *The database diagram from the NorthwindCS Project.*

Figure 12-6 shows the Properties dialog box for the selected relationship in Figure 12-5. The tabs present substantially more information about the relationships between tables than you get from the Relationships window in a classic Access/Jet database file.

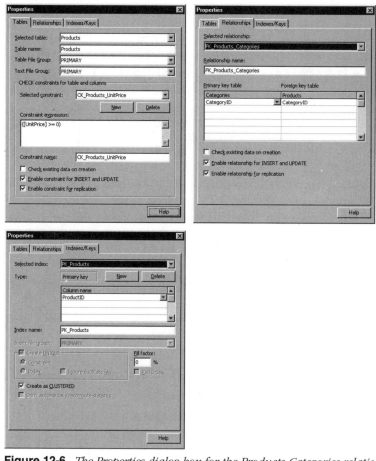

Figure 12-6. *The Properties dialog box for the Products-Categories relationship in the NorthwindCS database.*

You can use the Tables tab to control the validity specifications for data entering the table. You use constraints for this task. To select any constraint to edit or delete it, select it in the Selected Constraint drop-down list box. Click New to add a new constraint for a table. Click Delete to drop the currently selected constraint. The three check boxes at the bottom of the Tables tab determine when a constraint takes effect. The two selections at the top left of Figure 12-6 apply the constraint when a user adds or updates data in the table or when the table is copied to another database. Use the Selected Table drop-down list at the top of the Tables tab to select another table and add constraints for it.

The Relationships tab initially shows the relationship between the *Products* and *Categories* tables. However, you can use the Selected Relationship drop-down list box to examine the relationships that the *Products* table shares with the *Suppliers* table or the *Order Details* table. To accomplish the same result with a .mdb file, you must explicitly select that relationship from the Relationships window.

The Indexes/Keys tab shows the settings for the table's existing keys and indexes and lets you add new ones or delete existing ones. The *ProductID* field defines the primary key for the *Products* table. The index is clustered, which means that the physical order and the logical order of the rows are identical.

Managing Multiple Database Diagrams

Figure 12-7 highlights another potential use for database diagrams. It shows three different diagrams, all for the same database. Classic .mdb files do not permit multiple diagrams depicting the relationships in a database; each file has a single Relationships window. With SQL Server, however, you can have multiple database windows. Database diagram windows can have mutually exclusive or overlapping content. For example, both the *FamilyMembers* table and the *AdditionsToFamilyMembers* table appear in the MyDiagram and JustFamilyDiagram windows. You can copy a window to the Clipboard and paste it into another window. Since you can secure database diagram windows, you can control the views of a database that different groups of users have.

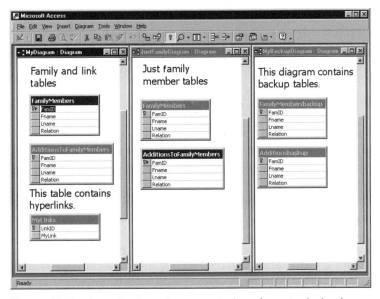

Figure 12-7. *Three database diagram windows for a single database.*

As you can see in Figure 12-7, you can add labels to diagrams to identify one or all of the tables. To modify the font style, size, color, or other features of a label, right-click in a label box to open the Font dialog box.

You can list the database diagram windows within a database by enumerating the members of the *AllDatabaseDiagrams* collection. Your programs can also read the *IsLoaded* property of the collection's members to report whether the window is open. However, you cannot set the *IsLoaded* property to open and close database diagram windows. The *AllDatabaseDiagrams* collection belongs to either the *CurrentData* or *CodeData* object within an application.

The following procedure writes out a list of all the database diagram windows and indicates whether they are open:

```
Sub listDatabaseDiagrams()
Dim obj As AccessObject, dbs As Object

'Set the hierarchical container for AllDatabaseDiagrams.
    Set dbs = Application.CurrentData

'List database diagrams by whether they are loaded.
    For Each obj In dbs.AllDatabaseDiagrams
        If obj.IsLoaded = True Then
            Debug.Print obj.Name; " is loaded."
        Else
            Debug.Print obj.Name & " is not loaded."
        End If
    Next obj

End Sub
```

Editing Tables in Database Diagram Windows

You can edit tables and enter new tables from either a database diagram window or the *Tables Objects* collection in the Database window. Each approach has merit for particular tasks.

Database diagram windows are great for performing data definition tasks graphically or in a table's Properties dialog box. To designate a primary key, you select the field's row selector in the database diagram. If your primary key relies on more than one field, hold down the Ctrl key as you select other fields that also define the primary key. Right-click the selected row or rows and choose Primary Key from shortcut menu to complete the task.

Database diagram windows are also helpful for defining relationships. Start by selecting the row selector for the primary key in the first table. You do not have to use a primary key, but the field must have unique values. Next, drag the selected field from the first table and drop it on the title bar for the second table. The Create Relationship dialog box (which resembles the top right panel in Figure 12-6) will appear. Modify the relationships specifications as needed, and then click OK.

You can enforce referential integrity using three check boxes in the lower part of the Create Relationship dialog box and on the Relationship tab of the Properties dialog box (shown in Figure 12-6). Select the Enable Relationship For Insert And Update check box to enforce referential integrity for all new data in the current database. If your existing data already obeys referential integrity or if it doesn't need to follow referential integrity, leave the Check Existing Data On Creation check box deselected. If following referential integrity in another database that will receive rows from your database will cause an unacceptable number of records to fail to transfer (because of key violations), leave the Enable Relationship For Replication check box deselected.

Editing and Creating Tables Using a Worksheet

You can add a new table to a database by right-clicking in a database diagram window and choosing New Table. After you accept the default system-generated name or assign a new name, you'll see a worksheet for naming fields, assigning data types, and making other data definition specifications. This same worksheet opens from the *Tables* collection in the Database window when you click New or Design. It exposes several important user-friendly table and field properties.

Figure 12-8 shows a pair of worksheets for the *FamilyMembers* and *MyLInks* tables from Figure 12-7. Actually, the relationship was updated from Figure 12-7 so that there is a one-to-many relationship between the tables. The *FamID* field in *MyLInks* relates to the primary *FamID* field in *FamilyMembers*. You can create a foreign key in one table that exactly matches a primary key in another table, just as you do in a classic Access .mdb file. Copy the primary key to the Clipboard from the first table and paste it into the second table.

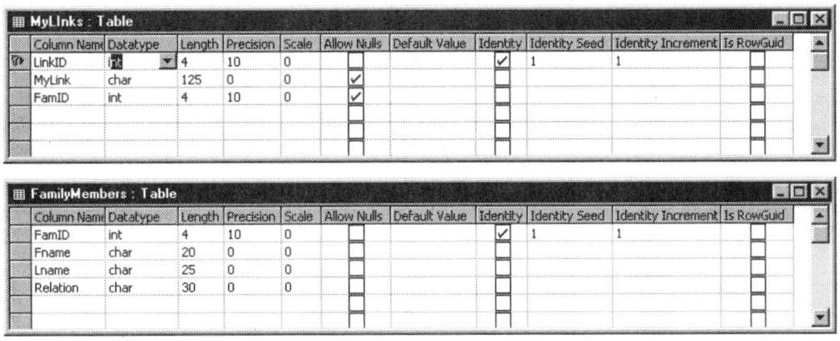

Figure 12-8. *Two worksheets that show settings for defining fields in tables for MSDE and SQL Server databases.*

The *FamID* primary key in *FamilyMembers* has the SQL Server Integer data type. This corresponds to the Long data type in Access/Jet databases. The *LinkID* primary key in *MyLInk* uses the Integer data type with an Identity column setting. Notice that this interface, unlike Access with Jet, provides a graphical interface for setting the identity start and step values. The *nvarchar* data type is a special designation for Unicode variable-length string fields. The comparable non-Unicode data type is *varchar*. Again, Access with Jet does not expose this data type distinction.

VIEWS AND STORED PROCEDURES

Although SQL Server does not offer queries for building custom applications, as Access does, it provides similar functionality in its views and stored procedures. A view is a SQL statement that returns rows without using parameters or an ORDER BY phrase. In contrast, a stored procedure can use both parameters and the ORDER BY phrase to specify a return a row set. Stored procedures can also perform SQL statements that do not return rows, such as INSERT, UPDATE, and DELETE.

Using Views

While the rules for writing queries change as you move from Jet to MSDE or SQL Server, the new Access Query Designer should help to ease the transition. It resembles the query designer for Jet-based queries. You can use the Query Designer to build views. (You have to write stored procedures without the help of a Builder wizard.) It consists of three panels that you can turn on or off. You can build a view in any panel. Entries in one panel automatically update the other two.

Figure 12-9 shows the Query Designer for a select query from the *authors* table in the Pubs database. The top panel is the diagram pane. You right-click in this pane to add any table or previously built view as an input source for your new view. Select the check box next to a field to add it to the grid pane in the middle. Use the check boxes in the output column to indicate whether a field appears in the return set for a view. You can also add criteria in the columns to the right to restrict the rows that a view returns. If you prefer to write SQL rather than point and click, you can use the SQL pane at the bottom to write SQL statements.

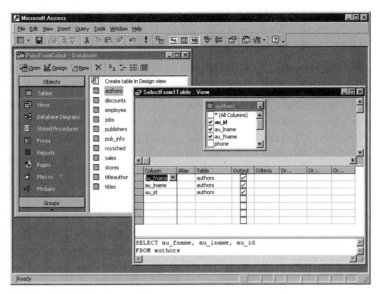

Figure 12-9. *The Query Designer.*

The View Design toolbar and the menu bar offer additional help for writing views. The SQL button turns the SQL pane on and off. In the default arrangement, the button to the left of the SQL button performs the same function for the grid and diagram panes. The button to the right with the check mark—the Verify SQL button—performs a syntax check for SQL that you enter directly into the SQL pane. The Group By button next to the Verify SQL button modifies the grid pane to start the design of an aggregate query. Its behavior mimics the Totals (Σ) button in the classic Jet query builder. After you have the view the way you want it, click the New Object button to automate the preparation of a form or report based on the view. (If the view is not already saved, you will be prompted to save it first.)

> **NOTE** The Query Designer offers the benefits of graphical query design for building views without the overhead of attaching remote tables (as is the case with classic .mdb files). The SQL statements for the views execute on the database server, and the Access Project merely displays the return set.

You are not restricted to building views that pull data from the active connection for an Access Project. You can use the OPENROWSET keyword to point a view at a different database on the same server or even another database server.

This can even be from a different type of database server, such as Oracle or Jet. The OPENROWSET keyword takes three arguments with comma delimiters. Enclose the first and second arguments in single quotes to designate them as strings. The third argument is a database object name. The first argument names the OLE DB provider for the alternate data source.

The two samples below use the OLE DB provider for ODBC-compliant data sources. This enables your custom view to connect to any ODBC-compliant data source. The second argument contains the connection string. The provider determines the correct syntax for this argument. The third argument is a database object name in SQL Server format. The general format for specifying the object is *linkserver.catalog.schema.object*. *linkserver* is the local SQL Server 7 name for the OLE DB provider that points at the remote, heterogeneous data source. If you are not performing a query for a non-SQL Server data source, you do not need this parameter. *catalog* is the database name, and *schema* is the database owner. *object* is the table name.

Figure 12-10 shows SQL pane representations of two views. Both are from the Project PubsFromCabxli.adp. For the test environment, this file resides on a computer named CABXLI, but its Data Link Properties dialog box indicates a connection with the Pubs database on a computer named cab2200. Each view uses the OPENROWSET keyword to connect to a data source other than Pubs on cab2200. The SelectFromAnotherDB view connects to the *Shippers* table in the NorthwindCS database on cab2200. The SelectFromAnotherServer view links to the *Shippers* table on the local server, CABXLI. The Query Designer automatically adds the *DerivedTable1* term at the end of both SQL statements.

Figure 12-10. *SQL syntax for the OPENROWSET keyword, which you use to connect to data sources outside the active connection.*

Using Stored Procedures

You can use stored procedures to build on and extend the power of views in custom SQL Server applications. There is no Query Designer for stored procedures. Stored procedures compensate for this lack by using an enhanced vocabulary based on Transact-SQL, a special dialect of SQL for SQL Server. The flexibility of Transact-SQL along with the power of its stored procedures make this SQL dialect a candidate for your second or third programming language after VBA and ADO, especially if you plan to develop with Access Projects.

Figure 12-11 shows the result of a union query in an Access Project. Recall that a union query concatenates one recordset behind another. In this case, the code (shown below) concatenates the *FamilyMembers* table with the *AdditionsToFamilyMembers* table. The code and sample data for the union query are in adp1.adp on the companion CD. The *AdditionstoFamilyMembers* table references the adp1SQL database.

```
SELECT FamID, Fname, Lname, Relation
FROM AdditionsToFamilyMembers
UNION
SELECT FamID, Fname, Lname, Relation
FROM FamilyMembers
```

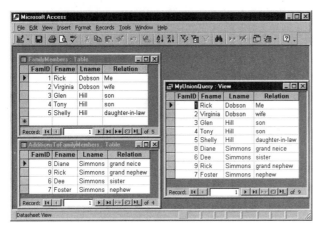

Figure 12-11. *A union query in SQL Server (and MSDE) can concatenate two or more tables, but it cannot sort them.*

This code is in a view named *MyUnionQuery*. Notice that the rows do not sort on *FamID*; there is no ORDER BY phrase in the SQL for the view. Recall that SQL Server views do not enable the ORDER BY phrase. If you want the records ordered by *FamID* or any other field, you must run a stored procedure.

The following sample adapts the SQL for the view and builds a stored procedure with more flexibility. In this case, a procedure named *StoredProcedure1* does the concatenation and sorts by *FamID*.

```
ALTER PROCEDURE StoredProcedure1 AS

SELECT FamID, Fname, Lname, Relation
FROM AdditionsToFamilyMembers

UNION

SELECT FamID, Fname, Lname, Relation
FROM FamilyMembers

-- Here's the ORDER BY phrase
ORDER BY FamID
```

The ALTER PROCEDURE phrase derives its name from its ability to change a procedure initially created with the CREATE PROCEDURE phrase. However, you can initially create a procedure with ALTER PROCEDURE. Notice that the syntax calls for the keyword AS after the ALTER PROCEDURE phrase. The balance of the stored procedure is exactly like the MyUnionQuery view, except for the last two lines. The next-to-last line shows the syntax for a comment that fits on one line. You start the line with two dashes. The final line contains the ORDER BY phrase that sorts the records by *FamID*.

There are many important reasons for becoming familiar with stored procedures when using Access Projects. The SQL Server and MSDE engines support a series of administrative functions through system stored procedures. These procedures reside in the master database. All these system procedures start with *sp_*. For this reason, you should avoid using *sp_* in the names of your custom stored procedures.

A stored procedure named *sp_server_info* gives feedback about all kinds of server functionality. (SQL Server Books Online offers information about this procedure.) You can run it as a stored procedure in your application to determine property settings for a SQL Server engine that can help you decide how to program it. For example, the 18th row of a normal return set can indicate whether your server sorts in a case-sensitive or case-insensitive fashion. The following sample builds a simple stored procedure in your application that taps the system-stored procedure *sp_server_info* to determine the collation convention on the server that you are currently connected to. This sample also shows the format for a comment that extends over more than one line.

```
ALTER PROCEDURE DetermineSortOrder
/*If row 18 shows sort_order - nocase,
then sorts are case insensitive.
*/
AS

EXEC sp_server_info 18
```

Another reason for learning about stored procedures is to use their parameters. You can pass parameters to them, and they can return values through output parameters. The *DetermineSortOrder* procedure pulls the 18th row from the return set generated by *sp_server_info*. The number *18* is a parameter that specifies which row the system procedure should display from its normal return set.

The two custom procedures below design stored procedures that accept parameters and programmatically pass them values. Custom stored procedures with parameters can automatically prompt for values if you do not pass them values programmatically. The first procedure performs two functions: It calls the procedure that generates a sales report, and then it passes values to the second procedure that designates start and end dates for the report as well as an employee name. You can edit the three parameters in the first procedure to vary the output of the second one.

```
ALTER PROCEDURE RunEmployeeSalesByDate
AS

EXEC "Employee Sales by Date" '1/1/95', '1/1/98', 'Buchanan'
```

The second procedure above accepts its parameters as part of the ALTER PROCEDURE statement. Each parameter specification has two arguments: the name, such as *@Beginning_Date*, and the data type designation, such as *datetime* or *varchar(20)*. The data type specification for an employee's name in the stored procedure must match the data type setting for Employee Name in the *Employees* table. The SQL statement joins three tables, and a WHERE clause puts the parameters to work.

```
/*This procedure accepts three parameters to determine the
content for a sales report.
    @Beginning_Date is the start date period.
    @Ending_Date is the end period.
    @lastname specifies the employee for which
    the report lists sales.
*/
```

(continued)

```
ALTER PROCEDURE [Employee Sales by Date]
@Beginning_Date datetime, @Ending_Date datetime,
@lastname varchar(20)
AS

SELECT Employees.Country, Employees.LastName, Employees.FirstName,
    Orders.ShippedDate, Orders.OrderID,
    "Order Subtotals".Subtotal AS SaleAmount
FROM Employees INNER JOIN (Orders INNER JOIN "Order Subtotals" ON
    Orders.OrderID = "Order Subtotals".OrderID)
    ON Employees.EmployeeID = Orders.EmployeeID

-- This format is for comments on a single line.
WHERE Orders.ShippedDate Between @Beginning_Date And @Ending_Date And
    Employees.LastName = @lastname
```

REPORTS AND FORMS

After connecting to one or more remote data sources and filtering, aggregating, or combining them with other sources, you can present your results with Access 2000. Because tables, views, and stored procedures are tightly integrated with forms, reports, and modules, you can easily deliver client/server data in the same way that Access has been serving up file-server data sources since its initial release. While prior Access releases made client/server data available, they never made true client/server processing so easy. Can .adp files do for client/server data sources what .mdb files did for file-server data sources? It depends on your interest and imagination. The upcoming samples might spark your creativity.

Sorting, Formatting, and More with Reports

The Query Designer makes it relatively easy to filter, combine, and aggregate data, but it does not offer much in the way of presentation capabilities. Recall that you cannot even sort the records in a view. Reports, on the other hand, have relatively limited processing capabilities but are great at sorting and formatting data for printers (and even the World Wide Web, if you consider snapshots—see Chapter 6).

Figure 12-12 shows how to use Access Project views with Access reports so that they complement each other. The report sorts records by *FamID*. It also conditionally formats the color for displaying a row based on the value of *FamID*: Values of less than 6 appear in black, but values of 6 or greater are in red. In addition, the display shows the normal report flourishes, including a title, a bar separating the title column headings from the column entries, and formatting for column headings and the report title that contrasts with the formatting of the body of the report.

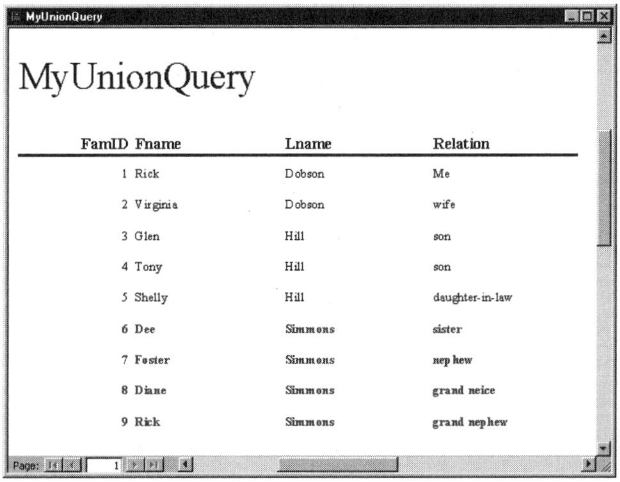

FamID	Fname	Lname	Relation
1	Rick	Dobson	Me
2	Virginia	Dobson	wife
3	Glen	Hill	son
4	Tony	Hill	son
5	Shelly	Hill	daughter-in-law
6	Dee	Simmons	sister
7	Foster	Simmons	nephew
8	Diane	Simmons	grand neice
9	Rick	Simmons	grand nephew

Figure 12-12. *A report based on the* MyUnionQuery *view shown in Figure 12-11.*

Aside from the union query coding for the view, this report requires no programming. After you build your view, you simply set the report's *Record Source* property to the name of the view. Except for the different colors based on *FamID*, all of the report features are default tabular report settings. The new Conditional Formatting command on the Format menu dramatically simplifies the task of conditionally applying colors to the contents of text boxes. (See Chapter 5 for details.) Such capabilities used to require *Format* event procedures. By bringing the view and report together, you can use each to do the task that it performs best. Since reporting is a major Access strength, the.adp file's ability to process client/server data sources can dramatically lower the cost of delivering informative, easy-to-read reports throughout an organization.

Adding Hyperlinks

There is no Hyperlink data type in SQL Server databases. (Recall that Jet supports this data type as an extension of the Memo data type—see Chapter 1.) However, you can still insert and follow hyperlinks in forms within Access Projects. There are four steps to doing this:

1. Assign a table column one of these data types: *char*, *nchar*, *nvarchar*, or *varchar*. These are fixed and variable-length string data types in Unicode or non-Unicode format.

2.   Open a form in Design view and make the table the record source for the form.

3.   Assign the field with the string data type to one of the form fields.

4.   Set the field's *IsHyperlink* property to *Yes*. This is a new property in Access 2000 that is explicitly for hyperlinks on forms in Access Projects.

After setting up the table and form, you can add hyperlinks to the table through the form using the Insert-Hyperlink command, which opens a dialog box for setting or editing the hyperlink's URL and its display text. Once the hyperlinks are formatted, users can follow them to designated Web locations by simply clicking the entry in a hyperlink field. Their default browser takes them there. Then they can return to Access by clicking the back arrow. Access 97 introduced this functionality; it is now available for SQL Server and MSDE databases through Access 2000.

Figure 12-13 shows the MyLinks Access form in the process of having its hyperlink entry edited. You can browse to the desired Web location so that you do not have to type the URL. In addition, you can use the Text To Display text box to enter text that appears instead of the URL. Notice also that you can use this dialog box to set hyperlinks for files on a local file server or even link to e-mail addresses. The latter option starts a browser workstation's default e-mail package with the name and e-mail address that you specify in the link.

Figure 12-13. *You can use the Edit Hyperlink dialog box to enter and edit hyperlinks into a shared client/server database of hyperlinks.*

Viewing and Editing Data Using Forms

Access Projects offer two *Recordset Type* property settings for working with forms and traditional data sources, such as tables of employees or customers. These settings are unique to .adp files. The traditional .mdb files have different *Recordset Type* property settings.

When you design an application that uses forms with data from a SQL Server or MSDE database, your client application always works with a snapshot of the original data on the server. Although the locally available data is a snapshot of the data on the server, you can update it on the server. To accommodate this functionality, Access 2000 offers *Updatable Snapshot* and *Snapshot Recordset Type* settings for Access Projects. You can set these properties on the Data tab of the form's Property dialog box. You can also manipulate the *Recordset Type* setting using VBA or an Access macro.

When you set a form's *Recordset Type* property to *Updatable Snapshot*, users can change the form's underlying data source as if the file were on a local file server. Using the *Lock* property for individual controls, you can selectively enable editing on a subset of a form's controls. In addition, you can control the type of changes permitted at client workstations. There are separate *Yes/No* settings for *Allow Edits*, *Allow Deletions*, and *Allow Additions* properties. Changes you make from the Access Project file propagate to the server. Each user of an Access Project should have a separate copy of the .adp file even though each user relates to a common client/server database. While data changes propagate from the client workstations to the server database, users must choose Records-Refresh to view changes made by others.

Figure 12-14 on the next page shows a sample form in an Access Project based on data in a remote server. Below the form is an excerpt from the form's property sheet. It exposes the two possible settings for the *Recordset Type* property. Since *Updatable Snapshot* is in effect, users can change the form's underlying record source. In fact, because of the *Yes* settings for *Allow Edits*, *Allow Deletions*, and *Allow Additions*, they can perform all three standard types of database revisions. You can turn off all three capabilities by setting the *Recordset Type* property to *Snapshot*.

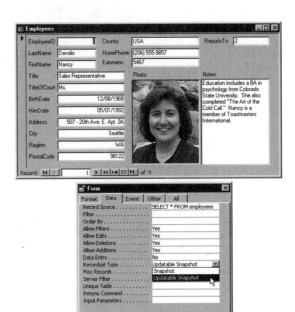

Figure 12-14. *You can use forms in Access Projects to modify data on a database server.*

The form was prepared using the AutoForm wizard (with a minor amount of editing). Moving to the next record passes any edits that a user makes to fields back to the server. If the *Recordset Type* setting is *Snapshot*, Access responds that the recordset is not updateable. The button marked with an X lets users abort a lengthy download of many records to a local workstation.

Resynchronizing a Form with its One-To-Many Data

When the source for a form in an Access Project is based on a recordset with a one-to-many relationship between two tables, you can automatically populate all the fields on the one side by setting the foreign key on the many side. This feature is especially convenient when you add new records. For example, if you are designing a form that presents employee and sales data, the one-to-many relation follows from the fact that each employee can have multiple sales. You simply enter the employee ID for the sales table and commit the record. This action automatically populates all the employee fields on the one side of the underlying record source. Then you enter the sales data on the many side of the record source. You can update the employee information for a previously existing record just as easily.

To enable this feature, your form must use *Updatable Snapshot* as the *Recordset Type* setting. You assign to the *Unique Table* property the table on the many side of the relationship. You must also set the *Resync Command* property to a string representing a SQL statement that enables the resynchronization. You'll learn a trick for quickly constructing this statement below.

Figure 12-15 shows the one-to-many Design view for the *vwForResynch* view. The top panel shows the one-to-many relationship in the line connecting the *Employees* and *Orders* tables. Notice that the view links the tables using the primary key in the *Employees* table and the corresponding foreign key (*EmployeeID*) in the *Orders* table. The bottom panel shows the SQL for the view. The form's *Resync Command* property requires a simple modification of this statement.

Figure 12-15. *This view represents a one-to-many relationship like that used for resynchronization on a form. The SQL statement forms the basis of the* Resync Command *property setting.*

Figure 12-16 on the next page shows a form just after the entry of 9 into the EmployeeID text box. The form is a standard AutoForm with some minor editing. Clicking the record selector brings up data automatically to all the other employee fields on the form. Entering a new value into the EmployeeID text box and clicking the record selector automatically brings up employee data corresponding to the new ID value. That is the benefit of the resynchronization function.

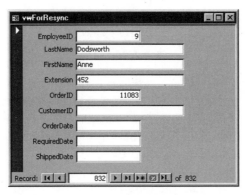

Figure 12-16. *A form that demonstrates resynchronization against a remote database.*

Figure 12-17 shows the form settings that enable this automatic resynchronization. The *Recordset Type* is *Updatable Snapshot*, and the form's *Unique Table* property points at the many side of the underlying recordset—namely, the *Orders* table. The zoomed *Resync Command* setting is exactly the same as the SQL for the underlying form with one extra line: *WHERE Orders.OrderID = ?*. This final step completes the tasks for enabling a form by using the resynchronization function.

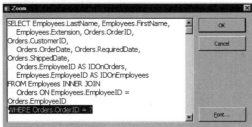

Figure 12-17. *The Data tab of the form's property sheet. The* Updatable Snapshot *and* Resync Command *settings are necessary for resynchronization.*

PROGRAMMATIC ISSUES

One way to extend the capabilities of your Access Projects is with SQL. This is particularly so for views and stored procedures. Several of the preceding samples have shown what you can do with SQL. However, you can also put your VBA and ADO knowledge to use. The remaining samples in this chapter show how to apply your expertise in these areas to working with Access Projects or even to working with SQL Server and MSDE databases without the convenient user interface of Access Projects.

Working with Forms

While the Access Project user interface delivers extraordinary functionality with remote data sources, you can automate and simplify processes by developing custom programmatic solutions. We'll look at three areas pertaining to Access Projects: opening a form, finding a record, and viewing changes made by other users.

Opening a form

When you open a form with the Access Project interface, the form populates a local copy of the remote data in the client workstation. This local copy is a snapshot, at a point in time, of the remote data for the form. When you open the form programmatically, you must create the local copy of the remote data. One advantage to programmatically opening a form is that you can dynamically assign values to the local cache of the remote data. Your application can do this because the recordset that you assign to the form with VBA overrides the *Record Source* setting on the form's property sheet.

The procedure below constructs a recordset for a form before opening it. It starts by setting a reference to a new recordset instance: It assigns *adUseClient* to the recordset's *CursorLocation* property to establish the location of the form's data. (Recall that the form gets the data from the local cache on the workstation, not from the remote server.) Next, it opens the recordset with a SQL statement that extracts data from the remote source into the local copy. The sample works with the form from Figure 12-14 on page 496. A commented line shows a SQL statement that can override the form's default record source. After making the local copy of the remote data, the procedure opens the form and assigns the local copy to the form's *Recordset* property. This new property possesses the functionality of the *RecordsetClone* property; in addition, changes to the recordset appear on the form automatically—the *RecordsetClone* property provides a read-only copy of a form's recordset. Like the *RecordsetClone* property, a form's *Recordset* property is available only programmatically.

```
Sub openForm()
Dim rst1 As ADODB.Recordset

'Establish a local recordset and populate it with values;
'can override property sheet settings.
    Set rst1 = New ADODB.Recordset
    rst1.CursorLocation = adUseClient
    rst1.Open "SELECT * FROM employees", _
        CurrentProject.Connection, adKeySet, _
        adLockPessimistic
'Optionally run with WHERE clause to demo override effect.
'    "SELECT * FROM employees WHERE employeeid>3"

'Open the form.
    DoCmd.openForm "frmemployees2"

'Assign recordset to the open form; can override a
'setting on the property sheet.
    Set Forms("frmemployees2").Recordset = rst1

End Sub
```

> **NOTE**   The recordset created for a recordset instance is available only if the form remains open. Closing and reopening the form manually causes the form to revert to the *Record Source* setting on its property sheet.

Finding a record

One common task when you work with data in a form is finding a specific record. The following two procedures accomplish this task. The *locateEmployee* procedure prompts for an employee ID value and passes that value along to the second procedure, *findByID*. The second procedure taps the *FindRecord* method of the *DoCmd* object to search for and position the form at a new record.

```
Sub locateEmployee()

'Ask for employee ID and pass it on to findByID.
    employeeNumber = InputBox("Type the ID for the employee you want", _
        "Programming Microsoft Access 2000")
    findById CLng(employeeNumber)

End Sub


Sub findById(eid As Long)
On Error GoTo findByIdTrap
```

```
'Set focus to employee ID field and launch find.
    Forms("frmemployees2").EmployeeID.SetFocus
    DoCmd.FindRecord eid

findByIdExit:
'Report mismatch before exiting.
    If Forms("frmemployees2").EmployeeID <> eid Then
        MsgBox "No employee with ID " & eid & ".", _
            vbExclamation, "Programming Microsoft Access 2000"
    End If
    Exit Sub

findByIdTrap:
    If Err.Number = 2450 Then
'Open form if it is closed and start find again.
        openForm
        Resume
    Else
        Debug.Print Err.Number, Err.Description
    End If

End Sub
```

The second procedure detects two potential problems. First, if there is no match, the procedure issues a message to that effect. Second, neither procedure is an event procedure, so they can be invoked from outside the form. If the form is closed, the procedure detects the problem and opens it so that it can try again to find the target record.

Viewing changes made by other users

Access is inherently a multi-user development environment, and Access Projects frequently serve multi-user purposes. Therefore, you need a way to refresh the local cache so that you can view updates, additions, and deletions made by others. The following procedure does this by repopulating the local recordset for the form from the remote data source. Like the preceding samples, this one is based on the form in Figure 12-14 on page 296.

```
Sub requeryRemoteRestoreID()
Dim int1 As Integer

'Turn off screen updates and save employee ID.
    DoCmd.Echo False
    int1 = Forms("frmemployees2").EmployeeID

'Requery local recordset from the server.
    openForm
```

(continued)

```
'Reposition to employee ID before requery and
'restore screen updating.
    Forms("frmemployees2").EmployeeID.SetFocus
    DoCmd.FindRecord int1
    DoCmd.Echo True

End Sub
```

The procedure refills the local data cache by invoking the *openForm* procedure (which was discussed earlier). If the form is already open, the call simply repopulates the cache. Since repopulating a form's recordset automatically makes the first record current, the procedure saves the current record position before repopulating the local cache from the remote data store. After repopulating the cache, the procedure searches through the records to find the preceding current record. This restores the old record position if that record is still available (that is, not deleted). If another user has deleted the former current record, the form displays the first record in the local cache.

Working with Standalone Modules

All the emphasis on ADO throughout this book will serve you well when you develop custom solutions against MSDE and SQL Server data sources. Chapter 4 shows some samples for dealing with remote data sources. Here, we'll revisit some programmatic issues in the context of Access Projects and MSDE.

Opening a table

The following sample integrates opening a table in a remote data source with writing the results to the Immediate window as a telephone directory. It uses ADO *Connection* and *Recordset* objects to do this. The procedure starts by creating a new instance of an ADO *Connection* object. Then it defines a connection string and uses that string to open a connection to the NorthwindCS database on the cab2200 server. Next, it opens a forward-only, read-only recordset based on the *Employees* table in NorthwindCS. This type of recordset is acceptable for a report that makes a single pass through a recordset. The procedure prints the employee directory in the Immediate window with the help of a *Do* loop for passing through successive records.

```
Sub openTableOnRemoteServer()
Dim cnn1 As ADODB.Connection
Dim rst1 As ADODB.Recordset

'Open connection to NorthwindCS database
'on cab2200 server.
    Set cnn1 = New ADODB.Connection
    strCnn = "Provider=sqloledb;" & _
```

```
            "Data Source=cab2200;" & _
            "Initial Catalog=NorthwindCS;" & _
            "User Id=sa;Password=;"
        cnn1.Open strCnn

    'Open employee table with a forward-only,
    'read-only recordset; this type is OK for a single
    'pass through the data.
        Set rst1 = New ADODB.Recordset
        rst1.CursorType = adOpenForwardOnly
        rst1.LockType = adLockReadOnly
        rst1.Open "employees", cnn1, , , adCmdTable

    'Print an employee telephone directory.
        Do Until rst1.EOF
            Debug.Print rst1.Fields("FirstName") & " " & _
                rst1.Fields("LastName") & " has extension " & _
                rst1.Fields("Extension") & "."
            rst1.MoveNext
        Loop

    'Close the connection and recover the resource.
        cnn1.Close
        Set cnn1 = Nothing

End Sub
```

The test environment for this chapter has an MSDE server on the local machine named CABXLI in addition to the SQL Server database manager on the machine named cab2200. The syntax for referring to local servers is slightly different than the syntax for referring to remote ones. Instead of having to designate a specific server by name, you can simply specify *(local)*. Since my local computer also has the NorthwindCS database installed, no other change in the procedure is necessary. The procedure is identical to the preceding one with the exception of the one block that appears below. Notice the new server name. In practice, you might want to have users designate their own login account name or have them use a limited one with fewer privileges than *sa*.

```
'Open connection to NorthwindCS database
'on the local server.
    Set cnn1 = New ADODB.Connection
    strCnn = "Provider=sqloledb;" & _
        "Data Source=(local);" & _
        "Initial Catalog=NorthwindCS;" & _
        "User Id=sa;Password=;"
    cnn1.Open strCnn
```

You can process views by using the same syntax that you use for tables. Simply enclose the view's name in quotes, just like you do for a table. You must still use the *adCmdTable* setting for the *Option* parameter. The companion CD includes a sample named *openViewOnRemoteServer* that demonstrates this approach.

Opening a stored procedure

Stored procedures can return recordsets. Your applications have more flexibility when they provide recordsets using stored procedures instead of tables because you are not restricted to the tables in the current data source or even exact copies of the tables in the current data source. With stored procedures, you can filter records, compute new values, and aggregate field values across the records in a table.

The following procedure invokes the stored procedure named *Ten Most Expensive Products* and prints in the Immediate window the 10 product names and prices. Because the procedure name includes spaces, it must be in brackets. Notice also that the procedure uses an *Options* argument of *adCmdStoredProc*. This tells the ADO processor to expect a procedure name that contains SQL, not an actual SQL statement. Since the procedure always processes 10 records, the procedure for printing out the records uses a *For* loop that goes from 1 through 10. In other respects, the procedure for printing the return set from a stored procedure is identical to the procedure for printing an entire table.

```
Sub openProcedureOnRemoteServer()
Dim cnn1 As ADODB.Connection
Dim rst1 As ADODB.Recordset
Dim int1 As Integer

'Open connection to NorthwindCS database
'on cab2200 server.
    Set cnn1 = New ADODB.Connection
    strCnn = "Provider=sqloledb;" & _
        "Data Source=cab2200;" & _
        "Initial Catalog=NorthwindCS;" & _
        "User Id=sa;Password=;"
    cnn1.Open strCnn

'Open employee table.
    Set rst1 = New ADODB.Recordset
    rst1.CursorType = adOpenForwardOnly
    rst1.LockType = adLockReadOnly
    rst1.Open "[Ten Most Expensive Products]", _
        cnn1, , , adCmdStoredProc
```

```
'Print prices for 10 products.
    For int1 = 1 To 10
        Debug.Print rst1.Fields(0) & " has a unit price " & _
            "of $" & rst1.Fields(1) & "."
        rst1.MoveNext
    Next int1

'Close the connection and recover the resource.
    cnn1.Close
    Set cnn1 = Nothing

End Sub
```

Assigning *CursorLocation* values

CursorLocation settings can profoundly affect performance, especially as table sources grow to even moderate size. The sample below demonstrates this with a recordset source of just over 19,000 records. It forms this recordset with a view based on the Cartesian product of the *Employees* and *Order Details* tables. The view's name is *vwLargeView*.

The sample opens its recordset source with either *adUseClient* or *adUseServer* as its *CursorLocation* setting. The *adUseServer* setting causes a procedure to progressively move through the records one at a time on the server. The *adUseClient* setting transfers the records to the local workstation so that procedures can access the records from a local workstation without returning to the server for each record.

The first procedure in the sample prompts for an instruction about which *CursorLocation* setting to use. The second procedure prepares a report and prints it in the Immediate window. It prints the cursor location and type as well as the start time, end time, and the duration for the task. You can adapt this general model for testing various combinations of database settings with your own data sources.

```
Sub openRemoteWithCursorLocation()
Dim cnn1 As ADODB.Connection
Dim rst1 As ADODB.Recordset
Dim start As Date, done As Date

'Open connection to NorthwindCS database
'on cab2200 server.
    strCnn = "Provider=sqloledb;" & _
        "Data Source=cab2200;" & _
        "Initial Catalog=NorthwindCS;" & _
        "User Id=sa;Password=;"
```

(continued)

```
    Set cnn1 = New ADODB.Connection
    If MsgBox("Use local cursor?", vbYesNo, _
        "Programming Microsoft Access 2000") = vbYes Then
        cnn1.CursorLocation = adUseClient
    Else
        cnn1.CursorLocation = adUseServer
    End If
    cnn1.Open strCnn

'Open vwLargeView view; create the view in the remote
'database server before running the procedure.
'The sample uses the Cartesian product of the
'Employees and Order Details tables.
'Notice that the connection setting for CursorType silently
'overrides the recordset property setting.
    Set rst1 = New ADODB.Recordset
    rst1.CursorType = adOpenKeyset
    rst1.LockType = adLockOptimistic
    rst1.Open "vwLargeView", cnn1, , , adCmdTable
    start = Now
    Do Until rst1.EOF
        temp = rst1.Fields(1)
        rst1.MoveNext
    Loop
    done = Now
    reportResults cnn1.CursorLocation, rst1.CursorType, _
        start, done

End Sub


Sub reportResults(cloc As Integer, ctype As Integer, _
    startedAt As Date, endedAt As Date)

    Debug.Print "Results for: "
    Select Case cloc
        Case adUseServer
            Debug.Print "    Cursor Location: adUseServer"
        Case adUseClient
            Debug.Print "    Cursor Location: adUseClient"
        Case Else
            Debug.Print "    Faulty Cursor Location setting"
    End Select
    Select Case ctype
        Case adOpenForwardOnly
            Debug.Print "    Cursor Type: adOpenForwardOnly"
```

```
        Case adOpenKeyset
            Debug.Print "        Cursor Type: adOpenKeyset"
        Case adOpenDynamic
            Debug.Print "        Cursor Type: adOpenDynamic"
        Case adOpenStatic
            Debug.Print "        Cursor Type: adStatic"
    End Select
    Debug.Print "Start time to nearest second: " & startedAt
    Debug.Print "End time to nearest second: " & endedAt
    Debug.Print "Difference in seconds: " & DateDiff("s", & _
        startedAt, endedAt)

End Sub
```

Figure 12-18 shows the results of running the procedures using an *adUseClient* setting and then an *adUseServer* setting. It took just 1 second to loop through the records with a local cursor, but it took 37 seconds to loop through the records with a server-side cursor. Results can vary depending on a wide range of factors, so it's a good idea to test for other settings and your particular databases.

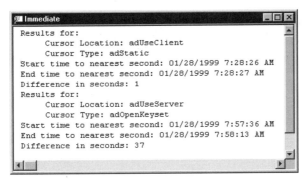

Figure 12-18. *Sample output showing results of processing the same data source with an* adUseClient *or an* adUseServer *setting.*

This sample is instructive for a few reasons. First, the performance outcomes are drastically different. Second, you can see that ADO changes your settings if they conflict. For example, the program sets the cursor type to *adOpenKeyset*, but this setting conflicts with *adUseClient*, so the ADO interpreter silently changes the cursor type setting to *adStatic*. This happens in other contexts as well. Third, this sample presents a simple model that you can readily adapt for exploring database settings in your own custom applications.

Chapter 13

Access 2000 Does the Web

Microsoft Access 2000 continues the dual traditions of innovative Internet technologies and serviceable yet easy ways to develop database solutions for the
World Wide Web. Access 2000 offers data access pages, fresh ActiveX controls,
improved database connectivity, and enhanced Dynamic HTML (DHTML).
These new capabilities mark the passing of the Publish To The Web wizard
from Access 97, which packaged an interface for the HTML Layout control.
This control was never more than an interim technology awaiting a standards-
based DHTML.

This chapter will review traditional Access Web technologies and then cover
hyperlink technology, including the *Hyperlink* object and the Hyperlink data type.
The bulk of the chapter is devoted to data access pages, which facilitate reporting
on and interacting with databases over the Web. The development environment
for data access pages can also serve as a host for Microsoft Office 2000 Web
Components.

TRADITIONAL APPROACHES

The traditional Access Web technologies are particularly appropriate for developing low-volume (around 10,000 visitors per day or fewer) Web and database solutions. Since browsers can be incompatible across manufacturers and versions, traditional approaches are safe and relatively easy to use.

Access 2000 offers three such approaches:

- Publishing datasheets in HTML, IDC/HTX, and ASP format.

- Using HTML forms. There is no built-in development environment within Access for HTML forms, but you can adapt your old HTML form solutions to OLE DB/ADO (ActiveX Data Objects) technology.

- Publishing reports in snapshot format to an FTP folder. This simplifies access to Access reports using Netscape browsers.

Publishing Datasheets

You can choose Export from the File menu in the database window to export an Access datasheet, such as a table. This command (which also publishes datasheets behind forms and reports) offers some of the functionality associated with the obsolete Publish To The Web wizard. It publishes datasheets in HTML, IDC/HTX, and ASP formats. The HTML format is static but easy to edit with standard HTML editors. The latter two formats are dynamic. They use the server to write out HTML content to reflect the most recent results in a datasheet.

The IDC/HTX format targets the first two releases of Microsoft Internet Information Server (IIS), but it also works with more recent releases. The ASP format works only with more recent releases, but it lets you mix Microsoft Visual Basic Scripting Edition and Microsoft JScript with HTML code. You should not automatically choose one of the dynamic formats. If you have large datasheets or many users, and if the content in a datasheet changes infrequently or if timeliness is not an issue, the static HTML format might be the best choice because static pages publish faster.

Publishing in HTML format

To publish a datasheet in HTML format, select a table, query, form, or report in the database window and then choose Export from the File menu. In the Export dialog box, use the Save In drop-down list box to select a location for the file. If you are publishing to an intranet, this can be a folder at the site. If you are publishing to a remote Web server, you can use any local folder to collect your HTML pages and then transfer the pages to a remote server using the File-Import command in FrontPage 2000. You can also use another route, such as File Transfer Protocol (FTP).

Figure 13-1 shows the Export dialog box for publishing the datasheet behind the Products form from the Northwind database. The Save As Type drop-down list box shows the HTML format. The Save In box designates the folder CAB_Office_2000, the root folder of a local intranet site with the same name. The Autostart check box is selected, so the page will appear as soon as it is published. This can cause a browser session to start with the Products datasheet open.

Figure 13-1. *The Export dialog box.*

When you click Save, the HTML Output Options dialog box appears. Here you can specify a template for the page containing the datasheet. If you have a theme set for the default.htm page, you can reference that page. Otherwise, you can reference a local file with formatting that you will use at a remote site.

One of the advantages of the HTML format is that you have an HTML table to edit. Figure 13-2 on the next page shows the published Products datasheet in FrontPage 2000 and the Table Properties dialog box, which shows some of the formatting options, including cell padding, cell spacing, and background color or image. You can also set properties for cells, rows, and columns to specify other formatting options. You can undo any custom formatting in FrontPage, and you can even select individual columns and rows and selectively delete them.

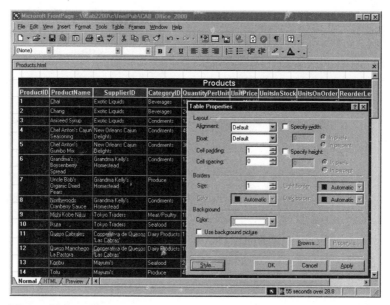

Figure 13-2. *After loading your datasheets into FrontPage, you can edit the resulting HTML table.*

Publishing in IDC/HTX format

When you publish a datasheet in either dynamic format, you need an open database connectivity (ODBC) Data Source Name (DSN). The DSN must reside on the Web server along with the database to which it refers. The file DSN approach is in theory more flexible since you can send it to the server, but ISPs often impose special rules that make it less than straightforward to run them. On the other hand, Internet service providers (ISPs) manage DSNs as a Web site resource. They routinely issue one or more DSNs for each Web site account with database usage privileges. Therefore, it's often easier to use system, rather than file, DSNs. In any event, system DSNs offer a performance advantage.

After selecting a datasheet source in the database window and choosing File-Export, select Microsoft IIS 1-2(*.htx;*.idc) in the Save As Type list box. Make other selections as you would for an HTML file. Clicking Save opens the HTX/ IDC Output Options dialog box (shown in Figure 13-3). You can use the Browse button to select a template that formats the page returning the results from the IDC file. In order to run, the IDC file needs a DSN name on the server. In the Data Source Name text box, enter the name of the DSN that your Webmaster set up for this task. The dialog box also includes user ID and password fields in case the database on the Web server runs with user-level security. (This is very rare, particularly in Internet applications.)

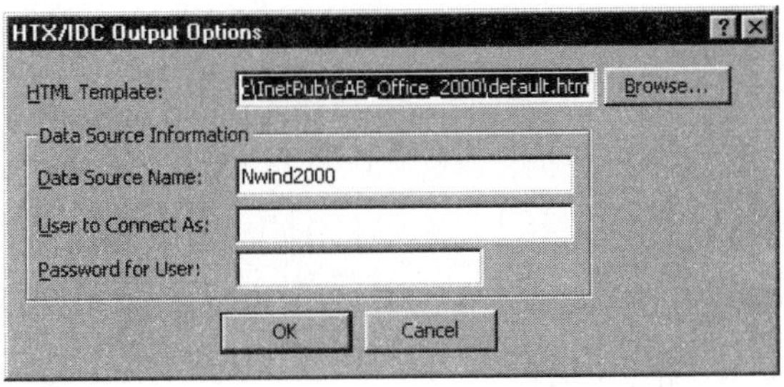

Figure 13-3. *The HTX/IDC Output Options dialog box.*

The IDC and HTX files complement one another. The IDC file runs a query against an Access database on the Web server. The HTX file uses HTML extensions to format the return set in HTML for viewing by a browser. While you can code the HTX file in an HTML extension, it returns pure HTML to the browser so that any browser can read its results. Because the only way that an IDC file can expose its return set is through an HTML file, this format processes datasheets. However, it is not appropriate for processing forms because the HTML return format does not serve as a good input for most HTML forms.

When you run an IDC/HTX pair from a Web server, browsers reference the IDC file, which must reside in a Web server folder that can run scripts. The IDC file automatically invokes the HTX file, which in turn processes the return set from the IDC file and sends HTML-formatted results back to the browser.

Publishing in ASP format

Like IDC and HTX files, ASP files require a reference to a DSN. In the Export dialog box, select Microsoft Active Server Pages (*.asp) in the Save As Type list box. In the Microsoft Active Server Pages Output Options dialog box, enter a DSN name. Other fields in the dialog box are optional and depend on your formatting preferences and database security settings. (These fields are optional in the IDC/HTX and HTML dialog boxes as well.)

The ASP format differs from the IDC/HTX format in that there is only one file. This ASP file performs the query and formats the result for the browser. The file runs its query and creates its HTML on the server, and then the Web server transports the HTML page back to the browser. The following ASP code writes the datasheet behind the Products form in the Northwind database to a browser:

```
<HTML><HEAD>
<META HTTP-EQUIV="Content-Type"
    CONTENT="text/html;charset=windows-1252">
<TITLE>Products</TITLE>
</HEAD><BODY>
```

(continued)

```
<%
If IsObject(Session("Nwind2000_conn")) Then
    Set conn = Session("Nwind2000_conn")
Else
    Set conn = Server.CreateObject("ADODB.Connection")
    conn.open "Nwind2000","",""
    Set Session("Nwind2000_conn") = conn
End If
%>
<%
If IsObject(Session("Products_rs")) Then
    Set rs = Session("Products_rs")
Else
    sql = "SELECT * FROM [Products]"
    Set rs = Server.CreateObject("ADODB.Recordset")
    rs.Open sql, conn, 3, 3
    If rs.eof Then
        rs.AddNew
    End If
    Set Session("Products_rs") = rs
End If
%>
<TABLE BORDER=1 BGCOLOR=#ffffff CELLSPACING=0 RULES=none>
<FONT FACE="Arial" COLOR=#000000><CAPTION><B>Products</B>
</CAPTION></FONT>

<THEAD><TR>
<TH BGCOLOR=#c0c0c0 BORDERCOLOR=#000000 >
<FONT SIZE=2 FACE="Arial" COLOR=#000000>ProductID</FONT></TH>
<TH BGCOLOR=#c0c0c0 BORDERCOLOR=#000000 >
<FONT SIZE=2 FACE="Arial" COLOR=#000000>ProductName</FONT></TH>
<TH BGCOLOR=#c0c0c0 BORDERCOLOR=#000000 >
<FONT SIZE=2 FACE="Arial" COLOR=#000000>SupplierID</FONT></TH>
<TH BGCOLOR=#c0c0c0 BORDERCOLOR=#000000 >
<FONT SIZE=2 FACE="Arial" COLOR=#000000>CategoryID</FONT></TH>
<TH BGCOLOR=#c0c0c0 BORDERCOLOR=#000000 >
<FONT SIZE=2 FACE="Arial" COLOR=#000000>QuantityPerUnit</FONT></TH>
<TH BGCOLOR=#c0c0c0 BORDERCOLOR=#000000 >
<FONT SIZE=2 FACE="Arial" COLOR=#000000>UnitPrice</FONT></TH>
<TH BGCOLOR=#c0c0c0 BORDERCOLOR=#000000 >
<FONT SIZE=2 FACE="Arial" COLOR=#000000>UnitsInStock</FONT></TH>
<TH BGCOLOR=#c0c0c0 BORDERCOLOR=#000000 >
<FONT SIZE=2 FACE="Arial" COLOR=#000000>UnitsOnOrder</FONT></TH>
<TH BGCOLOR=#c0c0c0 BORDERCOLOR=#000000 >
<FONT SIZE=2 FACE="Arial" COLOR=#000000>ReorderLevel</FONT></TH>
<TH BGCOLOR=#c0c0c0 BORDERCOLOR=#000000 >
<FONT SIZE=2 FACE="Arial" COLOR=#000000>Discontinued</FONT></TH>
```

```
</TR></THEAD>
<TBODY>
<%
On Error Resume Next
rs.MoveFirst
do while Not rs.eof
%>
<TR VALIGN=TOP>
<TD BORDERCOLOR=#808080 ><B>
<FONT SIZE=1 FACE="MS Sans Serif" COLOR=#000000>
<%=Server.HTMLEncode(rs.Fields("ProductID").Value)%><BR></FONT>
</B></TD>
<TD BORDERCOLOR=#808080 >
<FONT SIZE=1 FACE="MS Sans Serif" COLOR=#000000>
<%=Server.HTMLEncode(rs.Fields("ProductName").Value)%><BR>
</FONT></TD>
<TD BORDERCOLOR=#808080 >
<FONT SIZE=1 FACE="MS Sans Serif" COLOR=#000000>
<%=Server.HTMLEncode(rs.Fields("SupplierID").Value)%><BR>
</FONT></TD>
<TD BORDERCOLOR=#808080 >
<FONT SIZE=1 FACE="MS Sans Serif" COLOR=#000000>
<%=Server.HTMLEncode(rs.Fields("CategoryID").Value)%><BR>
</FONT></TD>
<TD BORDERCOLOR=#808080 >
<FONT SIZE=1 FACE="MS Sans Serif" COLOR=#000000>
<%=Server.HTMLEncode(rs.Fields("QuantityPerUnit").Value)%><BR>
</FONT></TD>
<TD BORDERCOLOR=#808080  ALIGN=RIGHT>
<FONT SIZE=1 FACE="MS Sans Serif" COLOR=#000000>
<%=Server.HTMLEncode(rs.Fields("UnitPrice").Value)%><BR>
</FONT></TD>
<TD BORDERCOLOR=#808080  ALIGN=RIGHT>
<FONT SIZE=1 FACE="MS Sans Serif" COLOR=#000000>
<%=Server.HTMLEncode(rs.Fields("UnitsInStock").Value)%><BR>
</FONT></TD>
<TD BORDERCOLOR=#808080  ALIGN=RIGHT>
<FONT SIZE=1 FACE="MS Sans Serif" COLOR=#000000>
<%=Server.HTMLEncode(rs.Fields("UnitsOnOrder").Value)%><BR>
</FONT></TD>
<TD BORDERCOLOR=#808080  ALIGN=RIGHT>
<FONT SIZE=1 FACE="MS Sans Serif" COLOR=#000000>
<%=Server.HTMLEncode(rs.Fields("ReorderLevel").Value)%><BR>
</FONT></TD>
```

(continued)

```
<TD BORDERCOLOR=#000000  ALIGN=RIGHT><B>
<FONT SIZE=2 FACE="System" COLOR=#000000>
<%=Server.HTMLEncode(rs.Fields("Discontinued").Value)%><BR>
</FONT></B></TD></TR>
<%
rs.MoveNext
loop
%>
</TBODY><TFOOT></TFOOT>
</TABLE></BODY></HTML>
```

Notice that the code mixes HTML with VBScript. It also uses ADO to create the connection to a data source, extract a recordset, and insert the results into an HTML table. A *Do* loop transfers the recordset contents to an HTML table. None of the VBScript code stays in the version that the server sends to the browser; the browser receives pure HTML. This makes ASP appropriate for many different kinds of browsers. The versatility of composing HTML on the fly is the cause for a pause when a browser launches an ASP file. Pages with more iterations and field translations require more composing time than those with just a few fields and rows. You should plan your ASP page contents so that they deliver sufficient information in a single page without incurring undue processing delays.

Using HTML Forms

One of the strengths of ASP technology is its support of HTML forms. This is important because all browsers support HTML forms. You can use these forms to gather information from site visitors or return database results in a record layout (as opposed to a datasheet layout). An HTML form consists of one or more controls for displaying or storing information. Typically, the form contains at least one button for submitting the form fields to the Web server. If the form requires a reply, a program on the server can process the form fields and generate a response page.

HTML forms often work like a call-and-response game between a browser and a Web server. The browser user fills in the fields and clicks the Submit button for the form. When the browser sends the form to the server, it transmits form field values and the name of a program on the server that knows what to do with those field values. This is the *call* part of the game. The Web server sends the form field values to the right processing program on the server. That program can echo the input values, check them for validity, append them to a record source, do a lookup of data from a record source, or more. It typically prepares some kind of return page for the browser. This is the *response*. ASP files can serve as both the initial form that accepts the call and the response program that replies to the call.

Figure 13-4 shows a pair of HTML forms that illustrate the call-and-response character of HTML form processing. The top form includes a drop-down list box with the names of employees in the Northwind database. A user can select a name, such as Buchanan, and click Get Extension to submit the form to the server. This is the call action. The Web server takes the input form and passes it to telereturn.asp, which reads the entry in the list box, looks up the telephone number for the employee, and writes a page with the information for the browser. The Web server sends the page back to the browser. This is the response action.

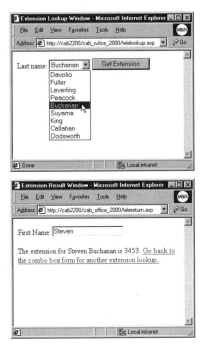

Figure 13-4. *The HTML form on top calls the Web server and invokes the reply page on the bottom.*

Access 2000 does not include built-in wizards for building these kinds of pages with HTML forms, but the process is straightforward. The main challenge is learning the syntax for a few HTML form controls and how to intermix HTML and script, such as VBScript, in an ASP file. The following code is all that the top page in Figure 13-4 requires. The filename for this code is telelookup.asp. Its name appears in the Address list box on the top page.

```
<%
set cnn1 = server.createobject("ADODB.Connection")
cnn1.Open "Provider=Microsoft.Jet.OLEDB.4.0;" & _
    "Data Source=C:\Program Files\Microsoft Office\Office\" & _
    "Samples\Northwind.mdb;"
set rs = Server.CreateObject("ADODB.Recordset")
rs.open "select * from employees", cnn1
%>
<html>
<head><title>Extension Lookup Window</title></head>
<body>
<form name=MyForm method=Post action=telereturn.asp>
Last name: <select name=DCombo>
<%
do while not rs.eof
%>
    <option value=<%=rs.fields("EmployeeID")%>>
        <%=rs.Fields("LastName")%>
<%
rs.MoveNext
Loop
%>
</select>
<input type="Submit" value="Get Extension"><br><br>
</form></body></html>
```

Notice that the script is delimited by <% and %>. The first script segment opens a connection to the Northwind database through OLE DB drivers that do not require a DSN. The first segment also creates a recordset with the information to populate the drop-down list box. Next, some HTML code starts a page and a form on the page. In the form declaration, the code assigns telereturn.asp as the program that processes the form. Just before starting a *Do* loop, the program declares a drop-down list box with the HTML *select* keyword. It names the control dcombo. (Names in HTML are not case sensitive.). The *Do* loop populates the list box with values from the recordset created by the first script segment. The form closes with a Submit button that has the label Get Extension.

The telereturn.asp file also starts by opening a connection and creating a recordset, as shown below. However, this open action has two important differences from the one in telelookup.asp. First, it uses a DSN to help create the connection. This is not necessary, but many legacy ASP files are designed this way. Second, the code reads the value of dcombo and uses it to form the SQL statement for the query that looks up an employee's telephone number.

```
<%
set rs = Server.CreateObject("ADODB.Recordset")
sql = "select * from employees"
sql = sql & " where employees.employeeid = "
sql = sql & request.form("dcombo")
rs.open sql,"DSN=Nwind2000"
%>
<html>
<head><title>Extension Result Window</title></head>
<body>
<form>
First Name: <input TYPE="TEXT" VALUE="
    <%=rs.fields("FirstName")%>">
</form>
The extension for <%=rs.fields("FirstName")%> 
    <%=rs.fields("LastName")%>
    is <%=rs.fields("Extension")%>.
    <a href="telelookup.asp">
    Go back to the combo box form for another extension lookup.
</a>
</body></html>
```

After creating a recordset with information for the employee selected in telelookup.asp, telereturn.asp formats a page. The page contains the employee's first name in an HTML text box, a simple HTML string with the name and extension, and a hyperlink for returning control to telelookup.asp. When the Web server passes this page back to the browser, the call-and-response cycle ends.

Using FTP Snapshots with Netscape Browsers

Chapter 6 discussed the snapshot format for reports and showed examples of its capabilities, but it did not mention using snapshots with FTP. When you place snapshots in an FTP folder for a Web server, Netscape browsers can open them remotely at the Web server. The user need not download the file and launch a separate viewer, as is the case with Hypertext Transfer Protocol (HTTP).

When a Netscape browser opens a snapshot of a report from an FTP folder, it automatically creates a new window for the report. This scenario assumes that you have installed the Snapshot Viewer and that the workstation has an association between .snp file types and that viewer. Figure 13-5 on the next page shows an excerpt from a snapshot of the Northwind Catalog report. It shows an image, multiple fonts, and other formatting touches, such as dividing lines. The order entry form at the end of the Catalog report also reproduces faithfully.

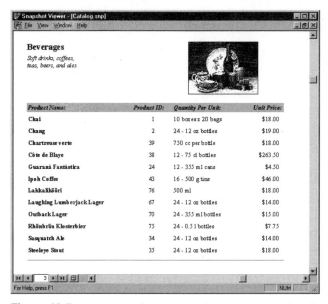

Figure 13-5. *An excerpt from a snapshot report opened with a Netscape browser.*

When you save the snapshot file, you simply place it in the FTPROOT folder for the Web server (or another FTP folder). Type *ftp://webserver/filename.snp* in the Netscape address Location box. Replace *webserver* with the name of your Web server. (For the samples in this chapter, the Web server is cab2200.) Since the FTP protocol is very popular, you can use this publishing mechanism with many different types of Web servers and Web browsers.

USING HYPERLINKS

In Chapter 5, you learned how to use hyperlinks to navigate around forms in a custom application. This is only a small portion of the functionality that hyperlinks can deliver. You can also navigate to other Access databases, to bookmarks in a Word document, or to intranet and Internet URLs. You can even use hyperlinks to open your e-mail software (such as Microsoft Outlook) with the address of a specific individual and a designated subject.

Types of Hyperlinks

Hyperlinks can appear as labels, command buttons, and unbound image controls on forms, reports, and data access pages. You can also create bound hyperlinks so that a table can contain a set of hyperlinks. You can assign a unique hyperlink to each record in a table. One obvious use for this is associating a URL with each record entity (for example, companies). After following either a bound or unbound hyperlink, you can use the Back control on the Office Web or browser toolbar to navigate back from a hyperlink target address to Access.

The Hyperlink Data Type

When you use bound hyperlinks, your application specifies the Hyperlink data type, which can contain up to four parts, each delimited by the number (#) sign. The display text part appears first if you specify it. This text appears in place of the address to which a hyperlink navigates. For example, instead of a hyperlink showing the address for the Microsoft Web site, it can say simply *Microsoft*.

The second part is the address—the URL or UNC address for a target file. The address can be absolute or relative. It is common at Web sites to specify hyperlinks relatively. In Access, a relative address extends from the *Hyperlink Base* setting in an Access file. You can examine this setting by choosing the Database Properties command from the File menu in the database window.

The third part is the subaddress, which names a part of a file to navigate to. The parts you can navigate to vary by Office component. In Access, you can navigate to database objects, such as forms, reports, tables, and queries. You can specify a database object type, such as table, and the name of a specific object, such as *Customers*. You do not have to specify an object type, but if a database contains multiple objects with the same name, Access navigates to them in an arbitrary order. If a hyperlink includes both address and subaddress parts, the link navigates to another file. If the address part is missing, the link navigates to an object in the current database.

The fourth part, a screen tip, is new in Access 2000. This text appears when you rest the cursor over a hyperlink. It can offer a reminder about the purpose of a hyperlink. These tips appear in hyperlinks on pages viewed with Internet Explorer 4 and later. They also appear in Access 2000 custom applications.

Inserting and Editing Hyperlinks

While you can type a new hyperlink address, it is simpler and safer to use the Insert Hyperlink tool or its corresponding menu command. You can invoke the Insert Hyperlink command from any point at which you can add a hyperlink to a document. For example, you can choose Insert Hyperlink from the Design view of a form to add a hyperlink as a label. You can give a command button navigational abilities by clicking the Build button next to its *Hyperlink Address* or *Hyperlink SubAddress* properties. You can assign navigational capabilities to an image in the same way.

All these actions open the Insert Hyperlink dialog box. Figure 13-6 shows this dialog box for creating a label hyperlink on a form. The label's caption value is the ASP sample at the fictional Programming Microsoft Access site, whose URL is http://samples.microsoft.com/telelookup.com. Click ScreenTip to open a second dialog box for entering text for the screen tip associated with the hyperlink.

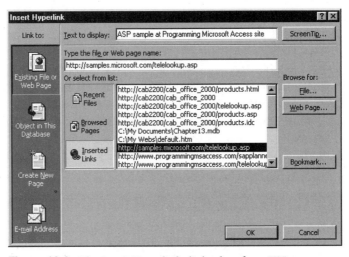

Figure 13-6. *The Insert Hyperlink dialog box for a URL.*

You can click the E-mail Address button on the Option bar to open the version of the dialog box for e-mail. (See Figure 13-7.) The dialog box automatically inserts the mailto protocol prefix to invoke a workstation's default e-mail package from a browser. You can also specify the recipient and the subject. Just as you can select from sites previously visited when you assign a hyperlink address, you can select a previously entered e-mail address and subject. The hyperlink that Figure 13-7 creates displays the phrase *mail the prez*. When a user clicks this phrase, it opens the user's e-mail software with the recipient rickd@cabinc.net and with *the scoop* as the subject.

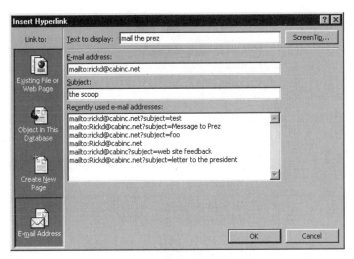

Figure 13-7. *The Insert Hyperlink dialog box for an e-mail message.*

After you insert a hyperlink in an application, you can right-click it and choose Hyperlink from the shortcut menu to see an array of options for processing existing hyperlinks. The Edit Hyperlink command is the most obvious choice for revising a hyperlink. This opens the Edit Hyperlink dialog box, which has the same layout as the Insert Hyperlink dialog box. You can use it to update any of the hyperlink fields. Over time, you might have to fine-tune the display text or the URL for a hyperlink. Similarly, you can add to the recipient list for links that send e-mail so that messages route to more recipients directly.

Hyperlink Samples

One of the most popular pages at many Web sites is the Favorites page, which points to sites that the author finds valuable or interesting. You can insert similar pages in your custom Access solutions. Such sites can include e-mail or Web links to your business and can include site addresses with free or low-cost technical support.

Figure 13-8 on the next page shows a Favorites page that is an Access form with two images and two labels. All four serve as hyperlinks. The first image is my company's logo. If users with a live connection to the Internet click the image, Access takes them to my firm's Web site. The second image is a Microsoft Access logo, which takes users to the Access site within the Microsoft site. The two label hyperlinks open e-mail links to employees of my firm.

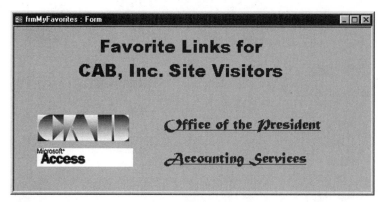

Figure 13-8. *A Favorites page with two images and two labels that serve as hyperlinks.*

Figure 13-9 shows a form with a bound hyperlink that is based on a table of hyperlinks. The table appears below the form in the figure. The screen tip, CAB Headquarters, appears for the first hyperlink. The bottom display presents that hyperlink in Edit mode, which exposes the hyperlink parts. Notice that there is display text and an address part, but no subaddress. The hyperlink concludes with the screen tip text.

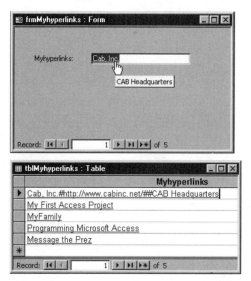

Figure 13-9. *The form with a bound hyperlink shows a screen tip for the first hyperlink in the table. The table exposes the full syntax for the first hyperlink.*

CREATING AND USING DATA ACCESS PAGES

Data access pages are data-bound HTML files. In many ways, they look and behave like a cross between a traditional Access report and a form because you can use it to browse through the records in a data source. The page's database connection enables users to add, update, and delete data. Typically, but not necessarily, the data is from a database object in the current database file. You can use the Sorting And Grouping tool to hierarchically display data—for example, in reports that have multiple, nested bands or group headings. The Pages icon in the database window represents the data access page objects associated with a database. But Access does not store pages in the database; they are separate DHTML files in the file system—for example, in a folder on your intranet server. The *Pages* collection in a database file is a collection of hyperlinks to the DHTML files. You create pages within Access, and users can then open them in Internet Explorer 5 or Access 2000.

> **NOTE**   If multiple users will launch a page from browsers on different workstations, you might have to revise the Data Source setting in the DHTML file so that it does not reference local drive letters. Use a Uniform Naming Convention (UNC) address instead.

Creating a Data Access Page

Access 2000 contains wizards for basing a new data access page on either a tabular or columnar layout. You can also base a new page on an existing Web page. However, many will prefer to create a data access page by opening a blank page in Design view and populating it with controls from the Field List dialog box (shown in Figure 13-10 on the next page).

To populate a page, you can open the Tables or Queries node to reveal the table names in the active connection. If you see a table from which you want to select values for the page, you can expand the table to view the individual fields. You can then select fields by dragging and dropping them on the page. Alternatively, you can populate a page with all fields in a table by dragging a table name to the page. You can then choose to arrange fields in a columnar or pivot table layout. You can perform the same kind of operations with queries.

NOTE The pivot table report layout (which originated in Excel) is a special kind of tabular layout that facilitates creating interactive, aggregate summaries of the information in a record source. The pivot table promises to become a popular front end for working with multidimensional data cubes.

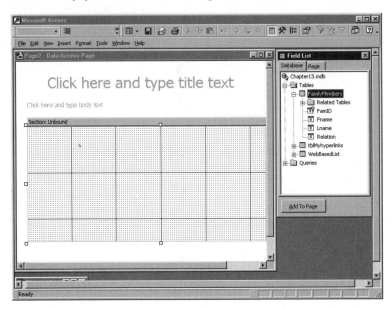

Figure 13-10. *You can use the Field List dialog box to populate a blank data access page with controls bound to database fields.*

To change the active connection, right-click on the database connector in the top left corner of the Field List dialog box and choose Connection from the shortcut menu. In the Data Link Properties dialog box that appears, select an OLE DB connection driver and a database consistent with that driver. When you close the dialog box, the Field List dialog box shows the tables and queries from the new database source.

Creating and Using a Simple Columnar Page

Figure 13-11 shows a simple data access page that serves as a form for the *FamilyMembers* table in a database file. Four fields appear on the form. A control below the fields supports navigation and other functions. Clicking the two navigator buttons on either side of the record indicator window moves the current record's position back and forth in the underlying recordset.

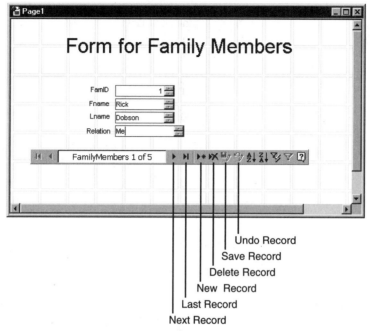

Figure 13-11. *This data access page serves as a form. Users can browse, add, delete, edit, sort, and filter records using the navigation control below the fields.*

The first six buttons to the right of the indicator for the record source and number are as follows, from left to right:

■ *Next Record button.* Moves to the next record.

■ *Last Record button.* Moves to the last record.

■ *New Record button.* Adds a record.

■ *Delete Record button.* Deletes the current record.

■ *Save Record button.* Saves any changes to the current record.

■ *Undo Record button.* Undoes any unsaved changes to the current record.

If you enter a record that you later want to remove, use the Delete button to delete it. You can also edit records by simply typing over them, adding new content, or removing existing content. If you want to preserve your revisions, click Save Record. Otherwise, click Undo Record.

The remaining buttons on the navigation control (except the Help button on the far right) are for sorting and filtering:

- *Sort Ascending and Sort Descending buttons.* Specify the sort direction. To sort on the values in a field, click in that field for any record, and then click one of these buttons.

- *Filter By Selection button.* Applies a filter based on the current value in a field. Click in the field to choose a value for filtering (for example, the *Lname* field with a value of Dobson), and then click Filter By Selection. The display changes to show just records matching the previously selected filter value. For example, if you choose Dobson for *Lname* in Figure 13-11, the record indicator changes from FamilyMembers 1 of 5 to FamilyMembers 1 of 2.

- *Toggle Filter button.* Applies or removes the filter.

All this functionality is available from within Access as well as from a browser on an intranet. Data access pages display best and have all their features function with Internet Explorer 5. Various degrees of degradation occur with Internet Explorer 4. Users of browsers other than Internet Explorer 5 must also obtain ActiveX controls for reading and working with a data access page.

Grouping Records

One powerful feature of data access pages is their ability to group records and conditionally expand a group to show the individual entries within. Figure 13-12 shows this capability. The page shown in the figure groups records from the *FamilyMembers* table by the *Lname* field. All records from the table with the same last name group together. When a user clicks the gray expand button (it changes from + to –), a second, nested navigation control appears for moving through the records with the same last name. Clicking the outer navigation control closes the expanded display and moves to the first record with the next last name.

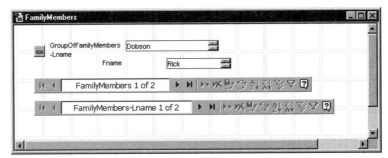

Figure 13-12. *You can group and conditionally expand records within groups on data access pages.*

You can show more than a single record on a page. You use the *Data Page Size* setting in the Sorting And Grouping window to specify how many records to show at a time. (See the bottom window in Figure 13-13.) This window lets you set the page size independently for the grouping field as well as the fields within a group. You can use the Grouping And Sorting window for data access pages to control whether groups have header and footer sections, just like you use the corresponding window for reports. You can use the *Group On* setting to specify intervals, ranges of values, and prefixes for grouping fields.

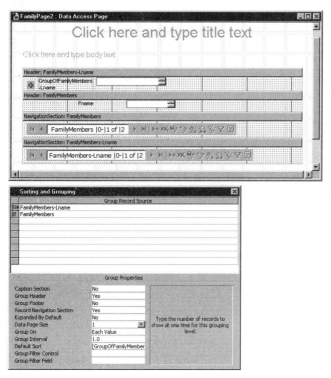

Figure 13-13. *In Design view, you can add Expand controls to let users interact with your pages and conditionally expand them to see the records within a group.*

The top window in Figure 13-13 shows the Design view of the page in Figure 13-12. Notice that it contains two navigation controls. You can assign a grouping function to a field by selecting the field and clicking the Promote button (the left-pointing arrow) on the Page Design toolbar. When the record source for a page derives from a one-to-many relationship, you can use the Sorting And Grouping tool to group all the fields from the one side of the relationship over the fields on the many side. Access sorts and groups the records by the primary key for the one side of the relationship in this case.

Office 2000 Web Components on Data Access Pages

Three Office 2000 Web Components ship with Office 2000 (the Standard, Professional, Premium, and Developer editions): spreadsheet, chart, and PivotTable list components. You can use these to complement and extend the basic database functionality provided by data access pages. If a site has a license that permits intranet distribution, the site administrator can configure browsers under the license to automatically download and configure the Office Web Components the first time they load a page using a component. (For more information on configuring Office Web Components, see the Microsoft Office 2000 Resource Kit.)

An Office spreadsheet sample

Figure 13-14 shows one use of a spreadsheet component on a data access page. Controls on the page show the *CategoryName*, *ProductName*, and *ProductSales* fields for the Sales By Category query from the Northwind database. This query computes sales by product in 1997 for each product. The query lists the category ID and name of each product along with its sales.

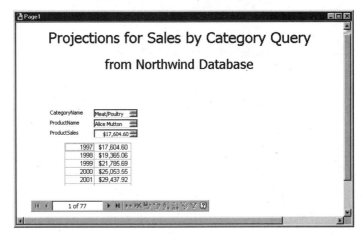

Figure 13-14. *The spreadsheet component on this data access page uses sales from the database for 1997 to project sales through 2001.*

The sample in Figure 13-14 extends the basic query by projecting sales from 1998 through 2001. First, the component copies the current value of the ProductSales control from the page to the spreadsheet. Then it applies a progressive series of growth rates to sales starting with 1997. These rates increase sales from one year to the next. While the growth rates are the same for all products, the actual sales levels vary between products because the 1997 sales are different for each product. Finally, to protect the formulas from damage, you can lock selected spreadsheets to block users from inadvertently changing them.

Figure 13-15 shows the Design view of the data access page in Figure 13-14. Notice that a spreadsheet appears below the ProductsSales control. You can insert an Office 2000 Spreadsheet Component using the Insert-Office Spreadsheet command and adapt the component for use in your application by right-clicking it and choosing Property Toolbox. The spreadsheet in Figure 13-15 hides the toolbar, title bar, column headers, and row headers. In addition, the component's horizontal and vertical scrollbar settings are set to *False*.

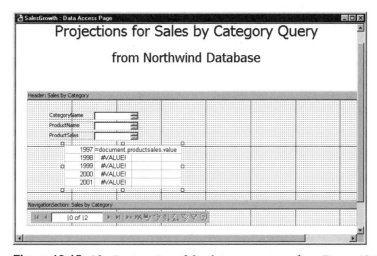

Figure 13-15. *The Design view of the data access page from Figure 13-14.*

The top sales cell in the spreadsheet shows a formula that updates with each new record on the data access page: *=document.productsales.value*. The term *document* references a data access page. The term *productsales* references a specific control on the page. Finally, the *value* property references the current value of the control on the data access page. This value changes only if the user moves to a new record in the page's underlying record source.

The sales entries for 1998 through 2001 all evaluate to #VALUE! in Design view. This is not an error. It results from the fact that there is no value for 1997 in Design view. Recall from Figure 13-14 that there are legitimate values for these cells in Page view. This results from the formula in the top spreadsheet cell evaluating to the current value of *productsales* on the data access page.

An Office chart sample

The sample that begins on page 534 builds on the preceding one by adding an Office 2000 Chart Component that charts the values in the spreadsheet. The chart shows a graphical depiction of how sales grow over time for each product. Figure 13-16 shows a product with its spreadsheet projections and graphical depiction to the right side of the page. The chart dynamically updates each time the values in the spreadsheet change.

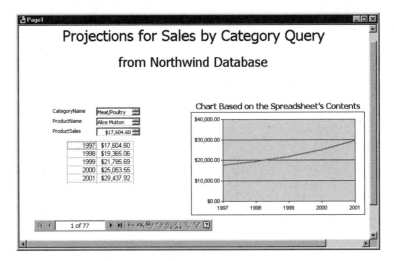

Figure 13-16. *The Office 2000 Chart Component on a data access page accepts values from a Spreadsheet Component that changes its sales projections when a user moves off the current record.*

To add a chart to a page, select the area of the page where you want the chart to appear, and then choose Insert-Office Chart. The command starts a wizard that walks you through the process of formatting a chart. You can select a chart type, choose a record source for the chart, and set values to display in the chart. After you finish using the wizard, you can right-click in the chart and choose Property Toolbox to edit your choices or specify other options that were not explicitly presented at setup time.

An Office PivotTable list sample

The PivotTable list control lets users sort, group, filter, outline, and manipulate data. It can also work with data from more providers than a normal data access page or other Office 2000 Web Components can. Its data sources can include a worksheet, a database, and a multidimensional data cube.

Figure 13-17 shows a PivotTable list control on a data access page that is based on the *Orders* table in the NorthwindCS database. It counts orders by *ShipCountry*, *CustomerID*, and *EmployeeID*. You can click the *Expand* control next to the *EmployeeID* and *CustomerID* fields to expand the table within that column or row. In addition, you can selectively show a subset of the table by opening the list of elements comprising all countries, customers, and employees and selecting just one or a few from each set. A toolbox along the top of the PivotTable list presents still more analysis options, such as filtering and sorting.

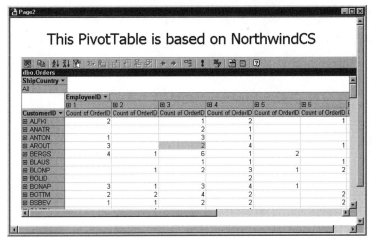

Figure 13-17. *A PivotTable list on a data access page that displays data from the NorthwindCS database.*

Programmatic Issues for Data Access Pages

You can program solutions with data access pages at several different levels. Data access pages can also serve as hosts for Office Web Components. Both data access pages and Office 2000 Web Components have object models that you can use to develop programmatic solutions. You can also code solutions in VBA or a Web scripting language, such as VBScript.

This section explores solutions based on VBA, the *AllDataAccessPages* collection, and the *DataAccessPage* object. The *AllDataAccessPages* collection works like the *AllForms* and *AllReports* collections. Its members are not database objects, but rather *AccessObject* objects. These objects are available whether or not a data access page is open. The *AllDataAccessPages* collection lets you track the full set of all data access pages associated with a database project. The following short VBA procedure lists all the data access pages in a project and notes whether they are open.

```
Sub listPages()
Dim myPage As AccessObject

    For Each myPage In _
        Application.CurrentProject.AllDataAccessPages
        Debug.Print myPage.Name & IIf(myPage.IsLoaded, _
            " is loaded.", " is not loaded.")
    Next myPage

End Sub
```

The *FullName* property of an *AccessObject* object in the *AllDataAccessPages* collection has a special meaning. Recall that pages are not stored as objects in the database file; they are separate DHTML files. The location of the pages can be anywhere on a LAN. The *FullName* property indicates the path and filename for a data access page. The next procedure lists all the pages in a project and itemizes them by their *Name* and *FullName* properties. The *Name* property value is the shortcut name for the data access page that appears in the database window.

```
Sub whereArePages()
Dim myPage As AccessObject
Dim obj As Object

    Set obj = Application.CurrentProject
    For Each myPage In obj.AllDataAccessPages
        Debug.Print "The link "; myPage.Name & " points at " & _
            myPage.FullName & "."
    Next myPage

End Sub
```

The only method for a *DataAccessPage* object is *ApplyTheme*. You can use this method to automate the application of a Microsoft Office theme to the pages that members of the *AllDataAccessPages* collection point to. This method works properly only if the page is open in design mode. The following two procedures assign a theme to all the data access pages in a project whether or not they are open and whether or not they are open in design mode. The procedures also restore each data access page to its former open and current view status before applying the theme. If you do not like a theme selection, you can rerun the *callSetTheme* procedure with an argument of *Blank*.

```
Sub callSetTheme()

'Test with Artsy or Blends.
'Clear with Blank.
```

```
        setTheme "Artsy"
End Sub


Sub setTheme(ThemeName As String)
Dim myPage As AccessObject
Dim obj As Object
Dim blnCloseit As Boolean
Dim blnMakePageView As Boolean

'Loop through all DataAccessPages.
    Set obj = Application.CurrentProject
    For Each myPage In obj.AllDataAccessPages

'Get Page open in Design view.
        If myPage.IsLoaded = False Then
            DoCmd.OpenDataAccessPage myPage.Name, _
                acDataAccessPageDesign
            blnCloseit = True
        Else
            If DataAccessPages(myPage.Name).CurrentView <> _
                acDataAccessPageDesign Then
                DoCmd.Close acDataAccessPage, myPage.Name
                DoCmd.OpenDataAccessPage myPage.Name, _
                    acDataAccessPageDesign
                blnMakePageView = True
            End If
        End If

'Apply Theme.
        DataAccessPages(myPage.Name).ApplyTheme ThemeName
        DoCmd.Save acDataAccessPage, myPage.Name

'If necessary, restore page.
        If blnCloseit = True Then
            DoCmd.Close acDataAccessPage, myPage.Name
            blnCloseit = False
        ElseIf blnMakePageView = True Then
            DoCmd.Close acDataAccessPage, myPage.Name
            DoCmd.OpenDataAccessPage myPage.Name, _
                acDataAccessPageBrowse
        End If
    Next myPage

End Sub
```

Chapter 14

The Office 2000 Developer Edition

The Microsoft Office 2000 Developer Edition (ODE) provides many important features for Microsoft Access development, including versatile setup and deployment options. ODE originally shipped with Office 97 as an outgrowth of the Access SDK. Longtime Access developers will recognize ODE as a vehicle for getting the Access run-time engine and the Setup wizard. ODE has since come a long way. Selected features that are new or greatly improved include

- A run-time version of the Microsoft Data Engine (MSDE)

- A Package And Deployment wizard

- Tools to facilitate data binding to Microsoft Forms used with the other Office applications (instead of Access Forms)

- The Code Librarian, for storing and retrieving code snippets and whole procedures

- Full-scale printed and electronic documentation for Office 2000 development

This chapter offers a brief overview of the ODE feature set and explores topics of interest to Access developers (and developers generally, in the case of digital signing).

ODE OVERVIEW

ODE delivers benefits in three main areas: Microsoft Visual Basic for Applications (VBA) productivity, data access, and deployment and management. ODE is for the millions of professional developers who build solutions with Office, VBA, and data access tools. Many of these solutions use the powerful data access capabilities of Access from within another Office application capabilities.

ODE include these Microsoft products:

- Microsoft Word 2000
- Microsoft Excel 2000
- Microsoft PowerPoint 2000
- Microsoft Access 2000
- Microsoft Outlook 2000
- Microsoft Publisher 2000
- Microsoft FrontPage 2000
- Microsoft PhotoDraw 2000
- Microsoft Small Business Tools

ODE includes documentation and samples that help you build solutions within and across these applications. VBA is available throughout the Office product line, but one difficulty in becoming productive with a new application is learning the object model. The ODE printed documentation includes a brochure with graphical representations of the object models for the above applications (except PhotoDraw, which does not have one). It documents 24 object models that are either for the major applications, shared by those applications, specialized for data access services, or targeted at Office Web technologies.

VBA Productivity Tools

The VBA productivity tools help you program faster in all the Office applications that support VBA. They range from a simple string editor for building SQL statements to the Component Object Model (COM) Add-In Designer, which simplifies the building of dynamic link libraries (DLLs) as add-ins in two or more Office applications.

The COM Add-In Designer offers an integrated approach to building and using add-ins across Office 2000 applications. Previous versions of Office required different approaches for building, storing, and invoking add-ins.

The Code Librarian is a database that shares code snippets, functions, and modules among members of a development team. An individual developer can also use it to retrieve previously built code. You can add your own custom code to the database and search it by keyword and other criteria. The Code Librarian comes with a starter kit of code for common programming tasks.

The VBA Code Commentator and VBA Error Handler automatically update your modules to perform standard tasks that are essential for many custom development efforts. The Code Commentator adds comments, such as your name, the date, and the parameters that you must send to procedures. It builds this information from a customizable template that lets developers within a large organization modify the basic process to meet their own requirements. The Error Handler builds standardized error-handling code for all the procedures in an application. Again, you can customize its template. Beyond that, of course, the Error Handler provides a framework for adding your own custom error-handling code.

The VBA String Editor is a dialog box for writing, editing, copying, and pasting custom SQL statements into VBA code. It is a simple tool that performs a single task that can become quite complicated.

ODE also simplifies team development by offering Microsoft Visual SourceSafe, whose check-out and check-in features let one member of a team work on one or more VBA modules while other members work on quality control or system integration features for the rest of the application. Visual SourceSafe also makes it easy to compare versions of VBA code as well as restore prior versions.

The VBA Multi-Code Import/Export add-in facilitates importing and exporting code from a module. You load this feature as a single add-in, but it has two separate user interfaces—one for importing code and one for exporting it.

The printed and online documentation available through the ODE helps you improve your development skills and explains cross-component application development techniques. In addition to the printed object models, there is a VBA Programmer's Guide. A special collection of Microsoft Developer Network (MSDN) CDs includes all the printed documentation as well as additional documents; all have search engine support.

Data Access

ODE offers a host of tools that support data access development. Perhaps the single, brightest jewel in this set is the redistributable MSDE (Microsoft Data Engine). You can ship a royalty-free, stand-alone version of your custom application that works with MSDE. This is especially appropriate for prototyping applications that might grow into full-scale SQL Server applications. The MSDE footprint is smaller than SQL Server's, so you can use it when SQL Server resource requirements are too demanding. You can also build custom forms and reports against SQL Server with the new Access Project. (See Chapter 12 for more on MSDE and Access Projects.)

For the best backward compatibility, you should build solutions with the Microsoft Access Run Time. This package emulates Access 2000 and Jet without the user interface. Your custom application is the only exposed interface. This royalty-free package lets you ship solutions that work at the department level and are unlikely to demand significantly more resources over time. For example, you can use the Access Run Time to build a solution for a utility plant. Utility plants have relatively long lifetimes, and they often operate at or near an optimal level. In this kind of environment, a system's requirements are unlikely to expand significantly over the lifetime of an application.

The ADO Data Control and the Data Environment Designer offer graphical access to ADO and ODBC data sources. The ADO Data Control is familiar to those who used the ActiveX User Connection Designer to create Remote Data Objects at design time. The ADO Data Control permits connection to one data source at a time, and you can navigate to the next, previous, last, and first records in its recordset. With the Data Environment designer, you can create multiple *Connection* objects, each of which has multiple *Command* objects with corresponding recordsets. The Data Environment Designer lets you drag and drop fields from a *Command* object to Microsoft Forms and to the Data Report Designer.

These graphical data access tools do not make ADO manual coding techniques obsolete. You can still use ADO code to build and manipulate data access connections to familiar data sources from the other Office applications. (Later in this chapter, you'll see a sample that does this with Excel).

You use the Data Report Designer in VBA applications along with the Data Environment Designer to build custom reports without any code. You can export these reports as Hypertext Markup Language (HTML) documents. While you can build reports in a graphical fashion, you get greater control with code by formatting, printing, previewing, and saving your hierarchical reports.

Deployment and Management

The Package And Deployment wizard in Office 2000 is a significant improvement over earlier setup and distribution wizards. It is completely menu driven. You can use it to produce a professional setup package that works like the one for Office 2000. One especially exciting feature is the ability to deploy custom solutions via the Internet so that remote clients can install your custom solutions without needing disks or CDs. You can even automate the packaging and deployment processes using custom scripts that eliminate the possibility of wrong selections in the wizard screens.

You can use the wizard to circulate solutions based on the redistributable MSDE or the Access Run Time. However, you should not overlook delivering solutions that use the full working version of Access 2000. One reason clients are motivated to use many custom solutions is that they are familiar with the Access implementation environment. Some clients want to participate in the maintenance of their systems to lower the total cost of ownership.

Microsoft Replication Manager, a graphical user interface that ships with ODE, lets you view and manage replicated Microsoft Jet databases over a network or the Internet. Replication Manager converts a database to a design master, creates additional replicas, and manages a replica set. You can use it to graphically manage the exchange of data and data structures across the members of a replica set. The Replication Manager permits three styles of synchronization: on demand, at the next connection, and on a regular schedule. In addition, it supports data exchange between Jet and SQL Server databases. (See Chapter 11 for more on database replication and for samples that illustrate how to manage replication.)

Any professional custom solution can benefit from some kind of help system or documentation. Users need a document that explains how to respond to system screens, and developers need flow charts and excerpts that illustrate how the code and database objects interact to support system performance. ODE ships with the HTML Help Workshop, which supports both of these functions. All of the screens shown in this chapter, as well as selected others throughout the book, were captured with the HTML Help Image Editor. This tool lets you display the cursor—a feature that many screen capture packages lack. It also supports capturing a whole screen as well as various windows within it based on a timer, mouse click, or keyboard event.

THE CODE LIBRARIAN

To reuse code, you need a place to store it, a way to find it, and a mechanism for retrieving it. The Code Librarian that ships with ODE lets you do all of this and more. To start the Code Librarian, you must perform two steps. (These steps are similar for the other ODE built-in add-ins.) The first time in a session that you want to invoke the Code Librarian, choose Add-Ins from the VBE Project window, and then double-click Code Librarian in the Add-In Manager dialog box. (See Figure 14-1 on the next page.) This places the word Loaded in the Load

Behavior column and selects the Loaded/Unloaded check box in the Load Behavior group. Double-click any other add-ins that you want to use during the session. You can select the Load On Startup check box to cause the add-in to start automatically when the Project window opens. After loading the add-in, you can start it from the Add-Ins menu.

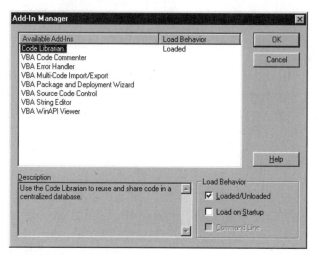

Figure 14-1. *The Add-In Manager dialog box.*

Figure 14-2 shows the Code Librarian window, which organizes code samples by category. The categories are expandable. You can associate a description with a code segment to help you identify it. On the Keywords tab, you can retrieve a list of code samples associated with a keyword. You can use the Search tab to retrieve samples that contain a keyword associated with the sample or that contain a keyword in the full text of the code.

The Code Librarian toolbar offers typical management features. For example, you can see the code behind a selected item by clicking the View Code button. (See Figure 14-2.) The Insert Code To Module button to the right adds the code to your code window. It does this at the cursor's current location in the window, so be sure that the cursor is not in the middle of another procedure (unless that is where you want to insert a snippet). You can also just drag and drop a code sample from the librarian to your code window. The Copy Code To Clipboard button lets you copy code to the Windows Clipboard. This is convenient when you want to copy code to another session that does not appear on the screen. Simply toggle to the session and then paste the contents of the Clipboard into the code window.

View Code
   Insert Code to Module
      Copy Code to Clipboard
         Add New Code

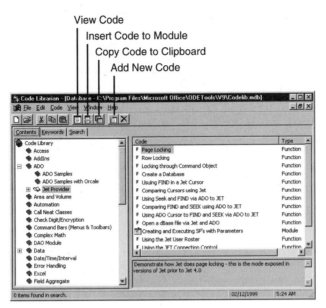

Figure 14-2. *The Code Librarian organizes its code samples by category, but you can also search for them by keyword or on a full-text basis.*

You can also modify existing code or add new code to the Code Librarian. To modify code, open it for viewing, make your changes, and then click Apply. Close the Code Librarian window to commit your changes. To add new code, click the Add New Code toolbar button to open a blank Code Librarian dialog box. Paste a code sample from the Clipboard into the dialog box, and assign a name to the sample in the Name text box. The Name text box is just above where you pasted the code. Use the Description tab to assign a type, such as code snippet, function, module, or class module. Enter a description for the sample in the text box below the Sample Type drop-down list box. You can also assign a category and one or more keywords to the sample. Click OK to save the sample.

Figure 14-3 on the next page shows a series of Jet provider ADO samples. As you can see, there are two other collections of ADO samples. These and many other samples ship with the Code Librarian as a starter kit. Some of these might be appropriate for your custom applications with little or no refinement. One of the samples in the figure computes the file size of the current file. The second sample computes a person's age, given the person's birthdate and the current date.

Figure 14-3. *These samples ship with the Code Librarian.*

PACKAGING AND DEPLOYING SOLUTIONS

The Package And Deployment wizard performs three functions:

- Package—Lets you create one or more compressed files with a .cab file type for distribution via disk, CD, a network, or the Internet.

- Deployment—Manages the distribution of your compressed setup files to a target media. There are as many as 23 screens that support both the Package and Deployment functions. The wizard automatically creates a script that records your choices each time you perform either function.

- Manage Scripts—Lets you save, rename, remove, and reuse scripts. Since there can be a large number of screens with multiple choices per screen, rerunning the scripts can save time and reduce the tendency for errors.

You launch the wizard in the same way that you start Code Librarian. Load the add-in and then select it in from the Add-Ins menu in the VBE window.

Before you start the wizard, you should load the custom application that you want to package and deploy. Figure 14-4 shows the wizard's first screen.

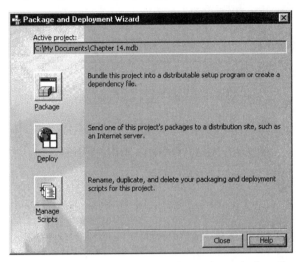

Figure 14-4. *The first screen of the Package And Deployment wizard.*

NOTE It can take several seconds to load an add-in. A progress meter appears to help you recognize that a process is in operation. If you attempt to invoke the add-in before it completes loading, you can generate a run-time error.

You can redistribute any custom solutions or components that you create with Office applications, except for those created with FrontPage and Outlook. In the latter two applications, project support is limited to user profiles instead of stand-alone projects. You can redistribute stand-alone projects for the remaining Office applications. You can also include additional files for the execution of a project, including bitmap images, DLL files, and ActiveX controls, and other Office document files.

Solutions that work with Jet or MSDE databases can include Access Run Time or the redistributable MSDE so that your custom solutions can perform database maintenance functions on machines that do not have Office 2000 installed. You can also include the Graph9.exe file in your .cab setup files to support the graphical display of data.

NOTE Applications that use Office 2000 Web Components require a workstation license for Office 2000. However, you can freely distribute applications using the components. There is also no run-time engine for the standard Office applications, except as noted above. Therefore, users must have Excel on their workstation to run a redistributed Excel project.

If you choose to distribute your custom application with Access Run Time, you might want to test your solution with the */runtime* command-line option to simulate the environment that users will see if they run your solution without Access. When your custom forms use Access Run Time they are more critical than ever because users do not have exposure to any built-in Access user interfaces, such as the database window or even error message dialog boxes. Therefore, you need a welcome switchboard form (see Chapter 5) and thorough error-trapping logic (see Chapter 1). Without this logic, errors will cause your solution to terminate abruptly and confuse its users.

You can create two kinds of packages with the Package function in the wizard. You can create a standard package if you plan to distribute your application via floppy disk, CD, or a network share. If you want to deploy to floppy disk media, select the Multiple Cabs option so that the wizard sizes your .cab files so that no one file is larger than a floppy disk. To distribute your application via the Internet, you should create an Internet package.

DATA ACCESS IN NON-ACCESS APPLICATIONS

Recall that ODE offers three routes to data: the Data Environment designer, the ADO Data Control, and the ADO object model. You might initially feel most comfortable with the ADO object model route. (See Chapter 2 for an introduction to the ADO object model; other chapters offer additional details). The following sample populates an Excel worksheet with ADO *Connection* and *Recordset* objects. It copies the field names from the Northwind *Products* table to the first row of an Excel worksheet. Then it copies field values for successive rows from the recordset down the worksheet. The sample runs from the VBA project associated with a workbook file.

```
Sub northwind2XL()
Dim cnn1 As ADODB.Connection
Dim rst1 As ADODB.Recordset
Dim RowCnt, FieldCnt As Integer

'Create instances of the connection and recordset objects.
    Set cnn1 = New ADODB.Connection
    Set rst1 = New ADODB.Recordset

'Set cnn1.ConnectionString to Northwind DSN.
    cnn1.ConnectionString = "DSN=Northwind"
```

```
'Open connection and recordset.
    cnn1.Open
    Set rst1.ActiveConnection = cnn1
    rst1.Source = "Select * FROM Products"
    rst1.Open , , adOpenStatic, adLockOptimistic

'Write in column headings in first row.
    RowCnt = 1
    For FieldCnt = 0 To rst1.Fields.Count - 1
        Cells(RowCnt, FieldCnt + 1).Value = _
            rst1.Fields(FieldCnt).Name
        Rows(1).Font.Bold = True
    Next FieldCnt

'Fill rows with records, starting at row 2.
    RowCnt = 2
    While Not rst1.EOF
        For FieldCnt = 0 To rst1.Fields.Count - 1
            Cells(RowCnt, FieldCnt + 1).Value = _
                rst1.Fields(FieldCnt).Value
        Next FieldCnt
        rst1.MoveNext
        RowCnt = RowCnt + 1
    Wend

End Sub
```

The connection string for the *Connection* object relies on a DSN object. The DSN in the sample points at the Northwind database, but it can specify any DSN . Using a DSN simplifies the design of the connection string syntax because you can use the graphical procedure from the ODBC icon in the Control Panel to specify the connection to a database. Also notice the standard syntax for specifying a connection and basing a recordset on it.

The procedure applies the *Cells* property, which implicitly refers to the *ActiveWorksheet* object in the Excel object model. You specify individual cells of a worksheet by denoting a row index followed by a column index. Setting the index values inside of loops lets the code move across columns within a row and down the rows of a worksheet.

DIGITALLY SIGNING VBA PROJECTS

The *Microsoft Office 2000/Visual Basic Programmer's Guide* is a rich source of documentation on many critical aspects of operation, including how to sign a project digitally. If you obtain an Authenticode certificate, you can digitally sign Word, Excel, PowerPoint, and Outlook VBA projects so that they do not display the macro warning message even when security is set to high.

Figure 14-5 shows a pair of warning messages. The top one appears for unsigned documents with VBA projects. The bottom one appears for documents with signed projects before they are trusted. You cannot add a digital signature to the trusted list directly—you must select the Always Trust Macros From This Source check box and enable its macros. Thereafter, all documents with the digital signature for that document are trusted, and no macro warning messages appear for properly signed VBA projects from that source.

Figure 14-5. *A typical macro warning message for an unsigned document and a warning message for the first document from a new digitally signed source.*

NOTE Authenticode verification works only on workstations that run Internet Explorer version 4 or later. Workstations running an earlier version of Internet Explorer or a different brand of browser will not have the Authenticode verification software installed on the workstation.

Authenticode technology relies on public-key cryptography to sign software publications, such as VBA projects. When an author saves a file, the Authenticode software performs a hashing operation to create a "digital fingerprint" for the document and encrypts the fingerprint with the private key. When a recipient receives the document, the Authenticode software attempts to unlock the fingerprint and decode it. Documents that pass this process can be opened without the macro warning message. Others bring up the message. If another user modifies the VBA project and saves it, that removes the digital signature, so a warning message will appear the next time someone tries to open the file.

To digitally sign a VBA project, you must first obtain a valid digital certificate. There are three ways to do this. The first way is to create your own with the Selfcert.exe utility that ships with Office 2000. This is appropriate for personal testing or for a small workgroup. The second way is to obtain a certificate from your organization's internal certification authority. This is appropriate for an enterprise or for a major enterprise and its suppliers. The third way is to obtain a digital certificate from a commercial certification authority. This is a good general solution.

The digital signature applies strictly to the VBA project and not its associated Office document, such as a workbook. This allows a user to modify a worksheet but not the associated VBA project. From the VBE window, select the project in the Project Explorer window. Then choose Digital Signature from the Tools menu. The first time that you use the certificate, select the certificate and click OK twice. Otherwise, just click OK.

The following pair of procedures shows how to determine whether a workbook file is digitally signed. The procedure *callIsDSigned* calls the function *isDSigned* twice. In the first call, *callIsDSigned* passes along the name for the current file. In the second call, *callIsDSigned* shows one way of gathering a file name from the user and passing it along to *isDSigned*. Since a workbook must be open to determine whether it is digitally signed, *callIsDSigned* opens the file with the name input by the user.

```
Sub callIsDSigned()
Dim myName As String

'Check whether current workbook is digitally signed.
    myName = Application.Workbooks(1).Name
    isDSigned (myName)

'Prompt user for workbook name and
'check whether that workbook is digitally signed.
    myName = InputBox("Type name as filename.xls", _
        "Programming Microsoft Access 2000", myName)
    Workbooks.Open myName
    isDSigned (myName)

End Sub


Public Function isDSigned(fileName As String)
    isDSigned = _
        Application.Workbooks(fileName).VBASigned
```

(continued)

```
If isDSigned Then
    Debug.Print fileName & " is digitally signed."
Else
    Debug.Print fileName & " is not digitally signed."
End If

End Function
```

The *IsDSigned* function stores the return value of the *VBASigned* property and then branches to one of two print statements based on that value. The property is set to *True* if the workbook is digitally signed. You can use similar code to determine whether Word documents and PowerPoint presentations have been digitally signed. (The precise syntax for opening a file varies across applications, but Word and PowerPoint also support the *VBASigned* property.)

Appendix

Third-Party Sample Applications and Demos

This book's companion CD includes content from three third-party vendors— Database Creations, FMS, and Visio—all of whom provide quality support for Microsoft Access developers.

The CD's content can expand your prospective development opportunities in two major directions. First, the sample applications and demos include accounting and statistics applications that you, as an Access developer, can leverage in expanding your Access development business into new markets. Accounting and statistics vertical market opportunities offer rich rewards for those who pursue them successfully. Second, the CD contains tools for Access and Microsoft Visual Basic developers that can enrich and simplify developing classic custom database applications.

DATABASE CREATIONS

The CD includes both sample applications and product demos from Database Creations (www.databasecreations.com). You can use the sample applications as is or upgrade to the full version or a related version, but each sample performs a basic chore without restrictions. For example, Check Writer 2000 lets you manage one or more checking accounts with Access 2000. The product demos simply show how you can use a product. For example, the Yes! I Can Run My Business demo illustrates a full-featured accounting package for a sample toy company. You can see the features of the package, but you cannot create a new company from the demo.

Check Writer 2000

Check Writer 2000 is a fully functional application that includes Check Register and Check Reconciliation modules. You can pay your bills, print checks, and balance your checkbook. This application won the Microsoft Network Access Product of the Year award and is part of the full accounting system called Yes! I Can Run My Business, which won the 1998 Readers Choice award from *Microsoft Access Advisor* magazine. A complete user guide is also included in the directory.

Check Writer 2000 normally costs $179.95. If you mention this book, you can buy it for only $99.95. To order, call Database Creations at (860) 644-5891, fax them at (860) 648-0710, or e-mail them at info@databasecreations.com.

You can install Check Writer 2000 and the documentation by running \Access 2000 Examples - Database Creations\Free Access Software \Check Writer (Award Winning)\Check Writer 2000.exe.

EZ File Manager Sampler

The EZ File Manager is one of eight products in the new EZ Access Developer Suite. The complete File Utilities tool, which helps you compile, compact, repair, and backup attached data databases, is included, along with the entire documentation set from the EZ Access File Manager. Install the sampler and then copy the form and module to your own application to add file management capabilities to your application.

You can install the EZ File Manager Sampler and documentation by running \Access 2000 Examples - Database Creations\Free Access Software\EZ File Manager Sampler\EZ File Manager.exe.

EZ Search Manager Sampler

The EZ Search Manager is another product in the EZ Access Developer Suite. The complete SmartSearch tool is included, along with the entire documentation set from the EZ Access Search Manager. Install the sampler and then copy the forms to your own application to add a flexible search interface to your application.

You can install the EZ Search Manager Sampler and documentation by running \Access 2000 Examples - Database Creations\Free Access Software\EZ Search Manager Sampler\EZ Search Manager.exe.

Business Forms Library Sampler

The Access Business Forms Library Sampler contains some of the Business Forms Library collection of 35 forms and reports. The library contains tables, forms, reports, and macros for each of the forms and reports. You can integrate them into your own applications to save hundreds of hours of work. Microsoft included an early version of forms in the Microsoft Access Welcome Kit with Access 2.0. These have been updated for Access 2000, and they come with a complete user guide.

You can install the Business Forms Library Sampler and documentation by running \Access 2000 Examples - Database Creations\Free Access Software \Business Forms Library Sampler\BusFrm2000.exe.

Cool Combo Box Techniques

This is a demonstration database of 25 of the coolest combo and list box techniques. Full documentation is included in the CD directory. The demo is from a highly acclaimed paper given by Cary Prague at the Microsoft Access conferences.

You can install the Cool Combo Box Techniques samples and the paper by running \Access 2000 Examples - Database Creations\Free Access Software \Cool Combo Box Techniques\coolcombo.exe.

Picture Builder Button Sampler

You can use these button faces on Access 2000 toolbars or on switchboard forms or on menus. Simply copy the files to your hard disk or use the bitmaps as is. The files named ACT*xx*.BMP are 32-by-32-pixel bitmaps for Access 2000 command buttons. The files named ACT*xx*.B24 are 24-by-23-pixel bitmaps for Access 2000 toolbars and any Microsoft Office–compatible application.

You can install the Picture Builder Button Sampler by running \Access 2000 Examples - Database Creations\Free Access Software\Picture Builder Button Sampler\Picture Builder Sampler.exe.

Yes! I Can Run My Business Demo

The Yes! I Can Run My Business demo package is fully customizable and includes all source code. It offers all typical accounting functions, including sales, customers, A/R, purchases, suppliers, A/P, inventory, banking, general ledger, and fixed assets, and it features multicompany accounting for businesses of any size. It costs less than $1,000 for a LAN version. A developer version is available with royalty-free distribution rights for around $2,000. The full product includes over 1500 pages of documentation.

You can copy Yes! I Can Run My Business Brochure.pdf in the directory referenced below to your hard drive to review the online brochure using Adobe Acrobat (which is included on the CD). The entire Yes! I Can Run My Business product retails for $599.95 for the end-user version and $2,295 for the developer version. Mention the code "BOOKCD," and you can get the developer version for just $2,095.95. You can also view additional samples at www.databasecreations.com.

You can install the Yes! I Can Run My Business demo by running \Access 2000 Examples - Database Creations\Demos\Yes! I Can Accounting \Yes4demo.exe.

PC-Payroll Demo

PC-Payroll from Pensoft is a standalone payroll package for small businesses written in Visual Basic. It interfaces with Yes! I Can Run My Business to provide complete employee, hour, tax, deduction, and benefit processing.

Run \Access 2000 Examples - Database Creations\Demos\PC-Payroll\PC Payroll Professional Demo.exe to install the PC-Payroll demo.

EZ Access Developer Suite Demo

The EZ Access Developer Suite consists of eight separate products. Each can be easily integrated into your Access application to provide new functions in a fraction of the time that it would take you to create them yourself. Think of them as a library of over 100 predesigned, preprogrammed interfaces.

The embedded reviewer's guides in the demo give a complete overview of each product. The entire EZ Access Developer Suite retails for $799.95; the individual products are $199.95. Mention the code "BOOKCD" and get the entire suite for just $699.95. You can also view additional samples at www.databasecreations.com.

The eight EZ Access Suite pieces are:

- EZ Report Manager
- EZ Support Manager

- EZ Search Manager

- EZ Security Manager

- EZ File Manager

- EZ Extensions

- EZ Application Manager

- EZ Controls

Run \Access 2000 Examples - Database Creations\Demos\EZ Access Suite\EZ Access Suite Demo.exe to install the EZ Access Developer Suite demo.

Access Product Catalogs

The CD also includes the latest catalogs from Database Creations (the full 1998 catalog, the 1999 supplement for Access and Office, and a Microsoft Visual FoxPro catalog). You can view them using the included Adobe Acrobat viewer. Mention the book code BOOKCD and receive an additional 5 percent off any software product in the catalogs. You can also view product updates and new products at www.databasecreations.com or call for new printed catalogs and product descriptions at (860) 644-5891. E-mail also works well. Mail info@databasecreations.com.

The files to run after you install Adobe Acrobat include:

- \Access 2000 Examples - Database Creations\Access Product Catalogs\1998 48 Page Access 97 Product Catalog.pdf

- \Access 2000 Examples - Database Creations\Access Product Catalogs\1999 20 Page Access 2000 Product Catalog.pdf

- \Access 2000 Examples - Database Creations\Access Product Catalogs\Visual FoxPro Product Catalog.pdf

Adobe Acrobat Reader

This free reader from Adobe lets you view and print files stored in the Abobe Acrobat .pdf file format. You can use virtually any product to create an output file by simply printing it, and then you can let anyone else view the output file without any special software except Adobe Acrobat.

In the future, instead of receiving a big catalog in the mail, you might get a .pdf file of the catalog by e-mail. The Access Product Catalogs directory of the CD includes several catalogs with .pdf filename extensions. To view them, you must first install the Adobe Acrobat reader. To install the Adobe Acrobat reader, run the file \Visio\Utilities\AcrobatReader.exe. Double-click on the installation file and follow the instructions. This file contains just the reader. To create your own .pdf files, you must purchase the full Acrobat program from Adobe.

FMS

The FMS (www.fmsinc.com) product demos address a broad range of developer-oriented topics, from custom ActiveX controls to maintaining Access databases. Most demos explicitly target Access developers. Many Visual Basic developers also use Microsoft Jet as a database engine for their custom solutions. Two of the FMS demos explicitly target Visual Basic development issues.

Total Access Agent

For optimal performance and stability, Access/Jet (.mdb) databases must be periodically repaired, compacted, backed up, and monitored. Total Access Agent schedules and automatically performs these tasks across multiple databases. You can perform these tasks at night or even back up data while users are working in the database. Total Access Agent can manage multiple databases across any network that supports Access—it even handles secured databases and lets you assign security workgroups, user names, and passwords. Total Access Agent lets you create hourly, daily, weekly, and monthly events, and you can even specify when processing should finish. Every task performed by Total Access Agent is recorded in Access tables with customizable reports. If any problems (such as corruption) occur, the error is recorded and the system administrator can be notified by e-mail.

Total Access Analyzer

Total Access Analyzer offers complete documentation, cross-referencing, error detection, enhancement suggestions, and reporting on your Access databases. You can generate complete documentation of tables, fields, indexes, relationships, forms, controls, reports, command bars, hyperlinks, macros, and modules. You select the objects and analysis to perform, and then you can view the results and use any of the more than 225 presentation reports. All of the output is stored in Access tables. You can query and sort the results or create your own reports.

Total Access Components

Total Access Components is the only collection of ActiveX controls specifically designed and tested for Access. It includes 27 ActiveX controls, which you can place on your forms and reports. Many controls provide new and enhanced display effects, while others let you use properties and methods to perform complex operations with little or no programming. You can modify most properties programmatically and invoke methods on some of the controls for additional functionality.

Total Access Memo

Total Access Memo lets Access users and developers add formatted memo fields to forms and reports. You can enhance your applications by adding support for features such as fonts, point sizes, boldface, italics, underline, bullet points, paragraph alignment, and tab stops. You can add the Total Access Memo control to your form or report and bind it to a memo field. You press Shift+F2 on the field to launch the FMS Rich Text Formatting (RTF) editor, and when you finish, it is automatically saved in your table and displayed on your form. You can save and maintain both an RTF and a nonformatted (text-only) memo field. You can even import text files in RTF format, export the current field to an RTF file, or export to a text-only file. The RTF editor lets you easily enter text and apply the styles you want. It also includes features such as Find, Search & Replace, and Spell Checking.

Total Access Statistics

Total Access Statistics offers a wide range of statistical functions for Access users and developers. It eliminates the need to export your data to other programs for statistical analysis. It is installed as an Access add-in and runs directly from your database through the File-Add-Ins menu. Using the Total Access Statistics wizard, you can quickly analyze your data without programming. You can analyze any Access table, linked table, or select query. You can analyze an unlimited number of records and multiple fields at one time. Best of all, the results are kept in Access tables. You can view, sort, or query the results, merge it with other data, or add it to forms and reports. You can also add Total Access Statistics to your Access applications. If you are a developer and need statistical analysis in your database, you can bypass the wizard and add all the statistical features directly to your application with a simple procedure call.

Total VB Statistics

Total VB Statistics offers a wide range of statistical functions for Visual Basic programmers who use Jet databases. It eliminates the need to export your data to other programs for statistical analysis. You can perform a wide range of statistical functions; all results are kept in Access tables. You can view, sort, query, or display the results. You can also add them to reports. Total VB Statistics has two parts: The interactive Statistics Scenario Designer, a standalone program, lets you specify the database, data, fields, and analysis to perform; the ActiveX DLL component performs the analysis. This DLL file, which is less than 1 MB, is the only file you need to include with your VB applications to add statistical analysis.

Total VB SourceBook

Total VB SourceBook is an extensive source code library for Visual Basic, with over 60,000 lines of code and more than 1700 procedures that you can add directly to your applications. It includes more than 100 classes and modules covering 27 major categories of Visual Basic application development. Each class and module is independent, so you can add one without others. Select the code you want from the FMS Code Explorer and insert it directly into your project. You can even add your own code so that all your important code is in one convenient place.

VISIO

The CD includes two product demos from Visio (www.visio.com). Visio Enterprise targets enterprise information applications. It works with both Jet and Microsoft SQL Server databases, and it can draw the relationships between entities in a database design within either database. Visio Professional targets information system and business applications. Both packages share a core set of drawing templates, and each has special templates as well. You can also use your Visual Basic for Applications (VBA) programming skills to extend either package. Visio Professional can also draw entity relationships diagrams, but it has additional interfaces for drawing business charts based on the contents of an Access database.

Visio Enterprise 5.0

You can design and model your enterprise information architecture using Visio Enterprise. You can reengineer databases, synchronize models with databases, and create customizable reports. You can model using UML 1.2, integrate with Microsoft Repository 2.0, and reverse-engineer Microsoft Visual C++ and Visual Basic code into UML models.

Visio Professional 5.0

You can use this package to diagram your information systems and business processes. Visio Professional is for business analysts who design applications and databases and communicate their relationships. You can choose from a selection of shapes and wizards developed specifically for network, software, and database diagramming. You can plan software development using leading methodologies, such as UML diagrams. You can also create database proposals using data flow diagrams or entity relationship diagrams.

Index

Note: Page numbers in italics refer to figures or tables.

A

AccessObject object
  enumerating, 299
  properties of, 327
AccessObject Type property, 330
Access Projects, 187, 475–81
  connecting to a database, 475–76
  forms and, 495–96
  hyperlinks and, 493–94
  learning from the NorthwindCS and
    Pubs databases, 476–81
  programmatic issues and, 499–507
    finding a record, 500
    opening a form, 499
    viewing changes made by other
      users, 501–2
  querying in, 238–40, *239, 240*
  reports and, 492–93
  resynchronizing a form with its
    one-to-many data in, 496–98
  standalone modules and, 502–7
  stored procedures and, 489–92
Access Run Time, 540
acForm constant, 5
action queries, 183–84, 211–19
  append queries, 214–15, *215*
  delete queries, 216–18, *217*
  hiding, 216

action queries, *continued*
  make-table queries, 218–19, *219*
  update queries, 212–14, *213*
ActionQueryDemo procedure, 217–18
Activate event, 292
ActiveConnection property
  Catalog object's, 116
  Connection object's, 83
  Recordset object's, 85, 92
  Replica object's, 454, 456, 457, 460,
    462, 468
ActiveDocument object, 404
ActiveX Data Objects. *See* ADO (ActiveX
  Data Objects)
ActualSize property, *Field* object's, 97
AddARecord procedure, 91–92
addCbrBtns procedure, 374–75
addContacts procedure, 399–400
AddFromFile method, 322
AddGroupToUser procedure, 430
AddIdx procedure, 167–68
Add-In Designer, Component Object
  Model (COM), 538
AddIndex procedure, 123–24
Add-In Manager dialog box, 541–42, *542*
AddNew method, 72, 89, 92, 168, 169
addOneContact procedure, 397–98
AddPKErr procedure, 165–67
AddPK procedure, 163–65

Rick Dobson

Rick Dobson, Ph.D., is an author, speaker, trainer, and developer. His areas of expertise include Microsoft Access and Microsoft Office, World Wide Web development, and database design and planning. His consulting practice, CAB, Inc., has been in full-time operation since 1991; he operated the practice on a part-time basis for six years before that. His wife, Virginia, participates in the practice by offering professional accounting and tax services. She also writes for such publications as *Microsoft Office and Visual Basic for Applications Developer* and *PC Novice*.

Rick used Access from its initial release, and he became active as an Access developer with the beta release of Access 2. Since then, he has lectured on Access development in Australia, Great Britain, Canada, and throughout the United States. Shortly after the release of Access 2, Rick authored his own five-day Access training course. Later, he became a Microsoft Certified Professional and Trainer and started offering the Microsoft courses to clients.

Rick's articles on Access, Web development, and database topics appear in a wide variety of publications, including *BYTE*, *ACCESS-OFFICE-VB ADVISOR* (formerly *Access/Visual Basic Advisor*), *Visual Basic Developer*, *Microsoft Interactive Developer*, *Visual Basic Programmer's Journal*, *Microsoft Office Developer's Journal*, *WEB Techniques*, and *Microsoft Office and Visual Basic for Applications Developer*. Early in his computer career, Rick wrote books for Que about Lotus 1-2-3 and Lotus Symphony.

Rick has built solutions for the utility, home care nursing, paper manufacturing, and engineering construction industries. Rick has based this book on his consulting experiences as well as on the shared experiences of his trainees and those who write to him with feedback on his articles.

Rick encourages you to share your Access development experiences with him. He particularly welcomes praise of the book, but constructive feedback is OK too. Rick has created a Web site for extra information about Microsoft Access and book updates at http://www.programmingaccess.com. His training and consulting business, CAB Inc., also has information that may be of interest to Access programmers at http://www.cabinc.win.net. You can e-mail Rick at rickd@cabinc.net.

The manuscript for this book was prepared using Microsoft Word 97. Pages were composed by Microsoft Press using Adobe PageMaker 6.52 for Windows, with text in Garamond and display type in Helvetica Black. Composed pages were delivered to the printer as electronic prepress files.

Cover Graphic Designer

Tim Girvin Design, Inc.

Cover Illustrator

Glenn Mitsui

Interior Graphic Artist

Joel Panchot

Principal Compositor

Elizabeth Hansford

Principal Proofreader/Copy Editor

Cheryl Penner

Indexer

Maro Riofrancos

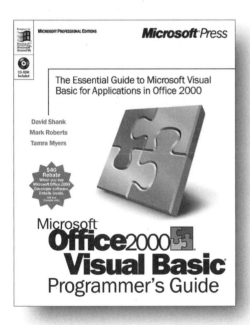

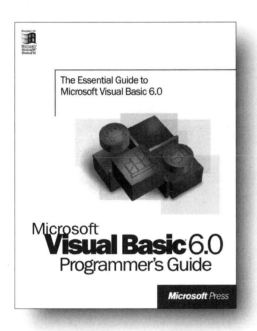

MICROSOFT LICENSE AGREEMENT
Book Companion CD

IMPORTANT—READ CAREFULLY: This Microsoft End-User License Agreement ("EULA") is a legal agreement between you (either an individual or an entity) and Microsoft Corporation for the Microsoft product identified above, which includes computer software and may include associated media, printed materials, and "online" or electronic documentation ("SOFTWARE PROD-UCT"). Any component included within the SOFTWARE PRODUCT that is accompanied by a separate End-User License Agreement shall be governed by such agreement and not the terms set forth below. By installing, copying, or otherwise using the SOFTWARE PRODUCT, you agree to be bound by the terms of this EULA. If you do not agree to the terms of this EULA, you are not authorized to install, copy, or otherwise use the SOFTWARE PRODUCT; you may, however, return the SOFTWARE PROD-UCT, along with all printed materials and other items that form a part of the Microsoft product that includes the SOFTWARE PRODUCT, to the place you obtained them for a full refund.

SOFTWARE PRODUCT LICENSE

The SOFTWARE PRODUCT is protected by United States copyright laws and international copyright treaties, as well as other intellectual property laws and treaties. The SOFTWARE PRODUCT is licensed, not sold.

1. **GRANT OF LICENSE.** This EULA grants you the following rights:

   a. **Software Product.** You may install and use one copy of the SOFTWARE PRODUCT on a single computer. The primary user of the computer on which the SOFTWARE PRODUCT is installed may make a second copy for his or her exclusive use on a portable computer.

   b. **Storage/Network Use.** You may also store or install a copy of the SOFTWARE PRODUCT on a storage device, such as a network server, used only to install or run the SOFTWARE PRODUCT on your other computers over an internal network; however, you must acquire and dedicate a license for each separate computer on which the SOFTWARE PRODUCT is installed or run from the storage device. A license for the SOFTWARE PRODUCT may not be shared or used concurrently on different computers.

   c. **License Pak.** If you have acquired this EULA in a Microsoft License Pak, you may make the number of additional copies of the computer software portion of the SOFTWARE PRODUCT authorized on the printed copy of this EULA, and you may use each copy in the manner specified above. You are also entitled to make a corresponding number of secondary copies for portable computer use as specified above.

   d. **Sample Code.** Solely with respect to portions, if any, of the SOFTWARE PRODUCT that are identified within the SOFT-WARE PRODUCT as sample code (the "SAMPLE CODE"):

      i. **Use and Modification.** Microsoft grants you the right to use and modify the source code version of the SAMPLE CODE, *provided* you comply with subsection (d)(iii) below. You may not distribute the SAMPLE CODE, or any modified version of the SAMPLE CODE, in source code form.

      ii. **Redistributable Files.** Provided you comply with subsection (d)(iii) below, Microsoft grants you a nonexclusive, royalty-free right to reproduce and distribute the object code version of the SAMPLE CODE and of any modified SAMPLE CODE, other than SAMPLE CODE, or any modified version thereof, designated as not redistributable in the Readme file that forms a part of the SOFTWARE PRODUCT (the "Non-Redistributable Sample Code"). All SAMPLE CODE other than the Non-Redistributable Sample Code is collectively referred to as the "REDISTRIBUTABLES."

      iii. **Redistribution Requirements.** If you redistribute the REDISTRIBUTABLES, you agree to: (i) distribute the REDISTRIBUTABLES in object code form only in conjunction with and as a part of your software application product; (ii) not use Microsoft's name, logo, or trademarks to market your software application product; (iii) include a valid copyright notice on your software application product; (iv) indemnify, hold harmless, and defend Microsoft from and against any claims or lawsuits, including attorney's fees, that arise or result from the use or distribution of your software application product; and (v) not permit further distribution of the REDISTRIBUTABLES by your end user. Contact Microsoft for the applicable royalties due and other licensing terms for all other uses and/or distribution of the REDISTRIBUTABLES.

2. **DESCRIPTION OF OTHER RIGHTS AND LIMITATIONS.**

   - **Limitations on Reverse Engineering, Decompilation, and Disassembly.** You may not reverse engineer, decompile, or disassemble the SOFTWARE PRODUCT, except and only to the extent that such activity is expressly permitted by applicable law notwithstanding this limitation.

   - **Separation of Components.** The SOFTWARE PRODUCT is licensed as a single product. Its component parts may not be separated for use on more than one computer.

   - **Rental.** You may not rent, lease, or lend the SOFTWARE PRODUCT.

   - **Support Services.** Microsoft may, but is not obligated to, provide you with support services related to the SOFTWARE PRODUCT ("Support Services"). Use of Support Services is governed by the Microsoft policies and programs described in the user manual, in "online" documentation, and/or other Microsoft-provided materials. Any supplemental software code provided to you as part of the Support Services shall be considered part of the SOFTWARE PRODUCT and subject to the terms and conditions of this EULA. With respect to technical information you provide to Microsoft as part of the Support Services, Microsoft may use such information for its business purposes, including for product support and development. Microsoft will not utilize such technical information in a form that personally identifies you.

- **Software Transfer.** You may permanently transfer all of your rights under this EULA, provided you retain no copies, you transfer all of the SOFTWARE PRODUCT (including all component parts, the media and printed materials, any upgrades, this EULA, and, if applicable, the Certificate of Authenticity), **and** the recipient agrees to the terms of this EULA.

- **Termination.** Without prejudice to any other rights, Microsoft may terminate this EULA if you fail to comply with the terms and conditions of this EULA. In such event, you must destroy all copies of the SOFTWARE PRODUCT and all of its component parts.

3. **COPYRIGHT.** All title and copyrights in and to the SOFTWARE PRODUCT (including but not limited to any images, photographs, animations, video, audio, music, text, SAMPLE CODE, REDISTRIBUTABLES, and "applets" incorporated into the SOFTWARE PRODUCT) and any copies of the SOFTWARE PRODUCT are owned by Microsoft or its suppliers. The SOFTWARE PRODUCT is protected by copyright laws and international treaty provisions. Therefore, you must treat the SOFTWARE PRODUCT like any other copyrighted material **except** that you may install the SOFTWARE PRODUCT on a single computer provided you keep the original solely for backup or archival purposes. You may not copy the printed materials accompanying the SOFTWARE PRODUCT.

4. **U.S. GOVERNMENT RESTRICTED RIGHTS.** The SOFTWARE PRODUCT and documentation are provided with RESTRICTED RIGHTS. Use, duplication, or disclosure by the Government is subject to restrictions as set forth in subparagraph (c)(1)(ii) of the Rights in Technical Data and Computer Software clause at DFARS 252.227-7013 or subparagraphs (c)(1) and (2) of the Commercial Computer Software—Restricted Rights at 48 CFR 52.227-19, as applicable. Manufacturer is Microsoft Corporation/One Microsoft Way/Redmond, WA 98052-6399.

5. **EXPORT RESTRICTIONS.** You agree that you will not export or re-export the SOFTWARE PRODUCT, any part thereof, or any process or service that is the direct product of the SOFTWARE PRODUCT (the foregoing collectively referred to as the "Restricted Components"), to any country, person, entity, or end user subject to U.S. export restrictions. You specifically agree not to export or re-export any of the Restricted Components (i) to any country to which the U.S. has embargoed or restricted the export of goods or services, which currently include, but are not necessarily limited to, Cuba, Iran, Iraq, Libya, North Korea, Sudan, and Syria, or to any national of any such country, wherever located, who intends to transmit or transport the Restricted Components back to such country; (ii) to any end user who you know or have reason to know will utilize the Restricted Components in the design, development, or production of nuclear, chemical, or biological weapons; or (iii) to any end user who has been prohibited from participating in U.S. export transactions by any federal agency of the U.S. government. You warrant and represent that neither the BXA nor any other U.S. federal agency has suspended, revoked, or denied your export privileges.

DISCLAIMER OF WARRANTY

NO WARRANTIES OR CONDITIONS. MICROSOFT EXPRESSLY DISCLAIMS ANY WARRANTY OR CONDITION FOR THE SOFTWARE PRODUCT. THE SOFTWARE PRODUCT AND ANY RELATED DOCUMENTATION ARE PROVIDED "AS IS" WITHOUT WARRANTY OR CONDITION OF ANY KIND, EITHER EXPRESS OR IMPLIED, INCLUDING, WITHOUT LIMITATION, THE IMPLIED WARRANTIES OF MERCHANTABILITY, FITNESS FOR A PARTICULAR PURPOSE, OR NONINFRINGEMENT. THE ENTIRE RISK ARISING OUT OF USE OR PERFORMANCE OF THE SOFTWARE PRODUCT REMAINS WITH YOU.

LIMITATION OF LIABILITY. TO THE MAXIMUM EXTENT PERMITTED BY APPLICABLE LAW, IN NO EVENT SHALL MICROSOFT OR ITS SUPPLIERS BE LIABLE FOR ANY SPECIAL, INCIDENTAL, INDIRECT, OR CONSEQUENTIAL DAMAGES WHATSOEVER (INCLUDING, WITHOUT LIMITATION, DAMAGES FOR LOSS OF BUSINESS PROFITS, BUSINESS INTERRUPTION, LOSS OF BUSINESS INFORMATION, OR ANY OTHER PECUNIARY LOSS) ARISING OUT OF THE USE OF OR INABILITY TO USE THE SOFTWARE PRODUCT OR THE PROVISION OF OR FAILURE TO PROVIDE SUPPORT SERVICES, EVEN IF MICROSOFT HAS BEEN ADVISED OF THE POSSIBILITY OF SUCH DAMAGES. IN ANY CASE, MICROSOFT'S ENTIRE LIABILITY UNDER ANY PROVISION OF THIS EULA SHALL BE LIMITED TO THE GREATER OF THE AMOUNT ACTUALLY PAID BY YOU FOR THE SOFTWARE PRODUCT OR US$5.00; PROVIDED, HOWEVER, IF YOU HAVE ENTERED INTO A MICROSOFT SUPPORT SERVICES AGREEMENT, MICROSOFT'S ENTIRE LIABILITY REGARDING SUPPORT SERVICES SHALL BE GOVERNED BY THE TERMS OF THAT AGREEMENT. BECAUSE SOME STATES AND JURISDICTIONS DO NOT ALLOW THE EXCLUSION OR LIMITATION OF LIABILITY, THE ABOVE LIMITATION MAY NOT APPLY TO YOU.

MISCELLANEOUS

This EULA is governed by the laws of the State of Washington USA, except and only to the extent that applicable law mandates governing law of a different jurisdiction.

Should you have any questions concerning this EULA, or if you desire to contact Microsoft for any reason, please contact the Microsoft subsidiary serving your country, or write: Microsoft Sales Information Center/One Microsoft Way/Redmond, WA 98052-6399.

Register Today!

Return this
Programming Microsoft® Access 2000
registration card today

Microsoft *Press*
mspress.microsoft.com

OWNER REGISTRATION CARD   **0-7356-0500-9**

Programming Microsoft® Access 2000

FIRST NAME	MIDDLE INITIAL	LAST NAME

INSTITUTION OR COMPANY NAME

ADDRESS

CITY	STATE	ZIP

E-MAIL ADDRESS	( ) PHONE NUMBER

U.S. and Canada addresses only. Fill in information above and mail postage-free.
Please mail only the bottom half of this page.

**For information about Microsoft Press®
products, visit our Web site at
mspress.microsoft.com**

Microsoft *Press*